CORRECTIONAL
MENTAL HEALTH

For information:

SAGE Publications, Inc.
2455 Teller Road
Thousand Oaks, California 91320
E-mail: order@sagepub.com

SAGE Publications Ltd.
1 Oliver's Yard
55 City Road
London EC1Y 1SP
United Kingdom

SAGE Publications India Pvt. Ltd.
B 1/I 1 Mohan Cooperative Industrial Area
Mathura Road, New Delhi 110 044
India

SAGE Publications Asia-Pacific Pte. Ltd.
33 Pekin Street #02-01
Far East Square
Singapore 048763

Printed in the United States of America

Library of Congress Cataloging-in-Publication Data

Correctional mental health : from theory to practice / Thomas J. Fagan, Robert K. Ax.
     p. cm.
Includes bibliographical references and index.
ISBN 978-1-4129-7256-7 (pbk. : acid-free paper)
    1. Mentally ill offenders—Mental health services. 2. Prisoners—Mental health services.
3. Prisoners—Medical care. I. Fagan, Thomas J., 1949- II. Ax, Robert Kirk, 1952-

RC451.4.P68C6683 2011
364.3′8—dc22   2010032324

This book is printed on acid-free paper.

10   11   12   13   14   10   9   8   7   6   5   4   3   2   1

Acquisitions Editor:	Jerry Westby
Editorial Assistant:	Nichole O'Grady
Production Editor:	Karen Wiley
Copy Editor:	Matthew Adams
Typesetter:	C&M Digitals (P) Ltd.
Proofreader:	Laura Webb
Indexer:	Jeanne Busemeyer
Cover Designer:	Candice Harman
Marketing Manager:	Erica DeLuca
Permissions Editor:	Karen Ehrmann

Brief Contents

Detailed Contents

Introduction

During the past 30 years there has been a dramatic rise in the number of incarcerated individuals in the United States. Current estimates are that more than 2.3 million individuals are housed in U.S. prisons and jails with an additional 5 million people on probation and/or parole (Glaze & Bonczar, 2009; Harrison & Beck, 2006; Sabol, West, & Cooper, 2009). In fact, the United States incarcerates more of its citizens per capita than any other country in the world (Hartney, 2006). Embedded in these figures are a growing number of mentally ill individuals who find themselves in correctional settings rather than community-based mental health treatment facilities. Reasons for this dramatic increase in the number of mentally ill criminal offenders are rooted in a series of social and legislative policy initiatives including the deinstitutionalization movement of the 1950s, the underfunded community mental health movement of the 1960s, the war on drugs that began in the 1970s, the "get tough on crime" legislative actions of the 1980s, and the increased legislation regarding sexual predators of the 1990s and 2000s.

Collectively, these initiatives have produced a prison population that now contains a significant number of mentally troubled individuals. Current estimates are that 20% of incarcerated individuals have a serious mental illness (e.g., schizophrenia, major mood disorders; James & Glaze, 2006), and 30% to 60% have substance abuse problems (Karberg & James, 2005). When other, less debilitating mental illnesses (e.g., anxiety disorders) and personality disorders (e.g., antisocial personality disorder or borderline personality disorder) are considered, these percentages grow significantly. As a result, any discussion of persons with serious mental illness must also include a discussion of corrections, and no discussion of corrections is complete without considering mentally ill criminal offenders. Correctional facilities have become major mental health care settings despite their primary missions of punishment, deterrence, and protecting the public.

A number of professional organizations have demonstrated recognition of this population by developing standards of care specifically related to correctional settings. For example, the National Commission on Correctional Health Care is a nonprofit organization dedicated to the health care needs of inmates. This organization has developed general health/mental health accreditation standards for jail and prison facilities and in 2008 published a separate set of accreditation standards defining care for mentally ill offenders (National Commission on Correctional Health Care, 2008). Other professional organizations such as the American Correctional Association and the Joint Commission (formerly the Joint Commission on Accreditation of Healthcare Organizations) also have accreditation standards related to the treatment of mentally ill individuals in correctional settings (American Correctional Association, 2008; Joint Commission, 2009). Court systems using consent decrees and court monitors, advocacy groups (e.g., National Alliance on Mental Illness), state legislatures, and professional organizations (e.g., American Psychiatric Association) have also demonstrated a growing interest in how individuals with mental illness are managed and treated in correctional systems.

Despite growing awareness of overlaps between the criminal justice and mental health systems, academic settings have been slow to respond to the growing need for mental health professionals trained in the unique aspects of correctional practice. Historically, correctional mental health issues have not received sufficient coverage in academic circles, and correctional practice has not been viewed as a desirable career choice. We have attempted to bridge the gap between academic training and correctional practice with two previous edited volumes that defined the challenges, opportunities, and unique nature of correctional practice. In *Correctional Mental Health Handbook* (Fagan & Ax, 2003), our goal was to raise the awareness of academics and entry-level practitioners regarding the unique aspects of correctional mental health practice. Additionally, we wished to inform and motivate readers about the challenges and benefits of correctional practice. In *Corrections, Mental Health, and Social Policy: International Perspectives* (Ax & Fagan, 2007), we discussed the global nature of corrections by highlighting the common problems and issues faced by correctional mental health practitioners in North American and other Western countries. We also presented various innovative strategies for addressing these problems and issues to enable readers to benefit from the efforts and experiences of other practitioners grappling with similar problems. It was our hope that readers of both of these volumes would take away a greater understanding of correctional mental health issues, their interrelationship with various social and political initiatives, and their commonality across Western countries. As well, we wanted to provide a largely American readership with perspectives, policies, and practices from the correctional and criminal justice systems of other nations that might have value and relevance for domestic correctional mental health practice in the coming years.

In the current volume, *Correctional Mental Health: From Theory to Best Practice*, we add another dimension to those already discussed. In this volume we provide readers with a guide to treating criminal offenders—a biopsychosocial guide that is firmly grounded in theory, professional literature/research, and the clinical experience of our contributors and editors. It represents a confluence of the theoretical and the practical. This volume is intended primarily for academic use in psychology, sociology, and criminal justice classes related to correctional mental health, but it will also have broad appeal to correctional practitioners—both those at the entry level and those with considerable experience. Additionally, correctional administrators who wish to expand their understanding regarding mental health issues would benefit from the contents of this book.

At this point, a comment on terminology is in order. Best practice is not identical with empirically supported practice. Ideally, best practices involve treatments that have substantial empirical support, interventions that have been investigated according to accepted research protocols and validated with the populations for whom they are intended. However, correctional populations and environments are historically understudied. Furthermore, the issues that inmates present are so varied and complex, and their environments so different from the "free world," that many treatments developed and assessed in other settings may not readily generalize to prisons and jails and to their residents. Hence, when clinicians practicing in corrections are confronted with the need to provide interventions in the absence of clear guidance as to a best practice, an aspirational guideline in this regard is to seek empirical support for new and existing interventions on an ongoing basis. Best correctional practice involves clearly identifying problem areas; designing potential treatment and/or management options that are realistic, pragmatic, ethical, and based on current research and practice standards, where available; and assessing these options to determine their effectiveness, thereby helping to identify through empirical research those options that are most effective.

The overall goal of the book is to present students and other readers interested in correctional mental health with practical information about how to establish and manage a correctional mental health practice. The book is divided into four sections with individual chapters written by correctional practitioners and/or administrators with extensive correctional experience at the federal, state, or local level or by academics with considerable interest and research experience in correctional settings.

Section 1, consisting of Chapters 1 to 3, sets the stage for the remainder of the book. Chapter 1 places correctional practice within the larger criminal justice context and discusses the limitations of correctional practice when viewed in isolation. Chapter 2 highlights the unique aspects of clinical practice in correctional settings by pointing out the similarities and differences between a community-based clinical practice and a corrections-based clinical practice. Chapter 3 presents a correctional administrator's perspective on the delivery of mental health services within a correctional setting.

Section 2 (Chapters 4–8) describes the essential nature of correctional practice with individual chapters devoted to each of the following topics: assessment, treatment, multiculturalism, psychopharmacologic treatment agents, and interdisciplinary collaboration. An understanding of the benefits and limitations of each of these elements is essential to a successful correctional practice. Section 3 (Chapters 9–15) contains individual chapters focused on specific offender populations and how best to address each population within the jail and prison setting. Each of these chapters describes the general characteristics of the specific population, discusses how the population interfaces with the correctional environment, notes correctional barriers that interfere with effective treatment delivery, and presents treatment and/or management strategies that have proven to be best practices for each group of offenders. The fourth section consists of the final chapter, which takes a critical look at where correctional mental health practice currently is and where it needs to go to realize a best practices future.

Throughout the book, an emphasis is placed on defining important issues, challenges, opportunities, and special populations commonly found in correctional mental health settings and practice. Current best practices and other practical tips are featured in each chapter. Each chapter concludes with a glossary of key terms and discussion questions related to relevant topics presented in the chapter. These questions can be used in academic settings to prompt more in-depth discussion regarding important aspects of correctional practice and the social, political, and ethical forces that impact it. The book also contains an appendix of relevant references for the interested reader including a sampling of books, articles, journals, and websites containing useful information about correctional and/or mental health issues.

Through this volume, our goal is to create a stronger link between correctional mental health practitioners and the academic community. The correctional community has a number of significant needs, especially as regards its growing mental health population, and needs to make itself more accessible and amenable to research designed to address these needs. The academic community has the resources and research interest to help address some of these issues but must increase its willingness to address both the practical considerations inherent in conducting research in a correctional facility and the difficult challenges presented by this complex population. If the corrections-academic gap can be bridged, the results could lead to improved management and treatment strategies; a safer, more humane correctional environment; and more effective reentry and reintegration processes.

We thank our contributing authors for taking time out of their busy schedules to prepare thoughtful chapters that reflect professional literature, best practices, and personal experiences. Their insights are formed by many years of work and/or research in the correctional arena and should serve as a guide for readers interested in correctional mental health issues and/or careers, correctional mental health practitioners, and correctional administrators wishing to gain a greater understanding of the correctional mental health population.

Thomas J. Fagan, Ph.D.

Robert K. Ax, Ph.D.

References

American Correctional Association. (2008). *2008 standards supplement*. Alexandria, VA: Author.

Ax, R. K., & Fagan, T. J. (Eds.). (2007). *Corrections, mental health, and social policy: International perspectives*. Springfield, IL: Charles C Thomas.

Fagan, T. J., & Ax, R. K. (Eds.). (2003). *Correctional mental health handbook*. Thousand Oaks, CA: Sage.

Glaze, L. E., & Bonczar, T. P. (2009, December). *Probation and parole in the United States, 2008* (Bureau of Justice Statistics Special Report NCJ 228230). Washington, DC: U.S. Department of Justice, Office of Justice Programs.

Harrison, P. M., & Beck, A. J. (2006, May). *Prison and jail inmates at midyear 2005* (Bureau of Justice Statistics Special Report NCJ 213133). Washington, DC: U.S. Department of Justice, Office of Justice Programs.

Hartney, C. (2006, November). *U.S. rates of incarceration: A global perspective*. Retrieved June 3, 2009, from National Council on Crime and Delinquency: http://www.nccdcrc.org/nccd/pubs/2006nov_factsheet_incarceration.pdf

James, D. J., & Glaze, L. E. (2006, September). *Mental health problems of prison and jail inmates* (Bureau of Justice Statistics Special Report NCJ 213600). Washington, DC: U.S. Department of Justice, Office of Justice Programs.

The Joint Commission. (2009). *2009 comprehensive accreditation manual for hospitals (CAMH): The official handbook*. Oakbrook Terrace, IL: Author.

Karberg, J. C., & James, D. J. (2005, July). *Substance dependence, abuse, and treatment of jail inmates, 2002* (Bureau of Justice Statistics Special Report NCJ 209588). Washington, DC: U.S. Department of Justice, Office of Justice Programs.

National Commission on Correctional Health Care. (2008). *Standards for mental health services in correctional facilities*. Chicago, IL: Author.

Sabol, W. J., West, H. C., & Cooper, M. (2009, December). *Prisoners in 2008* (Bureau of Justice Statistics Special Report NCJ 228417). Washington, DC: U.S. Department of Justice, Office of Justice Programs.

SECTION I

Correctional Practice

Introduction and Foundation

CHAPTER 1

Criminal Justice and Mental Health Systems

The New Continuum of Care System

Thomas J. Fagan and Dyona Augustin

The Criminal Justice System: An Overview

The criminal justice system in the United States consists of a loose confederation of more than 50,000 federal, state, and local government and private agencies. These agencies can be divided into four broad categories based on their primary mission and include the police, the courts, jails and prisons, and community corrections.

The Police

The primary mission of the police is to maintain public order through the prevention, detection, and/or investigation of crime. When crimes are reported to the police or when police discover the commission of a crime, they are tasked with investigating, typically through witness statements and evidence gathering, to determine what happened and who is culpable. When suspects are identified, the police arrest them and bring them to the police station where the arrest is recorded through the booking process.

Special appreciation is extended to Dr. Susan Williams, Community Corrections Mental Health Clinical Supervisor, Virginia Department of Corrections, who provided the composite case history and responses to interview questions that were used in this chapter. Views expressed by Dr. Williams are hers alone and do not necessarily represent those of the authors or the Virginia Department of Corrections.

The Courts

Once a suspect is booked, a prosecutor decides whether to charge him or her with a crime. Suspects not charged are released. Those who are charged begin the court process, which is often divided into pretrial and trial stages. During the pretrial stage, suspects, now known as defendants, are formally notified of the charges being brought against them and informed of their constitutional rights. For misdemeanant charges, the defendant may participate in an immediate trial without a jury. This is called a summary trial. When felony charges are involved, an initial appearance before a judge is held during which the judge determines if there is probable cause (i.e., presence of sufficient evidence to believe that the arrest is justified) to hold the person for a preliminary hearing and to determine if bail (i.e., a monetary guarantee that the defendant will appear during the subsequent criminal proceedings) is appropriate.

Following the initial appearance, a preliminary hearing occurs before a judge to determine if sufficient evidence exists to believe that the defendant actually committed the crime for which he or she is charged and to inquire about the appropriateness of arrest and search procedures used by the police. If the judge finds that sufficient evidence exists, then the defendant's case goes before a grand jury in states that use the grand jury system. Grand juries may choose to indict the defendant or not based on evidence presented by the prosecutor. If the grand jury decides not to indict, then the prosecutor must drop all charges and release the defendant. In states without a grand jury system, formal charges are written in a document called an information, which summarizes the formal charges, the laws that have been violated, and the evidence that supports the charges.

Once a grand jury indictment or an information document is filed with the trial court, the defendant is scheduled for an arraignment, during which the formal charges are presented and the defendant is allowed to enter a plea. During the arraignment, about 95% of all felony defendants plead guilty through plea bargaining arrangements made between the prosecutor, the defense attorney, the defendant, and the judge in many jurisdictions. If the defendant chooses to plead not guilty, then a trial date is set. About 2% of criminal cases involve jury trials. The remaining 3% of criminal cases are decided in bench trials (i.e., those with a judge and no jury; Bohm & Haley, 2008).

Defendants found not guilty through the trial process are released. Defendants found guilty are sentenced by the judge. Depending on the nature of the crime, sentences may involve a range of options including fines, community service, probation, intermediate punishments (i.e., more restrictive than probation but not as restrictive as incarceration—for example, home confinement or boot camps), incarceration, or death. Judicial discretion in sentencing is restricted to some degree by factors such as constitutional prohibitions against cruel and unusual punishment, statutory provisions (e.g., sentencing guidelines and mandatory minimum sentences), and prevailing judicial philosophy, and is influenced by the personal beliefs of the judge and by information provided to the judge about the defendant in presentence reports or other historical documents about the defendant.

Jails and Prisons

When bail is denied or cannot be paid, defendants are frequently housed in jails pending and during the trial. Jails are also used to house individuals who have been found guilty at trial but have not yet been sentenced by the judge, sentenced offenders who have been given relatively short sentences (i.e., traditionally less than one year), and probation and/or parole violators pending a dispositional hearing. By their nature, jails tend to be operated primarily by local governments or their surrogates (e.g., private companies) and house an extremely diverse group of individuals (e.g., males and females, dangerous versus nonviolent, young versus old, mentally ill versus mentally healthy, etc.) during a high-stress period in the lives of these individuals (i.e., the trial and sentencing process). Although most jails in the United States are relatively small, housing fewer than 50 people, some, such as those in Los Angeles, Chicago, or New York, are quite large, housing in excess of 10,000 individuals (Minton & Sabol, 2009). Additionally, some smaller jurisdictions have banded together to form regional jails in an effort to improve efficiency and cost saving. Whereas some individuals may remain in a jail setting for an extended period of time due to lengthy pretrial challenges or trial proceedings, most jails have extremely high turnover rates, making programming and rehabilitative services, other than basic crisis intervention, difficult (Tartaro & Ruddell, 2006).

Prisons are used primarily to house individuals who have been sentenced to a period of incarceration ordinarily exceeding one year. Prisons are tasked with multiple, sometimes competing, missions including protecting the general public; deterring future crime; punishing convicted felons for their crime(s); and rehabilitating offenders through various educational, vocational, and counseling programs. Prisons are typically operated by state or federal governments or by private companies contracted to manage all prison operations or specific prison services (e.g., food services, medical services, or mental health services). At the end of 2008, approximately 6.6% of state offenders and 16.3% of all federal offenders were housed in prisons operated by private vendors (West & Sabol, 2009).

Although it is generally true that most jails are operated by local governments and most prisons are operated by state or federal governments, any discussion of jails and prisons would not be complete without mentioning the presence of other ways in which the United States confines individuals. Private prisons and jails have already been mentioned. However, the military has its own system for trying and confining felons, as do Native American tribal courts. At the end of 2007, these facilities housed 1,794 and 2,163 offenders, respectively (West & Sabol, 2008). Additionally, the U.S. Immigration and Customs Enforcement Agency (ICE) operates a number of facilities for the detention of illegal immigrants and housed approximately 9,700 detainees in 2007, with an additional 20,785 detainees housed in local jails (West & Sabol, 2008). Finally, the U.S. government currently operates or has operated a number of prisons in foreign countries (e.g., Guantánamo in Cuba, Bagram in Afghanistan, Abu Ghraib in Iraq, CIA shadow prisons, etc.), which house individuals accused of crimes against the United States (e.g., terrorism).

Community Corrections

Community corrections have been defined broadly as "a range of programs, supervision, and punishments aimed at the criminal offender . . . [that] involve any treatment or punishment outside of the institution of the prison or jail" (Whitehead, Pollock, & Braswell, 2003, p. 155). As such, community correctional programs might include federal, state, or local programs such as probation, day reporting centers, community service activities, electronic monitoring, nonprison residential treatment facilities, and community supervision—programs or activities that are imposed on convicted adults or juveniles either by a court in lieu of a prison sentence or by a parole board following release from prison. The main focus of community corrections is threefold. First, it is designed to divert accused individuals from the criminal justice system or jail prior to prosecution. Second, it can consist of sentences and programs that impose restrictions on convicted offenders while maintaining them in the community. Third, community corrections programs can be used as part of the parole process to smooth the transition of inmates from prison back to the community (McCarthy, McCarthy, & Leone, 2001). Table 1.1 presents a summary of the criminal justice process.

Table 1.1 The Criminal Justice Process

Police	Judicial Pretrial	Judicial Trial	Posttrial Dispositions	Reentry Following Incarceration
Investigate crime	Police consultation with local/state prosecutor or U.S. attorney	Summary trial for misdemeanants	Released, if found not guilty	Release following completion of full sentence—no parole supervision
Interview suspects and witnesses	Initial appearance	Criminal trial for felonies	Hospitalization, if found not guilty by reason of insanity (NGRI)	Parole with regular supervision
Gather evidence	Bail or jail		Fines or other minor penalties like community service	Parole with regular supervision plus other aftercare requirements (e.g., mental health treatment)
Divert to community mental health	Preliminary hearing		Probation with regular supervision	Participation in specialized reentry programs
Arrest potential suspect	Grand jury or creation of the information		Probation with supervision plus other conditions (e.g., home confinement, restitution, etc.)	Civil commitment for violent sexual predators
Book suspect	Arraignment		Boot camp	
	Competency and criminal responsibility assessments		Posttrial diversion for mentally ill individuals or substance abusers	
	Pretrial diversion programs for substance abusers or mentally ill individuals		Incarceration in prison	
			Death penalty	

Criminal Justice/Mental Health Interface

Although not intended to be a substitute for the mental health system, the criminal justice system has slowly become inexorably entwined with the mental health delivery system over the past 40 years. Four social policy initiatives seem to be responsible in large part for this occurrence.

The first social policy initiative involved the closing of mental health beds in state hospitals—a phenomenon commonly referred to as deinstitutionalization. This process began in the 1950s and 1960s with the development of antipsychotic medications. These medications allowed seriously mentally ill patients to be effectively treated and released back into their communities for follow-up treatment. This was an optimistic time for the mental health community. State mental hospitals were able to significantly reduce their bed capacity, and community mental health centers were being developed to treat these former hospital patients in their respective communities. Whereas the concept of community-based treatment remains commendable, local, state, and federal funding was never sufficient to meet demand. Consequently, the number of individuals with serious mental illness in many communities has grown dramatically, swelling the ranks of the homeless and putting a strain on available mental health, social service, and law enforcement agencies. Charged with various crimes including vagrancy, disorderly conduct, and theft, the homeless mentally ill population has slowly migrated into jail and prison populations. Current estimates suggest that between 16% and 64% of incarcerated individuals in the United States have serious mental health concerns (Ditton, 1999; James & Glaze, 2006). Some have proposed that correctional facilities have assumed the roles of state mental hospitals as the primary providers of mental health services to the seriously mentally ill and now house significantly more mentally ill individuals than do state hospitals (McDonald, Dyous, & Carlson, 2008). They support this claim with the fact that state mental hospitals now house fewer than 55,000 individuals, whereas prisons and jails now manage more than 775,000 individuals with serious mental illness (James & Glaze, 2006; Lamb, Weinberger, & Gross, 2004; Perez, Leifman, & Estrada, 2003). In fact, the Los Angeles County Jail now houses more such persons than any traditional inpatient facility in the United States (Montagne, 2008). Some refer to this process as transinstitutionalization (i.e., the shift from state mental hospitals to correctional facilities).

The second social policy initiative, which began in the 1980s, was America's declared war on drugs. This policy criminalized many aspects of substance abuse and involved law enforcement in the apprehension of substance abusers, the courts in the prosecution of substance abusers, correctional systems in the incarceration of substance abusers, and community corrections with the supervision of substance abusers. Current estimates suggest that approximately 21% of state prisoners, 68% of jail inmates, and 60% of federal prisoners are currently confined for substance-related criminal offenses (Harrison & Beck, 2003; Karberg & James, 2005; Mumola, 1999).

A third social policy initiative that slowly evolved throughout the 1980s and 1990s is the growing attention being paid to domestic violence and sexually predatory behaviors. Based on a series of high-profile cases, various laws have been passed requiring legal consequences for instances of domestic violence, stiffer prison penalties for sexual offenders, community notification and registration for sexual offenders following their release from prison, and civil commitment for the most dangerous sexual predators following incarceration. Collectively, these laws resulted in a doubling of the annual rate of incarceration for sexual offenses compared to other criminal offenses between 1980 and 1996 (Greenfeld, 1997) and placed correctional systems in the position of providing treatment for sexual offenders.

A fourth social policy initiative is the "get tough on crime" mentality that was popularized in the 1970s and 1980s and continues to influence legislative agendas today. This mentality has spawned a number of legislative actions including the abolition of parole, the introduction of determinant and mandatory minimum sentences, the creation of "three strikes" laws, and changes in standards defining competency at the time of trial and mental state at the time of the crime (sometimes referred to as criminal responsibility or the insanity defense). Cumulatively, these laws have impacted all criminal offenders, including those with mental illness, and have resulted in criminal offenders, especially violent offenders, serving longer sentences without benefit of early release through parole. Since the mentally ill are incarcerated more often for violent offenses than non–mentally ill offenders (James & Glaze, 2006; McNeil, Binder, & Robinson, 2005), they have been disproportionately punished by these laws. Additionally, the cumulative effect of these laws has been a burgeoning incarcerated population that now exceeds 2.3 million offenders (Harrison & Beck, 2006) and a population in excess of 5 million who either require parole or probation supervision (Glaze & Pella, 2005; Pew Center on the States, 2009).

This series of social policy initiatives has led to a growing overlap between the criminal justice and mental health systems, forcing each to make significant adjustments to the ways in which their services are delivered or their primary missions implemented. How have each of the four criminal justice components addressed their increased involvement with the mentally ill population? While the next section addresses this question in more detail, Munetz and Griffin (2006) provide a framework by which to conceptualize this overlap. Their model, called the Sequential Intercept Model, identifies points along the criminal justice continuum where specific interventions might be taken to address the needs of the mentally ill. These intercept points are loosely defined as follows: law enforcement and emergency services in the community; judicial hearings and court proceedings; jails or prisons; and reentry from jails or prisons, community corrections, and community support services. To the extent that the needs of mentally ill individuals can be successfully treated at early interception points, then the number of mentally ill individuals in jails and prisons can be significantly reduced.

While each of these intervention points will be discussed below, Munetz and Griffin (2006) make the overarching point that an accessible, comprehensive, well-integrated, and effective mental health delivery system using evidence-based practices would go a long way toward preventing individuals with serious and persistent mental illness from ever entering the criminal justice system. They describe this ideal mental health system as one in which competent clinicians; community support services such as active case management, vocational training, and safe, affordable housing; available medications; and crisis intervention services are both available and easily accessible.

Munetz and Griffin's (2006) overarching point is very reminiscent of the primary, secondary, tertiary prevention philosophy commonly espoused during the early years of community psychology (Edelstein & Michelson, 1986; Felner, Felner, & Silverman, 2006; Gordon, 1983). Primary prevention was conceived to target at-risk populations and develop intervention strategies to prevent the development of problems before they had a chance to develop (e.g., after-school recreation programs in inner cities, high school driver's education programs, Head Start Program). Secondary preventive strategies were designed to screen for early signs of trouble and then intervene while problems were small and manageable (e.g., vision and auditory screening in kindergarten, preschool readiness testing). Tertiary prevention was designed to involve immediate intervention when more serious problems were identified so that the problem did not become more engrained and widespread. Both Munetz and Griffin and the early community psychology movement place significant value on prompt, early intervention as a strategy for reducing bigger, more long-term problems.

Police and Emergency Services Diversion Initiatives

Police officers are very often the first responders when individuals with mental illness are in crisis. These critical encounters have not been without incident. For example, Munetz, Fitzgerald, and Woody (2006) reported that in 2003, 52 mentally ill individuals were killed by law enforcement officers, and seven officers were killed by mentally ill individuals during these encounters. Even without serious injury, these encounters may result in arrest and incarceration of the mentally ill individual when referral and treatment might have been a better course of action. Such encounters have prompted a number of police departments to implement various collaborative efforts with mental health agencies in recognition of their increasingly important role in the management of mentally ill individuals in crisis. At a minimum, many police departments have mandated that all of their officers receive training on basic mental health issues. Although the amount of training varies widely across departments, Hails and Borum (2003) reported 6.5 hours as the median of mental health training for new police recruits with 1 hour of subsequent in-service training.

Lamb, Weinberger, and DeCuir (2002) have described several more involved collaborative strategies used by police departments to deal with mentally ill individuals in crisis. Among the strategies that they describe are law enforcement's use of either mobile mental health crisis teams, consisting of mental health professionals, who can quickly be brought on scene to deal with the mental health crisis, or mental health workers who work for the police and can provide either on-site or telephone consultation to the officer during a mental health crisis. Other strategies include either the use of joint police/mental health teams to address crises in the field or the use of police officers who have received specialty training in mental health issues and crisis de-escalation techniques from mental health practitioners. Hails and Borum (2003) reported that about 32% of the 84 law enforcement agencies in their research sample had some specialized response for dealing with mental health–related calls. They also noted that 21% of their sample had a specialized unit within the department to deal with these calls, and 8% had access to a mental health mobile crisis response team.

One of the first collaborations between a police department and a mental health agency occurred in 1988 in Memphis, Tennessee. In this collaboration, the Memphis police department created a crisis intervention team (CIT) consisting of specially trained police officers who could be deployed to address the needs of mentally ill individuals in crisis (Cochran, Deane, & Borum, 2000). CITs have spread throughout the country since 1988 and are currently used by a number of police departments. Frequently, CIT programs are paired with a psychiatric emergency room that responds immediately to individuals transported by CIT officers. This process helps reduce the bureaucracy and long waits that frequently frustrate officers and lead them to choose arrest rather than hospitalization (Skeem & Bibeau, 2008).

In the typical CIT training program, officers receive 40 hours of basic training including an introduction to mental health, mental illness, and how to access the local mental health delivery system. Other topics covered during the training include verbal de-escalation techniques, basic communication skills, and realistic role-play scenarios to allow officers an opportunity to practice their newly acquired skills. Following completion of this basic training course, CIT members also receive 1 to 2 days of annual refresher training focused on legal and mental health updates; current research findings; negotiation and suicide prevention techniques; and Taser techniques, procedures, and qualifications (Teller, Munetz, Gil, & Ritter, 2006).

Several studies have examined the effectiveness of CITs. For example, Steadman, Deane, Borum, and Morrissey (2000) found that implementation of the Memphis CIT resulted in lower arrest rates for mentally ill individuals, more frequent referrals to treatment, and high utilization rates by patrol officers. Dupont and Cochran (2000) reported a reduction in officer injuries for mental health–related calls when CITs were utilized. CIT officers reported increased knowledge of mental illness, decreased stereotyping of mentally ill individuals, greater empathy for mentally ill individuals and their caregivers, and more patience when dealing with the mentally ill (Hanafi, Bahora, Demir, & Compton, 2008). However, Skeem and Bibeau (2008) noted that most studies discussing the effectiveness of CITs to date have lacked adequate comparison groups and scientific rigor. Consequently, they propose additional, more scientifically rigorous studies on the question of CITs' effectiveness.

Perhaps related to police efforts to respond to mentally ill individuals with CITs are community mental health agency efforts to more aggressively target the needs of mentally ill individuals through assertive community treatment (ACT). ACT began in the 1970s as a way of preventing the revolving door of repeat hospitalizations for seriously mentally ill individuals in state hospitals (Stein & Santos, 1998). It is a service delivery model dictated by individual need. It provides a combination of treatment, rehabilitation, and support services for as long as the individual needs these services. Services are provided in the community by an interdisciplinary team including psychiatry, nursing, addiction counseling, and vocational rehabilitation and are available to individuals 24 hours a day, 7 days a week. ACT's primary goals are to provide more effective community outreach and to help participants generalize skills to their real-world settings. ACT is intended for the most seriously mentally ill individuals who often have high rates of co-occurring substance abuse disorders; medical problems like hepatitis and HIV; and social risk factors like poverty, homelessness, and jail detentions. ACT has been slow to spread throughout the United States primarily because of its high per capita cost and rich staffing needs (Morrissey, Meyer, & Cuddeback, 2007). The effectiveness of ACT has been well documented in terms of reducing days in the hospital and in improving symptoms (Bond, Drake, Mueser, & Latimer, 2001; Ziguras & Stuart, 2000).

Because of ACT's effectiveness, some have suggested that this treatment model be expanded to include mentally ill individuals who have become involved in the criminal justice system (Morrisey et al., 2007). These programs have been referred to as FACT (i.e., forensic assertive community treatment) and differ from ACT in that participants all have criminal histories and in that their primary goal is preventing arrests and incarcerations. To date, these FACT programs vary greatly in terms of whom they accept (e.g., misdemeanants vs. felons, violent vs. nonviolent offenders, only cases pleading insanity), at what stage of the criminal justice process they are situated (i.e., preadjudication, postadjudication, reentry following incarceration), how faithfully they follow ACT's originally proposed resource and staffing guidelines, the degree of involvement by probation and parole officers and other criminal justice case management officials, and under whose auspices the program operates (i.e., the criminal justice or mental health system).

As a result, early research on FACT programs has been equivocal. However, there are a few studies that show some promise. For example, Lamberti et al. (2001) found FACT was able to reduce jail days, arrests, hospital days, and hospitalizations for a group of Rochester, New York, participants who remained in the program for one year. McCoy, Roberts, Hanrahan, Clay, and Luchins (2004) found similar results in a community-jail linkage program in Chicago. Whereas these results are promising, other researchers suggest that additional interventions may be needed that specifically target reductions in criminal behavior (Calsyn, Yonker, Lemming, Morse, & Klinkenberg, 2005; Morrisey et al., 2007). These researchers discussed several possible interventions that could be added to FACT to make it more responsive to criminal behavior. They specifically mentioned cognitive-behavioral interventions that have shown promise with criminal offenders, therapeutic communities, and programs for mentally ill/substance-abusing offenders as possibly being beneficial for mentally ill criminal offenders, but they suggested the need for more empirical research on these hybrid models.

As an alternative to ACT/FACT, some communities have developed a forensic intensive case management (FICM) concept as a way of managing mentally ill individuals who have become involved with the criminal justice system (Morrissey et al., 2007). FICM is a less costly approach in that it utilizes case managers rather than multidisciplinary teams of mental health professionals to manage individuals who are being diverted from jails. Additionally, FICM brokers mental health services rather than providing them directly to the individual (Schaedle, McGrew, Bond, & Epstein, 2002). FICM has been shown to be effective at keeping mentally ill individuals in the community for more days, reducing the number of days these individuals spend in jail, and increasing the amount of service used by these individuals when compared to a group of comparable individuals who did not receive FICM. Interestingly, symptom relief and quality of life did not seem to be impacted significantly for individuals who received FICM when compared to individuals who did not (Boner, Lattimore, Cowell, & Schlenger, 2004).

From this brief discussion, it is evident that the police have begun to recognize the importance of dealing with mentally ill individuals with increased sensitivity, and community mental health agencies have come to realize that having services available in the community does not always guarantee that seriously mentally ill individuals will utilize them without more aggressive outreach. Both the police and community mental health agencies have begun separately to address these issues through such innovative programs as CITs and ACT and collaboratively through programs like FACT and FICM.

Judicial Diversion Initiatives

Even when prearrest diversion programs are in place and community mental health resources are available, some individuals with serious mental health problems will still be arrested. Typically, these individuals are those with weaker social functioning, more substantial substance abuse problems, and prior histories of criminal behavior (Lattimore, Broner, Sherman, Frisman, & Shafer, 2003). For these individuals, a second intercept point in the criminal justice system can occur at the initial hearing. At the initial hearing, courts have the option of hiring a mental health professional to assess the presence of mental illness and to make treatment recommendations that might include diversion to available community mental health resources. Such diversion could be made a condition of probation. Courts might also develop collaborative relationships with community mental health agencies that could provide assessment services and provide linkages to community treatment resources. The ideal candidate for these types of diversion programs (i.e., those that occur at the initial hearing) might include nonviolent misdemeanants whose crime is the direct result of their mental illness (Munetz & Griffin, 2006). Connecticut's statewide diversion program is illustrative of a diversion program that occurs at the initial hearing (Fisman, Sturges, & Baranoski, 2001). The city of Miami also offers a similar type of diversion program (Perez et al., 2003).

For individuals who are not diverted during the initial hearing, another intercept point for possible diversion and treatment occurs when individuals come before a criminal court for trial. A number of jurisdictions have established special court programs designed to focus on the specific needs of individuals with substance abuse and/or mental health problems. These courts are referred to as drug courts and mental health courts, respectively. Both operate on the premise of therapeutic jurisprudence—a belief that the law can serve as an active social change agent and can exert a therapeutic (or nontherapeutic) influence through its various procedures, rulings, and dispositions, which can have a profound impact on individuals coming before the court (Wexler & Winick, 1996).

Drug Courts

The first drug court was established in 1988 and began hearing cases in 1989. It was located in Florida's 11th Judicial Circuit (Miami/Dade County) and represented itself as an innovative program that emphasized teamwork, cooperation, and collaboration among members of the treatment team led by the judge and consisting of defense and prosecution attorneys as well as other court and treatment personnel. Participants had no histories of violence, drug trafficking, or felony convictions and participated in a community-based program consisting of detoxification, stabilization, and aftercare generally lasting from 12 to 18 months. Treatment team members were cognizant of the nature of addiction, relapse, and recovery and were focused on helping program participants remain drug free and crime free. Throughout the program, participants, the treatment team, and the judge met regularly, with the judge monitoring the participant's progress, offering encouragement, and dispensing sanctions for failure to comply with program requirements. Participants who successfully completed the program were eligible to petition the court to have their arrest expunged from their record. Program participants who failed to comply with treatment requirements were expelled from the program and/or prosecuted in criminal court (Lurigio, 2008).

Using the Miami court as the prototype, the number of drug courts has grown considerably since 1988. As of September 2004, there were more than 1,200 drug court programs operating in all 50 states with an additional 500 being planned (General Accounting Office, 2005). In general, most drug courts contain the following points of commonality: (a) prompt identification of clients and immediate placement in treatment; (b) a nonadversarial court proceeding; (c) regular contact between participants and the judge; (d) intensive supervision that includes close monitoring and frequent drug testing; (e) treatment interventions that are delivered on a continuum of care, evidence based, comprehensive, and integrated for individuals with co-occurring psychiatric disorders; (f) contingencies of rewards and punishments that encourage adherence to treatment; (g) ongoing evaluations to monitor program implementation and measure the accomplishments of program objectives and goals; (h) close working relationship with a range of community service providers and public agencies; and (i) interdisciplinary educational opportunities to help program staff stay current with the latest advances in offender drug treatment and case management strategies (Drug Strategies, 1999).

Drug courts have yielded promising results. For example, some studies have reported that program participants were less likely to be rearrested and consequently had fewer rearrests than did control subjects (Deschenes, Turner, Greenwood, & Chiesa, 1996; Gottfredson & Exum, 2002). Other studies found that program participants had lower incarceration rates compared to nonparticipants (Finn & Newlyn, 1993) and were able to maintain lower rearrest rates even 2 years after program completion (Gottfredson, Najaka, & Kearley, 2003). In comparing drug courts with regular criminal courts, Lindquist, Krebs, and Lattimore (2006) noted that drug courts identified more behaviors that would result in sanctions, used sanctions that were more treatment oriented, and were more sensitive to individual participant needs. Drug courts were also found to save jurisdictions money as a result of lower recidivism rates (Carey, Finigan, Crumpton, & Waller, 2006). When samples of male and female drug court participants were compared, female participants were found to have higher levels of problem recognition with more co-occurring mental health problems and a greater desire for help (Webster et al., 2006). Despite these favorable results, research is still needed to determine what specific operational and/or treatment components are most responsible for positive changes in offenders and to investigate the effects of race, gender, age, type of substance abuse, and beliefs about addiction and recovery on drug court success.

Mental Health Courts

Using the drug court model, mental health courts are specialty courts that attempt to expand legal leverage and enhance treatment access to individuals with severe mental illness who become involved in the criminal justice system. Mental health courts began to proliferate in the mid-1990s and got their impetus from the growing realization that persons with mental illnesses were overrepresented in the criminal justice system (Ditton, 1999). As of January 2005, there were approximately 90 operational mental health courts located in 34 states with Ohio having the largest number (Redlich, Steadman, Monahan, Robbins, & Petrila, 2006).

Similar to drug courts, mental health courts have several points of commonality. These points include (a) maintenance of a separate docket for people with severe mental illness; (b) diverting people with mental illness from the criminal justice system into community mental health treatment; (c) a court mandate that participants engage in treatment typically including medication and adherence to other conditions (e.g., find and maintain employment, report for all treatment appointments) imposed by the court and treatment provider; (d) continuing supervision through judicial reviews and direct community supervision; and (e) utilization of praise, encouragement, and incentives (e.g., graduation ceremony following program completion, dropping of all criminal charges, vacating conviction) for adherence and imposition of sanctions for nonadherence with treatment requirements (Redlich, 2005).

Regarding community supervision for mental health court participants, Griffin, Steadman, and Petrila (2002) described three types of community supervision. In the first type, supervision is provided by community mental health treatment providers who report participant progress back to the court. In the second type, probation officers and court personnel are responsible for community supervision; and in the third type, both community treatment providers and court personnel are jointly responsible for monitoring participants. Typical sanctions imposed by mental health courts for nonadherence include admonishments from the judge, increased community supervision, more frequent status hearings by the court, and program expulsion and a return to jail. Some have criticized the use of jail as a sanction by mental health courts, stating that the idea of returning people to jail for treatment nonadherence appears counter to the therapeutic philosophy of mental health courts and seems to punish people for their mental illness. However, in one study most of the courts surveyed (i.e., 92%) reported using jail as a sanction for nonadherence (Redlich et al., 2006).

Preliminary results on the effectiveness of mental health courts suggest that mental health courts are moderately successful in obtaining access to treatment for at least some mentally ill individuals who find themselves before a court (Trupin & Richards, 2003), in reducing recidivism (Boothroyd, Calkins-Mercado, Poythress, Christy, & Petrila, 2005), and in reducing the severity of rearrests when they do occur (Moore & Hiday, 2006). Despite these promising results, mental health courts do not currently have the capacity, with their relatively small caseloads, to serve all, or even a reasonable percentage, of those mentally ill individuals coming before the courts.

Two additional issues are worth mentioning regarding mental health courts. First, the term *mental health court* implies a single entity with a clearly defined mission. This is not the case. There is no single, coherent mental health court model. Different courts use different diagnostic criteria to determine admission into the program.

Some courts only accept misdemeanants into the program, whereas others allowed defendants charged with felonies. A small number of programs even accept defendants charged with violent felonies (Erikson, Campbell, & Lamberti, 2006). Second, about one quarter of all mental health courts could more accurately be described as co-occurring mental health–substance abuse courts in that participants need both types of problems to be admitted into the program (Redlich et al., 2006). These dual-diagnosis programs clearly recognize the increased risk of criminal behavior typical of this population (Peters & Hill, 1993). Given these two points, further research is clearly needed to look at similarities and differences across these courts, assess the efficacy of different court approaches, and continue to identify strengths and potential areas of concern.

Jail and Prison Initiatives

For mentally ill individuals who are not diverted prior to arrest or through court diversion programs, a third intercept point at which these individuals can receive therapeutic intervention within the criminal justice system is during their incarceration. As noted earlier in this chapter, jails are difficult places to offer significant mental health services other than crisis intervention because individuals are moving back and forth to court and tend to be somewhat transient. However, prisons offer an environment where the offender will be located for an extended period of time and where medical, mental health, and other rehabilitative services are available.

Whereas the remainder of this book is dedicated to the specific mental health services offered in prisons and jails, to discussions of specific diagnostic groups served by correctional mental health programs, and to issues raised by offering mental health services in jails and prisons, this section is reserved for a brief discussion of the broader issues with which correctional mental health concerns itself. To varying extents, correctional mental health is concerned with at least four distinct but overlapping domains: mental health services, rehabilitation, redemption, and staff consultation and training on mental health issues.

Mental health services are those that are provided to offenders who self-report or are assessed as having a definable disorder of thinking or behavior according to an accepted psychiatric taxonomy, such as the *Diagnostic and Statistical Manual of Mental Disorders–Fourth Edition, Text Revision* (*DSM-IV-TR*; American Psychiatric Association, 2000). Theoretically, the diagnosis and treatment of mental disorders among prison inmates translates to other settings in a fairly straightforward manner. Bipolar disorder and schizophrenia, for example, have the same diagnostic criteria in the community or a state psychiatric facility. A "best practices" standard would dictate that prisoners experiencing these disorders receive the same type and quality of treatment as their counterparts in the community or in hospitals, although this is not always true in practice. Mental health services are often provided in the community by individuals with professional degrees and licenses: psychologists, psychiatrists, clinical social workers, and others. However, in correctional settings these services are sometimes provided by paraprofessionals, such as drug treatment specialists, correctional counselors, volunteers, and even inmate peer counselors.

With some notable exceptions (for example, substance abuse, paraphilias, kleptomania), these disorders bear no direct or formal relationship to criminal behavior. Increasingly, however, they contribute indirectly to incarceration. More than anything, the criminalization of some aspects of mental illness (as mentioned earlier in this chapter) has compelled attention to this specific set of concerns. As state mental hospitals have downsized or closed, and community services have proved inadequate to their needs, increasing numbers of individuals with serious and persistent mental illness have been incarcerated. In fact, as noted earlier, the Los Angeles County Jail now houses more such persons than any traditional inpatient facility in the United States (Montagne, 2008).

Treatment for these disorders constitutes an end in itself, as a legally and ethically mandated obligation of the American criminal justice system, but such treatment may also be a necessary step toward the goal of rehabilitation. A person with schizophrenia, for example, whose behavior is stabilized in prison, may be better able to avoid the kinds of difficulties (often related to illegal drug use or other relatively minor offenses) that resulted in the original incarceration.

Rehabilitation is one of the four traditional missions of incarceration (along with punishment, incapacitation, and deterrence). Although many individuals in prison have no diagnosable mental disorder, all prisoners have broken the law and are, therefore, by definition in need of rehabilitation. However, mental health expertise is crucial to rehabilitation because of its fundamentally behavioral nature. To be considered rehabilitated in the eyes of society, an individual must behave in a law-abiding manner. Basically, that means developing and using appropriate employment, social, leisure, and self-care skills and inhibiting behaviors that are illegal or harmful to the individual or others. Helping individuals who have broken the law to develop self-control skills or, generally speaking, impulse control, is critical to rehabilitation. To remain at liberty, often as a condition of parole or probation, individuals must not behave aggressively, use illegal drugs, or exploit (e.g., steal from) others for personal gain.

Rehabilitation efforts could include individualized or small group approaches or large-scale interventions such as "de-ganging" (see Conley & Zobel, 2007, for a discussion of these approaches), which might take place in the prison or the community. Correctional mental health professionals are likely to be involved in rehabilitation through drug treatment or teaching a range of behavioral skills, such as anger management. However, teachers, vocational instructors, and the clergy also contribute to correctional rehabilitation efforts. Historically, incarceration itself was considered rehabilitative. Early penitentiaries were designed to isolate prisoners. It was thought that this, in conjunction with religious instruction, would promote repentance and a more prosocial orientation.

The effectiveness of rehabilitative treatments provided in correctional settings is best measured by the behavior of offenders after their release. Accordingly, fundamental to the concept of rehabilitation is the growing field of risk assessment, the use of a range of instruments such as the Violence Risk Appraisal Guide (see Chapter 4 for a review of violence risk and other assessment issues) to assess the likelihood that an individual, if released to the community, or diverted from incarceration, will reoffend. Theoretically, this provides some level of protection against releasing those inmates most likely to reoffend.

When rehabilitation efforts fail, the result may be catastrophic, if an ex-inmate reoffends violently, perhaps seriously injuring or killing another person. Historically, rehabilitation programs have been no more than moderately successful, with many ex-offenders returning to prison within a few years. Consequently, correctional rehabilitation has been quite controversial, and failures have led to scholarly and public calls for the abandonment of the prison system's rehabilitation mission in favor of longer periods of incarceration. When criminal defendants are sentenced to life imprisonment without the possibility of parole or to death, the court is implicitly acknowledging that rehabilitation is either unfeasible or irrelevant for these persons.

A third entity must be acknowledged at a minimum—redemption. Redemption is spiritual and ultimately personal in nature and is often, though not always, thought of in terms of the tenets of a formal religion and its belief system. However, the quest for redemption may also help an individual achieve control over some aspect of his or her own life. Indeed, religion and the early penitentiary were closely linked. (See Ax, 2007, for a history of the penitentiary system in the United States and elsewhere.) The most obvious example of a way in which religion and redemption are intertwined with personal change and contemporary concepts of rehabilitation is addictive behavior. Twelve-step programs based on the Alcoholics Anonymous (AA) model, which explicitly relies on a "higher power," have been increasingly used within the criminal justice system, both in the community and in prisons and jails, over the past several years, and have often become the responsibility of mental health departments within correctional facilities. As Peters and Matthews (2003) noted, legal decisions have characterized AA and Narcotics Anonymous (NA) as religion-based treatment. These programs are often based in prison mental health departments, with mental health professionals providing some level of oversight.

Faith-based prison programs are now supported in many correctional systems. An impetus for the recent growth of such programs was the establishment of the Office of Faith-Based and Community Initiatives by the George W. Bush administration and continued by the Obama administration as the Office of Faith-Based and Neighborhood Partnerships. Through this agency, funding is provided to support a range of prison and community initiatives. Faith-based and secular mental health services may prove complementary. Consistent with this is the fact that studies of faith-based correctional programs have begun to find their way into the correctional psychology literature. Daggett, Camp, Kwon, Rosenmerkel, and Klein-Saffran (2008) conducted an evaluation of completion rates for the Life Connections Program, which is based in several federal prisons. The study was published in the journal *Criminal Justice and Behavior*.

A fourth concern for correctional mental health involves the ongoing need to consult with and train all correctional workers on various mental health issues. For example, correctional mental health professionals are often asked to train correctional staff on issues related to suicide prevention and intervention, and this training requirement is frequently noted in various correctional accreditation standards (e.g., the National Commission on Correctional Health Care's [NCCHC's] *Standards for Mental Health Services in Correctional Facilities*, 2008). Through this training, correctional mental health providers are able to educate all staff regarding identification and referral procedures for suicidal inmates and may also be able to discuss various intervention strategies with which correctional staff may become involved. Mental health staff may also be a part of basic training for new employees and through that process educate staff about general signs and symptoms of mental illness, sensitize staff about mental health issues, and remove the stigma often associated with mental illness (Harowski, 2003). Additionally, mental health professionals may serve as institutional consultants and problem solvers. In this capacity, correctional mental health practitioners may provide input into classification decisions, case management decisions, disciplinary hearings, work/housing assignments, staff screening and selection, program evaluation, and assessments of institutional climate (Dvoskin, Spiers, & Pitt, 2003).

Community Corrections Initiatives

Another point of interception in the criminal justice system where mentally ill individuals may receive mental health services is postconviction and/or postincarceration. As was noted earlier, community corrections is that part of the criminal justice system that provides sanctions and services that maintain public safety while also keeping the criminal offender within the community. Its main focus is to divert accused individuals from the criminal justice system or jail prior to prosecution, impose restrictions on convicted offenders while maintaining them in the community postconviction on probation, or smooth the transition of inmates from prison back to the community (McCarthy et al., 2001). Since prearrest and judicial diversion programs have already been discussed, this section will focus primarily on the programs aimed at facilitating the reentry of criminal offenders, especially those with mental illness, following a period of incarceration (see Text Box 1.1 for a sample case history of an offender receiving community corrections services).

TEXT BOX 1.1
COMPOSITE CASE STUDY

Identifying Information

Mr. H is a 5'4," 130 lbs, 38-year-old Hispanic male. He was born in the United States and is fluent in English, but he also speaks Spanish. He was convicted of animate object penetration and sentenced to 15 years with 10 years suspended and indefinite supervised probation. He served 18 months of his sentence in a local jail and the remaining 3½ years in the Department of Corrections (DOC). Mr. H had three previous convictions for public intoxication, two convictions for trespassing, and one conviction for defrauding an innkeeper.

Mental Health History

Mr. H began receiving special educational services in the third grade when he was diagnosed with learning disabilities. By age 16, he was also receiving psychological services when he reported "hearing voices and seeing things that weren't there." He was first hospitalized at age 22 and has had at least 10 hospitalizations since that time. Over the course of his hospitalizations, he has been prescribed various antipsychotic medications including Navane, Haldol, Thorazine, and Prolixin.

During his incarceration, he was sent to the DOC psychiatric facility one time for stabilization. At that time, he was responding to internal stimuli, smearing feces, refusing to bathe, not attending to his grooming, and not eating his food because he believed it was poisoned. He was prescribed Haldol, which remains his current medication.

Mr. H's only substance abuse history involved alcohol. He began drinking at age 16 and, when not incarcerated or hospitalized, has continued to drink. It has been reported that he drinks approximately 80 ounces of beer per day when in the community.

Diagnosis

Mr. H has been diagnosed with schizophrenia (disorganized type), alcohol abuse, and borderline intellectual functioning.

(Continued)

(Continued)

Psychosocial Functioning

Since his first hospitalization, Mr. H has drifted between his mother's home, adult group homes, friends' houses, and periods of homelessness. Typically, he would get hospitalized, stabilized on medication, and discharged to his home. Once home, he would take his medication and remain stable for a while until he believed he no longer needed it. Then he would stop taking it, get into minor trouble, go to jail or the hospital, and start the cycle all over again.

His current offense represents his only felony and only sex offense conviction. At the time of the offense, he had not been taking his medication for approximately 6 months and was not seeing his case manager at the community service board (CSB). He went into a convenience store to buy a beer. He reported that he saw a spider on the pants of the 18-year-old, female clerk, who was bending over some boxes at the time. He stated that he brushed the spider off of the clerk's pants, and the clerk communicated to him "through her eyes" that she wanted him to touch her and check for webs. He then put his hand in her pants and fondled and assaulted her until a customer intervened. The clerk confirmed that he was speaking about spiders and other incoherent topics during the assault.

Community Corrections Plan of Supervision

Due to the sexual nature of the offense, Mr. H was evaluated to determine if he should be considered to be a sexually violent predator. However, he was determined to be a low risk, was not considered to be a sexually violent predator, and was discharged to the community. As a mentally ill sex offender, Mr. H was placed on intensive supervision status. He was required to receive mental health services, including medication and sex offender services, as recommended by his psychiatrist. The probation officer communicated and coordinated service delivery with the regional mental health clinician, the CSB case manager, and the sex offender treatment provider. As a sex offender, housing was a problem. His mother was deceased, and he could not stay at the Salvation Army homeless shelter because of his crime. The district paid for a motel room while he applied for benefits. Once received, the district continued to pay for his motel until an alternative housing arrangement was found.

Community reentry and reintegration is an essential criminal justice service for three reasons. First, treatment and rehabilitation, especially in maximum-security facilities, is sometimes difficult to accomplish, suggesting that successful treatment and rehabilitation may have to occur postrelease in the offender's community, utilizing such community supports as mental health centers, schools and vocational training centers, social services, and family members (Whitehead et al., 2003). Second, community corrections programs are more cost-effective than maintaining an offender in a high-security correctional facility, especially for nonviolent offenders (Whitehead et al., 2003). Third, roughly 93% of criminal offenders will eventually be released from prison after an extended period of incarceration (Petersilia, 2003; Travis & Visher, 2005). According to most estimates, nearly 600,000 prisoners are released from U.S. prisons every year or about 1,600 inmates per day (Austin, 2001; Freudenberg, 2001; Human Rights Watch, 2003; Mellow & Dickinson, 2006; Petersilia, 2003; Travis & Petersilia, 2001; Visher & Travis, 2003; Wilkinson, Rhine, & Henderson-Hurley, 2005). Glaze (2003) estimated that the number of parolees with significant mental health problems was approximately 37,650 at the end of 2002.

The process of transitioning from the prison to the community is a critical time for all offenders (Knollenberg & Martin, 2008), but especially for those with mental illness. Failure to make a successful transition frequently results in a return to prison. The fact that recidivism rates for prisoners are currently about 30% at 6 months postrelease (Knollenberg & Martin, 2008) and jump to 44% percent within 1 year and to nearly 68% within 3 years of release (Petersilia, 2003) suggests that an increased focus on community corrections programs is justified.

Prisoners face several specific challenges when transitioning back into the community. One of the most common is finding suitable housing because most offenders leave prison with limited financial resources and family support (Austin, 2001; Human Rights Watch, 2003; Osher, Steadman, & Barr, 2003; Roman, 2004; Visher & Travis, 2003). In addition, the law currently requires that public housing agencies deny certain offenders housing (e.g., sex offenders and drug offenders; Petersilia, 2003). Austin (2001) reported that only a minority of states currently provide ex-prisoners with housing assistance.

A second challenge that ex-prisoners face is finding a job (Human Rights Watch, 2003; Nelson & Trone, 2000; Petersilia, 2003; Travis & Petersilia, 2001; Visher & Travis, 2003). Researchers have documented both a positive relationship between lower recidivism rates and job stability and extremely low employment rates for ex-offenders (Petersilia, 2003; Travis & Petersilia, 2001). This is due to a number of factors including the stigma associated with being incarcerated, a lack of prior legitimate work experience, a lack of social networks that can help facilitate getting a job, employers' wariness at hiring ex-prisoners (Wilkinson, 2005), and the restrictions placed on offenders in regards to certain fields (e.g., education, nursing, child care; Petersilia, 2003; Travis & Petersilia, 2001).

A third challenge faced by ex-prisoners is that many, if not all, have trouble getting public assistance such as welfare or food stamps (Human Rights Watch, 2003; Petersilia, 2003). Being eligible to receive public assistance is important in terms of helping released offenders successfully reintegrate into the community. However, public assistance for ex-prisoners has been reduced/limited dramatically (Petersilia, 2003; Roman, 2004), and in some states, public assistance is permanently denied to prisoners convicted of certain offenses (e.g., a drug felony; Petersilia, 2003). Even offenders who received public assistance prior to their incarceration have their benefits temporarily suspended once they are incarcerated or found to be in violation of their probation. Once released, these offenders often face significant delays in getting their public assistance reinstated after release from prison (Human Rights Watch, 2003).

Ex-offenders also face the challenge of reconnecting with their families and gaining forms of legal identification (Nelson & Trone, 2000; Petersilia, 2003; Roman, 2004; Visher & Travis, 2003; Wilkinson et al., 2005). For instance, many ex-prisoners leave prison without having any form of legal identification (e.g., a passport, a social security card, a driver's license); this can in turn affect their ability to find employment (Nelson & Trone, 2000). Many offenders will also face some difficulties when it comes to reconnecting/reuniting with their family members (Human Rights Watch, 2003; Nelson & Trone, 2000; Travis & Petersilia, 2001; Visher & Travis, 2003).

TEXT BOX 1.2
INTERVIEW WITH SUSAN WILLIAMS, PH.D.
COMMUNITY CORRECTIONS MENTAL HEALTH
CLINICAL SUPERVISOR
VIRGINIA DEPARTMENT OF CORRECTIONS

1. What is the primary role of a community corrections psychologist?

Our role in community corrections is a little different than that of psychologists in correctional institutions who provide services like intakes, individual therapy, group therapy, or evaluations. Although community corrections psychologists do some therapy, we are mainly facilitators. We ease the transition from institution to community. We are often the ones getting the discharge medications straightened out because the offender left his much-needed medication on the transportation bus or because the offender who was receiving injectable medication in prison left the institution with no prescription for medication. Often there is a waiting list at the community services board (CSB), so we will see an offender prior to release and then again after release to help ensure stability while they wait for their first appointment with the CSB.

We speak "institution," "probation," and "mental health" languages, so we are able to cross traditional boundaries between mental health and correctional agencies. For example, if a probation officer is trying to get someone hospitalized, he might call the hospital's crisis line and say that someone is "acting crazy or schizo." This information may not be helpful to the hospital in determining if the person meets admission criteria. However, if the probation officer calls the community corrections psychologist, we can evaluate the person and make the same call to the hospital's crisis line and say, "This person has a diagnosis of paranoid schizophrenia. He has been receiving Haldol for the past 15 years. He was discharged from the institution 1 month ago and it appears that he has not been adherent with his medications. He appears to be responding to internal stimuli and arguing with the voices. He is delusional and believes that he must go save the president from Osama Bin Laden. He has threatened to cut anyone who gets in his way. He has a history of malicious wounding and we believe that he is a danger to others due to his mental illness and needs to be involuntarily hospitalized." This approach facilitates hospital admission. It also decreases the amount of probation violations and parole revocations due to mental health problems. Prior to having community corrections clinicians, probation officers didn't really know what to do with mentally ill offenders who were nonadherent with medications. Out of a concern for public safety, they would often violate their probation and send them back to jail where we know that mental health care is not always good. Now, they can call the clinician and the clinician can talk to the person and help the person become more medication adherent or facilitate changes in medication. The clinicians can also help the probation officer know when something is less serious or when something is more serious (e.g., missing a dose of Prozac isn't the same as missing a Haldol injection).

2. What are some of the biggest challenges that you face in your job?

The biggest challenge by far is securing mental health services for reentering offenders. The community mental health system is overwhelmed. They just don't have the resources to see everyone as much as they need to be seen. That includes daily structured activities, intensive case management, psychiatric appointments, etc. For those with some form of benefits (Medicaid, SSI, SSDI, or Veteran's), there are other providers that can help bridge the gap. But for those without benefits, it is very difficult to get them the care they need.

Additionally, the homeless population is difficult. Housing shortages, lack of alternative living facilities, and a general social attitude of "housing for these individuals can be anywhere, but not in my backyard" mentality, all contribute to the difficulty we face in placing some of these offenders. They do not have the same resources as similar clientele coming from a hospital might have. If they have committed a sex offense, it's even more difficult to find adequate housing.

3. What have you found are some of the biggest challenges for mentally ill offenders during the reentry process?

a. Housing—without a fixed address, CSB appointments are difficult to make and oftentimes the CSB will not take a walk-in, if the person is homeless.

b. Mental health care—as previously described.

c. Lack of a support system—many of these individuals have burned bridges with family members, have been incarcerated a long time, and do not have pleasant personalities, especially when not taking medications.

d. Difficulty navigating the system. Oftentimes, the offender would be eligible for benefits, but the application process can be time-consuming and is often not started prior to discharge. They do not have the mental capacity to understand and navigate through the various systems and sometimes get sent from one office to another with a boatload of paperwork to complete. We now have a memorandum of understanding with the Social Security Administration that allows offenders to apply for benefits prior to release so that they will have minimal paperwork and wait time after discharge.

Although all prisoners face challenges in transitioning back to the community, the challenges described above are especially daunting for offenders with mental health and substance abuse problems (Draine & Herman, 2007; Thompson, Reuland, & Souweine, 2003).

According to Osher et al. (2003), housing supports are especially important for mentally ill offenders because the stability of these individuals represents both a clinical and a public safety concern. Mentally ill offenders are also faced with the added challenge of ensuring continuity in their mental health care throughout the transition process.

One issue that is especially pertinent to mentally ill offenders is a lack of medication continuity once they are released from prison. Many mentally ill offenders, who have been taking medication while in prison, are released from prison with as little as one week's supply of medication (Human Rights Watch, 2003). Not surprisingly, this supply might not last until the offender can schedule an appointment with a community-based practitioner who can renew the prescription. Osher et al. (2003) state that medication adherence is an integral part of the reintegration process and that a plan must be put in place to ensure that inmates who are going to be released will have a continuous supply of their medication. In fact, without an ongoing plan for continued medication and clinical supervision, many inmates stop taking their medication completely.

In addition to their medication needs, mentally ill offenders will also need to be connected with community mental health services once they are released from prison. In fact, without the appropriate mental health treatment, mentally ill offenders have difficulty functioning satisfactorily (Nelson & Trone, 2000) and are more likely to recidivate (Couturier, Maue, & McVey, 2005; Human Rights Watch, 2003; Munetz & Griffin, 2006), with rates in excess of 70% (Ventura, Cassel, Jacoby, & Huang, 1998) in some jurisdictions. Interestingly, in a national survey, more than a third of correctional facilities reported offering no transitional aid to mentally ill offenders as they reenter the community (Beck & Maruschak, 2001). Among those correctional facilities that did offer assistance (i.e., about 66% nationwide), the percentage of prisoners who really did receive transitional care and the quality of that care was unknown (Human Rights Watch, 2003). In brief, whereas many offenders suffer from mental health problems, the majority do not receive adequate help with community reentry and reintegration. However, the *Brad H. v. City of New York* case (2000; see Text Box 1.3) has prompted a number of correctional systems nationwide to reassess their efforts to assist mentally ill inmates with their community reentry. Researchers have also proposed various models that they believe will lead to more effective community reentry.

TEXT BOX 1.3
THE CASE OF *BRAD H. V. CITY OF NEW YORK*

In August 1999, a group of mentally ill inmates filed a class-action lawsuit against the city of New York. In the lawsuit they alleged that they received inadequate discharge planning from the city's jail. They charged that they were released from jail between the hours of 2 a.m. and 6 a.m. with a $3.00 Metrocard and $1.50 in cash. The plaintiffs were not provided with any follow-up mental health services, government benefits assistance, housing referrals, other services, or help in planning their reentry into the community.

In January 2003, the parties settled the case with an agreement that the city would provide mentally ill offenders who had received mental health treatment or had taken medication for a mental health condition while in jail with discharge planning. The court found that without adequate discharge planning, class members would be harmed by a return to the cycle of mental decompensation, likely harm to themselves and/or others through substance abuse, mental and physical deterioration, indigence, crime, rearrest, and reincarceration. The settlement entitled class members to a discharge summary that explains the offender's mental health diagnosis, what services are needed, and the plan that is being set up while the offender is still in jail to make sure that the individual can get those services when he or she is released. Class members were also entitled to have family members, social workers, or case managers involved in the discharge planning process.

This lawsuit led correctional facilities nationwide to assess what, if anything, they were doing to help prepare inmates for release and served as an impetus for more thoughtful discharge planning from correctional facilities.

For example, Osher et al. (2003) proposed the APIC model to facilitate an inmate's community reentry. Their acronym represents the following four steps: (a) **A**—assess the inmate's clinical and social needs and public safety risks; (b) **P**—plan for the treatment and services required to address the inmate's needs; (c) **I**—identify required community and correctional programs responsible for postrelease services; and (d) **C**—coordinate the transition plan to ensure implementation and avoid gaps in care with community-based services. Another suggestion proposed by this model is that incentives be given to community providers so that they can do more "in reach" to correctional facilities, thus starting the transitional process prior to the inmate's release. Empirical research on this model has yet to determine which elements, if any, are most predictive of improved outcomes (Osher et al., 2003).

Lurigio, Rollins, and Fallon (2004) suggested the following strategies for mentally ill offenders being placed on parole. First, they stressed the importance of a comprehensive discharge plan documenting the inmate's need for community-based treatment, employment, housing, and financial and social support. Second, they emphasized the importance of effective postrelease services that are both intensive and ongoing. Third, they indicated the importance of parole officers' efforts to balance the monitoring and control of the offender in the interest of public safety with the offender's need for social and rehabilitative services in the community. They suggested that parole supervision can be an excellent tool for ensuring adherence to medication and other treatment conditions with the added leverage of a return to prison for nonadherence. Fourth, they advocated for active case management strategies with mentally ill offenders. Case management techniques proposed included active goal setting with the offender, assistance in establishing and maintaining income-supporting benefits, triaging the offender's service needs and serving as a broker between the parole officer and treatment providers, and advocating on behalf of the inmate. In short, active case management is seen as a formal support system for the offender where other more informal systems have failed the offender. Fifth, they proposed the use of a team approach consisting of the parole officer, case manager, and treatment provider—all collaborating on decisions regarding the selection, supervision level, treatment needs, and continuity of care issues for mentally ill offenders nearing release from prison, as well as sanctions to impose on mentally ill offenders who do not comply with parole and treatment requirements. Sixth, they suggested the liberal use of memorandums of understanding (MOUs) and frequent cross-training between community mental health agencies, correctional system staff, and parole officers. The ultimate goal of MOUs is to create lasting connections between mental health and correctional systems that will lead to more coordinated and continued care for mentally ill offenders as they reenter the community.

A number of criminal justice systems have begun to develop reentry programs that address many of the issues proposed by Lurigio et al. (2004). For example, the Ohio Department of Rehabilitation and Correction, along with the Richland County Common Pleas Court, uses a reentry court to help offenders transition back into the community. After an initial needs assessment is compiled, the offender periodically meets with prison staff and a case manager to make sure that the court orders and the offender's needs are being met; then the offender is enrolled in programs consistent with his or her reentry plan (Wilkinson, 2005).

The Illinois Department of Corrections created the Prisoner Aftercare Program (PAP) to serve the needs of a small number of the most seriously mentally ill offenders transitioning back into the community. The PAP uses the assertive community treatment (ACT) approach discussed earlier in this chapter. Once a referral is received from the prison, the PAP team visits the offender while he or she is still in prison to begin the discharge planning process. Once released, the offender receives intensive and comprehensive supportive services aimed at avoiding reincarceration, homelessness, and hospitalization. Offender engagement in community mental health treatment begins several weeks before the offender is released from prison with weekly meeting between the PAP team and the offender. On the day of release, the PAP team meets the offender at the front door of the prison and escorts the offender to safe housing; arranges for benefits to begin; and assists the offender in keeping treatment, parole, and other social service appointments. Even if the offender is rearrested, the PAP team continues to maintain contact, visiting the offender in prison and preparing for the offender's next release (Lurigio et al., 2004).

Pennsylvania's Departments of Corrections and Mental Health and Mental Retardation collaboratively developed a series of policies and programs to assist mentally ill offenders with their reentry efforts. For example, these agencies developed a continuity of care policy that mandates that an interdisciplinary correctional mental health treatment team meet with the offender 1 year prior to discharge and again 6 months prior to discharge to coordinate continuity of care planning. During these meetings, release of information forms are signed by the inmate so that community mental health agencies can be contacted and case information shared, entitlement applications are completed so that the offender can receive benefits immediately following discharge, and medication needs are assessed. Pennsylvania also developed a community orientation and reintegration program that is arranged as a two-stage program. Stage 1, which occurs while the inmate is still in prison, focuses on preparing the inmate for reentry by educating the inmate about parole responsibilities, employment preparation, personal finances, mental health and substance abuse treatment needs, housing, family and parenting issues, and so forth. Stage 2 occurs in a community corrections center and serves as a gradual transition for the offender back into the community. Lastly, Pennsylvania's Department of Corrections (DOC) entered into a collaborative partnership with county administrators in the Philadelphia and Pittsburgh areas (areas that receive about half of all released offenders). Through this partnership, the DOC provides the community mental health agency with rosters of mentally ill inmates who will be released in their areas during the next 12 months and allows representatives from these mental health agencies to visit the prison and review inmate records, discuss cases with correctional mental health providers, and begin "in-reach" efforts with these offenders (Couturier et al., 2005). Massachusetts has developed a similar "in-reach" program for its mentally ill offenders that allows community mental health providers to reach into the correctional facility and establish therapeutic contacts with offenders 3 months prior to their release and then to follow them for 3 months after release to assist in making a successful community transition (Munetz & Griffin, 2006).

The tragedy of many of these programs is that they target only a fraction of those inmates in need. However, they do represent a beginning and hold the promise of expansion, if success can be demonstrated. Although these programs are commendable and represent first steps in improving the prison to community reentry process, more collaborative efforts will be required to facilitate a more seamless reentry and ensure a successful community reintegration.

Summary and Conclusions

A few general summary statements seem appropriate from the topics presented in this chapter. First, the client population under discussion is a difficult population. Their problems are significant and complex. In addition to their mental health concerns, many have co-occurring substance abuse disorders; multiple medical problems; and legal difficulties resulting from their transient lifestyle, financial instability, and high-risk behaviors. Many lack health insurance, family support, adequate housing, suitable employment, and positive relationships in their lives. Even when treatment has been offered to this population, treatment adherence has not always been good.

Second, services for this population have historically been delivered in a fragmented fashion, if they were delivered at all. Different local, state, and/or federal governmental entities with their own missions, budgets, and priorities have been responsible for delivering an array of medical, mental health, and substance abuse treatment, as well as housing, educational, and income support to this population. This "silo" approach to treatment, where different agencies target different problems or identical problems at different points in time, has not proven to be a very effective strategy. In fact, many of these individuals with significant problems have fallen through the large gaps between these silos.

Third, a significant percentage of this population has entered the criminal justice system—a system whose original charge was public safety, not treatment and social support. Once in the criminal justice system, they have begun to cycle through the system much like they did in the past with the community mental health and state hospital systems.

Fourth, and perhaps most significant, there has been a growing social and political awareness over the past decade that the current fragmented system of service delivery is not effectively meeting the needs of this population. With this growing awareness has come a series of initiatives at all levels of the criminal justice and community mental health systems, some internal and some more collaborative, but all designed to more aggressively address the needs of this population. Many of these initiatives have been made possible through funding provided by federal grants or through the individual efforts of dedicated mental health and criminal justice professionals. Community mental health agencies have adopted ACT and intensive case management strategies. Police have developed crisis intervention teams and collaborative networks with mental health agencies. Courts have implemented various diversion programs collaboratively with community mental health organizations. Correctional systems have created an array of mental health and substance abuse treatment programs, specialized housing units, and transitional planning strategies. Community corrections has followed the lead of community mental health agencies or partnered with them to provide offenders reentering the community with more intensive supervision as well as assistance with treatment needs, housing, employment, and income support. A start has clearly been made. Boundaries between agencies are beginning to blur somewhat as collaborative projects are conceived, implemented, and evaluated.

What seems lacking at the moment is the leadership and political will needed to craft an overarching strategy for dealing with the seriously mentally ill (especially those who have entered the criminal justice system) in a comprehensive, well-integrated fashion. There is no one national or even statewide mental health policy that guides all necessary service delivery or that cuts across multiple agencies at the federal or state level. Instead, each agency currently does what it reasonably can to address the needs of this population until it leaves and moves on to another agency. There is no one person or entity, no single "mental health czar," in charge of mental health policy at the national or state level who can guide policy review, development, and change or who can cut across budgetary lines to redistribute mental health monies and staffing resources more efficiently and effectively. However, with strong leadership and political will, several areas would appear ripe for development and/or expansion. Innovations in these areas would clearly represent best practices in the mental health arena.

First, more collaboration and cross-training needs to be developed between agencies that have not historically shared common goals or missions. Correctional systems need to learn more about the needs of the mentally ill and substance-abusing populations. Mental health agencies need to become familiar with strategies for dealing with mentally ill offenders who are also criminally inclined. The simplest way to accomplish this is through cross-training among agencies and through collaboration on projects of joint interest and benefit. Whereas this process has begun in some areas, it needs to become the norm rather than the exception.

Second, a more uniform data collection system and data-sharing mechanism could be developed to replace the current fragmented data collection systems used by various agencies. This would require agencies to develop common language, classification systems, and labels that are recognized and accepted by all agencies. Although better integrating data systems will not transform the actual delivery or quality of services, it will make it easier for agencies to exchange information about shared clients, to understand issues of coordination better, and to evaluate the successes and failures of various policy decisions. With a more integrated system or with data collection systems that can talk to each other, fewer individuals will be lost during handoffs between agencies, disconnections between agencies will be reduced, and duplications of services (e.g., intake screening) and costs will be minimized. One promising best practice that may assist agencies in closing these gaps is the development of electronic medical/mental health records, which are portable, could follow the individual across these silos, could potentially reduce redundant assessments or failed treatment strategies, and could help eliminate corrections-community barriers.

Third, and perhaps related to the first point, is the need for better risk assessment and tracking procedures, especially for "high-risk" mentally ill, substance-abusing individuals. Once identified, these individuals could be offered treatment and necessary supportive services in the least restrictive environment possible. Obviously, for more violent individuals with criminal, substance abuse, and mental health histories, these services might need to be offered initially in a highly structured correctional setting. However, for nonviolent mentally ill or substance-abusing criminal offenders, interventions might be more appropriate and cost-effective if offered at the community level with appropriate supervision and support. Additionally, with better tracking procedures, individuals could be supervised more effectively across correctional, mental health, and social service systems.

Fourth, treatments need to be offered in a more holistic fashion. Individuals with medical, mental health, and substance abuse problems need to have all of their treatment needs addressed simultaneously, not sequentially. Additionally, the ancillary problems of safe, affordable housing; marketable vocational skills; acquisition of social service benefits; and development of a solid support system need to be satisfactorily addressed to ensure long-term success for these individuals in the community. Because each of these services is currently provided by different government agencies with individual budgets, more integrated services would by necessity require changes in how budgets are developed and funds distributed and would require the development of centers that could offer an array of integrated services under the auspices of one controlling, overarching agency or entity.

Fifth, more research is clearly needed to determine what works best with which individuals under what circumstances and in which surroundings. Once identified, effective strategies need to be applied, ineffective strategies need to be discarded, and hopeful strategies need to be further explored. Systems need to be developed to continuously evaluate programs and ensure that evidence-based practices are implemented and expanded.

Finally, collaborative projects that are evidence-based, cost-effective, and successful need to be applied to far greater numbers of mentally ill criminal offenders than is the current practice. Some of the more successful current programs are only working intensely with small groups of individuals, while the need is far greater.

KEY TERMS

Booking

Defendant

Prosecutor

Summary trial

Probable cause

Preliminary hearing

Bail

Grand jury

Information

Arraignment

Bench trial

Presentence report

Jails

Prisons

Community corrections

Deinstitutionalization

Transinstitutionalization

Sequential intercept model

Primary prevention

Secondary prevention

Tertiary prevention

Crisis intervention teams (CITs)

Assertive community treatment (ACT)

Drug court

Mental health court

Therapeutic jurisprudence

Community reentry

Community reintegration

Memorandum of understanding (MOU)

DISCUSSION QUESTIONS

1. Does having prosecutors and defense lawyers working together with judges, mental health clinicians, and parole officers in mental health courts subvert the adversarial nature of the judicial process?

2. In the larger context of homelessness, unemployment, general health care, and other pressing concerns of the American public, where should the needs and rights of offenders, particularly those with serious mental illness, rank as a priority?

3. In the face of community resistance (note especially the interview with Dr. Williams), are community programs for ex-offenders "designed to fail"; that is, effectively to ensure that these individuals are either marginalized within the community or returned to prison?

4. If simple drug possession were decriminalized, it might appreciably reduce the prison population in general and the number of incarcerated individuals with serious mental illness in particular. Should this be considered? What are other possible benefits and some of the risks associated with such an approach?

5. The largest prison system in the United States is the Federal Bureau of Prisons, with prisons all around the country. How can community-corrections linkages be created and maintained when the correctional facility is far away, perhaps in another state or across the country? Does this suggest that a national coordinator for community corrections is appropriate? How can technology aid in this endeavor?

References

American Psychiatric Association. (2000). *Diagnostic and statistical manual of mental disorders* (4th ed., Text Revision). Washington, DC: Author.

Austin, J. (2001). Prisoner re-entry: Current trends, practices, and issues. *Crime & Delinquency, 47*, 314–334.

Ax, R. K. (2007). An international history of American correctional psychology: The Enlightenment to 1976. In R. K. Ax & T. J. Fagan (Eds.), *Corrections, mental health and social policy: International perspectives* (pp. 5–40). Springfield, IL: Charles C Thomas.

Beck, A. J., & Maruschak, L. M. (2001). *Mental health treatment in state prisons, 2000.* Washington, DC: Bureau of Justice Statistics.

Bohm, R. M., & Haley, K. N. (2008). *Introduction to criminal justice* (5th ed.). New York, NY: McGraw-Hill.

Bond, G. R., Drake, R. E., Mueser, K. T., & Latimer, E. (2001). Assertive community treatment: Critical ingredients and impact on patients. *Disease Management and Health Outcomes, 9,* 141–159.

Boner, N., Lattimore, P. K., Cowell, A. J., & Schlenger, W. E. (2004). Effects of diversion on adults with co-occurring mental illness and substance use: Outcomes from a national multi-site study. *Behavioral Sciences and the Law, 22,* 519–541.

Boothroyd, R., Calkins-Mercado, C., Poythress, N. P., Christy, A., & Petrila, J. (2005). After mental health court: Do diverted defendants experience improved clinical outcomes? *Psychiatric Services, 56,* 829–834.

Brad H. v. City of New York, No. 117882/99 (N.Y. Sup. Ct. New York County, July 14, 2000).

Calsyn, R. J., Yonker, R. D., Lemming, M. R., Morse, G. A., & Klinkenberg, W. D. (2005). Impact of assertive community treatment and client characteristics on criminal justice outcomes in dual disorder homeless individuals. *Criminal Behavior and Mental Health, 15,* 236–248.

Carey, S. M., Finigan, M., Crumpton, D., & Waller, M. (2006, November). California drug courts: Outcomes, costs, and promising practices: An overview of Phase II in a statewide study. *Journal of Psychoactive Drugs,* SARC Supplement 3, 345–356.

Cochran, S., Deane, M. W., & Borum, R. (2000). Improving police response to mentally ill people. *Psychiatric Services, 51,* 1315–1316.

Conley, J. K., & Zobel, D. (2007). Prison gangs. In R. K. Ax & T. J. Fagan (Eds.), *Corrections, mental health and social policy: International perspectives* (pp. 275–294). Springfield, IL: Charles C Thomas.

Couturier, L., Maue, F., & McVey, C. (2005). Releasing inmates with mental illness and co-occurring disorders into the community. *Corrections Today, 67*(2), 82–85.

Daggett, D. M., Camp, S. D., Kwon, O., Rosenmerkel, S. P., & Klein-Saffran, J. (2008). Faith-based correctional programming in federal prisons. *Criminal Justice and Behavior, 35,* 848–862.

Deschenes, E. P., Turner, S., Greenwood, P., & Chiesa, J. (1996). *An experimental evaluation of drug testing and treatment interventions for probationers in Maricopa County, Arizona.* Santa Monica, CA: Rand.

Ditton, P. M. (1999). *Mental health and treatment of inmates and probationers* (Bureau of Justice Statistics Bulletin NCJ 174463). Washington, DC: National Criminal Justice Reference Service.

Draine, J., & Herman, D. B. (2007). Critical time intervention for re-entry from prison for persons with mental illness. *Psychiatric Services, 58,* 1577–1581.

Drug Strategies. (1999). *Drug courts: A revolution in criminal justice.* Washington, DC: Author.

Dupont, R., & Cochran, S. (2000). Police response to mental health emergencies: Barriers to change. *Journal of the American Academy of Psychiatry and the Law, 28,* 338–344.

Dvoskin, J., Spiers, E. M., & Pitt, S. (2003). In T. J. Fagan & R. K. Ax (Eds.), *Correctional mental health handbook* (pp. 251–271). Thousand Oaks, CA: Sage.

Edelstein, B. A., & Michelson, L. (Eds.). (1986). *Handbook of prevention.* New York, NY: Plenum.

Erikson, S. K., Campbell, A., & Lamberti, J. S. (2006). Variations in mental health courts: Challenges, opportunities, and a call for caution. *Community Mental Health Journal, 42,* 335–344.

Felner, R. D., Felner, T. Y., & Silverman, M. M. (2006). Prevention in mental health and social intervention: Conceptual and methodological issues in the evolution of the science and practice of prevention. In J. Rappaport & E. Seidman (Eds.), *Handbook of community psychology* (pp. 9–42). New York, NY: Springer.

Finn, P., & Newlyn, A. K. (1993). *Miami's Drug Court: A different approach.* Washington, DC: U.S. Department of Justice, Office of Justice Programs, National Institute of Justice.

Fisman, L., Sturges, G., & Baranoski, M. (2001). Connecticut's criminal justice diversion program: A comprehensive community mental health model. *Community Mental Health Report, 3,* 19–20, 25–26.

Freudenberg, N. (2001). Jails, prisons, and the health of urban populations: A review of the impact of the correctional system on community health. *Journal of Urban Health: Bulletin of the New York Academy of Medicine, 78*, 214–235.

General Accounting Office. (2005). *Adult drug courts: Evidence indicates recidivism reductions and mixed results for other outcomes* (GAO-05-219). Washington, DC: Author.

Glaze, L. E. (2003, August). *Probation and parole in the United States* (Bureau of Justice Statistics Bulletin NCJ 201135). Washington, DC: National Criminal Justice Reference Service.

Glaze, L. E., & Pella, S. (2005, November). *Probation and parole in the United States, 2004* (Bureau of Justice Statistics Bulletin NCJ 210676). Washington, DC: National Criminal Justice Reference Service.

Gordon, R. S. (1983). An operational classification of disease prevention. *Public Health Reports, 98*, 107–109.

Gottfredson, D. C., & Exum, M. L. (2002). The Baltimore City Drug Court: One-year results from a randomized study. *Journal of Research on Crime and Delinquency, 39*, 337–356.

Gottfredson, D. C., Najaka, S. S., & Kearley, B. (2003). Effectiveness of drug treatment courts: Evidence from a randomized trial. *Criminology and Public Policy, 2*, 171–196.

Greenfeld, L. A. (1997, February). *An analysis of data on rape and sexual assault: Sex offenses and offenders* (Bureau of Justice Statistics Special Report NCJ 163392). Washington, DC: National Criminal Justice Reference Service.

Griffin, P., Steadman, H. J., & Petrila, J. (2002). The use of criminal charges and sanctions in mental health courts. *Psychiatric Services, 53*, 1285–1289.

Hails, J., & Borum, R. (2003). Police training and specialized approaches to respond to people with mental illness. *Crime & Delinquency, 49*, 52–61.

Hanafi, S., Bahora, M., Demir, B. N., & Compton, M. T. (2008). Incorporating crisis intervention team (CIT) knowledge and skills into the daily work of police officers: A focus group study. *Community Mental Health, 44*, 427–432.

Harowski, K. J. (2003). Staff training: Multiple roles for mental health professionals. In T. J. Fagan & R. K. Ax (Eds.), *Correctional mental health handbook* (pp. 237–249). Thousand Oaks, CA: Sage.

Harrison, P. M., & Beck, A. J. (2003, July). *Prisoners in 2002* (Bureau of Justice Statistics Special Bulletin NCJ 200248). Washington, DC: National Criminal Justice Reference Service.

Harrison, P. M., & Beck, A. J. (2006, May). *Prison and jail inmates at midyear 2005* (Bureau of Justice Statistics Bulletin NCJ 213133). Washington, DC: National Criminal Justice Reference Service.

Human Rights Watch. (2003). Failure to provide discharge services. In *Ill equipped: U.S. prisons and offenders with mental illness.* New York, NY: Author.

James, D. J., & Glaze, L. E. (2006, September). *Mental health problems of prison and jail inmates* (Bureau of Justice Statistics Special Report NCJ 213600). Washington, DC: National Criminal Justice Reference Service.

Karberg, J. C., & James, D. J. (2005, July). *Substance dependence, abuse, and treatment of jail inmates, 2002* (Bureau of Justice Statistics Special Report NCJ 209588). Washington, DC: National Criminal Justice Reference Service.

Knollenberg, L., & Martin, V. A. (2008). Community re-entry following prison: A process evaluation of the accelerated community entry program. *Federal Probation, 2*(2), 54–60.

Lamb, H. R., Weinberger, L. E., & DeCuir, W. J. (2002). The police and mental health. *Psychiatric Services, 53*, 1266–1271.

Lamb, H. R., Weinberger, L. E., & Gross, B. H. (2004). Mentally ill persons in the criminal justice system: Some perspectives. *Psychiatric Quarterly, 75*, 107–126.

Lamberti, J. S., Weisman, R. L., Schwarzkopf, S. B., Price, N., Ashton, R. M., & Trompeter, J. (2001). The mentally ill in jails and prisons: Towards an integrated model of prevention. *Psychiatric Quarterly, 72*, 63–77.

Lattimore, P. K., Broner, N., Sherman, R., Frisman, L., & Shafer, M. S. (2003). A comparison of prebooking and postbooking diversion programs with mentally ill substance-using individuals with justice involvement. *Journal of Contemporary Criminal Justice, 19*, 30–65.

Lindquist, C. H., Krebs, C. P., & Lattimore, P. K. (2006). Sanctions and rewards in drug court programs: Implementation, perceived efficacy, and decision making. *Journal of Drug Issues, 3*, 119–145.

Lurigio, A. J. (2008). The first 20 years of drug courts: A brief description of their history and impact. *Federal Probation, 72*(1), 13–17.

Lurigio, A. J., Rollins, A., & Fallon, J. (2004). The effects of serious mental illness on offender re-entry. *Federal Probation, 68*(2), 45–52.

McCarthy, B. R., McCarthy, B. J., Jr., & Leone, M. C. (2001). *Community-based corrections* (4th ed.). Belmont, CA: Wadsworth/Thomson Learning.

McCoy, M. L., Roberts, D. L., Hanrahan, P., Clay, R., & Luchins, D. J. (2004). Jail linkage assertive community treatment services for individuals with mental illnesses. *Psychiatric Rehabilitation Journal, 27*, 243–250.

McDonald, D., Dyous, C., & Carlson, K. (2008). *The effectiveness of prisoner re-entry services as crime control: The fortune society.* Cambridge, MA: Abt Associates.

McNeil, D. E., Binder, R. L., & Robinson, J. C. (2005). Incarceration associated with homelessness, mental disorder, and co-occurring substance abuse. *Psychiatric Services, 56*, 840–846.

Mellow, J., & Dickinson, J. M. (2006). The role of prerelease handbooks for prisoner re-entry. *Federal Probation, 70*(1), 70–76.

Minton, T. D., & Sabol, W. J. (2009, March). *Jail inmates at midyear 2008—Statistical tables* (Bureau of Justice Statistics Special Report NCJ 225709). Washington, DC: National Criminal Justice Reference Service.

Montagne, R. (2008, August 14). *Inside the nation's largest mental institution* [Broadcast transcript]. Retrieved January 10, 2009, from National Public Radio: http://www.npr.org/templates/story/story.php?storyId=93581736

Moore, M. E., & Hiday, V. A. (2006, October). Mental health courts: A comparison of re-arrest and re-arrest severity between mental health court and traditional court participants. *Law and Human Behavior, 30*, 659–674.

Morrissey, J., Meyer, P., & Cuddeback, G. (2007). Extending assertive community treatment to criminal justice settings: Origins, current evidence, and future directions. *Community Mental Health Journal, 43*, 527–544.

Mumola, C. J. (1999, January). *Substance abuse and treatment, state and federal prisoners, 1997* (Bureau of Justice Statistics Special Report NCJ 172871). Washington, DC: National Criminal Justice Reference Service.

Munetz, M. R., & Griffin, P. A. (2006). Use of the sequential intercept model as an approach to decriminalization of people with serious mental illness. *Psychiatric Services, 57*, 544–549.

Munetz, M. R., Fitzgerald, A., & Woody, M. (2006). Police use of the Taser with people with mental illness in crisis. *Psychiatric Services, 57*, 883.

National Commission on Correctional Health Care. (2008). *Standards for mental health services in correctional facilities.* Chicago, IL: Author.

Nelson, M., & Trone, J. (2000). *Why planning for release matters. Issues in brief.* New York, NY: Vera Institute of Justice.

Osher, F., Steadman, H. J., & Barr, H. (2003). A best practice approach to community re-entry from jails for inmates with co-occurring disorders: The APIC model. *Crime & Delinquency, 49*, 79–96.

Perez, A., Leifman, S., & Estrada, A. (2003). Reversing the criminalization of mental illness. *Crime & Delinquency, 49*, 62–78.

Peters, R. H., & Hill, H. A. (1993). Inmates with co-occurring substance abuse and mental health disorders. In H. Steadman & J. Cocozza (Eds.), *Mental illness in America's prisons.* Seattle, WA: National Coalition for the Mentally Ill in the Criminal Justice System.

Peters, R. H., & Matthews, C. O. (2003). Substance abuse treatment programs in prisons and jails. In T. J. Fagan & R. K. Ax (Eds.), *Correctional mental health handbook* (pp. 73–99). Thousand Oaks, CA: Sage.

Petersilia, J. (2003). *When prisoners come home: Parole and prisoner re-entry.* New York, NY: Oxford University Press.

Pew Center on the States. (2009, March). *One in 31: The long reach of American corrections.* Washington, DC: Author.

Redlich, A. D. (2005). Voluntary, but knowing and intelligent? Comprehension in mental health courts. *Psychology, Public Policy, and Law, 11*, 605–619.

Redlich, A. D., Steadman, H. J., Monahan, J., Robbins, P. C., & Petrila, J. (2006). Patterns of practice in mental health courts: A national survey. *Law and Human Behavior, 30,* 347–362.

Roman, C. G. (2004). A roof is not enough: Successful prisoner reintegration requires experimentation and collaboration. *Criminology & Public Policy, 3,* 161–167.

Schaedle, R., McGrew, J. H., Bond, G. R., & Epstein, I. (2002). A comparison of experts' perspectives on assertive community treatment and intensive case management. *Psychiatric Services, 53,* 207–210.

Skeem, J., & Bibeau, L. (2008). How does violence potential relate to crisis intervention team responses to emergencies? *Psychiatric Services, 59,* 201–204.

Steadman, H. J., Deane, M. W., Borum, R., & Morrissey, J. P. (2000). Comparing outcomes of major models for police responses to mental health emergencies. *American Journal of Public Health, 51,* 645–649.

Stein, L. I., & Santos, A. B. (1998). *Assertive community treatment of persons with severe mental illness.* New York, NY: Norton.

Tartaro, C., & Ruddell, R. (2006). Trouble in Mayberry: A national analysis of suicides and attempts in jails. *American Journal of Criminal Justice, 31,* 81–101.

Teller, J. L. S., Munetz, M. R., Gil, K. M., & Ritter, C. (2006). Crisis intervention team training for police officers responding to mental disturbance calls. *Psychiatric Services, 57,* 232–237.

Thompson, M. D., Reuland, M., & Souweine, D. (2003). Criminal justice/mental health consensus: Improving responses to people with mental illness. *Crime & Delinquency, 49,* 30–51.

Travis, J., & Petersilia, J. (2001). Re-entry reconsidered: A new look at an old question. *Crime & Delinquency, 47,* 291–313.

Travis, J., & Visher, C. (2005). *Prisoner re-entry and crime in America.* New York, NY: Cambridge University Press.

Trupin, E., & Richards, H. (2003). Seattle's mental health courts: Early indicators of effectiveness. *International Journal of Law and Psychiatry, 26,* 33–53.

Ventura, L. A., Cassel, C. A., Jacoby, J. E., & Huang, B. (1998). Case management and recidivism of mentally ill persons released from jail. *Psychiatric Services, 49,* 1330–1337.

Visher, C. A., & Travis, J. (2003). Transitions from prison to community: Understanding individual pathways. *Annual Review of Sociology, 29,* 89–113.

Webster, J. M., Rosen, P. J., Krietemeyer, J., Mateyoke-Scrivner, A., Staton-Tindall, M., & Leukefeld, C. (2006). Gender, mental health, and treatment motivation in a drug court setting. *Journal of Psychoactive Drugs, 38,* 441–448.

West, H. C., & Sabol, W. J. (2008, December). *Prisoners in 2007* (Bureau of Justice Statistics Bulletin NCJ 224280). Washington, DC: National Criminal Justice Reference Service.

West, H. C., & Sabol, W. J. (2009, March). *Prisoner inmates at midyear 2008: Statistical tables* (Bureau of Justice Statistics Bulletin NCJ 225619). Washington, DC: National Criminal Justice Reference Service.

Wexler, D., & Winick, B. J. (Eds.). (1996). *Law in a therapeutic key: Developments in therapeutic jurisprudence.* Durham, NC: Carolina Academic Press.

Whitehead, J. T., Pollock, J. M., & Braswell, M. C. (2003). *Exploring corrections in America.* Cincinnati, OH: Anderson.

Wilkinson, R. A. (2005). Engaging communities: An essential ingredient to offender re-entry. *Corrections Today, 67*(2), 86–89.

Wilkinson, R. A., Rhine, E. E., & Henderson-Hurley, M. (2005). Re-entry in Ohio corrections: A catalyst for change. *Journal of Correctional Education, 56,* 158–172.

Ziguras, S., & Stuart, G. (2000). A meta-analysis of the effectiveness of mental health case management over 20 years. *Psychiatric Services, 51,* 1410–1415.

CHAPTER 2

Comparison of Correctional and Community Mental Health Service Delivery Models

Robert J. Powitzky

Introduction

This chapter will describe the unique nature of a correctional mental health practice and dispel preconceived negative images and prejudices that some may have about clinical practice in correctional settings. One of the underlying premises of this chapter is that the delivery of mental health services in a correctional setting represents a distinct mental health specialty with its own unique best practices and evidenced-based programs in addition to—not opposed to—those practices, ethical standards, and goals shared by other mental health specialties, such as community mental health and private practice. This chapter will describe correctional mental health services by exploring the similarities and differences between a community-based and corrections-based clinical practice. It is hoped that a comparison of correctional mental health services with the more familiar community-based mental health services will provide a clearer vision of the nature of correctional mental health services.

It is a central thesis of this chapter that the most effective correctional mental health services are those that incorporate certain best practices from other community-based mental health service delivery models along with best practices unique to the correctional setting—an appropriate combination of which will produce a distinctive, distinguishable mental health services delivery system called correctional mental health services. In other words, just as community psychiatry and psychology are areas of specialization, correctional psychiatry and psychology are also professional areas of specialized mental health services. Neither is better. They are simply different.

Community Mental Health Services

Although New York and a few other states began formalizing community mental health centers before 1960, the Community Mental Health Centers Act of 1963 is most commonly accepted as the official legitimization of the need for federally funded community mental health services. Prior to that time, without any of the psychotropic medications and best psychosocial practices that are available today, community mental health centers basically functioned as gatekeepers of state mental health hospitals (Cutler, Bevilacqua, & McFarland, 2003; Pollack & Feldman, 2003). Their role was to try to provide supportive therapy to those who could benefit. However, those patients who could no longer adequately function in the community due to their mental illness were committed to mental health hospitals, often for the rest of their lives, with no hope of reintegration into the community. From their early role as gatekeeper for state mental hospitals, community mental health centers have evolved considerably since the 1960s and are now the providers of a wide variety of services and service paradigms too numerous to adequately describe in this limited chapter (Cutler et al., 2003; Malone, Marriott, Newton-Howes, Simmonds, & Tyrer, 2009).

With the advent of new psychotropic medications in the 1950s and 1960s, many believed that individuals with serious mental illness could function better, at less cost—both financial and human—in the community, rather than being warehoused in hospital settings. Unfortunately, the resources and planning necessary to turn this theory into action were not put into place prior to emptying out the hospitals. So what happened to all those people who were released from mental health hospitals beginning in the 1960s, and what happens to those who experience acute mental health crises today but have no hospital beds available to them? Figure 2.1 dramatically illustrates one state's all too typical experience. As the graph indicates, whereas the state's rate of per capita mental health hospitalizations went from 274 per 100,000 in 1960 to only 9 per 100,000 in 2007,

| **Figure 2.1** | Per Capita Imprisonment Versus Mental Hospital Commitment |

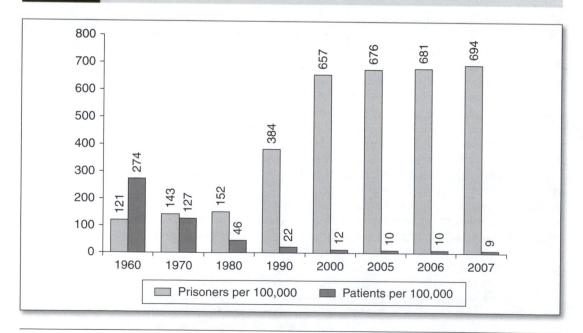

Source: Oklahoma Criminal Justice Resource Center (www.ocjrc.net).

during the same time period, the per capita rate of prison incarceration rose from 121 per 100,000 to an incredible 694 per 100,000.

Although there is no firm evidence of a direct cause-and-effect relationship, the data clearly demonstrate a dramatic decline in the number of mentally ill individuals housed in state hospitals coupled with an equally dramatic increase in the number of mentally disordered individuals housed in correctional facilities. Clearly, this implied transinstitutionalization of mentally disordered individuals from hospitals to prisons has changed the clinical profiles of today's incarcerated individuals compared to the typical offender profiles from 30-plus years ago. As a result of the growing numbers of mentally ill individuals in correctional facilities, correctional mental health delivery systems have had to adapt to accommodate the needs of this demanding population. It could be said that today's frontline mental health workers are law enforcement officers and today's mental health hospitals are jails and prisons (McDonald, Dyous, & Carlson, 2008; Powitzky, 2008).

Correctional Mental Health Services

Simple definitions of correctional mental health services are difficult to generate because of the great variability across correctional systems including organizational structure (private vs. public, internal vs. external provider services, lines of authority, etc.); mental health service management philosophy; institutional/cultural history; fiscal structure, source, and restrictions; and legal restraints or requirements (Cohen, 2008; Powitzky, 2008; Warlaw, 1983). The literature on correctional mental health services has focused on multiple factors including rehabilitation, criminogenic assessment and treatment, sex offender assessment and treatment, adherence to treatment for physical illnesses (also called medical psychology), substance abuse disorder treatment, habilitation programs for persons with developmental disabilities, geriatric services, neurological rehabilitation, and assessment and treatment of persons with mental illness.

For the purposes of this chapter, the term *correctional mental health services* will focus on the assessment and treatment of persons with mental illness, developmental disabilities, and/or co-occurring disorders associated with substance abuse. However, to be effective in providing care for these persons, mental health services must also include collaboration, training, and consultation with a wide spectrum of other disciplines that operate under the correctional umbrella. Participants in the four 1983 to 1984 National Institute of Corrections (NIC) Prison Mental Health Workshops reached a consensus on the following wording for the mission of correctional mental health services:

> The mission of mental health services in corrections is to provide those programs and services which are designed to evaluate, prevent, and treat mental health problems and which contribute to safe, humane corrections environments. (Powitzky, 2008, p. 5)

Three Levels of Services

Fagan (2003) described three levels of correctional mental health services, additive in nature, from required to desired:

- *Level 1*—services that are provided to all offenders and that are focused on the identification and treatment of mental disorders, especially those that may lead to suicidal and/or homicidal behavior. Frequently, these services are mandated by accreditation bodies such as the American Correctional Association (ACA; 2002, 2010) and the National Commission on Correctional Health Care (NCCHC; 2008).

- *Level 2*—services that are offered to specific targeted groups (e.g., substance abusers) and may or may not be mandated.
- *Level 3*—organizational/systemic or staff/administration-directed behavioral science intervention, training, and/or consultation.

Another way of describing Fagan's (2003) three levels is to think of various correctional mental health services located on a continuum of services ranging from individual-focused (consumer, client, patient, etc.) clinical services to systemic-focused intervention services. These levels will provide a useful framework in the following examination of correctional mental health services.

Fagan's (2003) Level 1 services can simply be described as basic services (e.g., intake screening, risk assessment, crisis intervention, and suicide intervention/prevention) that are often mandated by case law, which has accumulated over the past few decades. Perhaps the best resource for legal information regarding correctional mental health services can be found in Cohen's *The Mentally Ill Disordered Inmate and the Law* (2008). In discussing how complicated and difficult these legal issues are to apply, Cohen stated,

> For example, a constitutional right to treatment might be fashioned as a right to the most thorough diagnosis and the most skillful treatment currently available for the particular condition. Mentally retarded inmates might be entitled to such habilitative efforts that will maximize their human potential. On the other hand, the right to treatment could be construed to require only that some medical or professional judgment be brought to bear first to identify and then to provide minimally acceptable care in order to avoid needless pain and suffering. (p. 14)

What has become known as "best practices" in correctional mental health services are often those requirements mandated by the courts. Although there is not sufficient space in this chapter for a thorough discussion of these issues, suffice it to say that the most common legal issues that have to be addressed when designing and implementing correctional mental health services include issues of deliberate indifference, the disciplinary hearing process, use of forcible (involuntary) medication, treatment for serious medical need/medical necessity, use of restraints/seclusion, suicide prevention, accurate record keeping, conditions of confinement, segregated housing and isolation, and management of developmentally disabled offenders (Cohen, 2008).

To understand how the relative priorities of Fagan's (2003) levels of correctional mental health services have changed over time, one must first understand that the characteristics of incarcerated individuals are dramatically different today than they were 10, 20, and especially 30 years ago. Thirty years ago, when the incidence of mentally ill offenders was considerably lower in correctional settings, Level 2 services were often the primary focus of correctional mental health and were frequently viewed as part of correctional management best practices. It was in the provision of these and Level 3 services that correctional mental health services were especially distinguished from other non-correctional behavioral specialties. Today, correctional facilities are too often the repositories for mentally disabled and disordered people who cannot find community-based services. This relatively new social phenomenon has impacted various local, state, and federal correctional systems in different time periods and in different degrees. However, all systems across the United States have experienced this shift to some degree (James & Glaze, 2006; Steadman, Osher, Robbins, Case, & Samuels, 2009). It is this increase in mentally disordered offenders that has prompted the court's growing focus on and involvement in the delivery of mental health services in correctional settings. Given the large number of mentally ill offenders in correctional settings and the court's increased interest in the delivery of correctional mental health services in recent years, Level 1 services have typically supplanted Level 2 and 3 services as priorities for correctional administrators and mental health providers.

Despite this shift in focus by correctional administrators and mental health clinicians, Level 2 correctional mental health services continue to receive considerable attention from the general public and from politicians who often reflect the views of their constituents. Level 2 services address those areas of human behavior that are not necessarily directly related to the brain disease model of mental illness. These are the services that are typically thought of as psychosocial rehabilitation services (i.e., services that theoretically help a criminal become a noncriminal). Current research in this area has focused on the assessment of risk, need, and responsivity as core concepts in the development of effective programming in an effort to more scientifically analyze what methods best reduce "normal" criminal recidivism (see Chapter 9 for a more detailed discussion of this research).

Correctional managers, unlike other human service providers, are under constant political pressure to reduce crime, which means reducing recidivism. Therefore, Fagan's Level 2 services often receive greater political support than Level 1 services for the mentally ill, because these criminogenic factors are what citizens and politicians understand the most and on which they most focus.

Considering these competing needs and demands, how does a correctional professional decide what services should be provided? The most practical way is to list the desired services in order of priority as determined by court mandates, legislative mandates, and the correctional system's administration. This approach is helpful in educating all parties about needed services and is useful in requests for and allocation of resources. By referring to the prioritized services, correctional mental health clinicians and administrators can demonstrate what services can and cannot be provided with a specified staffing pattern and funding level. Table 2.1 lists one correctional system's mental health services duties in order of priority and groups them into primary, secondary, and tertiary duties.

Table 2.1	Duties and Responsibilities of Correctional Mental Health Professionals

1. Primary clinical duties and service responsibilities
   a. Crisis and suicide intervention services
   b. Mental health evaluations and assessments
   c. Individual treatment plan development and review
   d. Individual and group psychotherapy
   e. Monthly assessment contact with all offenders on antipsychotic medications for the treatment of major depression, bipolar, and psychotic disorders
   f. Required segregated housing unit reviews and 30/90-day assessments
   g. Specialized psychoeducational groups
   h. Maintenance of legible documentation for services rendered in accordance with OP-140106 entitled "Medical Record System," consistent with Department of Corrections (DOC) policy, procedure, and professional ethics

(Continued)

Table 2.1 (Continued)

i. Assessment of offenders on antipsychotic medications a minimum of every 90 days will be documented by use of the "Abnormal Involuntary Movement Scale (AIMS)" (OP-140201C)

j. Required reviews of offender disciplinary actions, as outlined in OP-060125 entitled "Department Offender Disciplinary Procedures"

2. Secondary duties and responsibilities

   a. Written special mental health evaluation reports and treatment plans as required

   b. Consultation with medical, support, and custodial staff on treatment and programming concerns

   c. Plan, direct, and coordinate special programs

   d. Provide screening, orientation, and record reviews

   e. Participate in professional development activities

   f. Provide staff training

3. Tertiary duties and responsibilities

   a. Supervise volunteers and student interns as appropriate

   b. Serve on committees

   c. Conduct research

   d. Write grants

Source: Oklahoma Department of Corrections Policy OP-140201C (2009).

In understanding the importance of Level 3 services, it must be understood that the provision of all possible individual clinical services (Level 1 services) will not be effective on a long-term basis if they are provided within an institutional living environment that does not accommodate the unique needs of the mentally ill offender. Therefore, correctional mental health service professionals are compelled to make an effective impact on the overall management of the individual correctional facility and the larger system through ongoing training of and consultation with correctional staff and administrators regarding mental health issues and concerns. These core principles will be discussed further in the section on comparisons between corrections- and community-based mental health services (see Chapters 8 and 14 for more discussion on correctional consultation).

Another domain that must be explored when describing correctional mental health services is organizational structure and culture. In American corrections, there are as many systemic structural/organizational variations of the correctional mental health delivery system as there are states, counties, and cities. Table 2.2 is one example of ways to categorize the different facets involved in describing the various organizational structures and issues of correctional mental health services delivery systems. These structural, cultural, and historical variables must be addressed in any thorough analysis of correctional mental health services.

Table 2.2	Organizational Differences in Correctional Mental Health Services Models

1. Department of Corrections (DOC) interagency administration line of command
   - *Cabinet-level DOC:* The DOC is a separate organizational unit whose director/commissioner/manager reports directly to the governor.
   - *Sub-cabinet-level DOC:* The DOC director/commissioner reports to some state official other than the governor.

2. DOC intra-agency and interagency functions
   - *Unified DOC:* The DOC operates all types of correctional facilities within the state, including jails, prisons, community facilities, etc.
   - *Umbrella DOC:* A DOC that operates more than incarceration facilities, including community sentencing, probation, and parole, etc.
   - *DOC for adjudicated incarceration only:* One or more separate agencies for each traditional correctional function and/or type of facility, for example, separate departments of institutions, probation, parole, state jails, county jails, community sentencing, community corrections, etc.

3. Structure of types of mental health services state systems
   - *Forensic mental health hospital:* The forensic mental health unit/hospital either as a separate unit within a DOC housing criminal competency/insanity ordered offenders or as a unit that also houses adjudicated offenders. Most states have forensic mental health hospitals under an agency other than the DOC.
   - *Mental health hospitals within another agency providing services to DOC offenders:* States with mechanisms for transferring and/or committing offenders with mental illness to the Department of Mental Health or Department of Forensic Mental Health.
   - *Private contract services:* Some states have part or all of their mental health services provided by one or more private contractors.
   - *The full range of services provided within DOC facilities:* Many states provide all mental health services within the DOC facilities equivalent in nature to those accessible in the community, ranging from involuntary acute/stabilization inpatient care to outpatient services. However, innumerable variations are found even within this category. Some systems may have government-certified psychiatric hospital facilities with traditional psychiatric staffing, whereas other systems simply have converted separate prison housing facilities with some increased security and professional staffing patterns. Some states have mental health services as a separate DOC organizational unit with its own staffing and budget, and others place mental health services organizationally under another organizational unit such as medical services or programs.

4. Differences within the system by nature of system components
   - *Mission:* Facilities have different types of mental health services depending on the mission. For example, a facility that performs assessment and reception duties on all newly admitted offenders would have different mental health requirements than a facility with one or more specialized housing/treatment units or with only general population offenders.
   - *Security level:* A maximum-security facility will have different mental health service needs than a minimum-security facility.

(Continued)

Table 2.2	(Continued)

5. History

- *Personnel:* Some facilities have staff who have worked there for decades and who may be very resistant to change, whereas other systems have high turnover with new staff.
- *Tradition:* Some facilities have deeply ingrained practices and traditions that make change difficult.
- *Trauma:* Many facilities have suffered tragedies such as riots and murders. If not properly debriefed and/or managed, the traumatic incident(s) may have long-lasting impact on staff attitudes, procedures, and overall philosophy.

As is evident from Table 2.2, correctional mental health services cannot be described by one simple template that fits all correctional settings and systems. However, it is clear that correctional mental health services comprise a unique mental health specialization distinct from specialized mental health services in other settings.

Correctional Mental Health Services: A Proposed Model

No thorough discussion of correctional mental health services would be complete without a proposed model of an ideal correctional mental health services delivery system that would most effectively address the simultaneous, complex demands discussed above: (a) medically necessary care for offenders with mental illness, (b) legal requirements, (c) criminogenic program requirements, and (d) organizational differences. This ideal model of correctional mental health services would provide an integrated system of mental health care aligned with good correctional management designed to empower offenders with mental illness to attain their maximum level of crime-free employment, self-care, interpersonal relationships, and community participation. It would promote individual recovery and resilience while protecting the public.

This correctional mental health recovery model would adapt current, evidence-based best practices from community settings (e.g., illness management and recovery, supported employment, family psychoeducation, assertive community treatment, integrated treatment for co-occurring disorders, and medication management) and apply them to a correctional setting. Illness management and recovery programs are structured cognitive-behavioral, psychoeducational groups that teach the client to understand mental illness and to develop a plan that will allow the client to manage his or her illness while living a stable, productive lifestyle. These programs have been developed in several different forms including Wellness Recovery Action Plan (WRAP; Copeland, 2000), the Peer-to-Peer Program (National Alliance on Mental Illness, 2009), and Illness Management and Recovery (Mueser & MacKain, 2006/2008; Substance Abuse and Mental Health Services Administration, National Mental Health Information Center, n.d.-a). Integrated or co-occurring disorder treatment services are for people who have co-occurring disorders (e.g., mental illness and a substance abuse addiction). This treatment approach helps people recover by offering both mental health and substance abuse services at the same time and in one setting. In addition to a practical guide by McKillip (2004), integrated services have been promoted by the National Mental Health Information Center of the Substance Abuse and Mental Health

Services Administration (n.d.-b). Assertive community treatment (Allness & Knoedler, 2003; Coldwell & Bender, 2007; Cuddeback, Morrissey, & Cusack, 2008) is a relatively new proactive team community mental health approach for assertively reaching out to and supporting persons with severe, persistent mental illness who would ordinarily get lost in the system of care (see Chapter 1 for more discussion on assertive community treatment). The other listed services (supported employment, family psychoeducation, and medication management) are straightforward, traditional services that are nonetheless important components of an offender's successful reentry into the community from incarceration.

This proposed model would be cost-efficient in utilizing a management information system (Powitzky, 2003) that facilitates a concentration of staffing and designated housing for those inmates with the most serious mental illness in the safest, yet least restrictive, conditions possible. Prototype individual plans, called "treatment tracks," would be developed with specified treatment objectives to be accomplished through evidence-based treatment protocols. These treatment tracks would include, but not be limited to, psychotic disorders, mood disorders, impulse control disorders, brain injury/disorders, and co-occurring disorders (e.g., mental retardation/mental illness, substance abuse/mental illness, etc.).

Within the prototype framework, an individualized treatment plan for each identified inmate would be developed that incorporates the elements of this model of care and the unique needs of the individual with the initial goal of integration back into the general prison population where possible and eventually into the community. Crucial to the success of this proposed model is the active participation of all relevant state and local agencies involved in the planning and provision of reentry services. Simply put, the agencies that provide the aftercare services have to take ownership of discharge plans to ensure successful reentry.

Comparisons of Mental Health Services in Community and Correctional Settings

By now it should be apparent that community-based and correctional-based mental health services systems cannot be described by one simple recipe or template. Many variables are at work to forge what each system or subsystem must provide to address its own unique mental health need. Even so, enough generalizations can be found that permit the following comparisons between community-based and correctional-based mental health services.

Purpose

Regardless of setting, the basic purposes for mental health delivery systems in both correctional and community settings are the same—to empower persons with mental illness or co-occurring disorders to attain their maximum level of crime-free employment, self-care, interpersonal relationships, and participation in the community or prison population. Power (2006) stated this shared goal in the following manner:

> Mental health recovery is an individual's journey of healing and transformation to live a meaningful life in a community of his or her choice, while striving to achieve maximum human potential. (Slide 11)

Population Served

In essence, both community and correctional mental health delivery systems serve the same population. It is only through a change in social policy that the housing of individuals with mental illness has shifted from containment in mental hospitals to containment in jails and prisons (James & Glaze, 2006; Lamb, Weinberger, & Gross, 2004; Perez, Leifman, & Estrada, 2003). Unfortunately, current social and political forces continue to support a containment model for those citizens who act in ways that make the community fearful, confused, or angry.

Some community-based mental health professionals would argue that there are definite differences between a criminal mentally ill person and a noncriminal mentally ill person. For example, there are some data to suggest that mentally ill individuals with violent backgrounds are incarcerated more often, suggesting that this subset of mentally disordered individuals may be different from those who remain in the community (James & Glaze, 2006; McNeil, Binder, & Robinson, 2005).

Based on these perceived differences, there continues to exist a mistaken we-they mentality, which suggests that community Department of Mental Health clients are inherently different from Department of Corrections offenders (Lurigio, Fallon, & Dincin, 2000; Wolff, 1998). Two points are worth making in reference to this perception. First, what differences may exist are further compounded by the mostly learned coping skills that a person who comes into contact with the criminal justice system acquires to survive within that setting. Even non–mentally ill persons are changed by the iatrogenic effects of experiencing the criminal justice system, from arrest to detention to court proceedings to incarceration to reentry (Tonry, 2004). Second, even if differences exist between criminal and noncriminal mentally disordered individuals, mentally disordered offenders were originally culled from the general community population and will eventually return to the community and require community-based services.

Having been changed by their correctional experience and labeled by the criminal justice and community mental health systems as felons, mentally disordered criminal offenders face greater challenges in readjusting to life in the community and require greater, not less, attention by community mental health providers. Without the active support of community mental health resources and without greater collaboration between corrections- and community-based practitioners, it is easy for mentally disordered offenders to become part of the revolving door of repeated incarcerations (Baillargeon, Binswanger, Penn, Williams, & Murray, 2009).

Accountability and Responsibility

One difference between mental health services in community and correctional settings may be in the degree of accountability and responsibility for patient care—a difference defined, in part, by societal and legal expectations. For example, consumers of mental health services in community settings can seek or refuse services as they wish. There is also no expectation that those services will include accountability for adherence to prescribed treatment, much less the assumption of any responsibility for food, lodging, clothing, medical/dental care, employment, or conflict with the law (Larsen, 1986). Additionally, there is no expectation that community mental health practitioners will actively go out into the community, assess citizens for mental health need, and provide services to those most in need.

People served by correctional mental health services, on the other hand, are adjudicated by the court as criminals and are sentenced to the care and custody of the correctional system, with all the legal and ethical requirements and implications that status involves. Included in these legal and ethical requirements is the need for the correctional system to assume responsibility for the provision of food, lodging, medical/mental health/dental care, education, vocational training, and so forth (Mears, 2008) and to be held accountable when these services are not sufficient or do not meet minimum professional standards or community expectations.

Legal Issues

Obviously, community mental health services also have to be aware of their legal obligations and restrictions. Many of these relate to the protection of the patient and the public. For example, following the Tarasoff rulings by the California Supreme Court in 1974 and 1976, most states have statutes or case law dictating a psychotherapist's duty to warn or protect potential victims from an imminently dangerous (assaultive or homicidal) patient and, in doing so, breaching therapist-patient confidentiality (Pabian, Welfel, & Beebe, 2009). In addition, the Health Insurance Portability and Accountability Act of 1996, known as HIPAA, imposes federal privacy protections for patient information, penalties for wrongful disclosure, and related obligations on providers, such as protection of patient information from theft.

Correctional mental health services, however, differ from community mental health services in the specific content and the volume of case law that uniquely applies to correctional settings. For example, if a patient in the community refuses treatment and never shows up for doctor's appointments, the health professional cannot be sued for deliberate indifference or negligence if he or she simply closes the file on the patient. Correctional mental health services, on the other hand, can be found guilty of deliberate indifference for allowing an incarcerated offender to die from a hunger strike or become vulnerable to physical harm due to an untreated psychosis. Involuntary psychotropic medication in correctional settings has to conform to specific case law, not only to ensure against unnecessary forced medication, but also to ensure that those in need are provided involuntary medication necessary for prevention of permanent physical and/or mental harm. Again, the reader is referred to Cohen (2008) for a detailed presentation of the complex issues involved.

Personal Versus Professional Credibility

The comments in this particular section about personal and professional credibility represent the author's subjective observations based on almost 40 years of correctional experience and may or may not ultimately be supported through empirical research. In essence, the author believes that there is a difference in the source of attributed credibility, at least initially, for a mental health professional in a community setting compared to one in a correctional setting. Most of the initial credibility and competency attributed to a mental health professional in a community setting is based on the professional's job title and credentials of the clinician. However, when a mental health professional first begins working in a correctional setting, he or she is judged more by personal attributes such as resiliency, honesty, self-confidence, maturity, and intelligence before anyone even cares to ask about job title or credentials. Only after the correctional mental health professional has proven himself or herself along these dimensions will those staff and offenders who genuinely want help actually seek help.

Multiple Roles

Much of the literature in the past few decades continues to focus on "role conflicts" in correctional settings that are somehow different from those found in community settings. These role conflicts are often presented as problematic (Weinberger & Sreenivasan, 1994). Mental health services in correctional settings are characterized by multiple roles—some of which may appear to be in conflict by their very nature. For example, a correctional mental health professional may at various times be a therapist, a systems interventionist, an advocate, a law enforcement officer, or any combination of the above. These roles certainly present correctional mental health clinicians with unique challenges and opportunities. However, community-based mental health professionals may also experience these different roles to a lesser degree. For example, when a therapist issues a Tarasoff warning because a patient has disclosed plans to harm a potential victim or a therapist is forced to call 911 because the patient is at home with the intention of committing suicide, the therapist is essentially in a law enforcement role. In other words, these are actually role issues that all mental health professionals must handle to some degree. Perhaps the fact that mental health clinicians must face these issues in an environment where treatment is not always the primary focus makes these issues seem more problematic or dramatic. However, these issues are not problematic simply because they exist. Rather, they become problematic only when poorly managed, ignored, or viewed out of context (see Bonner & Vandecreek, 2006; Dignam, 2003; and Haag, 2006, for more discussion on this topic).

Axis I Versus Axis II Disorders

The Diagnostic and Statistical Manual of Mental Disorders–Fourth Edition, Text Revision (*DSM-IV-TR*; American Psychiatric Association, 2000) is based on a multiaxial system of assessment, with Axis I diagnoses consisting of most mental disorders excluding personality disorders and intellectual, mental, and/or developmental retardation/disability. The *DSM-IV-TR* warns, "The coding of Personality Disorders on Axis II should not be taken to imply that their pathogenesis or range of appropriate treatment is fundamentally different from that for the disorders coded on Axis I" (p. 28). Even with this caveat, the prevailing view among practitioners, and one supported by traditional abnormal psychology textbooks (e.g., Comer, 2008), is the view that Axis II disorders are more entrenched, more permanent, and less amenable to treatment than the more fluid Axis I disorders. Although these traditional views are beginning to be challenged by research (e.g., Baker & Holroyd, 2009; Beck & Freeman, 2004; Heard & Linehan, 2005; Issa & Kantarjian, 2009; Kandel, 2009; Linehan, Cochran, & Kehrer, 2001), mental health professionals in both community and correctional settings still tend to view persons with personality disorders, or even those individuals with co-occurring Axis I and Axis II disorders, as less amenable to treatment. In an era of tight budgets and limited staff resources, it seems reasonable to conclude that clients most amenable to treatment are likely to take priority over clients who are either less amenable to treatment or simply refuse treatment.

Without adequate community-based treatment, some of these individuals ultimately find themselves in correctional settings, where their symptomatology can be problematic for both the offender and the correctional facility. For example, a common clinical picture in the correctional setting is a person with a diagnosis that falls within a "Cluster B Personality Disorder" combined with intermittent psychotic symptoms. Cluster B Personality Disorders include antisocial personality disorder, borderline personality disorder, histrionic personality disorder, and narcissistic personality disorder. When the psychotic symptoms are controlled successfully with medication, the underlying personality disorder becomes primary, resulting in behaviors that are difficult to treat and possibly unpleasant to work with. This difficult clinical picture has become even more complex in the past decade with the rapid increase of methamphetamine addiction, which in itself can create symptoms of a complicated psychotic disorder.

Further complicating the diagnostic picture is the fact that offenders with only Axis I diagnoses must also develop survival skills to adapt to the jail/prison environment. It is easy to misinterpret these behaviors as indicators of resistance to treatment and/or symptoms of Axis II personality disorders. Rotter, McQuistion, Broner, and Steinbacher (2005) summarize this point as follows:

> People with serious psychiatric disorders experience high rates of incarceration. Through their experience in the uniquely demanding and dangerous environment of jail and prison, many develop a repertoire of adaptations that set them apart from persons who have not been incarcerated. The so-called inmate code—which includes rules and values such as do not snitch, do your own time, and do not appear weak may be manifest in certain behaviors, such as not sharing any information with staff, minding one's business to an extreme, and demonstrating intimidating shows of strength. Although these behaviors help the person adapt during incarceration and act as survival skills in a hostile setting, they seriously conflict with the expectations of most therapeutic environments and thus interfere with community adjustment and personal recovery. Simultaneously, mental health providers are frequently unaware of these patterns and misread signs of difficult adjustment as resistance, lack of motivation for treatment, evidence of character pathology, or active symptoms of mental illness. As a result, providers often experience unwarranted concerns about safety and lose opportunities for early and empathic engagement. (p. 265)

Confidentiality

Confidentiality is often cited as a crucial element of counseling/psychotherapy, especially individual psychotherapy. However, in all clinical practices, confidentiality is not without limits. In community settings, these limitations include the duty to warn certain others when the patient becomes a threat to the safety and health of identifiable persons in the community and the duty to implement involuntary commitment/detention procedures when the patient becomes suicidal. These limits also include instances of child abuse or elder abuse (American Psychological Association, 2002).

In correctional settings, these limitations to confidentiality, especially those pertaining to danger and duty to warn, must be viewed from a broader, somewhat different context (Bonner & Vandecreek, 2006; Dignam, 2003; Haag, 2006). For example, in all communities, it is against the law by definition to possess illegal drugs. The community-based clinician commonly hears a client talk about recreational or even addictive drug usage as part of the therapeutic process, and yet the therapist certainly does not call 911 to report this activity. However, the correctional mental health professional knows that this behavior in certain situations might be very dangerous to the client, to other offenders, or to staff, due to the nature of the potentially volatile prison culture. As a result, the correctional mental health professional may need to violate the inmate's confidentiality to protect others. Similarly, if an offender reports a credible plan to escape the prison, the mental health clinician may need to report this plan to ensure public safety. In essence, this level of confidentiality is different only in degree from that typically provided in the community, yet it still follows an essential guiding principle for all mental health clinicians (i.e., protecting lives takes precedence over protecting the therapeutic alliance).

Power Differential

Power differentials between clinicians and patients exist in both community and correctional settings, and both types of settings can experience abuses of power between the clinician and the client. This author suspects that correctional settings with their paramilitary structure may have a more evident power differential that, in turn, provides clearer boundaries and expectations than those typically found in the community setting. This remains an empirical question that has not yet been addressed in the literature. Additionally, as noted in earlier sections, these differences between community and correctional settings may again be more a matter of degree and detail than a difference in core operating principles.

Coerced Versus Voluntary Treatment

Offenders often have fewer choices in correctional settings than they would have in the community, including whether to seek treatment and with which mental health professional they wish to work. Additionally, criminal offenders are often mandated to participate in specific treatment programs. For example, before a sentence is suspended or terminated, the courts and/or the correctional system may require successful participation in certain mental health programs such as anger management or substance abuse treatment. This forced or coerced treatment has raised the question of whether coerced treatment can be effective, especially in correctional settings.

In two meta-analytic studies, coerced drug abuse treatment was found to be no less effective than voluntary treatment (Anglin, Prendergast, & Farabee, 1998; Prendergast, Podus, Chang, & Urada, 2002; Scott & Crime and Justice Institute, 2008). Other studies have concluded that coerced treatment may even be more effective as a means of retaining an individual in treatment (Brecht, Anglin, & Jung-Chi, 1993; Gerstein & Harwood, 1990; Leukefeld & Tims, 1988; Wanberg & Milkman, 2004; Watson, Brown, Tilleskjor, Jacobs, & Pucel, 1988).

As with other differences between community and correctional settings, it should be noted that coercive treatment is not unique to correctional settings. One could argue, for example, that "coerced voluntarism" is common in both settings and that any differences represent a matter of degree and not a dichotomous distinction. For example, is a man voluntarily seeking treatment for alcoholism when he admits the only reason he came was because his wife said she would divorce him if he did not get help? Similarly, other clients come to treatment with some degree of external pressure, whether it comes from a boss, a spouse, a relative, or a judge.

Access to Total Healthcare

Correctional settings may provide better, more centralized access to all types of medical/mental health/dental care, housing, food, clothing, work, and educational opportunities than is found in the typical community setting, especially for those individuals who come from the lower or lowest socioeconomic strata and who are unable to afford adequate care and services in the community. In addition, most correctional mental health professionals have access to the same health records that medical providers have, and vice versa, an advantage that many community practitioners do not share. Also, in correctional settings more so than in community settings, it is possible for mental health clinicians to get almost constant, real-time feedback regarding offender conduct, hygiene, food consumptions, and so forth from correctional staff charged with the offender's supervision. This information helps the clinician assess offender progress and assists in uncovering problem areas.

Unfortunately, these correctional advantages can become liabilities for the offender following release back into the community, where these services are neither centralized nor proximate. Without easy access to these services, ex-offenders may lack the needed resources to acquire these services in the community and, therefore, may cease efforts to receive them, with relapse and reoffense likely consequences (Morrissey, Meyer, & Cuddeback, 2007; Schaedle, McGrew, Bond, & Epstein, 2002). Clearly, better integration between correctional and community care would be one way of remedying this issue.

Research

In March 2007, a national work group met to review the state of mental health research in correctional settings. One of their conclusions was, "An overarching theme of the discussion was the widely shared perception that research in correctional mental health in general has been sparse and often based on the questionable application of community-based methods or data to correctional settings" (Appelbaum, 2008, p. 269). Only a limited number of research articles (see Smith, Gendreau, & Goggin, 2007, for a summary of "what works" meta-analyses in correctional settings) related to the treatment of mentally ill offenders in correctional settings meet basic criteria for an acceptable empirical study. In part, the 1978 federal laws and regulations, which provide *Protections Pertaining to Biomedical and Behavioral Research Involving Prisoners as Subjects* (U.S. Department of Health, Education, and Welfare, 1978), have been responsible for limiting experimentally rigorous research possibilities in correctional settings. Despite these limitations, more rigorous, empirically sound research is needed on a variety of correctional mental health issues to determine what works best on which offender groups in which settings.

Summary and Conclusions

The twofold purpose of this chapter was to describe and to challenge. Any description of correctional mental health services has to be, by its very nature, a dynamic process. Correctional mental health services have evolved in response to social and political initiatives and changes in other mental health services delivery systems (e.g., community mental health delivery systems). In addition, the characteristics of each correctional system and/or system component impact the correctional mental health services delivery. These differences were discussed in this chapter and must be considered in understanding correctional mental health services.

Even with all the variations across correctional mental health delivery systems, correctional mental health constitutes a clear and distinct specialized field or model of mental health services. No longer should another model (i.e., the community model) be considered superior and simply imported into the criminal justice system; nor should its standards be uncritically adopted. Some of the similarities and differences between clinical services delivered in community settings and in correctional settings were also discussed in this chapter. Neither type of setting is better than the other. They are simply different. By understanding the differences and similarities between community-based and corrections-based mental health services, professionals from both of these environments will expand their repertoire of knowledge and skills in creating seamless continuity of care for all persons with mental illness and co-occurring disorders.

KEY TERMS

Community mental health services

Correctional mental health services

Community Mental Health Centers Act of 1963

Psychotropic medication

Criminogenic

Developmental disability

Levels of mental health services

Illness management and recovery programs

Integrated treatment co-occurring disorders

Supported employment

Substance Abuse and Mental Health Services Administration (SAMHSA)

Psychoeducation

Tarasoff ruling

Health Insurance Portability and Accountability Act of 1996 (HIPAA)

APA *Ethical Principles of Psychologists and Code of Conduct* (2002)

Multiple roles

Power differential

Axis I disorders

Axis II disorders

Personality disorders

Confidentiality

Coerced vs. voluntary treatment

DISCUSSION QUESTIONS

1. What were your perceptions about mental health services in correctional settings prior to reading this chapter? Have they changed as a result of this chapter? If so, how? If not, why not?

2. What is the need for mental health services with incarcerated persons? Has this changed over the years? If so, what was the change, and how and why has the change occurred?

3. This chapter emphasized the need to understand organizational differences between various correctional mental health services delivery systems. Why is understanding these differences important?

4. What are two similarities between mental health services in community settings and correctional settings?

5. What are three major differences between mental health services in community settings and correctional settings? A few of the differences discussed in this chapter were mostly the author's subjective perceptions that were not supported or refuted by empirical research. Are there any that you can help to prove or disprove? If so, which ones, and what is the research?

References

Allness, D. J., & Knoedler, W. H. (2003). *A manual for ACT start-up: Based on the PACT model of community treatment for persons with severe and persistent mental illnesses.* Arlington, VA: National Alliance for the Mentally Ill.

American Correctional Association. (2002). *Performance-based standards for correctional health care for adult correctional institutions.* Alexandria, VA: Author.

American Correctional Association. (2010). *2010 standards supplement.* Alexandria, VA: Author.

American Psychiatric Association. (2000). *Diagnostic and statistical manual of mental disorders* (4th ed., Text Revision). Washington, DC: Author.

American Psychological Association. (2002). *Ethical principles of psychologists and code of conduct.* Washington, DC: Author.

Anglin, M. D., Prendergast, M., & Farabee, D. (1998). *The effectiveness of coerced treatment for drug-abusing offenders.* Washington, DC: Office of National Drug Control Policy's Conference of Scholars and Policy Makers.

Appelbaum, K. L. (2008). Correctional mental health research: Opportunities and barriers. *Journal of Correctional Health Care, 14,* 269–277.

Baillargeon, J., Binswanger, I. A., Penn, J. V., Williams, B. A., & Murray, O. J. (2009). Psychiatric disorders and repeat incarcerations: The revolving prison door. *American Journal of Psychiatry, 166,* 103–126.

Baker, T. E., & Holroyd, C. B. (2009). Which way do I go? Neural activation in response to feedback and spatial processing in a virtual T-maze. *Cerebral Cortex, 19,* 1708–1722.

Beck, A. T., & Freeman, A. (2004). *Cognitive therapy of personality disorders* (2nd ed.). New York, NY: Guilford.

Bonner, R., & Vandecreek, L. D. (2006). Ethical decision making for correctional mental health providers. *Criminal Justice and Behavior, 33,* 542–564.

Brecht, M. L., Anglin, M. D., & Jung-Chi, W. (1993). Treatment effectiveness for legally coerced versus voluntary methadone maintenance clients. *American Journal of Drug and Alcohol Abuse, 19,* 89–106.

Cohen, F. (2008). *The mentally disordered inmate and the law* (2nd ed.). Kingston, NJ: Civic Research Institute, Inc.

Coldwell, C. M., & Bender, W. S. (2007). The effectiveness of assertive community treatment for homeless populations. *American Journal of Psychiatry, 164,* 393–399.

Comer, R. J. (2008). *Fundamentals of abnormal psychology* (5th ed.). New York, NY: Worth.

Community Mental Health Centers Act of 1963, Pub. L. No. 88-164 (1963).

Copeland, M. E. (2000). *Wellness recovery action plan.* West Dummerston, VT: Peach Press.

Cuddeback, G. S., Morrissey, J. P., & Cusack, K. J. (2008). How many forensic assertive community treatment teams do we need? *Psychiatric Services, 59,* 205–208.

Cutler, D. L., Bevilacqua, J., & McFarland, B. H. (2003). Four decades of community mental health: A symphony in four movements. *Community Mental Health Journal, 39,* 381–398.

Dignam, J. T. (2003). Correctional mental health ethics revisited. In T. J. Fagan & R. K. Ax (Eds.), *Correctional mental health handbook* (pp. 39–56). Thousand Oaks, CA: Sage.

Fagan, T. J. (2003). Mental health in corrections: A model for service delivery. In T. J. Fagan & R. K. Ax (Eds.), *Correctional mental health handbook* (pp. 1–19). Thousand Oaks, CA: Sage.

Gerstein, D. R., & Harwood, H. J. (1990). *Treating drug problems* (Vol. 1). Washington, DC: National Academies Press.

Haag, A. M. (2006). Ethical dilemmas faced by correctional psychologists in Canada. *Criminal Justice and Behavior, 33,* 93–109.

Health Insurance Portability and Accountability Act of 1996, Pub. L. No. 104-191, 110 Stat. 1962 (1996).

Heard, H. L., & Linehan, M. M. (2005). Integrative therapy for borderline personality disorder. In J. C. Norcross & M. R. Goldfried (Eds.), *Handbook of psychotherapy integration* (2nd ed., pp. 299–320). New York, NY: Oxford University Press.

Issa, J., & Kantarjian, H. (2009). Targeting DNA methylation. *Clinical Cancer Research, 15,* 3938–3946.

James, D. J., & Glaze, L. E. (2006, September). *Mental health problems of prison and jail inmates* (Bureau of Justice Statistics Special Report NCJ 213600). Washington, DC: National Criminal Justice Reference Service.

Kandel, E. (2009). *A biology of mental disorder.* Retrieved from http://www.newsweek.com/id/204320

Lamb, H. R., Weinberger, L. E., & Gross, B. H. (2004). Mentally ill persons in the criminal justice system: Some perspectives. *Psychiatric Quarterly, 75,* 107–126.

Larsen, J. K. (1986). Local mental health agencies in transition. *American Behavioral Scientist, 30,* 174–188.

Leukefeld, C. G., & Tims, F. M. (1988). *Compulsory treatment of drug abuse: Research and clinical practice. A final report to the National Institute of Drug Abuse.* Washington, DC: Government Printing Office.

Linehan, M. M., Cochran, B. N., & Kehrer, C. A. (2001). Dialectical behavior therapy for border-line personality disorder. In D. H. Barlow (Ed.), *Clinical handbook of psychological disorders* (3rd ed., pp. 470–522). New York, NY: Guilford.

Lurigio, A. J., Fallon, J. R., & Dincin, J. (2000). Helping the mentally ill in jails adjust to community life: A description of a postrelease ACT program. *International Journal of Offender Therapy and Comparative Criminology, 44,* 532–548.

Malone, D., Marriott, S., Newton-Howes, G., Simmonds, S., & Tyrer, P. (2009). Community mental health teams for people with severe mental illnesses and disordered personality. *Schizophrenia Bulletin, 35,* 13–14.

McDonald, D., Dyous, C., & Carlson, K. (2008). *The effectiveness of prisoner re-entry services as crime control: The Fortune Society.* Cambridge, MA: Abt Associates.

McKillip, R. (2004). *The basics: A curriculum for co-occurring psychiatric and substance abuse disorders* (2nd ed., Vols. 1 & 2). Spokane, WA: McKillip and Associates.

McNeil, D. E., Binder, R. L., & Robinson, J. C. (2005). Incarceration associated with homelessness, mental disorder, and co-occurring substance abuse. *Psychiatric Services, 56,* 840–846.

Mears, D. (2008). Accountability, efficiency, and effectiveness in corrections: Shining a light on the black box of prison systems. *Criminology & Public Policy, 7,* 143–153.

Morrissey, J., Meyer, P., & Cuddeback, G. (2007). Extending assertive community treatment to criminal justice settings: Origins, current evidence, and future directions. *Community Mental Health Journal, 43,* 527–544.

Mueser, K., & MacKain, S. (2006, May; updated 2008, August). *Illness management and recovery in criminal justice.* Retrieved October 3, 2009, from CMHS National GAINS Center: http://gainscenter.samhsa.gov/pdfs/ebp/IllnessManagement.pdf

National Alliance on Mental Illness. (2009). *Peer-to-peer: NAMI's recovery curriculum.* Retrieved October 4, 2009, from http://www.nami.org/template.cfm?section=Peer-to-Peer

National Commission on Correctional Health Care. (2008). *Standards for mental health services in correctional facilities.* Chicago, IL: Author.

Oklahoma Department of Corrections. (2009, January 23). *Duties and responsibilities of qualified mental health professionals.* Retrieved October 4, 2009, from http://www.doc.state.ok.us/Offtech/op140201.pdf

Pabian, Y. L., Welfel, E., & Beebe, R. S. (2009). Psychologists' knowledge of their states' laws pertaining to Tarasoff-type situations. *Professional Psychology: Research and Practice, 40,* 8–14.

Perez, A., Leifman, S., & Estrada, A. (2003). Reversing the criminalization of mental illness. *Crime & Delinquency, 49,* 62–78.

Pollack, D., & Feldman, J. M. (2003). Introduction to the special issue of Community Mental Health Journal commemorating the 40th anniversary of the Community Mental Health Centers Act of 1963. *Community Mental Health Journal, 39,* 377–379.

Power, A. K. (2006). *Mental health system transformation: Solving the mental health maze.* Retrieved from http://mentalhealth.samhsa.gov/newsroom/speeches/011306.asp

Powitzky, R. (2003). A useful management tool for understanding correctional mental health services. *Correctional Mental Health Report, 4*(5), 65–66, 77–80.

Powitzky, R. (2008, March). *Past, present, and future of correctional mental health services.* Paper presented at the Mental Health in Corrections Symposium, Kansas City, MO.

Prendergast, M. L., Podus, D., Chang, E., & Urada, D. (2002). The effectiveness of drug abuse treatment: A meta-analysis of comparison group studies. *Drug and Alcohol Dependence, 67,* 53–72.

Rotter, M., McQuistion, H. L., Broner, N., & Steinbacher, M. (2005). The impact of the "incarceration culture" on re-entry for adults with mental illness: A training and group treatment model. *Psychiatric Services, 56,* 265–267.

Schaedle, R., McGrew, J. H., Bond, G. R., & Epstein, I. (2002). A comparison of experts' perspectives on assertive community treatment and intensive case management. *Psychiatric Services, 53,* 207–210.

Scott, W., & Crime and Justice Institute. (2008). *Effective clinical practices in treating clients in the criminal justice system.* Washington, DC: U.S. Department of Justice, National Institute of Corrections.

Smith, P., Gendreau, P., & Goggin, C. (2007). "What works" in predicting psychiatric hospitalization and relapse: The specific responsivity dimension of effective correctional treatment for mentally disordered offenders. In R. K. Ax & T. J. Fagan (Eds.), *Corrections, mental health, and social policy: International perspectives* (pp. 209–233). Springfield, IL: Charles C Thomas.

Steadman, H. J., Osher, F. C., Robbins, P. C., Case, B., & Samuels, S. (2009). Prevalence of serious mental illness among jail inmates. *Psychiatric Services, 60,* 761–765.

Substance Abuse and Mental Health Services Administration, National Mental Health Information Center. (n.d.-a). *Evidence-based practices: Shaping mental health services toward recovery. Illness management and recovery.* Retrieved October 3, 2009, from http://mentalhealth.samhsa.gov/cmhs/CommunitySupport/toolkits/illness/

Substance Abuse and Mental Health Services Administration, National Mental Health Information Center. (n.d.-b). *Evidence-based practices: Shaping mental health services toward recovery. Co-occurring disorders: Integrated dual disorders treatment.* Retrieved October 3, 2009, from http://mentalhealth.samhsa.gov/cmhs/communitysupport/toolkits/cooccurring/

Tarasoff v. Regents of the University of California, 529 P.2d 553 (Cal. 1974).

Tarasoff v. Regents of the University of California, 551 P.2d 334 (Cal. 1976).

Tonry, M. (2004). Has the prison a future? In M. Tonry (Ed.), *The future of imprisonment* (pp. 3–24). New York, NY: Oxford University Press.

U.S. Department of Health, Education, and Welfare. (1978). Protection of human subjects, Subpart C, additional protections pertaining to biomedical and behavioral research involving prisoners as subjects. *Federal Register, 43*(222), 53651–53656.

Wanberg, K., & Milkman, H. (2004). *Criminal conduct and substance abuse treatment: Strategies for self-improvement and change* (2nd ed.). Thousand Oaks, CA: Sage.

Warlaw, G. (1983). Models for the custody of mentally disordered offenders. *International Journal of Law & Psychiatry, 15,* 164–165.

Watson, C. G., Brown, K., Tilleskjor, C., Jacobs, L., & Pucel, J. (1988). The comparative recidivism rates of voluntary- and coerced-admission male alcoholics. *Journal of Clinical Psychology, 44,* 573–581.

Weinberger, L. E., & Sreenivasan, S. (1994). Ethical and professional conflicts in correctional psychology. *Professional Psychology: Research and Practice, 25,* 161–167.

Wolff, N. (1998). Interactions between mental health and law enforcement systems: Problems and prospects for cooperation. *Journal of Health Politics, Policy and Law, 23,* 133–174.

CHAPTER 3

Managing the Mentally Ill From a Correctional Administrator's Perspective

Peter M. Carlson

Introduction

Managing the mentally ill population can be a difficult challenge in any setting. However, when individuals with mental illness are confined in a correctional setting, the routine demands associated with the management of their care can be greatly exacerbated. This chapter describes some of the daily challenges this population presents for correctional administrators such as wardens, superintendents, sheriffs, and other staff tasked with the ultimate responsibility for the secure and orderly operation of correctional facilities. In particular, it frames correctional mental health care in terms of competing priorities and the importance of staff training (a recurrent theme in this chapter) as a means of ensuring proper care for incarcerated persons with serious and persistent mental illness. Lastly, this chapter proposes a reframing of conventional thinking about some aspects of correctional management and proposes best practices for addressing common challenges regarding mental health care in correctional settings.

Mentally Ill Criminal Offenders: A Societal Failure

American society has not done an adequate job of caring for individuals with serious mental illness. As noted in Chapter 1, failed social and political initiatives over the past few decades (e.g., deinstitutionalization and aggressive criminal justice approaches to reducing crime, such as the so-called war on drugs) have led to an increase in the number of mentally disordered individuals in correctional settings.

In fact, correctional institutions across the United States have become the primary providers of mental health services. The three largest psychiatric institutions in the United States are urban jails: the Los Angeles County Jail, the Cook County Jail in Chicago, and the jail at Riker's Island in New York City (Insel, 2003). In the United States, more than half of all prison and jail inmates now have mental health issues, including more than 700,000 inmates in state prisons, more than 70,000 in federal prisons, and more than 400,000 in local jails (James & Glaze, 2006). This shift from mental hospitals to correctional facilities has created a number of significant problems for local, state, federal, and private correctional administrators.

Correctional Administrator Challenges Associated With Mentally Ill Offenders

Placement of mentally ill individuals in correctional settings raises several management issues for correctional administrators, only a few of which can be discussed here due to space limitations.

Competing Priorities

Perhaps the greatest correctional administrative challenge associated with the increased number of mentally ill offenders in jails and prisons is the need for more staff resources to ensure adequate care of these offenders and an agency commitment to provide these resources. Meeting the needs of this particular population is disproportionately costly in terms of both time and labor, as interventions are often individualized and may be required at a moment's notice, as when a mental health emergency occurs. Without additional resources, the growing numbers of mentally ill offenders place a drain on institutional resources—resources that are needed for a number of competing correctional demands and responsibilities. Foremost among these is the provision of safe and secure institutions 24 hours a day, 7 days a week. Carlson and DiIulio (2008) describe the demands of correctional leadership as follows:

> Leaders of state and federal correctional systems, chief executive officers of major institutions, and all those who work in developmental assignments under these senior leaders are responsible for millions of dollars of building and equipment, thousands of staff members, and many thousands of inmates within each facility or jurisdiction. (p. 193)

In addition to the management and treatment of mentally ill offenders, correctional leaders are responsible for a broad range of other vital functions, including ensuring public safety by maintaining all inmates in a secure environment; providing medical care; offering three meals each day; ensuring a safe and sanitary environment for offenders and staff; offering a full range of religious programs; training all staff in various topics relevant to corrections; maintaining positive labor-management relations; recruiting qualified staff; maintaining physical facilities; offering educational, vocational, and recreational opportunities; operating major industrial factories and other work sites for inmates; and providing other program services in support of an inmate population. Factor in other challenges, such as the management of inmate gangs, treatment of serious and chronic medical illnesses such as HIV or tuberculosis, separation of those offenders who need protection from other inmates, and issues associated with managing a large staff complement, and the daily concerns facing a correctional administrator become readily apparent.

To understand the dilemma of determining funding and personnel management priorities, one has first to consider the fiscal issues facing correctional executives, especially during periods of economic downturn. Managing the institution's budget is a pressing matter each and every day. The competing needs of all institutional departments are constant, and correctional administrators bear the responsibility for allocating limited resources to hire and train staff, purchase medical equipment and medications, maintain the physical plant (including housing units, plumbing, grounds, and perimeter fences), and provide nutritious food for each inmate. One surely cannot deny the need for healthcare and medication to control a life-threatening illness such as HIV/AIDS or hepatitis C. Yet as baby boomers retire from today's workforce, all labor-intensive organizations, including prisons, must recruit, train, and retain high-quality personnel. The need is especially great with regard to healthcare and mental health care workers, where shortages are growing more urgent and are projected to continue during the next several years (Fogg, 2008). Yet is this need more deserving of funding than cutting-edge technology in perimeter security? Imagine being a correctional administrator trying to explain to the state legislature an escape by a violent offender from the secure facility for which you are responsible, especially if you have spent vital funding on nonsecurity concerns.

How do these budget needs compare to the expense and extreme time commitment associated with institutional accreditation by such independent organizations as the American Correctional Association (ACA) or the National Commission on Correctional Health Care (NCCHC)? Is allocating financial resources to improving the inmate release transition program, as offenders complete their sentences and try to assimilate into their home communities, a high priority? In short, what are the truly critical needs in a tough budget climate? From the correctional administrator's perspective, mental health care is a priority, but only one of many to be accommodated to the extent available resources permit.

Beyond addressing the legitimate needs of inmates, prison administrators must attend to the concerns—and sometimes the demands—of staff. Labor unions may add to the daily pressure with their demands for safer work conditions or their recalcitrance in assuming additional job functions. For example, the influence of special interest groups such as the California Correctional Peace Officers Association (i.e., the state's prison officers' union) over California's prison policy is recognized by politicians and practitioners alike. With its ability to spend millions of dollars to defeat political enemies, this group has achieved unparalleled success in furthering its agenda. This union makes large-scale donations to political party candidates within the state, and this has resulted in very favorable treatment of union requests by many elected individuals (Macallair, 2009). When politicians such as Governor Arnold Schwarzenegger refuse to bow to this aggressive labor union, repercussions and payback appear in many forms, including attempts to recall the governor (Mitchell, 2008). This powerful labor union routinely tries to overturn the decisions of prison wardens and superintendents as correctional leaders grapple with complex and competing daily issues. To the extent that staff are adversarial in relationship to management, dealing with the fundamental concerns of running a prison, including, but not limited to, making sure mental health care is provided, becomes much more difficult.

The challenges of prison and jail management have never been greater than at present with expanding inmate populations, legal challenges, more aggressive and dangerous inmates, politicians who want to exert greater oversight over correctional institutions as correctional budgets are targeted, and staff issues that are complex and unending. When correctional administrators add the additional burden of managing a large mental health population to this list of responsibilities, it is easy to see how complex institution management can become. In brief, prison and jail leaders at the federal, state, and local levels are constantly asked to accomplish extremely tough tasks, often with less than adequate financial support. For example, the North Carolina Department of Corrections is facing unprecedented budget cuts; state agency officials say the budget will cost the agency 500 jobs over the next 2 years and require the agency to close seven prisons (Wig, 2009). In today's weak economy, other states are considering budget cuts that may close prisons, change sentencing practices, and generally reduce funding to correctional agencies. Washington State's lawmakers are considering nearly $4 billion in spending cuts, and such budget cuts would take a large percentage of funding from correctional agencies (Sullivan, 2009).

Few would argue that individuals with mental illness can be a clinically diverse and sometimes challenging group with which to work in the community. They are more problematic to manage in correctional institutions, which have now become the nation's default mental health care facilities. Although prisons were designed to rehabilitate, their medical and mental health care missions are incidental or ancillary to their primary public safety mission. Correctional administrators are faced with that subset of the larger mentally ill population who have been charged with and convicted of a crime. At the point of conviction or guilty plea, these individuals' primary status becomes that of a convicted offender, not a patient, and the correctional system must accommodate them accordingly.

Once incarcerated, these mentally ill offenders may be bullied by other, more aggressive, criminally sophisticated offenders or may respond to overtures from other offenders with aggression. Their vulnerability and unpredictability must be considered and balanced with their right to live in the least restrictive setting (i.e., not to be arbitrarily confined in a psychiatric hospital or segregation unit) as correctional administrators decide where to house and how to manage them.

Competing Missions

No matter where the mentally ill offender is housed or how he or she is managed, it is safe to say that correctional environments are less focused on the provision of mental health services than on safety and security concerns. Correctional leaders are expected to accomplish several potentially conflicting goals in dealing with criminal offenders: punishment, deterrence, incapacitation, and rehabilitation. They are expected to accomplish these goals while at the same time maintaining the safe and secure confinement of offenders, including those with mental illness. The organization and management structure of correctional facilities is significantly shaped by these very different goals. However, some believe that the conditions necessary to reform, treat, or otherwise rehabilitate an inmate conflict with the conditions that are necessary to punish offenders (Carlson & DiIulio, 2008; Craig, 2004). Is it possible for correctional officers responsible for security and inmate supervision also to be skilled therapists or drug treatment counselors? Most correctional administrators agree that whereas the missions of a correctional institution are often multipronged, staff members can successfully wear more than one hat. This philosophy is most prominent in the Federal Bureau of Prisons' (FBOP's) position that all correctional employees are correctional workers first and job specialists (e.g., case manager, psychologist, or administrator) second. As such, the FBOP emphasizes the cross-training of all employees in basic correctional management techniques so that all employees have a working knowledge of general correctional issues and management strategies.

Role Conflicts

Conflicting missions and priorities understandably result in role conflict. All correctional staff, including mental health professionals, have a responsibility to uphold and promote the institution's safety and security missions. Is it possible for a correctional counselor also to serve as a disciplinarian? In fact, it is often necessary. Can a correctional officer who is expected to control inmate behavior also provide advice and serve as a role model for prisoners? From an administrator's point of view, the ability to do both defines a good correctional officer. Should a mental health clinician report the suspected drug use of an inmate-patient to custodial staff? According to the rules of most correctional systems in the United States, he or she must. For instance, the FBOP program statement on inmate discipline specifies that all staff members are to report any known inmate misconduct (FBOP, 2003).

Certainly, it is desirable that inmates should respect and trust staff. They must feel they can approach staff with concerns about their own safety or that of the institution in general, or with their most personal mental health concerns. Given these contradictory pressures, perhaps the simplest way that correctional administrators can begin to address this issue is by acknowledging the difficulty staff have in confronting and resolving role conflicts and by supporting their efforts to resolve role conflicts through frequent consultation and guidance with senior administrators. Correctional administrators can also ensure that policies are in place that specify as much as possible the degrees of latitude staff have in working with inmates (e.g., in deciding whether to issue a formal sanction for a rule infraction).

Diagnostic Confusion

Correctional administrators are tasked with the smooth, orderly running of the institution. One factor that sometimes complicates this task is the inability of staff, including mental health staff, to come to a clear consensus regarding how to conceptualize and manage a particular inmate case. Without it, staff may not present a united front in their management of the inmate. This can result in increased staff frustration and in the inmate's ability to split staff—that is, to create differing perceptions of the inmate's mental status or trustworthiness—and thereby disrupt the smooth running of the facility.

All correctional employees who interact with offenders find themselves dealing with inmates who may or may not have mental health problems. Oppositional or resistant behavior in a correctional setting is frequent, and its causes can be multidimensional and easily misunderstood. Most institutional workers have little formal education in the identification and care of the mentally ill, other than what they may receive through on-site training. Yet they are routinely asked to differentiate between offender behaviors that may have at their roots either mental illness or criminal manipulation, or both, often for purposes of determining whether a mental health emergency exists. It is important to bear in mind that many institutions may have no mental health staff on-site at any given time, particularly at night or on weekends, so other staff must often be the "eyes and ears" of the mental health care professionals.

Even experienced clinicians may miss a diagnosis or disagree about a diagnosis of schizophrenia or other mental disorder when it is accompanied by antisocial behavior (i.e., an individual may be both psychotic and manipulative), so it is not surprising that correctional staff may have trouble making these behavioral distinctions. Additionally, many disruptive inmates come to prison with a history of various mental health diagnoses determined, in part, by the setting or circumstances in which the diagnosis was made. For example, an individual may be taken to a hospital emergency room with an amphetamine psychosis, treated, and released without a recognition that there is an underlying depressive disorder or antisocial tendency that may be contributing to the amphetamine use. With younger offenders, even those who have had encounters with the mental health system, psychotic disorders may not have emerged by the time they were old enough to be committed to an adult correctional facility.

In prison, inmates may display both Axis I (major mental illness) and Axis II (personality disorder) characteristics that potentially create confusion, both in identifying mental illness and in devising appropriate care. For example, imagine a correctional officer who observes a fight between two prisoners. The officer's responsibility is to break up the fight and then write incident reports (or "tickets" or "shots") based on what was observed. The cause might appear to be due to situation and circumstance (i.e., a chance disagreement that escalated out of control). However, the institution's mental health staff might have further information, indicating that one inmate has a diagnosis of antisocial personality disorder (Axis II) and a related predisposition to intimidate and victimize others. Perhaps in addition (or instead), the same inmate might have a diagnosis of paranoid schizophrenia (Axis I) and a history of psychotic episodes during which he is prone to acting on delusional beliefs that others intend him harm. Determining the causes of behavior is a serious challenge in a correctional environment and can be particularly difficult when inmates are reluctant to disclose information about themselves or, especially, to "snitch" (inform) on another inmate, or when an inmate malingers, pretending to have a serious mental illness (e.g., a psychosis) in hopes of avoiding the consequences of his or her misbehavior. When behavior is the direct result of mental illness, then a different staff response may be necessary and is likely to influence the institutional disciplinary process.

In brief, when an inmate's behavior is not clearly understood, staff conflict and frustration are distinct possibilities. They can occur when a mental health clinician provides a diagnosis for an inmate that is not credible to correctional staff, or when correctional workers observe behaviors that seem to reflect mental illness despite mental health staff's denials of such illness, or when inmates present different facades to different staff. Such confusion interferes with the smooth running of the institution and presents correctional administrators and their subordinates with an additional burden.

Establishing a Standard of Care

The standard of healthcare required in a correctional environment should not differ from the community standard of care. The 1976 U.S. Supreme Court case of *Estelle v. Gamble* established the constitutional right of inmates to adequate medical care. In defining what constitutes necessary and appropriate medical care, the courts have consistently included mental health needs (Moore, 2003).

Organizations such as the NCCHC (2008) and the ACA (2002) provide standards that may be used for assessing the quality of care provided in correctional facilities. Reviews, or audits, by these independent organizations of institutions' healthcare practices aid all staff, including administrators, in maintaining quality medical and mental health care for offenders. Correctional administrators have the ultimate responsibility to ensure that such care, according to these or other acceptable guidelines, including the agency's own regulations, is provided to inmates as appropriate to their needs. This means ensuring the provision of adequate resources, including qualified staff, office space, and equipment, as well as maintaining accountability for those practices.

Adequate Intake Screening Procedures

Fundamental to the establishment of appropriate standards of care is an appropriate mental health assessment procedure. The identification of incoming inmates suffering from a mental illness is truly the foundation of a high-quality mental health program (Fagan, 2003). There is no guarantee that adequate background information will be available on inmates newly committed to a jail or prison. They may readily acknowledge or perhaps deny previous mental health contacts, and records may be unavailable to corroborate their assertions. To ensure that inmates with mental illness are identified early in their incarceration, correctional administrators must ensure that they have adequate mental health staff or appropriately trained correctional staff to identify these offenders as they arrive at the institution. Intake screening procedures are also required by organizations (e.g., ACA and NCCHC) that accredit correctional programs. The American Psychiatric Association (2000) also recommends the screening of all new institution arrivals in its *Guidelines for Psychiatric Services in Jails and Prisons*. In establishing and/or maintaining adequate mental health screening protocols, correctional administrators should make sure their mental health supervisors use such guidelines.

Correctional administrators, as well as correctional mental health care providers, depend upon this screening program functioning well. Without an adequate intake screening process, mentally disordered offenders may enter the general population, where their behaviors may disrupt the orderly running of the institution or where they may be victimized by more criminally sophisticated inmates.

Therefore, the early identification of mental illness is clearly a critical need for correctional administrators. Concerning this point, Dr. Sally Johnson (2008), a nationally recognized correctional psychiatrist, has noted that historically the principal focus for most correctional mental health clinicians has been the identification of the more serious or major Axis I disorders such as bipolar disorder, major depression, or schizophrenia. Whereas this group is estimated to make up about 16% of prison populations (Ditton, 1999; Peters, LeVasseur, & Chandler, 2004), Johnson suggests that more time and attention must also be focused on identifying and meeting the needs of inmates with Axis II disorders such as borderline personality disorder and antisocial personality disorder—disorders that are represented in greater numbers in correctional settings than in the general population (Johnson, 2008). Such disorders can manifest themselves as highly disruptive behaviors like suicidal gestures, self-injury, or attempts to manipulate staff. Therefore, having good mental health information is an essential management tool for correctional administrators, as well as the foundation for high-quality treatment.

The Need for Staff Training About Mental Illness

Correctional administrators are tasked with determining how best to train all correctional workers. Most correctional systems now offer some staff training in recognizing the signs and symptoms of mental illness and how to refer individuals with these symptoms to mental health professionals. Institutional staff are trained to understand that a percentage of inmates with whom they interact at any given time are likely to suffer from serious mental illness and must be identified and offered treatment during their confinement. Staff throughout the facility must be trained to recognize that they are a critical element in identifying aberrant behavior and that, collectively, they are in the unique position of being able to observe inmates 24 hours a day. If all of these staff members are knowledgeable in identification and reporting procedures, then the institution's mental health program is enhanced and is better integrated into the fabric of the institution.

What may be more difficult for correctional staff to understand is that sometimes these inmates may need to be treated differently (i.e., in ways that may seem preferential) because of their mental illness. Most problematic from a correctional officer's perspective are situations in which offenders with serious mental illness commit institutional infractions, perhaps even assaulting a staff member. Such behavior may be entirely under the inmate's control, entirely a product of psychosis (e.g., an assault resulting from a paranoid delusion involving the victim), or a combination of both. Correctional administrators must make sure that mental health providers are available to assess the inmate, identify the basis of his or her behavior, and educate staff about the nature of these behaviors so that they more clearly understand the inmates they are ultimately responsible for managing on a daily basis.

In particular, however, it is vital to make sure all correctional workers understand that inmates with serious and persistent mental illness may at times need to be handled differently during the institutional disciplinary process. Failure to understand this point can create friction among custodial and treatment staff, can have implications for treatment planning, and can adversely impact the overall management of an already difficult group of offenders. When this point is understood, however, the integrity of the disciplinary process is maintained, and the institution's mental health mission and its primary safety and security missions are mutually supportive. (The disciplinary process, especially as it relates to the particular concerns of inmates with serious mental illness, will be discussed in more detail in a later section.)

This complementary state of affairs starts with training, which includes teaching staff constructive ways to interact with inmates. In fulfilling their daily institutional safety responsibilities, correctional officers regularly deal with recalcitrant and aggressive personalities. It is, therefore, very easy to perceive a challenge to one's authority in an inmate's unusual behavior. Historically, the response to aberrant behavior was more likely to be a physical response to control the offender. However, in the past 30 years there has been a growing emphasis on staff training focused on de-escalating emotionally charged, potentially violent situations and avoiding confrontations where possible.

Administrators also train through their own conduct. They require a high level of staff conduct and accountability, but to obtain this, senior correctional administrators must serve as role models. Correctional leaders must do what they say they are going to do, be consistent each and every day, and comport themselves in a manner that reflects the professional values and conduct desired of all employees. Ralph Waldo Emerson had it right when he said, *"What you are speaks so loudly I cannot hear what you say."*

Best Practices for Correctional Administrators

Housing for Mentally Disordered Offenders

Correctional administrators are in the unique position of being able to support innovative programs when they are presented or to lobby funding sources for monies to implement creative programs. Such programs not only benefit the inmate in terms of more responsive treatment in a safe, secure environment, they also benefit the institution through reducing the inmate misconduct that is the by-product of mental illness. In essence, both the mental health and security/safety missions of the institution are better served when correctional administrators support such programs.

Two examples of excellent practices regarding the housing of mentally ill offenders can be found in the state of Colorado and in the FBOP. Inmates in the Colorado prison system who need long-term mental health care can be transferred to the San Carlos Correctional Facility, a new 255-bed facility. In this institution, inmates participate in a wide range of therapeutic programs and activities. One key element in this program is the collaborative effort demonstrated by all staff—correctional officers, teachers, psychologists, nurses, and social workers—working together to treat inmates with serious mental illness (Correctional Association of New York, 2004).

The FBOP operates 115 federal correctional facilities across the United States for approximately 170,000 inmates. It also contracts with a variety of privately managed confinement facilities to house an additional 22,000 inmates (FBOP, 2009). The federal system mainstreams the vast majority of its mentally ill offenders in the general prison population of its correctional facilities, but it also has the option of transferring those in crisis to any one of several federal medical centers for inpatient treatment.

Access to Care: Staff and Program Availability

Inmates who suffer from mental illness must have the ability to access appropriate therapeutic programs and mental health professionals when necessary. Correctional administrators must ensure this access while still providing safe and secure housing and programs. Reasonable access is defined as institution administrators' ensuring that the facility has adequate mental health staffing, mental health screening for new arrivals, and procedures in place for a staff member or an inmate to request chronic or acute care without undue obstacles that preclude access to the caregivers (NCCHC, 2008). Correctional leaders must also ensure a continuum of mental health care, a process to monitor inmates in crisis, a suicide prevention program, and routine assessment for those offenders receiving psychiatric medication. This continuum extends to coordination for the provision of postrelease care.

Recruitment of Qualified Mental Health Professionals

One of the greatest challenges in ensuring access to care is that it is extremely hard to find qualified and motivated clinicians who are willing to work inside a correctional facility and create a quality mental health care program. The competing, though not mutually exclusive, interests of care and institution security/safety are difficult aspects of day-to-day operations that correctional facility leadership must resolve. Government career positions with limited pay options often present large obstacles to mental health hiring. Practitioners in this field are in great demand and command the ability to earn larger salaries than the government is sometimes authorized to pay. The geographic location of many correctional facilities complicates the recruitment efforts of correctional administrators. Many prisons are located in rural areas. Psychiatrists, psychologists, social workers, and other mental health professionals may not wish to live in such isolated communities away from professional contacts.

Various strategies have evolved to deal with these challenges in different state and federal jurisdictions. Many state and federal correctional agencies have chosen to identify one central facility as a mental health care center. All offenders with mental health issues are then referred to this facility for care and programming. This has the added advantage of potentially locating the facility near a large population center and may facilitate the hiring of quality staff, but it may also move the offender further away from family and community support.

The FBOP and some state systems have spent considerable resources in predoctoral psychology internship programs that have enjoyed positive recruitment results. Many jurisdictions have also developed forensic training programs for postdoctoral students in the form of psychology (Association of Psychology and Postdoctoral Internship Centers, n.d.) and psychiatry residency training programs (National Resident Matching Program, 2008)—programs that also assist with recruitment.

Correctional agencies have also experimented with telehealth technology to provide long-distance assessment and support programs over closed-circuit television lines (Magaletta, Ax, Bartizal, & Pratsinak, 1999; Magaletta, Fagan, & Ax, 1998). Some success has also been noted by agencies in using contract mental health resources (*locum tenens*; Moran, 2001). Correctional leaders have also successfully lobbied for the development of a pay differential for psychiatrists, who are particularly difficult to recruit.

The FBOP has sought and received approval from the Office of Personnel Management for improved pay rates for medical officers, especially psychiatrists, by citing recruitment difficulties.

Revisiting Correctional Justice: Changing Staff Perceptions

Inmate Disciplinary Process

One of the main concerns of correctional administrators, particularly with regard to inmates with serious and persistent mental illness, is prison discipline. Correctional workers judiciously exercise their formal and informal authority to maintain a safe and secure environment for all offenders. This is the foundation upon which all other institutional missions, including the provision of mental health care, are based. This means that all staff must consistently enforce institutional rules. All prison and jail facilities have established a disciplinary process to deal with unacceptable inmate behavior that violates institution regulations. All disciplinary infractions observed by staff are documented and referred to a disciplinary committee or a disciplinary hearing officer. All inmates have specified rights under these regulations and are entitled to a due process hearing for adjudication of the charges. Inherent in this disciplinary process is the premise that all will be treated fairly. Inmates expect fair treatment from staff, and staff expect the support of their colleagues throughout the disciplinary process. Essentially, this means all of the actors involved (i.e., the misbehaving inmate, the staff member reporting the unacceptable behavior, and the disciplinary hearing officer) expect a fair and reasoned outcome from the disciplinary process. In short, holding inmates accountable for their unacceptable behavior is key to the concepts of accountability, fairness, and institutional control. Although this process works for most offenders, is it the right procedure for mentally disordered offenders? Consider the composite case example illustrating minor inmate misconduct presented in Text Box 3.1.

TEXT BOX 3.1
MINOR MISBEHAVIOR IN THE CELL HOUSE

THE INCIDENT: James Phillips was having a bad day. The 43-year-old felon was serving a 10-year sentence for armed robbery and had been in the state penitentiary for 18 months. He had not been a management problem for correctional personnel, but today was very different. It seemed that everything he did was turning sour. His supervisor in the Food Service Department had told him this morning that his work quality had deteriorated this week, and when he returned to his cell after the noon meal he found that the institution shakedown team had gone through all of his property as part of their routine searches for contraband. They had left his cell in a mess. As Phillips looked at his bed sheets and blanket piled on the bed, and books scattered on the floor, he became angry. At this unfortunate moment, the cell house officer, Hank Turner, walked by Phillips's cell and sarcastically told him that his house looked like a pig lived in it. "Clean it up, Phillips!" This was the straw that pushed Phillips over the edge, and he retorted, "F__k you, Turner. Those a__holes messed it up, let them come clean it up!"

Officer Turner had never had any problems with Inmate Phillips before, but he knew he had to deal with this outburst. He turned back to the cell and said evenly, "What did you say?" The angry Phillips repeated his succinct thought: "I said f__k you. Your f__king crew made this mess, I'm not going to clean up after them!"

"OK, Phillips. You've just earned yourself a ticket for insubordination," replied the officer.

EXPECTATIONS OF THE ACTORS: Following this situation, both the staff member and the inmate have expectations of the institutional disciplinary system. The officer fully expects the disciplinary hearing officer to support his authority and sanction the offending inmate with a reasonable punishment, such as a loss of privileges (e.g., visits or phone calls) or a short time in disciplinary segregation.

Once Inmate Phillips cools down, he will fully expect staff members to punish his transgression. He will hope for a lighter sanction, but he understands that he has crossed the line and there will be some form of punishment.

In sum, all involved in this incident have expectations of fairness that must be enforced through the institutional disciplinary code. What would be the result if staff did not hold an inmate accountable for insubordination?

What if the inmate involved in this minor incident was known to be diagnosed with schizophrenia? In that case, should the correctional staff member and/or the disciplinary hearing officer treat him differently? Will other inmates view the offending inmate as "getting away" with misbehavior? If so, what impact will this view have on subsequent inmate behavior or on the orderly running of the institution? What about if the offending behavior is more serious (e.g., if the inmate assaulted the staff member) and the inmate was mentally ill? These questions are really at the heart of the dilemma faced by correctional administrators when they are crafting an inmate disciplinary process.

Although correctional staff can intellectually grasp that the mentally ill inmate may not be thinking clearly, most also believe there must be accountability for unacceptable behavior. This issue is further complicated by two additional factors. First, offenders have occasionally been known to prevaricate and fake mental illness. Differentiating between malingering and true illness is sometimes a difficult task, and some correctional workers can become somewhat jaundiced over the years after working with inmates who are perceived as having tried to manipulate staff. Second, labor-management relations often become strained when staff believe their authority is being diminished by senior managers as the disciplinary process is modified because of a mental health concern.

Correctional systems continue to struggle with establishing the right balance between firm, fair, and consistent treatment for all offenders (i.e., the bedrock on which all correctional systems are built) and recognizing and accommodating the special needs presented by mentally ill offenders. Some states have begun to alter significantly their procedures for dealing with mentally ill offenders who violate institutional rules. For instance, in New York State, where the management of mentally ill offenders is the joint responsibility of the Department of Correctional Services (DOCS) and the Office of Mental Health (OMH), these agencies have established Special Treatment Programs in their segregated disciplinary housing units, as well as a special multiphased Behavioral Health Unit. Both are designed for offenders with mental illnesses who have also violated institutional rules, and both try to balance the offender's need for treatment with the institution's need to create a safe, secure environment for all staff and inmates. Although innovative, these programs have not been without controversy. The union that represents correctional officers has complained about these special programs/units and refers to them as a serious security concern (Lehman, 2008). It is easy to see how these concerns can create rifts between correctional officers and mental health caregivers.

This potential to create friction between security staff and mental health workers must be dealt with in a forthright manner. First and foremost, all staff must understand that the problem of an increasing population with mental health issues is everybody's concern. This population presents as a very real problem that impacts the institutional operations of all departments and everyone working or living inside the correctional facility. It will be critical for all staff members to understand that everyone benefits from the proper care of those who have mental health concerns.

The issue is multifaceted, and staff members of all departments must come to understand that unique programs and procedures will have to be created to protect, control, and treat those with mental health problems professionally and effectively. The argument in support of this shift can be made in terms of creating a humane way to treat illness, developing a safer means of dealing with strange behaviors, or simply avoiding litigation and the perception of unprofessional care in the view of the public and the media.

Staff Training and Interdisciplinary Collaboration

As noted earlier, training is a key ingredient for the initial development and continued education of all correctional professionals. It also represents a major commitment of staff time and availability from a correctional administrator's perspective. As more and more staff members are exposed to inmates with mental health issues, training is of increasing importance. Training must emphasize that the issues presented by the mentally ill offender are not easily defined or solved. Complex problems require collaborative responses by all staff members.

First and foremost, it is extremely important that all correctional workers receive a consistent message from both correctional administrators and mental health professionals about the importance of recognizing the signs and symptoms of mental illness and about the necessity to appropriately respond to those offenders who are suffering from chronic mental disorders. Senior administrators must emphasize the need for all personnel to be sensitive to mental illness. This requires foundation knowledge that can assist in the recognition of symptoms of mental illness.

Although correctional personnel must be trained to understand the basics of identifying and dealing with the mentally ill offender, mental health professionals must also learn the basic tenets of correctional practices and operations. Educating mental health staff regarding the issues correctional officers confront in managing inmates with serious mental illness on a daily basis will help them to be more effective in practicing in prison and jail environments, both in working with inmates directly and in collaborating with correctional officers. Encouraging them to understand common terms and slang related to correctional life also enables them to work more effectively with other staff and inmates in the system.

All correctional organizations will benefit from collaboration and training relationships between correctional staff and mental health professionals. An outstanding example of such collaboration can be found in the New York DOCS, where an excellent working relationship has been developed between DOCS custodial staff and mental health staff employed by the state OMH (i.e., the separate organization responsible for the provision of mental health care to inmates). OMH training has been conducted in numerous maximum-security New York correctional facilities and focuses on the recognition of serious mental illness; the mental health service system; appropriate coordination procedures between correctional, medical, and OMH staff; and how to safely deal with an inmate in crisis. The goal of the training is to ensure the provision of effective mental health services while maintaining the safety and security of the prison operation.

Additionally, New York's correctional system has established Joint Case Management Committees in a number of its high-security facilities. These committees consist of senior administrative staff with day-to-day management authority (e.g., assistant warden), OMH mental health staff, and DOC case/unit management and correctional staff. They meet weekly to consider individual cases of problem inmate behavior, determine whether the behavior is the result of mental illness, and jointly decide on a management strategy. Collaboratively, this committee determines an individual course of action that meets the offender's treatment needs while maintaining institutional safety and security. These committees typically focus on cases of inmates housed in disciplinary units where, historically, a disproportionate number of disruptive, mentally disordered offenders have been housed. These committees are also authorized to modify unit security operations to accommodate treatment goals and to reduce or suspend disciplinary penalty times. New York utilizes these Joint Case Management Committees throughout its large correctional system, and the outcome has been a significant reduction in the number of offenders with the most serious mental health cases in special housing units (Fischer, 2009).

Two aspects of this program are particularly significant. First, it represents an acknowledgement by senior administrators that some flexibility may be needed when managing complex cases involving inmates with mental illness and/or disruptive behavioral patterns. Second, it achieves a "buy in" of all staff involved in managing the inmate by allowing them to be a part of the decision-making process regarding inmate treatment and to have their respective concerns aired and addressed.

Segregating Mentally Disordered Offenders

Segregation or special housing units (SHUs) are sometimes used to control the behavior of inmates and are a necessary part of prison management. In most prisons and jails, there are separate housing units, sometimes even entire buildings, for housing inmates who cannot reside in the general population. These SHUs are utilized for various purposes including as a disciplinary sanction for inmates who break institution rules and regulations, as a method of protecting offenders who request protective custody status, and as a temporary holding area for offenders awaiting adjudication for violating institutional rules.

This traditional means of dealing with inmates who choose to violate institutional regulations has the threefold purposes of separating these offenders as punishment for their misbehavior, ensuring the safety of other inmates and staff, and maintaining the normalcy of the institution's routine. Inmates who cannot or will not comply with staff rules or present a threat to others are segregated from the general population for specific periods of time. Those who present violent behavioral characteristics are typically placed in long-term, highly controlled, segregated housing units. This has proven to be a reasonable method of ensuring safety and security in most correctional environments and has successfully modified the problem behaviors of most inmates over time.

Whereas SHUs are essential to maintaining order in the correctional setting, it must be noted that the segregation of some inmates, especially those with depressive symptoms and other mental disorders, may lead to an increased risk of suicide or an exacerbation of mental health symptomatology (He, Felthous, Holzer, Nathan, & Veasey, 2001; Way, Miraglia, Sawyer, Beer, & Eddy, 2005). Lindsay Hayes (1995), a nationally recognized expert in preventing prison suicide, has suggested that isolation should be avoided for clinically depressed offenders. Mears and Watson (2006) have also argued that solitary confinement can create a negative effect on the human persona of most inmates.

How should correctional administrators and staff deal with mentally disordered offenders who violate institutional rules? Should these offenders be placed in SHUs similar to non–mentally ill offenders? This is a dilemma for most correctional administrators. Many of those who break institutional rules are likely to have treatment-resistant disorders, including personality disorders, impulse control disorders, and other mental disorders that compromise cognitive and behavioral functioning. Prisoner advocacy groups, mental health practitioners, and prison administrators have found that the segregation of an individual with mental illness can exacerbate the inmate's behavioral and emotional problems (Haney, 2003). Segregation itself can be an extreme stressor that may compound preexisting illness. The paradox is that the inmate presenting the greatest need for mental health services is often housed in the type of unit where it is most difficult to provide it.

Accordingly, a number of state correctional systems have adopted new regulations that govern the disciplinary policies for handling inmates that have been diagnosed with mental illness. A sampling of these regulations is given in Table 3.1.

Table 3.1   Disciplinary Procedures for Mentally Ill Offenders

1. Separating the mental health population through transfer to a medical/psychiatric unit or facility. This model can range from a full-service, correctional mental hospital to a specialized wing of a maximum-security prison or jail (Holton, 2003).

2. Training disciplinary hearing officers to mandate the mental health screening of all documented unacceptable behavior by inmates. If the documented behavior reflects mental health concerns, then professional evaluation can be requested before the incident is administratively adjudicated (Smith, Sawyer, & Way, 2004).

3. Establishing quality care programs for mentally ill offenders with the goal of facilitating appropriate behavior, clear thinking, and emotional stability for all patients (Smith et al., 2004).

4. Developing transitional care units to facilitate the return of inmates from SHUs to a general population unit (Holton, 2003; Cordelli, Bradigan, & Holanchock, 1997).

5. Developing alternatives to typical segregation or SHUs to avoid the problem of creating worse behavior in the mentally disordered offender. This approach may involve suspending a segregation sanction, creating a unique behavioral contract with the offender, and utilizing special positive reinforcement programs designed to shape improved behavior (Correctional Association of New York, 2004).

6. Establishing a special oversight committee to review and track the discipline and special confinement of all inmates whose mental state or intellectual capacity may be at issue. Such committees meet regularly and are required to identify and consider alternatives for any inmate on the mental health caseload or any offender involved in a disciplinary process who may be demonstrating that his or her mental state is an issue. This committee can track behavioral changes by anyone on its caseload and intervene when necessary (Smith et al., 2004).

7. Creating mental health programs that serve those in lock-down status. This may include various therapies (individual psychotherapy, group interaction using unique separation booths), and offenders may have the ability to earn more privileges and freedom with progressively good behavior. Some correctional mental health professionals have recommended "step-up" units, areas within the general population where those inmates in need of more structure or those feeling threatened by open population can receive an intermediate level of support and supervision. This places less strain on a disciplinary SHU and can provide more direct care for this specific population (Magaletta, Ax, Patry, & Dietz, 2005).

Arguments in favor of removing mentally ill offenders from a prison's SHU have gained more widespread acceptance in the past several years. For example, New York's state legislature recently passed legislation that will eventually phase out the placement of mentally disordered offenders in disciplinary units and mandate their confinement in therapeutic treatment program units such as the Special Treatment Programs or Behavioral Health Units mentioned above. Other states have passed similar prohibitions against the placement of mentally ill offenders in SHUs.

Passage of this type of legislation illustrates how some correctional initiatives come from outside of the correctional system. This particular legislation was championed by various advocacy groups such as Human Rights Watch and the National Alliance for the Mentally Ill (NAMI). Although this represents an advance for incarcerated mentally ill offenders, it presents a new set of issues for correctional administrators, who must now find a suitable treatment site for these offenders in a system that is already short on available treatment space. To accomplish this, additional funding must be requested from the state legislature, or other programs or services must sacrifice.

Rethinking Past Practices

It should be clear to most correctional administrators that some past management procedures simply do not apply to mentally disordered offenders who are not thinking clearly. For instance, it is against institutional regulations for an individual to attempt to commit suicide. In the past, someone who attempted suicide would be placed in special housing or be isolated from others—and the troubled inmate might again attempt to take his or her life. Additionally, these inmates were given an incident report or "ticket" for attempted suicide and were often denied telephone calls to family, contact with lawyers, outdoor time, and even clothing and showers. Correctional staff often had no choice but to place such inmates in segregation—even those at risk—because there were no alternative housing options. All of these practices work against professional and supportive treatment of those in crisis.

Historically, most correctional practitioners believed in classical criminological theory, which assumes that people are basically rational and make choices about how to live their lives, including whether they want to violate the law. In other words, criminological theory endorses the concept of free will and the notion that criminal behavior reflects the conscious exercise of free will. As Rothman (1998) noted when referring to the founding philosophy of the Auburn and Pennsylvania prison models,

> Reform, not deterrence, was now the aim of incarceration. The shared assumption was that since the convict was not innately depraved but had failed to be trained to obedience by family, church, school or community, he could be redeemed by the well-ordered routine of the prison. (p. 106)

In the context of this discussion, many correctional staff believe that all persons have the ability to decide how they will comport themselves on a daily basis. Again, in practice this means that each prisoner has the ability to choose conformity or misbehavior. If one accepts the concept that most individuals can plan and direct their actions, then it follows that a swift and severe consequence for acting out may deter unwanted behaviors in the future. However, this philosophy does not easily accommodate the vagaries of mental illness or tolerate other potential explanations for unacceptable behavior. Correctional administrators must train staff in the knowledge and skills necessary to work with inmates with serious and persistent mental illness (e.g., discerning unusual conduct by inmates). Once observed, staff must be trained to document these behaviors and refer offenders displaying these behaviors immediately to professional staff for further clinical assessment. These offenders cannot be left on their own in an open prison population or other inmates may prey upon them or vice versa.

Summary and Conclusions

Local, state, federal, and private correctional institutions across the United States have become de facto mental health facilities. This has created considerable additional demand on available resources—resources that are already seriously limited.

Correctional administrators are now expected to develop not only an effective security operation but also a comprehensive mental health program that promotes early identification, intervention, and extensive services for mentally ill inmates within a correctional environment that is both safe and secure. All of this must be accomplished while holding down the cost of care. This requires exceptional management of both fiscal and human resources in an environment where the mental health mission is one of many.

Leaders in the field of correctional management are expected to make a sustained commitment to the provision of mental health services. The interested constituents, including taxpayers, have very high expectations as to how persons with mental illness are managed and treated while confined. Correctional administrators, politicians, and other government leaders have begun to take responsibility for this special population, knowing that institutional operations will suffer if programs are not developed in a timely and efficacious manner.

Individual wardens and superintendents must personally emphasize the need for all staff to support mental health programming. Correctional administrators must be advocates for strong mental health programs if they expect their subordinates to value them as well. They should provide policy direction to personnel within their facility and policy advice to the political leadership of the government. Leadership expectations must be clearly established that result in continuous improvement in the continuity of care for those in custody. Safe and secure correctional operations depend upon it.

KEY TERMS

Access to care

Accreditation

American Correctional Association

National Commission on Correctional Health Care

Correctional administrator

Punishment

Deterrence

Incapacitation

Rehabilitation

Role conflicts

Diagnostic confusion

Estelle v. Gamble

General population

Intake screening

Inmate discipline process

Interdisciplinary collaboration

Segregation

Labor-management relations

Special housing unit (SHU)

Human Rights Watch

National Alliance for the Mentally Ill

DISCUSSION QUESTIONS

1. What is the importance of intake screening to the overall operation of a correctional facility?

2. Why do mentally ill offenders present unique challenges to staff members working in a prison or jail?

3. What is the difference between mad and bad behavior?

4. Why is it difficult to expect staff members to respond differently to those offenders diagnosed with mental illness?

5. Can you explain why training all correctional staff to recognize signs and symptoms of mental illness is critical to the mental health mission in a correctional facility?

References

American Correctional Association. (2002). *Performance-based standards for correctional health care for adult correctional institutions.* Alexandria, VA: Author.

American Psychiatric Association. (2000). *Guidelines for psychiatric services in jails and prisons* (2nd ed.). Washington, DC: Author.

Association of Psychology and Postdoctoral Internship Centers. (n.d.). *APPIC online directory.* Retrieved March 15, 2009, from http://www.appic.org/directory/4_1_directory_online.asp

Carlson, P. M., & DiIulio, J. J. (2008). Organization and management. In P. M. Carlson & J. S. Garrett (Eds.), *Prison and jail administration: Practice and theory* (2nd ed., pp. 193–212). Sudbury, MA: Jones and Bartlett.

Cordelli, W., Bradigan, B., & Holanchock, H. (1997). Intermediate care programs to reduce risk and better manage inmates with psychiatric disorders. *Behavioral Sciences and the Law, 15,* 459–467.

Correctional Association of New York. (2004). *Mental health in the house of corrections.* Retrieved May 26, 2009, from http://www.correctionalassociation.org/publications/download/pvp/issue_reports/Mental-Health.pdf

Craig, S. C. (2004). Rehabilitation versus control: An organizational theory of prison management. *The Prison Journal, 84,* 92–114.

Ditton, P. M. (1999). *Mental health and treatment of inmates and probationers* (Bureau of Justice Statistics Special Report NCJ 174463). Washington, DC: U.S. Department of Justice, Office of Justice Programs.

Estelle v. Gamble, 429 U.S. 97 (1976).

Fagan, T. J. (2003). Mental health in corrections: A model for service delivery. In T. J. Fagan & R. K. Ax (Eds.), *Correctional mental health handbook* (pp. 3–19). Thousand Oaks, CA: Sage.

Federal Bureau of Prisons. (2003). *Inmate discipline and special housing units* (Program Statement 5270.07). Retrieved March 15, 2009, from http://www.bop.gov/DataSource/execute/dsPolicyLo

Federal Bureau of Prisons. (2009, June 11). *Monday Morning Highlights population report.* Washington, DC: U.S. Department of Justice, Federal Bureau of Prisons.

Fischer, B. (2009, March 17). *Testimony of Brian Fischer, Commissioner New York State Department of Correctional Services before New York State Senate Committee on Crime Victims, Crime and Correction.* Retrieved May 26, 2009, from http://www.docs.state.ny.us/Commissioner/Testimony/SHUExclusionLaw.html

Fogg, J. G. (2008). Face the facts: We need to focus on recruitment. *Corrections Today, 70*(4), 8.

Haney, C. (2003). Mental health issues in long term and super-max confinement. *Crime & Delinquency, 49,* 124–156.

Hayes, L. M. (1995). *Prison suicide: An overview and guide to prevention.* Washington, DC: National Institute of Corrections, U.S. Department of Justice.

He, X. Y., Felthous, A. R., Holzer, C. E., Nathan, P., & Veasey, S. (2001). Factors in prison suicide: One-year study in Texas. *Journal of Forensic Sciences, 46,* 896–900.

Holton, S. M. B. (2003). Managing and treating mentally disordered offenders in jails and prisons. In T. J. Fagan & R. K. Ax (Eds.), *Correctional mental health handbook* (pp. 101–122). Thousand Oaks, CA: Sage.

Insel, T. R. (2003, March). *Beyond the clinic walls: Expanding mental health, drug and alcohol services research outside the specialty care system.* Symposium presented at a conference cosponsored by the National Institute of Mental Health and the National Institute on Alcoholism and Alcohol Abuse, Washington, DC.

James, D. J., & Glaze, L. E. (2006). *Mental health problems of prison and jail inmates* (Bureau of Justice Statistics Special Report NCJ 213600). Washington, DC: U.S. Department of Justice, Office of Justice Programs.

Johnson, S. (2008). Mental health. In P. M. Carlson & J. DiIulio (Eds.), *Prison and jail administration: Practice and theory* (2nd ed., pp. 113–124). Sudbury, MA: Jones and Bartlett.

Lehman, D. (2008, May 1). Union calls for removal of mental health unit at prison. *The Post Star.* Retrieved January 5, 2009, from http://www.poststar.com/articles/2008/05/01/news/latest/doc481a686ae3342466932628.prt

Macallair, D. (2009). *A modest proposal on prison costs.* Retrieved May 26, 2009, from Center on Juvenile and Criminal Justice: http://www.cjcj.org/post/alternatives/incarceration/modest/proposal/prison/costs/reign/overtime

Magaletta, P. R., Ax, R. K., Bartizal, D. E., & Pratsinak, G. J. (1999). Correctional telehealth. *Journal of the Mental Health in Corrections Consortium, 44,* 4–5.

Magaletta, P. R., Ax, R. K., Patry, M., & Dietz, E. F. (2005). Clinical practice in segregation: The crucial role of psychologists. *Corrections Today, 67*(1), 34–37.

Magaletta, P. R., Fagan, T. J., & Ax, R. K. (1998). Advancing psychology services through telehealth in the Federal Bureau of Prisons. *Professional Psychology: Research and Practice, 29,* 543–548.

Mears, D. P., & Watson, J. (2006). Towards a fair and balanced assessment of supermax prisons. *Justice Quarterly, 23,* 232–270.

Mitchell, J. (2008, September 8). *Prison guards union confirms Schwarzenegger recall effort.* Retrieved June 30, 2009, from http://www.politicker.com/california/3485/prison-guards-union-confirms-schwarzenegger-recall-effort

Moore, J. (2003). *Management and administration of correctional health care.* Kingston, NJ: Civic Research Institute.

Moran, M. (2001). More psychiatrists opt for life on the road. *Psychiatric News, 36*(18), 8.

National Commission on Correctional Health Care. (2008). *Standards for mental health services in correctional facilities.* Chicago, IL: Author.

National Resident Matching Program. (2008, July 16). *About the NRMP*. Retrieved August 13, 2009, from http://www.nrmp.org/about_nrmp/index.html

Peters, R. H., LeVasseur, M. E., & Chandler, R. K. (2004). Correctional treatment for co-occurring disorders: Results of a national survey. *Behavioral Sciences & the Law, 22,* 563–584.

Rothman, D. J. (1998). Perfecting the prison. In N. Morris & D. J. Rothman (Eds.), *The Oxford history of the prison: The practice of punishment in Western society* (pp. 100–116). New York, NY: Oxford University Press.

Smith, H., Sawyer, D., & Way, B. (2004). Correctional mental health services in New York: Then and now. *Psychiatric Quarterly, 75*(1), 21–39.

Sullivan, J. (2009, April 9). Closing prisons, slashing sentences eyed to balance budget. *The Seattle Times.* Retrieved July 21, 2009, from http://seattletimes.nwsource.com/html/politics/2009010460_criminaljusticecuts09m.html

Way, B. B., Miraglia, R., Sawyer, D. A., Beer, R., & Eddy, J. (2005). Suicide risk factors in New York State prisons. *International Journal of Law and Psychiatry, 28,* 207–221.

Wig, J. (2009, March 17). *Prison system hit hard with budget cuts.* Retrieved July 21, 2009, from My North Carolina.Com: http://politics.mync.com/2009/03/prison-system-hit-hard-with-budget-cuts/

SECTION II

Entering Correctional Practice

CHAPTER 4

Clinical Assessment in Correctional Settings

Daryl G. Kroner, Jeremy F. Mills,
Andrew Gray, and Kelly O. N. Talbert

Introduction

Clinical assessment is one of the most highly developed services that a psychologist can offer criminal offenders and correctional managers. Within the correctional environment, the purpose of clinical assessment is to address a clinical problem in a way that can assist the offender, as well as staff tasked with managing the offender. This chapter will begin with a discussion of some general issues and guidelines that impact clinical assessment in correctional settings, including barriers to optimal assessment, situations resulting in difficult assessments, and considerations regarding screening procedures. Then the chapter will focus on three areas within corrections where clinical assessment can make a value-added contribution. These areas involve the assessment of mental health problems, suicidality, and violence risk. The coverage of these specific areas of clinical assessment will include an overview of important issues, a review of sample instruments, and a checklist of general principles for choosing a specific instrument. The chapter will end with a discussion of socially desirable responding in clinical assessment.

General Issues and Guidelines

Barriers to Optimal Assessments

Physical Conditions

Optimal group testing will occur in a space designated for testing. Unless a space has been specifically designed for assessment procedures, less than optimal physical conditions are frequently the norm.

Testing crowdedness may contribute to undesirable testing results by compromising private responses and by unduly intensifying individual characteristics (Bonta & Gendreau, 1990). In group testing, offenders should be situated so that there is a sense of privacy. There should not be the opportunity for another inmate to easily see another person's responses.

One seemingly potential solution to overcrowdedness is to have offenders fill out tests in their cells. This is an unacceptable practice. First, test security is breached. Having copies of an instrument floating around in general population will undermine the validity of the instrument, the future use of the instrument, and the profession of psychology (American Psychological Association [APA], 2002, Ethics Code, Standard 9.11). Second, the conditions in a cell do not reflect standard test administration procedures. The administration will not be reflective of the normative test administration setting, which will be used to compare the current results. Usually offenders have cellmates with whom the items can be discussed, further contaminating the results.

Test Protocol Errors

Ensuring best practices through the use of appropriate instruments can be easily undermined by errors in administration, scoring, compiling scores, identification, administration, and applying correction scoring criteria. An instrument's reliability and validity become meaningless if scoring errors occur.

If an appropriate instrument is chosen for an assessment task, ease of use will not correct simple clerical errors. Research indicates that clerical scoring errors can range from 5.0% to 24.7% (Charter, Walden, & Padilla, 2000; Goddard, Simons, Patton, & Sullivan, 2004; Simons, Goddard, & Patton, 2002). Clerical errors were relatively common using hand-scoring templates with the Minnesota Multiphasic Personality Inventory–Second Edition (MMPI-2), a commonly used personality test, with 7% of the scales scored inconsistently (Iverson & Barton, 1999). The VRIN (Variable Response Inconsistency) scale of the MMPI-2, a difficult scale to score, was shown to have a 27% error rate. In one specific setting, Allard and Faust (2000) found an error rate of 51%!

One may think that using a scoring program/service would eliminate the error problem. Fewer errors are one of the results of computer scoring, but errors can still occur. The correct software and most current versions must be used. Allard and Faust (2000) found computer program errors with the MMPI. In one setting, this specific error altered MMPI profiles in 48 of 50 cases. The proper updates and answer forms are also necessary for correct scoring. In providing a legal overview of the MMPI-2, Pennuto (2004) cited a personal communication with Roger L. Greene, stating that Dr. Greene had never evaluated an MMPI-2 in court that had been correctly scored. A computer program should also be checked. If there are errors in a computer scoring program/service, these errors can be magnified when scoring programs are used. One way to hedge against scoring errors is to use instruments that are relatively easy to use. A difficult instrument may increase the likelihood of errors in administration, rating, and scoring of the scales.

There are four strategies that will serve as safeguards and reduce test scoring errors.

1. Emphasize accuracy. The main way of preventing scoring errors is to emphasize accuracy. Allard and Faust (2000) have presented evidence that an emphasis on accuracy can substantially reduce scoring error. Differences in actual errors between a strong and low commitment to accuracy occurred across multiple settings (VA outpatient, VA inpatient, private inpatient). The emphasis on accuracy starts by ensuring that names, ID numbers, birthdates, and so forth are fully correct. On paper forms, smudge marks need to be checked. Careful counting and recording need to occur. The emphasis on accuracy should be made throughout the full assessment. Whether it is the psychologist or an assistant scoring the test results, the goal of high accuracy is important, even if the task has the appearance of being mundane or unimportant. Although somewhat painful, keeping a list of the types of scoring errors will be beneficial. This list serves two purposes. First, it will be a reminder of which administration and scoring tasks are the most fallible. Second, when training others to administer and score tests, these examples will highlight potential areas of errors. Knowing that simple clerical scoring errors occur will help, but attention to detail is necessary for the simple and sometimes boring procedure of scoring tests. Providing examples of the common errors and how to prevent them will be beneficial. Such instructions will vary according to the type of test (e.g., self-report, computer-scored, rating, etc.), but the important point is to have the instructions accessible and in a written format.

2. Training and practice must occur. Adequate training is critical (APA, 2002, Ethics Code, Standard 2.01, "Boundaries of Competence"). Hall, Howerton, and Bolin (2005) noted that inadequate training is a major contributor to making errors. The nature of this training may vary considerably according to the nature of the instrument. For a standardized self-report inventory, basic training in psychometric principles and test administration, along with a working knowledge of the test manual, may provide a foundation for competent test administrations. Other instruments may require specialized training. Criminal justice rating instruments tend to require specific training. With certain rating instruments, such as the Psychopathy Checklist–Revised (PCL-R), it is optimal to obtain training from people endorsed by the original authors. If an instrument is complex, or deals with a unique population, additional training may be needed in areas such as interviewing skills or cross-cultural traditions.

Prior to administering a test, the manual/guide must be fully read and comprehended. Even if one of the tests looks similar to another, or a revised version has been released, one must have a working knowledge of the current instrument's manual. Scoring test results should be done the first time on a practice case, not on a current examinee. Not only should the practice cases be "former" cases, they need to have been checked for errors. If errors are in the practice cases, these errors will continue.

3. Test scoring needs to be checked. In other words, there needs to be an audit procedure built into the assessment process that will periodically check the accuracy of scoring. This includes both hand scoring and computer entry of data. An overconfidence may be placed in computers and scoring programs at the expense of ensuring that the correct information is being inputted. The specific time frame criterion for checking may vary according to how routine the testing is. For routine testing, an appropriate guideline to conduct a review is at every 20% point of the number of assessments. Thus, if 100 assessments are completed over a year, a review should occur after every 20 protocols. If few assessments occur, a more frequent review may be necessary.

4. A proper environment must be provided for test administrators to score tests. Recent research compared scoring errors by psychologists under a quota assessment, time-based, or self-managed system. The self-managed system had significantly lower scoring errors than the other two systems of conducting assessments (Goddard et al., 2004). Within correctional environments, psychological assessment competes with other institutional activities, usually resulting in a constant struggle to conduct routine assessments. Placing additional time-frame or quota pressures will likely increase scoring errors, as compared to allowing test administrators to structure their scoring activities.

Scoring tests while having other tasks to do also increases error (Allard & Faust, 2000). Having a self-managed space that can be used for scoring tests will be a best practice.

Difficult Assessments

Not all assessments will be completed smoothly. There are several contributors to difficult or incomplete assessments. Offender issues impeding the assessment process may include reading difficulties, belligerent attitudes, and the offender being under the influence of drugs or alcohol. A basic reading level is required for most self-report inventories. As pointed out by Rankin (2005), the view that offenders are highly illiterate is incorrect. But 20% to 28% of offenders read below a Grade 5 level, with the majority at a Grade 8 level or below (Muirhead & Rhodes, 1998; Rankin, 2005). This has implications in two areas of offender assessment. First, some instruments with a high reading level may not be appropriate with offender populations. For example, the MMPI-2 has a Grade 8 reading level and may not be appropriate for one half of offenders. Second, a systematic procedure for checking reading levels is necessary. This check needs to occur prior to proceeding with an assessment. Having offenders routinely not finish self-report inventories is not fair for the offenders and is a poor use of testing resources. For those offenders who do not have adequate reading levels, tests can be verbally read, and publishers often have audio versions available.

Related to reading level issues is the use of translated instruments. It is not a recommended practice to use a translated version unless the test has been backwards translated. For example, an English test is translated into Spanish. The Spanish version is translated back into English by someone who did not do the initial translation. Then the original English version is compared to the translated version. If similar, then the confidence can be high that the Spanish version is reflective of the original English version.

Occasionally an offender will become belligerent during an assessment. A firm approach is required to continue the testing session. In a one-on-one session, examining the reasons for acting out may assist in refocusing. Asking the offender permission to continue with the assessment can be a useful segue.

Developing good rapport with offenders will help promote their cooperation in the test process. Rapport development is considered one of the minimal competencies in the assessment process, and its quality may increase or decrease test performance significantly (Hall et al., 2005). In the above situations, good rapport will result in better cooperation in verbally administering individual test items, a process that admittedly can become boring. With belligerent offenders, an initial solid rapport may assist in continuing the assessment. Regarding offenders under the influence of drugs or alcohol, having an initial rapport may assist in their willingness to conduct the assessment at a later point in time. Thus, rapport development is necessary for any assessment, but it will prove to be a good resource when having to conduct difficult assessments.

Considerations Regarding Intake Screening Procedures

Intake units usually deal with a high volume of offenders and have to make speedy decisions with minimal resources. Often the initial contact is under 1 minute (Birmingham, Gray, Mason, & Grubin, 2000). Triage decision making occurs for a variety of reasons, including prison placement, healthcare needs, mental health needs, and, in some systems, rehabilitation needs. The purpose of screening is not to develop a definite course of action for an offender with mental disorder but, rather, to identify offenders who need a more in-depth assessment (Fagan, 2003; Morey, 1991; Ogloff,

Roesch, & Hart, 1993). There are four phases to the management of offenders with mental disorder within an intake context. The first is screening, the second is an in-depth assessment from the screening referrals, the third is intervention, and the fourth is reassessment to evaluate the intervention. Cohen (2008) outlines the legal responsibilities of (a) screening, (b) proper training of staff, and (c) the fact that screening does not violate the rights of offenders.

Fagan (2003) outlines three levels of services within corrections. At Level 1 are basic services offered to all offenders. Level 2 involves specialized interventions according to groups or categories of treatment needs. Level 3 involves the application of behavioral science principles to the organization. The first step of Level 1 services is intake assessments.

Clinical intake assessments are conducted for several reasons, according to Fagan (2003). These reasons include (a) assessing emotional, intellectual, and behavioral deficits; (b) identifying specialized treatment needs; (c) providing baseline data for future contacts; (d) assisting staff with offender management strategies; (e) providing offenders with information regarding mental health services that may be particularly relevant to them; (f) assessing risk of injury to self and others; and (g) assessing ability to participate in correctional treatment. Because the intake assessment process is by its definition a quick triage procedure, screening instruments should be brief and easy to administer. These assessment instruments are typically more factual in nature, targeting specific historical variables and behavioral/emotional characteristics and superficially assessing a broad range of topics (Reddon, Vander Veen, & Munchua, 2001).

In conducting a screening assessment, the development of a rapport with the offender is very important. Birmingham et al. (2000), in assessing screening measures for consecutive admissions, found that initial screening failed to identify three quarters of offenders with mental disorder. Similarly, other researchers have found 42% of offenders not disclosing past psychiatric involvement upon intake (Mitchison, Rix, Renvoize, & Schweiger, 1994). A potential contributor to low levels of self-disclosure is the perception offenders have of the screening process. After the screening, Birmingham et al. asked offenders about their experiences and views of the screening process. They found offenders to be critical of the screening, having the perception that healthcare staff did not have their best interests at heart. These perceptions prevented many from disclosing related mental health information. Some of the respondents from the Mitchison study indicated greater disclosure may have occurred if they were sitting down and the interview had been "more like seeing a doctor" (Mitchison et al., 1994, p. 328). Others felt pressure to get through the intake process and perceived that detailed responses would prolong it. Given the very real time pressures of the screening process, the development of rapport with offenders will be a major contributor to its effectiveness.

Assessment of Mental Health Problems

There is a legal obligation to identify offenders with mental health problems (Cohen, 2008; National Commission on Correctional Health Care, 2008). In addition to this obligation, the assessment of mental health problems has a direct benefit for correctional management and offenders alike. At the most basic level, knowing the number of mentally ill offenders in a facility gives administrators guidance on the number of beds necessary to manage this subsection of the offender population. Additionally, knowing this number will also assist with resource allocations. In certain contexts, conducting a diagnostic assessment also may have implications for funding and resources for offenders upon release.

The prevalence rate of serious mental disorder within the correctional system is conservatively estimated to be between 5% and 20% (Birmingham et al., 2000; Ditton, 1999; Fazel & Danesh, 2002). When assessing symptoms, the self-reported presence of one psychotic symptom varied from 7.8% in federal prisons to 11.1% in state prisons and 16.7% in local jails (James & Glaze, 2006). These rates among offenders are several times greater than the rates for the general public. It would seem that establishing the correctional prevalence would be straightforward, but this is not the case. There are issues of defining mental illness, using various techniques for assessment (e.g., file review, self-report, interviews), and range of sample issues (local, state, federal, sex, race, age, etc.; Ax et al., 2007).

Screening for mental health problems has multiple benefits, beyond gathering prevalence data. According to Fagan (2003), providing intake screening services is often the foundation upon which other Level 1 services are based within a correctional environment. Careful intake screening increases the likelihood of offenders' obtaining mental health services. If services are not offered upon intake, they are typically more difficult to obtain once offenders enter the general population. Associated with an intake screening procedure is a decision rule of who will have further assessment and/or services and who will not. But once within general population, the number of barriers to obtain services becomes an issue. First, will inmates voluntarily self-refer despite the stigma ascribed to mental illness by other offenders? Second, even if an inmate is willing to self-refer, will a staff person recognize signs of inmate distress and voluntarily act as a referral agent? With the less external indicators of a disorder, the task of convincing a staff person that an offender is experiencing psychiatric pain may be difficult to accomplish. Third, once within an institution, a set of clearly defined screening procedures with clearly defined criteria is usually not available (Birmingham & Mullee, 2005; Ogloff et al., 1993). There are referral procedures for mental health services, but these typically do not use a validated screening process, as may be found at intake.

Thus, it is best, both from management and clinical perspectives, that screening procedures are in place at intake to identify those who are having mental difficulties. Within the prison system, another intake point also occurs when an offender is placed in segregation. Problems with overreacting, behaving impulsively, and displaying odd behavior beyond the offender's control often result in a segregation placement. Several recent studies have used mental health screening instruments within segregation (O'Keefe, 2008; Zinger, Wichmann, & Andrews, 2001), suggesting mental health needs as offenders enter segregation.

Sample Intake Screening Instruments

In a four-phase assessment system including screening, full assessment, intervention, and reassessment, screening can be successfully accomplished by a brief instrument with basic psychometric properties. At times, screening instruments have been overly criticized for not having the same predictive validity as a full assessment instrument (Ferguson & Negy, 2006). However, the purpose of the screening phase is to determine whether to refer the offender for a full assessment. Below are three screening instruments with good empirical support.

1. The Holden Psychological Screening Inventory (HPSI; Holden, 1996). The HPSI is a screening instrument that evolved from three full-length instruments. It is a self-report instrument that takes about 5 to 7 minutes to administer. The items cover anxiety, depression, suicide risk, stress, and phobia (Book, Knap, & Holden, 2001). The test contains 36 items (using a 5-point Likert scale), with three scales of psychiatric symptomatology, social symptomatology, and depression.

The HPSI has been evaluated on multiple groups of offenders. These have included male inmates from six institutions (Book et al., 2001), psychiatric patients from a forensic unit of a psychiatric hospital (Holden & Grigoriadis, 1995), offenders entering an institution (Mills, Green, & Reddon, 2005), and young offenders (Starzyk, Reddon, & Friel, 2000).

In a study on the effects of administrative segregation, the HPSI was administered to both segregated offenders and a random sample selected from the general prison population (Zinger et al., 2001). Data collection occurred at three institutions. In addition, this was a multiwave study, with three testing times over 3 months. Segregated offenders did have higher HPSI scores than the control groups, but both groups improved over time.

2. The Brief Jail Mental Health Screen (BJMHS; Osher, Scott, Steadman, & Robbins, 2006). The BJMHS screens for the possible presence of serious mental illness such as schizophrenia, bipolar disorder, and/or major depression. It has eight yes/no rating questions, with six questions about current mental health problems and two questions about history of hospitalization and medication for mental or emotional problems The BJMHS takes about 3 minutes to administer (*http://gainscenter.samhsa.gov/ HTML/resources/MHscreen.asp*). *The development of the BJMHS emphasized brevity, explicit decision criteria, low false-negative rate, and no more than a modest false-positive rate.* Using multiple Axis I criteria, others have found the BJMHS to correctly identify approximately 83% to 100% of screened offenders (Ford, Trestman, Wiesbrock, & Zhang, 2007).

3. Brief Psychiatric Rating Scale (BPRS; Overall & Gorman, 1962; http://www.psychiatric times.com/clinical-scales/schizophrenia). The BPRS is the most commonly used instrument to measure psychiatric symptoms. The scale consists of 24 rated items that measure psychiatric symptom change over time and takes approximately 20 to 30 minutes to administer. Content areas include hostility, suspiciousness, hallucination, and grandiosity. The questions are asked about the individual's behavior for the previous 2 to 3 days. Items include rating both the client's self-report and behavioral observations.

Traditionally four subscales have been used (Anxiety, Depression, Suicidality, and Hallucinations), although a recent study with remanded psychiatric patients found a five-factor structure of the BPRS consisting of Psychoticism, Thought Disturbance, Depression, Withdrawal, and Mania (Jacobs, Ryba, & Zapf, 2008). Other offender research has also indicated a five-factor solution (Cloyes, Lovell, Allen, & Rhodes, 2006). Multiple studies have demonstrated the validity of the BPRS among offenders (Harris & Lovell, 2001; O'Keefe, 2008).

There are several screening instruments that have been used or developed with offenders and show promise for clinical use. Up to this point in time, however, these scales have minimal validity data.

1. Birmingham and Mullee (2005) developed an intake screening instrument consisting of six items. The development of these rated items involved surveying frontline staff, semi-structured interviews with offenders, and structured ratings and self-report instruments administered to offenders. Five of the items came from the data gathered, and the sixth item allowed officers to specify any other symptoms. In the initial evaluation, the officers found the tool easy to use. A doctoral researcher conducted a follow-up semistructured interview with those offenders identified by the six-item tool. The tool was able to distinguish those who had a mental illness from those who did not.

2. The Defendant and Offender Screening Tool (DOST; Ferguson & Negy, 2006). The DOST is a 67-item self-report inventory that includes subscales of Social Desirability, Malingering, Psychosis, Cognitive Impairment, and Aggressiveness. Adequate internal consistency (α = .77–.89) and test-retest (.71–.94) reliabilities were found. The DOST is calculated at a Grade 6 reading level. No differences were noted between male and female offenders.

3. Personality Assessment Screener (PAS; Morey, 1991). The PAS is a self-report 22-item scale with 10 subscales: Negative Affect, Acting Out, Health Problems, Psychotic Features, Social Withdrawal, Hostile Control, Suicidal Thinking, Alienation, Alcohol Problem, and Anger Control. With a jail sample, the PAS correctly identified more than 80% of the offenders as depressed by the Negative Affect subscale (Harrison & Rogers, 2007).

4. Correctional Mental Health Screens (CMHS; Ford et al., 2007). From the 56-item CMHS yes/no questions, an eight-item screen for women (CMHS-F) and a 12-item screen for men (CMHS-M) were developed. With the jail developmental sample, the CMHS-F had a coefficient alpha of .76 and test-retest correlation of .82. The CMHS-M had a coefficient alpha of .78 and a test-retest correlation of .84. When compared to the Referral Decision Scale (RDS; Teplin & Swartz, 1989) and the BJMHS, the CMHS scales consistently had incremental validity in predicting mental health outcomes.

Sample Full Assessment Instruments

The purpose of this section is to list four standardized inventories that have been used in correctional settings. The use of these instruments to screen inmates is not recommended. As noted in the previous section, there are multiple instruments available to adequately determine if an offender needs a full assessment. These four instruments would be considered in the full assessment phase.

1. Millon Clinical Multiaxial Inventory (MCMI-III; Millon, Davis, & Millon, 1997). The MCMI-III assesses for personality disorders (Axis II) and clinical syndromes (Axis I). The MCMI-III requires a Grade 8 reading level. The MCMI-III has been used extensively with offenders (O'Keefe, 2008; Retzlaff, Stoner, & Kleinsasser, 2002).

2. Basic Personality Inventory (BPI; Jackson, 1989/1996). The BPI is a 240-item, 12-scale self-report measure assessing the same traditional domain of psychopathology as the MMPI. However, the BPI has fewer items, does not permit item overlap between clinical scales, and requires a Grade 5 reading level. Past research with offenders at medium- and maximum-security levels has demonstrated adequate reliability (Kroner, Reddon, & Beckett, 1991), validity (Kroner, Holden, & Reddon, 1997; Kroner & Reddon, 1996), and capacity to detect malingering (Steffan, Kroner, & Morgan, 2007).

3. Minnesota Multiphasic Personality Inventory (MMPI; Butcher, Dahlstrom, Graham, Tellegen, & Kaemmer, 1989). The MMPI-2, the revised version presently in use, has validity, clinical, and content scales, as well as supplementary scales that have been shown to be useful in criminal justice settings.

4. Personality Assessment Inventory (PAI; Morey, 1991, 2007). The PAI is a 344-item, 22-scale, self-report measure. Similar to the BPI, there are no overlapping items among the scales. The PAI has been shown to be valid with offenders (Douglas, Guy, Edens, Boer, & Hamilton, 2007; Edens, 2009; Edens & Ruiz, 2005; Skopp, Edens, & Ruiz, 2007).

The Camberwell Family Interview (CFI; Leff & Vaughn, 1985). The CFI does not have the research base of the previous four instruments, but it does show considerable promise. In a structured review of the predictors of psychiatric relapse among offenders, Smith, Gendreau, and Goggin (2007) found the CFI to be the strongest predictor compared to other instruments.

Suicide Risk Assessment

According to Hayes (1995), prison suicide is the third-ranked cause of death in prisons, following natural causes and AIDS. Prison suicides often result in legal, procedural, and emotional consequences that challenge correctional mental health practitioners and managers.

Suicide Risk Factors

As research continues, the list of potential suicide risk factors increases (see Lewinsohn, Rohde, & Seeley, 1994). A Canadian study compared demographic and person-based risk factors of suicide attempters and nonattempters among prisoners (Wichmann, Serin, & Motiuk, 2000). Information on 731 prisoners who attempted suicide was compared with 731 randomly selected prisoners who did not attempt suicide. Differences between groups showed that prisoners who attempted suicide were more likely to be young; to be unmarried; to be serving sentences longer than 10 years; and to have committed offenses involving theft, robbery, and homicide. Attempters were more likely to be placed in a higher security prison upon arrival into custody. Higher security levels were generally associated with individuals who had institutional adjustment problems, were an escape risk, and represented higher criminal and violence risk in general.

This study also compared mental health, psychological functioning, and institutional adjustment in a subsample of 76 prisoners who attempted suicide with a matched subsample of 76 prisoners who had not. The prisoners who attempted suicide showed evidence of more dysfunction in the areas of social-cognitive problems (low self-awareness, empathy problems, impulsivity, anger), victimization with psychiatric problems (social isolation, victimization, psychiatric problems), dysfunctional relationships (predatory behavior, poor social support, dysfunctional family relationships), and high criminal risk. An analysis of institutional adjustment variables revealed that those prisoners who had attempted suicide had greater numbers of negative behavioral incidents within the prison in general, specifically more violent acts, disturbances, contraband, escape-related incidents, and requests for protective custody.

Depression's association with suicide-related thoughts and behaviors is well established across varied populations (Dieserud, Roysamb, Ekeberg, & Kraft, 2001; Konick & Gutierrez, 2005; Rudd, Joiner, & Rajab, 1996). Among 1,900 offenders in the Canadian federal correctional system, lifetime depressive disorders ranged from 21.5% (stringent criteria) to 29.8% (wide criteria ignoring severity and exclusions; Motiuk & Porporino, 1992).

Hopelessness, defined as "a system of negative expectancies concerning himself and his future life" (Beck, Weissman, Lester, & Trexler, 1974, p. 861) is also key in the assessment of suicide risk (Dieserud et al., 2001; Dixon, Heppner, & Rudd, 1994; Konick & Gutierrez, 2005; Rudd et al., 1996). Although some suicidal protocols ignore the measurement of depression and hopelessness (Correia, 2000), these two areas are essential to suicidal risk assessment.

A relatively recent but important conceptual addition to the assessment of suicide risk is the construct of psychological pain or psychache (Schneidman, 1993). Schneidman contended that psychiatric distress would never successfully predict suicide because the most important predictor of suicide is intolerable, unbearable psychological pain or psychache. Psychache is associated with many other negative emotions such as guilt, fear, shame, humiliation, grief, loneliness, and hopelessness (Schneidman, 1998). According to Schneidman, depression and hopelessness do not predispose one to suicidal manifestations. In its simplest form, Schneidman (1999) suggested the basic formula for suicide was "elevated psychache plus constricted perceptions of life's options plus thanatophilic thoughts (preference for being dead over being alive)" (p. 290).

Support for the use of the psychache construct comes from recent research that indicates that depression alone does not conclusively lead to suicide (Holden, Kerr, Mendonca, & Velamoor, 1998; Schneidman, 1993). In another study of the process of suicide, Holden, Mehta, Cunningham, and McLeod (2001) proposed that depression contributed to hopelessness, which in turn contributed to psychache, which then led, along with motivations to escape psychache, to suicide. This model is predicated upon their findings that hopelessness mediates the relationship between depression and psychache and that psychache mediates the relationship between hopelessness and suicide.

Mills and Kroner (2008) examined the interaction effect between suicide risk variables and suicidal ideation. The results underscored the multiplicative effect of current depressed/hopeless affect as they interacted with both a history of suicide and cognitions permissive of suicide in estimating the likelihood of suicidal ideation. Although not everyone who experiences suicidal ideation goes on to commit suicide, suicidal ideation may lead to eventual suicidal behavior (Fawcett et al., 1990). Therefore, suicidal ideation is an important point at which to intervene clinically. For clinicians practicing within correctional settings, identifying offenders who are at risk for experiencing suicidal ideation and the accompanying emotional distress is very important in the assessment process. Mills and Kroner (2008) found that hopelessness proved more predictive of suicidal ideation than depression, which is consistent with other research that has shown hopelessness to be strongly and consistently related to suicidal ideation and behavior (Bonner & Rich, 1990; Holden & Kroner, 2003).

Well-Researched Assessment Instruments

The Beck Depression Inventory (BDI) is likely the most widely used measure of depression across many settings. Thirteen percent of correctional psychologists report using the BDI, making it the instrument of choice when measuring depression (Boothby & Clements, 2000). A large sample of offenders was assessed upon admission to custody using the BDI, and the mean score on the BDI for offenders in general was found to be greater than that of the general population (Boothby & Durham, 1999). Between 65% and 70% of offenders were within the mild to severe categories for depression.

To compensate for higher offender scores, modifications to cutoff scores and interpretation ranges have been suggested (Boothby & Durham, 1999; Cochran, Buse, Brantley, Van Hasselt, & Sellers, 2002). However, modifying the cutoff scores and ranges to identify depressive offenders may introduce another set of problems. It would need to be determined if offenders are reporting more symptoms of depression specific to incarceration (i.e., feelings of being punished) or because of a depressed emotional state. If incarceration increases the occurrence of depression, then adjusting the cutoff score could result in not identifying the genuinely depressed. If, on the other hand, these symptoms are independent of depression (i.e., possibly feelings of punishment or guilt), then adjusting the ranges could be a reasonable solution.

Less Researched Instruments

Among the more recent instruments developed to assist in the assessment of suicide risk is the Depression Hopelessness and Suicide Screening Form (DHS; Mills & Kroner, 2002). The DHS is a 39-item instrument consisting of a Depression scale (17 items), a Hopelessness scale (10 items), and a Critical Item Checklist (12 items). The Critical Item Checklist does not measure a construct such as depression but contains a series of questions pertaining to suicide history, suicidal ideation, and cognitions permissive of suicide. The DHS was developed on offenders to measure multiple domains related to suicide. It was also developed to overcome the potential confound of certain items found in the BDI (feelings of punishment, loss of interest in sex, and guilty feelings) that may measure variance related to incarceration. The DHS has been shown to have good internal consistency (DHS Depression $\alpha = .87$ and DHS Hopelessness $\alpha = .75$), factor structure, and validity (Mills & Kroner, 2004). The DHS scores also showed construct validity in their robust correlations with other measures of depression and hopelessness. The DHS was very accurate in identifying offenders experiencing psychological distress (correctly classifying 96% of offenders) and was comparable with file review and interview in identifying offenders with a history of suicide attempts/self-harm (Mills & Kroner, 2005).

Holden et al. (2001) operationalized psychache through their development of a 13-item Psychache Scale. The Psychache Scale has been validated among samples of students and offenders (Flamenbaum & Holden, 2007; Mills et al., 2005). Among offenders, the Psychache Scale was related to previous suicidal acts (Mills et al., 2005).

One helpful suicide risk assessment protocol that has served well within correctional settings is the HELPER model authored by White (1999). The acronym stands for **H**istorical factors, **E**nvironmental factors, **L**ethality of suicidal thinking and behavior, **P**sychological factors, **E**valuation, and **R**eporting risk. This step-by-step system covers all of the areas relevant to a suicide risk assessment. Each letter in the acronym has its own chapter with details regarding the risk factors that should be documented and considered in making a suicide risk assessment. This model very easily adapts itself to a structured interview or checklist that will help minimize errors and oversights. The author is very aware of the litigious environment in which many clinicians work and has proposed a systematic approach that can serve as a very defensible decision-making model.

Violence Risk Assessment

Most mental health clinicians do not realize that they are required at one level or another to be competent to conduct a violence risk assessment. The well known case of *Tarasoff v. Regents of the University of California* (1976) makes explicit that clinicians have a duty to protect. By virtue of this ruling, mental health providers may very well have to assess, decide, and potentially report a client who may be a danger to another person. The process for conducting a Tarasoff violence assessment and a violence risk assessment are different, and the focus here is on the latter. Since the Tarasoff rulings (*Tarasoff v. Regents of the University of California*, 1974, 1976), an increasing number of states have statutory or case law requirements dictating a duty to protect from, or a duty to warn potential victims of, imminently dangerous patients (Pabian, Welfel, & Beebe, 2009). A Tarasoff decision usually comes into play within the context of clinical treatment when the act of violence is imminent and a specific victim or victims can be identified. A violence risk assessment generally covers a broad range of violent behavior that is not necessarily directed at a specific person and that focuses on the probability of violence occurring over time.

Advances in Violence Risk Assessment

The assessment of risk for violence has changed over time. For many years, clinicians were asked to determine if an individual was dangerous or not. Dangerousness is not a psychological term but rather has legal meaning. Also, answering the question "dangerous or not" puts the clinician in the position of responding in a dichotomous fashion. Over time, it became apparent that clinicians were not particularly good at making such determinations, and the evidence began to mount that clinicians' level of accuracy was little, if at all, better than chance.

Psychologists began to turn to the use of actuarial measures to assess violence risk. The actuarial approach is the application of statistics to a structured method of risk factors. The resurgence in violence risk assessment occurred when it became evident that actuarial methods consistently outperformed clinical judgment as reported by a number of meta-analyses (Aegisdottir et al., 2006; Grove & Meehl, 1996).

Some researchers rejected actuarial methods in favor of structured professional judgment (SPJ) as they observed that most actuarial assessments were based upon historical and static (unchanging) factors. A number of SPJ instruments have been developed and typically assess a broad range of empirically identified risk factors. The resulting score is not associated with a numerical or probability statement but, rather, with a descriptive classification of low, moderate, or high risk. Advocates of SPJ prefer to leave the final determination of risk with the clinician and allow for individual risk factors to be weighed more heavily than others. This would allow for risk to be adjusted based upon the clinical judgment of the assessor. Once a "clinical override" occurs, the assessor is back to making a clinical judgment. This view is also shared by others (Hilton, Harris, & Rice, 2006).

Not new, but often recommended, is an integration of actuarial risk information with dynamic risk factors (changeable factors related to risk, e.g., substance abuse, attitudes, associates) and risk management strategies (Dvoskin & Heilbrun, 2001). The actuarial risk information serves to anchor the risk assessment in terms of the likelihood to reoffend, and the inclusion of dynamic risk variables provides points for intervention and risk management strategies. This approach has been termed the *integrated actuarial risk assessment* and at present is a recommended method for conducting risk assessments. The integrated approach is more completely described in *The Clinician's Guide to Violence Risk Assessment* (Mills, Kroner, & Morgan, 2011) and includes the integration of actuarial risk estimates, with potentially dynamic risk factors, intervention/treatment recommendations, and risk management strategies.

Violence Risk Assessment Instruments

The more common instruments have been validated with offender populations. The Violence Risk Appraisal Guide (VRAG; Quinsey, Harris, Rice, & Cormier, 2006) is an actuarial instrument that utilizes psychiatric diagnoses in the scoring of items. The HCR-20 (Webster, Douglas, Eaves, & Hart, 1997) includes both historical and dynamic items. The Sex Offender Risk Appraisal Guide (SORAG; Quinsey et al., 2006) is similar to the VRAG but was developed for sex offenders. The Level of Service Inventory–Revised (LSI-R; Andrews & Bonta, 1995) is a general risk instrument that covers contributors to criminal offending, such as education, criminal associates, and substance abuse. The Static-99 (Hanson & Thornton, 2000) is the most used instrument measuring sexual recidivism. Specialized and newer instruments will be briefly covered.

Risk Matrix 2000 (RM2000). The RM2000 (Thornton, 2005) was developed to predict both sexual and violent reoffending among sex offenders and consists of three scales: the RM2000/S (sexual recidivism), the RM2000/V (nonsexual violence), and the RM2000/C (any violence). There are only a few studies to this point reporting on the RM2000. A retrospective study by Kingston, Yates, Firestone, Babchishin, and Bradford (2008) found the RM2000 to be correlated to the Static-99 and SORAG but not as predictive over the follow-up time of 11 years.

Spousal Assault Risk Assessment Guide (SARA). Like the HCR-20 and Sexual Violence Risk–20 (SVR-20), the SARA (Kropp, Hart, Webster, & Eaves, 1999) is scored and applied according to the rules of structured clinical judgment. The SARA has a moderate relationship with subsequent spousal assault in Canada (Hilton et al., 2004). A prospective study in the United States also reported a moderate level of predictive accuracy over an 18-month period (Williams & Houghton, 2004).

Ontario Domestic Assault Risk Assessment (ODARA). The ODARA (Hilton et al., 2004) was developed in similar fashion to the VRAG and SORAG, relying on purely statistical information regarding potential risk factors and their relationship with the physical assault of a man's current or former common-law partner or wife. In the original sample of development, the ODARA showed very good predictive accuracy, and a replication using a retrospective design also showed good predictive accuracy (Hilton et al., 2004). Table 4.1 contains a sample of the most commonly used assessment instruments in corrections.

Table 4.1 Instruments Used in Clinical Assessments in Corrections

Category	*Instruments*
Mental health problems	
Screening instruments	Holden Psychological Screening Inventory (HPSI)
	Brief Jail Mental Health Screen (BJMHS)
	Brief Psychiatric Rating Scale (BPRS)
Less researched, investigational	Birmingham and Mullee's (2005) intake screening instrument
	Defendant and Offender Screening Tool (DOST)
	Personality Assessment Screener (PAS)
	Correctional Mental Health Screens (for women, CMHS-F; for men, CMHS-M)
Full assessment instruments	Millon Clinical Multiaxial Inventory (MCMI-III)
	Basic Personality Inventory (BPI)
	Minnesota Multiphasic Personality Inventory (MMPI)
	Personality Assessment Inventory (PAI)

(Continued)

Table 4.1	(Continued)
Category	*Instruments*
Suicide risk assessment	
Well researched, validated, commonly used	Beck Depression Inventory (BDI)
Less researched, investigational	Depression Hopelessness and Suicide Screening Form (DHS) Psychache Scale
Violence risk assessment	
Well researched, validated, commonly used	Violence Risk Appraisal Guide (VRAG) HCR-20 Sex Offender Risk Appraisal Guide (SORAG) Level of Service Inventory–Revised (LSI-R) Static-99
Less researched, investigational	Risk Matrix 2000 (RM2000) Spousal Assault Risk Assessment Guide (SARA) Ontario Domestic Assault Risk Assessment (ODARA)

General Principles for Choosing a Specific Assessment Instrument

This section covers general principles to follow when choosing an assessment instrument. As noted in the previous sections, there are numerous instruments that can be used by psychologists in the correctional environment. The number of new instruments is an exciting advancement in the field; and some older ones (i.e., Brief Psychiatric Scale) have also been applied specifically to corrections. With numerous instruments available to correctional psychologists, a pressing issue is deciding which is most appropriate. The criteria presented below are not criteria to develop a test. Those criteria are outlined in *Standards for Educational and Psychological Testing* (American Educational Research Association, American Psychological Association, & National Council on Measurement in Education, 1999) and in many fine psychometric textbooks (Anastasi & Urbina, 1997; Devellis, 1991; Nunnally & Bernstein, 1994).

An assumption in employing the criteria below is that the available instruments meet some basic psychometric standard. This is reinforced by a principle-based approach to mental health assessment, which includes the principle to "assess clinical characteristics in relevant, reliable, and valid ways" (Heilbrun, Marczyk, DeMatteo, & Mack-Allen, 2007, p. 53). Structured procedures, structured case conferences, or screening guidelines for decision making are not assessment instruments (Hanson & Price, 2004). An instrument will have some basic reliability and validity data, which has preferably been published in an academic journal. The six criteria for choosing an instrument can be summarized with the TODATE acronym: **T**ype of client, nature of the **O**utcomes, **D**ecision assistance, guidance for **A**ction, **T**heory, and **E**ffort required.

Type of Client

The first question in evaluating an instrument needs to be, "What type of client is to be assessed?" Once this question is answered, the task becomes finding an instrument whose norms most closely match the type of client. This criterion essentially is a normative issue. The closer the match between a normative sample and the current type of client, the more defensible is the choice for this instrument, and the more robust the test results will be over time. The norms used in test interpretation do not necessarily need to be from the original test manual. Often, more recent research will include an adequate description of a sample that may function as norms for interpretation. If a more recent publication has age, race, sex, place of assessment, and purpose of assessment, along with means and standard deviations of the scales, then it may be appropriate to use that sample as the normative sample.

The benefit of using a more recent sample is a better interpretation of the client's scores. Over time, the meaning, utility, and base rates of variables can change. Items can be constructed with idioms, usually to increase meaning and simplicity, but with time they may lose their meaning. Potential contributors to a change in meaning include improved standard of living; increased education levels; increased questioning, discussing, and changing of moral, religious, and ethical views; and changes in family compositions and mobility patterns, just to name a few (Colligan, Osborne, Swenson, & Offord, 1984). For example, the Lifestyle Criminality Screening Form (Walters, White, & Denney, 1991) has one item that makes reference to tattoos, which is one of three items used to measure self-indulgence. The meaning and use of tattoos has substantially changed over the past 15 years. Tattoos may still have predictive value, but the rates of endorsement and how this item relates to other items has likely changed. Thus, recency of norms will likely result in a better match with a client. When the current context of the assessment is quite different from the normative sample, the results can be quite erroneous.

Choosing an instrument should involve the type of client being assessed and the normative samples available that will most accurately reflect the client. Within the criminal justice system, norms should be considered first by the assessment context (i.e., community vs. maximum security); then by recency of norms; and then by the coverage of basic demographic characteristics, such as race, age, and gender. An appropriate normative sample will help to increase the value of the test scores and, with the use of confidence bands, assist in outlining the applicability and utility of the test scores (Hanna, 1988).

Nature of Outcomes

Within the criminal justice system, an instrument will rarely be developed to map directly onto a referral question (Packer, 2008). In fact, it is not desirable that an instrument map directly onto a referral question. Instruments designed to answer referral questions based directly on policy or legislation have the following difficulties: (a) operationalizing the legal standard or policy, (b) allowing for changes in law or policy over time, and (c) jurisdictional variation of laws and policies (Otto & Heilbrun, 2002). The closer a research study is to the purpose of the clinical assessment, the more desirable is the instrument on this criterion. As previously noted, the purpose of a clinical assessment is to address a clinical problem. Correctional assessments fall into two basic categories: those that inform classification/intervention/understanding and those that assess future risk. Thus, the second criterion for choosing an instrument is the amount of documented validity present for the referral question or questions.

Ease of Interpretation for Decisions

Is the instrument's output designed to assist with the interpretation of the referral question? If understanding an offender's mental health problem is the main purpose, then the scores need to measure an easily understood construct. In addition, there needs to be sufficient information to derive a confidence interval based on the standard error of measurement in order to more fully understand the current level of functioning of the client. The weight placed on an interpretation increases if the instrument can rule out other related constructs. Thus, if there is an elevated depression score, the confidence that depression is the predominant mental health concern is increased if it is known that this scale is minimally related to anxiety or anger.

If risk assessment is the main purpose, then the instrument should have risk probabilities associated with the risk scores. With the appropriate confidence intervals, probabilities communicate more clearly the value of the score and the limits of a risk probability. Solely using high, moderate, or low levels of risk does not enhance the ease of interpretation for decision.

Guidance for Action

The majority of clinical assessments within a correctional context result in a recommendation for intervention. The better the instrument can inform the intervention, the greater the utility of the instrument. Assessments assist in making better decisions and providing guidance for further action (Einhorn, 1986). This criterion may seem similar to the previous two, but it differs in its emphasis on the potential intervention. As an example, consider an instrument designed for assisting with suicidal assessments. The instrument may relate to suicidal behaviors, meeting the nature of outcomes criterion, and may report the probability of suicidal behaviors, meeting the ease of interpretation for decision criterion. However, the scale may not be able to inform the psychologist of the content area that needs to be addressed to reduce the likelihood of the outcome behaviors. If this instrument measured hopelessness, then the guidance for action criterion would be met.

Theory

This criterion asks if the scales can be placed within a greater theoretical framework. Practically, this means using the scale to tell a story that will give greater meaning to the test results. For example, hopelessness is used in suicidal assessment, but this construct will have greater utility if placed within Seligman's learned helplessness model of suicidal behavior (Seligman, 1972).

Effort

The easier the instrument is to use the better. This will result in fewer administration and scoring errors. Applied reliability is an issue with the completion of instruments in an applied setting. Especially with rating instruments, an adequate level of reliability will be more difficult to achieve with a complex instrument. Thus, instruments that are relatively easy to use and do not require extensive training will be preferable (Philipse, Koeter, van der Stakk, & van den Brink, 2005).

Socially Desirable Responding

Clinical assessment commonly uses self-report in correctional settings. Given the general view that offenders engage in deceptive tactics while completing self-report inventories, clinicians must be cautious in their interpretations (Kroner & Weekes, 1996; Tan & Grace, 2008). Research literature has identified socially desirable responding (SDR) as a major threat to the validity of offender self-report and defines this concept "as the tendency to give overly positive self-descriptions" (Paulhus, 2002, p. 49). Despite the number of existing measures, none has been developed specifically for use with offenders.

One of the most widely used measures of SDR is the Paulhus Deception Scales (PDS; Paulhus, 1998), also known as the Balanced Inventory of Desirable Responding–7 (BIDR-7). Although initial validity for the BIDR was found among offenders (Kroner & Weekes, 1996), confidence in the use of the BIDR with offenders has begun to dwindle. Recent studies have indicated that statistically controlling for SDR did not improve upon the construct or predictive validity of crime-related self-report (Kroner, Mills, & Morgan, 2006), the relationship between self-reported anger and institutional misconducts (Mills & Kroner, 2003), or the relationship between antisocial attitudes and recidivism (Mills & Kroner, 2006). Questioning whether the possible contamination by SDR would decrease the predictive validity of self-report among offenders, Mills, Loza, and Kroner (2003) conducted a follow-up study with a sample of federally incarcerated male offenders. Offenders within the sample were administered both the Self-Appraisal Questionnaire (SAQ; Loza, 2005) and the BIDR-6 (Paulhus, 1994). Level of risk was calculated using the General Statistical Information on Recidivism (GSIR; Nuffield, 1982), whereas general and violent recidivism was based on file review and official police records. Interestingly, results from the study appeared counterintuitive, as the authors found significant negative correlations between the Impression Management (IM) scale and both general and violent recidivism. Only violent recidivism was found to be significantly negatively correlated with SDR. This significant negative relationship between the BIDR's IM scale and an offender's level of risk (as measured by the GSIR) and rate of recidivism has since been replicated using two additional independent samples of federally incarcerated male offenders (Mills & Kroner, 2005, 2006).

Other researchers have identified a significant negative relationship between the IM scale of the BIDR and recidivism (Brown, St. Amand, & Zamble, 2009; Hanson & Wallace-Capretta, 2004), whereas other research has found significant negative relationships between IM and a measure of general recidivism (Simourd & Hoge, 2000) and a measure of psychopathy (Simourd & Hoge, 2000). Interestingly, these concerns are not exclusive to the BIDR alone. Other researchers have identified a similar significant negative relationship between other measures of SDR and criminal outcome (Henning & Holford, 2006; Peersen, Sigurdsson, Gudjonsson, & Gretarsson, 2004). These findings appear consistent with the negative relationship between SDR and criminal justice outcomes.

Overall, the replicated findings reported within the research literature have become worrisome. Are these self-report inventories in fact measuring what was intended, namely SDR, or are they becoming too confounded by risk-related content, particularly when administered to offender populations? Taking into consideration the numerous issues concerning the construct validity of measures, such as the PDS/BIDR, as evidenced by items relating to criminal risk and the ongoing significant negative relationship between SDR and criminal risk/recidivism, the reality of the situation becomes dismally apparent: Clinicians are currently unable to appropriately measure SDR in male offenders. Accordingly, no evidence currently exists to support the efficacy of using measures of SDR such as the PDS/BIDR for determining the validity of self-report among male offenders. Until such time as a population-specific measure of SDR has been developed for use with offenders, clinicians working within correctional settings are advised to be cautious when relying on measures such as the PDS/BIDR.

Summary and Conclusions

Conducting high-quality clinical assessments is an opportunity to provide unique, value-added information for both the offender and correctional managers. Ensuring high quality will be achieved through paying attention to process issues (e.g., administration detail, developing a rapport with offenders) and content issues (choosing appropriate instruments). Moving forward, the next step is to develop theoretically driven, empirically based, and dynamic assessments that inform and guide intervention. Such accomplishments will ensure the added value of clinical assessment to the correctional system.

KEY TERMS

Reliability	Clinical judgment	Intake screening process
Validity	Actuarial data	
Internal consistency	Dynamic risk factors	Prevalence rates
Coefficient alpha	Static risk factors	Likert scale
Construct	Risk management strategies	Malingering
Normative sample		Suicide risk factors
Confidence interval	Test manual	Psychache
Standard error of measurement	Self-report inventory	Tarasoff rulings
	Rapport	

DISCUSSION QUESTIONS

1. Are there benefits to having a specific unit dedicated to the intake screening process from both a mental health and a correctional administrative perspective? What are the drawbacks to having such units from a correctional management perspective?

2. What are the benefits of using actuarial data to make predictions of risk? Are there limitations to the use of actuarial data in risk assessment?

3. Should specially trained correctional officers be allowed to conduct intake screening assessments, or should these assessments only be performed by mental health clinicians? Give reasons to support your answer.

4. Is there a role for clinical judgment in the assessment process? Explain your answer.

References

Aegisdottir, S., White, M. J., Spengler, P. M., Maugherman, A. S., Anderson, L. A., Nichols, C. N., et al. (2006). The meta-analysis of clinical judgment project: Fifty-six years of accumulated research on clinical versus statistical prediction. *The Counseling Psychologist, 34,* 341–382.

Allard, G., & Faust, D. (2000). Errors in scoring objective personality tests. *Assessment, 2,* 119–129.

American Educational Research Association, American Psychological Association, & National Council on Measurement in Education. (1999). *Standards for educational and psychological testing.* Washington, DC: Author.

American Psychological Association. (2002). Ethical principles of psychologists and code of conduct. *American Psychologist, 57,* 1060–1073. Available from http://www.apa.org/ethics/code2002.html

Anastasi, A., & Urbina, S. (1997). *Psychological testing* (7th ed.). Upper Saddle River, NJ: Prentice Hall.

Andrews, D. A., & Bonta, J. L. (1995). *The Level of Service Inventory–Revised.* Toronto, Ontario, Canada: Multi-Health Systems.

Ax, R. K., Fagan, T. J., Magaletta, P. R., Morgan, R. D., Nussbaum, D., & White, T. W. (2007). Innovations in correctional assessment and treatment. *Criminal Justice and Behavior, 34,* 879–892.

Beck, A. T., Weissman, A., Lester, D., & Trexler, L. (1974). The measurement of pessimisms: The Hopelessness Scale. *Journal of Consulting and Clinical Psychology, 42,* 861–865.

Birmingham, L., Gray, J., Mason, D., & Grubin, D. (2000). Mental illness at reception into prison. *Criminal Behavior and Mental Health, 10,* 77–87.

Birmingham, L., & Mullee, M. (2005). Development and evaluation of a screening tool for identifying prisoners with severe mental illness. *Psychiatric Bulletin, 29,* 334–338.

Bonner, R. L., & Rich, A. R. (1990). Psychosocial vulnerability, life stress, and suicide ideation in a jail population: A cross-validation study. *Suicide and Life-Threatening Behavior, 20,* 213–224.

Bonta, J., & Gendreau, P. (1990). Reexamining the cruel and unusual punishment of prison life. *Law and Human Behavior, 14,* 347–372.

Book, A. S., Knap, M. A., & Holden, R. R. (2001). Criterion validity of the Holden Psychological Screening Scale in a prison sample. *Psychological Assessment, 13,* 249–253.

Boothby, J. L., & Clements, C. B. (2000). A national survey of correctional psychologists. *Criminal Justice and Behavior, 27,* 716–732.

Boothby, J. L., & Durham, T. W. (1999). Screening for depression in prisoners using the Beck Depression Inventory. *Criminal Justice and Behavior, 26,* 107–124.

Brown, S. L., St. Amand, M. D., & Zamble, E. (2009). The dynamic prediction of criminal recidivism: A three-wave prospective study. *Law and Human Behavior, 33,* 25–45.

Butcher, J. N., Dahlstrom, W. G., Graham, J. R., Tellegen, A., & Kaemmer, B. (1989). *The Minnesota Multiphasic Personality Inventory-2 (MMPI-2): Manual for administration and scoring.* Minneapolis: University of Minnesota Press.

Charter, R. A., Walden, D. K., & Padilla, S. P. (2000). Too many simple clerical scoring errors: The Rey Figure as an example. *Journal of Clinical Psychology, 56,* 571–574.

Cloyes, K. G., Lovell, D., Allen, D. G., & Rhodes, L. A. (2006). Assessment of psychosocial impairment in a supermaximum security unit sample. *Criminal Justice and Behavior, 33,* 760–781.

Cochran, C. K., Buse, G. L., Brantley, K. L., Van Hasselt, V. B., & Sellers, A. H. (2002, August). *Norms for the Beck Depression Inventory (BDI) with incarcerated offenders.* Poster session presented at the 110th meeting of the American Psychological Association, Chicago, IL.

Cohen, F. (2008). *The mentally disordered inmate and the law* (2nd ed.). Kingston, NJ: Civic Research Institute.

Colligan, R. C., Osborne, D., Swenson, W. M., & Offord, K. P. (1984). The aging MMPI: Development of contemporary norms. *Mayo Clinic Proceedings, 59,* 377–390.

Correia, K. M. (2000). Suicide assessment in a prison environment: A proposed protocol. *Criminal Justice and Behavior, 27,* 581–599.

Devellis, R. D. (1991). *Scale development: Theory and applications.* Newbury Park, CA: Sage.

Dieserud, G., Roysamb, E., Ekeberg, O., & Kraft, P. (2001). Toward an integrative model of suicide attempt: A cognitive psychological approach. *Suicide and Life-Threatening Behavior, 31,* 153–168.

Ditton, P. (1999). *Mental health and treatment of inmates and probationers* (Bureau of Justice Statistics Special Report NCJ 174463). Washington, DC: National Criminal Justice Reference Service.

Dixon, W. A., Heppner, P. P., & Rudd, M. D. (1994). Problem-solving appraisal, hopelessness, and suicide ideation: Evidence for a mediational model. *Journal of Counseling Psychology, 41,* 91–98.

Douglas, K. A., Guy, L. S., Edens, J. F., Boer, D. P., & Hamilton, J. (2007). The Personality Assessment Inventory as a proxy for the Psychopathy Checklist-Revised. *Assessment, 14,* 255–269.

Dvoskin, J. A., & Heilbrun, K. (2001). Risk assessment and release decision-making: Toward resolving the great debate. *Journal of the American Academy of Psychiatry and the Law, 29,* 6–10.

Edens, J. F. (2009). Interpersonal characteristics of male criminal offenders: Personality, psychopathological, and behavioral correlates. *Psychological Assessment, 21,* 89–98.

Edens, J. F., & Ruiz, M. A. (2005). *PAI Interpretive Report for Correctional Settings (PAI-CS) professional manual.* Lutz, FL: Psychological Assessment Resources.

Einhorn, H. J. (1986). Accepting error to make less error. *Journal of Personality Assessment, 50,* 387–395.

Fagan, T. J. (2003). Mental health in corrections: A model for service delivery. In T. J. Fagan & R. K. Ax (Eds.), *Correctional mental health handbook* (pp. 3–19). Thousand Oaks, CA: Sage.

Fawcett, J., Scheftner, W. A., Fogg, L., Clark, D. C., Young, M. A., Hedeker, D., et al. (1990). Time-related predictors of suicide in major affective disorder. *American Journal of Psychiatry, 147,* 1189–1194.

Fazel, S., & Danesh, J. (2002). Serious mental disorder in 23,000 prisoners: A systematic review of 62 surveys. *Lancet, 359,* 545–550.

Ferguson, C. J., & Negy, C. (2006). Development and preliminary validation of a defendant and offender screening tool for psychopathology in inmate populations. *Criminal Justice and Behavior, 33,* 325–346.

Flamenbaum, R., & Holden, R. R. (2007). Psychache as a mediator in the relationship between perfectionism and suicidality. *Journal of Counseling Psychology, 54,* 51–61.

Ford, J. D., Trestman, R. L., Wiesbrock, V., & Zhang, W. (2007). Development and validation of a brief mental health screening instrument for newly incarcerated adults. *Assessment, 14,* 279–299.

Goddard, R., Simons, R., Patton, W., & Sullivan, K. (2004). Psychologist hand-scoring error rates on the Rothwell-Miller Interest Blank: A comparison of three job allocation systems. *Australian Journal of Psychology, 56,* 25–32.

Grove, W. M., & Meehl, P. E. (1996). Comparative efficiency of informal (subjective, impressionistic) and formal (mechanical, algorithmic) predict. *Psychology, Public Policy, and Law, 2,* 293–323.

Hall, J. D., Howerton, D. L., & Bolin, A. U. (2005). The use of testing technicians: Critical issues for professional psychology. *International Journal of Testing, 5,* 357–375.

Hanna, G. S. (1988). Using percentile bands for meaningful test score interpretations. *Journal of Counseling and Development, 66,* 477–483.

Hanson, R. K., & Price, S. (2004). Sexual abuse screening procedures for positions of trust with children. In R. K. Hanson, F. Pfaffin, & M. Lutz (Eds.), *Sexual abuse in the Catholic Church: Scientific and legal perspectives* (pp. 77–93). Vatican City: Libreria Editrice Vaticana.

Hanson, R. K., & Thornton, D. (2000). Improving risk assessments for sex offenders: A comparison of three actuarial scales. *Law and Human Behavior, 24,* 119–136.

Hanson, R. K., & Wallace-Capretta, S. (2004). Predictors of criminal recidivism among male batterers. *Psychology, Crime & Law, 10,* 413–427.

Harris, V. L., & Lovell, D. (2001). Measuring level of function in mentally ill prison inmates: A preliminary study. *Journal of the American Academy of Psychiatry and the Law, 29,* 68–74.

Harrison, K. S., & Rogers, R. (2007). Axis I screens and suicide risk in jails. *Assessment, 14,* 171–180.

Hayes, L. M. (1995). Prison suicide: An overview and a guide to prevention. *The Prison Journal, 75,* 431–456.

Heilbrun, K., Marczyk, G., DeMatteo, D., & Mack-Allen, J. (2007). A principles-based approach to forensic mental health assessment: Utility and update. In A. M. Goldstein (Ed.), *Forensic psychology: Emerging topics and expanding roles* (pp. 45–72). New York, NY: John Wiley.

Henning, K., & Holdford, R. (2006). Minimization, denial, and victim blaming by batterers: How much does the truth matter? *Criminal Justice and Behavior, 33,* 110–130.

Hilton, N. Z., Harris, G. T., & Rice, M. E. (2006). Sixty-six years of research on the clinical versus actuarial prediction of violence. *The Counseling Psychologist, 34,* 400–409.

Hilton, N. Z., Harris, G. T., Rice, M. E., Lang, C., Cormier, C. A., & Lines, K. J. (2004). A brief actuarial assessment for the prediction of wife assault recidivism: The Ontario Domestic Assault Risk Assessment. *Psychological Assessment, 16,* 267–275.

Holden, R. R. (1996). *The Holden Psychological Screening Inventory manual.* North Tonawanda, NY: Multi-Health Systems.

Holden, R. R., & Grigoriadis, S. (1995). Psychometric properties of the Holden Psychological Screening for a psychiatric offender sample. *Journal of Clinical Psychology, 51,* 811–819.

Holden, R. R., Kerr, P. S., Mendonca, J. D., & Velamoor, V. R. (1998). Are some motives more linked to suicide than others? *Journal of Clinical Psychology, 54,* 569–576.

Holden, R. R., & Kroner, D. G. (2003). Differentiating suicidal motivations and manifestation in a forensic sample. *Canadian Journal of Behavioural Science, 35,* 35–44.

Holden, R. R., Mehta, K., Cunningham, E. J., & McLeod, L. D. (2001). Development and preliminary validation of a scale of psychache. *Canadian Journal of Behavioural Science, 33,* 224–232.

Iverson, G. L., & Barton, E. (1999). Interscorer reliability of the MMPI-2: Should TRIN and VRIN be computer scored? *Journal of Clinical Psychology, 55,* 65–69.

Jackson, D. N. (1989/1996). *Basic Personality Inventory manual* (2nd ed.). London, Ontario, Canada: Sigma Assessment Systems.

Jacobs, M. S., Ryba, N. L., & Zapf, P. A. (2008). Competence-related abilities and psychiatric symptoms: An analysis of the underlying structure and correlates of the MacCAT-CA and the BPRS. *Law and Human Behavior, 32,* 64–77.

James, D. J., & Glaze, L. E. (2006). *Mental health problems of prison and jail inmates* (Bureau of Justice Statistics Special Report NCJ 213600). Washington, DC: National Criminal Justice Reference Service.

Kingston, D. A., Yates, P. M., Firestone, P., Babchishin, K., & Bradford, J. M. (2008). Long-term predictive validity of the Risk Matrix 2000: A comparison with the Static-99 and the Sex Offender Risk Appraisal Guide. *Sexual Abuse: A Journal of Research and Treatment, 20,* 466–484.

Konick, L. C., & Gutierrez, P. M. (2005). Testing a model of suicide ideation in college students. *Suicide and Life-Threatening Behavior, 35,* 181–192.

Kroner, D. G., Holden, R. R., & Reddon, J. R. (1997). Validity of the Basic Personality Inventory in a correctional setting. *Assessment, 4,* 141–154.

Kroner, D. G., Mills, J. F., & Morgan, R. D. (2006). Socially desirable responding and the measurement of violent and criminal risk: Self-report validity. *Journal of Forensic Psychology Practice, 6,* 27–42.

Kroner, D. G., & Reddon, J. R. (1996). Factor structure of the Basic Personality Inventory with incarcerated offenders. *Journal of Psychopathology and Behavioral Assessment, 18,* 275–284.

Kroner, D. G., Reddon, J. R., & Beckett, N. (1991). Basic Personality Inventory clinical and validity scales: Stability and internal consistency. *Journal of Psychopathology and Behavioral Assessment, 13,* 147–154.

Kroner, D. G., & Weekes, J. R. (1996). Balanced Inventory of Desirable Responding: Factor structure, reliability, and validity with an offender sample. *Personality and Individual Differences, 21,* 323–333.

Kropp, P. R., Hart, S. D., Webster, C. D., & Eaves, D. (1999). *Spousal Assault Risk Assessment: User's guide.* Toronto, Ontario, Canada: Multi-Health Systems.

Leff, J. P., & Vaughn, C. E. (1985). *Expressed emotion in families.* London, UK: Guilford.

Lewinsohn, P. M., Rohde, P., & Seeley, J. R. (1994). Psychosocial risk factors for future adolescent suicide attempts. *Journal of Consulting and Clinical Psychology, 62,* 297–305.

Loza, W. (2005). *Self-Appraisal Questionnaire (SAQ): A tool for assessing violent and non-violent recidivism.* Toronto, Ontario, Canada: Multi-Health Systems.

Millon, T., Davis, R. D., & Millon, C. (1997). *Manual for the Millon Clinical Multiaxial Inventory–III (MCMI-III)* (2nd ed.). Minneapolis, MN: National Computer Systems.

Mills, J. F., Green, K., & Reddon, J. R. (2005). An evaluation of the Psychache Scale on an offender population. *Suicide and Life-Threatening Behavior, 35,* 570–580.

Mills, J. F., & Kroner, D. G. (2002). *Depression, Hopelessness and Suicide Screening Form (DHS): User guide.* Unpublished user guide.

Mills, J. F., & Kroner, D. G. (2003). Anger as a predictor of institutional misconduct and recidivism in a sample of violent offenders. *Journal of Interpersonal Violence, 18,* 282–294.

Mills, J. F., & Kroner, D. G. (2004). A new instrument to screen for depression, hopelessness and suicide in offenders. *Psychological Services, 1,* 83–91.

Mills, J. F., & Kroner, D. G. (2005). Screening for suicide risk factors in prison inmates: Evaluating the efficiency of the Depression, Hopelessness and Suicide Screening Form (DHS). *Legal and Criminological Psychology, 10,* 1–12.

Mills, J. F., & Kroner, D. G. (2006). Impression management and self-report among violent offenders. *Journal of Interpersonal Violence, 21,* 178–192.

Mills, J. F., & Kroner, D. G. (2008). Predicting suicidal ideation with the Depression Hopelessness and Suicide Screening Form (DHS). *Journal of Offender Rehabilitation, 47,* 74–100.

Mills, J. F., Kroner, D. G., & Morgan, R. D. (2011). *The clinician's guide to violence risk assessment.* New York, NY: Guilford.

Mills, J. F., Loza, W., & Kroner, D. G. (2003). Predictive validity despite social desirability: Evidence for the robustness of self-report among offenders. *Criminal Behaviour and Mental Health, 13,* 140–150.

Mitchison, S., Rix, K. J. B., Renvoize, E. B., & Schweiger, M. (1994). Recorded psychiatric morbidity in a large prison for male remanded and sentenced prisoners. *Medical Science and the Law, 34,* 324–330.

Morey, L. C. (1991). *Personality Assessment Inventory professional manual.* Odessa, FL: Psychological Assessment Resources.

Morey, L. C. (2007). *Personality Assessment Inventory professional manual* (2nd ed.). Lutz, FL: Psychological Assessment Resources.

Motiuk, L. L., & Porporino, F. J. (1992). *The prevalence, nature and severity of mental health problems among federal male inmates in Canadian penitentiaries: User report.* Ottawa, Ontario: Correctional Service of Canada, Research and Statistics Branch.

Muirhead, J. E., & Rhodes, R. (1998). Literacy level of Canadian federal offenders. *Journal of Correctional Education, 49,* 59–60.

National Commission on Correctional Health Care. (2008). *Standards for mental health services in correctional facilities.* Chicago, IL: Author.

Nuffield, J. (1982). *Parole decision-making in Canada: Research towards decision guidelines.* Ottawa, Ontario: Solicitor General of Canada.

Nunnally, J. C., & Bernstein, I. H. (1994). *Psychometric theory* (3rd ed.). New York, NY: McGraw-Hill.

Ogloff, J. R. P., Roesch, R., & Hart, S. D. (1993). Screening, assessment, and identification of services for mentally ill offenders. In H. J. Steadman & J. J. Cocozza (Eds.), *Mental illness in America* (pp. 61–90). Washington, DC: U.S. Department of Health and Human Services.

O'Keefe, M. (2008). Administrative segregation for mentally ill inmates. *Journal of Offender Rehabilitation, 45,* 149–165.

Osher, F., Scott, J. E., Steadman, H. J., & Robbins, P. C. (2006). *Validating a brief jail mental health screen, final technical report (No. 2001-IJ-CX-0030).* Washington, DC: National Institute of Justice.

Otto, R. K., & Heilbrun, K. (2002). The practice of forensic psychology: A look toward the future in light of the past. *American Psychologist, 57,* 5–18.

Overall, J. E., & Gorman, G. R. (1962). The Brief Psychiatric Rating Scale. *Psychological Reports 10,* 799–812.

Pabian, Y. L., Welfel, E., & Beebe, R. S. (2009). Psychologists' knowledge of their states' laws pertaining to Tarasoff-type situations. *Professional Psychology: Research and Practice, 40,* 8–14.

Packer, I. K. (2008). Specialized practice in forensic psychology: Opportunities and obstacles. *Professional Psychology: Research and Practice, 39,* 245–249.

Paulhus, D. L. (1994). *Balanced Inventory of Desirable Responding: Reference manual for the BIDR Version 6*. Unpublished manuscript, University of British Columbia, Vancouver, British Columbia, Canada.

Paulhus, D. L. (1998). *Paulhus Deception Scales (PDS): The Balanced Inventory of Desirable Responding–7: User's manual*. Toronto, Ontario, Canada: Multi-Health Systems.

Paulhus, D. L. (2002). Socially desirable responding: The evolution of a construct. In H. Braun, D. N. Jackson, & D. E. Wiley (Eds.), *The role of constructs in psychological and educational measurement* (pp. 49–69). Hillsdale, NJ: Lawrence Erlbaum Associates.

Peersen, M., Sigurdsson, J. F., Gudjonsson, G. H., & Gretarsson, S. J. (2004). Predictive re-offending: A 5-year prospective study of Icelandic prison inmates. *Psychology, Crime & Law, 10*, 197–204.

Pennuto, T. O. (2004). Murder and the MMPI-2. *Golden Gate University Law Review, 34*, 349–391.

Philipse, M. W. G., Koeter, M. W. J., van der Stakk, C. P. F., & van den Brink, W. (2005). Reliability and discriminant validity of dynamic reoffending risk indicators in forensic clinical practice. *Criminal Justice and Behavior, 32*, 643–664.

Quinsey, V. L., Harris, G. T., Rice, M. E., & Cormier, C. A. (2006). *Violent offenders: Appraising and managing risk* (2nd ed.). Washington, DC: American Psychological Association.

Rankin, C. E. (2005). Illiterate prisoners? Myths and empirical realities. *Journal of Offender Rehabilitation, 41*, 43–55.

Reddon, J. R., Vander Veen, S., & Munchua, M. M. (2001). The hierarchical nexus of psychosocial adjustment and psychopathology: Relationship of the Holden Psychological Screening Inventory (HPSI) with the Basic Personality Inventory (BPI) and the Differential Personality Inventory (DPI). In F. Columbus (Ed.), *Advances in psychology research* (Vol. 3, pp. 91–125). Huntington, NY: Nova Science.

Retzlaff, P., Stoner, J., & Kleinsasser, D. (2002). The use of the MCMI-III in the screening and triage of offenders. *International Journal of Offender Therapy and Comparative Criminology, 46*, 319–332.

Rudd, M. D., Joiner, T., & Rajab, M. H. (1996). Relationships among suicide ideators, attempters, and multiple attempters in a young-adult sample. *Journal of Abnormal Psychology, 105*, 541–550.

Schneidman, E. S. (1993). Suicide as psychache. *Journal of Nervous and Mental Disease, 181*, 145–147.

Schneidman, E. S. (1998). Further reflections on suicide and psychache. *Suicide and Life-Threatening Behavior, 28*, 245–250.

Schneidman, E. S. (1999). The Psychological Pain Assessment Scale. *Suicide and Life-Threatening Behavior, 29*, 287–294.

Seligman, M. E. P. (1972). Learned helplessness. *Annual Review of Medicine, 23*, 407–412.

Simons, R., Goddard, R., & Patton, W. (2002). Hand-scoring error rates in psychological testing. *Assessment, 9*, 292–300.

Simourd, D. J., & Hoge, R. D. (2000). Criminal psychopathy: A risk-and-need perspective. *Criminal Justice and Behavior, 27*, 256–272.

Skopp, N. A., Edens, J. F., & Ruiz, M. A. (2007). Risk factors for institutional misconduct among incarcerated women: An examination of the criterion-related validity of the Personality Assessment Inventory. *Journal of Personality Assessment, 88*, 106–117.

Smith, P., Gendreau, P., & Goggin, C. (2007). "What works" in predicting psychiatric hospitalization and relapse: The specificity responsivity dimension of effective correctional treatment for mentally disordered offenders. In R. K. Ax & T. J. Fagan (Eds.), *Corrections, mental health, and social policy: International perspectives* (pp. 209–233). Springfield, IL: Charles C Thomas.

Starzyk, K. B., Reddon, J. R., & Friel, J. P. (2000). Need structure, leisure motivation, and psychosocial adjustment among young offenders and high school students. *Journal of Offender Rehabilitation, 31*, 163–174.

Steffan, J. S., Kroner, D. G., & Morgan, R. D. (2007). Effect of symptom information and intelligence in dissimulation: An examination of faking response styles by inmates on the Basic Personality Inventory. *Assessment, 14*, 1–13.

Tan, L., & Grace, R. C. (2008). Social desirability and sexual offenders: A review. *Sexual Abuse: A Journal of Research and Treatment, 20*, 61–87.

Tarasoff v. Regents of the University of California, 529 P. 2d 553 (Cal. 1974).

Tarasoff v. Regents of the University of California, 131 Cal., 551 P. 2d 334, R. 14 (1976).

Teplin, L., & Swartz, J. (1989). Screening for severe mental disorders in jails: The development of the Referral Decision Scale. *Law and Human Behavior, 13, 1–18.*

Thornton, D. (2005). *Scoring guide for the Risk Matrix: 2000.5.* Unpublished manuscript.

Walters, G. D., White, T. W., & Denney, D. (1991). The Lifestyle Criminality Screening Form: Preliminary data. *Criminal Justice and Behavior, 18,* 406–418.

Webster, C. D., Douglas, K. S., Eaves, C. D., & Hart, S. D. (1997). *The HCR-20 scheme: Assessing risk for violence: Version 2.* Vancouver, British Columbia, Canada: Simon Fraser University, Mental Health, Law and Policy Institute.

White, T. W. (1999). *How to identify suicidal people: A systematic approach to risk assessment.* Philadelphia, PA: The Charles Press.

Wichmann, C., Serin, R., & Motiuk, L. (2000). *Predicting suicide attempts among male offenders in federal penitentiaries.* Ottawa, Ontario: Correctional Service of Canada, Research Branch.

Williams, K. R., & Houghton, A. B. (2004). Assessing the risk of domestic violence reoffending: A validation study. *Law and Human Behavior, 28,* 437–455.

Zinger, I., Wichmann, C., & Andrews, D. A. (2001). The psychological effects of 60 days in administrative segregation. *Canadian Journal of Criminology, 22,* 47–83.

CHAPTER 5

Correctional Treatment

Donald A. Sawyer and Catherine Moffitt

Introduction

As reported in earlier chapters, the prevalence of mental health problems is substantial across all U.S. correctional populations. Specifically, the Bureau of Justice Statistics reports that 64% of jail inmates, 56% of state prisoners, and 45% of federal prisoners admitted to mental health issues and symptoms during the course of personal interviews (D. J. James & Glaze, 2006). Over time, the incidence of mental illness has been reported to be in the 8% to 24% range by a number of authors who have studied this phenomenon (Diamond, Wang, Holzer, Thomas, & des Anges, 2001; J. F. James, Gregory, Jones, & Rundell, 1980; Lamb & Weinberger, 1998; Metzner, Cohen, Grossman, & Wettstein, 1998; National Commission on Correctional Health Care, 2002; Steadman, Monahan, Hartsone, Davis, & Robbins, 1982; Teplin, 1990, 1994; Teplin, Abram, & McClelland, 1996). It is clear there is a compelling need for mental health assessment and treatment at all levels of incarceration. Treatment availability is first and foremost critical to the individual inmate, but it also has profound implications for the safe and effective operation of the correctional facility. Security staff frequently view mentally ill inmates as more challenging, more difficult, and more disruptive to day-to-day operations.

This chapter explores salient issues and treatment modalities, which are essential to the effective delivery of mental health treatment services in prison. It will (a) consider the requirements for effective correctional treatment, (b) share what works in correctional treatment, (c) explore the unique challenges of treating inmates with all levels and types of mental health service needs, and (d) consider the effectiveness of various treatment strategies.

Effective Correctional Treatment: General Considerations

Providing mental health treatment in prison is daunting. Prisons have long had as their mission "care, custody, and control." To effectively and safely manage hundreds and at times thousands of inmates in one facility requires a substantial amount of structure. Prisons are obviously not traditional treatment settings, but they have become in some respects the treatment setting of last resort. Despite this, they are not mental health–friendly settings. It is important for the mental health practitioner to recognize that although persons with serious and persistent mental illness are overrepresented in jails and prisons, it is rare that an individual is incarcerated only because of his or her mental illness. It is far more likely that mental illness was, at most, a contributing factor. Mentally ill inmates are incarcerated due to the commission of a crime and their proclivity to pursue illegal means to meet personal needs. In many instances, especially for those in state and federal prisons with longer sentences, crimes were directed toward people, not property, and were violent in nature (Baillargeon, Binswanger, Penn, Williams, & Murray, 2009; Sirotich, 2008; Taylor, 2008). It is critical for a provider of mental health services in a prison to realize that although inmates in custody may have legitimate mental health needs, they are incarcerated due to an inability to adhere to the laws of society.

The inability to adhere to societal expectations, norms, and laws is also related to an inability to adhere to prison-based expectations. Mental health practitioners and their interventions must account for the often unique blend of Axis I (i.e., clinical syndromes) and Axis II (i.e., more persistent and long-standing personality disorders) illness in the inmate population. That is, not only are there large numbers of offenders with traditional Axis I serious mental illnesses such as schizophrenia, bipolar disorder, and major depressive disorder (D. J. James & Glaze, 2006; Steadman, Osher, Robbins, Case, & Samuels, 2009; Way, Steinbacher, Sawyer, & Lilly, 2008), but also many offenders have Axis II diagnoses, such as antisocial personality disorder or borderline personality disorder, either alone or in combination with Axis I disorders (Rotter, Way, Steinbacher, Smith, & Sawyer, 2002). Successful intervention programs, therefore, will take into account the multidimensional nature of the population.

As mentioned above, inmates with mental health needs come in conflict with the rules, regulations, and structure of prison with greater frequency than their non–mentally ill counterparts. Several studies have confirmed that inmates with serious mental illness have more difficulty adapting to prison life than do their non–seriously mentally ill counterparts. For example, Morgan, Edwards, and Faulkner (1993) reported that the seriously mentally ill recorded one and a half times more prison-based disciplinary infractions per 100 inmates annually and that a significantly higher proportion of the infractions were characterized as violent. McShane (1989) reported that inmates with mental illness committed 5 times more staff assaults and other major infractions than inmates without mental illness. Lovell and Jemelka (1996, 1998) found that inmates with serious mental illnesses committed infractions at 3 times the rate of non–seriously mentally ill counterparts. Therefore, an important component of the skill set of a correctional mental health clinician is the ability to perform a functional assessment of behaviors that lead to disciplinary infractions and to include the reduction of such behaviors as treatment goals. In addition, optimal treatment approaches should include collaboration between correction staff and mental health professionals. Consultation with corrections staff, joint training initiatives, and the use of multidisciplinary treatment teams are all avenues through which corrections staff can be integrated into the treatment of inmates with mental illness (Dvoskin & Spiers, 2004).

It is not surprising that seriously mentally ill inmates are less able to successfully negotiate the challenges and complexity of prison environments, given the nature of their illness. Prisons are not infinitely adaptable and are in general unable to make major changes or concessions to meet the special needs of a small group of inmates (see Chapter 3 for a more detailed discussion of this topic). This complicates the treatment process and adds to the challenges faced by practitioners of prison-based mental health services.

A further complication is the challenge of ascertaining whether the signs and symptoms of mental illness an inmate is evidencing are real symptomatology, a manifestation of malingering, or an exaggeration of psychiatric symptomatology. Malingering is the intentional production of false or exaggerated physical or psychological symptoms, which is motivated by external incentives such as gaining some reward (e.g., financial compensation) or avoiding some aversive circumstance (e.g., criminal prosecution, placement in special disciplinary housing within a prison; American Psychiatric Association, 2000). Within the criminal justice system there are many possible motives for malingering or exaggerating mental health symptoms. In some instances, inmates who are malingering or exaggerating mental health symptoms may be trying to address their needs through one of the few routes available to them. Walters (2006) describes several discrete motives for malingering or exaggeration, including financial compensation; avoidance of negative consequences; separation from possible predators; relocation to a preferred setting, such as a forensic hospital; ability to gain special privileges and/or attention; and amusement.

Malingering is not necessarily an all-or-nothing issue. Malingering and exaggeration may fall along a continuum that includes significant mental health difficulties with no exaggeration, presence of genuine mental health symptomatology plus exaggeration, and pure malingering with no behavioral verification of symptomatology (Walters, 2006). The ability to assess inmates for malingering and exaggeration of symptoms, as well as to assist them in developing alternatives to malingering, is an important skill for the correctional mental health clinician.

Considering the points above, the skill set that successful correctional mental health clinicians must have is unique and considerable. It varies from their community-based colleagues' skill set in that the ability to effectively advocate within a highly structured setting is critical. Clinicians must be able to withstand the inevitable challenges security will bring to many cases. For example, clinicians might need to advocate with security staff for a cell move when an inmate with serious mental illness develops a conflict with another inmate or with security personnel. They may need to support mitigation of a consequence when a psychotic inmate receives a disciplinary infraction for violating prison rules. Additionally, merely getting corrections officers to understand that some behavior results from mental illness and not from the "criminal nature" of the inmate can be challenging. Because supports are limited in most prison settings (e.g., relatively few corrections counselors, few clergy, and a less than appropriate peer group), mental health staff will assume an even greater importance for the psychological well-being of the inmate population than do their community-based counterparts.

What Works in Correctional Treatment: Challenges and Effective Strategies

Various authors have commented on evidence-based treatments for offenders. For example, Smith and colleagues describe three principles of effective treatment for offenders in general (i.e., including, but not limited to, mentally disordered offenders; P. Smith, Gendreau, & Goggin, 2007). Effective treatment tends to target criminogenic needs, that is, attributes of offenders that are directly linked to criminal behavior (Andrews, Bonta, & Wormith, 2006). These are typically dynamic factors (factors that can be changed, such as attitudes, as opposed to static factors, those that cannot be changed, such as gender). Criminogenic needs that have been identified in the literature include antisocial values, criminal peers, low self-control, dysfunctional family ties, substance abuse, and criminal thinking. Reductions in these factors have been associated with reductions in recidivism (Day & Howells, 2002; see Chapter 9 for a more detailed discussion of this topic). Effective treatments also tend to be behavioral in nature and to focus on delivering the most services to the highest-risk offenders (P. Smith et al., 2007).

Although preventing future offending and reducing recidivism are important goals for those working within the criminal justice system, correctional treatment is often focused on more proximate goals. Among these are symptom reduction and assisting inmates with mental illness in coping with the correctional environment. Programs aimed at reducing recidivism are often aimed at all offenders, not only those with mental illnesses. These programs typically employ a psychosocial rehabilitation approach and are frequently delivered by corrections rather than mental health staff. In contrast, specialized programs such as those described below are focused on inmates with mental illness. As such, these programs are more analogous to treatment for mental illness that might occur in a community setting rather than to rehabilitative programs commonly found in correctional settings, which are aimed at reducing recidivism. As the scope of correctional treatment expands, however, a case can be made for incorporating the criminogenic model into more traditional mental health work (for a more extensive discussion on this point, see Howells, Day, & Thomas-Peter, 2004; and Chapter 9). The focus of this chapter will be the treatment of individuals with mental illness in correctional settings, not correctional treatment programs that aim to reduce recidivism in non–mentally ill offenders.

Correctional Treatment in Different Types of Correctional Facilities

Different types of correctional facilities serve different roles and unique populations, and mental health services must be targeted to the particular population and challenges of a specific setting. In this regard, local and county jails are short-term settings where adjudicated inmates are typically held for under a year. Instant offenses are less serious and often less violent. On the other hand, state and federal prisons deal with inmates facing longer sentences who have committed more serious crimes. Mental health practitioners and administrators need to focus services accordingly.

Local and County Jails

The inmate population in local and county jails is incarcerated for shorter sentences; therefore, interventions need to take into account the time-limited nature of the therapeutic relationship. In addition, it is important for mental health clinicians to recognize that local and county jails are more accessible to spouses, children, family, and friends, so inmates incarcerated in these settings are more likely to maintain close ties and communication with those they perceive as supportive. At times these close ties can lead to conflict, such as when children and a spouse are dealing with issues of abandonment or when families are dealing with the loss of income.

Given the shorter term nature of the incarceration, and the fact that first-time offenders are more likely to settle in local lockups and county jails, the focus of the mental health clinician begins with screening and crisis work. Standards require that inmates be thoroughly assessed for mental health needs and suicide upon arrival (National Commission on Correctional Mental Health Care, 2002, 2008a, 2008b), and if there are mental health needs, interventions should begin shortly thereafter. Brief individual and family therapy interventions are appropriate in these settings. Clinicians will need to work to maintain continuity of care and adherence to prescribed medication regimes for those inmates with serious mental illness. Contact with previous community providers of services will enhance the ability of the clinician to provide targeted and effective services. For inmates in local and county jails, making necessary discharge connections will be critical so that they can return to treatment with previous providers. This continuity of care is often essential to long-term adjustment and success (see Chapter 1 for a more detailed discussion of this topic).

A frequent challenge to providing adequate mental health services in local and county jails is the recruitment of skilled staff. Access to certified social workers, licensed psychologists, and board-certified psychiatrists is much more difficult in most rural and remote locations in the United States, where many of these facilities are typically located. At times administrators in these correctional settings will need to rely on other professionals and paraprofessionals to deliver interventions and support and on general medical practitioners or nurse practitioners to provide medication review and coverage. Despite the fact that many of these smaller jurisdictions experience problems with recruitment, it is critical and necessary that adequate mental health services be delivered to ensure the well-being of the inmate population. In rural sites, the use of telehealth has increased and can provide a standard of care heretofore unavailable. In these situations, the remote correctional facility will often contract with a provider or provider group from a more urban area of the state. These experts provide the specialty service (medication review, suicide assessment, etc.) unavailable in the local community (Magaletta, Ax, Bartizal, & Pratsinak, 1999; Magaletta, Dennery, & Ax, 2005; Magaletta, Fagan, & Ax, 1998).

State and Federal Prisons

State and federal prisons deal with a longer sentenced inmate population; therefore, services targeted to this group need to be more robust, and a full continuum of services must exist. Several authors (Cohen, 1985, 1993; Fagan, 2003; Metzner, 1997a, 1997b, 1998; Metzner & Dvoskin, 2006) have described what they see as the essential elements of a constitutionally adequate, correctional mental health continuum of care such as crisis intervention programs, acute care programs, residential programs for patients with chronic mental illness, outpatient treatment services, consultation services, and discharge/transfer planning. Federal courts have periodically weighed in on this issue as well. While a detailed review of case law is beyond the scope of this chapter, rulings have maintained that adequate assessment and treatment of medical needs, including mental health needs, must be provided (*Estelle v. Gamble*, 1976; *Jones 'El v. Berge*, 2001; *Madrid v. Gomez*, 1995). The present chapter proposes a continuum of mental health services that meets or exceeds what these authors recommend and the courts have ruled as constitutionally necessary.

As noted above, the Bureau of Justice Statistics indicates that a large percentage of inmates in state and federal prisons have a prior mental health treatment history, and a significant portion of those inmates with a prior history have a serious mental illness. To achieve best practice standards in prison, there is a need to re-create the continuum of mental health care and treatment services that exists in the community. This is not meant to imply that there should be a perfect correspondence between the community and prison mental health service systems (see Chapter 2 for a more detailed discussion of differences between community and correctional mental health practice). The service continuum will not precisely mirror its community counterpart, but all major program components should be available to comprehensively treat the mentally ill in prison.

An inmate population that spends years to decades in prison will present diverse and at times significant mental health needs. State and federal prison-based mental health providers will likely experience every diagnosis and level of service need within all diagnostic categories. For inmates incarcerated over a longer period, situational stressors precipitating a short-term treatment need will occur (death of a loved one, divorce, illness of a child, etc.). In other instances, inmates with a preexisting serious mental illness such as psychosis, bipolar disorder, or major depressive disorder will carry their ongoing service need with them from the community into the prison.

In large correctional systems, the potential value of pooling mental health programs in fewer prisons should be considered and may represent a best practice for efficient treatment delivery. When a full mental health treatment team is present, a richness and intensity of service can be delivered. Through greater numbers of mental health staff and programs, the prison culture can be attenuated somewhat. For example, in New York, there are 69 state prisons spanning the entire state from the Canadian border to New York City. Rather than spread services evenly throughout each prison, the bulk of services are concentrated in a subset of the prisons with the majority of mental health staff and programs (H. Smith, Sawyer, & Way, 2004). Other large states (e.g., Arizona, California, and Texas) employ a similar approach, as it would be cost-prohibitive to provide all mental health services in every location. By grouping inmates with mental health needs in fewer facilities, especially in those prisons closer to urban areas, cost-effective treatment can be provided, and recruitment of mental health specialists is more feasible.

In prisons with numbers of mental health practitioners and programs, a degree of "treatment intensity" can be achieved. In settings where a single mental health clinician travels between several prisons visiting individual prisons weekly or biweekly, it is more difficult to maintain the necessary rapport and communication with security staff to get the information needed to fully understand an inmate's needs and problems.

As a practical consideration, it is important to recognize that the security level (e.g., high, medium, or low) of a prison can complicate the provision of mental health services. Within many medium and minimum-security institutions, inmates experience greater freedom of movement without direct escort by uniformed staff; whereas in many maximum-security institutions, more movement is conducted under security escort. Because of this, arranging and completing a mental health appointment in maximum-security settings requires close cooperation with, and support of, security staff. Mental health clinicians often report that available clinical time is limited because of mandatory counts, structured meal times, and other required security functions. In many maximum-security settings clinicians find that they have about a 2-hour window to see patients in confidential settings in the morning and another 2-hour block in the afternoon. In many prisons, security-staffing levels make service delivery in the early evening and on weekends impossible because there is no available escort staff.

Essential Correctional Mental Health Services

Given the above caveats, specific mental health treatment services that should be available for inmates in correctional settings are presented below.

Clinic Services

Clinic services are similar to outpatient treatment in the community, whereby a patient receives counseling and possibly medication management during periodic appointments at a mental health clinic. The issue of assessment is more fully addressed elsewhere in this book (see Chapter 4), but it is important to begin any discussion of clinic services by noting that it is critical that there be sufficient resources to assess all inmates referred in a timely fashion. Broadly stated, corrections-based mental health services such as individual and group therapy appointments and medication prescription should be available to all inmates who have appropriately assessed need. Corrections-based services should be accessible either by referral from staff or by inmate self-referral. The latter point is critical because inmates typically are reluctant to disclose to security personnel their reasons for requesting mental health services. If a facility requires an inmate to request access to a mental health assessment through security personnel, a barrier to service is erected.

Clinic services will be the appropriate level of intervention for most inmates experiencing a host of issues and problems. Much clinic work in correctional facilities is routine and focuses on treatment concerns similar to those presented in outpatient community mental health clinics. There are, however, certain unique issues that are more frequently the focus of mental health treatment in correctional settings. A few examples include inmates who engage in self-injurious behavior or who go on hunger strikes. Inmates will also seek psychotropic medication for sleep disturbance. Although no published literature exists with regard to this issue, anecdotal reports from the New York State system indicate that issues of sleep disturbance occur frequently. Furthermore, although estimates vary, it has been reported that as many as 80% of the inmates on the mental health caseloads have a co-occurring substance abuse disorder that can complicate interventions (D. J. James & Glaze, 2006; H. Smith, Sawyer, & Way, 2002). The prevalence rates of traumatic brain injury, post-traumatic stress disorder, developmental disability, and many other diagnoses are higher in an inmate population than in the free community (Barnfield & Leathem, 1998; Denkowski & Denkowski, 1985; Goff, Rose, Rose, & Purves, 2007; Schofield et al., 2006). Mental health clinicians must be prepared to deal with complex and challenging cases, which are made even more difficult when one considers that a portion of the inmate patient population is seeking treatment for issues of secondary gain or to self-medicate. Although this is also true of community-based treatment, the stressors of the prison environment, coupled with the high levels of co-occurring Axis II and trauma history in the population, lead to a high concentration of such cases.

It is important to note that not all inmates in treatment will be there to address issues and to make personal improvements. In many cases inmates will be required to seek mental health treatment by the facility's classification committee or parole board, for example, as a condition for transfer to a less secure facility or to be considered for early release. In some prisons, required interventions are delivered by correctional staff, rehabilitation counselors, teachers, or clergy, and the mental health clinician is reserved for the more traditional therapeutic work. Additionally, as noted earlier, some inmates seeking mental health services may be feigning or exaggerating psychiatric symptoms.

It should be noted that in most jurisdictions, inmates have a constitutional right to refuse treatment without experiencing disciplinary action. A notable exception to this situation is the inmate with serious mental illness who becomes imminently dangerous to himself, herself, or others. Most systems have policies and procedures in place regarding the psychiatric treatment over objection process.

Services to Special Populations

Special services may need to be provided to subgroups of inmates with mental illnesses. For example, female inmates report much higher rates of mental illness than male inmates (D. J. James & Glaze, 2006), as well as higher rates of trauma and co-occurring substance abuse disorders (Levin, Blanch, & Jennings, 1998). Thus, at facilities for female inmates, staffing must take into account the greater proportion of inmates needing mental health services (see Chapter 10 for a detailed discussion regarding the assessment and treatment of female offenders). In addition, specialized programs are needed to meet the needs of inmates with co-occurring mental health needs and developmental disabilities (see Chapter 11 for a more detailed discussion of co-occurring disorders). For such patients, as for patients in general, an emerging best practice is dimensional assessment and treatment, where mental disorders are conceptualized as existing along a continuum of dimensions of functioning rather than as discrete categories that are qualitatively distinct from normal functioning (Moran, Coffey, Mann, Carlin, & Patton, 2006; Watson, 2005; Widiger & Lowe, 2008; Widiger & Samuel, 2005). A dimensional model lends itself to conceptualizing a patient's mental health problems in terms of functional deficits, as well as to conducting a functional analysis of those behaviors that are interfering with the patient's functioning. These behaviors then become treatment targets. For example, behaviors that have in the past led to a patient's incurring disciplinary infractions might be targeted in the treatment plan. The clinician would work with the patient to develop alternatives to the problematic behaviors (Haynes & Williams, 2003). A discussion of special populations is beyond the scope of this chapter, but several special populations are discussed in subsequent chapters of this book.

Residential Treatment for Offenders With Serious Mental Illness

There is widespread agreement that the continuum of services for persons with serious mental illness in prison must include residential treatment in a protective environment. Inmates appropriate for these units have significant difficulty functioning in a general population setting due to their serious mental illness. Intermediate Care Programs (ICPs) in the state of New York, which represent a best practice in the care of mentally ill inmates, have a special living area typically provided with the following characteristics (Condelli, Dvoskin, & Holanchock, 1994). The galleries (ranges, tiers, or cell clusters) are smaller and designed to house between 30 and 60 inmates. Security staff receive specialized training from clinicians to assist them in understanding and responding to the issues presented by the seriously mentally ill. In addition to a supportive living arrangement, inmates in these programs receive several hours of programming 5 days a week. This allows the system to provide a substantive treatment intervention while the inmate remains in the prison population. Specific treatment offerings should parallel those found in community-based day treatment programs for the seriously mentally ill with group sessions such as wellness, self-management, anger management, understanding medications, coping skills, problem solving, and activities of daily living.

Admission criteria will be an area of special interest. Typically, seriously mentally ill inmates with functional deficits are most appropriate for these settings, which provide more oversight than the prison general population, but which are also somewhat more restrictive. Typically, nearly all individuals in these programs require major psychiatric medication intervention. The settings themselves support medication adherence because emergent issues can be identified and dealt with quickly and encouragement is provided daily. In addition, the stigma associated with psychiatric medication for inmates in general population is less operative. There is a culture supporting treatment adherence and participation. Several authors have reported on the success of ICPs (Condelli, Bradigan, & Holanchock, 1997; O'Connor, Lovell, & Brown, 2002; Way, Mahoney, & Adams, 2002; Way & Nash, 2003). Other programs in New York State modeled on ICPs for different populations have not yet been evaluated in published literature, but have shown promising results in internal program evaluation reports (Moffitt, 2008; Moffitt, Way, & Sawyer, 2008).

Prison-Based Case Management

Not all inmates with serious mental illness want to live in specialized housing. As just described, many prefer to reside in the prison's general population, where prison life is more diverse and options for programming greater. In many cases, however, these inmates will cycle from general population to residential care or inpatient treatment because of stressors, an inability to consistently meet expectations, and a lack of medication adherence.

At times the number of prison-based residential treatment program slots is limited, so inmates with a significant degree of illness must live in general population. In New York, for example, there was recognition of the "gap" in the continuum of prison-based care, and a new prison-based case management program was designed and implemented in 2008 and has since served more than 200 inmates. The program model is straightforward: one certified social worker for a caseload of no more than 18 seriously mentally ill inmates, a ratio equivalent to most community-based case management programs. Inmates reside in general population, but case managers attempt to secure preferred housing for the inmate. Preferred housing is defined in general as smaller galleries within the larger prison and galleries where security staff show a willingness to engage with mental health staff to support inmates with serious mental illness (Metzner, 1998).

The case manager meets at least every other week with the inmates on the caseload and, in addition, runs groups that inmates attend at least twice a week. Groups are targeted toward helping inmates resolve and address issues they are facing when dealing with the prison's services and programs (e.g., work assignments). Security staff attend a portion of the group to discuss issues that require resolution and mediation. Case managers interact with prison program and security staff and function in the same way, as does a community-based case manager. Interactions with staff inform the case manager as to what issues the inmate is facing, so that the case manager can help resolve those that would previously have led to the inmate's removal from the program or may even have resulted in disciplinary action. Initial results are encouraging and indicate the majority of patients released from this program transitioned either to the general prison population or to a more intensive treatment program, rather than a disciplinary setting (Moffitt & Sawyer, 2009).

It is important to note that case management programs are flexible and fit easily within the prison, where space is often limited. No specialized rooms are required as groups can be held in any available space as long as confidentiality can be maintained. Inmates in a case management program experience relative freedom of movement and are able to maximally benefit from prison-based programming. The program is cost-effective compared to inpatient care. Whereas rates vary by state, where state or federal inpatient hospitals are operated, certified, and reviewed by The Joint Commission (2009), the annual cost for one inmate-patient bed is well over $150,000 (costs include full psychiatric hospital staffing plus sufficient security staff to maintain a secure perimeter to serve inmates with a minimum- to maximum-security designation). In contrast, case management programming adds only the cost of 1/18th of a social worker's salary to the cost of incarceration. Given the fiscal challenges facing most states, there is now an incentive to utilize the most cost-efficient and effective interventions available.

Crisis Intervention/Observation

To fully serve inmates, all prisons need to have access to appropriate crisis services. Local and county jails often use psychiatric wards at local hospitals. In these cases, it is important that there be a close relationship with the hospital staff, who will more often be treating a traditional psychiatric patient population. The special challenges that inmates will present when in crisis will be best resolved if there is good communication between clinical staff in the local or county jail and the mental health provider in the psychiatric ward at the local hospital.

In larger state and federal prisons, there is often an "in-house" crisis capacity to address emergent needs of the inmate population. The physical environment used for crisis intervention must be well suited to serving inmates who are reporting significant distress. In systems with a well-developed crisis capacity, there is a specialized physical environment that is critical to maintaining inmate safety. In some instances, this will be a small number of contiguous cells designed to be suicide-proof. Other systems will utilize medical infirmary beds (after modifications to suicide-proof the room).

There must be clear and consistent policies and procedures for the operation of crisis beds/cells. General population policies should not be applied to this specialized environment. For example, rounds in general population usually occur every half hour with a maximum of two or three officers for even the largest galleries. In crisis beds/cells, more frequent rounds are recommended, with at least one security staff person (apart from staff doing a one-to-one watch) constantly circulating around the gallery. Given the suspected acuity of the population, in no instance should rounds occur less often than every 15 minutes. Security staff assigned to crisis beds/cells must have specialized training provided by clinicians so that they can effectively observe, interact with, and report on inmates in distress.

In all instances, inmates admitted to crisis observation must be thoroughly assessed, and an initial treatment plan must be developed. If the assessment leads to a finding that the risk of suicide is significant, it is critical that clinical rather than security staff make the determination whether one-to-one observation is required. Likewise, clinical staff should determine which privileges and amenities are safe for the inmate to have. Whereas it is typical that in prison-based crisis observation units, security staff serve in a direct care function, decisions that are relevant to the inmate's condition in the crisis unit should be made by mental health staff unless there is a compelling security issue. Security staff often express concerns when segregation inmates (i.e., those who have been placed in disciplinary housing) are in crisis observation and will want to treat them differently. Mental health clinicians and administrators agree, however, that there should be one standard level of care for inmates in a crisis unit regardless of disciplinary status.

In general, lengths of stay in crisis cells should not be excessive but should fall within a maximum range of 4 to 7 days. For inmates who stay longer, clinical staff should have access to consultants to discuss the issues presented. Time in crisis should be utilized to stabilize and resolve inmate issues but should not substitute for inpatient treatment. Medication adjustment, individual sessions, and investigation of issues on the inmate's gallery that may have precipitated the admission should all occur.

It is important to note that crisis capacity in prison is used by inmates for many reasons, only some of which are related to mental health issues. A few examples of issues clinicians must contend with include inmates who gain access to crisis by threatening suicide but who are actually concerned about debts on the gallery, gang retaliation, and interpersonal conflicts with other inmates or with security staff. The composite case presented in Text Box 5.1 illustrates this type of case.

> ## TEXT BOX 5.1
> ## COMPOSITE CASE HISTORY
>
> Patient JG, male, age 23. He began serving his current prison sentence at age 21, after a conviction for armed robbery. According to his statement on the presentencing investigation, he had robbed a convenience store to obtain money to buy drugs. JG indicated that he had been in trouble with "the system" since age 12, when he was diagnosed with a conduct disorder and placed in special education classes. His drug use began at age 15 and, over time, his level of addiction increased. His drug of choice is crack cocaine, and although he preferred to deal to support his habit, he had resorted to robbery because his supplier was arrested.
>
> JG was admitted to a crisis observation cell within the prison at 11 p.m. one night after he threatened to commit suicide. Upon admission to the observation cell, he was placed on suicide precautions (e.g., not allowed any objects with which he could harm himself) and closely observed overnight. When interviewed by mental health staff the next morning, he confided that he had "purchased drugs" from another inmate on his housing block but did not have the money to pay what he owed. He also indicated that he was being threatened by the supplier (whose name he would not divulge), and so he threatened suicide to move off of the housing block.
>
> JG asked to be moved to another prison or, at the very least, to be placed in protective custody. Mental health staff pointed out that his urine test, administered upon admission to observation, would be positive, and that he would face disciplinary time for drug use. In addition, to be given protective custody, he would have to divulge the name of his source. JG indicated that he was not actually suicidal, and he wanted to return to the housing block to deal with this issue. After another 24 hours in observation, he was released back to his housing block. JG was placed on the mental health caseload and connected with mental health and substance abuse services.

Many admissions are due to clear and compelling mental health distress; thus, the clinician must carefully and thoroughly review every case and never presume the inmate's reason for seeking crisis services. Even when a crisis admission is precipitated by a non–mental health reason, for example, a gambling debt or fear of another inmate, there can be an adverse outcome. One study reported that 65% percent of inmates who successfully committed suicide in a state prison system were responding to real or perceived threats and stressors in the prison (Kovasznay, Miraglia, Beer, & Way, 2001).

Inpatient Psychiatric Hospital

A continuum of services for inmates must include the availability of inpatient psychiatric care either as a discrete operation within a larger correctional facility or as an independent maximum-security psychiatric hospital. As noted earlier, inpatient care is expensive, but at times it is critical to the treatment of the seriously mentally ill inmate. As in the community, the ideal role for inpatient care is to stabilize patients so that they can function in a less restrictive environment. The community for inmates is the prison, where they can live, learn, work, and recreate. A psychiatric hospital is an artificial environment where inmates cannot acquire the skills and abilities necessary to successfully return to the free community upon release. Hence the role of prison-based residential capacity addressed earlier is critical. The continuum of care must allow for a period of inpatient treatment, but the duration should be as short as can be appropriately arranged, with the inmate returning to the supports and programs available within the prison setting.

Inpatient care for inmates must be the equivalent of the care available for community-based patients; therefore, the facility/program should consider Joint Commission accreditation to ensure the quality of treatment services. Although American Correctional Association (ACA; 2002) review is necessary, it is not sufficient. Inpatient psychiatric care is technical, complex, and challenging to provide to any population, but especially to this group of patients with their blend of Axis I and Axis II diagnoses. Only an inpatient institution that meets all relevant national standards can meet the needs of this population. Whereas hospitals in the community are primarily short-term-stay settings, given the nature of the inmate population and the multidimensional nature of the patients' illnesses (high incidence of co-occurring disorders), length of stays in correctional/forensic inpatient facilities may necessarily be somewhat longer. Active treatment at the equivalent community standard (20 hours a week) should be the goal. A full multidisciplinary treatment team and use of treatment aides rather than security staff are ideal. The inpatient experience should be nearly an exact replica of what a community-based patient experiences, including family involvement, assessment of patient satisfaction, and a range of individualized interventions. Although much in the hospital experience is the same, it is important to mention special considerations.

First, it is critical that upon arrival to the hospital, inmate-patients are made aware that they are in a different setting from prison. The organizational culture should be one of treatment rather than containment and control. By helping inmates achieve this realization, the hospital will experience less violence and fewer outbursts than is typically the case with an inmate population. The hospital must have a comprehensive restraint/seclusion-reduction effort. Restraint and seclusion rates can be significantly reduced in civil psychiatric inpatient populations (Jonikas, Cook, Rosen, Laris, & Kim, 2004; Martin, Krieg, Esposito, Stubbe, & Cardona, 2008; McCue, Urcuyo, Lilu, Tobias, & Chambers, 2004). This remains an area to be investigated in forensic populations; however, programs similar to those described in the literature on civil inpatient populations have been implemented at a forensic psychiatric hospital in New York with good effect. Recommended components of a restraint- and seclusion-reduction policy include interviewing patients to determine their stress triggers and personal crisis management strategies and training staff members in crisis de-escalation and nonviolent intervention (Jonikas et al., 2004). In addition, a maximum-security psychiatric hospital should have a comprehensive conflict-mediation/resolution process. This population is inclined to disagree with each other and, as is evident from the literature, has a tendency at times to resolve issues violently. Caution must be used in implementing restraint-reduction programs because there is some evidence that interventions that reduce the rate of restraints and seclusions can lead to increased patient-related violence (Khadivi, Patel, Atkinson, & Levine, 2004). By carefully identifying and resolving interpersonal issues utilizing group and individual sessions, a hospital can significantly reduce and better manage incidents of violent outbursts.

Disciplinary Housing Treatment

During the past three decades, several states have constructed specialized prisons to house particularly dangerous or violent inmates. These facilities are commonly referred to as administrative maximum and supermax facilities. Likewise, units exist within prisons that segregate individuals from the general population. This segregation may exist for different reasons (sanctions for disciplinary infractions, protective custody, gang affiliation) and is referred to using a variety of terms (special housing units, intensive management units, solitary confinement). These facilities and units typically afford inmates limited access to exercise (usually 1 hour per day), and inmates are in lock-down for 23 hours every day. Often there are solid-front cell doors, and security staff work primarily in a control bubble and make infrequent rounds because much of the required observation is conducted through the use of video cameras. Although the names and specifics vary, in 1997 there were at least 57 supermax facilities operating in 34 states in the United States (U.S. Department of Justice, 1997). Most states reported that supermax facilities were required for management of violent and seriously disruptive inmates. Data indicate that between 1994 and 2001, the percentage of inmates in disciplinary housing nationwide increased from 4.5% to 6.5% (Camp & Camp, 2002). As the total number of inmates in disciplinary housing increased, so did the number of mentally ill inmates.

As noted earlier in this chapter, seriously mentally ill inmates experience greater difficulty in complying with prison rules and expectations and have demonstrated a tendency to engage in more acts of misbehavior that result in disciplinary time. The case history in Text Box 5.2 describes a typical scenario involving a mentally ill inmate and his involvement with disciplinary segregation and, ultimately, a successful treatment program. Literature on segregated housing has mixed conclusions regarding its effects on mental health. Whereas some research has suggested that segregation can cause serious psychological deterioration (Grassian & Friedman, 1986; Haney, 2003), other studies have reported no ill effects from short periods (Gendreau, 1984; Zinger & Wichmann, 2001). Many of these studies have been found to have methodological limitations, such as reliance on anecdotal evidence, use of conditions that are not analogous to disciplinary confinement (such as brief periods of confinement for volunteers), and making inferences based on laboratory conditions of sensory deprivation (Zinger & Wichmann, 2001). Indeed, in a recent review, Metzner and Dvoskin (2006) concluded that the enduring psychological effects of long-term segregation are still unknown.

TEXT BOX 5.2
COMPOSITE CASE HISTORY

Patient HM: Male, currently age 48. HM is currently serving his third sentence in state prison. He was convicted of murder at age 27 and received a life sentence. His two previous state sentences were for lesser crimes. Preincarceration treatment history included several psychiatric hospitalizations with various diagnoses, all of which indicate the presence of thought disorder, a serious mental illness. HM has not done particularly well adjusting to the prison rules; however, he avoided major difficulty with rules and expectations until an incident that occurred when he was 31 years old. At that time, HM assaulted a corrections officer when he was nonadherent with his antipsychotic medication regimen. Placed in disciplinary housing with a sanction of 1 year (half of which could be suspended for good behavior while in disciplinary), HM quickly amassed more than 20 years of additional disciplinary time. At age 38, HM had been in disciplinary housing for 7 years with more than two decades to serve and was selected for a program that provides services to seriously mentally ill inmates in disciplinary housing.

(Continued)

(Continued)

HM's adjustment to the program was not initially successful. It took more than 18 months of staff consistently attempting to engage, encourage, and motivate HM before he became more aware of his personal risk factors and worked to develop coping skills that would transfer to a nondisciplinary setting. Over the course of the next 3 years, HM attended programs and developed appropriate relationships with both clinical and corrections staff. HM regularly received reductions in his accumulated disciplinary time as a reward for program attendance and appropriate behavior. At the age of 43, he was released from disciplinary housing and he transitioned to a prison-based residential program for seriously mentally ill inmates, where he remains today.

There is general agreement, however, on one position. Placement of inmates with serious mental illness in disciplinary housing is contraindicated, whenever possible, because for many of these inmates, their mental illness will be exacerbated by the experience (American Psychiatric Association, 1997). In large part, the deterioration is believed to be associated with the decreased or altered social interactions experienced by inmates in disciplinary settings. For inmates experiencing difficulty maintaining reality contact, the isolation and the negative interactions so common in disciplinary settings can be difficult indeed.

Courts have recognized the importance of providing adequate treatment to the mentally ill inmate in disciplinary settings and note that for at least some inmates with serious mental illness, placing them in disciplinary housing is or may be unconstitutional. An extensive discussion of past and present litigation regarding the mentally ill in disciplinary settings is beyond the scope of this chapter, but for more information readers should consult *Madrid v. Gomez* (1995); *Ruiz v. Johnson* (1999); *Jones 'El v. Berge* (2001); and Private Settlement Agreement, *Disability Advocates Inc. v. NYS Office of Mental Health et al.* (2007).

It is important to consider one case in detail, that of *Jones 'El v. Berge* (2001). In this case, the court ruled that it was the actual conditions of disciplinary confinement and not inadequate treatment that made the confinement of seriously mentally ill unconstitutional. Most states and the federal government maintain that a disciplinary housing option is critical to maintaining the safe and effective operation of correctional facilities and that, on occasion, it is appropriate to place offenders with serious mental illnesses in disciplinary settings.

To afford facilities the option of placing the seriously mentally ill inmate in disciplinary housing while still meeting required standards of care, best practice program models have evolved to treat the mentally ill effectively in disciplinary settings (e.g., Moffitt, Way, Maxymilian, & Fraser, 2007; Moffitt et al., 2008). Model programs in the state of New York, for example, have included the Specialized Treatment Program and the Behavioral Health Unit (Moffitt et al., 2007, 2008). Program models share similar characteristics and can be summarized as follows: The programs are highly structured, offering at least 10 hours a week of treatment time, and focus on inmate-patients' developing improved social and interactional skills as an initial step toward improved functioning. Behavioral reinforcements are utilized involving increased privileges such as property beyond minimums, access to additional exercise, commissary purchases, television, and radios. After a period during which clinical staff foster an initial relationship, and subsequent to efforts to enhance social and interactional abilities, higher level clinical work begins.

As with any other prison mental health treatment program, collaboration between mental health and custody staff is essential to the workings of such programs. This is especially true in the highest-security settings, such as disciplinary housing, where custody staff must be enlisted to get inmates out of their cells and move them to programming areas. It is helpful to have custody staff who are specially recruited to work in the mental health programs, who receive extra training in dealing with mentally ill offenders, and who are considered a part of the treatment team.

Structured interventions focus on treatment readiness, behavior management, interpersonal relationships, structured recreation, mental health wellness/self-care, and healthful habits. Due to the highly volatile and reactive nature of this population, early phases of treatment occur with a significant amount of protection in place for inmate-patients, mental health clinicians, and security staff. Patients are escorted to group in restraints and during group are secured in various ways (therapeutic cubicle, security chair, leg chain) to ensure that they cannot aggress toward one another or the mental health clinician. As treatment continues and improvements are noted, the multidisciplinary treatment team (which includes security personnel) can determine that the inmate can be released from restraint during transport and/or during group. One of the major rewards for active program participation is disciplinary time cuts, which can be substantial. Inmates with serious mental illness often amass significant amounts of disciplinary time. Specialized disciplinary housing treatment programs have a capacity to break the cycle of maladaptive behavior, resulting in disciplinary time.

Support must be provided to clinicians working with this difficult population, including training regarding manifestations of personality disorders and strategies for dealing with typical behaviors. From the clinician's perspective, every successful discharge from one of these specialized programs leads to the admission of another seriously mentally ill inmate who is typically not motivated to accept treatment but is often quite angry and verbally abusive. Doing skilled clinical work and using techniques for developing rapport with these disciplinary inmates is not easily taught and falls into the category of "art form" as much as "learned skill." Clinical staff must help inmates understand that they have a different role than security staff and must sidestep the frequent attempts to engage in power struggles, challenges to rules and expectations, and requests for special favors. Clear limits, specific expectations, and consistency are keys to success. Clinical staff working with this group of inmates will be exposed to threats, violence, and incidents involving the use of force, as well as self-injurious behaviors. The patient population is without doubt the most stressful a correctional mental health clinician can treat. This makes mentoring, supervision, debriefing, and strategies to minimize burnout all the more important.

Prerelease Treatment Services

The vast majority of inmates in custody eventually leave prison and return to the free community. It is critical that comprehensive discharge planning services be provided for all inmates on the caseload but in particular for those inmates with serious mental illnesses. Standard discharge planning services should follow community standards and include a guaranteed supply of medication (30-day supply at a minimum) and appointments with outpatient clinics, psychiatrists, or other counseling services as indicated (for example, substance abuse counselors). For those who are seriously mentally ill, there is a need to engage in additional, specialized discharge planning. For example, in many jurisdictions these inmates may qualify for case management or assertive community treatment team services on release (see Chapter 1 for a more detailed discussion of this topic). In addition, it is this group that is most likely to qualify for entitlements such as

Supplemental Security Income (SSI) or Social Security Disability Income (SSDI), which are federal programs available to individuals unable to work due to physical or psychiatric disability. An additional challenge to discharge planning exists in large states such as Texas and California, as well as in the federal prison system, where staff are often attempting to arrange for services in locations hundreds of miles from the prison.

For the most seriously mentally ill who have been incarcerated for some time, a specialized program tailored to their specific needs is a desirable component. A program in the New York State prison system, the Community Orientation and Re-Entry Program, has demonstrated that program participants are less likely to be reincarcerated than individuals with serious mental illness who were released from prison without these enhanced services (Way et al., 2008). This program treats inmates about to be released from prison for about 90 days prior to discharge. The inmates live on a gallery together and program together for several hours, 5 days a week. Therapeutic groups and educational groups explore community survival skills, medication self-management, illness coping skills, and life skills. This program also includes an in-reach component wherein community-based providers, some peer-run and operated, dispatch staff to run groups within the correctional setting prior to the inmate's release. This in-reach serves several purposes but at a minimum helps the inmate develop a rapport with and acceptance of the agency/staff who will be in a position to provide direct help and support upon release from prison. In addition, in-reach services can be motivational and assist the inmate with a realization that community success is a real possibility, especially when the in-reach peer is a former inmate himself or herself. The composite case summarized in Text Box 5.3 exemplifies the benefits of transition planning.

TEXT BOX 5.3
COMPOSITE CASE HISTORY

Patient CS: female, age 23. CS is being released on parole after serving 4 years of her second sentence in state prison. CS was convicted of drug possession with intent to distribute and admits to a long history of drug use, as well as prostitution, petty theft, and forgery—acts she committed to support her drug habit. CS has a history of childhood physical and sexual abuse. She reports that she has three children, two of whom she gave up for adoption. Her last child is age 3 and is in foster care. The child was born while CS was in prison and stayed with CS for the first 9 months after birth as part of a novel, prison-based mother-child program. CS has a lengthy history of homelessness and is returning to a major metropolitan area, where she is intent on becoming a mother.

During her entire sentence, CS has participated actively in mental health treatment, carrying diagnoses of depression, borderline personality disorder, and substance abuse. She has been adherent to her antidepressant medication regimen. She is leaving prison in 2 weeks and has been working the past 6 months with a social worker at the prison who coordinates prerelease services. Given her diagnosis, an SSI application has been submitted, as well as applications for other entitlements such as food stamps, a housing voucher, and public assistance. In addition, CS has met with the person who will be her case manager and with her dedicated parole officer (one with a lower caseload and specialized training to carry a caseload of mental health–involved prison releases). CS will also be provided with a 30-day supply of her medication and a scheduled clinic appointment within her first 10 days in the community.

A similar program in Massachusetts, the Forensic Transition Team (FTT), serves offenders with serious mental illness and provides services for 3 months prior to and 3 months following their release from prison. This voluntary program provides services such as reestablishing entitlement benefits as well as linkages to community services (Haimowitz, 2004; Hartwell, 2008; Hartwell & Orr, 1999). Metzner (2002) indicates that these specialized programs have become the standard of care for seriously mentally ill inmates in supermax prisons if they are not excluded from confinement in these settings by policy.

Summary and Conclusions

In conclusion, mental health treatment in correctional settings provides unique challenges. A system of care within a correctional system must take into account not only the mental health needs of the inmate-patients but also the environment within which that care is delivered. To provide best practices care, systemic barriers must often be managed. Whereas the focus in settings with a relatively short length of stay, such as local and county jails, is on stabilization and discharge planning for continuity of care; the focus in settings where there is a longer term population, such as federal and state prisons, is on re-creating, with some modifications and to the extent possible, the continuum of care that exists in the community. This enables treatment to be provided at the level of intensity that is medically necessary to meet the needs of each inmate-patient. Furthermore, the continuum of care described in this chapter can be utilized to address the functional deficits of individual patients in a targeted manner. Self-defeating, criminogenic behaviors that present the greatest risk to the individual and the public can be targeted at every step along the way in the treatment process.

KEY TERMS

Axis I mental disorders

Axis II mental disorders

Malingering

Secondary gain

Criminogenic needs

Dimensional vs. categorical assessment

Clinical services

Case management

Residential treatment

Crisis intervention/observation

Inpatient psychiatric hospital

Disciplinary housing

Supermax prison

Administrative detention

Special housing unit (SHU)

National Commission on Correctional Health Care

American Correctional Association

The Joint Commission

Prerelease treatment services

Segregation

DISCUSSION QUESTIONS

1. Is it realistic to require correctional facilities to provide a standard of mental health care equivalent to that of the community? Is it desirable, that is, that inmates *should* have access to this level of care?

2. Should inmates with serious mental illness be held responsible for their behavior if it results in harm to someone else?

3. Should prison inmates with serious mental illness have the right to refuse treatment?

4. Consider malingering from an inmate's standpoint. Is such behavior reasonable under the circumstances, perhaps a coping skill for negotiating an environment that offers few rewards or reinforcers? Could such behavior be expected where threats, for example, from other inmates, are common?

5. Do you think the programs described in this chapter provide inmate-patients with a reasonable chance of recovery and successful transition to the free community? Why or why not?

6. Do you think the type of facility from which an inmate is being released—a local jail, state prison, or federal prison—might make a difference in terms of putting prerelease treatment services in place?

References

American Correctional Association. (2002). *Performance-based standards for correctional health care for adult correctional institutions.* Alexandria, VA: Author.

American Psychiatric Association. (1997). Practice guideline for the treatment of patients with schizophrenia. *American Journal of Psychiatry, 154*(Suppl. 4), 1–63.

American Psychiatric Association. (2000). *Diagnostic and statistical manual of mental disorders* (4th ed., Text Revision). Washington, DC: Author.

Andrews, D. A., Bonta, J., & Wormith, S. (2006). The recent past and near future of risk and/or needs assessment. *Crime & Delinquency, 52,* 7–27.

Baillargeon, J., Binswanger, I. A., Penn, J. V., Williams, B. A., & Murray, O. J. (2009). Psychiatric disorders and repeat incarcerations: The revolving prison door. *American Journal of Psychiatry, 166,* 103–126.

Barnfield, T. V., & Leathem, J. M. (1998). Incidence and outcomes of traumatic brain injury and substance abuse in a New Zealand prison population. *Brain Injury, 12,* 455–466.

Camp, G. G., & Camp, G. N. (2002). *Corrections yearbook 2001: Adult systems.* Middletown, CT: Criminal Justice Institute.

Cohen, F. (1985). Legal issues in the mentally disordered inmate. In F. Tracy (Ed.), *Sourcebook on the mentally disordered prisoner* (pp. 31–90). Washington, DC: National Institute of Corrections.

Cohen, F. (1993). Captives' legal right to mental health care. *Law Psychological Review, 17,* 1–39.

Condelli, W. S., Bradigan, B., & Holanchock, H. (1997). Intermediate care programs to reduce risk and better manage inmates with psychiatric disorders. *Behavioral Sciences & the Law, 15,* 459–467.

Condelli, W. S., Dvoskin, J. A., & Holanchock, H. (1994). Intermediate care programs for inmates with psychiatric disorders. *Bulletin of the American Academy of Psychiatry and the Law, 22,* 63–70.

Day, A., & Howells, K. (2002). Psychological treatments for rehabilitating offenders: Evidence-based practice comes of age. *Australian Psychologist, 37,* 39–47.

Denkowski, G. C., & Denkowski, K. M. (1985). The mentally retarded offender in the state prison system: Identification, prevalence, adjustment, and rehabilitation. *Criminal Justice and Behavior, 12,* 55–70.

Diamond, P. M., Wang, E. W., Holzer, C. E., Thomas, C., & des Anges, C. (2001). The prevalence of mental illness in prison. *Administration and Policy in Mental Health, 29,* 21–40.

Dvoskin, J., & Spiers, E. (2004). On the role of correctional officers in prison mental health. *Psychiatric Quarterly, 75,* 41–59.

Estelle v. Gamble, 429 U.S. 97 (1976).

Fagan, T. J. (2003). Mental health in corrections: A model for service delivery. In T. J. Fagan & R. K. Ax (Eds.), *Correctional mental health handbook* (pp. 3–19). Thousand Oaks, CA: Sage.

Gendreau, P. (1984). Solitary confinement is not cruel and unusual punishment: People some-times are. *Canadian Journal of Criminology and Criminal Justice, 26,* 467–478.

Goff, A., Rose, E., Rose, S., & Purves, D. (2007). Does PTSD occur in sentenced prison popula-tions? A systematic literature review. *Criminal Behavior and Mental Health, 17,* 152–162.

Grassian, S., & Friedman, N. (1986). Effects of sensory deprivation in psychiatric seclusion and solitary confinement. *International Journal of Law and Psychiatry, 8,* 49–65.

Haimowitz, J. D. (2004). Slowing the revolving door: Community reentry of offenders with men-tal illness. *Psychiatric Services, 55,* 373–375.

Haney, C. (2003). Mental health issues in long-term solitary and "supermax" confinement. *Crime & Delinquency, 49,* 124–156.

Hartwell, S. (2008, May). *Community reintegration of persons with SMI post incarceration* (CMHSR Research Brief, Vol. 5, No. 4). Worcester, MA: Center for Mental Health Services Research, Department of Psychiatry, University of Massachusetts Medical School.

Hartwell, S., & Orr, K. (1999). The Massachusetts Forensic Transition Program for mentally ill offenders reentering the community. *Psychiatric Services, 50,* 1220–1222.

Haynes, S., & Williams, A. (2003). Case formulation and design of behavioral treatment programs. *European Journal of Psychological Assessment, 19,* 164–174.

Howells, K., Day, A., & Thomas-Peter, B. (2004). Changing violent behaviour: Forensic mental health and criminogenic models compared. *Journal of Forensic Psychiatry and Psychology, 15,* 391–406.

James, D. J., & Glaze, L. E. (2006, September). *Mental health problems of prison and jail inmates* (Bureau of Justice Statistics Special Report NCJ 213600). Washington, DC: National Criminal Justice Reference Service, Office of Justice Programs.

James, J. F., Gregory, D., Jones, R. K., & Rundell, O. H. (1980). Psychiatric morbidity in prisons. *Hospital and Community Psychiatry, 31,* 674–677.

The Joint Commission. (2009). *2009 comprehensive accreditation manual for hospitals (CAMH): The official handbook.* Oakbrook Terrace, IL: Author.

Jones 'El v. Berge, 164 F. Supp. 2d 1096 (W.D. Wis. 2001).

Jonikas, J. A., Cook, J. A., Rosen, C., Laris, A., & Kim, J. (2004). A program to reduce the use of physical restraint in psychiatric inpatient facilities. *Psychiatric Services, 55,* 818–820.

Khadivi, A. N., Patel, R. C., Atkinson, A. R., & Levine, J. M. (2004). Association between seclusion and restraint and patient-related violence. *Psychiatric Services, 55,* 1311–1312.

Kovasznay, B., Miraglia, R., Beer, R., & Way, B. (2001). Reducing suicides in New York State cor-rectional facilities. *Psychiatric Quarterly, 75,* 61–70.

Lamb, R. H., & Weinberger, L. E. (1998). Persons with severe mental illness in jails and prisons: A review. *Psychiatric Services, 49,* 483–492.

Levin, B. L., Blanch, A. K., & Jennings, A. (1998). *Women's mental health services: A public health perspective.* Thousand Oaks, CA: Sage.

Lovell, D., & Jemelka, R. (1996). When inmates misbehave: The costs of discipline. *The Prison Journal, 76,* 165–179.

Lovell, D., & Jemelka, R. (1998). Coping with mental illness in prison. *Family & Community Health, 21,* 54–66.

Madrid v. Gomez, 889 F. Supp. 1146 (N.D. Cal. 1995).

Magaletta, P. R., Ax, R. K., Bartizal, D. E., & Pratsinak, G. J. (1999). Correctional telehealth. *Journal of the Mental Health in Corrections Consortium, 44,* 4–5.

Magaletta, P. R., Dennery, C. H., & Ax, R. K. (2005). Telehealth: The future of correctional health-care. In S. Stokovic (Ed.), *Managing special populations in jails and prisons* (pp. 20-1 to 20-12). New York, NY: Civic Research Group.

Magaletta, P. R., Fagan, T. J., & Ax, R. K. (1998). Advancing psychology services through telehealth in the Federal Bureau of Prisons. *Professional Psychology: Research and Practice, 29,* 543–548.

Martin, A., Krieg, H., Esposito, F., Stubbe, D., & Cardona, L. (2008). Reduction of restraint and seclusion through collaborative problem solving: A five-year prospective inpatient study. *Psychiatric Services, 59,* 1406–1412.

McCue, R. E., Urcuyo, L., Lilu, Y., Tobias, T., & Chambers, M. J. (2004). Reducing restraint use in a public psychiatric inpatient service. *Journal of Behavioral Health Services and Research, 31,* 217–224.

McShane, M. D. (1989). The bus stop revisited: Discipline and psychiatric patients in prison. *Journal of Psychiatry and the Law, 17,* 413–433.

Metzner, J. L. (1997a). An introduction to correctional psychiatry: Part I. *Journal of the American Academy of Psychiatry and the Law, 25,* 375–381.

Metzner, J. L. (1997b). An introduction to correctional psychiatry: Part II. *Journal of the American Academy of Psychiatry and the Law, 25,* 571–579.

Metzner, J. L. (1998). An introduction to correctional psychiatry: Part III. *Journal of the American Academy of Psychiatry and the Law, 26,* 107–115.

Metzner, J. L. (2002). Class action litigation in correctional psychiatry. *Journal of the American Academy of Psychiatry and the Law, 30,* 19–29.

Metzner, J. L., Cohen, F., Grossman L. S., & Wettstein, R. M. (1998). Treatment in jails and prisons. In R. M. Wettstein (Ed.), *Treatment of offenders with mental disorders* (pp. 211–264). New York, NY: Guilford.

Metzner, J. L., & Dvoskin, J. (2006). An overview of correctional psychiatry. *Psychiatric Clinics of North America, 29,* 761–772.

Moffitt, C. E. (2008). *BHU annual report 2008.* Marcy: Central New York Psychiatric Center.

Moffitt, C. E., & Sawyer, D. A. (2009). *Transitional Intermediate Care Program: Annual report 2009.* Marcy: Central New York Psychiatric Center.

Moffitt, C. E., Way, B. B., Maxymilian, T., & Fraser, S. (2007, March). *Behavioral health unit for inmates in special housing units: Evaluation report.* Marcy: Central New York Psychiatric Center.

Moffitt, C. E., Way, B. B., & Sawyer, D. A. (2008). *Special treatment programs at Attica and Five Points correctional facilities: One-year post-discharge follow-up.* Marcy: Central New York Psychiatric Center.

Moran, P., Coffey, C., Mann, A., Carlin, J. B., & Patton, G. C. (2006). Dimensional characteristics of DSM-IV personality disorders in a large epidemiological sample. *Acta Psychiatrica Scadanavica, 113,* 233–236.

Morgan, D. W., Edwards, A. C., & Faulkner, L. R. (1993). The adaptation to prison by individuals with schizophrenia. *Bulletin of the American Academy of Psychiatry and the Law, 21,* 427–433.

National Commission on Correctional Health Care. (2002). *The status of soon-to-be-released inmates: A report to Congress.* Chicago, IL: Author.

National Commission on Correctional Health Care. (2008a). *Standards for health services in jails.* Chicago, IL: Author.

National Commission on Correctional Health Care. (2008b). *Standards for mental health services in correctional facilities.* Chicago, IL: Author.

O'Connor, F. W., Lovell, D., & Brown, L. (2002). Implementing residential treatment for prison inmates with mental illness. *Archives of Psychiatric Nursing, 16,* 232–238.

Private Settlement Agreement, *Disability Advocates, Inc. v. NYS Office of Mental Health et al.,* 02 Civ. 4002 (GEL) (2007).

Rotter, M., Way, B., Steinbacher, M., Smith, H., & Sawyer, D. (2002). Personality disorders in prison: Aren't they all antisocial? *Psychiatric Quarterly, 73,* 337–349.

Ruiz v. Johnson, 37 F. Supp. 2d 855 (S.D. Tex. 1999).

Schofield, P. W., Butler, T. G., Hollis, S. J., Smith, N. E., Lee, S. J., & Kelso, W. M. (2006). Neuropsychiatric correlates of traumatic brain injury (TBI) among Australian prison entrants. *Brain Injury, 20,* 1409–1418.

Sirotich, F. (2008). Correlates of crime and violence among persons with mental disorder: An evidence-based review. *Brief Treatment and Crisis Intervention, 8,* 171–194.

Smith, H., Sawyer, D., & Way, B. (2002). Central New York Psychiatric Center: An approach to the treatment of co-occurring disorders in the New York State correctional mental health system. *Behavioral Sciences and the Law, 20,* 523–534.

Smith, H., Sawyer, D., & Way, B. (2004). Correctional mental health services in New York: Then and now. *Psychiatric Quarterly, 75,* 21–39.

Smith, P., Gendreau, P., & Goggin, C. (2007). What works in predicting psychiatric hospitalization and relapse: The specific responsivity dimension of effective correctional treatment. In R. K. Ax & T. J. Fagan (Eds.), *Corrections, mental health and social policy: International perspectives* (pp. 209–223). Springfield, IL: Charles C Thomas.

Steadman, H. J., Monahan, J., Hartsone, E., Davis, S. K., & Robbins, P. C. (1982). Mentally disordered offenders: A national survey of the patient and facilities. *Law and Human Behavior, 6,* 31–38.

Steadman, H. J., Osher, F. C., Robbins, P. C., Case, B., & Samuels, S. (2009). Prevalence of serious mental illness among jail inmates. *Psychiatric Services, 60,* 761–765.

Taylor, P. J. (2008). Psychosis and violence: Stories, fears, and reality. *Canadian Journal of Psychiatry, 53,* 647–659.

Teplin, L. A. (1990). The prevalence of severe mental disorder among male urban detainees: Comparison with the epidemiologic catchment area program. *American Journal of Public Health, 80,* 663–669.

Teplin, L. A. (1994). Psychiatric and substance abuse disorders among male urban jail detainees. *American Journal of Public Health, 84,* 290–293.

Teplin, L. A., Abram, K. M., & McClelland, G. M. (1996). Prevalence of psychiatric disorders among incarcerated women: I. Pretrial jail detainees. *Archives of General Psychiatry, 53,* 505–512.

U.S. Department of Justice. (1997). *Supermax housing: A survey of current practice.* Longmont, CO: National Institute of Corrections Information Center.

Walters, G. D. (2006). Coping with malingering and exaggeration of psychiatric symptomatology in offender populations. *American Journal of Forensic Psychology, 24,* 21–40.

Watson, D. (2005). Rethinking the mood and anxiety disorders: A quantitative hierarchical model for DSM-IV. *Journal of Abnormal Psychology, 114,* 522–536.

Way, B., Mahoney, K., & Adams, K. (2002). *Review of the intermediate care program.* Marcy: Central New York Psychiatric Center.

Way, B., & Nash, R. (2003). *CNYPC patient demographic and diagnostic profile: Year 2003.* Marcy: Central New York Psychiatric Center.

Way, B., Steinbacher, M., Sawyer, D., & Lilly, S. (2008). *The community orientation and re-entry program (CORP): An innovative in-prison pre-release program that develops community independent living skills for inmates with serious mental illness: Three year return to prison rates.* Unpublished manuscript.

Widiger, T. A., & Lowe, J. R. (2008). A dimensional model of personality disorder: Proposal for DSM-IV. *Psychiatric Clinics of North America, 31,* 363–378.

Widiger, T. A., & Samuel, D. B. (2005). Diagnostic categories or dimensions? A question for the Diagnostic and Statistical Manual of Mental Disorders–Fifth Edition. *Journal of Abnormal Psychology, 114,* 494–504.

Zinger, I., & Wichmann, C. (2001). The psychological effects of 60 days in administrative segregation. *Canadian Journal of Criminology and Criminal Justice, 43,* 47–84.

CHAPTER 6

Issues in Multicultural Correctional Assessment and Treatment

Corinne N. Ortega

Introduction

Increasing diversity in the United States has widened the base populations to whom psychologists provide services. Various divisions of the American Psychological Association (APA) have recognized the importance of multicultural competencies for more than 25 years (notably, Division 17—Counseling Psychology and Division 45—The Society for the Psychological Study of Ethnic Minority Issues). In 2002, APA formally recognized the evolution of the science and practice of psychology in a diverse society by adopting as policy the *Guidelines on Multicultural Education, Training, Research, Practice, and Organizational Change for Psychologists* (APA, 2002b).

Nowhere is the changing face of the United States reflected more clearly than in its correctional systems. Blacks and Hispanics make up 62% of the incarcerated population, although they comprise only 25% of the national population (Human Rights Watch, 2002). Hispanics represent 40% of all sentenced federal offenders, although they account for only 13% of the total U.S. population (López, 2000). According to the Bureau of Justice Statistics (2007), the lifetime chance of a person going to prison is higher for Blacks (18.6%) and Hispanics (10%) than for Whites (3.4%). Furthermore, Blacks represent approximately 40% of the death row population in the United States (Amnesty International, 2003).

The sociopolitical and socioeconomic explanations for this phenomenon are complex and far beyond the scope of this chapter. It is clear, however, that given the disproportionate confinement of minorities in the United States, any meaningful discussion of correctional mental health must necessarily include a discussion of multicultural issues. This chapter will first focus on a general overview of multicultural counseling and its applications in correctional

---

Editor's note: The views expressed in this chapter are those of the author and do not necessarily reflect the views or opinions of the Department of Justice or the Federal Bureau of Prisons.

settings. Second, the use of psychological tests and assessments with multicultural correctional populations will be explored with an emphasis on forensic evaluations. Finally, the issue of cultural competence with religious minorities and religious extremists will be addressed.

Multicultural Counseling

Jackson (1995) succinctly defines multicultural counseling as counseling that takes place between or among individuals from different cultural backgrounds. Although a simple enough definition, the implications of this in the mental health field are far-reaching. The increased racial, ethnic, and cultural diversity in the United States creates a demand for professional services, including mental health, that meet the needs of people from a wide variety of backgrounds (Barrett & George, 2005). The issues involved in providing culturally competent services are as complex and varied as clients themselves (Sue & Sue, 2007). Cookbook approaches to multicultural counseling cannot be utilized without contradicting the very concept. López (2000) discusses this in terms of culturally critical thinking. Multicultural awareness allows the counselor to think about diversity in nonjudgmental ways without polarizing issues into "right and wrong" and should take into consideration all of the complex dimensions of clients in a pluralistic society (Corey & Corey, 1998).

Unidimensional concepts of race, ethnicity, and culture allow practitioners to conceptualize their clients as having more than just a singular notion of self. Most people have more than just one definition of who they are. People often define themselves by criteria such as gender, race, ethnicity, sexual orientation, socioeconomic status, citizenship, and religious affiliation. Multicultural counseling is the understanding that individuals exist and behave in a larger context that includes all of these notions of self. Indeed, cultural identity is fluid and often changes according to social context (Monk, Winslade, & Sinclair, 2008). A complex undertaking is made more challenging with the realization that cultures are not static and should be understood in terms of their own dynamic processes (López, 2000). Multicultural counseling competency is the ability to understand and conceptualize a client through multiple worldviews, the ability to see the ways in which clients' cultural experiences may or may not influence their presenting problems, the clients' understanding of the source of their problems, and the understanding of what it will mean for the problems to be adequately addressed through the counseling process. The conceptualization of multicultural counseling competency understood in this light becomes, to coin a phrase, not a destination, but a journey.

To make matters more confusing, there are many ways in which to define mental health. The *Diagnostic and Statistical Manual of Mental Disorders–Fourth Edition, Text Revision* (*DSM-IV-TR*; American Psychiatric Association, 2000) recognizes this by stating,

> A clinician who is unfamiliar with the nuances of an individual's cultural frame of reference may incorrectly judge as psychopathology those normal variations in behavior, belief, or experience that are particular to the individual's culture. For example, certain religious practices or beliefs (e.g., hearing or seeing a deceased relative during bereavement) may be misdiagnosed as manifestations of a Psychotic Disorder. Applying Personality Disorder criteria across cultural settings may be especially difficult because of the wide cultural variations in concepts of self, styles of communications, and coping mechanism. (p. xxxiv)

Likewise, the *DMS-IV-TR* recognizes the term *culture-bound syndrome*, which "denotes recurrent, locality-specific patterns of aberrant behavior and troubling experience that may or may not be linked to a particular DSM-IV diagnostic category"

Table 6.1	Culture-Bound Syndrome	

Name	*Culture*	*Description*
Amok	Malaysia, Laos, Philippines, Polynesia, Papua New Guinea	A dissociative episode involving violent outbursts and aggressive or homicidal behavior directed at objects or people. Episodes may be precipitated by minor slights or insults.
Ataques de nervios	Hispanics (particularly those from the Caribbean)	A general sense of being out of control, occurring as a result of a stressful event, usually relating to family (e.g., death of a family member or conflict with a family member). Symptoms of ataques include trembling, crying, and fainting episodes.
Brain fag	West Africa	A condition resulting from mental exhaustion as a result of problems with schooling. Symptoms include difficulty concentrating, headaches, neck pains, and blurry vision.
Dhat	India	Severe anxiety and hypocondriasis associated with a sense of weakness and exhaustion, discharge of semen, and discoloration of the urine.
Ghost sickness	Native Americans	Bad dreams, loss of appetite, anxiety, confusion, and weakness associated with a preoccupation with death or the deceased, sometimes associated with witchcraft or evil forces.
Koro	Asians	An acute feeling of anxiety related to the fear that the external genitals (males) or breasts (females) will retract into the body, causing death.
Latah	Indonesia, Malaysia	A bout of hysterics, shouting of obscenities, or imitation of the movement or speech of others brought about by being startled or surprised.
Mal de ojo	Hispanics, Mediterranean	Literally translated as "evil eye," this disorder can cause a wide variety of somatic concerns, including loss of appetite, fever, diarrhea, and malaise. Caused by the malevolent intentions of another, who casts "mal de ojo" about the victim; children are particularly susceptible.
Taijin kyofusho	Japan	Included in the official Japanese diagnostic system for mental disorder, this phobia refers to the intense fear that the odor, appearance, and facial expressions of the individual are offensive to others.
Zar	North Africa and Middle Eastern cultures	This term refers to spirits possessing an individual, causing dissociative episodes of singing, weeping, withdrawal, apathy, or loss of willingness/ability to carry out daily activities.

Source: Adapted from American Psychiatric Association (2000); see also Paniagua (2000).

(p. 898). The *DSM-IV-TR* goes on to suggest that culture-bound syndromes are generally limited to specific cultural areas. Thus, abnormal or psychopathological behaviors should be viewed in their cultural context (see Table 6.1 for examples of culture-bound syndromes).

People from various cultures and backgrounds will also approach and respond to the therapeutic process differently. For example, Gonzalez (1997) notes that traditional Hispanic Americans are accustomed to being treated by physicians and may be unclear as to the role of a psychologist or other mental health provider, expecting medication and a quick solution to their problems. African Americans may be distrustful of the counseling process, based on historical hostility due to their prolonged inferior treatment by American society (Evans & George, 2008). They may prefer to use prayer, faith, spirituality, and religious figures to assist with personal problems (Toldson, 2008). Asian Americans tend not to seek psychological services and tend to terminate prematurely when they do (Kim & Park, 2008), as there is a cultural norm against sharing private matters with outsiders (Sue & Sue, 2007). Furthermore, in some Southeast Asian countries, a mental health problem is considered the same as being insane and is an admission of inferiority (Nguyen, 1985), thus reducing the likelihood of seeking treatment.

Communication styles also vary widely across racial and ethnic groups. For example, African Americans may speak loudly and be more animated than their non–African American counterparts (Evans & George, 2008). Asian Americans may communicate through indirect means, use apology to maintain and build "face," acknowledge and defer to hierarchy, be more modest and allow for more silence, and place a high value on emotional control and stoicism (Kim & Park, 2008). Native Americans may emphasize nonverbal communication and avoid direct eye contact out of respect for an elder or person in authority (Garrett, 2008).

Multicultural Applications in Corrections

Correctional mental health is practiced in a fast-paced environment and requires specialized training focused on the unique needs of the criminal population. This challenge is increased when it is also necessary to apply the principles of multicultural counseling to the offender population. Criminal offenders are as diverse as the racial, cultural, and socioeconomic backgrounds from which they come. The APA *Ethical Principles of Psychologists and Code of Conduct* (2002a) mandates that psychologists practice only in areas in which they maintain competence and, unless it is an emergency, refer clients with whom they do not have the necessary understanding of racial, socioeconomic, cultural, ethnic, and/or other issues essential to providing services. The ethical codes of the American Counseling Association and the National Association of Social Workers have similar expectations for providing services to diverse populations. Although this is a noble aspiration, it may be impractical at best and impossible at worst in a correctional setting.

Imagine that a new inmate, who was recently arrested at an international airport, arrives at a facility. The inmate is from South Africa and speaks Bantu. He reports he is part of the Lemba tribe. After tackling the first challenge of finding a translator, cultural competence requires an understanding of this inmate's background. Where does a clinician start—with his South African culture or with his tribal background? How many clinicians know anything about the Lemba tribe? In the absence of this cultural information, the APA ethical guidelines say that psychologists must refer the client to someone who does know about the tribe. How likely is it that there will be another clinician in the institution who is familiar with the Lemba tribe? (See Lerner & Lerner, 2006, for more information about the Lemba tribe). The pragmatic issues of referring are obvious. Just as unrealistic is trying to become educated and trained in every cultural group and all of their variations.

To make matters more confusing, the issue of prison culture must also be considered. Brodsky (1975) describes the process of adapting to the prison culture as *prisonization.* The prison subculture has its own set of values and beliefs, which are different from the culture of the communities and families from which inmates come (Gordon, 1999).

So, what is the solution? As with most aspects of correctional mental health, the key to successfully navigating the maze of cultural competence lies in flexibility. McAuliffe (2008) suggests three broad guidelines for flexibility in working with culture: recognizing the fluidity in culture; making measured, tentative generalizations; and adapting traditional counseling theories to cultures, but doing so flexibly.

Individuals from the same racial, ethnic, and/or cultural background will have tremendous variability in the degree to which they adhere to those values. The culturally competent correctional mental health practitioner must balance an awareness of the variety of cultural influences prisoners bring with them to the correctional institution. They must also have an understanding of the impact of the prison culture and the ways in which prisonization modifies behavior as individuals adapt to their incarceration. Finally, they must attempt to provide meaningful interventions and services that are both culturally competent and appropriate to address underlying criminogenic tendencies such as antisocial and narcissistic beliefs and attitudes and criminal thinking errors (e.g., "I'm not hurting anyone" and "Everybody does it, they just don't get caught").

As one can imagine, this is not an easy task, as the following sample case study illustrates.

Composite Case Study

Reason for Referral

"M" was referred to mental health services by another staff member. The staff member reported that during routine phone monitoring of inmate calls, M was overheard being informed of his mother's unexpected death in an auto accident. The staff member requested that mental health staff offer services to M based on his recent loss.

Background

M is a 33-year-old Black male. He is currently serving a 10-year sentence for armed robbery. This is his second adult felony. His arms and neck are heavily covered in gang tattoos. He has a few institutional disciplinary infractions for gambling. Other than a routine intake screening, he has had no contact with mental health services during his incarceration.

Findings

Because it was unclear if M wanted or desired mental health services, he was seen briefly on his unit. He was called into a private office on the unit. The door to the office had a window that faced the common area. M came into the office and closed the door. Although his back faced the window of the door, he left one hand on the doorknob, as if preparing to leave. He initiated the conversation by stating, "What you need? I didn't ask for no Psych." He was informed that it was a routine visit to offer services in light of his mother's passing. He stated, "I don't need nuthin.' I'm straight." A final attempt was made to engage M by offering him condolences and expressing that it must be very hard for him to have lost his mother so unexpectedly, especially while he is incarcerated. At this point, M's eyes began to tear up, and it appeared as though he might cry. Cognizant that the interview was still on the unit and in the presence of his peers, he was offered the opportunity to be taken to a private office off of the unit. M declined and continued to stand with one hand on the doorknob. However, M began to discuss the difficulty of his mother's loss, and he was provided with supportive counseling. When offered the opportunity to come to the mental health department at a later date to talk further, he declined. However, when asked if it would be okay if a mental health clinician came back to the unit to check on him, he stated that would be "alright." He was provided with an additional session that occurred in much the same manner as the first, with his hand never leaving the doorknob.

Discussion

Understanding the dynamics of this encounter requires viewing the situation from multiple lenses. First, the presenting issue of bereavement takes many forms. People grieve differently, and talking is not necessarily helpful to everyone. So, M's initial response that he was not interested in services is not indicative of anything in particular. However, as a Black male, multicultural awareness requires cognizance of the fact that M may have some inherent distrust of the mental health system. Therefore, it is possible that he may desire services but is apprehensive of availing himself of them. Finally, M's affiliation with the prison culture must also be considered. As a second-time felon, he is a more experienced inmate. His tattoos indicate he has led an antisocial and criminal lifestyle. Thus, he is less likely to view services established by "the man" as something useful to him. Additionally, to "save face" with other inmates on the unit, he needs to minimize his emotions regarding his mother's death and appear to remain "strong" by rejecting offers of help.

By standing at the door with his hand on the doorknob, M gave the appearance to others on the unit that he did not want to be there and, in fact, was "trying" to leave the office. This shifted the responsibility onto the mental health staff for "keeping" him there, rather than his desire for services. Choosing to stay on the unit also sent a clear message to his peers that he was not voluntarily going anywhere with mental health staff. Because his back was to the unit, he was able to express himself, without being seen, while giving the impression that he did not want to be talking to the clinician.

Psychological Tests and Assessments With Multicultural Correctional Populations

A variety of considerations are important in making determinations about the use of psychological assessments. Among the most important are standardization, reliability, and validity. These issues are essential in determining if the assessment being considered for administration to a client will be useful for the therapeutic goals.

Most psychological tests were developed in the United States and are based on the assumption that people can easily make judgments about psychological and social stimuli, can order and rank stimuli linearly, and are capable of self-reflection and self-appraisal (Trimble, Lonner, & Boucher, 1983). People from other cultures may have significantly less, if any, familiarity with such concepts, or even familiarity with test taking.

The appropriate use of any test begins with an understanding of the population on which it was standardized or normed. The validity and reliability of the test results extend only to populations with similar social, cultural, and demographic profiles. Dana (2000) stresses the importance of this and suggests that ethnic and racial comparisons cannot be made against a standard provided by the dominant or mainstream culture. He goes on to state that such comparisons are demeaning and prejudicial because they are made on the erroneous assumption that the measures and their interpretations are universal. Handel and Ben-Porath (2000) indicate that some research suggests that African Americans score higher on the Minnesota Multiphasic Personality Inventory–2 (MMPI-2) scales L (Lie), F (Infrequency), 7 (Psychasthenia), 8 (Schizophrenia), and 9 (Hypomania). Because culture is dynamic, it would be an impossible task to continually renorm all psychological assessments to all possible cultural groups. Even so, many psychological assessments have never been normed for a multicultural population. For this reason, López (2000) argues that multiculturally competent psychological assessment requires multiple perspectives, multiple observations, and multiple assessment instruments as the keys to determining the ways in which culture may be a salient factor in the assessments.

Finally, issues of reliability and validity are important to address when selecting appropriate assessment tools. Thorndike (1997) states,

> Reliability refers to the accuracy and precision of a measurement procedure. Indices of reliability give an indication of the extent to which the scores produced by a particular measurement procedure are consistent and reproducible. Validity has to do with the degree to which the test scores provide information that is relevant to the inferences that are to be made from them. (p. 96)

As mentioned previously, reliability and validity extend only to populations with characteristics similar to the norm group. Giving a test to a group on which it was not normed can have a profound impact on the results of the test (see, for example, the case of *Washington v. Davis*, 1976). Tatum (1997) argues that when the dominant group sets the parameters by which minority groups are measured, the results are often that the minority group is labeled as substandard. This was illustrated with the development of the *Black Intelligence Test of Cultural Homogeneity* (BITCH-100; Williams, 1972), a culture-specific test designed to assess the test taker's ability to function symbolically within his or her own culture. The author developed the test in response to the widespread use of IQ tests that were normed on White children to assess the intelligence of Black children. Williams' test assessed the test taker's ability to define and comprehend common urban language and experiences (e.g., What is playing the dozens? What is an Alley Apple? What is a deuce-and-a-quarter?). Research found that Black test takers showed clear superiority over White test takers (Williams, 1972).

Applications in Corrections

In correctional settings, psychological tests are most commonly used for forensic assessments. Forensic questions are usually raised during the pretrial and trial stages of the criminal justice process and typically focus on competency to stand trial and/or mental status at the time of the offense (i.e., the insanity defense). Although minorities make up a disproportionate number of those involved in the criminal justice system, the issue of cultural competence is often neglected in the area of forensic assessment. Indeed, Tsytsarev and Landes (2008) note that the American Academy of Forensic

Psychology regularly offers training programs for forensic psychologists but has never offered courses on multicultural assessment.

Cultural dimensions have seldom been added to research in the area of competency to stand trial (Tsytsarev & Landes, 2008). However, bias has been found to exist in competency evaluations. Research has found that African Americans are more likely to be found incompetent (Caldwell, Mandracchia, & Ross, 2003; Hicks, 2004). Ho (1999) contends that differences in case outcome are attributed to socioeconomic status (SES), rather than race. Caldwell et al. (2003) and Hicks (2004) also acknowledged that SES may account for the differences found in their studies. Whereas SES may account for some of the variance found in research on the differences in findings of competency, racial and ethnic minorities are also disproportionately affected by poverty in the United States. Therefore, whether due to race or SES, or some combination of these and other variables, the effects are the same.

Forensic evaluations are the formulation of a clinical answer to a legal question (e.g., competency to stand trial). They rely on multiple clinical tools, including testing, to arrive at a diagnosis. These diagnoses help form the basis of the clinical opinion. However, research has consistently shown that African Americans are overdiagnosed with psychotic disorders, such as schizophrenia, and underdiagnosed with mood disorders, such as depression (Baker & Bell, 1999; Borowsky et al., 2000; U.S. Department of Health and Human Services, 2001).

Test-taking attitudes, beliefs about psychological testing, and experience in test taking will all impact approaches and, ultimately, performance on a given test. For example, some Russians may respond "I don't know" to a test item, rather than risk giving an incorrect response (Judd & Beggs, 2005). An excess of these responses may result in a test being deemed invalid or a lack of effort on the part of the test taker. The F (Infrequency) scale on the MMPI-2 measures the degree to which a person endorses unusual or infrequent responses. High scores on the F scale indicate a person has answered in an atypical manner or is reporting a large number of unusual symptoms. High scores are often viewed as an indication of malingering or exaggerating symptoms. Scores on the F scale, a measure of the validity of the profile, may be elevated in Latino groups due to cultural tendencies toward the dramatic (Carbonell, 2000), which may result in exaggeration in the presentation of their clinical symptoms.

The *DSM-IV-TR* (American Psychiatric Association, 2000) provides an outline for cultural formulations. The outline recommends providing a narrative summary of several areas to provide a cultural context. The areas include the cultural identity of the individual, cultural explanations of the individual's illness, cultural factors related to psychosocial environment and levels of functioning, cultural elements of the relationship between the individual and the clinician, and an overall cultural assessment for diagnosis and care.

Forensic evaluations have high stakes for those being evaluated. The opinion and testimony of the evaluating clinician can impact potentially life and death decisions regarding the legal status of the accused, trial outcome, sentencing, and postrelease planning. Given the enormity of the consequences, forensic evaluators must be aware of the cultural influence of diagnosis, testing taking, and behavioral interpretations of diverse clients, as the following case study illustrates.

Composite Case Study

Reason for Referral

"P" was referred for a psychological evaluation by the parole board. P is up for her first parole hearing, and the board is interested in finding out if there are any underlying psychological concerns or issues that would be salient to the hearing.

Background

P is a 39-year-old Hispanic female. She is serving a 10- to 15-year sentence for possession of cocaine. She reported that this is her first felony incarceration and that she is bilingual. Although her first language is Spanish, she noted that she attended school in the United States and that all of her primary and secondary education was in English. She reported that she completed her associate's degree, and her program of study was also in English. She stated that she is comfortable speaking in English, and all sessions of the evaluation were conducted in English. She reported that she communicates with her family and children in Spanish. She indicated that she attends religious services at the institution in Spanish, but all other institutional programming she attends is in English.

Findings

During the clinical interview, she denied any history of treatment for mental health problems or concerns prior to her incarceration. Records indicate she has been seen by mental health staff three times during her 10 years of incarceration. She was seen once for brief counseling related to adjustment concerns after her initial arrest. She was seen a second time for bereavement counseling after the death of her father. Finally, she was seen for a brief counseling session at her request due to concerns she was having about one of her children whose school performance had begun to decline. No significant concerns were noted during those sessions. P denied ever being prescribed psychotropic medication. However, she reported she struggles with feelings of guilt and bouts of depression related to her incarceration. She reported she feels as though she has been a bad mother, because she has been incarcerated for much of her children's lives, and they have been raised by P's mother.

During her incarceration, P has actively participated in a variety of self-help and vocational programming. She has been involved in a drug treatment program and participates in Narcotics Anonymous (NA) groups. The unit officers reported that she is generally a well-behaved inmate and does not cause problems on the unit. Disciplinary records indicate she has had a few minor infractions during her incarceration but has never received a sanction harsher than "extra duty" (being assigned extra work on the unit) for her misconduct.

As a routine part of the evaluation process, P was administered the MMPI-2, English version. The results of the MMPI-2 showed clinical elevations on Scales 6 (Paranoia), and 8 (Schizophrenia). Additionally, the validity profiles were suggestive that P was exaggerating her symptoms ("faking bad"), or making a "cry for help."

Discussion

The results of the MMPI-2 were inconsistent with P's clinical interview and overall institutional adjustment. If P were truly suffering from paranoid or psychotic processes, she would have had difficulty successfully participating in institutional programming, following rules, and engaging in vocational classes. Furthermore, it is unlikely P would be severely psychotic and go unnoticed by the unit officers and other institutional staff, or that she would be able to present as stable during multiple contacts with mental health staff. Finally, because the evaluation was being done for a parole board hearing, P would have very little motivation to exaggerate her symptoms or "fake bad." Indeed, one would expect her to minimize any underlying problems or concerns, and perhaps even present herself in an overly virtuous manner (i.e., "faking good"). When the results of the MMPI-2 were shared with P, she appeared genuinely confused and insisted she took the test as carefully and honestly as possible.

In the presence of clearly inconsistent data between her presentation and the test results, P was administered the MMPI-2 a second time. For the second administration, she was given the Spanish version of the exam. The results of the second administration were markedly different. There were no elevations on any of the validity indices. There were no clinical elevations on Scales 6 or 8. Instead, the second administration showed slight elevations on Scales 2 (Depression) and 7 (Psychasthenia—a measure of anxiety). The second administration represented a much more consistent clinical picture of P between her presentation and the test results.

Although P was fluent and comfortable communicating in English, much of her important affective communication (i.e., communication regarding her feelings and psychological experiences on such topics as family and religion) was done in Spanish. Thus, her ability to articulate her feelings and psychological experiences was probably easier for her in Spanish.

This case study underscores two very important points. First, test data should never be used in isolation. Psychological assessments are very helpful tools, but they should not be used alone to draw diagnostic conclusions without the consideration of other essential data (e.g., history, clinical interview, etc.). Second, the role of language and culture can never be overestimated. There was no evidence to suggest that the English version of the MMPI-2 was inappropriate. Because P was fluent in both languages and had received all of her formal education in English, it was appropriate to give her the English version of the test. It would be easy to assume that P had either completed the test in an invalid manner or was severely psychotic. However, cultural awareness not only allows for the opportunity to explore other possible explanations for the findings but also can lead to alternative means of obtaining more meaningful clinical data.

Cultural Competence With Religious Minorities and Extremists

In the aftermath of the September 11, 2001 events, there has been an increased amount of attention focused on terrorism and acts of violence committed by religious extremists. Whereas there has been increased attention focused on the acts of violence committed by some members of the Islamic community, terrorist activities are better understood as political aggression rather than religious violence. It is important to recognize that the specific acts of terrorism committed by one or more individuals who practice any given religion do not represent the beliefs of the entire religion, or even a majority. It is no more accurate to consider the events of 9/11 to be a reflection of Islam than it is to consider the actions of David Koresh to be a reflection of Protestantism.

Crimes committed under the auspice of religion are not limited to international terrorist activities. They may also originate within the United States. For example, Warren Jeffs, the prophet of the Fundamentalist Church of Jesus Christ of Latter-day Saints, is currently serving a 10-year to life sentence for accessory to rape after arranging extralegal marriages between adult male followers and underage girls. Eric Rudolph, a Roman Catholic, was convicted of the 1996 bombing at the Atlanta Olympics and admitted to bombing several abortion clinics. James Kopp affiliated with an antiabortion group called the Lambs of Christ and was on the FBI's Most Wanted List from 1998 until his capture in 2001 for the murder of a doctor who performed legal abortions.

Similarly, religious cult leaders may also convince their followers to engage in any number of criminal activities as a way to salvation. David Koresh, mentioned earlier, led the Branch Davidian sect in Waco, Texas, whose female members, some underage, were encouraged to have sexual relationships with Koresh as a divine act. They also stockpiled illegal weapons and munitions, resulting in the siege at the cult's ranch in 1993. Individuals involved in fringe religious groups may be engaging in illegal activities with the belief that they are preserving their way of life or helping to ensure their entry into heaven.

A final category of spiritual-based criminal behavior involves indigenous and non-Western healing practices. This is arguably a more complicated issue. Sue and Sue (2007) describe the Southeast Asian healing method of *thuõc nam*. This traditional method of healing involves steaming bamboo tubes so the insides are low in pressure, applying them to a part of the skin that has been cut, and sucking out the "bad air." It also involves using coins or spoons to lightly strike or scrape along the ribcages and sides of the neck or shoulder. These techniques are meant to rid a person of maladies. However, they often leave bruises and marks on the patients (Sue & Sue, 2007). Immigrant parents who use these methods on their children risk being accused of child abuse. Chan and Lee (2004) note that some Asian families change dosages of medication or stop taking medicines when symptoms have ameliorated. The traditional view of illness is seen as an imbalance of yin and yang. Medicines are seen as yang, and the illness is yin. If medicines are taken too long, they may create an abundance of yang, causing further imbalance and more problems (Chan & Lee, 2004). Thus, rejection of Western medical care may not be due to child neglect, other than in the narrow legal sense, but rather due to cultural beliefs (Fontes & O'Neill-Arana, 2008).

Applications in Corrections

Although religious extremists receive a significant amount of media attention due to the nature and severity of their crimes, they still represent a very small percentage of the prison population. Criminal acts committed under the auspice of religious fundamentalism are rarely due to mental illness. Terrorist organizations exclude persons with serious mental illness because they create a security risk (Post, 2005). Most of the acts are done with the conviction that the acts are justified, or even sanctioned, within the context of their religious beliefs.

From a pragmatic view, these individuals are relatively easy for mental health staff to deal with because they rarely seek mental health services (Alderdice, 2007). Because they are not suffering from a mental illness, they understand that they are being punished for violating the "laws of man." However, they often see their punishment as inconsequential in the larger picture, as they believe they are following a law higher than man. As Alderdice (2007) notes, "The failure of the struggle, rather than their personal capture or death, is the ultimate disaster" (p. 203). They may also be reticent to use mental health services based on the gender and educational attainment of the practitioner. For example, a female psychologist related to this author that she was told by an alleged terrorist she was "a disgrace to Allah" because she worked outside of the home, and the inmate refused to talk to her because she was "just a woman."

Although religious extremists will often decline the offer of services, mental health clinicians should be mindful of salient religious and cultural issues to maximize the chance that an inmate in need will use mental health services. Notably, unit rounds should not be made during prayer times. If inmates are observed to be participating in religious activities (e.g., praying), mental health staff should return at a later time or wait until they have completed their ritual. Additionally, special attention should be given to major non-Christian holidays, and attempts should be made to acknowledge them to the inmates in an effort to build rapport.

For other types of religion-related criminal behavior, it is first necessary to distinguish if the behavior occurred in the context of sincere religious beliefs and long-practiced religious behavior (Tseng, Matthews, & Elwyn, 2004). Even if the criminal behavior occurs in the context of a sincere religious belief, it does not excuse or mitigate the behavior. Arguably, immigrants have an affirmative obligation to learn and obey the rules of the host country and should be held accountable for violating those rules. Nevertheless, it is important to have a basic understanding of the ways in which religion and spirituality affect the lives of those with whom the clinician works (Fukuyama, Sevig, & Soet, 2008).

The previously mentioned guidelines for flexibility in working with individuals from different cultural backgrounds proposed by McAuliffe (2008) are equally applicable in working with religious minorities. Additionally, practitioners must be especially aware of their own biases and religious beliefs to reduce the influence they have on the inter-action with the individual. The ability to understand the behavior of another within his or her cultural and/or religious framework does not require endorsement of the behavior or the religious practice. Correctional mental health clinicians do not have to make a determination regarding the degree to which an inmate's religious beliefs impacted the criminal behavior. The judge and/or jury have already made that determination during the trial and sentencing phases of the judicial process. The personal beliefs of the correctional mental health care provider as to the degree, if any, of mitigation these factors should play regarding criminal responsibility are irrelevant to the provision of mental health services to prisoners. Rather, culturally competent correctional mental health clinicians must be mindful of the degree to which religious beliefs impact the behavior and institutional adjustment of the inmate, as well as future behavior.

Whereas most people in the United States are familiar with the basic tenets of Christianity, it is equally important to be familiar with the tenets of other major religions, such as Judaism and Islam, as well as less familiar religions, such as Santería (a belief system that combines the Yoruba religion, brought by African slaves to the Caribbean, with Roman Catholic and Native American traditions) and Asatru (a Norse pagan religion with polytheistic beliefs worshiping major and minor deities). As mentioned previously, familiarity does not require an in-depth understanding of the religion. Most people would be unable to informatively explain the differences between the various divisions of Christianity, much less have a comprehensive understanding of religions that may be virtually unknown to many people. However, it takes little effort to ask an inmate who practices an unfamiliar religion about his or her belief system. The institution's religious services staff can also be a source of tremendous knowledge, and an informal chat in the lunch room can provide a wealth of information.

It is important to remember that for many ethnic groups, religion is an important means of asserting cultural identity (Bosworth, 2002). In a study of the Mariel Cuban detainees, Santería was found to be an important means of community building and proved to be one of the only means for the prisoners to try to improve their own situation (Hamm, 1995). Bosworth (2002) noted many religious rituals pose difficulties for prison administrators due to potential security concerns. For example, Native American prisoners may carry medicine bags that may be inspected but not touched by staff; Santería involves the use of food offerings, which may create rodent problems; and Orthodox Jews must not have any physical contact of any sort with a member of the opposite sex other than a wife or close relative (Bosworth, 2002).

There is a delicate balance between the security needs of the institution and a prisoner's First Amendment right to practice the religion of his or her choice. Awareness and sensitivity to the variety of ways in which religious practices impact behavior not only assist the counseling process but may allow the correctional mental health clinician the opportunity to provide education and training to staff members who may misconstrue religious behaviors as a challenge to institutional authority. The following case study highlights the interrelationship among religious beliefs, behaviors, and the criminal justice system.

Composite Case Study

Reason for Referral

"A" was referred to mental health services by his Unit Team. A's case manager was preparing programming recommendations and requested that mental health staff interview A to determine his eligibility for specialized sex offender programming.

Background

A is a 28-year-old Arab male. He reports himself to be a devout Muslim. He is serving a 1- to 3-year sentence for child sexual abuse and lewd and lascivious acts with a child. He has no prior criminal history. He was born in the Middle East but moved to the United States when he was 10 years old. He reported that he completed college. He denied any history of mental health treatment.

Findings

Upon interview, A gave the following account of the events that led to his arrest. He reported he was raised in rural Pakistan. When he was 8 years old, his parents and another couple engaged in the custom of *Pait likkhi*. In this custom, two families agree to marry their children when the children are still young, or even before they are born. A reported that the other family agreed to marry their first daughter to A, although they did not yet have any daughters. Soon after entering into the agreement, A and his family moved to the United States, so that A could get an education and job to properly provide for his wife under the Sharia (Islamic law). It was not until several years after they moved to the United States that the other family had their first daughter.

When the daughter turned 15, A and his family traveled to Pakistan, so that he could marry. Also raised a devout Muslim, the daughter understood her obligations to her family under the Sharia and consented to the marriage. After the *nikah* (ceremony), the couple returned to the United States because A had a good job and believed he would be better able to support his wife by staying in the United States. Several months after returning to the United States, a neighbor contacted the police to report that an underage girl was living with an older man. A was subsequently arrested and convicted of the aforementioned charges.

During the interview, A acknowledged that he married the girl. He also acknowledged engaging in sexual relations with his wife, as lawful under the Sharia. His wife testified in his defense at his sentencing and reported he was a good husband.

Discussion

This case presents a complex picture of the clash between religions, culture, and law. A's practice of Sharia is not universal among Muslims. As with other religions, there is great variability in the manner in which people follow their faith. For example, not all Catholics refrained from eating meat on Friday when it was prohibited, and many Jews drive their vehicles on the Sabbath (while strict adherence to either religion would require their respective abstinence).

Although the specifics of this case may not be a common occurrence in the field of correctional psychology, the issues for a culturally aware practitioner are transferable to other cases. The original referral question in this case asked the clinician to make a determination as to whether specialized sex offender programming was indicated for A. Ultimately, clinicians may disagree as to whether he meets the diagnostic criteria for pedophilia or another paraphilic disorder. It is not uncommon for professionals with the same information to come to different clinical opinions. As a culturally aware clinician, the diagnostic determination must be made by looking at the case holistically.

Given the highly sensitive nature of the issues in this scenario, it is critical that practitioners identify their own biases, so that they may objectively assess both the behavioral and cultural data. Remember that one's views of what constitutes sexually appropriate or deviant behavior are shaped by one's personal cultural and/or religious beliefs. Although one's personal beliefs may condemn a particular behavior, it does not stand to reason that the behavior must therefore be due to some underlying psychopathology.

Likewise, psychological treatment also exists in a context. The theories and empirical evidence used to support a specific treatment modality may not be appropriate for someone from another culture. This remains true even if the underlying problem behavior is the same. Therefore, even if a clinician diagnosed A with pedophilia, it is not clear that the treatment offered would be appropriate for A based on his cultural and religious background.

It is equally important to recognize that cultural influences also shape individual views related to family and community. In most Western cultures, the dominant world-view centers on individual decision making and autonomy. Children are raised to think independently and to make their own decisions. Indeed, that is one measure of developmental and psychological maturity. In the United States, most people might think that a 25-year-old who relied on his or her parents to help make decisions about whom to marry is weak-minded and overly enmeshed. However, in cultures where collective decision making is valued, psychological maturity is measured by a person's ability to forgo individual desires for what is best for the family. Thus, in those cultures, a person who agrees to an arranged marriage may be considered a mature and responsible member of the family.

A clearly engaged in unlawful behavior by U.S. standards, and he is therefore legally accountable for his actions. However, it is important to recognize that he did not engage in any criminal act within the context of his culture or religion. Accordingly, any clinical assessment or psychotherapy undertaken with A must take this considerable and highly sensitive difference in perspectives into account.

Putting It All Together: Best Practices for Culturally Competent Correctional Mental Health

In spite of the difficulties in providing culturally competent services in a correctional setting, there are successful strategies. The correctional environment is fast-paced and requires the ability to constantly adapt traditional skills for a unique population in a unique setting. Concerning cultural competence in a correctional mental health practice, language is often the first barrier mental health staff must overcome when interviewing an inmate from a different culture. Some institutions keep a list of multilingual staff available in case they are needed to help with a translation. Other institutions may subscribe to a "language bank" that allows staff to phone a toll-free number to be connected with an interpreter who can be used to interview an inmate via speaker phone. Similarly, telehealth and virtual meetings may allow staff from different institutions to share resources across the country. Certainly, these methods are helpful, but they create their own set of issues.

Language is often confused as synonymous with culture. It is easy to assume that because people speak the same language, they are also familiar with the culture. However, there are often huge differences between cultures sharing the same language. It would be a mistake to assume that a Mexican national is familiar with Puerto Rican, Ecuadorian, or European Spanish culture.

As a practical matter, other staff members are often used as interpreters for mental health staff. Staff interpreters should be provided with basic information about the importance of translating verbatim. A colleague once asked an officer to assist him with a Spanish translation. After a few moments, the psychologist, who knew a little Spanish, realized that the officer was not translating exactly what the inmate said. When asked, the officer explained that the inmate was "rambling" and "not making any sense." The officer did not want to "waste the psychologist's time" and was attempting to "make some sense of the gibberish." In actuality, the inmate had a serious thought disorder, and the circumstantial and tangential speech was a symptom.

It can also be difficult to locate staff to assist with translations, as they may be assigned to a different shift or in another time zone if located at a different institution. In an effort to increase the ability to obtain basic mental health information from inmates, standardized mental health questionnaires should be available in a variety of languages. Utilizing the foreign language department of a local college or university is an easy way to get basic, yet critical, mental health questions translated (e.g., Have you ever tried to commit suicide? Are you thinking of committing suicide now? Are you taking any psychotropic medication?). At the very least, this allows a practitioner to gather enough information to determine if safety precautions (i.e., suicide watch) are necessary until a formal interpreter can be arranged.

Inmates themselves can also be a great source of information about cultural beliefs and practices. When doing rounds or interacting with inmates, the clinician should take a moment to ask them the meaning of a religious symbol or medallion. Most people are happy to talk about their backgrounds or native country and can be queried by a simple question or statement (I've never been to your country. What has been the biggest culture shock for you between there and the U.S.?).

Perhaps most importantly, multicultural competence should be seen as an approach or paradigm rather than a specific skill or tool. Much like theoretical orientation, multiculturalism is about the lens through which one views the behavior of others. Culture-centered approaches to counseling see culture as a central and fundamental part of the process, rather than something marginal and exotic (Pederson, 2002). Clinical interviews and interactions should be approached with the underlying assumptions that race and culture do matter and are impacting the person's behavior. A clinician does not have to be buried in a library, becoming an academic expert on race and culture, to be culturally competent. It is more practical to use daily interactions and clinical contacts with inmates as an opportunity to ask questions and become educated based on their experiences. This is not incongruous with the brief therapy and behavioral models often used in prison. Indeed, B. F. Skinner, one of the founding fathers of behavior therapy, recognized that behavior is shaped and maintained by culture. He stated, "Individuals shape each other's behavior by arranging contingencies of reinforcement, and what contingencies they arrange, and hence what behavior they shape are determined by the evolving environment, or culture, responsible for that behavior" (Skinner, 1988, p. 48). Brief therapy often focuses on finding what has been helpful in the past to get through a crisis and using those past successes in the present situation.

A brief therapy counselor may ask, "What have you done in the past to help you through times of stress?"

A culturally competent approach would be, "In your culture or community, what traditional methods of healing are used for this type of problem?"

A practitioner with more familiarity with the inmate's culture may be able to add more, by stating, "In the past I've talked to some people who are from your country (or share your religion, etc.), who have said that they used treatment/healing method 'X' to help. Is that something that you have done?"

In almost all cases, the inmate will be more of an expert on his or her culture than the therapist is. Allowing the inmate an opportunity to educate the therapist will not only increase his or her cultural awareness but will also assist in building rapport.

Behaviors that are unfamiliar and different from the clinician's own behavior may be viewed as strange. In a correctional setting, some culture-bound behaviors may be not only illegal in this country but offensive to the clinician's own personal morals and ethics. As a correctional mental health provider, it is important to be mindful that although these behaviors may be personally abhorrent, to provide effective treatment it is critical to understand the context and culture in which these behaviors occur. Culture competence does not mean unconditional positive regard or acceptance of all behaviors. Rather, it requires openness to understanding the complexity of the behavior and an appreciation of the role culture plays in shaping and reinforcing human behavior.

Summary and Conclusions

Racial and ethnic minorities are disproportionately represented in U.S. correctional systems. Sociologists and social psychologists have long discussed the various contributing factors to this disparity. Regardless of the reasons, as a practical matter, correctional mental health clinicians are working with a diverse population. Therefore, they must be educated accordingly.

Multicultural counseling comprises an entire field of study within mental health. This chapter provides a general overview of multicultural counseling and the correctional applications. A discussion of the culturally competent use of psychological tests and assessments emphasized the implications and stakes in forensic evaluations. Finally, cultural competence with religious minorities and religious extremists in the correctional system illustrated that religious beliefs and practices are often an important part of cultural identity. However, at times there is a conflict between religious beliefs and the law. Correctional mental health clinicians must understand the cultural context of religious behaviors and exercise tolerance of beliefs and practices different from the mainstream.

The causes of differential incarceration rates are rooted in politics, history, and current economic realities. Although the ethical responsibilities of correctional mental health practitioners require practice that recognizes these differences, the realities and responsibilities of correctional mental health clinicians are more modest than comprehensive systemic change. They must provide services that are sensitive to all of these underlying dimensions but focus their efforts on maximizing individual functioning within the context of legal standards, institutional security, and public safety.

KEY TERMS

Multicultural counseling

Diagnostic and Statistical Manual of Mental Disorders–Fourth Edition, Text Revision

American Psychological Association ethical guidelines

Prisonization

Cultural competence

Indigenous healing practices

Culture-bound syndromes

Cultural identity

American Psychological Association multicultural guidelines

Cultural fluidity

DISCUSSION QUESTIONS

1. There is often a conflict between psychology and the law. Lawmakers, politicians, and policy makers are not always, or even usually, educated in social scientific methods. Even fewer have an understanding of the complexities of the impact of race and culture on the use and interpretation of social science data. What are some methods of effectively educating the key decision makers on the limitations of psychological testing?

2. For many people and in many cultures, religion is not seen as a "choice" per se but, rather, is a way of life that is passed down from generation to generation. Consider Jews, whose Jewish ancestry is passed down maternally. Do they "choose" to be Jewish? Islam is also considered to be a way of life rather than simply a religious preference. Should the law mandate the degree to which people are able to follow their faith and make personal choices about their own, or their children's, health and well-being?

3. Cultural identity is a fluid process. How does your own cultural identity change? What was your cultural identity on September 11, 2001? What is your cultural identity when you attend a religious worship service? Go to a sporting event? Attend a family gathering? In what ways might the approach to counseling change if you were receiving services for difficulties adjusting to college? Anxiety about introducing your biracial partner to your family?

4. People detained in correctional facilities often have backgrounds, experiences, and cultural identities vastly different from the correctional mental health professionals providing services. Even with similar racial backgrounds, educational attainment and socioeconomic status create a significant cultural barrier between service providers and the populations they serve. Being mindful of the security and ethical issues involved, what are some strategies to overcome some of the barriers in order to build rapport and increase the efficacy of the mental health services?

References

Alderdice, J. T. (2007). The individual, the group and the psychology of terrorism. *International Review of Psychiatry, 19*, 201–209.

American Psychiatric Association. (2000). *Diagnostic and statistical manual of mental disorders* (4th ed., Text Revision). Washington, DC: Author.

American Psychological Association. (2002a). *Ethical principles of psychologists and code of conduct.* Washington, DC: Author.

American Psychological Association. (2002b). *Guidelines on multicultural education, training, research, practices, and organizational change for psychologists.* Washington, DC: Author.

Amnesty International. (2003, April). *United States of America: Death by discrimination—The continuing role of race in capital cases* (Amnesty International Reports). Retrieved April 15, 2009, from http://web.amnesty.org/library/index/ENGAMR510462003

Baker, F. M., & Bell, C. C. (1999). Issues in the psychiatric treatment of African Americans. *Psychiatric Services, 50,* 362–368.

Barrett, K. H., & George, W. H. (2005). Psychology, justice, and diversity: Five challenges of culturally competent professionals. In K. H. Barrett & W. H. George (Eds.), *Race, culture, psychology, and law* (pp. 3–17). Thousand Oaks, CA: Sage.

Borowsky, S., Rubenstein, L. V., Meredith, L. S., Camp, P., Jackson-Triche, M., & Wells, K. B. (2000). Who is at risk of nondetection of mental health problems in primary care? *Journal of General Internal Medicine, 15,* 381–388.

Bosworth, M. (2002). *The U.S. federal prison system.* Thousand Oaks, CA: Sage.

Brodsky, S. L. (1975). *Family and friends of men in prison.* Lexington, MA: Lexington Books.

Bureau of Justice Statistics. (2007). *Criminal offender statistics.* Retrieved April 30, 2009, from http://www.ojp.usdoj.gov/bjs/crimoff.htm#lifetime

Caldwell, R. M., Mandracchia, S. A., & Ross, S. A. (2003). Competency to stand trial and criminal responsibility: An examination of racial and gender differences among African American and Caucasian pretrial defendants. *American Journal of Forensic Psychology, 21,* 367–381.

Carbonell, S. I. (2000). An assessment practice with Hispanics in Minnesota. In R. Dana (Ed.), *Handbook of cross cultural assessment* (pp. 547–572). Mahwah, NJ: Lawrence Erlbaum.

Chan, S., & Lee, E. (2004). Families with Asian roots. In E. W. Lynch & M. J. Hanson (Eds.), *Developing cross-cultural competence: A guide for working with young children and their families* (3rd ed., pp. 219–298). Baltimore, MD: Brookes.

Corey, M. S., & Corey, G. (1998). *Becoming a helper* (3rd ed.). Pacific Grove, CA: Brooks/Cole.

Dana, R. H. (2000). *Handbook of cross-cultural and multicultural personality assessment.* Mahwah, NJ: Lawrence Erlbaum.

Evans, K. M., & George, R. (2008). African Americans. In G. McAuliffe & Associates (Eds.), *Culturally alert counseling: A comprehensive introduction* (pp. 146–187). Thousand Oaks, CA: Sage.

Fontes, L. A., & O'Neill-Arana, M. R. (2008). Assessing for child maltreatment in culturally diverse families. In L. A. Suzuki & J. G. Ponterotto (Eds.), *Handbook of multicultural assessment: Clinical, psychological, and educational applications* (3rd ed., pp. 627–650). San Francisco, CA: John Wiley.

Fukuyama, M. A., Sevig, T., & Soet, J. (2008). Spirituality in counseling across cultures: Many rivers to the sea. In P. B. Pedersen, J. G. Draguns, W. J. Lonner, & J. E. Trimble (Eds.), *Counseling across cultures* (6th ed., pp. 345–361). Thousand Oaks, CA: Sage.

Garrett, M. T. (2008). Native Americans. In G. McAuliffe & Associates (Eds.), *Culturally alert counseling: A comprehensive introduction* (pp. 220–254). Thousand Oaks, CA: Sage.

Gonzalez, G. M. (1997). The emergence of Chicanos in the twenty-first century: Implications for counseling, research, and policy. *Journal of Multicultural Counseling and Development, 25,* 94–106.

Gordon, J. (1999). Debate 2: Are conjugal and familial visitations effective rehabilitative concepts? *The Prison Journal, 79,* 119–135.

Hamm, M. S. (1995). *The abandoned ones: The imprisonment and uprising of the Mariel boat people.* Boston, MA: Northeastern University Press.

Handel, R. W., & Ben-Porath, Y. S. (2000). Multicultural assessment with the MMPI-2: Issues for research and practice. In R. H. Dana (Ed.), *Handbook of cross-cultural and multicultural personality assessment* (pp. 229–245). Mahwah, NJ: Lawrence Erlbaum.

Hicks, J. W. (2004). Ethnicity, race, and forensic psychiatry: Are we color-blind? *Journal of the American Academy of Psychiatry and the Law, 32,* 21–33.

Ho, T. (1999). Examination of racial disparity in competency to stand trial between White and African American retarded defendants. *Journal of Black Studies, 29,* 771–789.

Human Rights Watch. (2002, February). Race and incarceration in the United States. *Human Rights Watch Backgrounder.* Retrieved August 15, 2009, from http://www.hrw.org/legacy/backgrounder/usa/race/

Jackson, M. L. (1995). Multicultural counseling: Historical perspectives. In J. G. Ponterotto, J. M. Casas, L. A. Suzuki, & C. M. Alexander (Eds.), *Handbook of multicultural counseling* (pp. 3–16). Thousand Oaks, CA: Sage.

Judd, T., & Beggs, B. (2005). Cross-cultural forensic neuropsychological assessment. In K. H. Barett & W. H. George (Eds.), *Race, culture, psychology, and law* (pp. 141–162). Thousand Oaks, CA: Sage.

Kim, B. S. K., & Park, Y. S. (2008). East and Southeast Asian Americans. In G. McAuliffe & Associates (Eds.), *Culturally alert counseling: A comprehensive introduction* (pp. 188–219). Thousand Oaks, CA: Sage.

Lerner, K. L., & Lerner, B. W. (2006). *African Lemba tribe.* Retrieved May 28, 2009, from eNotes.com: http://www.enotes.com/forensic-science/african-lemba-tribe

López, S. R. (2000). Teaching culturally informed psychological assessment. In R. H. Dana (Ed.), *Handbook of cross-cultural and multicultural personality assessment* (pp. 669–697). Mahwah, NJ: Lawrence Erlbaum.

McAuliffe, G. (2008). What is culturally alert counseling? In G. McAuliffe & Associates (Eds.), *Culturally alert counseling: A comprehensive introduction* (pp. 2–44). Thousand Oaks, CA: Sage.

Monk, G., Winslade, J., & Sinclair, S. (2008). *New horizons in multicultural counseling.* Thousand Oaks, CA: Sage.

Nguyen, S. D. (1985). Mental health services for refugees and immigrants in Canada. In T. C. Owen (Ed.), *Southeast Asian mental health: Treatment, prevention, services, training, and research* (pp. 261–282). Washington, DC: National Institute of Mental Health.

Paniagua, F. A. (2000). Culture-bound syndromes, cultural variations, and psychopathology. In I. Cuellar & F. A. Paniagua (Eds.), *Handbook of multicultural mental health* (pp. 139–169). San Diego, CA: Academic Press.

Pederson, P. B. (2002). Ethics, competence, and other professional issues in culture-centered counseling. In P. B. Pederson, J. G. Draguns, W. J. Lonner, & J. E. Trimble (Eds.), *Counseling across cultures* (5th ed., pp. 3–27). Thousand Oaks, CA: Sage.

Post, J. M. (2005). When hatred is bred in the bone: Psycho-cultural foundations of contemporary terrorism. *Political Psychology, 26,* 615–636.

Skinner, B. F. (1988). Selection by consequences. Commentaries and responses. In A. C. Catania & S. Harnad (Eds.), *The selection of behavior: The operant behaviorism of B. F. Skinner* (pp. 11–76). New York, NY: Cambridge University Press.

Sue, D. W., & Sue, D. (2007). *Counseling the culturally diverse: Theory and practice* (5th ed.). New York: Wiley.

Tatum, B. D. (1997). *Why are all the Black kids sitting together in the cafeteria? And other conversations about race.* New York, NY: Basic Books.

Thorndike, R. M. (1997). *Measurement and evaluation in psychology and education* (6th ed.). Upper Saddle River, NJ: Prentice Hall.

Toldson, I. A. (2008). Counseling persons of Black African ancestry. In G. McAuliffe & Associates (Eds.), *Culturally alert counseling: A comprehensive introduction* (pp. 161–179). Thousand Oaks, CA: Sage.

Trimble, J. E., Lonner, W. J., & Boucher, J. (1983). Stalking the wily emic: Alternatives to cross-cultural measurement. In S. Irvine & J. W. Berry (Eds.), *Human assessment and cultural factors* (pp. 259–273). New York, NY: Plenum.

Tseng, W. S., Matthews, D., & Elwyn, T. S. (2004). *Cultural competence in forensic mental health: A guide for psychiatrists, psychologists, and attorneys.* New York, NY: Brunner-Routledge.

Tsytsarev, S. V., & Landes, A. (2008). Competency to stand trial: A multicultural perspective. In L. A. Suzuki & J. G. Ponterotto (Eds.), *Handbook of multicultural assessment: Clinical, psychological, and educational applications* (3rd ed., pp. 651–665). San Francisco, CA: John Wiley.

U.S. Department of Health and Human Services, Substance Abuse and Mental Health Services Administration, Center for Mental Health Services. (2001). *Mental health: Culture, race, and ethnicity.* Rockville, MD: Author.

Washington v. Davis, 96 S. Ct. 2040 (1976).

Williams, R. L. (1972, September). *The BITCH-100: A culture specific test.* Paper presented at the 80th annual convention of the American Psychological Association, Honolulu, HI.

CHAPTER 7

Clinical Psychopharmacology in Correctional Settings

Gollapudi Shankar

Introduction

Many inmates in American prisons have serious and persistent mental disorders that are treatable with psychotropic medications. The purpose of this chapter is to provide an overview of the various classes of psychotropic medications, the disorders they treat, and some of the concerns related to the use of these medications in correctional populations. Treatment of mental health problems with psychotropic medications is common among individuals who go to prison. In a federal government survey, 18% of state prisoners, 10% of federal prisoners, and 14% of jail inmates reported they had taken prescribed medication in the year before arrest or since their incarceration (James & Glaze, 2006).

All those who work in correctional settings should have some knowledge of these medications and their effects, as well as their proper use and potential for misuse. This chapter is for general educational purposes and is not intended as a clinical guide. Neither is it implied that pharmacological treatment should be provided to the exclusion of behavioral, cognitive, and other psychosocial interventions. Indeed, combined therapies may often be warranted (Sammons & Schmidt, 2001). In other cases, medications may not be warranted at all.

One point deserves mentioning here, if only briefly. The history of psychotropic medications has not been without controversy. These include alleged abuses of psychiatric patients, such as through forced or otherwise inappropriate medication, resulting in irreversible damage; or through medication being used in simple attempts to control and quiet patients, rather than treat them (Breggin, 1991). However, it is not the purpose of this chapter to defend past abuses but, rather, to consider the ways in which these medications can be properly and prudently used to the benefit of inmate-patients. In that regard, it is acknowledged that prisoners are, by their status, relatively powerless, but not without rights under the law. Among these is the right of prisoners to refuse treatment, including the right not to be given psychotropic medications against their will except in rare circumstances, which involve imminent dangerousness to themselves or others by reason of a mental disorder (e.g., Federal Bureau of Prisons, 2008).

In fact, just as with psychotherapeutic interventions, the use of psychotropic medications should be based on a good therapist-patient relationship, one wherein the patient trusts that the prescribing mental health professional—often but not always a psychiatrist—is acting in his or her best interests. Ideally, a prescription for psychotropic medication is the result of a procedure that begins with a proper assessment by a trained and credentialed mental health professional and that may include tests to ensure the patient is healthy enough to take the medication being considered. This is followed by patient education about the drug and his or her informed consent to take it. The patient then begins the regimen and sees the healthcare professional regularly for follow-up appointments. Standard psychiatric practice and adherence require that there be no interruption of medications. Interruption in the availability of psychiatric medications leads to decreases in therapeutic drug levels and reduced drug efficacy.

Pharmacotherapy: An Overview

To understand pharmacotherapy, one has to be familiar with two terms, pharmacodynamics and pharmacokinetics. Pharmacodynamics deals with what a drug does to the body at the cellular level. Concentration at the receptor, permeability, receptor number, and binding characteristics are some of the influencing factors. Pharmacokinetics has to do with what the body does to the drug. Once the drug is introduced, the body starts working immediately with the processes of absorption, distribution, metabolism, and elimination. Age, kidney function, liver function, disease state, and nutritional state are some of the influencing factors of pharmacokinetics.

Many people suffering from mental illnesses have imbalances in the way their brains metabolize certain chemicals, called neurotransmitters. Because neurotransmitters are the messengers the nerve cells use to communicate with one another, these imbalances may result in the emotional, physical, behavioral, and/or cognitive problems from which persons with mental illness suffer. Psychotropic medications work at the neuronal junction, called the synapse, on presynaptic and/or postsynaptic receptor systems. All psychotropic medications act on various neuronal pathways in the brain, and their impact may be affected by other psychotropic drugs and other factors, including illness, alcohol or specific food intake, or other nonpsychotropic drugs the patient is taking. In some cases, drug-drug interactions can be life-threatening. Because many of these medications have the potential to cause adverse effects, monitoring patients who take psychotropic drugs must be done regularly by healthcare staff.

Typically, medications are approved by the Food and Drug Administration (FDA) for the treatment of specific disorders. FDA approval is usually meant for manufacturers, not for healthcare practitioners. A manufacturer cannot advertise a particular drug for a particular disorder unless it is approved by the FDA, whereas a healthcare practitioner can still use it based on his or her best judgment. Hence, groups of medications are classified as "antipsychotics" or "antidepressants" because the government has approved their use specifically to treat psychosis or depression. However, medications are sometimes used "off-label" to treat other types of disorders. For example, newer antipsychotics are sometimes used to treat depression at the prescribing professional's discretion.

Classes of Psychotropic Medications and Their Uses

During the past 50 years, there have been major leaps in the field of psychopharmacology. Psychotropic drugs have now taken the lead among treatments for mental disorders such as bipolar disorder, depression, and schizophrenia (Schatzberg & Cole, 1991; Shorter, 1997). Psychotropic medications are often required to maximize the quality of life and functional status of psychiatric patients. The psychotropic medications that will be discussed in this section are the drugs most commonly used to ameliorate psychosis and emotional discomfort and to manage problem behaviors (e.g., by enhancing impulse control). For present purposes, these drugs are grouped into the following five general classes: antipsychotic agents, antidepressants, mood stabilizers, antianxiety or anxiolytic agents, and drugs used to treat substance abuse, as these are particularly relevant to inmate populations.

- Antipsychotic agents are used most commonly to treat forms of schizophrenia. Classical antipsychotics are called typical antipsychotics, and the newer generation medications are called atypical antipsychotics (AA).
- Antidepressant agents are used to treat severe forms of major depression and bipolar (depression and mania) disorder. Drugs in this class include selective serotonin reuptake inhibitors (SSRIs), serotonin/norepinephrine reuptake inhibitors (SNRIs), monoamine oxidase inhibitors (MAOIs; rarely used due to their potential for adverse effects), tricyclics (TCAs; seldom used these days), and other unclassified drugs.
- Mood stabilizers or antimanic agents are used to modulate symptoms of mania and aggressive impulses in patients with bipolar disorders. Drugs in this category include lithium and anticonvulsants.
- Antianxiety agents are used in instances when anxiety symptoms significantly impact functionality. Some drugs in this category (i.e., benzodiazepines) are restricted in correctional settings due to their potential for abuse. Also included are azapirones, antidepressants, antihistamines, and antihypertensives.
- Agents used in the treatment of substance abuse assist in facilitating a pain-free withdrawal from alcohol or other drugs (e.g., benzodiazepines) or to treat addiction through drug replacement.

Antipsychotic Agents

These medications are commonly used to treat a group of psychotic disorders that include the various classes of schizophrenia, delusional disorders, schizophreniform disorder, brief psychotic disorder, and psychotic disorders not otherwise specified. In these disorders, thought processes and/or content are compromised, resulting in impaired reality contact. In general, symptoms may include confusion, hallucinations (usually auditory: "voices"), blunted emotions or (in acute phases) excitability, disorientation, an impairment in the ability to think logically, and/or delusional beliefs of a persecutory or grandiose nature. These disorders tend to be chronic, and medications may be required throughout the lifespan (American Psychiatric Association, 2000).

Generally, there are two classes of psychotic symptoms (i.e., positive and negative symptoms) that are relevant to the use of psychotropic medications. Positive symptoms are pathological excesses or bizarre additions to an individual's behavior. These behaviors include the presence of odd behaviors, bizarre speech, and labile affect. They may also reflect internal stimuli, such as irrational thoughts, delusional beliefs, and/or hallucinations. Negative symptoms describe pathological deficits in an individual's behavior, such as blunted affect, impairment in goal-directed behavior, or poverty of speech/thought content (Koda-Kimble et al., 2008).

There are two general classes of antipsychotic medication: typical and atypical (or first and second generation, respectively) antipsychotics (see Table 7.1). The typical antipsychotics were discovered first. The first typical antipsychotic agent, chlorpromazine, eventually to be marketed under the brand name Thorazine®, was approved for use in the United States in 1954. Typical antipsychotics have been widely used and shown to be effective in the treatment of positive symptoms of schizophrenia and related psychoses, as well as in preventing psychotic relapses (Kane, Honigfeld, Singer, & Meltzer, 1988).

The absence of effect of typical antipsychotics on the negative symptoms and the severity of their adverse effects prompted the development of second-generation antipsychotics that became known as atypical antipsychotics (AAs; Grilly, 2002). The first atypical antipsychotic medication was clozapine, introduced in 1970. The term "atypical" describes their different dominant characteristics compared to "typical" or "conventional" antipsychotics. The AAs appear to cause far fewer extrapyramidal symptoms (EPS), such as pseudoparkinsonism and dystonia, yet have efficacy in controlling positive symptoms (Chakos, Lieberman, Hoffman, Bradford, & Sheitman, 2001; Citrome, Bilder, & Volavka, 2002; Csernansky & Schuchart, 2002; Grilly, 2002; Wander, Nelson, Okazaki, & Richelson, 1987).

Table 7.1	Currently Used Typical and Atypical Antipsychotic Agents
First-Generation (Typical) Antipsychotics: Generic (Brand)	Second-Generation (Atypical) Antipsychotics: Generic (Brand)
chlorpromazine (Thorazine®)	aripiprazole (Abilify®)
thioridazine (Mellaril®)	clozapine (Clozaril®)
mesoridazine (Serentil®)	olanzapine (Zyprexa®)
perphenazine (Trilafon®)	quetiapine (Seroquel®)
trifluoperazine (Stelazine®)	risperidone (Risperdal®)
fluphenazine (Prolixin®)	ziprasidone (Geodon®)
thiothixene (Navane®)	paliperidone (Invega®)
haloperidol (Haldol®)	iloperidone (Fanapt®)
molindone (Moban®)	asenapine (Saphris®)
loxapine (Loxitane®)	
pimozide (Orap®)	

Antidepressant Medications

Major depressive disorder (MDD) is an acute and sometimes severe episode of depression with unrelenting symptoms persisting for at least 2 weeks. Depressive symptoms can manifest themselves in behavior (e.g., social withdrawal, loss of productive activity), emotion (e.g., sadness, loss of pleasure from anything, anger, agitation), motivation (e.g., lack of drive, initiative, and spontaneity), cognition (e.g., pessimism and hopelessness, negative views of self, memory deficits, attentional deficits), and physical (e.g., headaches, indigestion, pain, sleep and/or appetite disturbance) symptoms. To receive a diagnosis of depression, the symptoms cannot be secondary to a medical illness, substance abuse, or other psychological disorders, even though it may coexist with these conditions. A major depressive episode can be further classified into one of several subgroups: psychotic, melancholic, atypical, seasonal, and postpartum (American Psychiatric Association, 2000).

The pharmacological treatment of depression occurs in three phases: acute, continuation, and maintenance. Acute phase goals are to eliminate symptoms of depression and restore psychosocial and occupational function. The continuation phase is the middle stage in which the initially effective drug dosage is sustained. The treatment goal during the maintenance phase is to prevent recurrence of the depression. Some patients with more than one episode will require maintenance medication indefinitely (American Psychiatric Association, 2000). Antidepressant medications are described below and are summarized in Table 7.2 on page 151.

First-Generation Antidepressants: Monoamine Oxidase Inhibitors (MAOIs) and Tricyclic Antidepressants (TCAs)

The first drugs used to treat depression were the MAOIs and the TCAs. These drugs are sometimes called first-generation or traditional antidepressants. MAOIs prevent the enzyme monoamine oxidase from breaking down the neurotransmitters norepinephrine, serotonin, and dopamine in the brain. With more of these neurotransmitters in the brain, it is believed that depressive symptoms are alleviated. However, individuals who take MAOIs are required to remain on a very strict diet or risk a hypertensive crisis and even death. As a result, MAOIs are only used rarely, when an individual does not respond to other antidepressant medications.

TCAs were first discovered in the 1950s and work by preventing the reuptake of various neurotransmitters in the brain, especially serotonin and norepinephrine. Patients typically take the medication for 6 to 8 weeks, and if the response is positive, the medication may need to be taken for many months to prevent relapse (Ebmeier, Donaghey, & Steele, 2006). TCAs have been shown to be effective with about 60% to 65% of depressed individuals (Gitlin, 2002). However, they are no longer the first choice in the treatment of depression because of their multiple side effects including dry mouth, dizziness, constipation, sexual problems, daytime dizziness, increased heart rate, and blurred vision (Gartlehner et al., 2005).

Among TCAs, amitriptyline and doxepin are very sedating and may be a good choice when psychomotor agitation and insomnia accompany the depression. Protriptyline is the least sedating. Desipramine has an energizing effect and is a good choice for depression with psychomotor retardation and pronounced fatigue, but it may cause insomnia if taken too late in the day and can sometimes be implicated in the rise of blood pressure. TCAs may produce lethal cardiovascular toxicity in overdose. As little as 1 week's supply can be lethal, and this should be considered when working with potentially suicidal patients.

Second-Generation Antidepressants: Selective Serotonin Reuptake Inhibitors (SSRIs) and Serotonin and Norepinephrine Reuptake Inhibitors (SNRIs)

It is theorized that second-generation antidepressants work by inhibiting the reuptake of serotonin (SSRIs) or the reuptake of serotonin and epinephrine (SNRIs).

Research suggests that second-generation antidepressants are similar in treatment efficacy to first-generation antidepressants (Gartlehner et al., 2005; Gitlin, 2002), but have fewer and milder side effects and are better tolerated by patients (Hansen, Gartlehner, Lohr, Gayles, & Carey, 2005; Taylor, Freemantle, Geddes, & Bhagwager, 2006). The most frequently reported SSRI side effects are insomnia, nausea, headache, dizziness, agitation, and sexual dysfunctions. Because side effects tend to be worse at the beginning of treatment, they can be minimized if doses are kept low for the first 2 to 3 weeks.

In the early 2000s, several highly publicized cases raised concerns over the contributing effects of SSRIs to the suicidal thinking of children and adolescents. These concerns prompted the FDA to issue a warning label notifying users of the possible effects of the drug and prompted physicians to more closely monitor patients during the first several weeks of SSRI usage, especially among children and adolescents.

Among SSRIs, fluoxetine tends to be energizing; thus, it may be a good choice for patients presenting with a loss of energy or weakness and melancholia. However, it can also cause agitation, restlessness, and insomnia, particularly if patients present with anxiety. Among SNRIs, venlafaxine may provide the broadest spectrum of therapeutic effect across the full range of depressive symptoms. Patients may experience early-onset side effects. Initial nausea and vomiting occasionally can be problematic, and slower introduction of the drug is necessary. It is better tolerated when the dose is gradually increased. Desvenlafaxine is an active metabolite of venlafaxine. It is an extended-release tablet that only needs to be taken once a day. Its side effect profile is very similar to venlafaxine with the same intensity but lower incidence rates. Duloxetine is an SNRI that is effective in severe and treatment-resistant depression. It is FDA-approved for diabetic neuropathic pain. It shows promise in the management of fibromyalgia-type chronic pain. Duloxetine is the most effective drug compared to other classes of antidepressants.

Miscellaneous Antidepressants

Other drugs have shown promise in the treatment of depression. Among these medications, bupropion has fewer sexual side effects than the SSRIs or TCAs and also can cause weight loss instead of weight gain (Koda-Kimble et al., 2008). However, bupropion probably should be avoided in depressed patients with psychotic features or in individuals with schizophrenia-like disorders because the dopaminergic effects of the agent may give rise to an increase in psychotic symptomatology. Bupropion is implicated in causing insomnia and should be carefully used in inmates with the history of hypertension. Trazodone has hypnotic effects, which are prominent. Currently, its primary use is in the treatment of insomnia. Priapism (sustained, continuous painful erection in males sometimes requiring surgical intervention) is a rare adverse effect of trazodone that occurs in approximately 1 in 6,000 males treated with the drug. Nefazodone is useful for depressed patients who also have symptoms of anxiety. Some patients will have difficulty tolerating its sedative and orthostatic effects and will complain of sleepiness, lightheadedness, and/or dizziness. The side effects of the agent can often be made more tolerable by gradual dose increases. Because of its relatively sedative pharmacology, mirtazapine may be preferentially used in depressed patients with significant anxiety and/or insomnia. Mirtazapine's most common side effects are dry mouth, weight gain, somnolence, asthenia, and constipation.

Table 7.2	Major Classes of Antidepressants

First-Generation Antidepressants
Tricyclics (TCAs):
amitriptyline (Elavil®)
imipramine (Tofranil®)
doxepin (Sinequan®)
Monoamine oxidase inhibitors (MAOIs):
phenelzine (Nardil®)
tranylcypromine (Parnate®)
isocarboxazid (Marplan®)
Second-Generation Antidepressants
Serotonin selective reuptake inhibitors (SSRIs):
fluoxetine (Prozac®)
sertraline (Zoloft®)
paroxetine (Paxil®)
citalopram (Celexa®)
escitalopram (Lexapro®)
Serotonin/norepinephrine reuptake inhibitors (SNRIs):
venlafaxine (Effexor®)
desvenlafaxine (Pristiq®)
duloxetine (Cymbalta®)
Miscellaneous Antidepressants
trazodone (Desyrel®)
nefazodone (Serzone®)
bupropion (Wellbutrin®)

Mood Stabilizers or Antimanic Agents

The term *mood stabilizer* applies to a group of medications used in the treatment of bipolar disorder. Bipolar disorder is a cyclic disorder with alternating episodes of depression and mania. Mania is characterized by a compilation of emotional, motivational, behavioral, cognitive, and physical symptoms. Among the emotional symptoms are an elated mood with extreme joy and well-being not consistent with events in the person's life and irritability and anger when others get in the way of the person's unrealistic ambitions. Motivational symptoms common in mania include a constant need for excitement, social involvement, and companionship coupled with little awareness of the overwhelming nature of the person's social style. Behavioral symptoms often reflect the person's sense of time urgency, that is, quick movement, rapid speech, risk-taking activities, financial irresponsibility, and flamboyance. Poor judgment and planning, inflated self-esteem approaching grandiosity, and occasional loss of contact with reality are common cognitive symptoms of mania. Physically, people with mania often report feeling extremely energetic and require little sleep (American Psychiatric Association, 2000). Bipolar disorder is a complex mood disorder, and its clinical presentation differs among individual patients.

There are two types of bipolar disorder. Bipolar disorder I is characterized by at least one manic episode and one major depressive episode. Bipolar disorder II is characterized by at least one major depressive episode accompanied by one hypomanic (i.e., a milder form of mania) episode (American Psychiatric Association, 2000). Treatment for bipolar disorder has three phases: acute, continuation, and maintenance. During the acute phase of treatment, symptom control is the primary focus. During the continuation phase, relapse prevention and dose adjustments are primary goals. Preventing recurrence is the primary goal of the maintenance phase. During this last phase, the patient usually is on the lowest dosage of medication possible to effectively control symptoms. General treatment goals are to decrease the frequency, severity, and recurrence of episodes and to improve the patient's functioning between episodes. Most patients remain on a mood stabilizer indefinitely. Polypharmacy for bipolar disorder is the norm and monotherapy is the exception.

At present, lithium, valproate, carbamazepine, lamotrigine, and the atypical antipsychotic medications are used for the treatment of bipolar disorder (see Table 7.3). Mood stabilizers as a group are much more diverse with respect to their pharmacokinetic and pharmacodynamic properties, side-effect profiles, and potential for drug interactions. When prescribing mood stabilizers, it is clinically important to distinguish between bipolar and unipolar mood disorders when selecting pharmacotherapeutic agents because antidepressants may precipitate mania in patients with bipolar disorder. Also, manic symptoms can be induced from stimulants or adrenergic drugs, such as amphetamines, cocaine, levodopa, ephedrine, tricyclic antidepressants, and monoamine oxidase inhibitors, as well as by high doses of corticosteroids and various other over-the-counter (OTC) drugs. Therefore, a careful review of drug use, including OTC medications, should be undertaken before a diagnosis of mania or bipolar disorder is given.

Lithium

Lithium is the drug of choice for pure mania. First reported to have antimanic effects in 1949, it has been used for acute and preventive treatment of bipolar disorder in the United States since the mid-1960s. Lithium has been proven effective for acute and prophylactic treatment of both manic and depressive episodes in patients with bipolar disorder (Cusack, 2002; Viguera et al., 2000). It is a drug with a narrow therapeutic range; that is, too low a dosage results in no symptom relief, and too high a dosage results in lithium poisoning—a toxic reaction consisting of nausea, vomiting, sluggishness, tremors, dizziness, slurred speech, seizures, kidney dysfunction, and even death (Moncrieff, 1997). To avoid lithium poisoning, periodic assessment of lithium blood levels is necessary.

Anticonvulsants

Anticonvulsants like carbamazapine and valproic acid were originally used in the treatment of epileptic seizures. These drugs are also effective alternatives to lithium for the treatment of bipolar disorder and are used primarily for treating acute mania in patients who respond poorly to lithium (e.g., substance abuse–related mania, mixed episodes, or rapid cycling) or who are unable to tolerate lithium (Keck & McElroy, 2002a). Carbamazepine produces a better antidepressant response in patients with bipolar disorder than in those with unipolar depression and appears to be effective in controlling both manic and depressive episodes. Side effects include drowsiness, dizziness, unsteadiness, nausea, and diplopia. Valproic acid has potent antimanic properties but minimal or no antidepressant properties. In controlled trials, valproic acid was found to be as effective as lithium in pure mania (Emilien, Maloteaux, Seghers, & Charles, 1996). Nausea, vomiting, and diarrhea are common side effects during early therapy but usually resolve and rarely require discontinuation of the drug. Valproate has few serious side effects other than a dose-related thrombocytopenia and rise in liver function tests that may require discontinuing the drug. This drug is marketed in the United States as valproate, divalproex, and valproic acid.

Atypical Antipsychotic Agents

Second-generation (atypical) antipsychotics were introduced to treat psychosis in patients with schizophrenia and have been found to be effective when used both alone and in combination with mood stabilizers to treat acute mania in bipolar disorder, especially when the patient also exhibits signs of psychosis (Keck & McElroy, 2002b; Rothschild et al., 2004). All atypical antipsychotics are FDA-approved for acute mania as monotherapy, and all but ziprasidone are also approved for combination therapy.

Table 7.3	Mood Stabilizers

Generic (Brand)
lithium (Eskalith®, Lithane®)
Anticonvulsants: divalproex (Depakote®)   carbamazepine (Tegretol®)   lamotrogine (Lamictal®)
Atypical antipsychotic drugs: See Table 7.1 for list

Antianxiety (Anxiolytic) Agents

Anxiety disorders are the most common mental disorders in the United States, with approximately 18% of the adult population suffering from one or more of the six anxiety disorders (Kessler, Berglund, Demler, Jin, & Walters, 2005). The anxiety disorders include generalized anxiety disorder (GAD), characterized by chronic, uncontrollable worry; panic disorder, in which the patient suffers from discrete episodes of intense fear or even terror; phobias, in which the patient experiences intense anxiety associated with exposure to specific objects (e.g., spiders) and/or situations (e.g., social situations); obsessive compulsive disorder (OCD), in which obsessive ideas (e.g., contamination) lead to compulsions (such as hand-washing) to reduce the associated anxiety; and acute stress disorder and post-traumatic stress disorder (PTSD), both involving the continual subjective reexperiencing of an event in which the person experienced actual or potential harm, such as combat (American Psychiatric Association, 2000).

A variety of biological, psychological, and social factors have been used to explain the development and maintenance of anxiety disorders. From a biological perspective, anxiety is likely the result of multiple interactions among the central nervous system (CNS) and the neurotransmitters norepinephrine, serotonin, and gamma-aminobutyric acid (GABA). The excitatory and inhibitory effect of these neurotransmitters function together to regulate CNS activity, and it is on these neurotransmitters that the antianxiety or anxiolytic drugs act (Wetherell, Lang, & Stein, 2006). Psychopharmacologic treatment of anxiety disorders occurs in two phases: stabilization and management. Antianxiety drugs are most needed during the stabilization phase of treatment to help the patient become more comfortable and to resume normal daily activities. Anxiolytics facilitate psychotherapy, which is the foundation of treatment in the management phase. During this phase, the patient learns to control fears and deal with residual phobias, cognitions, and psychosocial problems. A variety of medications have been found effective in treating anxiety disorders. These are discussed below and summarized in Table 7.4 on page 156.

Benzodiazepines

Benzodiazepines (BZDs), the largest class of antianxiety agents, were the pharmacologic treatment of choice for anxiety disorders in the 1970s and 1980s and were prescribed freely. They primarily exert their antianxiety effects by enhancing the inhibitory action of GABA. However, chronic use of BZDs can result in both physical and psychological dependence and can cause a withdrawal syndrome upon abrupt discontinuation. As a result, these pharmacologic agents are no longer considered the first choice for the treatment of anxiety disorders. Of particular note for correctional populations, inmate-patients with a history of substance abuse or unstable personalities are not good candidates for BZDs.

Azapirones

Currently, buspirone is the only azapirone available in the United States. Buspirone decreases anxiety without the sedative effects of BZDs. Moreover, it has no abuse potential and may be taken for an extended period of time without bringing about dependency or withdrawal upon discontinuation (Julien, 2005). These characteristics make buspirone an attractive anxiolytic, particularly because substance abuse is frequently seen as a co-occurring condition in anxiety disorders among the prison population.

Miscellaneous Agents

Other classes of medications are sometimes used in treating anxiety including antidepressants, antihistamines, and antihypertensives. Among antidepressants, various SSRIs have been FDA-approved for treating GAD, panic disorder, social phobia, OCD, and PTSD (Ball, Kuhn, Wall, Shekhar, & Goddard, 2005; Stein, 2002; Stein & Hugo, 2004; Stein, Seedat, van der Linden, & Zungo-Dirway, 2000; Stein, Westerberg, Yang, Li, & Barbato, 2003). Extended-release venlafaxine, an antidepressant, has been FDA-approved for treatment of GAD (Liebowitz, Mangano, Bradwejn, & Asnis, 2005). TCAs that are generally sedative in their pharmacology (e.g., doxepin, amitriptyline) may also be used as anxiolytics. Because of the sedative, orthostatic, and anticholinergic effects of these agents, tolerance may be a problem, especially in the elderly. Moreover, because GAD and clinical depression can coexist, special attention should be paid to the potential danger of a TCA overdose in depressed patients with suicidal ideation.

Antihistamines are typically used to treat allergic responses. These medications, including hydroxyzine and diphenhydramine, can also be useful in treating anxiety, largely because of their sedative effects. Antihistamines are not substances of abuse and may be preferentially used for patients in whom anxiety is intermittent and when the clinician is concerned about prescribing a BZD because of these medications' abuse potential and "street value."

Antihypertensives treat high blood pressure. Among these, beta blockers (propranolol, atenolol) blunt the physiologic response to anxiety and are used for occasional performance anxiety and in some cases for panic disorder. Clonidine, an antihypertensive, is used as an adjunctive medication to reduce hyperarousal symptoms often found in PTSD.

From this author's experience, the following drugs have proven effective in the treatment of specific anxiety disorders. For GAD, a non-BZD anxiolytic such as buspirone or venlafaxine or escitalopram can be used. Drugs with secondary anxiolytic properties such as antihistamines, beta blockers, and antipsychotics are also prescribed for GAD. Currently, SSRIs are recommended as standard first-line agents for treating panic disorder, followed by TCAs. In fact, paroxetine and sertraline are FDA-approved for treatment of panic disorder. SSRIs and BZDs are used in treating social phobia. Most of the SSRIs appear to be effective, and paroxetine has received FDA approval for this disorder. Clonazepam and alprazolam are effective BZDs in treating the disorder. Alprazolam may be used for occasional performance anxiety on an "as-needed" basis. Although beta blockers are ineffective for treating generalized social phobia, they are quite effective for performance anxiety. Various types of psychotropics have been used to treat OCD although none have controlled symptoms completely. Thus, cognitive behavioral therapy and pharmacotherapeutic agents in combination have achieved the best treatment outcomes. SSRIs are the mainstay of OCD symptom relief, and higher doses are required than for the treatment of depression. For PTSD, pharmacotherapeutic agents provide relief from recurring nightmares and reduce psychological and physical distress. They make the patient more comfortable and enhance response to psychotherapeutic modalities. SSRIs are effective in reducing intrusive "flashbacks" (instances in which the individual reexperiences or relives the traumatic event, often with emotional concomitants) and anxiety related to the initial traumatic event. Antidepressants (TCAs, MAOIs, SSRIs), BZDs (clonazepam), and buspirone are often used for PTSD, but the SSRIs are most effective. Paroxetine and sertraline have been FDA-approved for treatment of PTSD. Clonidine is used to minimize the physiologic hyperreactivity associated with PTSD.

Table 7.4	Antianxiety (Anxiolytic) Agents

Generic (Brand)
Benzodiazepines:
diazepam (Valium®)
alprazolam (Xanax®)
chlordiazepoxide (Librium®)
chlorazepate (Tranxene®)
halazepam (Paxipam®)
lorazepam (Ativan®)
oxazepam (Serax®)
prazepam (Centrax®)
clonazepam (Klonopin®)
temazepam (Restoril®)
Azapirones:
buspirone (BuSpar®)
Miscellaneous agents:
Antidepressants:
See Table 7.2 for list
Antihistamines:
diphenhydramine (Benadryl®)
hydroxyzine (Atarax®)
Antihypertensives:
propranolol (Inderal®)
atenolol (Tenormin®)

Agents Used in the Treatment of Substance Abuse

This section reviews medications used to address several aspects of alcohol and drug abuse and dependence, including withdrawal and overdose, opiate replacement therapy, and relapse prevention (see Table 7.5). Drug dependence syndromes for which drug therapies are sometimes or regularly useful involve stimulants, opiates, sedative-hypnotics, and alcohol. Some classes of illicit drugs do not cause any serious degree of physical dependence (as distinguished from psychological dependence or emotional craving). These include cannabis, inhalants, and the hallucinogens (e.g., lysergic acid diethylamide [LSD] and mescaline). Withdrawal symptoms are also seldom seen with phencyclidine (PCP) use. Such drugs can be abruptly discontinued, even in heavy and frequent users. Nevertheless, a drug therapy that would decrease or stop the use of these agents might well be clinically useful.

Medical Emergencies Related to Substance Abuse

Prisoners are most likely to present medical emergencies because of substance abuse through either withdrawal or an overdose. Both are probably more likely to be encountered in jails, which house high-turnover populations, including many individuals who have just been arrested. They may have used drugs or alcohol only a few hours or even minutes prior to their arrest. However, these situations also occur in prisons because street drugs are often smuggled inside the security perimeter, because alcohol ("hooch," "pruno," or "homebrew") is illicitly manufactured and consumed inside the facility, and/or because other prescription drugs are abused.

Among the more problematic drugs from a prison perspective are alcohol, cocaine, and PCP because these substances are most likely to cause aggressive behavior (Weigel, Purselle, D'Orio, & Garlow, 2009). In more extreme cases, sedation with a benzodiazepine and possibly haloperidol may be necessary to manage these cases. Withdrawal from alcohol and sedative-hypnotics can result in a potentially fatal delirium and should be treated with a long half-life benzodiazepine (Oslin, 2006). Delirium tremens due to alcohol withdrawal has a high mortality rate and develops in 48 to 72 hours after alcohol intake stops. It should be treated in a medical intensive care unit (Weigel et al., 2009; see Table 7.5). Where overdose or withdrawal is suspected, medical staff should be informed immediately.

Opiate Replacement Therapy (ORT)

For heroin-dependent prisoners, ORT is a potential alternative to total abstinence. Two medications, methadone and buprenorphine, are available as substitutes for heroin. These prevent the physiological symptoms of withdrawal from heroin. In contrast to heroin, methadone and buprenorphine have gradual onsets of action and produce stable levels of the drug in the brain. As a result, patients maintained on these medications do not experience a rush, while they also markedly reduce their desire to use opioids. If an individual treated with these medications tries to take an opioid such as heroin, the euphoric effects are usually dampened or suppressed. Patients undergoing maintenance treatment do not experience the physiological or behavioral abnormalities from rapid fluctuations in drug levels associated with heroin use. Maintenance treatments save lives—they help to stabilize individuals, allowing treatment of their medical, psychological, and other problems so they can contribute effectively as members of families and society (O'Brien, Woody, & McLellan, 1995).

ORT is not routinely employed in U.S. prisons, and the usage rates in jails are not presently known. However, in one survey (Nunn et al., 2009) it was found that 55% of prison systems do offer methadone maintenance therapy under some circumstances. However, in more than half of these instances, it was available only to pregnant, opiate-dependent prisoners or for chronic pain management, with buprenorphine provided much less often. Fewer than half of these systems offered community referrals for ORT (either methadone or buprenorphine) to releasing inmates. The most common reason for not offering ORT in prison or community referrals was the stated preference for drug-free detoxification. Notably, another common reason for not making community referrals was "limited partnerships with community providers" (Nunn et al., 2009, p. 86; see Chapter 1 concerning continuity of care issues). The U.S. Federal Bureau of Prisons employs methadone only for opiate withdrawal, with an exception for pregnant, opiate-dependent women (Federal Bureau of Prisons, 2009). However, in the Canadian federal prison system, inmates addicted to heroin may receive methadone maintenance treatment throughout their incarceration (Correctional Service of Canada, 2003/2009).

Relapse Prevention

When inmates are released from custody, they may be highly motivated to remain alcohol and drug-free. Community mental health and social services can support these goals, and medications may also be helpful in this regard. Methadone maintenance (as opposed to the time-limited use of methadone for aiding in opiate withdrawal) may be a part of helping opiate addicts stay clean. Other medications have been shown to be helpful in preventing a return to using alcohol and a range of illegal drugs (see Table 7.5).

Cannabis

Medications are rarely required for the treatment of cannabis intoxication. The most common symptom requiring intervention is severe anxiety. This anxiety can usually be managed by one or two modest doses of oral benzodiazepines such as lorazepam. Likewise, if psychotic symptoms are present, one or two oral doses of haloperidol will control these symptoms, which occasionally have been reported in frequent users of high-potency cannabis. States of withdrawal from long-term cannabis dependence are quite uncommon except in chronic daily users of high-potency or high-dose cannabis. The withdrawal state can include mild insomnia, irritability, tremor, and nausea. These symptoms usually do not require treatment. The treatment of choice for long-term dependence is a combination of education, drug counseling, and support programs.

Hallucinogens

The hallucinogens include LSD, mescaline, psilocybin, and related drugs whose principal effects are increased perceptual sensitivity, derealization, visual illusions, and hallucinations. Occasionally, these perceptual changes are associated with a frank panic reaction (called a "bad trip"), depression, or paranoid ideation. The symptoms of hallucinogen intoxication usually begin 1 hour after the last dose and typically last for 8 to 12 hours. BZDs such as diazepam will decrease the anxiety and commonly contribute to the patient's being able to sleep off the effects of the hallucinogen. Antipsychotics have also been used, but they are rarely necessary. Withdrawal states for chronic hallucinogen use are very rarely reported, and no detoxification is necessary. Chronic hallucinogen use is best managed through psychosocial interventions.

Stimulants

Stimulants, including cocaine, amphetamine, and their various forms, are among the most common drugs of abuse. The U.S. National Institute on Drug Abuse (NIDA) estimates that at least 1% to 2% of the population currently abuses cocaine but that rates of amphetamine abuse are lower (NIDA, n.d.).

Stimulant overdose or abuse represents a fairly common reason for emergency room (ER) visits and hospitalization. When a patient who is dependent on stimulants is hospitalized, stimulant administration should be stopped abruptly. Cocaine withdrawal often has no visible physical symptoms like the vomiting and shaking that accompanies withdrawal from heroin or alcohol. However, patients who have been taking stimulants in large amounts (e.g., more than 50 milligrams of D-amphetamine or several doses of cocaine a day) often have a withdrawal syndrome consisting of depression, fatigue, hyperphagia, hypersomnia, and cardiovascular manifestations. Imipramine, desipramine, and venlafaxine have shown some benefit in treating depression in cocaine-dependent

Table 7.5	Pharmacological Agents Used in Treating Substance Abuse
Substance of Abuse	*Pharmacological Intervention*
Alcohol overdose	Medical as indicated
Alcohol withdrawal (acute)	chlordiazepoxide (Librium®)
Alcohol relapse prevention (abstinence)	disulfuram (Antabuse®) acamprosate (Campral®) naltrexone (ReVia®)
Opioid overdose	Medical as indicated Naloxone (Narcan®)
Opioid withdrawal	methadone
Opioid relapse prevention (maintenance)	methadone buprenorphine (Buprenex®)
Opioid relapse prevention (abstinence)	methadone buprenorphine (Buprenex®)
Cocaine overdose	Cocaine overdose presents various cardiovascular symptoms including hypertension, arrhythmias, and myocardial infarction, and treatment is symptomatic
Cocaine withdrawal	Several classes of drugs based on patient presentation, like antidepressants for depression, usually upon withdrawal
Cocaine relapse prevention (abstinence)	Cocaine vaccine is under investigation Relapse prevention is usually based on psychosocial approach, and currently no drug therapy is available
Other (cannabis, hallucinogens, methamphetamine)	Currently no effective pharmacological treatment for withdrawal of these drugs and treatment is based on clinical presentation

patients with major depression. Even aspirin has been used to prevent platelet aggregation and improve brain blood flow and, in one study, to improve neuropsychological function (Johnston et al., 2004).

Psychotropic Medications in Correctional Environments

In this section, selected topics of particular relevance to correctional practice are discussed in some detail. The emphasis here is on considering the practical aspects of treatment, particularly the challenges presented by prison and jail settings.

Combined Pharmacological and Psychotherapeutic Interventions

Available information indicates an increased reliance on psychotropic medications as treatments for mental illnesses. For example, there was an increased use of psychotropic medications among American psychotherapy patients between 1987 and 1997 (Olfson, Marcus, Druss, & Pincus, 2002). According to James and Glaze (2006), psychotropic medication was the most common intervention for prisoners with mental health problems in state and federal prisons and jails as of 2004. The same data showed a slight increase in the proportion of state prisoners who had taken psychotropic medication while incarcerated between 1997 and 2004 (from 12% to 15%). This may have to do in part with the portability of pharmacotherapy (i.e., with appropriate documentation, a prescription written in the community can be continued subsequent to arrest; see below).

However, some patients may benefit from both psychotropic medications and psychosocial intervention. As Sammons (2001) has pointed out, the research in this area is of questionable utility in guiding clinicians to one or the other such intervention, or a combination approach. Sammons further notes the meaningfulness of preference (both the clinician's and the patient's) in the choice of treatment. This may be particularly true with respect to patient choice when that individual is a prison or jail inmate. The roles of prisoner and (clinician) staff with their inherent power differential may exacerbate existing levels of distrust on the part of inmate-patients, perhaps based in part on the patient's previous unfortunate encounters with authorities that resulted in arrest and/or involuntary hospitalization. Further complicating matters are the potentially unpleasant side effects of some medications. These concerns may be overcome in many instances when the clinician takes the time to develop a good therapeutic relationship with the patient, such that patient education can take place in an atmosphere of trust. Ultimately, the choice of therapeutic intervention should be guided by a thorough and accurate assessment of the patient and must take into consideration the patient's willingness to consider pharmacotherapy and/or psychotherapy, as appropriate, based on informed consent.

The Portability and Standardization of Pharmacological Treatment

Prisons and jails function well as healthcare facilities in one particular respect. Treatment, for the most part, is centralized and proximate, in contrast to services provided in the community, where services may be spread out and quite distant from patients' homes, especially in rural areas. In prisons and jails, outpatient medical, dental, and mental health services are typically no more than a few hundred feet from the patients' housing units.

However, there are obstacles to treatment in correctional facilities, including literal barriers. In such circumstances, at a purely practical level, pharmacological treatment has one distinct advantage over psychosocial interventions. When inmate-patients must be confined to special housing units (SHUs), or are transferred to other facilities (a process that can take days or weeks in some prison systems), it is often a fairly straightforward matter to ensure the continuity of their prescribed medications, whereas other therapeutic interventions must either be temporarily discontinued or provided intermittently. In restricted-access units, such as SHUs, inmates are often kept in their cells up to 23 hours a day. It can be an extended, time-consuming process to have an inmate escorted (perhaps in handcuffs) to a private room for an appointment with a therapist, and it is simply not a feasible accommodation for the unit officers to make on a regular basis, given their other duties.

When inmates are transferred from one facility to another, their medical files, documenting their prescriptions, will typically accompany them (but see below), such that medications will be available to them during the transfer process and can be continued without interruption at the receiving facility. Psychotherapy on any regular basis, on the other hand, may be unavailable during the transfer process and perhaps for several weeks after inmates arrive at their new prisons.

Then there is the related issue of the standardization of psychopharmacological treatment. Twenty milligrams of fluoxetine, a standard dose of the SSRI antidepressant, is the same intervention regardless of the setting: prison, hospital, or community. However, provider bias (e.g., racial) in prescribing may reduce the effectiveness of medications and perhaps result in a counterproductive impact of treatment. Accordingly, prescribing algorithms ("if depression criteria *a*, *b*, and *c* are present, prescribe such-and-such specific medication") are sometimes used to make the process more objective (Hills, Siegfried, & Ickowitz, 2004). In some respects, this parallels the manualized treatment initiative, the purpose of which is to increase the quality and effectiveness of psychosocial treatments by standardizing their implementation across therapists and maintaining fidelity to the empirically supported components of these interventions (e.g., Sanderson & Woody, 1995). For example, Vallina-Fernández and his colleagues (2001) used a manualized cognitive-behavioral intervention combined with medication in treating schizophrenics (see "Combined Pharmacological and Psychotherapeutic Interventions," above). However, following Sammons's (2001) comments (earlier), the wisdom of rigid adherence to such protocols is questionable.

Barriers to Treatment

Whether it is a long-standing order for psychiatric medications for a chronic disorder or the treatment of an acute psychiatric episode, a system that delivers the right drug with the right dosage to the right person at the right time and in the right manner is the goal. However, there are obstacles to best practices in prison environments that may not exist outside these settings. Prison inmates have scant control over the healthcare they receive and are less able to act as advocates on behalf of their own healthcare needs when compared to individuals in the community. A common problem in prisons and jails is a delay in providing psychotropic medications or their outright unavailability. This may happen because an individual is arrested and admitted to a jail, and cannot or will not provide information about medications he or she has been prescribed, or because documentation of the prescription cannot be quickly obtained. When individuals are transferred between correctional facilities (e.g., from jail to prison or between prisons), medication orders may not accompany them, resulting in a delay. A similar problem can occur when an individual resides in general population and then is placed in an administrative segregation unit. Most psychotropic medications are controlled, and patients must pick up each dose from the pharmacy pill line. If the health services department is not informed that the inmate is no longer on the compound, staff may simply assume that he or she has decided to discontinue the medication when he or she does not appear at the pill line for several days. In essence, the difference between the potential for treatment portability and the reality is often considerable. Hence, communication is vital between correctional and community mental health services, between correctional facilities, and between staff at the same facility for optimal patient care.

Mental health coverage in prisons and jails may be limited, and patients might have to wait longer than is desirable for appointments with a mental health specialist. A particular facility may employ a psychiatrist, a physician specializing in mental health assessment and treatment, on a full-time or part-time basis. In some localities, especially rural and frontier areas, these specialists may not be readily available (see Ax et al., 2008, for a discussion of this topic). If so, the institution's primary care physicians may write the prescriptions. In some states, pharmacists, nurse practitioners, and psychologists with advanced training can prescribe psychotropic medications (Fox et al., 2009). The department of corrections' pharmacy and therapeutic committee can develop guidelines for the screening staff as to which medications' timely continuation is of an urgent concern.

On a more routine basis, it is important to spend time with patients and educate them about the medications they are being prescribed. Providing information about the drugs, which includes their intended effects as well as possible side effects or adverse effects, can promote adherence to treatment. Interdisciplinary collaboration can be particularly helpful in correctional settings, where healthcare staff shortages may be pronounced and chronic. For example, to avoid difficulties related to changing medications too frequently, often before they have had a chance to work, clinical pharmacists working in mental health can develop protocols to guide prescribing clinicians' decision making in this regard. Pharmacists can alert prescribers to new drugs or new findings regarding established drugs and can research information on a drug with which the prescriber is unfamiliar. Psychologists, nurse practitioners, social workers, and other mental health professionals who see patients regularly can provide information to the prescriber and the pharmacist about medication effects, perhaps alerting them to early indications of adverse effects of a prescribed medication.

Finally, there is the issue of cost. Prisons and jails are regularly under pressure to contain costs, and medications can be expensive. This may result in the unavailability of some newer psychotropics, when they are available only in brand form and not yet in the cheaper, generic version. Release issues must also be considered in this regard. Prisoners often lack health insurance, and unless they have recourse to public funds (e.g., Medicaid, Supplemental Security Income [SSI]) after their return to the community, they may be unable to afford more expensive medications, mainly those still under patent, and for which no generic alternative is available. In such cases, prescribing professionals must seek the most clinically appropriate and affordable alternative for the patient. Fortunately, many generic psychotropic medications are now available at greatly reduced prices in the community.

Abuse Potential and Nonadherence

Some medications are potentially toxic. As little as 1 week of regular doses of TCAs taken together can be fatal. In a study of completed suicides in the Texas prison system during a 1-year period, all three of the 25 suicides in which prescription medication was the method involved this class of antidepressants (He, Felthous, Holzer, Nathan, & Veasey, 2001). Patients considering suicide may store their medications and take several doses at once. For this reason, regular monitoring of the patient, directly observed therapy (see below), and adjunctive psychotherapy are necessary to assess proneness to suicidal acting out. Those medications with the greatest potential to be misused in this way would ordinarily not be first-line pharmacological interventions.

High percentages of inmates in state prisons and jails have substance abuse problems. More than 40% of those without mental illness and more than 60% of those with co-occurring mental disorders used drugs in the month prior to their arrest (James & Glaze, 2006; see also Chapter 11). Given their lack of access, in relative terms, to street drugs, inmate-patients may engage in drug-seeking behavior, particularly for BZDs and other psychotropics such as stimulants, which can induce hedonic mental states similar to those they experienced with their street drugs of choice. They may either seek to use these medications themselves or to sell or trade them for other goods or services in the prison environment. Accordingly, these particular medications may be barred from the prison formulary or available only after additional screening measures have been undertaken to reduce the likelihood of abuse or misuse.

Screenings (usually of urine and/or breath) are standard procedure in correctional facilities to detect the ingestion of street drugs and alcohol. Screens can also be done for prescription drugs if abuse is suspected, as when an inmate is believed to have obtained someone else's medication through coercion or the institutional "black market."

A different situation exists when patients are suspected of nonadherence. This may occur when medications such as antipsychotics have unpleasant side effects. The patient may miss several pill lines, for example. In such cases, simply discussing his or her concerns may elicit a frank unwillingness to take the prescribed medication, and it can be discontinued (as patients cannot ordinarily be forced to take medications). However, patients may feel pressured to take medications; this is often the case with patients experiencing psychosis, where insight into the nature of their illnesses is lacking. If so, they may pick up their medications, even place them in their mouths, and then spit them out after leaving the pill line, or save them for later use, as in a suicide attempt. (This is popularly known as "cheeking.") A best practice whenever medications are being given out is called directly observed therapy, in which the staff member observes the patient taking and swallowing the medication. This has been found to be an effective intervention with patients suffering from tuberculosis (Chaulk, Moore-Rice, Rizzo, & Chaisson, 1995) and HIV/AIDS (Macalino et al., 2004). If the patient declines under these circumstances, then further counseling by the prescriber is warranted. Some antipsychotic medications come in long-acting injectable form. These can be useful for patients who are simply forgetful or find the public nature of the pill line embarrassing. However, patients ultimately have the right to refuse treatment.

Mental Health Staff: Caring for Patients Taking Psychotropic Medications

In corrections, it is likely that patients taking psychotropic medications will be referred to the mental health staff for monitoring and possible psychotherapeutic intervention. As noted above, pharmacotherapy is often provided in combination with psychotherapy, and mental health professionals (e.g., psychologists, counselors, and social workers) can collaborate with prescribing professionals by being alert to signs of adverse reactions to these agents. Some of these signs may be observable. Information about others may be elicited by asking patients how they are feeling and specifically inquiring about problems they may have noticed with their medications. Listed here are the most common side effects of psychotropic medications that all mental health professionals can monitor in their patients:

- Weight gain.
- Sedation (most of the psychotropic medications except stimulants).
- Dryness of mouth (most of the psychotropic medications).
- Constipation (most of the psychotropic medications).
- Vulnerability to heatstroke (antipsychotics and some antidepressants). Patients taking these medications may be advised to limit sun and heat exposure and asked if they have experienced recent fainting.

- Cardiovascular problems. Orthostatic hypotension and tachycardia (antipsychotics and TCAs); patients may be asked if they have experienced lightheadedness on standing or after urination, or racing heartbeat.
- Controlling salt intake and caffeine with lithium therapy. Patients taking lithium may be reminded to watch these substances.

Supportive Roles for Non-Healthcare Staff

To promote optimal response to treatment, all staff should maintain good communication with medical staff regarding patients taking psychotropic medications. Training should include an overview of medication side effects, suicide potential for untreated mental illness, and so on. Correctional staff will often know which patients are taking psychotropic medications because patients will tell them, or they will have to release patients for medication pill lines. In some cases, it will be appropriate to inform correctional and other staff who have regular contact with inmates (e.g., teachers, work detail supervisors) that a particular patient is taking a medication, because of the tenuous nature of the patient's stability. When inmates represent a potential security threat because of compromises in their emotional stability, confidentiality issues may become secondary.

Summary and Conclusions

With so many individuals with serious mental illness now incarcerated, the appropriate use of psychotropic medications is a vital component of best practices correctional mental health care. Many major mental illnesses must, for the present, be treated as chronic. These are conditions with which patients must live, and some will require ongoing pharmacological treatment.

The future, in the form of the emerging field of pharmacogenomics, holds the promise of improved psychotropic medications that more precisely target patient symptoms, based on the patient's genetic makeup, reducing the wide variation currently seen in patient response to various drugs, while improving efficacy and decreasing the potential for harm (Meyer, 2002). As side effects are decreased, it is reasonable to expect that adherence would accordingly be increased. As medications become more effective, it becomes increasingly incumbent on a best practice healthcare system to make them available to those individuals who need them. For many persons, they are necessary, though not sufficient, to a successful readjustment to the community. However, given the secondary priority of the healthcare mission of correctional facilities, the benefits of these medications may be more elusive for inmate-patients than for many in the general population.

Finally, caution is urged against a facile reliance solely on psychotropic medications to treat inmate-patients with serious mental illness. They can help lift psychoses, stabilize moods, and enhance impulse control, and they may quiet the craving for alcohol or street drugs. As such, their appropriate use may be a necessary component of treatment, but it is certainly not in itself sufficient to ensure the recovery of a group of individuals, many of whom have lost years of their lives to dysfunctional lifestyles, and who must learn or relearn appropriate interpersonal skills, as well as prosocial attitudes and behaviors, if they are to make successful transitions to the free world community.

KEY TERMS

Pharmacodyamics

Pharmacokinetics

Neurotransmitters

Directly observed
   therapy

Antipsychotics

Side effects

Extrapyramidal
   symptoms

Antidepressants

Mood stabilizers

Anxiolytics

FDA-approved

Off-label

Opiate replacement
   therapy (ORT)

Relapse prevention

Pharmacogenomics

DISCUSSION QUESTIONS

1. Are there ethical considerations with prescribing psychotropic medications for acutely psychotic individuals? What are some of the risks that might occur from taking these medications?

2. Should all correctional staff have some training in psychotropic medications, or is this asking too much of busy correctional officers and work detail supervisors? Should medication monitoring be left entirely to the healthcare professionals who prescribe these agents?

3. Do you think that giving someone a pill for a mental illness is appropriate, or do you believe that it reduces motivation for psychotherapy, where the patient could confront and modify the maladaptive patterns of thinking and behaving that led or contributed to the problem? Are there other possibilities besides these "either/or" options?

4. Should prisoners with a history of opiate dependence be offered opiate replacement therapy while incarcerated? Upon release? Why or why not?

5. If you were a prisoner, would you trust a mental health professional, who was employed by the facility in which you were housed, who wanted you to take a powerful medicine? What factors would increase or decrease your sense of trust in that person?

References

American Psychiatric Association. (2000). *Diagnostic and statistical manual of mental disorders* (4th ed., Text Revision). Washington, DC: Author.

Ax, R. K., Bigelow, B., Harowski, K., Meredith, J., Nussbaum, D., & Taylor, R. R. (2008). Prescriptive authority for psychologists: Serving underserved health care consumers. *Psychological Services, 5*, 184–197.

Ball, S. G., Kuhn, A., Wall, D., Shekhar, A., & Goddard, A.W. (2005). Selective serotonin reuptake inhibitor treatment for generalized anxiety disorder: A double-blind prospective comparison between paroxetine and sertraline. *Journal of Clinical Psychiatry, 66*, 94–99.

Breggin, P. R. (1991). *Toxic psychiatry*. New York, NY: St. Martin's.

Chakos, M. H., Lieberman, J. A., Hoffman, E., Bradford, D., & Sheitman, B. (2001). Effectiveness of second-generation antipsychotics in patients with treatment-resistant schizophrenia: A review and meta-analysis of randomized trials. *American Journal of Psychiatry, 158*, 518–526.

Chaulk, C. P., Moore-Rice, K., Rizzo, R., & Chaisson, R. E. (1995). Eleven years of community-based directly observed therapy for tuberculosis. *Journal of the American Medical Association, 274*, 945–951.

Citrome, L., Bilder, R. M., & Volavka, J. (2002). Managing treatment resistant schizophrenia: Evidence from randomized trials. *Journal of Psychiatric Practice, 8*, 205–215.

Correctional Service of Canada. (2003/2009). *Specific guidelines for methadone maintenance treatment.* Retrieved November 24, 2009, from http://www.csc-scc.gc.ca/text/pblct/methadone/index-eng.shtml

Csernansky, J. G., & Schuchart, E. K. (2002). Relapse and rehospitalization rates in patients with schizophrenia: Effects of second generation antipsychotics. *CNS Drugs, 16*, 473–484.

Cusack, J. R. (2002). Challenges in the diagnosis and treatments of bipolar disorder. *Drug Benefit Trends, 14*(10), 34–38.

Ebmeier, K. P., Donaghey, C., & Steele, J. D. (2006). Recent developments and current controversies in depression. *Lancet, 367*, 153–167.

Emilien, G., Maloteaux, J. M., Seghers, A., & Charles, G. (1996). Lithium compared to valproic acid and carbamazepine in the treatment of mania: A statistical meta-analysis. *European Neuropsychopharmacology, 6*, 245–252.

Federal Bureau of Prisons. (2008, November 25). *Legal resource guide to the Federal Bureau of Prisons.* Retrieved November 6, 2009, from http://www.bop.gov/news/PDFs/legal_guide.pdf

Federal Bureau of Prisons. (2009, August). *Federal Bureau of Prisons clinical practice guidelines: Detoxification of chemically dependent inmates.* Retrieved October 13, 2009, from http://www.bop.gov/news/PDFs/detoxification.pdf

Fox, R. E., DeLeon, P. H., Newman, R., Sammons, M. T., Dunivin, D. L., & Baker, D. C. (2009). Prescriptive authority and psychology: A status report. *American Psychologist, 64*, 257–268.

Gartlehner, G., Hansen, R. A., Carey, T. S., Lohr, K. N., Gaynes, B. N., & Randolph, L. C. (2005). Discontinuation rates for selective serotonin reuptake inhibitors and other second generation antidepressants in outpatients with major depressive disorder: A systematic review and meta-analysis. *International Clinical Pharmacology, 20*, 59–69.

Gitlin, M. J. (2002). Pharmacological treatment of depression. In I. H. Gotlib & C. L. Hammen (Eds.), *Handbook of depression* (pp. 360–382). New York, NY: Guilford.

Grilly, D. M. (2002). *Drugs and human behavior* (4th ed.). Boston, MA: Allyn & Bacon.

Hansen, R. A., Gartlehner, G., Lohr, K. N., Gayles, B. N., & Carey, T. S. (2005). Efficacy and safety of second generation antidepressants in the treatment of major depressive disorder. *Annals of Internal Medicine, 143*, 415–426.

He, X.-Y., Felthous, A. R., Holzer, C. E., Nathan, P., & Veasey, S. (2001). Factors in prison suicide: One year study in Texas. *Journal of Forensic Sciences, 46*, 896–901.

Hills, H., Siegfried, C., & Ickowitz, A. (2004, May). *Effective prison mental health services: Guidelines to expand and improve treatment.* Washington, DC: U.S. Department of Justice, National Institute of Corrections. Retrieved November 6, 2009, from http://www.nicic.org/pubs/2004/018604.pdf

James, D. J., & Glaze, L. E. (2006, September). *Mental health problems of prison and jail inmates* (Bureau of Justice Statistics Special Report NCJRS 213600). Retrieved November 5, 2009, from http://www.ojp.usdoj.gov/bjs/pub/pdf/mhppji.pdf

Johnston, S. C., O'Meara, E. S., Manolio, T. A., Lefkowitz, D., O'Leary D. H., Goldstein, S., et al. (2004). Cognitive impairment and decline are associated with carotid artery disease in patients without clinically evident cerebrovascular disease. *Annals of Internal Medicine, 140*, 237–247.

Julien, R. M. (2005). *A primer of drug action* (10th ed.). New York, NY: Worth.

Kane, J., Honigfeld, G., Singer, J., & Meltzer, H. (1988). Clozapine for the treatment-resistant schizophrenic: A double blind comparison with chlorpromazine (clozaril collaborative study). *Archives of General Psychiatry, 45*, 789–796.

Keck, P. E., & McElroy, S. L. (2002a). Carbamazepine and valproate in the maintenance treatment of bipolar disorder. *Journal of Clinical Psychiatry, 63*, 13–17.

Keck, P. E., & McElroy, S. L. (2002b). Pharmacological treatments for bipolar disorder. In P. E. Nathan & J. M. Gorman (Eds.), *A guide to treatments that work* (2nd ed., pp. 323–350). New York, NY: Oxford University Press.

Kessler, R. C., Berglund, P., Demler, O., Jin, R., & Walters, E. E. (2005). Lifetime prevalence and age-of-onset distributions of DSM-IV disorders in the national co-morbidity survey replication. *Archives of General Psychiatry, 62*, 593–602.

Koda-Kimble, M. A., Young, L. Y., Alldredge, B. K., Corelli, R. L., Guglielmo, B. J., Kradjan, W. A., et al. (2008). *Applied therapeutics: The clinical use of drugs* (9th ed.). Philadelphia, PA: Lippincott, Williams, and Wilkins.

Liebowitz, M. R., Mangano, R. M., Bradwejn, J., & Asnis, G. (2005). A randomized controlled trial of venlafaxine extended release in generalized social anxiety disorder. *Journal of Clinical Psychiatry, 66*, 49–66.

Macalino, G. E., Mitty, J. A., Bazerman, L. B., Singh, K., McKenzie, M., & Flanigan, T. (2004). Modified directly observed therapy for the treatment of HIV-seropositive substance users: Lessons learned from a pilot study. *Clinical Infectious Diseases, 38*(Suppl. 5), S393–S397.

Meyer, U. A. (2002). Introduction to pharmacogenomics: Promises, opportunities, and limitations. In J. Licinio & M.-I. Wong (Eds.), *Pharmacogenomics: The search for individualized therapies* (pp. 1–8). Weinheim, Germany: Wiley-VCH.

Moncrieff, J. (1997). Lithium: Evidence reconsidered. *British Journal of Psychiatry, 171*, 113–119.

National Institute on Drug Abuse. (n.d.). *Infofacts on cocaine and methamphetamine use.* Retrieved November 22, 2009, from www.nida.nih.gov/Infofacts.cocaine.html and www.nida.nih.gov/Infofacts/methamphetamine.html

Nunn, A., Zaller, N., Dickman, S., Trimbur, C., Nijhawan, A., & Rich, J. D. (2009). Methadone and buprenorphine prescribing and referral practices in US prison systems: Results from a nationwide survey. *Drug and Alcohol Dependence, 105*, 83–88.

O'Brien, C., Wo__ G., & McLellan, A. (1995). Enhancing the effectiveness of methadone using ___ic interventions. *NIDA Research Monograph, 150*, 5–18.

___ C., Druss, B., & Pincus, H. A. (2002). National trends in the use of outpa-___y. *American Journal of Psychiatry, 159*, 1914–1920.

___dictions. In D. V. Jeste & J. H. Friedman (Eds.), *Psychiatry for neurologists* ___wa, NJ: Humana Press.

___on, D. J., Tohen, M. F., Schatzberg, A., Anderson, S. W., VanCampen, L. E., ___le-blind, randomized study of olanzapine and olanzapine/fluoxetine com-___epression with psychotic features. *Journal of Clinical Psychopharmacology,*

___ Combined treatments for mental disorders: Clinical dilemmas. In ___ B. Schmidt (Eds.), *Combined treatments for mental disorders: A guide ___ and pharmacological interventions* (pp. 11–32). Washington, DC: American Psychological Association.

Sammons, M. T., & Schmidt, N. B. (Eds.). (2001). *Combined treatments for mental disorders: A guide to psychological and pharmacological interventions.* Washington, DC: American Psychological Association.

Sanderson, W. C., & Woody, S. (1995). Manuals for empirically validated treatments. *The Clinical Psychologist, 48*(4), 7–11.

Schatzberg, A. F., & Cole, J. O. (1991). *Manual of clinical psychopharmacology* (2nd ed.). Washington, DC: American Psychiatric Press.

Shorter, E. (1997). *A history of psychiatry: From the era of the asylum to the age of Prozac.* New York, NY: John Wiley.

Stein, D. J. (2002). Obsessive-compulsive disorder. *Lancet, 360*, 397–405.

Stein, D. J., & Hugo, F. J. (2004). Neuropsychiatric aspects of anxiety disorders. In S. C. Yudofsky & R. E. Hales (Eds.), *Essentials of neuropsychiatry and clinical neurosciences* (pp. 1049–1068). Washington, DC: American Psychiatric Association.

Stein, D. J., Seedat, S., van der Linden, G. J. H., & Zungo-Dirway, N. (2000). SSRIs in the treatment of PTSD: A meta-analysis of randomized controlled trials. *International Clinical Psychopharmacology, 15*(Suppl. 2), 31–39.

Stein, D. J., Westerberg, H. G. M., Yang, H., Li, D., & Barbato, L. M. (2003). Fluvoxamine CR in the long-term treatment of social anxiety disorder: The 12- to 24-week extension phase of a multicenter, randomized, placebo-controlled trial. *International Journal of Neuropsychopharmacology, 6*, 317–325.

Taylor, M. J., Freemantle, N., Geddes, J. R., & Bhagwager, Z. (2006). Early onset selective serotonin reuptake inhibitor antidepressant action: Systematic review and meta-analysis. *Archives of General Psychiatry, 63*, 1217–1223.

Vallina-Fernández, O., Lemos-Giráldez, S., Roder, V., García-Saiz, A., Otero-García, A., Alonso-Sánchez, M., et al. (2001). An integrated psychological treatment program for schizophrenia. *Psychiatric Services, 52*, 1165–1167.

Viguera, A. C., Nonacs, R., Cohen, L. S., Tondo, L., Murray, A., & Baldessarini, R. J. (2000). Risk of recurrence of bipolar disorder in pregnant and nonpregnant women after discontinuing lithium maintenance. *American Journal of Psychiatry, 157*, 179–184.

Wander, T. J., Nelson, A., Okazaki, H., & Richelson, E. (1987). Differential effects of atypical and typical antipsychotic drugs. *European Journal of Pharmacology, 143*, 279–282.

Weigel, M. B., Purselle, D. C., D'Orio, B., & Garlow, S. J. (2009). Treatment of psychiatric emergencies. In A. T. Schatzberg & C. B. Nemeroff (Eds.), *The American Psychiatric Publishing textbook of psychopharmacology* (4th ed., pp. 1287–1308). Washington, DC: American Psychiatric Publishing.

Wetherell, J. L., Lang, A. J., & Stein, M. B. (2006). Anxiety disorders. In D. V. Jeste & J. H. Friedman (Eds.), *Psychiatry for neurologists* (pp. 43–58). Totowa, NJ: Humana Press.

CHAPTER 8

Interdisciplinary Collaboration in Correctional Practice

Dean Aufderheide and John D. Baxter

"As you ought not to attempt to cure the eyes without the head, or the head without the body, so neither ought you to attempt to cure the body without the mind . . . for the part can never be well unless the whole is well."

—Plato's Charmides, 380 BC

Introduction

At perhaps no other time in the history of corrections has the role of correctional mental health staff in interdisciplinary collaboration been more important. The reason is simple—the exponential growth in the number of individuals with mental illness populating jails and prisons throughout the United States. Ironically, the transinstitutionalization of this population, as described in previous chapters, appears to have created an inadvertent opportunity for mental health professionals to play an increasingly important role in interdisciplinary collaboration within the correctional setting. Because untreated mental illness impacts institutional security and is a salient risk factor of recidivism, interdisciplinary collaboration to ensure access to necessary treatment, continuity of care, and reentry planning for offenders with mental illness is emerging as a critical component for successful outcomes. High numbers of offenders with mental illness and often limited staffing have created the necessity for psychologists and other mental health providers to collaborate with allied healthcare staff, security staff, and other correctional professionals in identifying and responding to the needs of persons with mental illness housed in correctional facilities. The interdisciplinary collaboration between mental health staff, correctional staff, and other institutional staff, therefore, has become crucial for treatment outcome success and effective inmate management (Bonner, 2006).

This chapter will discuss ways in which the correctional mental health professional plays an integral role in fulfilling critical mission requirements that call for interdisciplinary collaboration in jails and prisons. From improving offender conduct and treatment outcomes to reducing recidivism, this chapter will explore the ways in which correctional mental health professionals can be model participants of interdisciplinary collaboration. Accordingly, this chapter will address a number of best practices informed by the principles of collaboration in correctional mental health.

Defining Interdisciplinary Collaboration

"Coming together is a beginning. Keeping together is progress. Working together is success."

—Henry Ford

Like any organization, correctional systems are composed of people working together to achieve a common goal or purpose. The purpose of a correctional system is defined by its mission statement, which is public safety and which, increasingly commonly, includes strategies to reduce recidivism. The necessary activities to achieve its goal are accomplished by individuals working interdependently. To illustrate, consider a football team:

> The football team's output depends synergistically on how well each player does his particular job in concert with his teammates. The quarterback's performance depends on the performance of his linemen and receivers, and ends on how well the quarterback throws the ball, and so on. (Margulies & Wallace, 1973, p. 99)

Interdisciplinary collaboration requires a group of people with complementary skills who are committed to a common purpose, a set of performance goals, and an approach for which they hold themselves mutually responsible. Correctional mental health professionals, therefore, must understand the importance of interdisciplinary collaboration as a way of improving offender conduct in prison, enhancing treatment efficacy, and reducing recidivism.

The Importance of Interdisciplinary Collaboration in Correctional Practice

"We may have all come on different ships, but we're in the same boat now."

—Martin Luther King Jr.

Although the role of mental health providers is different from that of other correctional staff, they often need help from other staff in producing positive treatment outcomes, assisting an inmate in successfully adjusting to the incarceration environment, and effecting prerelease continuity of care planning for community reentry. For example, enhanced supervision of inmates with mental illness, crisis intervention and interventions with special needs offenders, discretionary discipline for rule infractions, use of segregation, job and housing assignments, and an array of other programs are all critically important in facilitating successful mental health treatment. Thus, the provision of mental health services within jails and prisons requires a multidisciplinary workforce to provide assessment and treatment services. Often referred to as a "multidisciplinary treatment team," it usually comprises a group of staff members representing different professions, disciplines, or service areas. The team, which may include representatives from security, classification, substance abuse, unit management, work supervisors, and institution management, in addition to the medical, nursing, and mental health staff, works together to ensure the timely and appropriate provision of assessment, care, and treatment to the inmate. Although a designated case manager may be tasked with writing the draft treatment plan with input from members of the treatment team, the responsibility for the implementation, review, and updating of the treatment plan is shared by the entire multidisciplinary treatment team.

For those engaged in providing mental health services in correctional settings, it is not so much a question of whether to collaborate with others, but under what circumstances and to what ends. Correctional psychologists and other mental health staff collaborate with nonclinical staff in several arenas including identification and management of individuals with mental illness, implementation of evidence-based programs that reduce misconduct and recidivism, and intervention with severely behaviorally disordered inmates.

At all points of collaboration, the relationship with security staff is the sine qua non of interdisciplinary collaboration in the incarceration environment. Security is the responsibility of all institutional staff, and mental health staff must accept the basic security principles to provide effective treatment in the institution. Correspondingly, effective treatment facilitates effective inmate management, which is essential for effective security:

> Effective treatment of inmates who have mental disorders can alleviate the stress experienced by the mentally ill patients and by the correctional staff who supervise them. Such treatment often requires the involvement and skills of a multidisciplinary treatment team. As is the case in community mental health care settings, psychiatrists, psychologists, social workers, psychiatric rehabilitation professionals, and other mental health professionals all contribute to the assessment and treatment of patients. However, in a prison setting correctional officers also play a central role in the care of psychiatric patients. (Applebaum, Hickey, & Packer, 2001, p. 1344)

In addition to providing a safe and secure environment, correctional officers are a rich source of observational data that can enhance treatment interventions. They play an important role in defusing crises and in preventing potential escalation. They are with the inmates 24 hours a day, which allows them to see and hear much more than mental health staff can. Thus, correctional officers play an indispensable role in detecting and reporting debilitating symptoms of a mental illness.

Interdisciplinary Collaboration for Improving Offender Conduct in Prison

"Union gives strength."

—Aesop

Mental health professionals collaborate with others in group and individual efforts to reduce misconduct in a prison setting. Individual-level interventions consist of identification of persons with mental illness and collaborating with others to provide care, which results in better functioning in a correctional setting. These interventions are described later in this chapter.

At the group level, mental health practitioners provide and involve others in supporting behavioral treatment programs known to reduce misconduct. It is important to note that the behavioral programs that reduce misconduct by as much as 26% have also been shown to reduce recidivism by an estimated 23% (Andrews & Bonta, 2003; French & Gendreau, 2006). It is clear that collaboration in providing evidence-based behavioral programs not only reduces misconduct but also has a significant benefit in reducing recidivism upon release.

Because most treatment programming occupies less than 8 hours per day, program participants typically are involved in additional work or educational assignments throughout the facility. Staff supervising program participants in work details or other activities can support treatment in meaningful ways. Similar to correctional staff, they can reinforce program principles in interpersonal communication, encourage the application of treatment principles to work or other activities (e.g., task-relevant cognitive skills, attitudes and behavior related to honesty and responsibility), and address behavior issues in ways consistent with treatment principles.

None of these ideals of staff support occurs independently of the efforts of clinical staff. Given coexisting objectives related to care and custody (Adams & Ferrandino, 2008), correctional mental health providers must work effectively with staff across departmental lines and at all levels to facilitate understanding, trust, and agreement to reinforce program goals and principles. Simply explaining program rules and principles is insufficient. Helping staff understand how an evidence-based treatment program reduces misconduct and problem behaviors and ultimately leads to a safer prison and to lower recidivism can create a willingness on the part of staff to try supporting the program. As these principles are consistently applied and staff observe inmate behaviors change for the better, stronger and more consistent support for a treatment program occurs. Gendreau, Goggin, and Smith (1999) have summarized principles related to program implementation that bear on the essential elements of collaboration. These principles include staff involvement; absence of interdepartmental or staff conflict; belief of stakeholders that the program is congruent with organizational and facility goals and matches the needs of the clientele; and the change agent engaging in persuasion, advocacy, and brokerage.

Communication from correctional mental health clinicians involved in treatment programs must be consistent and presented across a variety of facility settings. Treatment staff must leave the treatment unit, visit work details or education areas, interact with inmate participants in multiple settings, and speak with staff in ways that reinforce their understanding and involvement in support of treatment goals. In short, they must model the collaboration they seek from others. This modeling is evident in supporting the goals of security staff, work detail supervisors, education staff, and unit staff. Annual staff training and new employee training programs offer opportunities to provide an overview of treatment programs, philosophy, and concrete examples of ways all staff can support treatment activities. Consider the hypothetical example of interdisciplinary collaboration described in Text Box 8.1.

TEXT BOX 8.1
CASE EXAMPLE

A facility underwent a sudden mission change that involved radically increasing the number of sex offenders in the institution. Some of these sex offenders volunteered for treatment, but a significant percentage did not. Over several months, as this transition in population occurred, the facility in question made practical preparations and worked through the emotional reaction of staff to this challenging mission. Facility managers created an implementation workgroup consisting of key staff and managers across facility departments that met regularly to discuss and solve issues related to program implementation. A number of sex offenders housed in the facility continued to engage in problematic sexually motivated behaviors. Staff were faced with addressing the behavior management needs of these inmates in several anticipated and unanticipated areas: behavior in the visiting room, inappropriate correspondence or telephone behavior, supervision in work assignments throughout the facility, and creation or collection of inappropriate stimulus material through mail. Staff found their assumptions about behavior norms tested repeatedly. As an example, some staff were surprised to find that inmates convicted of sex offenses involving children were coming to the education department library to watch videos featuring children. Staff in each department of the facility prepared for and implemented the mission change through discussion at regular meetings, asking questions, and working to resolve concerns. These active steps did not eliminate apprehension regarding the mission change or eliminate every challenge, but they created a climate of collaboration and understanding that allowed staff to work through issues as they arose during implementation. As a result of this collaboration, facility staff currently share a common understanding of issues and a commitment to professionalism in implementing sex offender treatment and management of problem behaviors in their facility.

Contrast this case with a treatment program unsupported or opposed by other staff in the facility. Staff can undermine treatment progress by failing to support and enforce behavior norms and expectations. A failure to communicate regarding inmates in treatment, whether due to choice or benign neglect, results in less effective treatment. When work supervisors or unit management staff fail to inform treatment staff about inmate behavior problems, changes in assignments, changes in behavior or demeanor, or other issues of concern (e.g., family problems at home), an opportunity to address these issues in the context of treatment is missed. Under these circumstances, treatment is compartmentalized and tangential to the inmate's day-to-day experience, rather than reinforced as an essential process necessary for preparing for release to the community.

One effective approach to fostering communication across departmental lines involves the principle of reinforcement (e.g., draw positive public attention to examples of the desired communication when they occur). For example, a staff member who informs treatment staff of a significant change in inmate behavior can be recognized at a general staff meeting, or a positive note regarding the communication can be sent to his or her supervisor for inclusion in an employee performance appraisal log. This approach can be supplemented with private, one-on-one discussion between treatment staff and other institution staff about a missed opportunity for intervention when communication about an inmate's issues is neglected.

At other times, and for various reasons, staff may actively undermine treatment. Consider the hypothetical case example presented in Text Box 8.2.

TEXT BOX 8.2
CASE EXAMPLE

An inmate's record indicates that he first began engaging in suicidal behaviors at age 15. Prior to incarceration, his suicidal behaviors included drug overdose, ingesting pesticides, and attempted hanging. Since incarceration, the inmate had received psychiatric care, mostly with antidepressant medications. During his years of incarceration, he has had multiple admissions to suicide watch as well as many inpatient admissions. Almost all of his inpatient admissions were the result of self-laceration. His primary diagnosis was borderline personality disorder.

At the time of the most recent incident, the inmate was already on observation status for a "superficial" self-laceration. Following his return from the outside hospital, he stated in the interview that he was having a particularly "bad day" and gave in to the urge to cut. He reported being angry/frustrated by a member of the nursing staff who allegedly made rude statements directed at him. "I tried to talk with her about a problem I was having in the dorm. She said that she was not interested in hearing about the problems of a 'child molester' and that as far as she was concerned I needed to stop 'whining.'" A nursing note by the referenced nurse described the inmate as manipulative and attention seeking. In consultation with the nurse, she acknowledged that she cannot tolerate these kinds of inmates and that "all they need is a good whipping."

As this case example illustrates, sometimes the stereotypes of inmates who have mental health or behavior problems may result in inappropriate responses to behaviors. Effective programming is only as successful as the staff's ability to communicate appropriately within the collaborative relationship.

Interdisciplinary Collaboration to Improve Treatment Efficacy

"The most important single ingredient in the formula of success is knowing how to get along with people."

—Theodore Roosevelt

In addition to programs, misconduct can be reduced through offender-specific mental health interventions. The goal of such collaboration is to ensure that inmates with mental health treatment needs are identified at the earliest possible opportunity and that staff work together to provide care and management in the interest of the inmate. To this end, correctional mental health providers collaborate with other healthcare professionals, security officers, unit management staff, work detail supervisors, discipline hearing staff, and others to identify and address mental health needs of inmates. In some cases, the indirect result of these mental health and behavioral interventions is the reduction of misconduct.

Collaboration in Identification of Individuals With Mental Illness

The responsibility for correctional systems to identify persons with mental illness and to provide care for their needs is constitutionally established and well defended in application through case law such as the Supreme Court ruling regarding deliberate indifference in *Estelle v. Gamble* (1976) and subsequent rulings in state courts regarding the provision of care for persons with serious medical needs (*Dean v. Coughlin*, 1985; *Duran v. Anaya*, 1986). Accrediting agencies such as the National Commission on Correctional Health Care (NCCHC) and the American Correctional Association (ACA) have long included standards that address screening for mental illness, monitoring of vulnerable populations, and standards of intervention and care (ACA, 2003; NCCHC, 2008).

Initial screening of arriving inmates is conducted by a multidisciplinary team. Critical to this process is communication between members of the team to address patient care issues. Unit management or other staff conduct social screening of arriving inmates to ensure that they are appropriately identified, that their security and management needs are addressed, and that their housing placement will not result in risk of harm to themselves or others. As part of this screening, staff notify healthcare or mental health staff of any documented healthcare needs or notations regarding suicide risk conveyed by transporting officers. Most correctional systems have established policies (for an example of such policy, see Federal Bureau of Prisons, 2007) that result in identification of inmates with serious mental health care needs at the time of arrival, so that immediate mental health screening occurs prior to placement in general population. Medical screening is conducted at the time of arrival by trained healthcare staff. The purpose of medical screening is to ensure that a health history is completed, patients are assessed or observed to determine any current healthcare needs, and an appropriate medical disposition of each person occurs (ACA, 2003; NCCHC, 2008). Typically, nursing staff conduct arrival healthcare screenings and notify mental health staff of any urgent or emergent mental health issues at the time of arrival. Mental health staff conduct an intake assessment of arriving sentenced offenders ordinarily within 14 days.

All staff working in correctional facilities are trained in the recognition of signs and symptoms of suicide risk and mental illness. As a result, referrals to mental health staff are common under a variety of circumstances including evidence of mental illness, low cognitive functioning, changes in mood or adaptation, concern regarding potential for suicide, and/or concern for victimization. Such collaboration greatly extends the ability of mental health staff to respond to emerging needs of inmates throughout their incarceration.

Segregation units are another critical area where ongoing identification of mental illness is essential. Ideally, nurses or other healthcare staff conduct presegregation screening of inmates for active treatment needs and mental health concerns and rule out health-related contraindications to placement in segregation. If referral thresholds are met, contact with a physician, midlevel provider, or mental health staff member occurs. In a small number of cases, presegregation screening identifies medical and/or mental health issues that should preclude placement in segregation, and the inmate is placed on medical or mental health observation status. While an inmate is in segregation, accreditation standards require that mental health rounds are routinely made and that mental health evaluations are conducted at least upon the initial 30 days of placement and at a 90-day minimum thereafter to screen for deterioration of mental status or for other mental health treatment needs (ACA, 2003; NCCHC, 2008). As a best practice, some facilities conduct such screenings at every 30-day interval. During regular rounds, mental health staff ask security staff about changes in behavior, conduct concerns, and other potential indicators of the need for mental health services. In addition to information provided by the security officers, who are typically vigilant and observant of behavior nuances, mental health staff can access information in the form of segregation activity records for each inmate. In doing so, they can identify gradual changes in patterns of behavior related to meals, hygiene, recreation opportunities, and other activities, which may be subtle indicators of adjustment problems or mental illness.

Collaboration in Treatment

Mental health services in correctional systems must be integrated if they are to succeed in addressing patient care needs. Psychiatrists, psychologists, and other mental health practitioners collaborate as a team in delivering a range of assessment and treatment interventions to inmates. In most correctional facilities, mental health staffing consists of a psychologist or supervisory social worker, with one or more subordinate mental health staff. Usually, psychiatrists are part-time adjuncts to the correctional mental health team. Given the scarcity of psychiatric resources in corrections, psychologists and other mental health staff serve as a primary assessment resource in identifying patients who have a potential need for pharmacotherapy. These patients are typically seen by a psychiatrist or a primary care provider during scheduled clinics, or by means of telepsychiatry (Ax et al., 2007). Prescribing providers routinely collaborate with mental health staff members in delivery of care to the individuals with serious mental illness in a correctional facility. Practice in many correctional settings mirrors the literature regarding the efficacy of combining medication interventions with evidence-based psychological and behavioral interventions (Sudak, 2009). The goal of the mental health team is primarily to identify and provide clinically indicated services and access to necessary mental health treatment to individuals suffering from mental illness. Under ideal circumstances, mental health staffing is adequate to provide ancillary evidence-based treatment services consisting of group and individual treatment to assist with medication adherence, interventions with anxiety and depression, and other group activities related to anger management and basic life skills (NCCHC, 2008).

Close collaboration between medical and mental health staff in a primary care or outpatient setting has been shown to result in improved treatment outcomes in a number of studies related to treatment of depression (Schulberg et al., 1996; Unutzer et al., 2002). Proximity and access to mental health staff have been speculated to help some patients overcome their reluctance to see mental health staff (Uebecker, Weisberg, Haggarty, & Miller, 2009). Regular interactions between healthcare staff in different disciplines result in better integrated care overall and in regular referral of patients who have co-occurring conditions. In corrections settings, patients who have been recently diagnosed with communicable diseases or other significant medical conditions may benefit from psychological counseling as they adjust to this news and as they deal with ongoing healthcare issues and concerns. Similarly, mental health staff may see patients whose presenting issues fall within their purview but who warrant assessment and treatment for an underlying medical condition (e.g., mood issues or disorientation in an inmate who has an undiagnosed diabetic condition).

Mental health and medical staff regularly collaborate with other facility staff in issues related to patients receiving care. Collaboration occurs around facility schedules, ensuring inmates have access to medication at scheduled times; ensuring inmates are in the medical department area when they have been scheduled to be seen by a psychiatrist or other outside specialist; and ensuring mental health and other healthcare staff have access to inmates in secure units such as segregation so that assessment, care, or medication delivery occurs. In some cases, limited sharing of healthcare information is necessary with non-healthcare staff to ensure patients receive care or are monitored for specific health issues. Recognizing this need to collaborate in the interest of patient care, the Health Insurance Portability and Accountability Act (HIPAA) of 1996 has specific exemptions related to the confidentiality of patient healthcare information, which allow treatment providers to disclose information necessary for the provision of healthcare or the health and safety of the inmate or others in the correctional environment (U.S. Department of Health and Human Services, 1996).

Collaboration With Substance Abuse Staff

Because incarcerated individuals have a significantly higher rate of co-occurring disorders than the general population (Beckett & Sasson, 2000), inmates with a diagnosed co-occurring disorder provide a unique opportunity for mental health staff collaboration with substance abuse staff. In fact, inmates have about 4 times the rate of mental health disorders and 4 to 7 times the rate of substance abuse disorders than the general population (National GAINS Center, 1997). Unfortunately, most mental health and substance abuse treatment systems operate independently of one another, each with its own treatment philosophies, clinical approaches, administrative structures, and funding sources. Services are often uncoordinated, which can compromise the potential for effective treatment outcomes (National Association for State Mental Health Program Directors/National Association of State Alcohol and Drug Abuse Directors, 1998; Substance Abuse and Mental Health Services Administration, 2008).

However, research has demonstrated that an integrated approach to assessment and treatment, where a single clinician is providing the treatment for both the mental health and substance abuse disorders, is the most effective mode of treatment for co-occurring disorders. Services that are integrated provide support for each condition in one setting concurrently. For individuals under the supervision of the criminal justice system, integrated treatment is also the treatment of choice and should be considered a best practice in corrections (Edens, Peters, & Hills, 1997; Hurwitz, 2000; Peters, 2000). Interdisciplinary collaboration to provide treatment for individuals with co-occurring disorders supports the concept concerning the efficacy of integrated services (Mangrum, Spence, & Lopez, 2006; see Chapter 11 for more discussion on co-occurring disorders).

Collaboration With Special Needs Populations

Some correctional facilities have established special needs treatment teams or committees to ensure that patients with significant healthcare needs have access to care and are placed in appropriate housing, work, and program assignments. These multidisciplinary treatment teams usually have representatives from mental health, medical, unit management, and administrative ranks. On a monthly basis, or more frequently as needed, they review the care and management needs of identified inmates (American Correctional Association, 2003). Some decisions that must be made by this group of concerned staff involve identifying and implementing solutions to unique challenges presented by these inmates' conditions; improving their access to needed care; or placement in program, work, or housing assignments that improve staff monitoring of their adjustment and minimize vulnerability to victimization. The hypothetical case example presented in Text Box 8.3 provides an example of this type of collaboration.

TEXT BOX 8.3
CASE EXAMPLE

A high-security facility identified a concern regarding the management of offenders with mental illness and other vulnerable inmates in the facility. Observant staff noted that when inmates with mental illness engaged in behavior that was disruptive (e.g., angry verbal outbursts) or failed to meet expected norms (e.g., poor sanitation or hygiene, timeliness in reporting to assignments), other inmates were sometimes intolerant and tried to create circumstances that resulted in the inmates' removal from the unit. Similarly, some staff who were concerned about unit sanitation scores or other issues related to the smooth running of the unit were intolerant of low-level noncompliant behaviors in inmates with mental illness and responded in ways that resulted in an inmate's removal from the unit or placement in segregation.

The facility responded to these concerns by creating a special needs unit that provided a sheltered living space for inmates with mental illness, as well as others who were vulnerable due to low functioning or prior victimization. Inmates housed in the unit were assigned work within their abilities, escorted as a group to and from the commissary or laundry to reduce the chance others would attempt to take their possessions, and received other accommodations as their abilities and conditions warranted. The facility saw a reduction of the number of altercations and other negative incidents involving inmates with mental illness and a reduction in the number of inmates with mental illness who were transferred between units or into segregation units for low-level misconduct. Staff and inmates worked together in this unit to address problem behaviors and other concerns in a constructive manner.

Collaboration in Protecting the Vulnerable

Staff collaborate across disciplines within correctional facilities to identify and respond to the needs of at-risk or vulnerable populations. In the case example in Text Box 8.3, staff worked creatively to establish a sheltered living unit for inmates with serious mental illness or developmental disability. At times, correctional facilities have seen the wisdom of making special accommodations for several types of at-risk or vulnerable populations including older inmates, cognitively impaired or developmentally disabled inmates, physically disabled inmates, and inmates who have been victims of trauma.

Accommodations can include housing, work or program assignments, enhanced monitoring by mental health or medical staff, enhanced monitoring by security staff, or inclusion in the facility's special needs treatment program. The reasons for providing sheltered housing units or separate facilities for older inmates are generally applicable to other at-risk, or vulnerable, segments of the inmate population. These include cost savings accruing from access to centralized healthcare, reduction or avoidance of civil liability related to disability service issues, enhancement of safety, and advancing treatment opportunities appropriate to the population in question (Kerbs & Jolley, 2009). By consolidating groups of inmates with common needs, staff are provided with greater clarity of focus in support of inmate care.

Collaboration by Mental Health Staff Serving as Behavioral Consultants

It is not uncommon for a warden to request consultation from the correctional mental health clinicians about a specific component of the mental health delivery system or guidance concerning the management of a problematic inmate. The management of inmates who engage in serial self-harm acts, for example, poses challenges in terms of time and staff involvement and requires accurate communication and close coordination (Fagan, Cox, Helfand, & Aufderheide, 2010).

Whether considered by trained mental health staff, facility administrators, or security staff, basic principles of behavior analysis have been found useful as ways of thinking about and intervening with problem inmate behaviors. The concepts of behavioral baselines, understanding behavior trends, and positive and negative reinforcers of behavior have been useful to practitioners working in corrections. Collaboration is as essential as it is natural in developing understanding of and effective interventions regarding inmate behavior. This process requires mental health practitioners to be actively engaged throughout the facility in identifying and addressing behavior issues (see Chapter 14 for a more detailed discussion of behavior management plans).

Just a Cup of Coffee

Reciprocal communication is essential to the development of interdisciplinary collaboration. It is important that stereotypical labels that undermine the working relationship be addressed. For example, security officers may perceive the mental health staff as inmate advocates or "do-gooders." Mental health staff may see the officers as insensitive and unresponsive to the mental health needs of the inmates and lacking professionalism. Whatever the source of friction, it is imperative that the two talk. Mental health staff need to educate the officers about what they do and the reasons for why they do it. Mental health staff should actively solicit opinions and insights from officers about the problems they deal with on a daily basis. More often than not, correctional and mental health staff can learn more over "just a cup of coffee" than in a formal training setting. The approach to behavioral consultation noted in Text Box 8.4 illustrates the importance of mentoring the principles of awareness and visibility.

> **TEXT BOX 8.4**
> **CASE EXAMPLE**
>
> Both Drs. Tom Fagan and Jack McWay (retired psychology administrators from the Federal Bureau of Prisons) have served as mentors to many new psychologists working in federal corrections over the years. They independently advocated a similar approach to beginning each day in a correctional facility.
>
> 1. Upon entering the facility, have a first cup of coffee in the shift lieutenant's office while reading the security log regarding inmate issues taking place overnight. Make note of any issues involving inmates with mental illness or incidents that suggest mental health follow-up is needed.
>
> 2. Have a second cup of coffee in the segregation unit. Talk to staff about any inmates who are exhibiting behavior concerns, show a significant change in routine or demeanor, or have received bad news recently. Address any issues requiring immediate intervention and take note of other issues requiring routine follow-up.
>
> 3. Prioritize the issues noted during this early morning routine. As time permits between meetings or scheduled patients, follow up on these issues.

The merit of the approach outlined in Text Box 8.4 is evident in active identification of needs and prioritizing interventions. Over time, staff accept and appreciate the mental health clinician's interest and involvement, viewing him or her as a professional resource to help in problem solving and management of challenging issues in the facility.

Collaboration with staff provides insight into specific inmate behaviors as well as inconsistencies in staff response that reinforce negative behaviors. Brief interactions with inmates by specific staff usually do not provide a comprehensive understanding of an inmate. Staff in various disciplines and roles have unique opportunities to observe inmates and develop insights into factors that are salient motivators for their behavior. The most skilled mental health practitioners in corrections realize the inherent limits of time and circumstance in their interactions with inmates. They draw out these observations and insights about inmate behavior through conversations with the inmate and with multiple staff.

At times, details emerge that suggest staff are giving incongruent messages or are being inconsistent in their approach to addressing behavior. In secure units such as segregated housing units, differences between staff on one shift and a succeeding shift can have a profound effect on the interactions in the unit as well as specific inmate behaviors. Gradually, observations regarding the complex interplay between a specific inmate's behavior and the varied reinforcements presented in a correctional setting emerge.

Behavioral Excess?

Historically, objections have been raised regarding application of classical and operant conditioning principles in a correctional setting (American Psychological Association, 1975). For decades, if not centuries, prisons have been replete with examples of the use of sanctions and incentives to motivate inmates to engage in positive behavior. Correctional professionals, whether they are trained mental health staff, facility administrators, or security officers, observe behavior and attempt to engage inmates with sanctions and incentives to address behavior problems. Attention is given to behavior trends over time. Whether formally or informally, correctional staff consider salient incentives to address emerging behavior trends. In this context, psychologists and other correctional mental health staff have a unique opportunity to bring their observational skills and insights into human behavior to bear on complex issues that affect individual inmates, staff, safety, and security. The ability of mental health practitioners to observe behavior, draw conclusions, and intervene appropriately can lead to better outcomes for inmates, staff, and the facility.

Collaboration in Reducing Recidivism

"The way a team plays as a whole determines its success. You may have the greatest bunch of individual stars in the world, but if they don't play together, the club won't be worth a dime."

—Babe Ruth

In response to the myriad challenges faced by offenders with mental illness when being released back to their communities, correctional agencies have begun adding reentry planning to their public safety mission statements. At the federal level, initiatives are spurring the development of programs (Pogorzelski, Wolff, Pan, & Blitz, 2005) that will facilitate interdisciplinary collaboration between mental health delivery systems and community corrections programs (see Chapter 1 for a more detailed discussion of this topic). At the state and local levels, policy makers and mental health care providers are focusing their efforts on improving outcomes for individuals with mental illness by providing requisite transition assistance for released inmates to successfully reenter their communities.

In Florida, for example, the Department of Corrections (DC) and the Department of Children and Families (DCF) established an Interagency Agreement that significantly improved the prerelease planning process to ensure continuity of care for inmates with mental illness reentering the community (see Figure 8.1). Subsequently, DC partnered with the DCF to develop a web-based electronic referral system, called the Mental Health and Substance Abuse Referral System. The system was implemented across the state in 2008. This system allowed for the electronic interchange of confidential information between DC, DCF, and community mental health centers (CMHCs). The result was an intake appointment at a CMHC for every inmate who consented to receive the recommended continuity of care at the time of his or her release.

The system shown in Figure 8.1 is used to maximize the successful reentry of inmates with mental illness returning to their communities (Florida Department of Corrections, 2008).

Additionally, DC assigned aftercare specialists at institutions with inmates who were receiving psychiatric care. When an inmate's date of release is within 180 days, the aftercare specialists initiate their mental health reentry planning. Eligible inmates who consented to aftercare planning receive a 30-day supply of their prescribed medication, treatment on the day of their release, and an appointment with a community mental health provider. This initial intake appointment is always scheduled within the first 30 days of their release to provide continuity of care for their mental health treatment and continued medication treatment. The mental health reentry program also initiates

Figure 8.1 The Mental Health and Substance Abuse Web-Based Electronic Aftercare Referral System

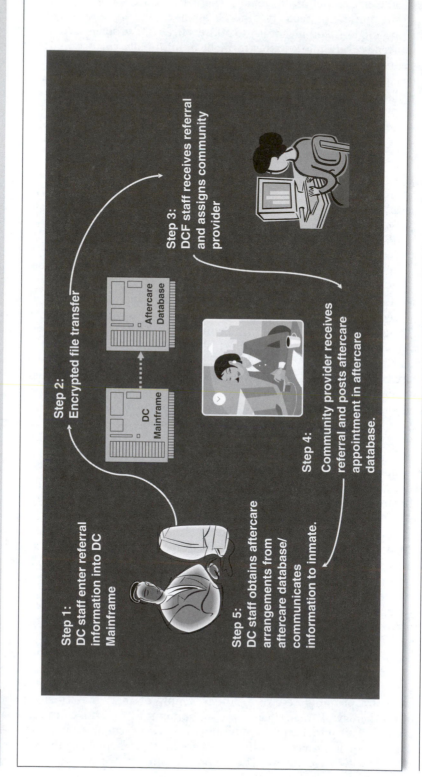

Source: Florida Department of Corrections (DC)/Department of Children and Families (DCF).

Social Security SSI/SSDI applications on all inmates that have been diagnosed with a severe and persistent mental illness 45 days prior to their release.

Mental health interventions and services can be an important component in the overall strategy to reduce recidivism (Pearson, Lipton, Cleland, & Yee, 2002). But successful efforts to reduce recidivism must incorporate linkages with an array of institutional programming and aftercare planning such as education (Zgoba, Haugebrook, & Jenkins, 2008), vocational training (Saylor & Gaes, 1997), and substance abuse treatment (Wexler, Lipton, & Johnson, 1988). By working together and implementing the principles of interdisciplinary collaboration, there is the opportunity for correctional mental health to be part of the solution that stops the relentlessly revolving door of arrest, incarceration, release, and reincarceration and, thereby, contribute to the public safety and welfare of our communities.

Summary and Conclusions

There is no doubt that correctional professionals work in a unique environment. From the security officer to the mental health professional, individuals who work in corrections are dedicated to a career of courage and honor in one of the most challenging settings imaginable. An excerpt from a message to departmental staff from Walter McNeil, secretary of the Florida Department of Corrections, illustrates the commitment to excellence and the innate importance of being part of something that is bigger than the individual correctional employee:

> Explorer Ernest Shackleton was known primarily for his expeditions to Antarctica, and for establishing all kinds of new records in exploring the continent. His was a life of exploration, adventure and challenge. Before taking one of his trips to the Antarctic, he assembled his crew by putting the following ad in a London newspaper: "Men wanted for hazardous journey. Small wages; bitter cold; long months of complete darkness; constant danger; safe return doubtful; honor and recognition in case of success." Thousands responded. It wasn't the job for everyone, but you can't say that those who signed on didn't know what they were getting into. The same could be said for our profession. (McNeil, 2009, p. 1)

As part of a team that "signed on" to work in a correctional setting, mental health professionals must understand the value of interdisciplinary collaborations as a way of improving offender conduct in prison, enhancing treatment efficacy, and reducing recidivism. While embracing a "what works" principle of management that focuses on ensuring treatment services match the level of assessed needs, it is imperative that mental health staff recognize that they are part of the correctional team and understand their role on the team. Interdisciplinary collaboration engenders credibility, and credibility is the touchstone for mental health leaders to be effective in ensuring the integrity of their mental health delivery systems.

Thus, whether at the practitioner or the administrative level, it is necessary to understand the importance of integrating mental health mission requirements into overall correctional programming. Although the core mission of correctional agencies is public safety (Kroner et al., 2007), it is crucially important that mental health clinicians collaborate with the correctional leadership to surmount the challenges associated with providing constitutionally adequate care with limited resources to a high number of inmates with mental illness. Examining the obstacles impacting the practice of correctional psychology during his 37-year career, the reflections of a retired correctional psychologist underscore the importance of interdisciplinary collaboration:

> These variables range from the availability of economic resources, the facility administrator's management and correctional philosophy and opinion about psychologists and their appropriate role in the facility, strained relationships with security and other institutional staff who may harbor anti-offender attitudes and biases, numbers and qualifications of other mental health services providers, limited availability of treatment and support resources, controlled access to inmates, stressed relationships with community agents, and limited availability of community mental health resources. (Althouse, 2009, p. 13)

There are, without a doubt, problems and obstacles that will emerge in the challenges associated with developing durable and productive interdisciplinary collaborations. But obstacles are opportunities in work clothes. By working together to strengthen partnerships, appreciating the needs and capabilities of all correctional staff, and understanding that the whole is greater than the sum of its parts, correctional mental health professionals can be model participants in interdisciplinary collaboration. Mental health providers must seize the opportunity because, in the end, the success of a correctional system's mission will always depend on the effective interdisciplinary collaboration of all its stakeholders.

KEY TERMS

Interdisciplinary collaboration

Treatment efficacy

Recidivism

Treatment outcome

Institutional adjustment

Continuity of care

Institutional rule infraction

Classification

Unit management

Case manager

Treatment team

Evidence-based programs

Evidence-based research

Defusing crises

Principles of reinforcement

Estelle v. Gamble

American Correctional Association

Behavioral consultation

National Commission on Correctional Health Care (NCCHC)

Segregation units

Segregation rounds

Telehealth

Health Insurance Portability and Accountability Act (HIPAA) of 1996

Co-occurring disorders

Integrated treatment approach

Special needs population

DISCUSSION QUESTIONS

1. Can you think of other ways in which correctional mental health and security staff can collaborate to improve the safe, smooth, and orderly running of the correctional institution?

2. Can correctional mental health providers be effective in treating inmates without regular consultation with other correctional workers? Explain your answer.

3. Is it unethical for correctional mental health staff to share inmate information with other correctional workers such as teachers, work detail supervisors, and correctional administrators? Explain your answer.

4. What do you think might be the effect on the patient-therapist relationship if information obtained in treatment is shared with other staff? Should inmate-patients be advised that confidentiality does not exist within correctional settings?

5. Do you see any basis for collaboration between mental health care and religious services staff?

6. Imagine that you are a community mental health care provider. How do you feel about the prospect of having ex-offenders assigned to your case load and seeing them in a nonsecure environment? How should the Department of Corrections support your work with these patients?

References

Adams, K., & Ferrandino, J. (2008). Managing mentally ill inmates in prisons. *Criminal Justice and Behavior, 35*, 913–927.

Althouse, R. (2009). Reflections and perspectives. *The Correctional Psychologist, 41*(2), 12–15.

American Correctional Association. (2003). *Standards for adult correctional institutions* (4th ed.). Lanham, MD: Author.

American Psychological Association. (1975). Behavior mod in federal prisons: GAO reports on a vanishing act. *Monitor on Psychology, 6*, 12.

Andrews, D., & Bonta, J. (2003). *The psychology of criminal conduct* (3rd ed.). Cincinnati, OH: Anderson.

Applebaum, K. L., Hickey, J. M., & Packer, I. (2001).The role of correctional officers in multidisciplinary mental health care in prisons. *Psychiatric Services, 52*, 1343–1347.

Ax, R. K., Fagan, T. J., Magaletta, P. R., Morgan, R. D., Nussbaum, D., & White, T. W. (2007). Innovations in correctional assessment and treatment. *Criminal Justice and Behavior, 34*, 893–905.

Beckett, K., & Sasson, T. (2000). *The politics of injustice: Crime and punishment in America.* Thousand Oaks, CA: Pine Forge Press.

Bonner, R. L. (2006). Stressful segregated housing and psychosocial vulnerability in prison suicide ideators. *Suicide and Life-Threatening Behavior, 36*, 263–267.

Dean v. Coughlin, 623 F. Supp. 392, 404 (S.D.N.Y. 1985).

Duran v. Anaya, 642 F. Supp. 510, 524 (D. N.M. 1986).

Edens, J. F., Peters, R. H., & Hills, H. A. (1997). Treating prison inmates with co-occurring disorders: An integrative review of existing programs. *Behavioral Sciences and the Law, 15*, 439–457.

Estelle v. Gamble, 429 U.S. 97 (1976).

Fagan, T. J., Cox, J., Helfand, S., & Aufderheide, D. (2010). Self-injurious behavior in correctional settings. *Journal of Correctional Health Care, 16*(1), 48–66.

Federal Bureau of Prisons. (2007). *SENTRY psychology alert function.* Washington, DC: Author.

Florida Department of Corrections. (2008). Mental health re-entry aftercare planning services in *Health Services Bulletin,* No. 15.05.21. Retrieved May 25, 2009, from http://dcweb/co/Health/hsb/15-05-21.doc

French, S., & Gendreau, P. (2006). Reducing prison misconducts: What works! *Criminal Justice and Behavior, 33*, 185–218.

Gendreau, P., Goggin, C., & Smith, P. (1999). The forgotten issue in effective correctional treatment: Program implementation. *International Journal of Offender Therapy and Comparative Criminology, 43*, 180–187.

Hurwitz, J. E. (2000). *Mental illness and substance abuse in the criminal justice system*. Cincinnati, OH: The Health Foundation of Greater Cincinnati.

Kerbs, J., & Jolley, J. (2009). A commentary on age segregation for older prisoners: Philosophical and pragmatic considerations for correctional systems. *Criminal Justice Review, 34*, 119–139.

Kroner, D., Mills, J., Reitzel, L., Dow, E., Aufderheide, D., & Railey, M. (2007). Directions for violence and sexual risk assessment in correctional psychology. *Criminal Justice and Behavior, 34*, 906–918.

Mangrum, L. F., Spence, R., & Lopez, M. (2006). Integrated versus parallel treatment of co-occurring psychiatric and substance abuse disorders. *Journal of Substance Abuse Treatment, 30*, 79–84.

Margulies, N., & Wallace, J. (1973). *Organizational change: Techniques and applications*. Glenview, IL: Scott, Foresman.

McNeil, W. (2009, July 3-10). Secretary's message: Doing the right thing. *Correctional Compass Weekly*, 1.

National Association for State Mental Health Program Directors/National Association of State Alcohol and Drug Abuse Directors. (1998). *The new conceptual framework for co-occurring mental health and substance use disorders*. Washington, DC: National Association for State Mental Health Program Directors.

National Commission on Correctional Health Care. (2008). *Standards for mental health services in correctional facilities*. Chicago, IL: Author.

National GAINS Center for People with Co-Occurring Disorders in the Justice System. (1997). *The prevalence of co-occurring mental and substance abuse disorders in the criminal justice system: Just the Facts Series*. Delmar, NY: Author.

Pearson, F. S., Lipton, D. S., Cleland, C. M., & Yee, D. S. (2002). The effects of behavioral/cognitive-behavioral programs on recidivism. *Crime & Delinquency, 48*, 476–496.

Peters, R. H. (2000). *Screening, assessment, and treatment strategies for offenders with co-occurring disorders* (SAMI Training Series). Hamilton, OH: SAMI.

Pogorzelski, W., Wolff, N., Pan, K., & Blitz, C. (2005). Behavioral health problems, ex-offender reentry policies, and the "Second Chance Act." *American Journal of Public Health, 95*, 1718–1724.

Saylor, W. G., & Gaes, G. G. (1997). Training inmates through industrial work participation and apprenticeship instruction. *Corrections Management Quarterly, 1*, 32–43.

Schulberg, H., Block, M., Madonia, M., Scott, C., Rodriguez, E., Imber, S., et al. (1996). Treating major depression in primary care practice: Eight month clinical outcomes. *Archives of General Psychiatry, 53*, 913–919.

Substance Abuse and Mental Health Services Administration, Office of Applied Studies. (2008). *The NSDUH Report: Serious psychological distress and receipt of mental health service*. Rockville, MD: Author.

Sudak, D. (2009). Training in cognitive behavioral therapy in psychiatry residency: An overview for educators. *Behavior Modification, 33*, 124–137.

Uebecker, L., Weisberg, R., Haggarty, R., & Miller, I. (2009). Adapted behavior therapy for persistently depressed primary care patients: An open trial. *Behavior Modification, 33*, 374–397.

Unutzer, J., Katon, W., Callahan, C., Williams, J., Hunkeler, E., Harpole, L., et al. (2002). Collaborative care management of late-life depression in the primary care setting: A randomized controlled trial. *Journal of the American Medical Association, 288*, 2836–2845.

U.S. Department of Health and Human Services. (1996, August 21). Health Insurance Portability and Accountability Act of 1996, Pub. L. No. 104-191, 104th Congress, Sections 164.51 (k) and (h). Washington, DC: Author. Retrieved June 3, 2009, from http://aspe.hhs.gov/admnsimp/pL104191.htm

Wexler, H. K., Lipton, D. S., & Johnson, B. D. (1988). The drug-crime connection: Rehabilitation shows promise. *Corrections Today, 50*(5), 144–147.

Zgoba, K. M., Haugebrook, S., & Jenkins, K. (2008). The influence of GED obtainment on inmate release outcome. *Criminal Justice and Behavior, 35*, 375–387.

SECTION III

Working With Special Populations

CHAPTER 9

Offenders With Severe and Persistent Mental Illness

Rebecca L. Bauer, Robert D. Morgan, and Jon T. Mandracchia

Introduction

The purpose of this chapter is to review prevalence and epidemiological issues affecting offenders with mental illness (OMIs). Specifically, the population of OMIs in all correctional arenas including probation, jail, prison, and parole will be discussed. The iatrogenic effects of criminal justice sanctions for OMIs will also be reviewed. The remainder of the chapter will focus on treatment-related issues including barriers to OMIs' utilizing mental health services, evidenced-based treatments for OMIs, and treatment issues with regard to community reentry. The chapter will conclude with a brief review of a promising new program specifically designed for this population of offenders.

Prevalence of Mental Illness in the Criminal Justice System

The United States continues to have high incarceration rates with well over 2 million offenders incarcerated in federal and state prisons, as well as in local jail systems (Minton & Sabol, 2009; West & Sabol, 2009). In addition, there are more than 5 million offenders supervised in the community (i.e., probation and parole; Glaze & Bonczar, 2008).

Development of this chapter was supported in part by the National Institute of Mental Health (R34 MH070401–01A1).

Recent Bureau of Justice Statistics survey results suggest that approximately 14% to 24% of these incarcerated offenders (i.e., including jail, state, and federal inmates) reported a history of mental health problems, including either being diagnosed with a mental disorder, having been admitted to a hospital due to mental health symptoms, having been prescribed medication, or receiving psychotherapy (James & Glaze, 2006). Additionally, it has been estimated that 16% of probationers have a mental illness or have been psychiatrically hospitalized (Ditton, 1999). An estimated 10% of parolees have a severe mental illness (Lurigio, 2001).

Individuals with severe mental illness are at a greater risk of being arrested and incarcerated than individuals without a severe mental illness (Munetz, Grande, & Chambers, 2001; Teplin, 1984, 1990), resulting in major mental disorders being 4 times more prevalent among incarcerated offenders than the general population (Hodgins, 1995). In fact, there are 3 times more individuals with severe mental illnesses in the U.S. prison system than in our mental health hospitals (Abramsky & Fellner, 2003). Although recently criticized as a theory for increased incarceration rates for OMIs, one historical theory has suggested the overrepresentation of OMIs in criminal justice settings has been a consequence of deinstitutionalization (Lamb & Bachrach, 2001; Lamb & Weinberger, 1998; Teplin, 1984). The deinstitutionalization movement sought to reduce the number of individuals with mental illness admitted to state psychiatric hospitals. Although this goal was accomplished, the development of appropriate community treatment alternatives has not been realized (Lamb & Bachrach, 2001), resulting in insufficient and limited outpatient treatment options and, at times, inadequate care (Lamb & Bachrach, 2001; Lamb & Weinberger, 1998). As a result, correctional facilities are currently the leading mental health care providers in the United States (Abramsky & Fellner, 2003).

Population Descriptions for Probation, Jail, Prison, and Parole

OMIs present with co-occurring disorders, including severe mental illnesses (e.g., schizophrenia, bipolar disorder, and major depression), substance abuse, and antisocial personality disorder (Abram & Teplin, 1991). Prior to incarceration, many OMIs have had previous psychiatric hospitalizations (Fisher et al., 2002), as well as multiple contacts with the criminal justice system (Lamb & Weinberger, 1998), including a history of incarceration in state prisons (Lamb, Weinberger, Marsh, & Gross, 2007). Not surprisingly, the majority of OMIs have been psychiatrically hospitalized during incarceration (Lamb et al., 2007).

OMIs' pattern of cycling in and out of both the mental health and criminal justice systems may be explained by the results put forth by Morgan, Fisher, Duan, Mandracchia, and Murray (2010). Their investigation showed that OMIs present with psychological symptoms similar to those demonstrated by psychiatric inpatients (see Figure 9.1), which is congruent with the notion that OMIs should receive mental health treatment similar to that provided to nonoffenders with mental illness. Additionally, OMIs show similar, and frequently more elevated, levels of criminal thinking (see Figure 9.2) and criminal attitudes (see Figure 9.3) compared to offenders without mental illness. Thus, OMIs may present as a challenge to mental health and criminal justice professionals because of their dual treatment needs (i.e., mental health and criminogenic needs).

Within corrections, OMIs present challenges to correctional management while incarcerated. Specifically, OMIs average more disciplinary infractions per year than

| Figure 9.1 | Comparison of Mentally Ill Inmates' MCMI-III Scores With a Psychiatric Inpatient Sample |

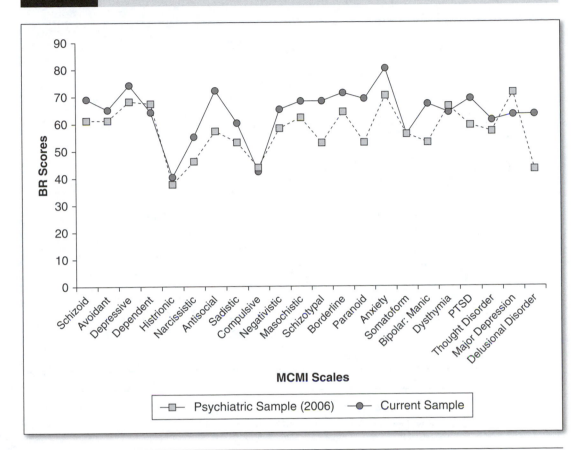

Source: Schoenber, Dorr, and Morgan (2006).

Note: MCMI = Millon Clinical Multiaxial Inventory; BR = Base Rate; PTSD = post-traumatic stress disorder.

nondisordered offenders (Feder, 1991; James & Glaze, 2006; O'Keefe & Schnell, 2008), resulting in their inability to qualify for early release options (i.e., parole; Lurigio, 2001). For example, due to institutional misconduct, OMIs are often prevented from participating in programs in which they can acquire good time, thus limiting their ability to go before parole boards (Lurigio, 2001). Additionally, Feder (1994) found offenders psychiatrically hospitalized during incarceration were much less likely to be granted parole. Thus, it appears OMIs are more likely to serve out a maximum sentence than offenders without mental illness (Jemelka, Trupin, & Chiles, 1989; Lurigio, 2001).

OMIs supervised in the community present unique challenges to probation and parole officers. As with incarcerated offenders, OMIs on probation or parole also present with co-occurring disorders. In fact, it has been estimated that approximately 75% of probationers with mental illness have a substance abuse disorder in addition to a severe mental illness (Lurigio, 2001). Probationers and parolees with mental illness are more likely to have their probation or parole revoked than their nondisordered counterparts. In fact, OMIs on probation were almost 2 times

| **Figure 9.2** | Comparison of Mentally Ill Male Inmates' PICTS Scales With Two Samples of Non–Mentally Ill Male Prison Samples |

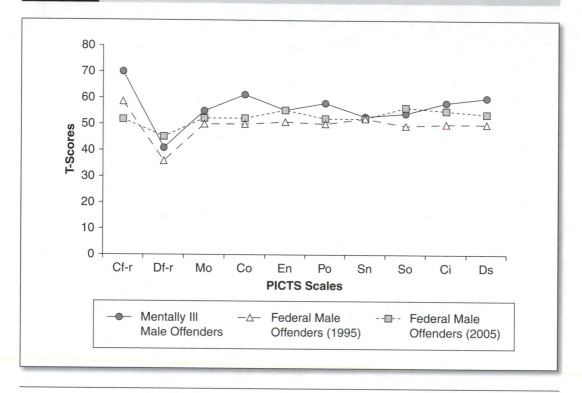

Source: Walters (1995); Walters and Geyer (2005).

Note: PICTS = Psychological Inventory of Criminal Thinking; Cf-r = revised Confusion scale; Df-r = revised Defensiveness scale; Mo = Mollification; Co = Cutoff; En = Entitlement; Po = Power Orientation; Sn = Sentimentality; So = Superoptimism; Ci = Cognitive Indolence; Ds = Discontinuity.

more likely to have been rearrested over a 3-year period than probationers without mental illness (Dauphinot, 1997). Additionally, OMIs on parole were twice as likely to have their parole suspended without committing a new offense (Porporino & Motiuk, 1995), likely due to more intensive supervision (Skeem & Eno Louden, 2006; Solomon, Draine, & Marcus, 2002).

Notably, OMIs may present with impairments due to the presence of mental health symptoms, which nondisordered offenders do not evidence, that lead to revocations (Dauphinot, 1997; Skeem & Eno Louden, 2006). For example, obtaining and maintaining employment, as well as paying community supervision fees, are often requirements of probation or parole. However, an individual with a severe mental illness may find complying with these requirements a difficult task (Dauphinot, 1997; Skeem & Eno Louden, 2006). Furthermore, as noted above, a majority of OMIs present with substance abuse disorders, potentially leading to drug-testing failures and subsequent revocations (Skeem & Eno Louden, 2006). Lastly, the mere presence of psychiatric symptoms may place OMIs on probation and parole at increased risk for rearrest (Munetz et al., 2001; Teplin, 1984, 1990).

Figure 9.3   Comparison of CSS-M Scale Scores for Male and Female Offenders With Mental Illness With a Non–Mentally Ill Offender Sample

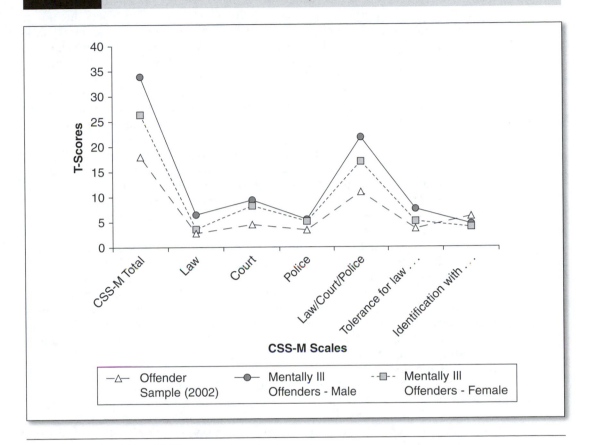

CSS-M Scales

Legend:
- —△— Offender Sample (2002)
- —●— Mentally Ill Offenders - Male
- -■- Mentally Ill Offenders - Female

Source: Simourd and Olver (2002).

Iatrogenic Effects of Criminal Justice Sanctions

With more than 2 million offenders housed in U.S. jails and prisons (Minton & Sabol, 2009; West & Sabol, 2009), overcrowding results. Oftentimes, overcrowding negatively impacts the psychological well-being of offenders within corrections, promoting, for example, high levels of self-reported stress, hypertension, and behavior problems (Bonta & Gendreau, 1990). Confinement is a stressful event as well. Inmates (both male and female) experience stress in reaction to the transition from the outside world to prison life, as evidenced by an increase in blood pressure, anxiety, and depression (Islam-Zwart, Vik, & Rawlins, 2007; MacKenzie & Goodstein, 1985). Although symptoms decrease over time (Islam-Zwart et al., 2007; MacKenzie & Goodstein, 1985; Paulus & Dzindolet, 1993; Zamble, 1992) prisonization may also occur. A recent study by Walters (2003) suggested that newly incarcerated offenders (with no prior history of incarceration) evidenced increased criminal thinking and the development of a criminal identity during incarceration, as a way of coping with the prison environment. This seemingly adaptive response is likely maladaptive once the offender returns to society (Walters, 2003).

As OMIs receive more disciplinary infractions (see earlier), they are more likely to be placed in administrative segregation, which may be particularly damaging to general mental health functioning (Coid et al., 2003; Zinger, Wichmann, & Andrews, 2001). Segregated inmates may develop a wide range of psychological problems, including social withdrawal (Miller & Young, 1997); disturbed appetite and sleep (Haney, 2003); delusional beliefs, depressed mood, and aggressive behavior (Kupers, 1996); anxiety, hallucinations, memory and concentration impairments, and suicidal and homicidal ideation (Grassian & Friedman, 1985), often resulting in psychiatric hospitalization (Rold, 1992). Others have suggested that the effects of segregation are not so deleterious. Psychological problems resulting from placement in segregation can be avoided by limiting duration (Bonta & Gendreau, 1990) and by creating a humane segregation environment, including proper nutrition, opportunities to participate in some activities or programs, and nondetrimental treatment from prison staff (Suedfeld, Ramirez, Deaton, & Baker-Brown, 1982). In particular, Zinger et al. (2001) found no evidence of psychological deterioration in inmates who had been segregated for 2 months. The authors, however, recognized that this finding was not applicable across all settings; in fact, they specified that offenders in the United States tend to be segregated much longer and under more desolate conditions.

The findings regarding the effects of segregation, however, were limited to offenders not suffering from severe mental disorders (e.g., schizophrenia, bipolar disorder, major depressive disorder). In fact, there has been a paucity of research conducted on the effects of incarceration on individuals with severe mental illness. Individual differences and institutional variables may impact how well an inmate adjusts to long-term incarceration (Bonta & Gendreau, 1990; Bukstel & Kilmann, 1980; Paulus & Dzindolet, 1993; Wright, 1993), and OMIs may not have the skills necessary to adjust to the prison environment while simultaneously trying to cope with and manage their psychiatric symptoms.

In fact, it appears that OMIs do function differently than non-OMIs in prison. For example, as a result of the presence of severe psychiatric symptoms, some OMIs display deficits in behavioral and emotional control, social skills, and problem-solving skills, as well as distorted cognitions and perceptions (Abramsky & Fellner, 2003). Therefore, OMIs may display disruptive, noncompliant, and at times aggressive behaviors in reaction to the demands and requirements of prison life (Abramsky & Fellner, 2003).

Of additional and perhaps greater concern is the potential for victimization. OMIs are more likely to be physically and sexually assaulted by non–mentally disordered inmates while in prison (Abramsky & Fellner, 2003). Wolff, Blitz, and Shi (2007) found that 1 in 12 male OMIs reported sexual victimization by another inmate over a 6-month period, compared with 1 in 33 nondisordered inmates. Furthermore, it was found that female OMIs report sexual assault at a 3 times higher rate. Victimization may result in psychiatric instability, decreased ability to function in the environment, and increased institutional suffering.

In the only investigation of the effects of long-term incarceration on OMIs, preliminary findings from Morgan, Bauer, and colleagues (2009) indicated that for female OMIs, the amount of time served in prison was significantly associated with more mental health symptoms, including increased symptoms associated with severe clinical syndromes (e.g., mood, thought, and delusional disorders). Additionally, as the amount of time spent in prison increased, so did the female OMIs' criminal thinking and criminal attitudes, as well as the number of disciplinary infractions received. These preliminary findings suggested that some OMIs evidence an increase in psychiatric symptomatology, criminal thinking and attitudes, and poorer institutional behavior the longer they are incarcerated.

Although questions remain regarding the effects of incarceration, solitary confinement, and overcrowding among prisoners (Bonta & Gendreau, 1990; Bukstel & Kilmann, 1980), OMIs have not generally been included in these investigations. Notably, it does appear OMIs experience incarceration differently (Abramsky & Fellner, 2003; Morgan et al., 2010). Thus, it is necessary to further examine the potential impact criminal justice sanctions have on OMIs to better serve this population and maintain individual and public safety.

Barriers to Treatment Utilization for Offenders With Mental Illness

Despite efforts to maintain pace with offenders' needs for mental health services, the dilemma in ensuring that offenders with psychological problems receive proper mental health services may derive more from characteristics of the offenders than those of the correctional institutions in which they are housed. There are several reasons that inmates with psychological problems may not participate in mental health treatment. Some of these appear to be their preferences, attitudes, perceptions, and past experiences related to mental health (Steffan & Morgan, 2005). Regarding inmates' preferences for specific aspects of mental health services, most inmates who receive mental health services while incarcerated prefer individual treatment versus a group treatment format (Morgan, Rozycki, & Wilson, 2004). Given this preference, it is encouraging to note that despite the general sentiment that mental health resources are limited in correctional settings, Boothby and Clements (2000) found that conducting individual sessions accounts for more than half of correctional psychologists' treatment provision time, compared to less than one-sixth for group sessions. In addition to differential preference for type of treatment modality, inmates also seem to have a preference for type of treatment provider. Specifically, inmates have indicated that they primarily prefer receiving mental health services from psychologists or professional counselors and then, in order of decreasing preference, from psychiatrists, addiction counselors, and social workers (Morgan et al., 2004).

Beyond preferences related to how and by whom mental health treatment is provided, individual demographics appear to be an important consideration in offenders' seeking or avoiding mental health treatment. An inmate's race and ethnicity is one area that has consistently been examined as potentially related to attitude toward and willingness to engage in mental health treatment. Studies across time and location have found that racial and ethnic minorities, when in prison, report more negative attitudes about mental health services and are less likely to initiate engagement in mental health services, but they do not report different intentions to seek help for psychological problems from mental health providers (Deane, Skogstad, & Williams, 1999; Skogstad, Deane, & Spicer, 2006; Steadman, Holohean, & Dvoskin, 1991).

In addition to race, other characteristics of inmates appear to be related to their attitudes and behaviors related to mental health services. Evidence suggests that inmates who are male (Reinsmith-Meyer, 2008; Steadman et al., 1991), inmates who are younger (Reinsmith-Meyer, 2008; Skogstad et al., 2006), and inmates without previous positive experiences receiving mental health treatment (Deane et al., 1999) report more concerns about receiving, and are less apt to access, mental health services. Of particular interest related to this last aspect (i.e., prior mental health treatment), Skogstad et al. (2006) found that inmates who had previously received mental health services while incarcerated reported lower intentions to seek assistance for suicidal ideation compared to inmates who had not. However, inmates who had previously received mental health services while in the community reported higher intentions to seek such assistance compared to inmates who had not.

Inmates recently incarcerated also reported significantly higher concerns about mental health services (Morgan et al., 2004). Specifically, those recently incarcerated were less aware of how and when to appropriately seek mental health services, were apprehensive about the length and quality of treatment they might receive, were concerned about the influence that receiving services would have on their reputations amongst other inmates (e.g., seen as weak or a snitch), were afraid that receiving psychological treatment would signify that they were "crazy," and were uneasy about issues of confidentiality. Morgan et al. (2004) suggested that newly incarcerated inmates may be more conservative in their approach to mental health services because of preconceptions about life in prison, and they may be cautious as a form of self-protection (Morgan et al., 2004). Although being overly cautious can be adaptive for inmates who are adjusting to the prison subculture, their avoidance of seeking and participating in mental health services may be perpetuating high rates of untreated mental illness in correctional institutions.

Inmates' participation in mental health services may also be influenced by the type of problems they experience. Steadman, McCarty, and Morrissey (1989) found that inmates were more willing to ask for assistance with personal and emotional issues than for suicidal ideation. This is particularly troublesome, considering the severity of potential negative consequences of untreated suicidal ideation. Steadman et al. (1989) reasoned that inmates who experience suicidal ideation may be attempting to avoid being placed in seclusion, have low motivation to engage in treatment due to feelings of hopelessness and depression, fear negative perceptions from staff and other inmates, distrust mental health providers, or believe that the institution will implement aversive conditions to manage suicidal inmates. Nearly two decades later, Skogstad et al. (2006) provided similar explanations in stating that inmates who were suicidal may intentionally hide their mental state because conveying suicidality may result in a restriction on allowable possessions, close monitoring of their behavior, special housing status that is worse than general population housing, and perceptions of weakness from other inmates. A qualitative study with English prisoners also provided similar findings (Howerton et al., 2007).

Although perceptions about, and intentions and willingness to engage in, mental health services are attenuated by numerous factors, overall, prisoners have shown to be hesitant to seek mental health services despite being a population with disproportionately high rates of mental health problems (Brinded, Simpson, Laidlaw, Fairley, & Malcolm, 2001). Reinsmith-Meyer (2008) found that nearly 20% of inmates with significant mental health concerns participated in no mental health treatment programming offered throughout the entirety of their sentence. Some of these inmates indicated that they were hesitant to become involved in mental health services because of stigmatization of mental illness, concerns that treatment would not be effective, or a lack of motivation to engage in any programming or other activities during their incarceration. Other inmates, however, indicated that they had been willing, but unable, to utilize mental health services because they would not be housed in the institution long enough to receive treatment, they had been placed on a waitlist but had not begun receiving services, they were denied treatment, or the programs they wanted were not available (Reinsmith-Meyer, 2008). Although inmates with severe mental illness are more likely to receive mental health services than inmates with little or no mental health concerns, about half of the most disturbed inmates in one study received no services for a period of up to 1 year (Steadman et al., 1991).

Although the discrepancy between the prevalence of mental health problems and participation in mental health services in prison is alarming, the situation may be even worse in jails. Steadman and Veysey (2007) reported that less than 10% of inmates in jail received mental health services, which is a rate much lower than that seen amongst prison inmates. This finding is especially poignant given that the rate of suicide amongst jail inmates is approximately 3 times higher than for prison inmates (Mumola, 2005).

Offenders' reasons to avoid mental health services have been reduced to four primary factors: self-preservation (e.g., issues of confidentiality, negative perceptions from other inmates), procedural issues (e.g., not knowing when, how, or why to request mental health services or how long they could expect to receive services), maintaining self-reliance (e.g., relying only on themselves or close associates for help), and concerns about mental health providers (e.g., the training and qualification of mental health staff, previous negative experiences receiving mental health services [Morgan, Steffan, Shaw, & Wilson, 2007]). Morgan et al. (2004) found that despite inmates' propensity to report an array of reasons why they may not want to initiate participation in mental health services, inmates generally did not identify these reasons as being strongly prohibitive of seeking services. Skogstad et al. (2006), however, warn that research in the area of barriers to mental health treatment in correctional settings may not adequately represent reality. They suggest the inmates who agree to participate in this area of research are likely to be more trusting of mental health workers than those who decline to participate, which may be creating a bias towards positive attitudes and increased willingness to seek mental health services, thus underrepresenting the barriers to mental health services for inmates. Therefore, even Morgan et al.'s (2004) findings of "neutral" feelings towards services may be overly positive for the entire inmate population.

Overall, however, general themes consistently arise as barriers to inmates seeking mental health services. Therefore, efforts to address these barriers should focus on increasing inmates' trust in mental health professionals, educating inmates about the nature of mental illness and the process and proper procedures for receiving mental health services, combating negative perceptions about the outcomes of reporting mental health concerns, and decreasing stigma associated with mental illness. Efforts to better educate inmates are likely to be particularly warranted when inmates first arrive at an institution, particularly a jail, and when inmates have had negative prior experiences receiving mental health services.

In addition to educating inmates about mental illness and mental health services in correctional institutions, efforts to improve how correctional and mental health staff deal with inmates' mental health issues may increase inmates' willingness to seek and participate in mental health services. For example, correctional officers may benefit from receiving education about mental illness and basic training on interacting with inmates with mental illness. In addition, mental health staff may benefit from being made aware of how their behavior can perpetuate potential negative consequences for inmates who receive mental health treatment. All staff working in correctional institutions should promote an atmosphere in which inmates' mental health issues are understood, dealt with professionally, and kept confidential.

Best Practices for Offenders With Mental Illness

Services for OMIs include basic mental health services and/or rehabilitation services. Basic mental health services include general assessment or treatment services that are available to all inmates (Morgan, 2003). These services are not specifically defined and are available to meet a variety of offender needs (e.g., symptom reduction, coping with incarceration) as they arise. Rehabilitation services, on the other hand, focus specifically on reducing criminal behavior and recidivism (return to the criminal justice system because of failure on release or new charges; Morgan, 2003; Morgan, Winterowd, & Ferrell, 1999).

There is a dearth of empirical research guiding effective treatment strategies for OMIs. In fact, "treatment outcome research on mentally ill offenders specifically is almost nonexistent" (Rice & Harris, 1997, p. 164), and such studies "are as scarce now as they were 30 years ago. . . . Too few programs are being developed and too few promising programs are being tested with the rigor that would yield the proof needed to label them as evidence-based" (Snyder, 2007, p. 6). Thus, clinicians treating OMIs are without efficacy or effectiveness data on which to base their practices. In fact, the therapeutic needs of OMIs are so neglected that there is limited data to guide the design of interventions. Consequently, clinicians are left searching for the most effective correctional treatment and rehabilitative methods for OMIs to alleviate suffering (e.g., reduced symptomatology, improved subjective well-being) during periods of confinement and subsequently reduce psychiatric and criminal recidivism (rehabilitation) when released back into society (i.e., reentry). Although there is a paucity of specific treatment interventions designed and scientifically tested for OMIs, there is promise when one examines the two growing bodies of research in the criminal justice and mental health sectors suggesting effective treatment strategies. Both will be discussed below. The key is to combine both bodies of research to develop integrated treatment strategies that can be empirically evaluated and ultimately proven beneficial for OMIs.

Evidence-Based Criminal Justice Interventions for Offenders

The most effective correctional rehabilitative programs adhere to the theory of Risk-Need-Responsivity (R-N-R; Andrews & Bonta, 2006). R-N-R, as outlined by Andrews, Bonta, and Hoge (1990), presents three principles of effective interventions. According to the Risk principle, services are more effective when provided to offenders at high risk for reoffending. Thus, offenders should be matched to services based on their level of risk for criminal recidivism (Andrews, Bonta, et al., 1990). Consequently, those at highest risk receive the most intensive rehabilitation services. The Need principle dictates that rehabilitative services must target the specific risks associated with criminal recidivism. These risk factors, known as criminogenic needs, are dynamic (changeable) and include, for example, antisocial cognitions, peer associations, substance use, work or school functioning, and leisure activities (Andrews, Bonta, et al., 1990; Gendreau, 1996a). Effective rehabilitation programs specifically target these needs (Andrews & Bonta, 2006; Gendreau, 1996a). The principal of Responsivity asserts that rehabilitative services should be based on behavioral, cognitive-behavioral, and social learning theories (Andrews & Bonta, 2006) to match offenders' needs and learning styles (Gendreau, 1996a). That is, to be effective, service providers need to consider the needs (e.g., learning style, personality, cognitive ability, etc.) of offenders to develop prosocial skills and ultimately be responsive to these needs.

Is R-N-R effective? A well-reasoned theory with high face validity is of minimal practical utility if it does not produce improved outcomes. In other words, does the implementation of the principles of R-N-R produce behavioral change such as reduced criminal behavior and criminal recidivism? A comprehensive meta-analytic review demonstrated a significant reduction in criminal recidivism of 10% (estimated percentage based on 443 effect sizes; note that effect size is a measure of the magnitude of a treatment effect) with treatment variables related to principles of risk and responsivity (Lipsey, 1989, as cited in Andrews & Bonta, 2006). Subsequent studies provided direct examination of principles of R-N-R and produced similarly positive results. Examination of a therapeutic program grounded in principles of R-N-R within the Texas Department of Criminal Justice resulted in reduced disciplinary infractions, staff assaults, and inmate assaults (Wang, Owens, Long, Diamond, & Smith, 2000). A meta-analytic review of 68 studies (104 effect sizes) found that programs adhering to principles of R-N-R effectively improved institutional behavior (French & Gendreau, 2006). Andrews and Bonta (2006) examined treatments consistent with the principles of R-N-R and found a reduction of criminal recidivism of approximately 50% (phi coefficient = .26) when compared to programs that departed from principles of R-N-R.

A comprehensive meta-analytic review of the adult and juvenile correctional rehabilitation literature indicated that sanctions alone (i.e., traditional punishment with no rehabilitative services offered) resulted in *increased* criminal recidivism (mean phi coefficient = –.07), with inappropriate services (i.e., rehabilitative services that did not adhere to principles of R-N-R) only slightly better but still resulting in *increased* criminal recidivism (mean phi coefficient = –.06; Andrews, Zinger, et al., 1990). Conversely, appropriate services (i.e., rehabilitative services that adhered to principles of R-N-R) resulted in a significant *reduction* of 30% in criminal recidivism (mean phi coefficient = .30).

Andrews and Bonta (2006) further summarized correctional rehabilitation programs and concluded that programs including all three principles produced significantly greater reductions in criminal recidivism than programs adhering to two principles or only one (mean correlation coefficients of .26, .18, and .02, respectively). Criminal justice sanctions and inappropriate rehabilitative programs, on the other hand, resulted in average mean correlation coefficients of .03 and –.01, respectively. Based on these results, it is clear that the greater the number of principles adhered to in R-N-R, the more favorable the outcomes. Andrews and Bonta further elaborated on the benefits of R-N-R by showing that the greatest reductions in criminal recidivism were attained when R-N-R was provided in community-based settings (mean correlations coefficient = .35). Others have noted the benefits of correctional rehabilitation programs utilizing principles of R-N-R with special populations of offenders when compared to therapeutic programs not utilizing principles of R-N-R, including female offenders, with a mean reduction in recidivism of 17% (Dowden & Andrews, 1999a); youthful offenders, with a mean reduction in recidivism of 22% (Dowden & Andrews, 1999b); sex offenders, with a mean reduction in recidivism of 12% (Hanson et al., 2002); with an average reduction in violent recidivism of 12% (Dowden & Andrews, 2000). Clearly, not only is R-N-R superior to sanctioned approaches to crime, but implementation of correctional rehabilitation services without adherence to R-N-R (referred to as "inappropriate services") is no better than not providing services and results in increased rates of criminal recidivism.

In fact, the evidence is so overwhelming for the effectiveness of R-N-R that not utilizing these theoretical principles in correctional rehabilitation programs may be considered negligent. As recommended by Andrews and Hoge (1995), to effectively reduce recidivism with offenders, practitioners must utilize individualized risk/need assessments, tailor treatments to the needs of offenders (or develop generic programs for special groups of offenders such as those high in antisocial attitudes), consider issues of responsiveness and incorporating principles of cognitive social learning theory (including reinforcement, modeling, etc.), and implement follow-up strategies including incorporating the offenders social support network, while maintaining focus on therapeutic integrity and exercising professional discretion.

Beyond the principles of R-N-R, research has identified treatment processes that have proven effective with offenders, including cognitive-behavioral theoretical approaches, structure in treatment programs, intensive services, and the use of homework. Cognitive-behavioral interventions are employed to change offenders' antisocial cognitions, attitudes, and values as well as to develop prosocial problem-solving and reasoning skills (Gendreau, 1996a). Cognitive-behavioral interventions have proven effective with a range of offenders, including violent (Berry, 2003) and nonviolent offenders (Bonta, Wallace-Capretta, & Rooney, 2000), sex offenders (Hanson et al., 2002; Polizzi, MacKenzie, & Hickman, 1999; Valliant & Antonowicz, 1992), and substance abusers (Vaughn & Howard, 2004). Furthermore, the effectiveness of cognitive-behavioral therapy is evidenced in meta-analytic reviews for criminal justice outcomes such as recidivism (Pearson, Lipton, Cleland, & Yee, 2002) as well as general psychological functioning (Morgan & Flora, 2002).

An important component of cognitive-behavioral interventions with offenders is relapse prevention. Relapse prevention is necessary for maintenance of change in addictive behaviors, such as substance abuse (Marlatt & Gordon, 1985), and criminal activity is similar in presentation to substance abuse (see Pithers, Kashima, Cumming, & Beal, 1988). Not surprisingly, then, relapse prevention programs help offenders maintain treatment gains and highlight the significance of treating "all areas of offending behavior" (Fisher, Beech, & Browne, 2000, p. 181), as well as the necessity of assessing for deterioration. Relapse prevention plans with offenders should identify those factors and situations that place offenders at high risk for committing crime and identify strategies for offenders to avoid high-risk situations, as well as to navigate high-risk situations when they occur (Henning & Frueh, 1996). Notably, these strategies must be overlearned so they become a natural instinct that replaces former antisocial instincts when the offender confronts real-world problems (Morgan, Kroner, & Mills, 2006). Homework is an effective strategy for helping offenders overlearn information by reaching out into their real world, and it significantly improves their mental health outcomes (Morgan & Flora, 2002).

Correctional rehabilitative services are also more effective when they are intensive in nature and incorporate structure. Intensive services are more effective than nonintensive services, and the more treatment offenders receive, the better the outcomes (see Aytes, Olsen, Zakrajsek, Murray, & Ireson, 2001; Bourgon & Armstrong, 2005; Fisher et al., 2000; Gossop, Marsden, Stewart, & Rolfe, 1999; Westhuis, Gwaltney, & Hayashi, 2001; Wexler, Falkin, & Lipton, 1990). The treatment to outcome ratio was recently quantified in a study of 4,155 substance-abusing offenders such that criminal recidivism (defined as return to prison) was reduced by 4% for every month spent in treatment (Burdon, Messina, & Prendergast, 2004). As a rule of thumb, empirically supported interventions are those that occupy between 40% and 70% of an offender's time (Gendreau, 1996b) and must be of significant duration (i.e., between 3 and 12 months). Consistent with findings that cognitive-behavioral interventions result in greater treatment gains, structured interventions or interventions that incorporate structure tend to produce the most favorable results (Andrews, Zinger, et al., 1990; Leak, 1980; Morgan & Flora, 2002; Saunders, 1996), including those obtained for juvenile offenders (Pomeroy, Green, & Kiam, 2001).

To summarize, clinicians electing to provide services in compliance with evidence-based practice with offenders should attend to the principles of R-N-R, while providing structured (or semistructured) services that incorporate cognitive-behavioral treatment strategies. These services should be intensive in nature and require homework that requires offenders to practice and overlearn treatment strategies in their real-world environments.

Evidence-Based Mental Health Interventions for Persons With Mental Illness

Psychiatric rehabilitation is a therapeutic approach that encourages a person with mental illness to develop his or her fullest capacities through learning and environmental supports (Bachrach, 1992; Garske & McReynolds, 2001). The most recent development of interest within psychiatric rehabilitation is the availability of Illness Management and Recovery (IMR), an evidence-based program specifically designed to meet the needs of persons with mental illness. IMR utilizes psychoeducational materials to enhance knowledge, psychotropic medication adherence training, relapse prevention training, social skills training, and coping skills training (Mueser et al., 2002) to promote the ability of persons with mental illness (referred to as "consumers") to self-manage their illness and strive for recovery (return to pre-illness levels of independence and prosocial functioning). The aim of IMR is to guide professional services aimed at facilitating collaboration between the consumers and providers, reducing risk for relapse (psychiatric recidivism), and increasing consumers' ability to cope with their illness (i.e., illness management [IM]; Mueser et al., 2004). Recovery (R) in IMR aims to facilitate enhanced self-esteem and self-efficacy for dealing with an illness, thereby allowing consumers to pursue their life goals (Mueser et al., 2004). To accomplish this goal, IMR provides a variety of treatments to facilitate consumers' management of their illness and thereby to allow them to achieve recovery.

The IMR curriculum (Gingerich & Mueser, 2005; available from the U.S. Department of Health and Human Services) includes the following treatment modules:

1. Recovery Strategies: Introduces consumers to the concept of "recovery" as pursuit of their personal goals and achieving pre-illness levels of functioning and independence. This module helps consumers accept responsibility for their recovery and define their lifelong personal goals.

2. Practical Facts About Mental Illness: Educates consumers about their illness, including prevalence rates, etiological factors, symptoms, and treatment-related information to foster active participation in their own recovery.

3. Stress-Vulnerability Model and Treatment Strategies: Educates consumers about the role of stress in their illness, particularly as it relates to vulnerability to relapse. Consumers are also taught treatment strategies and encouraged to actively participate in their treatment and treatment related decisions.

4. Building Social Support: Educates consumers about the role and benefits of an effective social support network. Consumers learn how to access their social support network to alleviate stress and actively participate in their relapse prevention plan.

5. Using Medication Effectively: Aims to educate consumers about psychotropic medications and the role of medications in their recovery. This education includes the anticipated benefits and side effects of psychotropic medications, as well as practical everyday strategies for remaining medication compliant.

6. Reducing Relapse: Helps consumers evaluate previous occurrences of relapse including antecedents to relapse, as well as coping strategies that were and were not effective. Consumers develop a formalized relapse prevention plan that identifies triggers to relapse, early warning signs of relapse, strategies to prevent relapse, and role responsibilities for members of the relapse plan.

7. Coping With Stress: Educates consumers about how to identify warning signs of stress, as well as strategies for effectively coping with stress.

8. Coping With Problems and Symptoms: Helps consumers cope with problems in an effective manner to avoid the onset of stress. Specifically, consumers are taught a step-by-step problem-solving process, as well as strategies for dealing with specific problems and symptoms.

9. Getting Your Needs Met in the Mental Health System: Provides consumers an overview of the mental health system, including what services and programs are available, types of service providers available to the consumer, and strategies for consumers to assume responsibility for their recovery.

10. Drug and Alcohol Use: Educates consumers on the impact of substance abuse on mental illness, as well as strategies for abstinence.

Preliminary investigations of the effectiveness of IMR are very encouraging. A small ($n = 33$), multisite (two U.S. sites and one site in Australia) feasibility study found that 70% of participants completed the program and evidenced significant symptom improvement as well as positive outcomes in other domains of interest to persons with persistent and serious mental illnesses (Mueser et al., 2006). Considering the high rate of treatment dropout for persons with severe mental illnesses (see Bruce et al., 2007; Herinckx, Kinney, Clarke, & Paulson, 1997), the 70% treatment retention rate is a promising finding. A randomized controlled trial provided even more compelling evidence of the effectiveness of IMR (Hasson-Ohayon, Roe, & Kravetz, 2007). In this trial, approximately 72% of participants completed the IMR program. Compared to participants receiving treatment as usual, consumers in the IMR condition evidenced significantly more knowledge of mental illness, as well as being better able to identify and work toward achieving personal goals. Finally, service providers also noted significant improvements in overall outcomes for consumers participating in IMR as opposed to treatment as usual. Although this randomized controlled study provided support for the effectiveness of IMR, much work remains to be done, and additional trials are needed. Nevertheless, for the first time, service providers have a systematic, structured, curriculum-based intervention based on evidence-based services, and evaluation of the effectiveness of aspects of IMR with incarcerated offenders are currently in progress (contact R. D. Morgan for more information, robert.morgan@ttu.edu).

Community Reentry of Offenders With Mental Illness

Research has shown that OMIs recidivate at the same rate as offenders without mental illness. However, they are at risk for psychiatric hospitalization within a short period of time (i.e., less than 2 years) after reentry (Feder, 1991). Bonta, Law, and Hanson (1998) found that long-term predictors of recidivism for OMIs are no different than the predictors of nondisordered offenders. These predictors include criminal history, antisocial personality, and substance abuse. Additionally, this research suggests that psychopathology is not related to the long-term prediction of recidivism for OMIs. However, the authors noted that psychotic symptoms may trigger antisocial behavior and, therefore, may serve as short-term predictors of recidivism.

Recent research has also shown that, in addition to criminal history, a history of mental health services is related to poorer short-term outcomes for OMIs released from incarceration (Hartwell, 2003). More specifically, 87% of OMIs with a history of mental health services prior to incarceration are reincarcerated within 3 months of release (Hartwell, 2003). In terms of criminal history, OMIs who have been incarcerated for misdemeanors are more likely to be reincarcerated within 3 months of being released than OMIs incarcerated for felonies. OMIs who were serving time for felonies are more likely to be hospitalized within 3 months of being released, compared with all other OMIs (Hartwell, 2003). Perhaps those who suffer from severe mental illness have a difficult time transitioning from a highly structured facility, like jail or prison, into a less structured environment in the community, and end up cycling back into hospitals and the criminal justice system (Lamb & Weinberger, 2005).

Additionally, as discussed above, if a subset of OMIs are evidencing an increase in psychiatric symptoms, as well as an increase in criminal thinking and attitudes, as a result of serving lengthy prison sentences (as indicated by the preliminary results put forth by Morgan, Bauer, et al., 2009), then upon release they may have difficulties reentering the community, perhaps resulting in psychiatric and criminal recidivism. Initiatives have been taken to improve offenders' ability to transition from incarceration back into society in an attempt to reduce high criminal recidivism rates. However, OMIs present with dual issues of mental illness and "criminalness." Criminalness involves behaviors that are antisocial, are nonproductive by avoiding responsibility, and that violate the rights and well-being of others. These behaviors may or may not lead to arrestable offenses such as indictable felonies/misdemeanors and nonarrestable activities like abuse of sick leave (Morgan, Kroner, & Mills, 2010). Consequently, they may be in need of more services upon release. This becomes problematic given findings that OMIs' lives are influenced more by the criminal justice system after release than the mental health system (Wilson & Draine, 2006). That is, decisions for treatment are shaped through the criminal justice system's goal of maintaining public safety and not necessarily the mental health system's goal of improving the quality of life and promoting recovery from mental illness (Wilson & Draine, 2006). Thus, reentry strategies must adequately incorporate both systems to ensure the offender is receiving the appropriate services to reduce psychiatric recidivism, as well as to ensure public safety and reduce criminal recidivism.

One aspect of treatment that has been shown to be an important component in improving outcomes among individuals with severe mental illness is continuity of services (see Chapter 1). Those who receive fewer gaps in service are more likely to achieve better rehabilitative outcomes (Brekke, Ansel, Long, Slade, & Weinstein, 1999). Additionally, research has suggested that continuity of services is a more important component for individuals with severe mental illness who are in transition periods of service (Greenberg & Rosenheck, 2005). For example, those who are transitioning from inpatient to outpatient status, or those who are initially without care when beginning outpatient services, may benefit more from fewer gaps in service than those who are continuing outpatients (Greenberg & Rosenheck, 2005). In addition to better treatment outcomes, continuity of care also contributes to lower healthcare costs by reducing the rate of psychiatric hospitalization (Chien, Steinwachs, Lehman, Fahey, & Skinner, 2000; Mitton, Adair, McDougall, & Marcoux, 2005). OMIs who are incarcerated encounter a significant disruption in environment and care (i.e., transitioning from the "free world" into a correctional facility), and if they do not continue to receive appropriate services on a consistent and regular basis during incarceration, as well as before and after incarceration, this may contribute to poorer outcomes. Research has also shown that the individuals with severe mental illness who have an arrest history are more likely to self-terminate outpatient services (Prince, 2005). Perhaps continuing treatment while incarcerated may help to reduce the dropout risk for outpatient services, once OMIs are released. Notably, 70% of U.S. citizens believe that to effectively facilitate community reentry, rehabilitative services should be available to offenders both during and after periods of confinement (Krisberg & Marchionna, 2006). Moreover, if OMIs receive care while incarcerated, eliminating gaps in service may decrease the likelihood of rehospitalization during incarceration and during reentry.

Aftercare or postrelease follow-up significantly improves criminal justice outcomes for offenders. The aim of aftercare programs is to ensure that offenders, posttreatment, maintain therapeutic gains. It has been speculated that without appropriate aftercare that is specific and supportive of offenders needs, treatment success is reduced (Carich & Stone, 2001). Based on a limited number of offenders ($n = 18$), the authors further postulated that effective aftercare programs included residential placement, treatment, and criminal justice supervision (Carich & Stone, 2001). In sum, continuity of services continues to be an important consideration for mental health professionals when preparing OMIs to reenter the community after incarceration (Solomon & Draine, 1995; Veysey, Steadman, Morrissey, & Johnsen, 1997).

Changing Lives and Changing Outcomes

There is good evidence of what works with offenders and what works with consumers involved in the mental health system (i.e., persons with serious and persistent mental illnesses). Why, then, have mental health and criminal justice professionals been unable to bridge the divide between these two systems to provide a comprehensive and holistic treatment targeting the needs of this special population of offenders with evidence-based practices from both sectors? The information has been published in the psychological, psychiatric, mental health, and criminal justice literature. The literature, as previously discussed, suggests that R-N-R is effective with offenders; that psychiatric rehabilitation and a specific derivative, IMR, are effective with persons with serious and persistent mental illnesses; and that specific treatment modalities will improve outcomes for offenders as well as consumers of mental health services. With this information readily at hand, why have there been so few attempts to integrate evidence-based practices?

The correctional treatment literature has primarily focused on rehabilitation with nondisordered offenders; however, as demonstrated in this chapter, OMIs are a unique population for whom mental health professionals need to treat both psychiatric symptoms and criminalness (e.g., antisocial thinking, criminal associations, substance abuse; Hodgins et al., 2007). Simply treating the mental illness does not reduce criminal recidivism (Bonta et al., 1998); however, correctional rehabilitative efforts must not ignore the mental health issues presented by OMIs. The goal of correctional interventions for OMIs must focus on dual issues of criminalness and mental illness, rather than solely on reducing criminal recidivism. Specifically, interventions for OMIs need to focus on the joint goals of reducing psychiatric hospitalization days and time spent incarcerated, as well as increasing the number of functional days. When providing treatment, mental health professionals need to be cognizant of how environmental factors and the presentation of mental illness (e.g., psychiatric symptoms) impact the delivery of services to OMIs. In other words, as noted by Senator Edward Kennedy, evidence-based practices need to "improve the lives of young people and make sure they do not commit further crimes" (Kennedy, 2007, p. 25).

This lack of integration reflects a systemic divide between the mental health and criminal justice systems that permeates service providers' thinking. When treating OMIs in the United States, the historical emphasis has been on treating these offenders as mentally ill patients and focusing more readily on issues of mental illness awareness and medication adherence. In other countries, Canada, for example, providers are more likely to focus on issues of criminalness (that is, offending behavior), such as criminal thinking, substance abuse, and antisocial associates, and less on symptoms of mental illness, which is a "minor" risk factor for recidivism (Andrews & Bonta, 2006). Paul Gendreau, a noted Canadian researcher, indicated this in a discussion when he said (paraphrasing) that mental illness is not relevant as it pertains to recidivism (personal communication, April 2007). However, it is this chapter's contention that service providers treating offenders with severe and persistent mental illnesses should be exactly that—concerned with *both* criminal and psychiatric recidivism. To focus on one and negate the other ignores half of the equation. If an offender is kept out of jail or prison only to find himself or herself in a secure hospital, has the system really succeeded? To truly be successful, mental health professionals need to reduce criminal and psychiatric recidivism and increase the quality of life (an issue of particular relevance in the mental health system but ignored in the criminal justice system) for this marginalized clinical population.

To accomplish this goal, Morgan, Kroner, Mills, and Bauer (2009) developed *Changing Lives and Changing Outcomes*, a comprehensive and holistic intervention designed for the specific needs of OMIs. *Changing Lives and Changing Outcomes* incorporates a bi-adaptive model: a two-pronged treatment approach (i.e., criminalness and mental illness) that is adaptive by focusing not only on reducing negative behaviors (e.g., criminal and psychiatric recidivism) but increasing positive behaviors (e.g., subjective well-being, prosocial behavior; see Morgan, Kroner, & Mills, 2010, for further explication of this model). To accomplish this goal, the intervention integrates evidence-based practices from the psychiatric rehabilitation and corrections literature. Part I of the treatment protocol is targeted specifically to issues of mental illness but integrates issues of criminalness and includes three treatment modules: Mental Illness and Criminalness Awareness, Medication Adherence, and Coping With Mental Illness and Criminalness. Part II of the treatment protocol is targeted to issues of criminalness but integrates issues of mental illness and includes Problematic Thinking, Attitudes and Cognitive Processes, Problematic Associates, and Emotions Management. Three additional modules are relevant for both a population with mental illness and offenders and are included as overlapping treatment targets. These overlapping modules include Preparation for Change, Skill Development (i.e., problem-solving skills, social and recreational skills, and vocational/housing skill development), and Substance Abuse. The aim of this treatment model is not to cure mental illness but, rather, to maximize adaptive behaviors to optimize functioning. Preliminary evaluation of this program is in progress; however, notably, this is the first program to offer service providers a holistic program based on evidence-based practices from both the criminal justice system as well as mental health best practices.

Summary and Conclusions

As discussed, there is an increasing prevalence of OMIs in corrections, including jail, probation, prison, and parole. This has led correctional facilities to become the nation's leading mental health care providers (Abramsky & Fellner, 2003). It appears the criminal justice system has become burdened with providing care and treatment to this special population, particularly because of the multiple treatment issues with which OMIs present. Incarcerated OMIs present as management challenges with increased disciplinary infractions (Feder, 1991; James & Glaze, 2006; O'Keefe & Schnell, 2008), as well as increased potential for victimization (Wolff et al., 2007), as compared to nondisordered offenders. The same trends can be seen when OMIs are supervised in the community—increased probation and parole violations and revocations compared with their nondisordered counterparts (Dauphinot, 1997; Porporino & Motiuk, 1995). Thus, there is a continuing need for research to identify the needs of OMIs as well as the needs and limitations of the correctional system to develop better supervision strategies that ensure public safety while simultaneously meeting the unique demands of OMIs.

In addition to examining supervision strategies, research needs to keep in mind the potential for iatrogenic effects of criminal justice sanctions for this special population. It is important for researchers to examine the impact incarceration, both short- and long-term, has on the psychological well-being of OMIs. Historically, OMIs have been left out in this line of research. Once researchers gain a better understanding of the impact criminal justice sanctions have on the mental health and behavioral functioning of OMIs, mental health professionals can become better equipped to develop interventions that increase stable long-term functioning and decrease criminalness during incarceration. This will allow for more humane treatment of OMIs while incarcerated, subsequently reduce institutional suffering, and perhaps reduce the challenge of managing this special population.

Although a main goal of the correctional system is to reduce criminal recidivism among offenders, strategies for OMIs must include reducing psychiatric recidivism as well. If the strategy in place aids in the reduction of criminal recidivism, but an OMI becomes psychiatrically hospitalized following release from incarceration, the overall system does not win. Thus, it becomes essential for both the criminal justice system and the mental health system to develop an effective working relationship to ensure both criminal and psychiatric recidivism are targeted. It is important not to lose sight of these dual treatment issues. It is important for treatment interventions and rehabilitation strategies to target the "whole" OMI, which includes both criminalness and mental illness. *Changing Lives and Changing Outcomes* (Morgan, Kroner, et al., 2009) is one potential program offering a holistic approach that utilizes empirically based treatments for targeting both criminalness and mental illness.

There has been much progress and great research conducted in the treatment of OMIs within the correctional system. However, as this special population continues to grow, work still needs to be done. Researchers, mental health professionals, and criminal justice professionals alike need to continue to work together towards unified goals. There needs to be continuity of care across agencies, as well as across the stages within the correctional system (e.g., from incarceration to parole) to ensure public safety, promote humane practices, and reduce *both* criminal and psychiatric symptomatology among OMIs. With continued research, and the devotion of the professionals within the field, the gap can continue to be bridged between the correctional and mental health systems, and effective strategies can be implemented and modified that target the unique needs of OMIs while taking into account the demands on both systems.

KEY TERMS

Offenders with mental illness (OMIs)

Prisonization

Iatrogenic effects of criminal justice sanctions

Treatment utilization

Risk-Need-Responsivity (R-N-R)

Illness Management and Recovery (IMR)

Relapse prevention

Criminalness

Continuity of services

Bi-Adaptive Model of Change

DISCUSSION QUESTIONS

1. Why do you think inmates might be reluctant to seek mental health services? What does this suggest about their perceptions of correctional mental health providers? What could be done to change those perceptions so as to promote appropriate help-seeking?

2. Imagine that you are in charge of developing a system to coordinate reentry services in your state for released OMIs. What challenges must be met to ensure that both the criminal justice system's public safety concerns and the mental health system's goals of recovery and quality of life are considered?

3. Could services such as those described in this chapter be successfully implemented in jails, where stays are often fairly short (days, weeks, or months), as well as in prisons? Why might such interventions be more important to offer in jails than in prisons?

4. The use of Risk-Need-Responsivity principles has been shown to result in improved treatment outcomes, including lower recidivism rates. Are these good enough to justify their use, in light of the costs (e.g., staff time) devoted to this intensive treatment and, perhaps, to warrant the early release (i.e., for "good behavior") of inmates who complete these programs successfully? Why or why not?

5. If there are so many inmates in prison because of deinstitutionalization and the lack of adequate community services, how likely do you think it is that OMIs being released from prison will receive the aftercare services they need to avoid returning to prison? What could be done in prison to help OMIs deal with less than ideal community services they might encounter after release?

References

Abram, K. M., & Teplin, L. A. (1991). Co-occurring disorders among mentally ill jail detainees: Implications for public policy. *American Psychologist, 46,* 1036–1045.

Abramsky, S., & Fellner, J. (2003). *Ill equipped: U.S. prisons and offenders with mental illness.* New York, NY: Human Rights Watch.

Andrews, D. A., & Bonta, J. (2006). *The psychology of criminal conduct* (4th ed.). Cincinnati, OH: Anderson.

Andrews, D. A., Bonta, J., & Hoge, R. D. (1990). Classification for effective rehabilitation: Rediscovering psychology. *Criminal Justice and Behavior, 17,* 19–52.

Andrews, D. A., & Hoge, R. D. (1995). The psychology of criminal conduct and principles of effective prevention and rehabilitation. *Forum on Corrections Research, 7*(1), n.p.

Andrews, D. A., Zinger, I., Hoge, R. D., Bonta, J., Gendreau, P., & Cullen, F. T. (1990). Does correctional treatment work? A clinically relevant and psychologically informed meta-analysis. *Criminology, 28,* 369–404.

Aytes, K. E., Olsen, S. S., Zakrajsek, T., Murray, P., & Ireson, R. (2001). Cognitive/behavioral treatment for sexual offenders: An examination of recidivism. *Sexual Abuse: Journal of Research and Treatment, 13,* 223–231.

Bachrach, L. L. (1992). Psychosocial rehabilitation and psychiatry in the care of long term patients. *American Journal of Psychiatry, 149,* 1455–1463.

Berry, S. (2003). Stopping violent offending in New Zealand: Is treatment an option? *New Zealand Journal of Psychology, 32,* 92–100.

Bonta, J., & Gendreau, P. (1990). Reexamining the cruel and unusual punishment of prison life. *Law & Human Behavior, 14,* 347–372.

Bonta, J., Law, M., & Hanson, K. (1998). The prediction of criminal and violent recidivism among mentally disordered offenders: A meta-analysis. *Psychological Bulletin, 123*, 123–142.

Bonta, J., Wallace-Capretta, S., & Rooney, J. (2000). A quasi-experimental evaluation of an intensive rehabilitation supervision program. *Criminal Justice and Behavior, 27*, 312–329.

Boothby, J., & Clements, C. (2000). A national survey of correctional psychologists. *Criminal Justice and Behavior, 27*, 716–732.

Bourgon, G., & Armstrong, B. (2005). Transferring the principles of effective treatment into a "real world" prison setting. *Criminal Justice and Behavior, 32*, 3–25.

Brekke, J. S., Ansel, M., Long, J., Slade, E., & Weinstein, M. (1999). Intensity and continuity of services and functional outcomes in the rehabilitation of persons with schizophrenia. *Psychiatric Services, 50*, 248–256.

Brinded, P., Simpson, A. I. F., Laidlaw, T. M., Fairley, N., & Malcolm, F. (2001). Prevalence of psychiatric disorders in New Zealand prisons: A national study. *Australian and New Zealand Journal of Psychiatry, 35*, 166–174.

Bruce, M. L., Koch, J. R., Laska, E. M., Leaf, P. J., Manderscheid, R. W., Rosenheck, R. A., et al. (2007). The prevalence and correlates of untreated serious mental illness. *Health Services Research, 36*, 987–1007.

Bukstel, L. H., & Kilmann, P. R. (1980). Psychological effects of imprisonment on confined individuals. *Psychological Bulletin, 88*, 469–493.

Burdon, W. M., Messina, N., & Prendergast, M. (2004). The California treatment expansion initiative: Aftercare participation, recidivism, and predictors of outcomes. *The Prison Journal, 84*, 64–80.

Carich, M. S., & Stone, M. H. (2001). Using relapse intervention strategies to treat sexual offenders. *Journal of Individual Psychology, 57*, 26–36.

Chien, C. F., Steinwachs, D. M., Lehman, A., Fahey, M., & Skinner, E. A. (2000). Provider continuity and outcomes of care for persons with schizophrenia. *Mental Health Services Research, 2*, 201–211.

Coid, J., Petruckevitch, A., Bebbington, P., Jenkins, R., Brugha, T., Lewis, G., et al. (2003). Psychiatric morbidity in prisoners and solitary cellular confinement: Disciplinary segregation. *Journal of Forensic Psychiatry & Psychology, 14*, 298–319.

Dauphinot, L. (1997). The efficacy of community correctional supervision for offenders with severe mental illness. *Dissertation Abstracts International: Section B: The Sciences and Engineering, 57*, 5917.

Deane, F., Skogstad, P., & Williams, M. (1999). Impact of attitudes, ethnicity and quality of prior therapy on New Zealand male prisoners' intentions to seek professional psychological help. *International Journal for the Advancement of Counseling, 21*, 55–67.

Ditton, P. M. (1999). *Mental health treatment of inmates and probationers* (Bureau of Justice Statistics Special Report NCJ 174463). Washington, DC: Department of Justice.

Dowden, C., & Andrews, D. A. (1999a). What works for female offenders: A meta-analytic review. *Crime & Delinquency, 45*, 438–452.

Dowden, C., & Andrews, D. A. (1999b). What works in young offender research: A meta-analysis. *Forum on Corrections Research, 11*, 21–24.

Dowden, C., & Andrews, D. A. (2000). Effective correctional treatment and violent reoffending. *Canadian Journal of Criminology, 42*, 449–467.

Feder, L. (1991). A comparison of the community adjustment of mentally ill offenders with those from the general prison population. *Law & Human Behavior, 15*, 477–493.

Feder, L. (1994). Psychiatric hospitalization history and parole decisions. *Law and Human Behavior, 18*, 395–410.

Fisher, D., Beech, A., & Browne, K. (2000). The effectiveness of relapse prevention training in a group of incarcerated child molesters. *Psychology, Crime & Law, 6*, 181–195.

Fisher, W. H., Packer, I. K., Banks, S. M., Smith, D., Simon, L. J., & Roy-Bujnowski, K. (2002). Self-reported lifetime psychiatric hospitalization histories of jail detainees with mental disorders: Comparison with a non-incarcerated national sample. *Journal of Behavioral Health Services & Research, 29*, 458–465.

French, S. A., & Gendreau, P. (2006). Reducing prison misconducts. *Criminal Justice and Behavior, 33*, 185–218.

Garske, G. G., & McReynolds, C. (2001). Psychiatric rehabilitation: Current practices and professional training recommendations. *Journal of Prevention, Assessment and Rehabilitation, 17,* 157–164.

Gendreau, P. (1996a). Offender rehabilitation: What we know and what needs to be done. *Criminal Justice and Behavior, 23,* 144–161.

Gendreau, P. (1996b). The principles of effective intervention with offenders. In A. T. Garland (Ed.), *Choosing correctional options that work: Defining the demand and evaluating the supply* (pp. 117–130). Thousand Oaks, CA: Sage.

Gingerich, S., & Mueser, K. T. (2005, October). *Evidence-based practice for justice involved individuals.* Discussion paper presented at the Evidence-Based Practice for Justice-Involved Individuals: Illness Self-Management, Bethesda, MD.

Glaze, L. E., & Bonczar, T. P. (2008). *Probation and parole in the United States, 2007 statistical tables* (Bureau of Justice Statistics Special Report NCJ 224707). Washington, DC: Department of Justice.

Gossop, M., Marsden, J., Stewart, D., & Rolfe, A. (1999). Treatment retention and 1 year outcomes for residential programmes in England. *Drug and Alcohol Dependence, 57,* 89–98.

Grassian, S., & Friedman, N. (1985). Effects of sensory deprivation in psychiatric seclusion and solitary confinement. *International Journal of Law and Psychiatry, 8,* 49–65.

Greenberg, G. A., & Rosenheck, R. A. (2005). Continuity of care and clinical outcomes in a national health system. *Psychiatric Services, 56,* 427–433.

Haney, C. (2003). Mental health issues in long-term solitary and "supermax" confinement. *Crime & Delinquency, 49,* 124–156.

Hanson, R. K., Gordon, A., Harris, A. J. R., Marques, J. K., Murphy, W., Quinsey, V. L., et al. (2002). First report of the Collaborative Outcome Data Project on the Effectiveness of Psychological Treatment for Sex Offenders. *Sexual Abuse: A Journal of Research and Treatment, 14,* 167–192.

Hartwell, S. (2003). Short-term outcomes for offenders with mental illness released from incarceration. *International Journal of Offender Therapy and Comparative Criminology, 47,* 145–158.

Hasson-Ohayon, I., Roe, D., & Kravetz, S. (2007). A randomized controlled trial of the effectiveness of the illness management and recovery program. *Psychiatric Services, 58,* 1461–1466.

Henning, K. R., & Frueh, B. C. (1996). Cognitive-behavioral treatment of incarcerated offenders. *Criminal Justice and Behavior, 23,* 523–541.

Herinckx, H. A., Kinney, R. F., Clarke, G. N., & Paulson, R. I. (1997). Assertive community treatment versus usual care in engaging and retaining clients with severe mental illness. *Psychiatric Services, 48,* 1297–1306.

Hodgins, S. (1995). Assessing mental disorder in the criminal justice system: Feasibility versus clinical accuracy. *International Journal of Law and Psychiatry, 18,* 15–28.

Hodgins, S., Müller-Isberner, R., Freese, R., Tiihonen, J., Repo-Tiihonen, E., Eronen, M., et al. (2007). A comparison of general adult and forensic patients with schizophrenia living in the community. *International Journal of Forensic Mental Health, 6,* 63–75.

Howerton, A., Byng, R., Campbell, J., Hess, D., Owens, C., & Aitken, P. (2007). Understanding help seeking behaviour among male offenders: Qualitative interview study. *British Medical Journal, 334,* 303.

Islam-Zwart, K. A., Vik, P. W., & Rawlins, K. S. (2007). Short-term psychological adjustment of female prison inmates on a minimum security unit. *Women's Health Issues, 17,* 237–243.

James, D. J., & Glaze, L. E. (2006). *Mental health problems of prison and jail inmates* (Bureau of Justice Statistics Special Report NCJ 213600). Washington, DC: Department of Justice.

Jemelka, R. P., Trupin, E. W., & Chiles, J. A. (1989). The mentally ill in prison: A review. *Hospital and Community Psychiatry, 40,* 481–490.

Kennedy, P. (2007). Mental health issues burden the juvenile justice system. *Corrections Today, 69*(5), 24–26.

Krisberg, B., & Marchionna, S. (2006, April). Attitudes of US voters toward prisoner rehabilitation and reentry policies. *FOCUS: Views From the National Council on Crime and Delinquency,* pp. 1–6.

Kupers, T. (1996). Trauma and its sequelae in male prisoners: Effects of confinement, overcrowding, and diminished services. *American Journal of Orthopsychiatry, 66,* 189–195.

Lamb, H. R., & Bachrach, L. L. (2001). Some perspectives on deinstitutionalization. *Psychiatric Services, 52,* 1039–1045.

Lamb, H. R., & Weinberger, L. E. (1998). Persons with severe mental illness in jails and prisons: A review. *Psychiatric Services, 49,* 483–492.

Lamb, H. R., & Weinberger, L. E. (2005). One-year follow-up of persons discharged from a locked intermediate care facility. *Psychiatric Services, 56,* 198–201.

Lamb, H. R., Weinberger, L. E., Marsh, J. S., & Gross, B. H. (2007). Treatment prospects for persons with severe mental illness in an urban county jail. *Psychiatric Services, 58,* 782–786.

Leak, G. K. (1980). Effects of highly structured versus nondirective counseling approaches on personality and behavioral measures of adjustment in incarcerated felons. *Journal of Counseling Psychology, 27,* 520–523.

Lurigio, A. (2001). Effective services for parolees with mental illness. *Crime & Delinquency, 47,* 446–461.

MacKenzie, D. L., & Goodstein, L. (1985). Long-term incarceration impacts and characteristics of long-term offenders: An empirical analysis. *Criminal Justice and Behavior, 12,* 395–414.

Marlatt, G. A., & Gordon, J. R. (1985). *Relapse prevention: Maintenance strategies in the treatment of addictive behaviors.* New York, NY: Guilford.

Miller, H. A., & Young, G. R. (1997). Prison segregation: Administrative detention remedy or mental health problem? *Criminal Behaviour and Mental Health, 7,* 85–94.

Minton, T. D., & Sabol, W. J. (2009). *Jail inmates at midyear 2008—Statistical tables* (Bureau of Justice Statistics Special Report NCJ 225709). Washington, DC: Department of Justice.

Mitton, C. R., Adair, C. E., McDougall, G. M., & Marcoux, G. (2005). Continuity of care and health care costs among persons with severe mental illness. *Psychiatric Services, 56,* 1070–1076.

Morgan, R. D. (2003). Basic mental health services: Services and issues. In T. J. Fagan & R. K. Ax (Eds.), *Correctional mental health handbook* (pp. 59–71). Thousand Oaks, CA: Sage.

Morgan, R. D., Bauer, R. L., Gaines, M. V., Fisher, W. H., Duan, N., Mandracchia, J. T., et al. (2009). *What happens to offenders with mental illness during incarceration? Effects of imprisonment on mental health and criminal risk factors.* Manuscript in preparation.

Morgan, R. D., Fisher, W. H., Duan, N., Mandracchia, J. T., & Murray, D. (2010). Prevalence of criminal thinking among state prison inmates with serious mental illness. *Law & Human Behavior, 34*(4), 324–326.

Morgan, R. D., & Flora, D. B. (2002). Group psychotherapy with incarcerated offenders: A research synthesis. *Group Dynamics: Theory, Research, and Practice, 6,* 203–218.

Morgan, R. D., Kroner, D. G., & Mills, J. F. (2006). Group psychotherapy in prison: Facilitating change inside the walls. *Journal of Contemporary Psychotherapy, 36,* 137–144.

Morgan, R. D., Kroner, D. G., & Mills, J. F. (2010). *Treating the mentally disordered offender: A model and guide for empirically supported practice.* Manuscript in preparation for Oxford University Press.

Morgan, R. D., Kroner, D. G., Mills, J. F., & Bauer, R. L. (2009). *Changing lives and changing outcomes: A treatment program for offenders with mental illness.* Treatment manual in preparation.

Morgan, R. D., Rozycki, A., & Wilson, S. (2004). Inmate perceptions of mental health services. *Professional Psychology: Research and Practice, 35,* 389–396.

Morgan, R. D., Steffan, J., Shaw, L. B., & Wilson, S. (2007). Needs for and barriers to correctional mental health services: Inmates perceptions. *Psychiatric Services, 58,* 1181–1186.

Morgan, R. D., Winterowd, C. L., & Ferrell, S. W. (1999). A national survey of group psychotherapy services in correctional facilities. *Professional Psychology: Research and Practice, 30,* 600–606.

Mueser, K. T., Clark, R. E., Haines, M., Drake, R. E., McHugo, G. J., Bond, G. R., et al. (2004). The Hartford Study of supported employment for persons with severe mental illness. *Journal of Consulting and Clinical Psychology, 72,* 479–490.

Mueser, K. T., Corrigan, P. W., Hilton, D. W., Tanzman, B., Schaub, A., Gingerich, S., et al. (2002). Illness management and recovery for severe mental illness: A review of the research. *Psychiatric Services, 53,* 1272–1284.

Mueser, K. T., Meyers, P. S., Penn, D. L., Clancy, R., Clancy, D. M., & Salyers, M. P. (2006). The Illness Management and Recovery Program: Rationale, development, and preliminary findings. *Schizophrenia Bulletin, 32*(Suppl. 1), S32–S43.

Mumola, C. J. (2005). *Suicide and homicide in state prisons and local jails* (Bureau of Justice Statistics Special Report NCJ 210036). Washington, DC: Department of Justice.

Munetz, M. R., Grande, T. P., & Chambers, M. R. (2001). The incarceration of individuals with severe mental disorders. *Community Mental Health Journal, 37*, 361–372.

O'Keefe, M. L., & Schnell, M. J. (2008). Offenders with mental illness in the correctional system. *Journal of Offender Rehabilitation, 45*, 81–104.

Paulus, P. B., & Dzindolet, M. T. (1993). Reactions of male and female inmates to prison confinement: Further evidence for a two-component model. *Criminal Justice and Behavior, 20*, 149–166.

Pearson, F. S., Lipton, D. S., Cleland, C. M., & Yee, D. S. (2002). The effects of behavioral/cognitive-behavioral programs on recidivism. *Crime & Delinquency, 48*, 476–495.

Pithers, W. D., Kashima, K. M., Cumming, G. F., & Beal, L. S. (1988). Relapse prevention of sexual aggression. *Annals of the New York Academy of Sciences, 528*, 244–260.

Polizzi, D. M., MacKenzie, D. L., & Hickman, L. J. (1999). What works in adult sex offender treatment? A review of prison and non-prison based treatment programs. *International Journal of Offender Therapy and Comparative Criminology, 43*, 357–374.

Pomeroy, E. C., Green, D. L., & Kiam, R. (2001). Female juvenile offenders incarcerated as adults: A psychoeducational group intervention. *Journal of Social Work, 1*, 101–115.

Porporino, F. J., & Motiuk, L. L. (1995). The prison careers of mentally disordered offenders. *International Journal of Law and Psychiatry, 18*, 29–44.

Prince, J. D. (2005). Predicting outpatient mental health program withdrawal among recently discharged inpatients with schizophrenia. *Psychological Services, 2*, 142–150.

Reinsmith-Meyer, C. L. (2008). Barriers to mental health and substance abuse treatment among incarcerated offenders. *Dissertation Abstracts International: Section B: The Sciences and Engineering, 69*, 1970.

Rice, M. E., & Harris, G. T. (1997). The treatment of mentally disordered offenders. *Psychology, Public Policy, and Law, 3*, 126–183.

Rold, W. J. (1992). Consideration of mental health factors in inmate discipline. *Journal of Prison & Jail Health, 11*, 41–49.

Saunders, D. G. (1996). Feminist-cognitive-behavioral and process-psychodynamic treatment for me who batter: Interaction of abuser traits and treatment models. *Violence and Victims, 11*, 393–414.

Schoenber, M. R., Dorr, D., & Morgan, C. (2006). Development of discriminant functions to detect dissimulation for the Millon Clinical Multiaxial Inventory (3rd ed.). *Journal of Forensic Psychiatry and Psychology, 17*, 405–416.

Simourd, D. J., & Olver, M. E. (2002). The future of criminal attitudes research and practice. *Criminal Justice and Behavior, 29*, 427–446.

Skeem, J. L., & Eno Louden, J. (2006). Toward evidence-based practice for probationers and parolees mandated to mental health treatment. *Psychiatric Services, 57*, 333–342.

Skogstad, P., Deane, F. P., & Spicer, J. (2006). Social-cognitive determinants of help-seeking for mental health problems among prison inmates. *Criminal Behaviour and Mental Health, 16*, 43–59.

Snyder, H. (2007). Nothing works, something works—But still few proven programs. *Corrections Today, 69*(5), 6–28.

Solomon, P., & Draine, J. (1995). Issues in servicing the forensic client. *Social Work, 40*, 25–33.

Solomon, P., Draine, J., & Marcus, S. C. (2002). Predicting incarceration of clients of a psychiatric probation and parole service. *Psychiatric Services, 53*, 50–56.

Steadman, H. J., Holohean, E., & Dvoskin, J. (1991). Estimating mental health needs and service utilization among prison inmates. *Bulletin of the American Academy of Psychiatry and Law, 19*, 297–307.

Steadman, H. J., McCarty, D. W., & Morrissey, J. P. (1989). *The mentally ill in jail: Planning for essential services.* New York, NY: Guilford.

Steadman, H. J., & Veysey, B. M. (2007). *Research in brief: National Institute of Justice: Providing services for jail inmates with mental disorders.* Washington, DC: U.S. Department of Justice, Office of Justice Programs, National Institute of Justice. Retrieved June 1, 2009, from www.mcjrs.gov/pdffiles/162207.pdf

Steffan, J. S., & Morgan, R. D. (2005). Meeting the needs of mentally ill offenders in the criminal justice system: Inmate service utilization. *Corrections Today, 67*(1), 38–41.

Suedfeld, P., Ramirez, C., Deaton, J., & Baker-Brown, G. (1982). Reactions and attributes of prisoners in solitary confinement. *Criminal Justice and Behavior, 9,* 303–340.

Teplin, L. A. (1984). Criminalizing mental disorder: The comparative arrest rate of the mentally ill. *American Psychologist, 39,* 794–803.

Teplin, L. A. (1990). The prevalence of severe mental disorder among male urban jail detainees: Comparison with the Epidemiologic Catchment Area Program. *American Journal of Public Health, 80,* 663–669.

Valliant, P. M., & Antonowicz, D. H. (1992). Rapists, incest offenders, and child molesters in treatment: Cognitive and social skills training. *International Journal of Offender Therapy and Comparative Criminology, 36,* 221–230.

Vaughn, M. G., & Howard, M. O. (2004). Adolescent substance abuse treatment: A synthesis of controlled evaluations. *Research on Social Work Practices, 14,* 325–335.

Veysey, B. M., Steadman, H. J., Morrissey, J. P., & Johnsen, M. (1997). In search of the missing linkages: Continuity of care in U.S. jails. *Behavioral Sciences and the Law, 15,* 383–397.

Walters, G. D. (1995). The Psychological Inventory of Criminal Thinking Styles. Part I: Reliability and preliminary validity. *Criminal Justice and Behavior, 22,* 307–325.

Walters, G. D. (2003). Changes in criminal thinking and identity in novice and experienced inmates: Prisonization revisited. *Criminal Justice and Behavior, 30,* 399–421.

Walters, G. D., & Geyer, M. D. (2005). Construct validity of the Psychological Inventory of Criminal Thinking Styles in relationship to the PAI, disciplinary adjustment, and program completion. *Journal of Personality Assessment, 84,* 252–260.

Wang, E. W., Owens, R. M., Long, S. A., Diamond, P. M., & Smith, J. L. (2000). The effectiveness of rehabilitation with persistently violent male prisoners. *International Journal of Offender Therapy and Comparative Criminology, 44,* 505–514.

West, H. C., & Sabol, W. J. (2009). *Prison inmates at midyear 2008—Statistical tables* (Bureau of Justice Statistics Special Report NCJ 225619). Washington, DC: Department of Justice.

Westhuis, D. J., Gwaltney, L., & Hayashi, R. (2001). Outpatient cocaine abuse treatment: Predictors of success. *Journal of Drug Education, 31,* 171–183.

Wexler, H. K., Falkin, G. P., & Lipton, D. S. (1990). Outcome evaluation of prison therapeutic community for substance abuse treatment. *Criminal Justice and Behavior, 17,* 71–92.

Wilson, A. B., & Draine, J. (2006). Collaborations between the criminal justice and mental health systems for prisoner re-entry. *Psychiatric Services, 57,* 875–878.

Wolff, N., Blitz, C. L., & Shi, J. (2007). Rates of sexual victimization in prison for inmates with and without mental disorders. *Psychiatric Services, 58,* 1087–1094.

Wright, K. N. (1993). Prison environment and behavioral outcomes. *Journal of Offender Rehabilitation, 20,* 93–113.

Zamble, E. (1992). Behavior and adaptation in long-term prison inmates: Descriptive longitudinal results. *Criminal Justice and Behavior, 19,* 409–425.

Zinger, I., Wichmann, C., & Andrews, D. A. (2001). The psychological effects of 60 days in administrative segregation. *Canadian Journal of Criminology, 43,* 47–84.

CHAPTER 10

Mental Health Needs of Female Offenders

Ann Booker Loper and Lacey Levitt

Introduction

There are more women in prison today than at any other point in U.S. history. The number of female offenders has climbed steadily since the early 1990s, with an increase of approximately 25% between the years 2000 and 2008 (Greenfeld & Snell, 1999; West & Sabol, 2009). Although still a minority compared to male offenders, the increasing presence of women in correctional settings raises the question, What is bringing women to prison? One early answer to this question was the simple one—with women becoming more liberated and therefore more "man-like," they were increasingly emulating masculine behavior (Adler, 1975). However, this easy answer was quickly disputed by overwhelming evidence that the new brigade of women entering prison was anything but liberated.

As a group, women in prison are poor, financially stressed, and tend to adhere to traditional role models of femininity (Bunch, Foley, & Urbina, 1983; Widom, 1979). Moreover, female patterns of offending do not resemble the patterns for men. Men account for more than 80% of the arrests for violent offenses, and proportionately fewer of the arrests of women are for violent crimes (Federal Bureau of Investigation, 2009). In the cases of violent offending committed by women, the gender patterns likewise differ: When a woman commits a violent offense, she is relatively more likely than a male to aggress against a family member or intimate, usually in the context of an emotional relational conflict (Loper & Cornell, 1996). Closer examination of the lives of women in prison reveals one obvious pathway—women in prison suffer from high levels of mental illness, substance abuse, and emotional distress, both before and during their time in prison, that can perpetuate criminal patterns. The heightened mental distress among a large portion of female offenders interacts with the broader societal changes in prison policies that have served to increase the entire prison population, such as abolition of parole, criminalization of drug possession, and stricter sentencing legislation. The net result is not only more women in prison today, but a population of women who face numerous emotional difficulties.

Mentally III Women in Prison: Why So Many?

Prevalence of Mental Illness in Female Offenders

Numerous women in prison experience mental illness (James & Glaze, 2006). Magaletta, Diamond, Faust, Daggett, and Camp (2009) documented several indicators of mental illness among approximately 2,900 newly committed federal offenders. For each indicator, women exceeded the rates among men. Relative to men, proportionately more female offenders suffered from a serious mental illness (9.6% versus 17.4%), had previously received inpatient psychiatric care (8.8% versus 15%), and had previously used psychotropic medications (11.4% versus 24.3%). This pattern of higher levels of mental illness among female offenders likewise extends to prison and jail populations (James & Glaze, 2006), as well as to offenders with known substance abuse problems (Zlotnick et al., 2008). As shown in Table 10.1, levels of mental illness among female offenders far exceed those found in population estimates of mental illness among women in the community (Lewis, 2006).

Table 10.1   Lifetime Prevalence of Psychiatric Diagnosis in Female Offenders

Disorder	Teplin [7][a] N = 1,272 (%)	Jordan et al [4][b] N = 805 (%)	Lewis [5][c] N = 136 (%)	National Comorbidity Survey[d] (%)
Schizophrenia	1.4	NR	2.4	0.8
Manic	2.4	NR	4.1	1.7
Major depressive disorder	16.9	13.0	36.2	21.3
Dysthymia	9.6	7.1	4.6	8.0
Substance abuse/dependence	70.2		65.4	
Alcohol abuse	32.3	38.0	22.3	6.4
Alcohol dependence			43.8	8.2
Drug abuse	63.6	44.2	14.0	3.5
Drug dependence			56.6	5.9
Panic disorder	1.6	5.8	3.8	5.0
Generalized anxiety disorder	2.5	2.7	5.4	6.6
PTSD	33.5	30.0	40.8	10.4
Antisocial personality disorder	13.8	11.9	32.3	1.2

Source: Reprinted from "Treating Incarcerated Women: Gender Matters," by C. Lewis, 2006, *Psychiatric Clinics of North America, 29,* p. 777.

[a]Newly admitted female felons.
[b]Female jail detainees.
[c]Female felons serving sentence.
[d]National sample of women in community.

The high level of mental illness among female offenders begs the question, "Why?" Understanding mental illness among this population requires understanding the typically troubled histories of women who offend as well as the particular stressors of incarceration. What are the gendered experiences in the lives of female offenders that account for these high levels of mental illness?

Childhood and Adult Victimization

Childhood Maltreatment

Although both men and women in prison report high levels of childhood maltreatment, the level of maltreatment and sexual abuse is generally higher among female offenders (Harlow, 1999; McClellan, Farabee, & Crouch, 1997; Messina, Grella, Burdon, & Prendergast, 2007). Greenfeld and Snell's (1999) report on female offenders revealed that approximately 44% of women under correctional authority reported sexual or physical abuse at some time in their lives, typically before age 18. Browne, Miller, and Maguin (1999) reported similar findings of physical and sexual abuse after interviewing 150 incarcerated women at Bedford Hills Correctional Facility in New York State. Approximately 70% of the interviewed inmates reported instances of severe physical violence during childhood and adolescence, and nearly 60% revealed instances of sexual abuse prior to 18 years, perpetrated by someone at least 5 years their senior. Moreover, there appeared to be a relationship between childhood victimization and later adult victimization, as high levels of childhood trauma were associated with high levels of later domestic violence victimization.

In one of the few prospective studies of the impact of child sexual abuse on offending, Siegel and Williams (2003) followed 206 women who, as children, had been treated in a hospital emergency room following a report of sexual abuse. Thus, unlike other studies that relied on the recollections of sexual abuse, this study was grounded in well-documented medical records. Siegel and Williams then examined official arrest records for each individual and compared criminal outcomes for the sexually abused group to a matched comparison group who had been seen in the emergency room for other, non–abuse-related incidences (e.g., intestinal illness). They also obtained information regarding juvenile dependency hearings that may have occurred. These dependency hearings reflected official concerns about the suitability of the girl's home life, including the likelihood of inadequate supervision, absence of care, or overt abuse. As expected, girls who were involved in these dependency hearings were more likely to be arrested later, confirming the expectation that an adverse childhood history predicts offending. However, they also found that sexual abuse as a child was associated with adult offending, even when the adverse childhood (dependency hearing) was statistically controlled. Sexual abuse as a girl was therefore a very potent event in many of these girls' already troubled lives and an obvious part of their pathway to prison.

Adult Victimization

The pattern of abuse and victimization experienced as children continues for many incarcerated women into their adult lives. McClellan et al. (1997) surveyed more than 1,000 incarcerated men and 500 incarcerated women regarding their childhood and adulthood maltreatment experiences. Women not only experienced more childhood abuse than did the men, but the abuse was more likely to continue into adulthood. As the men reached adulthood, their rates of victimization decreased, in contrast to the continuing patterns of victimization for the women. Approximately half of the women reported that during their adulthood they were beaten, and nearly one third reported sexual maltreatment or abuse, levels that were beyond those reported by men. In cases of severe physical violence committed against women, the most likely perpetrator was the inmate's male spouse or partner. In a descriptive study of female offenders in West Virginia, Douglas (2000) found that approximately half reported prior domestic violence committed by a spouse or ex-spouse. Similarly, based on interviews of 195 female inmates, Warren, Loper, and Komarovskaya (2009) reported that approximately half of the sample indicated prior domestic violence.

Victimization and Mental Illness

The pervasiveness of child and adult victimization among female offenders is a likely precursor to the high levels of mental illness that have been observed in this population. Moreover, the mental illness that women experience as a consequence of such victimization may itself be related to poor patterns of adaptation that can lead to prison. Recently, Salisbury and Van Voorhis (2009) examined how child and adult victimization, among several other variables, contributed to female offending among a sample of 313 female probationers who had committed felony offenses but were not immediately incarcerated. Thus, they were a group at high risk for coming to prison. The purpose of the study was to determine what pathways best described those who ended up in prison. Its results showed the importance of child and adult victimization as key variables in understanding the population.

A "childhood victimization model" described an indirect pathway between early maltreatment and later prison admission among female offenders. In this model, childhood victimization was not directly associated with prison admission. Rather, victimization was associated with a history of mental illness that in turn related to substance abuse and continuing depression and anxiety. In combination, current and previous mental illness and substance abuse paved the road to prison admission. This model supports a notion that early child victimization can "start the ball rolling" for female inmates by leading to mental and emotional distress that directly, or indirectly via substance abuse, increases the likelihood of offending.

A second distinct pathway identified by Salisbury and Van Voorhis (2009), termed the "relational model," included the inmate's adult victimization experiences. In this model, relational distress, as measured by self-reported involvement in painful, unsatisfying, and unsupportive relationships, was the "starting point" on a path to incarceration. A sense of unhappiness in interpersonal relationships was associated with adult victimization. This experience of victimization during adulthood was related to depression and anxiety that was, in turn, directly related to prison admission. As was the case with childhood victimization, mental illness was also associated with substance abuse, which linked to prison admission. Taken together, both of these models reflect the importance of childhood and adult victimization in the experiences of incarcerated women. The high levels of mental illness found among incarcerated women reflects, in part, these troubled histories of victimization that contribute to offending.

Trauma and Mental Illness

Childhood and adult victimization are two examples of traumatic experiences that can influence adaptive behavior. A particularly pernicious outcome that can ensue from traumatic experiences is post-traumatic stress disorder (PTSD). This disorder is a consequence of a perceived life-threatening event in which the individual recurrently experiences distress and arousal associated with the event. The individual copes with this turmoil through cognitive and behavioral avoidance such as memory lapse, detachment, flattened affect, and diminished social interaction. PTSD is more frequently observed in women than men, both in incarcerated and nonincarcerated samples (Kessler, Sonnega, Bromet, Hughes, & Nelson, 1995; Tolin & Foa, 2006; Zlotnick, 1997).

Warren et al. (2009) examined levels of PTSD and trauma among a sample of 195 female offenders. Consistent with other investigations, they observed high levels of previous violent victimization (74%), previous sexual victimization (61%), and domestic violence (46%), among other possible traumatic experiences. As part of their interview, the women were asked to identify the "worst" of any of the painful experiences they reported and then detail the emotional reactions that ensued. Warren and associates evaluated the women's reports of their reactions using standardized procedures for diagnosis of PTSD. Approximately half of the sample met criteria for PTSD during their lifetime. Approximately 14% of the women experienced PTSD as a direct consequence of sexual assault. Moreover, diagnosis of PTSD was associated with borderline personality disorder (BPD). BPD represents a long-standing pattern of poor emotional regulation and dysfunctional social relationships and is frequently diagnosed in women in prison (Jordan, Schlenger, Fairbank, & Caddell, 1996). Thus, for many of the interviewed women, their previous traumas continued to play a role in their lives in prison, via associated mental illness and poor emotional regulation. In sum, studies converge on the conclusion that the high levels of victimization and trauma among many female offenders lead either directly or indirectly to mental illness, substance abuse, and chronic patterns of emotional dysregulation.

Women who have been victimized can be *re*traumatized by prison experiences such as pat searches, internal physical searches, privacy violations, and verbal belittlement. If coupled with a disrespectful and devaluating attitude, the power imbalance between prison staff and inmates can evoke prior victimization events, instances which may themselves influence how women are able to cope in prison (Moloney, van den Bergh, & Moller, 2009). Moreover, women who have experienced lifetime sexual assault or domestic violence may be unaccustomed to seeking recourse against such abuse and may be at increased risk of abuse while incarcerated (Human Rights Watch Women's Rights Project, 1996).

Substance Abuse Disorders Among Incarcerated Women

Consistent with high risk patterns for mental illness, female offenders suffer high levels of substance abuse problems. Greenfeld and Snell (1999) drew on multiple national surveys of offenders and reported that approximately 40% of the female offenders, in contrast to 32% of the male offenders, were under the influence of drugs at the time of their offense. Approximately one third of the women acknowledged that obtaining money to support their drug habit was the motivation for their criminal acts.

Some scholars have argued that the high level of substance abuse found among female offenders represents a form of "self-medication" used to deal with the chronic pain of mental illness (Chesney-Lind, 1997; Sacks, 2004). It is a reasonable conclusion. Among female offenders, there is considerable overlap in the experiences of mental illness and substance abuse. In a study of more than 1,200 jail detainees in Chicago, Abram, Teplin, and McClelland (2003) found that 8% had a co-occurring severe mental disorder, such as schizophrenia or major depression, with substance abuse. Of those with severe mental disorders, nearly 75% met criteria for substance use disorders. Consistent with the pathways to offending models previously described (Salisbury &

Van Voorhis, 2009), mental illness and substance abuse interact dynamically with each other in female offenders. Treatment of women in prison requires a lens that includes an understanding of this complexity.

Financial, Social, and Familial Problems Among Female Prisoners

Financial Hardship

Female offenders have numerous financial stressors, often at levels that exceed the high levels of such stress among male offenders. Among parents in prison, more incarcerated mothers than fathers report homelessness prior to prison (Glaze & Maruschak, 2008), and female offenders report higher levels of financial hardship than do male offenders (Heilbrun et al., 2008). Moreover, financial instability appears to be a particularly potent risk factor in the prediction of female offending. Manchak, Skeem, Douglas, and Siranosian (2009) contrasted male and female offenders using the Level of Service Inventory (LSI-R; Andrews & Bonta, 1995), a well-established measure that is frequently used to assess the risk of recidivism. They found that the instrument, composed of 10 separate subscales, did a good job of predicting recidivism for both men and women. However, the particular scales that best accounted for the measure's predictive power differed. Whereas the best predictors for men were the criminal history scale, financial scale, and alcohol/drug scale, only the financial scale accounted for the measure's ability to predict the women who would return to prison.

The reasons for the potency of financial risk is likely related to its central role in the interplay of adverse circumstances for women offenders. The mental health and substance abuse problems that are frequent in this population can make the women poor candidates for financial stability and good candidates for engaging in activities to finance drug use, for becoming emotionally attached to criminal peers, and for making poor judgment calls (Alemagno, 2001).

Parenting Stress

Parents in prison, both men and women, routinely report that the separation from children represents one of the most painful aspects of incarceration (Arditti & Few, 2008; Hairston, 1991; Loper, Carlson, Levitt, & Scheffel, 2009; Magaletta & Herbst, 2001). However, the experiences and associated problems can differ. Mothers in prison are more likely than fathers to have been in a single-parent household prior to separation from children (Glaze & Maruschak, 2008). Consequently, children with mothers in prison are much less likely to reside with their other parent (37%) than children with fathers in prison (88.4%). Instead, children of female offenders tend to live with relatives, typically a grandparent. The reverberating consequences for the affected families can be severe. Burton (1992) interviewed 60 grandparents who were rearing the children of drug-addicted parents and documented that many of these seniors' lives were dramatically changed by the onus of raising their grandchildren. Grandparents expressed concerns regarding their own loss of freedom, their difficulty in keeping up with the emotional and physical demands of parenting, and their questionable ability to handle such a long-term obligation given their own health needs. With an estimated 45% of the children of incarcerated mothers residing with grandparents, the imprisoned mothers have good reason to be concerned about their child's welfare as well as for their own parents.

There are other gender-specific stressors for mothers in prison. Because there are fewer female offenders than male offenders, there are fewer prisons for women. Consequently, there is often a considerable distance between home and prison for a female offender, making it difficult and expensive for her family to visit (Bloom, 1995). There is a greater likelihood of adverse child outcomes among children of incarcerated mothers relative to children of incarcerated fathers (Johnson & Waldfogel, 2002), possibly reflecting the greater disruption in the lives of children of incarcerated mothers. Proportionately more children of incarcerated mothers (11%) in contrast to those of imprisoned fathers (3%) reside in foster care or another equivalent agency, possibly reflecting the greater likelihood of the imprisoned mothers' single-parent status (Glaze & Maruschak, 2008).

The stress associated with inmate mothers' compromised parental role is linked to symptoms of mental distress and dysfunction that can have implications for women's adjustment and mental health in prison. In a study of 362 female offenders, Houck and Loper (2002) found that women who reported higher levels of parenting stress regarding their children were more likely to experience symptoms of anxiety and depression. Moreover, stress regarding their children was associated with higher levels of "tickets" or official reports of institutional misconduct. This pattern was largely replicated in a later study with both men and women (Loper et al., 2009), in which parenting stress among the women was associated with heightened depression symptoms as well as increased self-reported violence during incarceration. Based on a series of interviews of mothers recently released on parole, Brown and Bloom (2009) noted that inmate mothers are acutely aware that their children face hardships, mental illness, and dangers that they themselves experienced as children. The frustration that, as prisoners, they were unable to protect their children on a familiar path to prison represented a major source of anxiety for interviewed mothers.

The Relevance of Relational Support

The importance of relationships within the lives of women has been highlighted by several feminist theorists who emphasize the role of social support and connection for women (e.g., Gilligan, 1982; Lorber, 2001), a theme that is echoed by several scholars who emphasize the importance of social and familial networks for female offenders (Chesney-Lind, 1997; Marcus-Mendoza & Wright, 2004). A recent study (Benda, 2005) provides some support for this gendered emphasis on relationships. Three hundred men and 300 women who had participated in a boot camp program for offenders were followed up for 5 years in an attempt to better understand what makes individuals reoffend. The best predictors for the men were job satisfaction, association with criminal peers, carrying weapons, and aggression during the boot camp experience. These findings are not surprising and are in line with much research concerning criminal prediction of recidivism (Andrews & Bonta, 2006). However, for the women, the predictors of returning to prison included a large number of social and interpersonal features. These included recent sexual and physical maltreatment, living with a criminal partner, depression, and a history of child abuse. Having children and satisfying romantic relationships reduced the probability of return to prison. Although the men likewise showed high levels of disruption on social and relational variables, such adversities were less potent as predictors of a return to prison than was the case for women. This study is consistent with the body of research that attests to the focal role of problematic relationships among female offenders.

Illness

Consistent with financial hardship, mental illness, and relational distress, disproportionately more female offenders suffer poor health, particularly in terms of infectious diseases, than is the case for male offenders. For example, a recent report indicated that an estimated 12.2% of women in New York state prisons are HIV-positive, a rate that doubles that of male inmates (6.0%; Maruschak, 2006) and is approximately 80 times higher than rates for the general public (Correctional Association of New York, 2009). Along similar lines, levels of hepatitis C infection are proportionately higher among women in correctional settings than among men, with some states reporting infection levels that are as much as double among women (DeGroot, Stubblefield, & Bick, 2001). The pain and potential stigma associated with these diseases can link to feelings of isolation and depression. Interventions that help inmates learn how to deal with their disease appear to be beneficial not only in imparting health information, but also in improving emotional well-being (Pomeroy, Kiam, & Abel, 1999).

Mentally Ill Women in Prison: What Can Be Done?

"Why do so many female offenders suffer from mental illness?" can be answered by the consistent body of scholarship that converges on the conclusion that a large portion of this population has experienced traumatic histories, patterns of victimization, substance abuse, and numerous financial and social problems. This leads to the next question: "What can be done?" Based on an assumption that many women come to understand their world in a context that emphasizes relationships and affiliations with loved ones, it is a reasonable leap to assume that optimal treatment takes place within a relational framework and emphasizes the importance of social support to address trauma histories, substance abuse, and parenting issues (Covington & Bloom, 2006; Morash, Bynum, & Koons, 1998; Sorbello, Eccleston, Ward, & Jones, 2002). Although there are, to date, few clinical trials regarding treatments for female offenders (Haywood, Kravitz, Goldman, & Freeman, 2000; Lewis, 2006), there is emerging evidence in support of this premise. There are promising nascent interventions that directly target offenders' histories of victimization, as well as an emerging body of treatments that focus on the social, familial, and relational stressors that so many female offenders face.

Mental Health Treatments Focused on Trauma and Victimization

Dialectical Behavior Therapy

Linehan (1993) conceptualized BPD as a long-standing pattern of emotional dysregulation caused, in part, by highly aversive early experiences that invalidate the individual's basic sense of safety. The high levels of BPD among female offenders may be mediated by the early victimization that is so prevalent among this population. Accordingly, Linehan's well-established treatment for BPD in outpatient samples, termed Dialectical Behavior Therapy (DBT), has been utilized in prisons in multiple countries (Nee & Farman, 2005). DBT is a skills-based cognitive behavioral program that focuses on self-regulation and coping. Individuals are taught to accept and validate themselves and their situation while simultaneously understanding the need for and becoming comfortable with change (Eccleston & Sorbello, 2002). The first stage of DBT involves individual therapy and group-skills training sessions focused on increasing behavioral control. These group sessions involve four modules: Core Mindfulness, Distress Tolerance, Emotional Regulation, and Interpersonal Effectiveness. Subsequent stages focus on post-traumatic stress, self-esteem, and the individual's personal treatment goals (Nee & Farman, 2005).

Nee and Farman (2005) launched a pilot DBT program for 14 women diagnosed with BPD in three British prisons. All of the participants were White women convicted of serious offenses. Results revealed statistically significant improvement on the Borderline Syndrome Index (a global measure of BPD features), as well as on the measures of impulsivity, locus of control, and emotion regulation.

However, the use of DBT with women prisoners has its critics. For example, Kendall and Pollack (2003) argue that, when applied in a prison environment, cognitive-behavioral approaches like DBT tend to assume that offenders have failed to develop particular cognitive skills and are characterized by thinking deficits. They point out that these cognitive-behavioral approaches are typically designed by White, middle-class researchers and may discredit legitimate prisoner protests against an oppressive institutional regime. Moreover, Kendall and Pollack question the appropriateness of asking prisoners to discuss very personal and distressing life events in a less than private setting, particularly when they are not guaranteed confidentiality. They point to consent forms that indicate that group facilitators must report significant information about the participant's past or present criminal behavior disclosed in treatment. Instead, the authors suggest feminist treatment approaches (e.g., Warner, 2001) and argue that inmates should be permitted to utilize community mental health services.

Furthermore, Pollack (2005) questions the very label of BPD when applied to disenfranchised inmates. She argues that behaviors such as angry outbursts, substance abuse, self-injury, and dissociation that may earn a woman the BPD diagnosis should be assessed in the context of systemic inequalities (poverty, racism). The behaviors may be regarded as self-protective measures for women who have been traumatized, then retraumatized by a prison environment in which abusive dynamics are replicated. She argues that correctional mental health policy "should not define the consequences of gender, class and racial discrimination as mental health needs" (p. 83) and that characterizations of female inmates as irrational, emotional, angry, needy, and sick should thus be challenged.

The Therapeutic Community

As is the case with DBT, therapeutic communities (TCs) are increasingly being adopted in correctional settings (Eliason, 2006; Messina & Prendergast, 2001) and represent another intervention aimed at addressing the negative outcomes of trauma, addiction, and associated emotional and behavioral dysregulation. These communities are highly structured treatment programs intended to provide containment, facilitate communication and attachment formation, and involve and empower participants in the community. TCs address mental health issues including trauma, antisocial personality traits, and psychopathy, as well as substance use and vocational needs (Lewis, 2006). The aim is to develop close-knit, prosocial, supportive groups by using a social learning model. Participants are isolated from the prison's general population. Through peer-counseling they confront and provide feedback to one another in a constructive manner in an effort towards "mutual self-help." Typical TCs include morning and evening meetings, a system of verbal and written notifications of negative behaviors ("pull-ups") and positive acknowledgements ("push-ups"), and a sense of community responsibility for upholding morals and values that are conducive to recovery (Pan, Scarpitti, Inciardi, &

Lockwood, 1993). A few evaluations of TCs in women's prisons indicate that they have resulted in reduced recidivism, but studies of the communities' overall effectiveness are mixed and still uncertain (Messina & Prendergast, 2001).

In one of the few studies to examine mental health effects of TCs, Sacks and colleagues (2008) randomly assigned 314 traumatized women to a TC. Alternately, 151 inmates received the standard outpatient program used at the institution, which involved a 90-hour, 15-week, cognitive-behavioral recovery and relapse-prevention course, as well as access to a number of prison offerings (e.g., a trauma-reduction class, adult education, a community reintegration program) and to psychopharmacological treatment.

The TC in Sacks and colleagues' (2008) study, called "Challenge to Change," involved individual and group counseling and addressed participants' mental health, trauma and abuse histories, relationships, parenting, substance abuse, criminal behaviors, education, and employment. Interventions were provided for 4 hours each day, 5 days per week; inmates spent the remaining 4 hours per day working within the prison. Peer-led groups and other activities took place on weekends. To make the community sensitive to women's unique needs, counselors focused on mutual respect, trust, affiliation, leadership, and becoming a positive role model. Efforts were made to avoid authoritarianism and the repetition of past abusive relationships. Participants remained in the TC for an average of 6 and one-half months. Consistent with the study expectations, Sacks and colleagues found that the TC group reported significantly greater reduction of depressive and post-traumatic symptoms 6 months after being released from prison compared to the control group, and both groups reported significant decreases in substance use.

However, like DBT, TCs have been criticized as being potentially harmful to inmates. Not only is the little research on their effectiveness mixed (Messina & Prendergast, 2001), but some argue that such communities are better suited to male offenders, who are much more likely to have antisocial personality disorder, than to female offenders, who are more likely to have borderline personality, mood, and/or anxiety disorders. Eliason (2006) argues that the confrontational nature of TCs may provide needed structure and boundaries for men but contribute to feelings of helplessness and trigger PTSD symptoms in depressed women. She argues that women, who are socialized to communicate indirectly, may take this direct communication and criticism as a devastating insult to their self-worth, particularly when it is presented in the very public setting of the community. Eliason also suggests that TCs present relational issues for women by instructing them to be open and vulnerable in the community but also telling them to resist forming strong bonds with individual peers. Finally, according to Eliason, notifications of negative behavior (or "pull-ups") can be misused to retaliate or threaten women who have no option of presenting their side.

Women Helping Women Turn Abuse Around (Esuba)

Both DBT and TC represent intensive treatments for female inmates. The criticisms raised by Eliason (2006) and Kendall and Pollack (2003) point to potential dangers in the implementation of the programs in a setting that is, by definition, punitive. Without careful implementation and sensitivity to the conundrum of providing relational support in the context of a punitive environment, the programs may be particularly susceptible to being skewed away from the original intent. Esuba is an alternate program, also directed toward abuse and victimization. However, as a psychoeducational group treatment, rather than an intensive milieu treatment, it may be less prone to the problems identified by critics of DBT and TC.

Esuba was developed for incarcerated women with histories of abuse (Bedard, Pate, & Roe-Sepowitz, 2003). It is a psychoeducational therapy group that follows Herman's (1992) stages of trauma recovery model by providing an emotionally and physically safe environment, remembrance and mourning for past experiences, and finally reconnection or movement toward the future (Ward & Roe-Sepowitz, 2009). It is designed to educate participants about childhood abuse and interpersonal violence, encourage discussion of past experiences, and teach anger management and communication skills (Bedard et al., 2003). Importantly, Esuba emphasizes relationships between participants and the importance of social support while attempting to decrease isolation, shame, and fear (Ward & Roe-Sepowitz, 2009).

Ward and Roe-Sepowitz (2009) documented positive effects of Esuba in an evaluation of a 12-week program for 18 women (who self-identified as having prostituted themselves) in a moderate-security southern prison. Consistent with patterns for most female offenders, the majority of the women had experienced significant childhood and domestic abuse, had substantial substance abuse problems, and had a high level of depression and suicidal episodes. Preassessments and postassessments revealed significant reductions of trauma-related symptoms (e.g., dissociation, nightmares, flashback), as well as reductions in anxiety and depression. Participants also reported improved self-awareness and self-confidence. Bedard et al. (2003) likewise documented positive effects for Esuba in a study of the effect of a two-phase, 24-week program on the self-esteem of traumatized inmates (96 females and 61 males). Results indicated that the Esuba program significantly improved offenders' mean self-esteem scores. Furthermore, female inmates reported decreased sensitivity to criticism and increased trust in others, stability of self, and self-satisfaction.

Summary: Trauma-Focused Intervention

Given the high levels of trauma and victimization among female offenders, and the pathways between such trauma and offending, it is sensible to position treatment within a context for dealing with grief and anger stemming from past victimization. For women with long-standing problems with associated emotional dysregulation, intensive treatments such as DBT or TC make sense. The rationale and theoretical assumptions that focus on the importance of relationships, healing, and intensive support likewise are reasonable. However, if implemented improperly, these treatments may cause more harm than good. The less intensive treatments, such as Esuba, may be less prone to these problems but are plausibly less effective with highly traumatized inmates. This is a clear area where more clinical trials are needed to document both positive and negative outcomes of trauma-focused treatments and to determine whether and for whom "high-dosage" treatments, such as DBT and TC, are appropriate.

Interventions That Indirectly Address the Mental Health Needs of Female Offenders

The negative effects of victimization and abuse (i.e., mental illness, substance abuse, and emotional dysregulation) are the targets of several previously described trauma-focused interventions. Often the women in these interventions have substantial and well-documented mental illness that captures the attention of the correctional institution.

However, many women in prison may suffer from depression and anxiety that can become "normalized" in a context where there are so many women with clear evidence of mental distress. For many women in prison, their most likely form of mental health intervention may come not so much from a designated mental health intervention, but from an intervention designed to treat or ameliorate other stressors. For example, most women's prisons have parenting classes for inmates (Pollock, 2002) that can serve to indirectly improve the stress among the affected mothers (Loper & Turek, 2006). Interventions that address prominent stressors for incarcerated women, such as separation from children, physical illness, and lack of relational support, can provide mental health benefits in the correctional setting.

Parenting Programs

Loper and Novero (in press) reviewed 23 parenting education interventions for incarcerated parents. Although the interventions differed in length and content, they shared a focus on improving communication patterns between inmate parents and their children within the context of a prison separation. Most of the interventions measured outcomes in terms of parenting attitudes and communication patterns with children and caregivers. However, 10 of the interventions also included measures of emotional well-being, such as self-esteem, parenting stress, and mental health symptoms. In 9 of these 10 studies, there were reported beneficial effects. For example, Loper and Turek (in press) evaluated a parenting program designed for mothers in prison that taught inmates a strategy for dealing with parenting stress through brief relaxation to reduce impulsive reactions, followed by cognitive reframing of negative thoughts about themselves and their relationships with children. The intervention taught strategies for having positive connections with children in the viable communications open to long-term offenders (i.e., phone calls, letters, personal visits, and contact with caregivers). In an evaluation of the program with 106 imprisoned mothers, Loper and Turek found significant reductions in parenting stress, depression, anxiety, and other mental health indices. Other studies of parenting interventions likewise point to mental health benefits for the inmates. For example, in a study of women in a state prison, Harm, Thompson, and Chambers (1998) found that inmates with serious drug or alcohol problems, as well as inmates who had reported previous physical abuse, showed significant improvements on measures of self-esteem after participation in a parenting education program.

Parenting programs may enhance the mental health of female inmates in other ways. Houck and Loper (2002) found that women with higher levels of parenting distress also had more "tickets" or official documentation of infractions at the prison. If parenting programs are successful in reducing incarcerated mothers' parenting stress, and associated feelings of emotional turmoil, these women may be more able to be good citizens of the institution and better adjust to the constraints of prison life. Parenting programs may also offer an opportunity for connection and community with other offenders that can likewise serve to heal. For example, in Virginia, Mothers Inside Loving Kids (MILK) continues to operate as a community of incarcerated women who meet weekly to discuss difficulties and stressors related to being a mother in prison, plan activities for upcoming visits, and receive educational information regarding parenting (Moore & Clement, 1998).

Community Engagement Through Religious Activities

The sense of community and personal support that can be important to the mental health of female inmates is not always easily available in prisons. Depending upon the security level of the institution, the formation of community may be overtly discouraged to ensure safety. Although education programs, such as parenting classes, may offer such a community, inmates often have to wait a long time to enroll in these activities, which are usually time-limited.

Religious participation, though not a mental health intervention in itself, can enable the creation of a community for offenders that is reliably offered and accessible. The Religious Land Use Act and Institutionalized Persons Act of 2000 protects prisoners' right to exercise their religion. Like other prosocial educational opportunities, it has been shown to have positive effects on inmates' mental health. O'Connor, Ryan, Sakovich, and Parikh (1997) surveyed 23 inmates who recently attended Prison Fellowship Bible study sessions in a maximum-security women's prison in South Carolina. The women stated that religious programs were more helpful than their family, friends, work, education, and psychiatric programs for adjustment to prison life. Similarly, during interviews with 35 female inmates in a medium-security prison in the Midwest, Greer (2002) found that religious experiences reportedly helped 16 of the women address the emotional discord they felt while in prison. Several women stated that their belief in a "higher power" helped them cope with their traumatic past, their volatile emotions (which they had previously suppressed with drugs), and the uncertainty of their future. During a focus group with 15 African American mothers in a midwestern prison, many of the women reported depending on their spirituality to make sense of their imprisonment and provide hope for the future (Stringer, 2009). Finally, in a study of 213 women incarcerated in central Virginia, Levitt and Loper (2009) found that women who reported receiving a high degree of support from their participation in religious activities reported less depression and fewer instances of feeling angry than those who did not attend religious activities.

Religious activities, like parenting programs or healthcare educational programs, are not designed specifically as mental health interventions. However, the reported improvements in emotional well-being of women involved in such programming fits with the findings about the key ingredient of successful mental health intervention: a supportive network that provides an opportunity to safely process previous traumas and learn prosocial behaviors.

Prison Animal Programs

An unconventional, but potentially effective, mental health intervention is a prison animal program. Such programs are increasingly being incorporated into correctional offerings (Furst, 2006). Prison animal programs operate in at least 36 U.S. states, Canada, Australia, New Zealand, and Italy, and most commonly follow a community service model in which homeless animals (usually dogs) at risk for euthanasia are trained by inmates so that they are more adoptable and then returned to the shelter. In other programs, inmates train service dogs for disabled people. Although animals are not necessarily included as a therapeutic intervention for the inmate or used in conjunction with clinical methods, anecdotal reports typically reflect the value of these programs on prisoners' mental health (Furst, 2006). For example, in a study at a maximum-security psychiatric hospital for the criminally insane, patients on a ward with pets required "half as much medication, had drastically reduced incidents of violence, and had no suicide attempts during the year-long comparison period" (Lee, 1987, p. 232, as cited in Furst, 2006). By contrast, the ward without pets had eight documented suicide attempts during the same year.

The therapeutic value of the animals seems to result from several factors, among them the sometimes tumultuous relationships inmates have with one another and their limited opportunities to develop relationships with noninmates. Animals provide unconditional positive regard. They do not care about the inmates' past mistakes. They also provide a sense of security, an outlet for physical affection (Furst, 2006), and fulfillment of an individual's need to nurture. Animal programs sometimes include vocational training and/or employment for prisoners as well (Walsh & Mertin, 1994).

Although the theorized mental health benefits of animal programs make sense, to date there are few studies that systematically evaluate the benefits of such intervention. A welcome exception is a recent study of dog training programs at a women's prison in Kansas. Britton and Button (2007) reported that many women found the routines and schedules that caring for an animal imposed to be useful because it forced them to get out of bed and tend to the dogs despite their depression. Importantly, caring for abused animals provided a unique way for the women, many of whom had also been abused, to work through their own trauma issues by identifying with the animal's own difficult past. Both inmates and staff reported that the presence of the dogs seemed to have a "normalizing" effect on the prison, making it seem like a calmer, less sterile environment. The dogs' presence improved relationships between staff members and inmates by providing a neutral context for interactions in which normally authoritarian staff might soften. Furthermore, training dogs was one of the only opportunities for meaningful work offered by the prison, which tended to employ inmates in institutional maintenance. The graduation ceremonies, in which trained dogs were given to recipients who expressed nonjudgmental gratitude, were particularly emotional for the inmates; the authors noted the necessity of receiving this kind of feedback for women. One inmate reflected on the parallel between her own lack of freedom and the freedom provided to the disabled individuals who would be given the service dogs she trained: "We're locked up inside a fence, those people are locked up in their own bodies. I am glad that I can give them some freedom to live" (p. 206).

Case History

Consider the case of Sue Kennon, a 59-year-old woman who spent 15 years behind bars at the Virginia Correctional Center for Women in Goochland, Virginia (see Text Box 10.1). Like many female inmates, Sue experienced trauma and struggled with drug addiction prior to entering prison. In an interview with the authors, Sue describes her pathway to prison, as well as her efforts to overcome sadness and to find meaning during her years in prison.

TEXT BOX 10.1
SUE'S STORY

1. Tell us about your life before coming to prison.

   I came from a nice home, and I moved to Richmond, Virginia, where I met my husband, C. He was beautiful to look at, funny, got a little crazy streak. We were married for 2 years when I became pregnant. Life was good. And then the stress happened. It was July—real hot days. He went to the boat landing to go for a swim and cool off. I got a call from one of the neighbors down there and they wanted me to come because he was hurt. I was 7 months pregnant. I went to the dock and I saw an ambulance. I jumped in the ambulance and there he was. Not a scratch on him. Didn't look dead. He had hit a submerged log and severed his spinal chord. That was the big stressor.

2. So what did you do next?

C was a disabled vet and he would get these severe migraine headaches and take some painkiller. I started taking them. I started going to all these doctors in Richmond [for prescriptions] and I started hanging out at the cemetery all the time, thinking of C. At that point, I had been to about 50,000 doctors, for prescriptions. But you rationalize it because you are taking a prescription and it was legal. After 3 years, I ran into a guy I went to high school with and I started living with him. We had two little boys together. So, now I had three children and I was scared because I knew I was going to get caught. I tried to detox myself. But you cannot do that alone. I ran into a girl I knew from school. I told her I was calling in scripts and I was scared to death of getting caught, and she explained to me it was easy to get heroin. So I did.

3. How did you pay for the drugs?

I stole from everybody, my mother and father, my children's piggy banks, stores. Pawn shops all knew me. I pawned everything I had. I loaned my car out to the dope man for a weekend. It didn't even take 6 months before getting a big habit. All I wanted to do was feel good on my own without this wrenching, awful pain about C. I did not go to a psychologist or a psychiatrist. It was a family thing. We do not let anybody see our emotions kind of thing.

4. How were you arrested?

I decided, okay, you are going to have to end it [her life]. In the meantime, I am going through withdrawal. I went to the shopping center, got a little toy gun, and robbed three little dress shops. I was a stupid robber. On all three robberies I got only $180 total.

Then after that came the day. It was a beautiful July Saturday, and I knew that I could not wait to die. The gut-wrenching part was trying to figure out how to say goodbye to my children. So I decided when they were taking their naps I would write each of them a little letter trying to explain as best I could that it was nothing they did, that Mommy was sick and they could forgive me. So I did that.

There was a guy in the neighborhood who repaired old guns and so I went to visit his wife. When she stepped out of the room for a minute, I pulled a gun down and put it in my pocketbook—no bullets, though. Then I went to this pharmacy with it. I pulled the gun out, said I was an addict and wanted to die, and just "give me all of your narcotics." It all happened so fast. He rushed toward me and I heard this noise, and I start running out the door. I remember feeling that I was wet and like I was on an escalator. For a minute I thought I was dead, and then I thought, "Well, I am wet, maybe he threw a pail of water on me." I look over and my arm is hanging off of me, blood everywhere. I had been shot and I didn't even feel it. So I did a 180 and ran back at him, put my hands up and cried and begged him to put a bullet in my head before the police came. I said "I can't live like this anymore, please don't make me live like this anymore."

(Continued)

(Continued)

5. What was it like when you were arrested?

I walked into the jail. I was looking all crazy and I had my arm in a sling. All I could do was cry. Turns out the women there were like a sisterhood, and they just wanted to help out another addict. For 6 days they took care of me. It was nasty and gross, and horrible and painful. When I finally got to my own mind and realized how I had failed, the only thing that came to my head was something my grandmother used to say, "If you ever feel like you just can't draw another breath, just go tell the truth and shame the devil." So, I had a court appointed lawyer and I told him, "Let's just say that I am guilty." I ended up with 48 years. When I got up here to the prison, I found out that I did not have parole. [Under an interpretation of the Virginia "three-strikes" law, Sue was considered a repeat offender as she confessed to multiple robberies, and she received the maximum sentence with no parole.]

6. What was the hardest part of prison?

Being separated from my children was the worst thing. The sickness that stays with you in your heart and your stomach, knowing that one day they are going to want to talk to you about this, and why do they have to see Mommy by going up to this prison. They were just too little to understand. That was the worst pain that I have ever felt in my life. I'd look at pictures and then go through and look at pictures again. And then some days I couldn't look—too hard. And hearing these little voices. You miss everything—every graduation, proms, first dates, events. Oh God! The guilt will just eat you alive if you are not careful.

7. Did you ever get mental health treatment in prison?

I had a counselor. She was the most kind, understanding, and supportive person I have ever met in my life. We found these crazy hats one day—all kinds of ladies hats with the little veil that goes over your nose. We put them on and laughed, like we were at a tea or something. It felt so human and fun.

In year 12 [of her sentence], I remember clear as a bell waking up that day thinking, "I have only done 12 years of this sentence—just a part. I have so many more." I lost my appetite, became lethargic, dark circles under my eyes, because I couldn't sleep. I dumped off weight. Finally, I sent a message to Dr. T, our psychiatrist. She got me in real quick, and things got better.

8. What made the biggest difference in your mental health and adjustment in prison?

Well, education. This wonderful little old woman met the chaplain from the prison and she wrote to me and she asked what she could do to help me want to live. I only had a high school degree, and I thought maybe she can help me with a long-distance learning course, Psych 101. That's how this started. [Sue continued her online education and went on to receive her AA degree, and then a BA from Ohio University. She became the first offender in Virginia to receive a BA degree while incarcerated. After release, she completed work initiated during prison on a master's degree in developmental psychology from Virginia Commonwealth University.]

Also the women I knew in prison made a difference. When my daughter got married, I wanted to get her something real personal. The lady in the gym gave me some beautiful blue satin, lace, and elastic. I brought it back and called everybody, "Let's do the garter thing for my daughter." Oh, they made the most beautiful garter. She still has it to this day. I put it in a box and sent it to her with this poem that my sister-in-law read at the shower. Then I wrote the assistant warden to see if a family member could make a video and send it to me. She worked it out so I could. Then the whole rec room, they fixed a big thing of popcorn and we all watched my daughter. We are jumping up and crying. When we heard "You may kiss the bride," everybody started throwing popcorn and singing. It was just wonderful. The next day my daughter and her new husband, instead of going on their honeymoon, came to see me. So much to be grateful for. A lot of pain and a lot of good stuff.

9. Your master's thesis was on the parenting education program you developed?

Yes. I am really interested in child development, what's going on with kids, so I focused my studies on that. I looked for a parenting program for mothers in prison, but there was none. So that's when I got the idea to write my own. It took a couple years trying different things out in classes I taught with the women, and once it was done, the DCE [Virginia Department of Correctional Education] accepted it and thought it was really good and made it part of the curriculum.

During Sue's 15th year, there was growing pressure from numerous individuals inside and outside of the correctional system to reevaluate the appropriateness of the "three-strikes" law for Sue's sentencing. Based on her achievements in prison, she was subsequently not only granted parole but was shortly thereafter hired by the DCE as coordinator of parenting education. The parenting curriculum she developed in prison is in use today by Virginia inmates (Virginia Department of Correctional Education, 2007). In 2006, the governor of Virginia presented Suzanne Kennon with a special award in recognition of her innovative programming and contribution to correctional education. While on the stage to receive her award, she reports that Governor Kaine leaned over and quietly asked, "Did you ever imagine you would be here?"

Like the majority of female offenders, Sue's pathway to prison involved an initial traumatic event—the sudden loss of her husband. She medicated her depression and pain with prescription drugs and eventually heroin. She stole to obtain money to buy drugs. Her offense was itself a suicide attempt. Once in prison, her greatest anguish was separation from her beloved children. These are experiences she shares with many of the women in prison today.

Unlike many women in prison, Sue's story has a happy ending. The relationship she formed with her counselor, her community with other offenders, and most of all, the opportunity to pursue an education and then offer the benefits of that education to other inmates led Sue to her current success. Other women in prison who suffer from mental distress can likewise find relief through interventions that provide a safe and supportive environment, the chance to deal with emotional pain, and educational programs that teach new skills and engender a sense of self-worth.

Summary and Conclusions

More research is needed regarding the effectiveness of interventions for female offenders. With some exceptions, there are few intervention studies that include stringent benchmarks for learning what works, such as random assignment to treatments, inclusion of control groups, adequate sample size, and attention to measuring treatment integrity. But the theoretical basis for designing gender-specific and effective intervention is available, drawing from the mounting body of research attesting to the intersection of mental illness with previous victimization and trauma, substance abuse, and numerous social and familial stressors, as well as the importance of supportive relationships and community. The road from theory to practice for treating mental illness in female offenders still needs some paving. But the groundwork is strong, the need is clear, and more and better interventions are emerging.

KEY TERMS

Prevalence rates

Victimization

Physical and sexual abuse

Domestic violence

Substance abuse

Mental illness

Childhood Victimization Model

Relational Model

Trauma

Post-traumatic stress disorder (PTSD)

Borderline personality disorder (BPD)

Emotional dysregulation

Self-medication

Co-occurring mental disorders

Parenting stress

Social support

Dialectic Behavior Therapy (DBT)

Therapeutic community

Trauma-focused interventions

Parenting programs

Community engagement programs

Prison animal programs

DISCUSSION QUESTIONS

1. How is the prison experience different for male and female offenders? Are there different issues or factors that influence or impact prison adjustment for male and female offenders?

2. Describe two common pathways that lead women to prison.

3. What are the obstacles, ethical concerns, benefits, or drawbacks to importing therapy programs that have been demonstrated to be effective in the community into the prison environment?

4. Should female offenders receive the same program and service opportunities that male offenders receive, or should they receive different programs and services?

5. Discuss the merits and drawbacks of the "three-strikes" legislation described in Sue's story. In Sue's case, was it an appropriate sanction? Should there be exceptions to the legislation? If so, under what circumstances?

References

Abram, K. M., Teplin, L. A., & McClelland, G. M. (2003). Comorbidity of severe psychiatric disorders and substance use disorders among women in jail. *American Journal of Psychiatry, 160*, 1007–1010.

Adler, F. (1975). *Sisters in crime.* New York, NY: McGraw-Hill.

Alemagno, S. A. (2001). Women in jail: Is substance abuse treatment enough? *American Journal of Public Health, 91*, 798–800.

Andrews, D., & Bonta, J. (1995). *The Level of Service Inventory—Revised user's manual.* Toronto, Ontario, Canada: Multi-Health Systems.

Andrews, D. A., & Bonta, J. (2006). *The psychology of criminal conduct* (4th ed.). Newark, NJ: LexisNexis.

Arditti, J., & Few, A. (2008). Maternal distress and women's re-entry into family and community life. *Family Process, 47*, 303–321.

Bedard, L. E., Pate, K. N., & Roe-Sepowitz, D. E. (2003). A program analysis of Esuba: Helping turn abuse around for inmates. *International Journal of Offender Therapy and Comparative Criminology, 47*, 597–607.

Benda, B. B. (2005). Gender differences in life-course theory of recidivism: A survival analysis. *International Journal of Offender Therapy and Comparative Criminology, 49*, 325–342.

Bloom, B. (1995). Imprisoned mothers. In K. Gabel & D. Johnston (Eds.), *Children of incarcerated parents* (pp. 21–30). New York, NY: Lexington Books.

Britton, D. M., & Button, A. (2007). "This isn't about us": Benefits of dog training programs in a women's prison. In S. Miller (Ed.), *Criminal justice and diversity: Voices from the field* (pp. 195–209). Boston, MA: Northeastern University Press.

Brown, M., & Bloom, B. (2009). Re-entry and renegotiating motherhood: Maternal identity and success on parole. *Crime & Delinquency, 55*, 313–336.

Browne, A., Miller, B., & Maguin, E. (1999). Prevalence and severity of lifetime physical and sexual victimization among incarcerated women. *International Journal of Law & Psychiatry, 22*, 301–322.

Bunch, B. J., Foley, L. A., & Urbina, S. P. (1983). Psychology of violent female offenders: A sex-role perspective. *Prison Journal, 63*, 66–79.

Burton, L. M. (1992). Black grandparents rearing children of drug-addicted parents: Stressors, outcomes, and social service needs. *Gerontologist, 32*, 744–751.

Chesney-Lind, M. (1997). *The female offender: Girls, women, and crime.* Thousand Oaks, CA: Sage.

Correctional Association of New York. (2009, April). *Incarcerated women & HIV/hepatitis C fact sheet.* New York, NY: Author. Retrieved November 15, 2009, from http://www.correctional association.org/publications/download/wipp/factsheets/HIV_Hep_C_Fact_Sheet_2009_FINAL .pdf

Covington, S., & Bloom, B. (2006). Gender responsive treatment and services in correctional settings. *Women & Therapy, 29*, 9–33.

DeGroot, A. S., Stubblefield, E., & Bick, J. (2001). Hepatitis C: A correctional-public health opportunity. *Medscape Infectious Disease, 3*, 1–14. Retrieved November 11, 2009, from http://www.medscape.com/viewarticle/408298

Douglas, B. (2000). *Adult female inmates: Crime and demographics.* Charleston: West Virginia Division of Corrections. Retrieved November 16, 2009, from http://www.wvdoc.com/wvdoc/ Portals/0/documents/female.pdf

Eccleston, L., & Sorbello, L. (2002). The RUSH program—Real Understanding of Self-Help: A suicide and self-harm prevention initiative within a prison setting. *Australian Psychologist, 37*, 237–244.

Eliason, M. J. (2006). Are therapeutic communities therapeutic for women? *Substance Abuse Treatment, Prevention, and Policy, 1*(3), 1–7. Retrieved October 30, 2009, from http://www.substanceabusepolicy.com/content/1/1/3

Federal Bureau of Investigation. (2009). *Crime in the United States 2008.* Washington, DC: Government Printing Office.

Furst, G. (2006). Prison-based animal programs: A national survey. *The Prison Journal, 86*, 407–430.

Gilligan, C. (1982). *In a different voice: Psychological theory and women's development*. Cambridge, MA: Harvard University Press.

Glaze, L., & Maruschak, L. (2008). *Parents in prison and their minor children* (Bureau of Justice Statistics Special Report NCJ 222984). Washington, DC: National Criminal Justice Reference Service.

Greenfeld, L., & Snell, T. L. (1999). *Women offenders* (Bureau of Justice Statistics Special Report NCJ 175688). Washington, DC: National Criminal Justice Reference Service.

Greer, K. (2002). Walking an emotional tightrope: Managing emotions in a women's prison. *Symbolic Interaction, 25*, 117–139.

Hairston, C. F. (1991). Mothers in jail: Parent-child separation and jail visitation. *Affilia, 6*, 9–27.

Harlow, C. W. (1999). *Prior abuse reported by inmates and probationers* (Bureau of Justice Statistics Special Report NCJ 172879). Washington, DC: National Criminal Justice Reference Service.

Harm, N. J., Thompson, P. J., & Chambers, H. (1998). The effectiveness of parent education for substance abusing women offenders. *Alcoholism Treatment Quarterly, 16*(3), 63–77.

Haywood, T. W., Kravitz, H. M., Goldman, L. B., & Freeman, A. (2000). Characteristics of women in jail and treatment orientations: A review. *Behavior Modification, 24*, 307–324.

Heilbrun, K., DeMatteo, D., Fretz, R., Erickson, J., Yasuhara, K., & Anumba, N. (2008). How "specific" are gender-specific rehabilitation needs? An empirical analysis. *Criminal Justice and Behavior, 35*, 1382–1397.

Herman, J. L. (1992). *Trauma and recovery*. New York, NY: Basic Books.

Houck, K. D., & Loper, A. B. (2002). The relationship of parenting stress to adjustment among mothers in prison. *American Journal of Orthopsychiatry, 72*, 548–558.

Human Rights Watch Women's Rights Project. (1996). *All too familiar: Sexual abuse of women in U.S. state prisons*. New York, NY: Human Rights Watch.

James, D. J., & Glaze, L. E. (2006, September). *Mental health problems of prison and jail inmates* (Bureau of Justice Statistics Special Report NCJ 213600). Washington, DC: National Criminal Justice Reference Service.

Johnson, E. I., & Waldfogel, J. (2002). Parental incarceration: Recent trends and implications for child welfare. *Social Service Review, 76*, 460–479.

Jordan, B. K., Schlenger, W. E., Fairbank, J. A., & Caddell, J. M. (1996). Prevalence of psychiatric disorders among incarcerated women: Convicted felons entering prison. *Archives of General Psychiatry, 53*, 513–519.

Kendall, K., & Pollack, S. (2003). Cognitive behaviorism in women's prisons: A critical analysis of therapeutic assumptions and practices. In B. Bloom (Ed.), *Gendered justice: Addressing female offenders* (pp. 69–96). Durham, NC: Carolina Academic Press.

Kessler, R. C., Sonnega, A., Bromet, E., Hughes, M., & Nelson, C. B. (1995). Posttraumatic stress disorder in the national comorbidity survey. *Archives of General Psychiatry, 52*, 1048–1060.

Levitt, L., & Loper, A. (2009). The influence of religious participation on the adjustment of female inmates. *American Journal of Orthopsychiatry, 79*, 1–7.

Lewis, C. (2006). Treating incarcerated women: Gender matters. *Psychiatric Clinics of North America, 29*, 773–789.

Linehan, M. (1993). *Cognitive-behavioral treatment of borderline personality disorder*. New York, NY: Guilford.

Loper, A. B., Carlson, W., Levitt, L., & Scheffel, K. (2009). Parenting stress, alliance, child contact and adjustment of imprisoned mothers and fathers. *Journal of Offender Rehabilitation, 48*, 483–503.

Loper, A. B., & Cornell, D. G. (1996). Homicide by juvenile girls. *Journal of Child and Family Studies, 5*, 323–336.

Loper, A. B., & Novero, C. (in press). Parenting programs for prisoners: Current research and new directions. In J. M. Eddy & J. Poehlmann (Eds.), *Children affected by parental incarceration*. Washington, DC: Urban Institute Press.

Loper, A. B., & Turek, E. H. (2006). Parenting programs for incarcerated parents: Current research and future directions. *Criminal Justice Policy Review, 17*, 407–427.

Loper, A. B., & Turek, E. H. (in press). Improving the emotional adjustment and communication patterns of incarcerated mothers: Effectiveness of a prison parenting intervention. *Journal of Child and Family Studies.*

Lorber, J. (2001). *Gender inequality: Feminist theories and politics.* Los Angeles, CA: Roxbury.

Magaletta, P. R., Diamond, P. M., Faust, E., Daggett, D., & Camp, S. (2009). Estimating the mental illness component of service need in corrections: Results from the mental health prevalence project. *Criminal Justice and Behavior, 36,* 229–244.

Magaletta, P. R., & Herbst, D. P. (2001). Fathering from prison: Common struggles and successful solutions. *Psychotherapy: Theory, Research, Practice, Training, 38,* 88–96.

Manchak, S. M., Skeem, J., Douglas, K. S., & Siranosian, M. (2009). Does gender moderate the predictive utility of the Level of Service Inventory–Revised (LSI-R) for serious violent offenders? *Criminal Justice and Behavior, 36,* 425–442.

Marcus-Mendoza, S., & Wright, E. (2004). Decontextualizing female criminality: Treating abused women in prison in the United States. *Feminism & Psychology, 14,* 250–255.

Maruschak, L. M. (2006). *HIV in prisons, 2006.* Washington, DC: U.S. Department of Justice, Bureau of Justice Statistics. Retrieved December 8, 2009, from http://www.ojp.usdoj.gov/bjs/pub/pdf/hivp06.pdf

McClellan, S. D., Farabee, D., & Crouch, M. (1997). Early victimization, drug use and criminality: A comparison of male and female prisoners. *Criminal Justice and Behavior, 24,* 455–476.

Messina, N., Grella, C., Burdon, W., & Prendergast, M. (2007). Childhood adverse events and current traumatic distress: A comparison of men and women drug-dependent prisoners. *Criminal Justice and Behavior, 34,* 1385–1401.

Messina, N. P., & Prendergast, M. L. (2001, July/August). Therapeutic community treatment for women in prison: Some success, but the jury is still out. *Offender Substance Abuse Report, 1*(4), 49–64.

Moloney, K. P., van den Bergh, B. J., & Moller, L. F. (2009). Women in prison: The central issues of gender characteristics and trauma history. *Public Health, 123,* 426–430.

Moore, A. R., & Clement, M. J. (1998). Effects of parenting training for incarcerated mothers. *Journal of Offender Rehabilitation, 27*(1-2), 57–72.

Morash, M., Bynum, T. S., & Koons, B. A. (1998, August). *Women offenders: Programming needs and promising approaches* (Research in Brief). Washington, DC: National Institute of Justice.

Nee, C., & Farman, S. (2005). Female prisoners with borderline personality disorder: Some promising treatment developments. *Criminal Behaviour and Mental Health, 15*(1), 2–16.

O'Connor, T. P., Ryan, P., Sakovich, P., & Parikh, C. (1997). *Women inmates, prison fellowship, and adjusting to prison life in South Carolina.* Washington, DC: Center for Social Research.

Pan, H., Scarpitti, F. R., Inciardi, J., & Lockwood, D. (1993). Some considerations on therapeutic communities in corrections. In J. Inciardi (Ed.), *Drug treatment and criminal justice* (pp. 30–43). Newbury Park, CA: Sage.

Pollack, S. (2005). Taming the shrew: Regulating prisoners through women-centered mental health programming. *Critical Criminology, 13,* 71–87.

Pollock, J. (2002). *Women, prison, and crime* (2nd ed.). Belmont, CA: Wadsworth.

Pomeroy, E. C., Kiam, R., & Abel, E. M. (1999). The effectiveness of a psychoeducational group for HIV-infected/affected incarcerated women. *Research on Social Work Practice, 9,* 171–187.

Religious Land Use Act and Institutionalized Persons Act of 2000, 42 U.S.C §§ 2000cc-2000cc-5 (2000).

Sacks, J. Y. (2004). Women with co-occurring substance use and mental disorders (COD) in the criminal justice system: A research review. *Behavioral Sciences and the Law, 22,* 449–466.

Sacks, J. Y., Sacks, S., McKendrick, K., Banks, S., Schoeneberger, M., Hamilton, et al. (2008). Prison therapeutic community treatment for female offenders: Profiles and preliminary findings for mental health and other variables (crime, substance use and HIV risk). *Journal of Offender Rehabilitation, 46,* 233–261.

Salisbury, E. J., & Van Voorhis, P. (2009). Gendered pathways: A quantitative investigation of women probationers' paths to incarceration. *Criminal Justice and Behavior, 36,* 541–566.

Siegel, J. A., & Williams, L. M. (2003). The relationship between child sexual abuse and female delinquency and crime: A prospective study. *Journal of Research in Crime and Delinquency, 40,* 71–94.

Sorbello, L., Eccleston, L., Ward, T., & Jones, R. (2002). Treatment needs of female offenders: A review. *Australian Psychologist, 37,* 198–205.

development of COD, but neither in itself is a sufficient cause. The stressor and diathesis must both be present for CODs to occur and manifest themselves, and the presence of one disorder constitutes vulnerability for the development of other disorders and CODs. Consider how this model applies to the composite case study presented in Text Box 11.1.

TEXT BOX 11.1
CASE STUDY

E.S. is a White female who is nearing completion of a third prison term. She became involved in illegal activities during middle school, when she shoplifted from Wal-Mart stores because she thought it was exciting and it provided her with money for drugs. She noted that all of her friends were shoplifting, and they had a competition to see who could steal the most merchandise.

She experienced sexual abuse, first from her father and then from a series of stepfathers, beginning at age 5 and continuing until she left home at the age of 16. In addition to the sexual abuse, she was physically abused by her father and one of her stepfathers. Her mother was addicted to alcohol and was never able to keep a job or to provide E.S. with a supportive environment. E.S. dropped out of school at 16, was convicted of shoplifting, and was sent to prison, where she worked on her GED. Unfortunately, she did not complete the GED before being released from prison. Even though she reported a long history of poly-substance abuse and dependence, she stated she was more addicted to crime than she was to drugs. She liked the "adrenaline rush" of stealing from stores and believed it was okay because it did not hurt anyone. She indicated that she lost custody of her three children as a result of her substance use and her criminal behavior.

Although she was diagnosed with bipolar disorder when she entered the prison system, it took a period of time to establish the diagnosis because prior to her most recent incarceration, she inconsistently took appropriate psychotropic medications for this disorder and never had a period of abstinence from methamphetamine and alcohol for longer than 3 weeks. The fact that she had never been diagnosed in the community, and only took medication when she was in jail, made the accuracy of the diagnosis uncertain. She has a family history of mental illness, with both her biological mother and father having been diagnosed with bipolar disorder. After observation in the correctional facility, a review of treatment records from the jail, and a careful diagnostic evaluation, her diagnosis of bipolar disorder was confirmed. She was also diagnosed with post-traumatic stress disorder and poly-substance dependence.

The treatment she received in prison included 9 months in the prison's Special Needs Unit—an inpatient unit for women with COD. During her time in this program, she participated in treatment groups for post-traumatic stress, substance abuse, parenting, women's issues, and relationship issues. She also participated in individual treatment and psychotropic medication management.

She refused to participate in any reentry planning during her previous incarcerations but became involved in an "in-reach" program for women with COD who would soon be returning to the community. She completed the "in-reach" portion of the program and continued treatment in the community. She got a job, has maintained sobriety and psychiatric stability, and has not engaged in any further criminal activity since her release from prison.

This case highlights a number of issues commonly experienced by those with COD in the correctional system and illustrates the diathesis-stress model. E.S. has a family history (i.e., genetic vulnerability) for both substance abuse disorders and mental illness. The sexual abuse she suffered along with the other life stressors she experienced may have served as a catalyst for the development of her co-occurring mental and substance abuse disorders. E.S.'s history of physical and sexual abuse, her early alcohol and drug use, her educational difficulties, and her association with other kids who engage in criminal behavior are common patterns found among many individuals who eventually come through the criminal justice system. Once in the system, they are frequently unmotivated for treatment and only become so after several episodes of incarceration and unsuccessful attempts at remaining in the community. Similar to E.S., treatment has to focus on all aspects of offenders' COD and teach skills necessary to maintain stability, achieve relapse and recidivism prevention, and move towards recovery.

Practical Considerations: Treatment Goals and Strategies

The treatment goals and strategies for criminal offenders with COD in correctional settings are very similar to those for individuals with COD in the community. Community goals and strategies typically include appropriate identification of all disorders, motivation enhancement, relapse and recidivism prevention, and achievement of recovery (Drake, Xie, McHugo, & Shumway, 2004; Mead & Copeland, 2000; Torrey & Wyzik, 2000). These community goals and strategies might be redefined somewhat to better suit the correctional environment and might include (a) appropriate screening, assessment, and diagnosis; (b) multidisciplinary treatment planning; (c) enhanced treatment motivation through assertive outreach efforts; (d) active treatment and medication management; and (e) reintegration or reentry services, which incorporate social support interventions, a long-term perspective, and comprehensiveness of services (Drake, Xie, et al., 2004). Each of these treatment goals and strategies will be discussed briefly.

Screening, Assessment, and Diagnosis

Correctional facilities utilize a variety of screening techniques and instruments to determine the presence of mental illness, substance use disorders, personality disorders, developmental disability, and traumatic brain injury (see Chapter 4 for a more detailed discussion of correctional screening and assessment). The outcome of the screening and assessment process should be the identification and diagnosis of those individuals with one or more mental health problems. Good assessment is clearly the first step in providing appropriate treatment. The second step is to assess the offender's level of motivation for treatment of each diagnosed disorder. This can be accomplished by utilizing a variety of motivation assessment instruments. Table 11.1 lists specific instruments that can be used to assess motivation for COD treatment.

Frequently there are varying levels of motivation for change across the COD. For example, an individual who has just gotten a charge of driving while intoxicated may be quite motivated to avoid further criminal behavior and legal system involvement but may not be motivated to discontinue drinking or to address any underlying mental illness. The goal of assessing motivation levels is to increase motivation for recovery across all disorders, regardless of which one the person is most motivated to address at the point of entry into the criminal justice system.

Table 11.1	Assessment Instruments for COD
Co-Occurring Disorder	*Motivation Assessment Instrument*
Mental illness	Readiness to Change Questionnaire (Heather, Luce, Peck, Dunbar, & James, 1999)
	Treatment Motivation Questionnaire (Ryan, Plant, & O'Malley, 1995)
Substance use	Stages of Change Readiness and Treatment Eagerness Scale (SOCRATES; W. R. Miller & Rollnick, 1991)
	Adult Self Assessment Questionnaire (ADSAQ; Wanberg & Milkman, 1993/2004)
	University of Rhode Island Change Assessment (URICA; DiClemente & Hughes, 1990).
Developmental disabilities	General assessment of readiness for change in "Changing for Good" (Prochaska, Norcross, & DiClemente, 1994)
Criminal conduct	General assessment of readiness for change in "Changing for Good" (Prochaska et al., 1994)

Multidisciplinary Individualized Treatment Planning

The information gained from the initial assessment process should be used to develop a multidisciplinary, individualized treatment plan. Multidisciplinary, individualized treatment planning is an essential element of improving quality of care (Davis, Barnhill, & Saeed, 2008; Pringle & Brittle, 2008). Additionally, correctional healthcare accrediting bodies, such as the National Commission on Correctional Health Care (NCCHC), require individualized treatment plans for inmates with mental health, substance abuse, developmental disabilities, medical conditions, and other relevant conditions (NCCHC, 2008a, 2000b, 2000c).

The multidisciplinary treatment plan should reflect input from the various professional disciplines (e.g., psychiatry, psychology, professional counselors, social workers, substance abuse professionals, education, vocational rehabilitation, case management, correctional officers, etc.). It should reflect not only the data collected specific to each disorder or clinical issue but also the person's readiness to enter the treatment process. Clinical interventions should be planned consistent with the offender's readiness for change (a concept that will be explained in more detail below).

The treatment plan should be modified periodically to reflect the offender's progress through treatment stages, changes in the offender's motivation level, or when there are changes in the clinical condition of any of the CODs. Even when no changes are apparent, an update of the treatment plan should occur every 6 months at a minimum, as is consistent with NCCHC standards.

Enhancing Treatment Motivation Through Assertive Outreach

Drake, Essock, et al. (2004) described several stages of treatment that seem appropriate for correctional settings. They note that treatment begins by forming a trusting relationship with the incarcerated person. They refer to this process as engagement. Engagement is particularly difficult in the correctional environment, because the life experience of offenders has frequently included negative interactions with authority figures including parents, teachers, social services agencies, treatment agencies, employers, and law enforcement and criminal justice professionals. For this reason, it is critical to recognize that trust will continue to be a prominent issue and may extend throughout the course of treatment and incarceration. In essence, the engagement process begins, by necessity, with the first contact that mental health staff have with the offender. An important part of engaging persons in the treatment process is helping them realize the importance of making changes relating to their COD, as well as to consider actually engaging in the change process.

Assertive outreach (Drake, Essock, et al., 2004) is a process whereby mental health and case management staff actively seek out offenders with mental health treatment needs and encourage them to become involved in treatment. This outreach can occur throughout the treatment process, but it may be especially beneficial when the offender is still ambivalent about entering treatment. Assertive outreach early in the treatment process may involve some degree of persuasion to motivate the offender to become involved in recovery-oriented activities (Drake, Essock, et al., 2004) and is designed to assist the offender to resolve ambivalence about making positive changes. At this stage of the treatment process, it is necessary to engage in interventions that assist and persuade the offender to move toward more active involvement in treatment for each of the COD. One example of an appropriate intervention in this stage of treatment is asking the offender to identify the pros and cons of not addressing the mental illness or continuing to engage in substance use or criminal behavior. It is important to also ask the offender to identify the pros and cons of making positive changes in these areas at the same time. This will help the person accurately assess the reasons that changes have not been made and increase the motivation for change.

Active Treatment and Medication Management

Once the offender is committed to the treatment process, then active treatment is the next step. This is the stage that is typically considered to be treatment and includes helping the person acquire and practice skills to manage the symptoms of his or her COD and move toward recovery (Drake, Essock, et al., 2004). Interventions in this stage include cognitive-behavioral individual and group therapies (including for those with histories of trauma, such as physical and sexual abuse); gender-specific interventions for women; interventions for those with developmental disabilities or traumatic brain injury; continued motivational interventions; strategies to address criminogenic needs; relapse prevention plans for mental illness, substance abuse, and criminality; and dialectical behavior therapy. This stage may also incorporate social support interventions, primarily in the form of therapeutic communities or other group treatments that assist the offender in developing social networks to achieve and maintain recovery.

The issue of medications in the correctional system is a difficult one in general and becomes much more complicated in the context of addressing COD. A number of issues need to be addressed when considering this important topic. These issues include the role of psychotropic medications in the prison (Gravier & Chevry, 1993; Kjelsberg & Hartvig, 2005), psychotropic medications and alleviation of stress (Cartwright & Gordon, 2007; Gray, Bressington, Lathlean, & Mills, 2008), psychotropic medications and substance abuse (Burns, 2009), and psychotropic medications and reentry. Despite the importance of this topic as it pertains to COD and the fact that psychotropic medications are appropriately utilized in prison to treat mental illness and other COD, there is little literature specifically addressing how these issues should be addressed in the correctional setting (but see Chapter 7 for a discussion of psychopharmacological treatment of specific disorders in prisons and jails).

Although psychotropic medications are appropriate to use in correctional settings, some concerns exist:

- The high prevalence of substance use disorders.
- The role of psychotropic medications in suicide attempts.
- Psychotropic medications as currency. Psychotropic medications are bought and sold illicitly by inmates, used to pay debts, and used to avoid physical violence.
- The role of psychotropic medications in reentry. Even when the medications are needed to maintain stability and recovery, inmates will often discontinue taking their psychotropic medications, often immediately upon release.

Existing algorithms and guidelines for the prescription of psychotropic medications, which encourage caution and restraint in prescriptive practices, should be followed closely. This will reduce the inappropriate utilization of psychotropic medications in correctional settings and can assist offenders in the process of reintegration/reentry. Many correctional systems and facilities provide inmates with up to a 30-day supply of medication upon their release or discharge, which assists them in maintaining stability until they can see a psychiatrist in the community.

Reintegration/Reentry

The final stage of treatment involves reentry, reintegration, relapse prevention, and maintenance of therapeutic gains. This stage may also utilize social support interventions to facilitate the reentry process (Drake, Essock, et al., 2004). When preparing an inmate for reentry to the community, it must be remembered that offenders can be at different points in the treatment process for each COD and may regress somewhat as they anticipate their return to the community. For this reason, continued multidisciplinary treatment planning must address the current stages of treatment and readiness for change and incorporate that information into the recommendations and planning for the offender as he or she reenters society.

Correctional Barriers to Effective Treatment

Correctional systems pose several barriers to effective treatment for offenders with COD. These barriers include correctional management procedures, inadequate treatment resources, lack of adequate screening procedures, attitudes of correctional workers and administrators, and inadequate training in correctional mental health care for the professionals who provide these services. These barriers are discussed next.

The Correctional System as a Treatment Barrier

The correctional system itself can sometimes serve as a primary barrier to effective treatment. Correctional systems have as their main objective preserving the safety of the correctional facility, its occupants, and the community. Assisting offenders with COD in their recovery efforts is often an important, yet secondary, mission. Although the primary goal of staff and offender safety is absolutely appropriate, it can result in decisions being made that complicate and/or create challenges to the effective delivery of treatment. Consider these examples.

Although strip searches and other searches are absolutely necessary for safety, they may complicate treatment for those who have been sexually abused. The need to observe offenders in their cells at night requires the maintenance of a low level of lighting and the occasional shining of a flashlight beam into the cell. This practice can disrupt the sleep of those who have sleep difficulties resulting from depression or other mental disorders. Also, the need to periodically count all offenders in the facility is certainly necessary for security purposes, but it can make it difficult to schedule and conduct psychotherapeutic activities or limit the times when these activities can be scheduled. These examples illustrate the impact that a correctional system can have on the treatment of offenders with COD and suggest how the system can present a significant barrier to the provision of treatment services.

Additionally, the physical plant of most correctional facilities was not designed to accommodate the treatment needs of those who are incarcerated. Whereas some systems are now developing physical plants or specialized treatment units that are more amenable to the treatment needs of offenders, many remain unfriendly to the treatment needs of offenders with COD. For example, it is not unusual for facilities to have inadequate space for individual and group counseling sessions. It is also sometimes difficult to find appropriate places to provide confidential treatment for those who are in segregation.

Screening and Treatment Barriers

Amazingly, despite the requirements of *Ruiz v. Estelle* (1980), the standards of the NCCHC (2008a, 2008b, 2008c), and the proliferation of lawsuits related to inadequate screening and treatment (R. D. Miller & Metzner, 1994) for those with mental disorders, inadequate screening still exists in many facilities and systems. The U.S. Department of Justice (2001) published a study that revealed the following:

- Nearly 25% of prisons in the United States do not screen inmates at intake to determine their mental health needs.
- Nearly 20% do not conduct any psychiatric assessment of inmates (Haney, 2006).

When screening for developmental disabilities is considered, a national survey revealed that only 36 states routinely screened inmates at intake for these issues (Metzner, Cohen, Grossman, & Wettstein, 1998). Although no formal study exists that has reviewed the screening practices for those with traumatic brain injury (TBI), it is virtually certain that even fewer state systems specifically screen for the presence, type, and degree of TBI. A more complete discussion of this is presented in Chapter 15.

Attitudes of Correctional Workers and Administrators

Another important barrier to effective treatment in correctional systems is the attitude of correctional officers and administrators toward treatment. The needs of those with COD can be confusing, puzzling, and even frightening for those who are not specifically trained to understand and address them. As has been previously noted, inmates with COD are often treated more harshly than others (Howard, 1997), prison systems do not respect the need for specialized housing (F. Cohen & Gerbasi, 2005), counseling and treatment programs are sometimes considered to be "coddling" inmates (Haney, 1998), and often prison officials consider inmates with COD to be more dangerous than other inmates (Haney, 2006). See Chapter 3 for more discussion on attitudes of correctional staff about mental illness and about the benefits of training on mental health issues.

Inadequate Correctional Training for Mental Health Professionals

Finally, inadequate training of mental health professionals regarding the specific issues and needs of criminal offenders, especially those with COD, as well as the effect of the correctional environment on these offenders, is a significant barrier to the provision of effective treatment. Magaletta, Patry, Dietz, and Ax (2007) described the importance of adequate academic and continuing education/training for correctional mental health professionals, if they wish to be effective in their correctional practice. These same authors and others (e.g., Harowski, 2003) have indicated that most of the training needs of mental health professionals as they enter the correctional arena for the first time are currently met by on-the-job training rather than through a more formal academic program or course of study.

Virtually all correctional settings require that all new employees go through some version of a training academy, which introduces new employees to the correctional environment, provides them with key instruction on how to maintain their safety and the safety of others in the facility, teaches them correctional professionalism, and dispenses other important information. Some systems have a section in the initial training curriculum devoted to introducing medical and mental health professionals to important correctional issues, such as different confidentiality requirements and challenges presented by the criminality of many of those who are incarcerated.

Unfortunately, very seldom do these training programs address the iatrogenic effects of the correctional environment on the offender population, particularly those with COD. These programs also do not train new employees in the multiple issues related to substance abuse and its complex implications, such as the role of psychotropic medications for those who are substance dependent and feigning mental illness or substance dependent and wanting to use psychotropic medications inappropriately. Finally, little or no training time or material is devoted to such critical issues as (a) the feigning of mental illness and the reasons for it, (b) the sophisticated ways in which inmates engage in feigning behaviors, (c) the appropriate role of psychotropic medications in the correctional environment, (d) the high prevalence of traumatic brain injuries, (e) the high prevalence of physical and sexual abuse, (f) the reality and role of criminogenic needs for those with COD, and (g) the reentry challenges for criminal offenders and how they manage them when they return to the community.

The expectation is often that mental health professionals will practice in much the same way as they did in the community or other agency settings, with very little emphasis on the specific issues and challenges of COD treatment in the correctional setting (see Chapter 2 for more discussion of similarities and differences between community and correctional practice). The net effect of this faulty expectation is that the individualized treatment needs of criminal offenders with COD are not adequately addressed.

Best Practices

This section will first discuss evidence-based practices for the treatment of COD that target individuals and groups and will conclude with a discussion of evidence-based practices for the treatment of COD that target correctional systems.

Evidence-Based Individual and Group Treatments for Co-Occurring Disorders

The primary evidence-based practice for COD involves integrated treatment (Drake, Xie, et al., 2004; Ho et al., 1999; Minkoff, 1989, 1991; Osher & Kofoed, 1989). Integrated treatment has been defined by Drake, Essock, et al. (2004) as follows:

The same clinicians or teams of clinicians, working in one setting, provide appropriate mental health and substance abuse interventions in a coordinated fashion. In other words, the caregivers take responsibility for combining the interventions into one coherent package. For the individual with a dual diagnosis (COD), the services appear seamless, with a consistent approach, philosophy, and set of recommendations. The need to negotiate with separate clinical teams, programs, or systems disappears. (p. 471)

Historically, most systems treated mental illness, developmental disabilities, and substance use disorders in separate ways and ignored the role of criminality altogether. Treatment was often conducted in a serial or sequential manner, with the disorder that was considered "primary" being treated first, followed by the "secondary" disorder(s) (Ries, 1992). In most cases, criminogenic needs were ignored.

More recently, the sequential model of COD treatment has been supplanted in some systems by parallel treatment models. Parallel treatment models provide treatment services simultaneously, but by separate agencies that are devoted to the treatment of one specific disorder. Many correctional systems continue to utilize either the separate/sequential or parallel treatment model, and in fact often have separate divisions within their system for substance abuse, mental health, and developmental disabilities treatment, while continuing to ignore the criminality/criminogenic needs.

Current thinking is that a more integrated treatment model may be the most appropriate and that earlier modes of COD treatment are too fragmented and, consequently, provide ineffective care (Jerrell & Ridgely, 1999). This recognition has resulted in some states' moving toward and/or adopting an integrated treatment model for COD. For example, Colorado has combined its state-level substance abuse and mental health treatment divisions into a single Division of Behavioral Health in an effort to become more integrated in its provision of care for COD. Other states (e.g., Missouri, Oklahoma, and New Mexico) have adopted similar administrative structures for their state treatment services. However, most states still do not provide integrated treatment for COD, and those that do have considerable room for improvement (Drake, Xie, et al., 2004).

As states begin to implement more integrated treatment models, they will also need to address the criminogenic needs of offenders if they are to be successful. The importance of this last point has been discussed earlier in the chapter and in previous chapters and is also reinforced by Drake, Morrissey, and Mueser (2006).

The following represent examples of specific emerging best practices for treating COD:

- Integrated Dual-Disorder Treatment (Drake, Antosca, Noordsy, Bartels, & Osher, 1991).
- Dialectical Behavior Therapy (DBT; Linehan, 1993). DBT has been rigorously researched and has been identified as the treatment of choice for borderline personality disorder. It includes a combination of cognitive-behavioral techniques, including the use of mindfulness, and Eastern philosophy to address appropriate emotional regulation.
- Strategies for Self-Improvement and Change (Wanberg & Milkman, 1998). This is a manualized curriculum designed for the substance-abusing offender. It incorporates motivational interviewing, a transtheoretical approach, relapse-prevention techniques, and cognitive-behavioral treatment to reduce relapse and recidivism.
- Thinking for a Change (TFC; Bush, Glick, & Taymans, 1997). TFC was developed by the authors for the National Institute of Corrections and is designed to address and reduce criminal behavior.
- Modified Therapeutic Community for Persons with Co-Occurring Disorders (Sacks, Sacks, & DeLeon, 1999). This approach deserves particular emphasis. It has recently been included in the Substance Abuse and Mental Health Services Administration's (2008) National Registry of Evidence-Based Programs and Practices, and it includes a focus on mental illness, substance use, and criminality. It has been implemented in prison systems with considerable success (French, McCollister, Sacks, McKendrick, & DeLeon, 2002; Sacks, McKendrick, Sacks, Banks, & Harle, 2008; Sullivan et al., 2007).

Evidence-Based System-Level Practices

Minkoff (1991) has developed the Comprehensive, Continuous, and Integrated System of Care (CCISC) Model. It will be discussed below in the context of providing integrated treatment for COD within correctional systems. Minkoff designed this model to "improve treatment capacity for these individuals in systems of any size and complexity, ranging from counties or regions to entire states, networks of agencies, individual complex agencies, or even programs within agencies" (p. 13). The model has four basic characteristics, which are

- system-level change,
- efficient use of existing resources,
- incorporation of best practices, and
- integrated treatment philosophy.

There are eight principles that guide the implementation of the CCISC Model. They are as follows:

1. Dual diagnosis (COD) is an expectation, not an exception.

2. All individuals with co-occurring psychiatric and substance disorders (ICOPSD) are not the same. The National Consensus Four Quadrant Model can be used for categorizing COD and as a guide for planning services at the systemic level (National Association of State Mental Health Program Directors/National Association of State Alcohol and Drug Abuse Directors, 1998). The four-quadrant model divides ICOPSD according to high and low severity for each disorder. The model is presented in Table 11.2.

Table 11.2	The Minkoff Model

Quadrant IV: High mental health/high chemical dependence	Quadrant III: Low mental health/high chemical dependence
Quadrant II: High mental health/low chemical dependence	Quadrant I: Low mental health/low chemical dependence

This model can be extended into eight categories for use in the treatment of criminal offenders with COD. Table 11.3 describes these eight categories.

Table 11.3	The Minkoff Model (Modified by the Author to Address Criminality)

Category	Mental Health	Substance Use	Criminal Conduct
1	Low	Low	Low
2	Low	Low	High
3	High	Low	Low
4	High	Low	High
5	Low	High	Low
6	Low	High	High
7	High	High	Low
8	High	High	High

Implementation of this extended model for those in the correctional system can focus the treatment planning process, help define specific programs in which offenders should participate, and assist with the appropriate utilization of resources.

3. Empathic, hopeful, integrated treatment relationships are some of the most important contributors to treatment success in any setting (including corrections). Provision of continuous integrated treatment relationships is an evidence-based best practice for individuals with the most severe combinations of psychiatric, developmental disabilities, criminal conduct, and substance abuse difficulties.

4. Case management and care must be balanced with empathic detachment, expectation, contracting, consequences, and contingent learning for each client and in each service setting. This is particularly true in the correctional environment, where these factors are most useful in addressing both criminal conduct and specific features of mental disorders. The Modified Therapeutic Community for Persons With Co-Occurring Disorders (Sacks et al., 1999) is an excellent example of this principle.

5. When other disorders (serious mental illness, substance abuse, developmental disabilities, and/or behavioral dysfunctions) coexist with criminal conduct, all disorders should be considered primary, and integrated dual (or multiple) primary diagnosis-specific treatment is recommended.

6. Both mental illness and addiction (and developmental disability and criminal conduct) can be treated within the philosophical framework of a disease and recovery model (Minkoff, 1989) with parallel phases of recovery (acute stabilization, motivational enhancement, active treatment, relapse and recidivism prevention, and rehabilitation/recovery), in which interventions are not only diagnosis-specific but also specific to phase of recovery and readiness/receptivity for change.

7. There is no single correct intervention for ICOPSD. For each individual, interventions must be individualized according to quadrant/category, diagnoses, level of functioning, external constraints or supports, and phase of recovery/readiness for change. The external constraints or supports are particularly important in the correctional setting. Interventions may have to be modified depending on custody level, available out-of-cell time, segregation status, and other factors. The utilization of homework, for example, is appropriate in any context but can be particularly beneficial in the correctional system. It should not be used as a substitute for individual or group face-to-face treatment, but it is a valuable adjunct to the treatment of inmates in correctional facilities.

8. Clinical outcome measures and goals for ICOPSD must also be individualized, based on similar parameters for individualizing treatment interventions. Relapse/recidivism prevention is usually a long-term goal that begins in the correctional facility and continues through the reentry process to the community, but short-term outcomes must be individualized and can include elimination of substance use in the correctional facility, appropriate use of and adherence to psychotropic medications, reduction of self-injurious behaviors, reduction of conduct violations as evidence of better managed mental illness and reduced criminality, movement through the stages of change, ability to live in general population as opposed to a special needs unit, ability to obtain and keep employment in the facility, and appropriate reductions in utilization of service due to increased stability.

The eight principles for COD treatment are summarized and divided into two categories in Table 11.4.

Table 11.4 Co-Occurring Disorder (COD) Treatment

Principle	Category	Summary
1. COD is an expectation in this population	Treatment philosophy	High frequency of all disorders in corrections
2. All people with COD are not the same	Treatment philosophy	Individual needs vary based on combination of disorders
5. All COD should be considered primary	Treatment philosophy	Each disorder must be addressed actively, and all given the same treatment priority

Principle	Category	Summary
7. There is no single, correct intervention for COD	Treatment philosophy	Must use evidence-based practices, but cannot rely on single intervention
3. Empathic, hopeful, integrated treatment relationships are very important to success	Treatment practice	Therapeutic relationship is primary in COD, as in all mental health issues
4. Case management and care must be balanced with behavioral expectations	Treatment practice	Addressing inappropriate or destructive behavior is very important in COD treatment
6. All COD (including criminality) can be treated from a disease and recovery perspective	Treatment practice	Focus on recovery process for all disorders
8. Clinical interventions must be individualized	Treatment practice	Individualized treatment plan and interventions critical for success

Reentry Issues

There has been a growing recognition over the past several years of the need to provide reentry services to inmates incarcerated in both jail and prison facilities (Gordon, Barnes, & VanBenschoten, 2006; Knollenberg & Martin, 2008; Osher, Steadman, & Barr, 2002; Sacks & Pearson, 2003). P. B. Burke (2008) suggested that most offenders released from correctional institutions do not successfully reintegrate into the community but, rather, return to the criminal justice system because of new crimes or parole violations. Based on the fact that 95% of incarcerated individuals eventually return to the community (Glaze & Bonczar, 2007; Glaze & Palla, 2005; Harrison & Beck, 2006), coupled with the currently high recidivism rates across state, city, and county jurisdictions, President George W. Bush initiated the Prisoner Re-entry Initiative in 2004. The goals of this initiative included the need to expand job training and placement services for releasing offenders and to provide them with transitional housing and mentoring assistance (Hogan, 2003).

A number of state correctional systems, including Kansas, Massachusetts, Missouri, Oklahoma, Oregon, West Virginia, Wisconsin, and Colorado have made reentry an agency priority. Each of these states has made a commitment to reentry as a central component of agency mission. Through work with the Center for Effective Public Policy, they have identified four components to consider when implementing an effective offender reentry strategy (Burke, 2008):

- leadership and organizational change,
- rational planning process,
- collaboration, and
- effective offender management practices.

As is the case with all inmates, those with COD are likely to return to the community. Inadequate transition planning is associated with very negative outcomes, such as relapse of mental health and substance use disorders (Daniel, 2007; Draine, Wolff, Jacoby, Hartwell, & Duclos, 2005), recidivism (Basile, 2005), and a crisis level of functioning (Osher et al., 2002). Inmates with COD returning to the community need assistance with a number of issues such as housing, medications, treatment services, culturally competent assistance and services, financial support, employment, medical treatment, and transportation (Listwan, Cullen, & Latessa, 2006; Osher et al., 2002; Peters, Sherman, & Osher, 2008; Pittman, 2005; Vogel, Noether, & Steadman, 2007).

The anticipation and process of reentry planning is a time of very high stress for all inmates, can be especially stressful for offenders with COD, and can lead to the occurrence or reappearance of suicidal thoughts and other manifestations of mental illness. Many offenders have been out of society for a number of years and are quite unfamiliar with current transportation systems, technology, community services, and other aspects of societal functioning. This is quite intimidating and can lead to relapse, risk of suicide, or recidivism, because many of these offenders may feel more comfortable with the structure and familiarity of the correctional setting. As a result, every effort should be made to assist all offenders in preparing for the stresses of reentering and acculturating to contemporary society.

The APIC model has been identified as a best practice approach to community reentry from jails for those with COD (Osher et al., 2002; see Chapter 1 for a more detailed description of this model). Although it is specific to jails and has not been specifically studied with reference to prisons, the process is an appropriate and helpful one for all people with COD who are leaving incarceration and returning to the community.

As noted above, the releasing inmate's clinical needs include continued treatment for each disorder, which involves enrollment in and access to individual and group therapy or related clinical services, ensuring access to appropriate medical care, and ensuring that there is no gap in the provision of psychotropic medications. Social needs include housing, clothing, adequate nutrition, financial assistance, enrollment in Medicare/Medicaid and other social services, employment, and transportation. Addressing these needs is critical to helping the offender avoid relapse, recidivism, self-injurious and/or suicidal behaviors, and the stressors that can lead to these conditions. Additionally, public safety risks are addressed through providing for the offender's clinical and social needs, as well as by including ongoing treatment for and management of criminogenic needs.

The process of planning for the inmate's release should include a multidisciplinary development of the probation or parole plan, which utilizes input from treatment providers, social service agencies, and the probation or parole officer. This multidisciplinary plan will help ensure that all of the offender's treatment needs are met, that all individuals and agencies involved in the delivery of postrelease services are identified, and that gaps in care are avoided.

Addressing all of these needs should occur before the inmate is released from incarceration. Ideally, this will begin on the first day of incarceration for those who are in jail, due to the short periods of confinement and the unpredictable nature of jail discharges (Osher et al., 2002), and begin 6 months prior to release for those in prison. In-reach services, which consist of having treatment providers from the community establish connections and relationships with inmates prior to release, can increase the success of the reentry process and transition back to the community.

Effective treatment and movement towards recovery cannot occur without a primary emphasis on reentry or transition back to the community. The stresses associated with returning to a very unstructured, foreign, technologically advanced society, many times without the support of family or friends, adequate lodging or housing, certain access to food or nutrition, transportation, required psychotropic or other medications, are very obviously enough to induce a state of panic and lead to relapse and recidivism. Any treatment gains made during the period of incarceration can very quickly disappear if these basic human needs are not met or if these basic supportive services are not readily available and accessible.

Summary and Conclusions

Correctional settings face numerous challenges, including identifying and providing appropriate treatment for offenders with COD. A conservative estimate of the prevalence of those with some combination of these COD in correctional systems is 10% to 15%, with combinations such as substance abuse and criminality occurring in 75% or more.

Recognition of the phenomenon of COD is relatively recent in the history of the mental health professions. More recent still is the notion of the need to treat these disorders in an integrated fashion. Despite these advances in identification and treatment, the field has not provided a comprehensive theoretical formulation to explain the development and course of COD. In similar fashion, the recognition of the need to provide mental health services to those incarcerated in the nation's jails and prisons is relatively new, and there is even less awareness and acknowledgement of COD on the part of many correctional mental health providers.

This chapter was written with several goals in mind. The first goal was to provide the reader with an overview of COD and to provide a new theoretical formulation that applies to all CODs in any clinical setting. The second goal was to identify the necessity of including criminogenic factors in any discussion of COD within correctional settings. Criminogenic factors can interfere with an offender's ability to achieve recovery from all CODs, including the ability to live a crime-free, prosocial life. The final goal was to identify the primary issues involved in providing appropriate treatment and support for those who are incarcerated, both while they are in correctional facilities and throughout the process of their reentry to the community.

The correctional mental health provider is faced with many challenges on a daily basis, including providing care in an environment that, even when it is functioning optimally, is stressful and strains the often limited or ineffective coping abilities of those who are incarcerated. The stresses of the correctional environment provide daily triggers for alcohol or drug use, often tax the resources of those with limited intellectual ability or cognitive impairment, and actively encourage the development or further entrenchment of criminal thinking and behavior patterns. Correctional mental health providers should be aware that every interaction they have with offenders with COD should encourage the offenders to develop greater motivation and skills to progress toward recovery from all the CODs from which they suffer. The extent to which this happens will have a significant impact on how aptly correctional systems are named.

KEY TERMS

Dual diagnosis

Co-occurring disorders (CODs)

Mental illness

Developmental disabilities

Substance abuse

Substance dependence

Criminality

Personality disorder

Traumatic brain injury

Diathesis-stress theory for COD

Motivational assessment

Stages of change readiness

Assertive outreach

Stages of treatment

Medication management

Comprehensive, continuous, integrated system of care model for COD

Separate/sequential treatment for COD

Parallel treatment for COD

Modified therapeutic community for persons with COD

DISCUSSION QUESTIONS

1. Why is it so important to consider criminogenic factors when treating offenders with co-occurring disorders?

2. Why has it been historically so difficult to offer integrated services to individuals with co-occurring disorders?

3. Are all individuals ready to actively seek behavior change when they enter therapy? Explain your answer.

4. In the chapter, it is suggested that, "Every effort should be made to assist all offenders in preparing for the stresses of re-entering and acculturating to contemporary society." Do you agree with this? Should this be one of our society's priorities? Why or why not?

5. Explain the diathesis-stress model and how it has been applied to COD. How does each disorder interact with the others to result in a person's being more vulnerable to the development of COD?

References

Abram, K. M., & Teplin, L. A. (1991). Co-occurring disorders among mentally ill jail detainees: Implications for public policy. *American Psychologist, 46,* 1036–1045.

Basile, V. D. (2005). Getting serious about corrections. *Federal Probation, 69*(2), 29–31.

Burke, H. M., Zautra, A. J., Schultz, A. S., Reich, J. W., & Davis, M. C. (2002). Arthritis. In A. J. Christensen & M. H. Antoni (Eds.), *Chronic physical disorders: Behavioral medicine's perspective* (The Blackwell Series in Health Psychology and Behavioral Medicine, pp. 268–287). Malden, MA: Blackwell.

Burke, P. B. (2008). *TPC re-entry handbook: Implementing the NIC transition from prison to the community model.* Washington, DC: U.S. Department of Justice, National Institute of Corrections.

Burns, K. A. (2009). Commentary: Top ten reasons to limit prescription of controlled substances in prisons. *Journal of the American Academy of Psychiatry and the Law, 37,* 50–52.

Bush, J., Glick, B., & Taymans, J. (1997). *Thinking for a change.* Washington, DC: U.S. Department of Justice, National Institute of Corrections.

Cartwright, J., & Gordon, H. (2007). Beyond the "quick fix": The role of medication in readiness for psychological treatment of severe personality disorder. *Issues in Forensic Psychology, 7,* 55–61.

Cohen, F., & Gerbasi, J. B. (2005). Legal issues regarding the provision of mental health care in correctional settings. In C. L. Scott & J. B. Gerbasi (Eds.), *Handbook of correctional mental health* (pp. 259–283). Arlington, VA: American Psychiatric Publishing.

Cohen, S., & Rodriguez, M. S. (1995). Pathways linking affective disturbances and physical disorders. *Health Psychology, 14,* 374–380.

Daniel, A. E. (2007). Care of the mentally ill in prisons: Challenges and solutions. *Journal of the American Academy of Psychiatry & the Law, 35,* 406–410.

Davis, E., Barnhill, L. J., & Saeed, S. A. (2008). Treatment models for treating patients with combined mental illness and developmental disabilities: An overview. *Psychiatric Quarterly, 79,* 157–170.

DiClemente, C. C., & Hughes, S. O. (1990). Stages of change profiles in alcoholism treatment. *Journal of Substance Abuse, 2,* 217–235.

Draine, J., Wolff, N., Jacoby, J. E., Hartwell, S., & Duclos, C. (2005). Understanding community re-entry of former prisoners with mental illness: A conceptual model to guide new research. *Behavioral Sciences & the Law, 23,* 689–707.

Drake, R. E., Antosca, L. M., Noordsy, D. L., Bartels, S. J., & Osher, F. C. (1991). New Hampshire's specialized services for the dually diagnosed. *New Directions for Mental Health Services, 50,* 57–67.

Drake, R. E., Essock, S. M., Shaner, A., Karey, K. B., Minkoff, K., Kola, L., et al. (2004). Implementing dual diagnosis services for clients with severe mental illness. *Psychiatric Services, 52,* 469–476.

Drake, R. E., Morrissey, J. P., & Mueser, K. T. (2006). The challenge of treating forensic dual diagnosis clients: Comment on "Integrated treatment for jail recidivists with co-occurring psychiatric and substance use disorders." *Community Mental Health Journal, 42,* 15–22.

Drake, R. E., Xie, H., McHugo, G. J., & Shumway, M. (2004). Three-year outcomes of long-term patients with co-occurring bipolar and substance use disorders. *Biological Psychiatry, 56,* 749–756.

Fazel, S., & Danesh, J. (2002, February 16). Serious mental disorder in 23,000 prisoners: A systemic review of 62 surveys. *The Lancet, 359,* 545–550.

Fazel, S., Xenitidis, K., & Powell, J. (2008). The prevalence of intellectual disabilities among 12,000 prisoners—A systematic review. *International Journal of Law & Psychiatry, 31,* 369–373.

Feder, L. (1994). Psychiatric hospitalization history and parole decisions. *Law and Human Behavior, 18,* 395–410.

French, M. T., McCollister, K. E., Sacks, S., McKendrick, K., & DeLeon, G. (2002). Benefit-cost analysis of a modified therapeutic community for mentally ill chemical abusers. *Evaluation and Program Planning, 25,* 137–148.

Glaze, L. E., & Bonczar, T. P. (2007, December). *Probation and parole in the United States, 2006* (Bureau of Justice Statistics Special Report NCJ 220218). Washington, DC: National Criminal Justice Reference Service.

Glaze, L. E., & Palla, S. (2005, November). *Probation and parole in the United States, 2004* (Bureau of Justice Statistics Special Report NCJ 210676). Washington, DC: National Criminal Justice Reference Service.

Gordon, J. A., Barnes, C. M., & VanBenschoten, S. W. (2006). The dual treatment track program: A descriptive assessment of a new "in-house" jail diversion program. *Federal Probation, 70*(3), 9–18.

Gravier, B., & Chevry, P. (1993). About the good use of psychotropic drugs in prison environment. *L'Evolution Psychiatrique, 58,* 93–107.

Gray, R., Bressington, D., Lathlean, J., & Mills, A. (2008). Relationship between adherence, symptoms, treatment attitudes, satisfaction, and side effects in prisoners taking antipsychotic medication. *Journal of Forensic Psychiatry & Psychology, 19,* 335–351.

Haney, C. (1998). Riding the punishment wave: On the origins of our devolving standards of decency. *Hastings Women's Law Journal, 9,* 27.

Haney, C. (2006). *Reforming punishment: Psychological limits to the pains of imprisonment.* Washington, DC: American Psychological Association.

Harowski, K. (2003). Staff training: Multiple roles for mental health professionals. In T. J. Fagan & R. K. Ax (Eds.), *Correctional mental health handbook* (pp. 237–249). Thousand Oaks, CA: Sage.

Harris, V., & Dagadakis, C. (2004). Length of incarceration: Was there parity for mentally ill offenders? *International Journal of Law and Psychiatry, 27,* 387–393.

Harrison, P. M., & Beck, A. J. (2006, November). *Prisoners in 2005* (Bureau of Justice Statistics Special Report NCJ 215092). Washington, DC: National Criminal Justice Reference Service.

Heather, N., Luce, A., Peck, D., Dunbar, B., & James, I. (1999). The development of a treatment version of the Readiness to Change Questionnaire. *Addiction Research, 7*(1), 63–68.

Ho, A. P., Tsuang, J. W., Liberman, R. P., Wang, R., Wilkins, J. N., & Eckman, T. A., et al. (1999). Achieving effective treatment of patients with chronic psychotic illness and comorbid substance dependence. *American Journal of Psychiatry, 156,* 1765–1770.

Hogan, M. F. (2003). *Achieving the promise: Transforming mental health care in America. New Freedom Commission on Mental Health. Executive summary* (Publication No. SMA-03-3831). Washington, DC: Substance Abuse and Mental Health Services Administration.

Howard, T. (1997). Therapeutic implications of incarceration for persons with severe mental disorders: Searching for rational health policy. *American Journal of Criminal Law, 24,* 283.

James, D. J., & Glaze, L. E. (2006). *Mental health problems of prison and jail inmates* (Bureau of Justice Statistics Special Report NCJ 213600). Washington, DC: National Criminal Justice Reference Service.

Jerrell, J. M., & Ridgely, M. S. (1999). Impact of robustness of program implementation on outcomes of clients in dual diagnosis programs. *Psychiatric Services, 50,* 109–112.

Kaplan, H. I., Sadock, B. J., & Grebb, J. A. (1994). *Synopsis of psychiatry: Behavioral sciences, clinical psychiatry.* Baltimore, MD: Williams & Williams.

Khantzian, E. J. (1985). The self-medication hypothesis of addictive disorders: Focus on heroin and cocaine dependence. *American Journal of Psychiatry, 142,* 1259–1264.

Kjelsberg, E., & Hartvig, P. (2005). Too much or too little? Prescription drug abuse in a nationwide prison population. *International Journal of Prisoner Health, 1,* 75–87.

Knollenberg, L., & Martin, V. A. (2008). Community re-entry following prison: A process evaluation of the accelerated community entry program. *Federal Probation, 72*(2), 54–60.

Linehan, M. M. (1993). *Cognitive-behavioral treatment of borderline personality disorder.* New York, NY: Guilford.

Listwan, S. J., Cullen, F. T., & Latessa, E. J. (2006). How to prevent prisoner re-entry programs from failing: Insights from evidence-based corrections. *Federal Probation, 70*(3), 19–25.

Magaletta, P. R., Patry, M. W., Dietz, E. F., & Ax, R. K. (2007). What is correctional about clinical practice in corrections? *Criminal Justice and Behavior, 34,* 7–21.

Matson, J. L., & Sevin, J. A. (1994). Theories of dual diagnosis in mental retardation. *Journal of Consulting and Clinical Psychology, 62,* 6–16.

Mead, S., & Copeland, M. E. (2000). What recovery means to us: Consumers' perspectives. *Community Mental Health Journal, 36,* 315–328.

Metzner, J. L., Cohen, F., Grossman, L. S., & Wettstein, R. M. (1998). Treatment in jails and prisons. In R. M. Wettstein (Ed.), *Treatment of offenders with mental disorders* (pp. 211–264). New York, NY: Guilford.

Miller, R. D., & Metzner, J. L. (1994). Psychiatric stigma in correctional facilities. *Bulletin of the American Academy of Psychiatry and the Law, 22,* 621–628.

Miller, W. R., & Rollnick, S. (1991). *Motivational interviewing: Preparing people to change addictive behavior.* New York, NY: Guilford.

Minkoff, K. (1989). An integrated treatment model for dual diagnosis of psychosis and addiction. *Hospital and Community Psychiatry, 40,* 1031–1036.

Minkoff, K. (1991). Program components of a comprehensive integrated care system for serious mentally ill patients with substance disorders. *New Directions for Mental Health Services, 50,* 13–27.

Mueser, K. T., Drake, R. E., & Wallach, M. A. (1998). Dual diagnosis: A review of etiological theories. *Addictive Behaviors, 23,* 717–734.

National Association of State Mental Health Program Directors/National Association of State Alcohol and Drug Abuse Directors. (1998). *The new conceptual framework for co-occurring mental health and substance use disorders.* Washington, DC: Author.

National Commission on Correctional Healthcare. (2008a). *Standards for health services in jails.* Chicago, IL: Author.

National Commission on Correctional Healthcare. (2008b). *Standards for health services in prisons.* Chicago, IL: Author.

National Commission on Correctional Healthcare. (2008c). *Standards for mental health services in correctional facilities.* Chicago, IL: Author.

National Institute of Justice. (2002). *Epidemiological trends in drug abuse: Advance report.* Washington, DC: Author.

National Institute of Justice. (2003). *Drug and alcohol use and related matters among arrestees.* Washington, DC: Author.

O'Keefe, M. L., Cooney, H. Z., & Schnell, M. J. (2008). *Overview of substance abuse treatment services: Fiscal year 2007.* Colorado Springs: Colorado Department of Corrections.

Osher, F. C., & Kofoed, L. L. (1989). Treatment of patients with psychiatric and psychoactive substance use disorders. *Hospital & Community Psychiatry, 40,* 1025–1030.

Osher, F. C., Steadman, H. J., & Barr, H. (2002). *A best practice approach to community re-entry from jails for inmates with co-occurring disorders: The APIC model.* Delmar, NY: National GAINS Center.

Penick, E. C., Nickel, E. J., Cantrell, P. F., Powell, B. J., Read, M. R., & Thomas, M. M. (1990). The emerging concept of dual diagnosis: An overview and implications. *Journal of Chemical Dependency Treatment, 3,* 1–54.

Peters, R. H., Sherman, P. B., & Osher, F. C. (2008). Treatment in jails and prisons. In K. T. Mueser & D. V. Jeste (Eds.), *Clinical handbook of schizophrenia* (pp. 354–364). New York, NY: Guilford.

Pittman, B. L. (2005). Offender and community reintegration: An exploratory and descriptive study of cultural competency within community treatment and correctional re-entry program. *Dissertation Abstracts International, Section A: Humanities and Social Sciences, 59,* 53–54. (UMI No. AAI3169486)

Pringle, A., & Brittle, R. (2008). Care planning across professional and organizational boundaries. In A. Hall, M. Wren, & S. Kirby (Eds.), *Care planning in mental health: Promoting recovery* (pp. 46–62). Malden, MA: Blackwell.

Prochaska, J. O., Norcross, J. C., & DiClemente, C. C. (1994). *Changing for good.* New York, NY: Avon Books.

Ries, R. K. (1992). Serial, parallel, and integrated models of dual-diagnosis treatment. *Journal of Health Care for the Poor and Underserved, 3,* 173–180.

Rosenthal, D. (1963). Possible inherited factors: Patterns of behavioral disturbance, premorbid personality, and test performance. In D. Rosenthal (Ed.), *Schizophrenia* (pp. 530–540). New York, NY: Basic Books.

Ruiz v. Estelle, 503 F. Supp. 1265 S.D. Texas (1980).

Ryan, R. M., Plant, R. W., & O'Malley, S. (1995). Initial motivations for alcohol treatment: Relations with patient characteristics, treatment involvement, and dropout. *Addictive Behaviors, 20,* 279–297.

Sacks, S., McKendrick, K., Sacks, J. Y., Banks, S., & Harle, M. (2008). Enhanced outpatient treatment for co-occurring disorders: Main outcomes. *Journal of Substance Abuse Treatment, 34,* 48–60.

Sacks, S., & Pearson, F. S. (2003). Co-occurring substance use and mental disorders in offenders: Approaches, findings, and recommendations. *Federal Probation, 67*(2), 32–39.

Sacks, S., Sacks, J. Y., & DeLeon, G. (1999). Treatment for MICA's: Design and implementation of the modified TC. *Journal of Psychoactive Drugs, 31,* 19–30.

Steadman, H. J., Osher, F. C., Robbins, P. C., Case, B., & Samuels, E. (2009). Prevalence of serious mental illness among jail inmates. *Psychiatric Services, 60,* 761–765.

Substance Abuse and Mental Health Services Administration. (2008). *SAMHSA's National Register of Evidence Based Programs and Practices: Modified therapeutic community for persons with co-occurring disorders.* Rockville, MD: Author.

Sullivan, C. J., McKendrick, K., Sacks, S., & Banks, S. (2007). Modified therapeutic community treatment for offenders with mica disorders: Substance use outcomes. *American Journal of Drug & Alcohol Abuse, 33,* 823–832.

Teplin, L. A., Abram, K. M., & McClelland, G. M. (1996). Prevalence of psychiatric disorders among incarcerated women: Pretrial detainees. *Archives of General Psychiatry, 53,* 505–512.

Torrey, W. C., & Wyzik, P. (2000). The recovery vision as a service improvement guide for community mental health center providers. *Community Mental Health Journal, 36,* 209–216.

Vogel, W. M., Noether, C. D., & Steadman, H. J. (2007). Preparing communities for re-entry of offenders with mental illness: The ACTION approach. *Journal of Offender Rehabilitation, 45,* 167–188.

Wallace, C., Mullen, P. E., & Burgess, P. (2004). Criminal offending in schizophrenia over a 25-year period marked by deinstitutionalization and increasing prevalence of comorbid substance abuse disorders. *American Journal of Psychiatry, 161,* 716–727.

Wanberg, K. W., & Milkman, H. B. (1993/2004). *The Adult Self Assessment Questionnaire (AdSAQ).* Arvada, CO: Center for Addictions Research and Evaluation.

Wanberg, K. W., & Milkman, H. B. (1998). *Criminal conduct and substance abuse treatment: Strategies for self-improvement and change: The providers guide.* Thousand Oaks, CA: Sage.

Wittchen, H. U., Hofler, M., & Merikangas, K. (1999). Toward the identification of core psychopathological processes? *Archives of General Psychiatry, 57,* 859–866.

CHAPTER 12

Assessment and Treatment of Incarcerated Sex Offenders

Shelia M. Brandt and Michael Thompson

Introduction

Of all categories of criminal behavior, there are few, if any, offenses that have the potential to evoke more public concern and outrage than sexual crimes. Furthermore, crimes of a sexual nature cut across all cultures and have been documented, though not necessarily classified as such, as long as humans have been actively assessing and attempting to modify human behavior. Yet the empirical understanding of these complex phenomena is only in its infancy.

In a review of some 2,000 references, Soothill (2009) noted that 30% of the work in this area was from the 1990s, 15% from the 1980s and 1970s, and only 32 references related to work were published before 1970. Thus, despite the provocative nature and complexity of crimes involving sexual violence, the corresponding body of significant literature has only emerged within the past two to three decades.

Whereas other chapters (e.g., Chapter 5) focus on general treatment in correctional settings, this chapter will focus on the description, assessment, and treatment of persons committing sexual offenses.

Population Description

Prevalence Rates

The most current data on the sex offender population in federal prisons comes from the U.S. Sentencing Commission (USSC; 2009). Two offense categories, "sexual abuse" and "pornography/prostitution," comprise the defendants sentenced for sexual offenses in federal courts. Combined, these categories accounted for only 3.1% of all offenders ($N = 37,792$) sentenced during the study period. For the period from October 1, 2008, to March 31, 2009, 219 individuals were sentenced for crimes within the category of sexual abuse, which includes "sexual abuse of a minor, sexual abuse of a ward, criminal sexual abuse, and abusive sexual contact" (p. A-7). Contact offenses are much more often handled in state courts.

Within the offense category of pornography/prostitution (a range of other offenses including the sexual exploitation of minors, e.g., through pornography and transportation of minors for prostitution/sex), crimes often transcend the jurisdiction of individual states, due, for example, to the use of the Internet or the transportation of minor and adult victims across state lines. Accordingly, more than 4 times as many defendants within this category were sentenced during the same period. Of these, 930 were sentenced to prison (only), 14 to split sentences (both incarceration and probation), 17 to probation plus confinement, and 5 to probation (only; USSC, 2009). Further data indicate that the majority of offenders in both categories were White (54.8% among those sentenced for sexual abuse, 85.3% for pornography/prostitution) and male (96.3% for sexual abuse, 98.3% for pornography/prostitution; USSC, 2009).

Motivans and Kyckelhahn (2007) reported data on federal prosecution of sexual offenses against children (i.e., child pornography, sex abuse, and sex transportation) in 2006. During that year, 3,661 suspects were referred to U.S. attorneys. About 7 in 10 of these were for child pornography. Nearly 6 in 10 defendants were prosecuted, and 9 out of 10 were convicted or pled guilty. Between 1994 and 2006, percentage increases in suspects referred were 82.1% for child pornography, 1.1% for sex abuse, and 16.8% for child transportation. Of all defendants arraigned in federal courts on the specific charge of sex abuse during 2006, nearly 3 in 4 were Native American or Alaska Native. (This is likely due to the fact that so many of these individuals live on federal government land.) However, they constituted only 1.3% of all child sex exploitation defendants. Whites accounted for 88.9% of child pornography defendants and 70.2% of those charged with sex transportation. Males constituted 97.0% of all defendants, and 95.8% were U.S. citizens.

Obtaining accurate information about the number of individuals incarcerated in state prisons or local jails is very difficult. There is the broad "funneling issue," which demonstrates that of all the sexual offenses that occur, only some are reported. Greenfeld (1997) stated reporting rates are so low that of all the offenders under some type of correctional authority in the United States, approximately 90% live in the community. Of those that are reported, only a fraction are indicted and possibly convicted. Even the concept of "conviction of a sexual offense" is skewed in that many sexual offenses are pled down to nonsexual charges (i.e., burglary instead of sexual assault in someone's home). Finally, for those individuals convicted of sexual crimes, there is great variability in how states use probation, county jail time, and state prison sentences.

Thus, data from state corrections typically only include adult inmates (juveniles convicted of sexual offenses are most often in other facilities) convicted of the most serious offenses with the longest sentences. Overall, most states are seeing an increase in the number of individuals incarcerated for sexual offenses against juveniles, though there does appear to be some discrepancy in the sentences conferred on offenders with adolescent victims, as opposed to victims 12 and younger, with the former receiving somewhat lighter sentences (Finkelhor & Ormrod, 2001). This is most likely related to the myth that adolescents are somehow more responsible for their own sexual assaults.

Characteristics of Sexual Offenders

Although general criminal offenders have traits in common with sexual offenders (e.g., antisocial traits), there are reasons to believe that the two groups are dissimilar in nature. Moreover, sex offenders themselves are a heterogeneous group. The dynamics, psychopathology, treatment approaches, and recidivism rates differ across individuals convicted of incest, rape, sexual offenses against children, and noncontact offenses such as creation and distribution of child pornography and exhibitionism. As a result, traditional risk assessment instruments may not adequately predict sexual recidivism in some offenders (cf. Hanson & Bussiere, 1998). Whereas general risk assessment instruments may be adequate for the prediction of violent or nonviolent recidivism among sex offenders, unique instruments may be needed for the prediction of sexual recidivism (Hanson & Bussiere, 1998).

Sexual Offenses and Substance Abuse

The presence of co-occurring disorders or substance abuse concerns is seen with some frequency among the sexual offender population. Peugh and Belenko (2001) found that two thirds of incarcerated sexual offenders were substance-involved (defined as being under the influence of alcohol or drugs at the time of the crime, had committed a crime to get money for drugs, had histories of regular illegal drug use, had received treatment for alcoholism, or shared some combination of these characteristics). Långström, Sjöstedt, and Grann (2004) found alcohol abuse spectrum disorders were the most frequent co-occurring diagnosis in incarcerated sexual offenders, followed by drug abuse disorders, personality disorders, and psychosis. Additionally, they found that pathology requiring admission to a hospital was more common in rapists as compared to child molesters. Contrary to these findings, Marshall and Marshall (2006) found that sexual offender sex addicts were no more likely than sexual offender nonaddicts to report co-occurring addiction problems with drugs or alcohol. (The concept of sexual addiction will be discussed in more detail below.)

Sexual Offenses and Mental Illness

Berlin, Saleh, and Malin (2009) noted that although sexual offending and mental illness are often talked about together, this is inaccurate and misleading in most cases. In most incarcerated sexual offenders, there is no Axis I condition present. Sex offenders may commit their acts during an acute phase of a serious mental illness or an Axis I paraphilic disorder, an Axis II personality disorder, any combination of these conditions, or the absence of any Axis I or II condition. Major mental illnesses do not cause sexual offending, but they can predispose or set the stage for increased likelihood in some individuals. If offenders only participate in treatment designed to look at cyclical patterns of sexual abuse, Axis I conditions can be missed. Co-occurring disorders that are left untreated may contribute to increased risk of recidivism. In the cases of non-paraphilic mental disorders, the primary target needs to be the mental illness, without ignoring sexual offenses just because they occurred within the context of the active phase of mental illness.

Paraphilias are Axis I conditions (American Psychiatric Association, 2000). From a purely psychological standpoint, therefore, offenses involving paraphilias are not voluntary, in the sense that the person does not choose the paraphilic attraction. However, the criminal justice system considers them as volitional in the sense that the person can choose to act or not act on the attraction. This volitional component is often used in terms of juror sympathy and sentencing consideration. Interestingly, the presence of paraphilias often serves as the justification for civilly committing some persons for treatment at the end of their prison terms based upon the condition of volitional impairment. This complicated psycho-legal paradox presents offenders, clinicians, and courts with conflicting perspectives based more upon where the offender is within the criminal and civil justice processes (i.e., adjudication and sentencing vs. treatment amenability and consideration for civil commitment) than upon an actual clinical conceptualization (see Text Box 12.1).

TEXT BOX 12.1
LEGAL STRATEGIES FOR COMBATING SEXUAL VIOLENCE

Eric Janus, J.D.

Legal strategies for combating sexual violence have undergone important development over the past three decades. Reflecting a number of influences, the developments range from well-founded innovations that reject outmoded and harmful myths about sexual violence, to highly popular and politically attractive approaches that are counterempirical, misdirecting limited prevention resources, and, at times, undermining the methodical but less flashy approaches that have been shown to reduce sexual violence.

Feminist theorists and empirical researchers, beginning in the 1970s, helped define and expose key myths about sexual violence. Their work led to a series of positive changes in the law and justice system, often referred to as "rape reform." These reforms reflected the new knowledge that much sexual violence was perpetrated by intimates and that old-fashioned ways of thinking—myths about rape—had too often made the legal system a hostile experience for victims of sexual violence. As a result of the reforms, the legal system tended to take sexual violence more seriously across the range of its manifestations.

Beginning in 1990, a set of markedly less useful changes began to develop. These changes have come to be known as "sexual predator" laws. The common flaw characterizing these laws is their indifference to empirical knowledge and their rejection of the key teachings of the feminist movement. Based on a distorted view of sexual violence, these laws are alternately hugely expensive or vastly underfunded. Their chief flaw is that they concentrate resources and public attention at small fractions of the problem of sexual violence while undercutting proven approaches in other areas.

Sexually violent predator (SVP) laws adapt a venerable legal tool—mental health commitment—to incarcerate sex offenders who are deemed "too dangerous" to release at the completion of their criminal sentences. Though fundamental constitutional provisions prohibit extending the criminal sentence after it is imposed (this would violate the double jeopardy and ex post facto clauses), the Supreme Court has upheld these laws because they are limited to sex offenders whose mental abnormality makes it "difficult" for them to control their behavior. In practice, this "control" test is an elastic one, providing little legal constraint on the states' ability to circumvent the normal constitutional rules limiting physical detention.

Because SVP laws depend for their constitutionality on the concept that they are really mental health commitments, they are exceedingly expensive. States must provide treatment. In practice, once committed, individuals remain committed; thus, these residential populations grow without short-term limit. These programs, which are explicitly aimed at only the "worst of the worst," consume most of the resources for violence prevention, though they prevent only a small fraction of sexual violence.

In addition to resource misallocation, SVP laws also distort our ways of framing the problem of sexual violence. They define the "worst of the worst" as mentally disordered individuals who cannot control their sexual behavior. This strengthens the popular image of the "predator" as the archetypal sex offender and casts into the shadows the much more common experience of victimization by acquaintances and intimates whose abusive behavior is allowed to flourish because of societal norms and practices.

Similarly, community notification laws and residential restrictions embody the assumption that the solution to sexual violence lies in segregating offenders from potential victims. These laws are attractive because they seem to be cost-free while addressing in a highly visible manner community fear and outrage. Yet because these laws are based on counterfactual assumptions about the nature of sexual violence, they are of dubious utility. Worse, by impairing the reentry process for offenders, these laws may actually impede the efficacy of supervision and treatment, interventions that most experts agree can be effective in reducing recidivism.

Note: Eric S. Janus is the president and dean of the William Mitchell College of Law. His focus is on the law and health sciences. He has spent the past 10 years focused on the state's ability to use civil commitment to protect public safety.

Sexual Offenses and Psychopathy

Although some sex offenders, especially those with a primary interest in child victims who have otherwise unremarkable criminal histories, may not be psychopathic, incarcerated sexual offenders occasionally do present with high levels of psychopathy. Psychopathy is a highly researched construct characterized by a deeply ingrained personality tendency to violate social norms without guilt, remorse, or the restraint of conscience. Individuals labeled as psychopaths often have a grandiose sense of self-worth and lack the ability to form genuine emotional attachments to others. People who are psychopathic prey on others using charm, deceit, violence, or other methods that allow them to get what they want. The symptoms of psychopathy also include a lack of empathy, egocentricity, pathological lying, disregard for the law, shallow emotions, and a history of victimizing others (Hare, 1999, 2006).

The construct of psychopathy and its relationship to offense type, recidivism, and sexual deviance have been studied extensively. Rates of psychopathy in sexual offenders have been estimated at anywhere from 10% (Serin, Malcolm, Khanna, & Barbaree, 1994) to 35% (Brown & Forth, 1997). Whereas some of these traits are evident across most sex offenders, those who prey on children are often actually seeking to form a type of emotional attachment to their victims beyond that which is typically seen in serial rapists of adults. Porter et al. (2000) found that 64% of mixed offenders (those who offended against both adults and children) and 35.9% of rapists met the definition of psychopathy, though only 6.3% of incest offenders and 9.4% of child molesters with any extrafamilial victims met the criteria for psychopathy.

The connection between psychopathy and sexual recidivism is less clear. A significant body of research (Hanson, 1998; Hanson & Harris, 2000; Hildebrand, de Ruiter, & de Vogel, 2004; Quinsey, Rice, & Harris, 1995; Rice, Harris, & Quinsey, 1990) suggests a link between psychopathy and sexual recidivism. However, others (Barbaree, Seto, Langton, & Peacock, 2001; Firestone, Bradford, Greenberg, Larose, & Curry, 1998; Långström & Grann, 2000; Sjöstedt & Långström, 2002) have not produced similar findings. It is most likely that these conflicting results reflect the complex and heterogeneous nature of sexual offenses.

Hare (1999) has postulated a connection between the presence of psychopathy and deviant sexual arousal and a subsequent increase in risk for sexual reoffense. Hare's notion was supported by Rice and Harris (1997) and Harris et al. (2003). Both of these studies found that rapists and child molesters who scored in the moderately high range on the construct of psychopathy (above 25 on the Hare Psychopathy Checklist–Revised) and had a deviant sexual preference (assessed through penile plethysmography) tended to have higher and faster failure rates for both violent and sexual recidivism. Sexual deviance or sexual preferences considered to be deviant are defined as both statistically unusual and, when acted upon, likely to inflict unwarranted harm on oneself or others, such as child molestation, forcible sexual contact, exhibitionism, and sexual sadism. It is generally accepted practice that sexual deviance can only be confirmed through use of the penile plethysmograph. Hildebrand et al. (2004) found that deviant psychopathic offenders showed a significantly higher sexual recidivism failure rate than did nondeviant psychopathic offenders and nonpsychopathic offenders in general.

L. E. Marshall and Marshall (2006) found sexual offenders were significantly more likely than a comparison group to be classified as sexual addicts. Those sexual offenders who were also sexual addicts were more likely than nonaddicts to report a preoccupation with sex and having been a victim of childhood or adolescent sexual abuse.

Sexual Offenders and Their Victims

Many sexual offender treatment providers believe that offenders' preferred victim pools remain generally static across offenses. However, a growing body of literature supports the notion that many sexual offenders do not exclusively offend against a preferred victim type. These "crossover" offenses are defined as those in which victims are from multiple age, gender, and relationship categories (Abel & Osborn, 1992; English, Jones, Pasini-Hill, Patrick, & Cooley-Towell, 2000; Heil, Ahlmeyer, & Simons, 2003; Heil & Simons, 2008; O'Connell, 1998; Wilcox, Sosnowski, Warberg, & Beech, 2005). Research has established that sex offenders' victim preferences may not be age-, gender-, or relationship-specific (Levenson, Becker, & Morin, 2008). Heil et al. (2003) found that the majority of incarcerated offenders admitted to sexually assaulting both children and adults from multiple relationships and to sexually assaulting victims from both genders. Research completed using confidential questionnaires suggest that a significant number of offenders assault victims of both sexes, that some abuse acquaintances or strangers as well as family members, and that some commit both hands-on and noncontact offenses (Abel et al., 1987; Abel, Becker, Cunningham-Rathner, Mittelman, & Rouleou, 1988; Ahlmeyer, Heil, McKee, & English, 2000; English et al., 2000; Heil et al., 2003).

Assessment

When assessing the general psychological functioning (i.e., mood states, intellectual ability) of individuals incarcerated for sexual offenses, conventional psychological testing can be utilized. However, risk assessment (i.e., "Which offenders are most likely to reoffend?") is somewhat different from assessment for general psychological functioning and is the area of assessment about which the public is most concerned. Over the years, there has been significant controversy and evolving beliefs about what information is valid in predicting a person's risk for recidivism. The factors that contribute to sexual offender reoffense and recidivism are among the most extensively researched areas in the field. Numerous factors have been identified as contributing to the risk of sexual offender reoffense, though the development of a model, test, or statistically based instrument with anything but modest predictive validity has been elusive.

Meta-analyses such as those of Hanson and Bussiere (1998) and Hanson and Morton-Bourgon (2004, 2005) provide the foundation for what is known about risk factors for sexual recidivism. Risk factors are generally classified as static or dynamic. *Static risk factors* are unchangeable factors in the individual's history. Those most closely related to sexual offending include age at first offense (with younger being more strongly correlated with risk); single marital status; lifestyle instability; and histories of rule violations, alcohol and substance abuse, antisocial behavior, and the commission of violent crimes. Among these factors, those signaling an antisocial orientation and rumination on sexually deviant themes are most strongly correlated with recidivism (Hanson & Morton-Bourgon, 2005).

Dynamic risk factors, by definition, are amenable to change and may be further divided into two subcategories: stable and acute dynamic risk factors. *Stable dynamic risk factors* are relatively stable over time but have the potential to change. The most recognized stable dynamic factors associated with sexual offending are sexual deviance, sexual dysregulation, deviant social influences, attitudes supportive of sexual offending, intimacy deficits, and lack of cooperation with supervision. *Acute dynamic risk factors* are relatively fluid and include emotional collapse, increased hostility, substance abuse, sexual preoccupation, collapse of social support, victim access, and rejection of supervision (Hanson & Morton-Bourgon, 2005).

Often, this model of risk is thought of in terms of static factors providing information about *which* offenders are more likely to reoffend and dynamic factors predicting *when* an individual may be more likely to reoffend. There are several instruments for assessing violence and/or sexual risk; however, none have been normed for assessing risk of violence within correctional settings, so a full discussion of these instruments is not warranted here (see Chapter 4 for a review of assessment in correctional settings, including instruments specifically for prediction of sexual offending risk).

Other specific areas of assessment related to sexual offenders include sexual deviance, psychopathy, and sexual addiction. Sexual deviance is assessed in a variety of ways, including offender interview, a thorough examination of criminal history and sexual offense history, self-report paper-and-pencil measures, physiological measurements, and visual reaction time. Offender interviews and paper-and-pencil measures in which an individual is asked about his or her sexual fantasies, attraction patterns, and preferences may be quite transparent and subject to deception. Physiological measures of arousal, such as the penile plethysmograph, and measurements of sexual interest based on visual reaction time, such as the Abel Assessment of Sexual Interest, are seen as less susceptible to deception and, as such, powerful and valid adjunctive measurements in assessing sexual deviance.

The standard for assessing psychopathy is the Hare Psychopathy Checklist–Revised (PCL-R). This instrument involves a comprehensive record review and clinical interview to assess an individual in various domains related to the concept of psychopathy.

Sexual addiction is a more nebulous construct. It is not a recognized diagnosis found in the *Diagnostic and Statistical Manual of Mental Disorders–Fourth Edition, Text Revision* (American Psychiatric Association, 2000), the most recent edition of the diagnostic manual as of this writing. As such, many clinicians do not recognize sexual addiction as a mental disorder. Other clinicians have formulated their own theories regarding the etiology of sexual addiction and have constructed diagnostic criteria and procedures to assess sexual addiction. Current "diagnostic" frameworks follow various models borrowed from the chemical dependency field, an integrated chemical dependency/biological/social learning perspective (Goodman, 1998) and obsessive/compulsive models (Coleman, 1996; Irons & Schneider, 1996). Patrick Carnes, a leading proponent of the construct of sexual addiction, suggests a 10-point behavioral criterion-based scale similar to those used to diagnose other, more accepted mental disorders. For example, Carnes (1983) lists as indicators of sexual addiction, in part, a recurrent pattern of failure to resist impulses to engage in extreme acts of lewd sex; frequently engaging in those behaviors to a greater extent or over a longer period of time than intended; persistent desire or unsuccessful efforts to stop, reduce, or control those behaviors; and an inordinate amount of time spent in obtaining sex, being sexual, or recovering from sexual experience.

Treatment

Sexual offender treatment is often ordered as a condition of sentence to reduce and, if possible, prevent risk of sexual reoffense. Sex offender programs/strategies represent various approaches used to prevent convicted sex offenders from committing future sex offenses. These approaches include different types of therapy, community notification, and standardized assessments. Sex offender programs/strategies are administered in prison and/or in the community to manage sex offenders.

Treatment targets are often offense-specific, meaning they can be directly linked to offense behaviors. These targets include self-esteem, life history, acceptance of responsibility, offense pathways, coping and mood management, social and relationship skills, sexual interests, and self-management plans. Targets may also be offense-related, suggesting they may not contribute directly to the commission of an offense but may set the stage for problematic or inappropriate interpersonal relationships. These target areas often include substance use and abuse, anger management, cognitive skills, and other psychological problems. The following summarizes the primary treatment approaches utilized within sexual offender treatment.

Relapse Prevention

In correctional settings, most prison-based sexual offender programs have historically focused on teaching relapse-prevention (RP) strategies. The RP model was adapted from the substance abuse field, the idea being that if substance abuse relapse could be prevented, perhaps the same approach could be applied to sexually deviant behavior. Conceptually, however, there is no precise correspondence. In the RP model for alcohol and drugs, lapses and relapses were viewed as expected and manageable. With sexual offending, lapses are viewed as willful returns to thinking or being in situations related to old offense cycles, but not engaging in any type of sexual offending behavior. Whereas lapses may be managed, relapses must never occur.

Furthermore, controversy exists in this area, as practitioners idiosyncratically apply variant forms of RP models, yielding results that have not been shown to be more effective than others in decreasing recidivism (Laws, Hudson, & Ward, 2000). This is particularly true when RP models are utilized in accordance with a zero-tolerance philosophy. Laws (1999a, 1999b) proposed utilizing constructs from the RP model within a harm-reduction model. Harm-reduction models acknowledge the limits of organized mental health's ability to eliminate sexual victimization, though affirming that this is a goal for which civilized societies ought to continue to strive. A harm-reduction approach to treatment maintains the philosophy that any steps toward decreased risk are steps in the right direction.

Cognitive-Behavior Therapy

Cognitive-behavior treatment focuses on changing thinking patterns related to sexual offending and changing deviant patterns of sexual behavior. This approach analyzes, challenges, and ultimately teaches an offender how to intervene on the distorted thoughts that allowed him or her to sexually offend. Typically, an offender is directed to detail his or her offending behaviors in an "offense grid" or "cycle," which graphically illustrates the behavioral components of the offense but also matches concurrent thoughts and feelings associated with each action. In this, it is expected that the offender will see links between his or her thoughts, feelings, and actions, and then work to modify them accordingly (Association for the Treatment of Sexual Abusers, 2005).

Risk-Needs-Responsivity Model

The Risks-Needs-Responsivity (RNR) Model was developed by Andrews and Bonta (2001) and has been discussed in a previous chapter (see Chapter 9). This is based on meta-analyses of what works in rehabilitation programs for all offenders. The risk principle maintains that treatment intensity should be adjusted according to each offender's risk level (low, moderate, or high). The most intensive treatment is offered to the highest-risk offenders, with less treatment or no treatment offered to low-risk offenders because they are at lower risk to reoffend anyway (Andrews & Dowden, 2006). The need principle requires treatment to be focused on individualized, modifiable factors (as contrasted with an approach in which everyone gets all aspects of treatment) shown to predict risk (i.e., dynamic risk factors, criminogenic needs). The responsivity principle suggests that treatment approaches need to be adjusted to the unique features of the individual (e.g., learning style, culture, motivation). Andrews and Bonta (2001) advocate using the RNR principles in determining the course of treatment for a particular individual.

Harkins and Beech (2007) echo the importance of assessing each patient's individual risk level so that treatment is effectively administered and criminogenic needs are addressed. However, they provide an expanded discussion of the principle of responsivity. Even if treatment is focused on dynamic risk factors and offered at the intensity commensurate with risk level, responsivity issues (including therapeutic environment and motivation to change) are considered pivotal in determining what change will occur within the individual.

Good Lives and Self-Regulation

The Good Lives Model (GLM; Ward, 2002; Ward & Brown, 2004; Ward & Gannon, 2006) is a humanistic/social-cognitive conceptualization of sexual offender motivation that suggests treatment must regard participants as whole beings in need of focus in many principal life areas. The GLM is based on the notion that all humans strive to achieve nine primary human "goods" (Ward & Stewart, 2003). Primary goods include (a) life, including healthy living, optimal physical functioning, and sexual satisfaction; (b) knowledge; (c) excellence in play and work; (d) excellence in agency, such as personal autonomy and self-directedness; (e) inner peace, as evidenced in freedom from emotional turmoil and stress; (f) relatedness and community, including intimate, romantic, and family relationships; (g) spirituality, particularly in the broad sense of finding meaning and purpose in life; (h) happiness; and (i) creativity (McMurran & Ward, 2004). The GLM agrees that traditional sexual offender treatment focusing on risk factors and RP within a cognitive-behavioral framework is a worthwhile endeavor. However, the GLM also notes that this traditional treatment approach has lacked a broader focus on the positive human "goods," or goals all humans seek to live satisfying and good lives; therefore, it shifts the focus of their treatment to the positive pursuit of these goals.

Best Practice: A Comprehensive Treatment Model

From a theoretical standpoint, the above approaches are often portrayed in contrast to one another because of the emphasis on approach goals in Ward's (2002) GLM framework and the perceived similarity of RP models and RNR. However, in practice, the factors identified as salient dynamic risk factors for sexual recidivism are considered appropriate treatment targets in both the GLM and RNR approaches. As such, the best practice for treatment is currently viewed as a comprehensive model that includes elements of the above models but also includes motivational interviewing (i.e., assessing and engaging a person based upon intensity of desire to change) and an emphasis on therapeutic process (i.e., the use of therapeutic relationships to address interpersonal deficits; W. L. Marshall, Marshall, Serran, & Fernandez, 2006). To date, substantial variability has been found in outcome studies examining treatment effectiveness for sex offenders (Hanson, Broom, & Stephenson, 2004).

Management Issues

Institutional Infractions

Among incarcerated sexual offenders, there are modest correlations between psychopathy ratings and institutional rule infractions (Buffington-Vollum, Edens, & Johnson, 2002). Incarcerated sexual offenders can be a challenge within a correctional institution. Some lack the social skills of more streetwise offenders. Some are looked at with derision and scorn by other inmates and even correctional staff. It is commonly reported by incarcerated sexual offenders that they are considered "the bottom of the barrel" within the informal but nonetheless rigid prisoner social hierarchy. Sexual offenders within correctional institutions are often the target of verbal and even physical abuse. The extent of physical abuse is unknown due to the inherent underreporting of such acts within correctional institutions (see Text Box 12.2, pages 268–269).

Staff Perceptions

Weekes, Pelletier, and Beaudette (1995) studied the perceptions of sexual offenders by prison correctional staff within a Canadian institution. They found that correctional staff perceived sexual offenders, in general, to be more dangerous, harmful, violent, tense, bad, unpredictable, mysterious, unchangeable, aggressive, weak, irrational, and afraid when compared to nonsexual offenders. The authors also found that correctional staff perceived sexual offenders with child victims to be significantly more immoral and mentally ill than sex offenders against women. Sexual offenders against women were perceived to be more immoral and mentally ill than inmates without sexual offenses.

Management of Exhibitionism

Exhibitionism toward correctional staff is a relatively common occurrence. Offenders expose their genitals to correctional staff for numerous reasons. Whereas some offenders expose in service to anger, authority, and powerlessness, others expose in service to a deviant sexual urge, sexual arousal, or other sexual proclivity. Prison inmates often use exposure of their genitals as angry reactions to the regimentation of the correctional system or loss of perceived personal power. Offenders with poor coping skills and strategies will often use exposure as an indirect method of exerting power through forcing inevitable staff reactions to their actions.

In considering incarcerated exhibitionists it is necessary, though difficult, to discern the motives of their actions. It is helpful from a treatment and management perspective to differentiate exposing behavior that has an instrumental foundation (exposing that is goal-directed and purposeful, such as using exposure of one's genitals to force a move to a segregated unit) from exposing behavior that has a reactive foundation (exposing as a hostile response to perceived provocation and anger).

One strategy to reduce inmate exhibitionism is to remove incentives to its occurrence. Understanding an offender's motivation for exposing, especially in terms of gaining a desired outcome, will assist correctional staff in developing a plan to reduce such behavior. In this, utilization of behavioral psychology principles of extinction may limit repetition of the behavior. For instance, inmates who desire administrative segregation or another punitive sanction for their own reasons may use exposing behavior to force correctional staff to act. Conversely, an exaggerated staff reaction may result in an increase in exposing behaviors, especially if the subsequent sanction imposed was desired by the inmate. If correctional staff understand the offender's specific motives for exposing, sanctions other than those desired by the inmate may be instituted. Of course, if an inmate desires a significant punitive consequence, such as segregation, the inmate may ultimately commit an act that must result in segregation (see Chapter 14 for a more detailed discussion of behavioral treatment strategies).

Inmate-on-Inmate Sexual Assault

The Prison Rape Elimination Act (PREA) of 2003 established the need to protect incarcerated individuals from sexual abuse. The PREA called for a commission to study prison rape, including causes, consequences, and prevention. Congress affirmed the right of incarcerated individuals to be protected against sexual abuse (see Text Box 12.2 for further discussion of the PREA.)

Sexual abuse in correctional settings makes these environments less safe for everyone, consumes resources, undermines rehabilitation, and devastates the lives of the victims. Sexual abuse is not an inevitable feature of incarceration, nor should it be accepted as part of the penalty imposed on offenders. However, certain characteristics including youth, small stature, lack of correctional experience, mental disability or mental illness, nonheterosexual orientation, and transgender identity are correlated with higher risk for being sexually victimized while incarcerated (Fagan, Wennerstrom, & Miller, 1996).

TEXT BOX 12.2
INTERVIEW WITH ROBERT W. DUMOND

1. Based on post-PREA (Prison Rape Elimination Act of 2003) data, is sexual assault in prison as significant a problem as previously thought?

Since the passage of PREA, the Bureau of Justice Statistics (BJS) has gathered data indicating that sexual assault in U.S. correctional settings is a serious and significant issue. For example, BJS (Beck, Harrison, & Adams, 2007) reported that in 2006, 6,528 sexual assault incidents were formally reported to correctional authorities. Of these sexual assault incidents, 961 (i.e., 15%) were investigated and substantiated, including 262 incidents of inmate-on-inmate rape, 158 incidents of nonconsensual sexual acts, 471 staff sexual misconduct incidents, and 70 staff sexual harassment incidents. For each of the 3 years of formal reports (Beck & Harrison, 2006; Beck et al., 2007; Beck & Hughes, 2005), the two primary types of prisoner sexual violence being reported have consistently involved incidents of staff sexual misconduct and inmate-on-inmate nonconsensual sexual acts (acts comparable to rape in most jurisdictions).

Comparing anonymous community with correctional survey data (Beck & Harrison, 2006, 2007, 2008; Beck et al., 2007; Beck & Hughes, 2005; Rand & Catalano, 2007) has revealed substantially higher incident rates of sexual violence in prisons. Whereas the national rate of sexual assault in the community is 1.1 per 1,000 U.S. citizens (Rand & Catalano, 2007), the national rate of sexual assault in U.S. prisons is 123 per 1,000 U.S. prisoners (Beck & Harrison, 2007). More specifically, of the 146 federal and state prisons surveyed, 10 facilities had overall prevalence rates of 9.3% or greater and 11 facilities had rates of inmate-on-inmate nonconsensual sexual acts greater than 300 per 1,000 prisoners (Beck & Harrison, 2007).

These results provide strong evidence that prisoner sexual violence is a serious, devastating crime which affects a large number of inmates in U.S. correctional facilities. Consistent with reporting problems noted in the collection of community data, some believe that reports of prison sexual assault are similarly underreported, suggesting that incidence rates may be even higher than those currently reported.

2. What have been some of the benefits of PREA?

Recognition of a problem is often the first step in effectively crafting a solution. For decades, the issue of sexual threats, intimidation, and against the incarcerated, by other prisoners and staff, has remained unsubstantiated and often not reported. Despite potential problems in this area, few concrete steps had been taken to systematically address the problem. The advent of PREA and a national discussion about prisoner sexual violence has prompted a reexamination of all areas of correctional management and practice, including initial inmate assessment, orientation, classification, as well as staff selection, training and accountability, investigations and intervention. PREA has also been helpful in improving the initial and ongoing training received by all correctional staff. Additionally, PREA has fostered more collaboration between healthcare and correctional staff and has helped to strengthen the interdisciplinary intervention and care provided to victims/survivors.

PREA prompted a national review of corrections in the United States, including a reexamination of the difficulties faced by prisoners with mental illness; developmental disabilities; as well as juveniles; women; and those who are lesbian, gay, bisexual, and transgendered. All of these issues continue to challenge correctional authorities. However, the work of the National Prison Rape Elimination Commission and their proposed national standards has provided a forum in which to examine and discuss these issues and has resulted in a growing awareness of issues surrounding prison sexual assault.

3. Have there been any unintended consequences (positive and/or negative) resulting from the legislation?

Some correctional practitioners have argued that one unintended negative consequence of PREA is that it has given inmates another "tool" to manipulate the system, by providing another reason to seek alternative housing, cell assignments, etc. This, however, can be managed effectively if agencies investigate and evaluate incidents with due diligence.

Perhaps the most important unintended positive consequence has been that PREA has been the catalyst for a national discussion about correctional policies and practices in U.S. jails and prisons in general. As a result of PREA, many correctional agencies have rededicated themselves to the principles of *"care, custody, control, safety, security, and rehabilitation."* There has been a renewed emphasis on institutional safety and security, resulting in a safer environment for inmates, detainees, prisoners, and juveniles, and the staff responsible for their care.

Note: Robert W. Dumond was a consultant to Congress during their deliberations on PREA and is an international consultant on prisoner rape. He has nearly 40 years of experience involving criminal justice and mental health issues.

References

Beck, A. J., & Harrison, P. M. (2006, July). *Prison Rape Elimination Act of 2003—Sexual violence reported by correctional authorities, 2005* (Bureau of Justice Statistics Special Report NCJ214646). Washington, DC: National Criminal Justice Reference Service.

Beck, A. J., & Harrison, P. M. (2007, December). *Prison Rape Elimination Act of 2003—Sexual victimization in state and federal prisons reported by inmates, 2007* (Bureau of Justice Statistics Special Report NCJ 219414). Washington, DC: National Criminal Justice Reference Service.

Beck, A. J., & Harrison, P. M. (2008, June). *Prison Rape Elimination Act of 2003—Sexual victimization in local jails reported by inmates, 2007* (Bureau of Justice Statistics Special Report NCJ 221946). Washington, DC: National Criminal Justice Reference Service.

Beck, A. J., Harrison, P. M., & Adams, D. B. (2007, August). *Prison Rape Elimination Act of 2003—Sexual violence reported by correctional authorities, 2006* (Bureau of Justice Statistics Special Report NCJ 218914). Washington, DC: National Criminal Justice Reference Service.

Beck, A. J., & Hughes, T. A. (2005, July). *Bureau of Justice Statistics—Prison Rape Elimination Act of 2003: Sexual violence reported by correctional authorities, 2004* (Bureau of Justice Statistics Special Report NCJ 210333). Washington, DC: National Criminal Justice Reference Service.

Rand, M., & Catalano, S. (2007, December). *Bureau of Justice Statistics Bulletin: Criminal victimization, 2006* (Bureau of Justice Statistics Special Report NCJ 219413). Washington, DC: National Criminal Justice Reference Service.

All individuals must be informed of their rights to be safe, and specifically to be protected against sexual abuse during incarceration, and of how to report it if it occurs. Providing such information should be an ongoing process and made part of the institutional climate via posters, handbooks, and other means. These materials must take into account the inmate population, language diversity, and the wide variability in cognitive abilities when providing this information. Staff must be educated about the type of information they might hear or receive in writing, trained in how to respond to allegations of abuse, educated about clear signs that abuse might be occurring, and held accountable for not reporting incidents according to established procedures. Furthermore, all reports must be taken seriously and investigated. Once victims come forward, it is often common practice to place them in a segregation unit to "remove them" from further potential victimization. However, isolation can often cause additional psychological distress or be experienced as pejorative; thus, this intervention must be utilized with caution and additional support provided for the inmate.

Reentry Issues

Successful community reentry programs sort offenders by public safety threat level, adjust interventions according to dynamic risk factors, appreciate the benefits and limitations of technology, impose swift and certain sanctions, create incentives for success, and measure progress. Supervision for sex offenders should be structured like that of other offenders who are reintegrating, in the sense that it should be based on RNR. Evidence-based practices decrease crime 10% to 20%, whereas non–evidence-based practices show no decrease (Andrews & Dowden, 2006). Of course, "what works" is less clear with sexual offenders as compared to general offenders.

Electronic Monitoring

As early as 1996, electronic monitoring, along with other resources and strategies (such as intensive supervision, surveillance, and polygraphs), was found to enhance the quality of sex offender supervision (Cumming & Buell, 1996). Morgan and Glover (2008) replicated the findings of Cumming and Buell (1996). They found electronic monitoring to be enhanced when employed with additional tools, such as the utilization of a task force to assist personnel in surveillance, sharing of information between agencies (law enforcement, treatment providers, and supervision), regular face-to-face contacts, regular contacts with those associated with the offender, and unannounced home and work visits (Morgan & Glover, 2008). Additionally, they found electronic monitoring to be effective only when paired with trained supervisory staff. In this, the authors pointed out that it is trained staff monitoring GPS equipment that leads to effectiveness, not the GPS equipment working in isolation. Though much research has been done concerning the relative cost-effectiveness of electronic monitoring and even offenders' perceptions of its relative punitive value, there is not yet a significant body of empirical research demonstrating the effectiveness of electronic monitoring as it pertains to sexual offenders.

Other Community Programming Issues

Community corrections departments are vastly understaffed. Officers struggle with high caseloads, limited community sanctions, and repeated administrative hurdles as they try to hold supervisees accountable. As a result, many wait until an offender has several violations before pursuing a sanction to ensure the time is worth the efforts (i.e., results in a penalty). Communities leading the way in this area have moved to systems of graduated sanctions including community service programs, day reporting centers, and short stays in jail without returning to court. Otherwise, these offenders may spend time in jail just waiting for a disposition hearing regarding their violations.

Rewards work better than punishments for motivating people. Some states, such as Arizona, have created performance incentives for offenders and the county-based supervision system. For every month the offender complies with terms of supervision (including community service assignments, abstinence, paying restitution, etc.), legislation authorizes the probation period to be reduced by 20 days. Slipups result in a loss of earned time. The county is then awarded 40% of the money the state saves by not having to house repeat offenders and probation rule violators in prison. The refund is used by the county to improve victim services and expand drug treatment and other recidivism-reducing programs. Even if revocations were reduced by 10%, the state could save about $10 million, with 40% of the money returning to the local level (Pew Center on the States, 2009).

Best practices in reentry suggest management of this transition is better accomplished through collaborative relationships and services through multiple agencies versus the traditional single agency management (Wormith et al., 2007). However, multiagency collaboration is challenging, especially when the political stakes are high (see Chapter 1 for a more detailed discussion of multiagency collaboration). There is little research on these programs for sex offenders.

Public Perception, Community Notification, and Sex Offender Registration

Laws and public policy are often greatly influenced by the public's perception of sexual offenders, regardless of the accuracy of these viewpoints. For example, one stereotype is of the sexual offender luring children at public parks or lying in wait in the bushes for child victims. These views have been formed as a result of a few rare but highly publicized cases and have served as the impetus for several sexual predator laws (e.g., community notification and registration laws). However, the reality is that most sex crimes involving children are committed by individuals known to the child, not by strangers (Lieb, Quinsey, & Berliner, 1998; Snyder, 2000).

Community notification and *sexual offender registration* are indistinct terms with meanings varying between states and municipalities. All states have some form of sexual offender registration. In general, sexual offender registration requires name, address, physical description, and other pertinent demographic and criminal history data to be retained in a database accessible to law enforcement and other authorized individuals. Offenders are required to keep their registration current. Many state sexual offender registration systems require an offender to register even after the expiration of his or her sentence. Failure to maintain registration is often prosecuted as a new offense and sometimes as a felony.

Community notification is different from sexual offender registration. Community notification involves making a sex offender's personal information, including such factors as location of residence and offense, available to the community in which the offender lives. Following their release from prison, sex offenders provide police with information such as their residence and employment for tracking/monitoring purposes. This type of registration typically accompanies community notification.

Interestingly, a cottage industry in community notification has grown in the past few years (see, e.g., http://www.sexoffender.com/, http://www.familywatchdog.us/ or https://www.neighborhoodscan.com/). Using publicly accessible (and usually free) data, Internet websites have appeared listing offenders by city or state. Such websites often offer the opportunity to search for registered offenders by zip code or city, and may charge a fee. There is even a downloadable application for the "iPhone" that offers a listing of registered offenders searchable by zip code. Such registration databases, whether maintained publicly or posted on the Internet, often possess flawed or incorrect data. Inaccurate addresses or lack of information on absconders can leave the public with a false sense of security or alarm the community. Additionally, many registration databases accessible to the public do not differentiate between offender type, risk of recidivism, or general dangerousness. As a result, the public tends to categorize all sexual offenders as similar in offense and victim type.

Policies that ostracize and disrupt the stability of sex offenders are unlikely to be in the best interest of long-term public safety, because housing and employment problems, social stigma, and a sense of vulnerability are factors commonly associated with recidivism (Mustaine, Tewksbury, & Stengel, 2006, as cited in Levenson, 2007). Empirically based risk assessment can assist in identifying the registered sex offenders who are more likely to reoffend, and this can be useful in determining specific offenders about whom to alert concerned citizens. This would utilize fiscal resources more responsibly and reduce collateral consequences experienced by sex offenders and their families during reentry while maintaining low probability of compromising public safety.

Sexual offender registration is a significant reentry issue. Public support for registration laws is strong. All states have sexual offender registration laws. The Pam Lychner Sex Offender Tracking and Identification Act of 1996 required the creation of a national database to ensure registration and address verification for sex offenders residing in states with insufficient registries. The Jacob Wetterling Act (1994) requires registration for persons convicted in federal and military courts, requires sex offenders who relocate to register in the new state of residence, and mandates sex offenders to register in the state in which they work or attend school. The Sexual Offender Registration and Notification Act (SORNA), Title I of the Adam Walsh Child Protection and Safety Act of 2006, requires states to adopt a uniform federal standard for sexual offender registration. The Adam Walsh Act standards of sexual offender registration include listing, on an Internet website, an offender's name, address, offense history, physical description, and automobile and employment information. To date, the federal government has not vigorously pursued the implementation of these standards.

Interface Between Treatment Providers and Supervision Agents

Another issue that often compromises the effectiveness of release plans is the interface between community supervision personnel and treatment providers (if an offender is required to enter or continue outpatient treatment postincarceration). McGrath, Cumming, and Holt (2002) found that probation officers and community-based sexual offender treatment providers value frequent and meaningful communication and see mutual benefit in it. However, these researchers found differing opinions about probation officers coleading or leading treatment groups, which is required in some states. The issue of cofacilitated groups (i.e., groups led in tandem between a treatment provider and a probation agent) is a contentious and controversial one.

Many corrections departments have found such groups invaluable in offender management. Corrections departments often cite the convenience of agents in cofacilitated groups being able to monitor dynamic risk factors on a regular and frequent basis, thereby ostensibly reducing the risk of reoffense. However, considering the general reluctance of many offenders to discuss their offending behaviors (Frost, 2004), many therapists believe that offenders will be reluctant to share issues in a group with a probation officer present for fear that their behavior will be constantly scrutinized for violations of probation. Many therapists also believe that a treatment group should offer the offender a place to discuss probation issues, and even possible probation violations, and strategize appropriate ways in which to broach the subject with their probation officer. Additionally, many probation agents do not possess the clinical skills or education required of a sexual offender treatment provider.

Housing

Mercado, Alvarez, and Levenson (2008) found that a high percentage of postrelease offenders perceived residence restriction and community notification legislation to negatively affect employment, housing, and social relations. These authors also suggested that residency restriction policies and community notification may actually hamper offenders' efforts toward community reintegration. Of course, it is arguable whether positive community reintegration and an offender's ultimate success are the goals of such policies. Instead, ostracism appears to be the unstated intent, leading to a de facto social stratification that a sexual offender may never be able to move past.

Jill Levenson and her colleagues (Levenson, 2007; Levenson, Brannon, Fortney, & Baker, 2007; Levenson & Cotter, 2005a, 2005b; Levenson & D'Amora, 2007; Levenson & Hern, 2007) have done extensive research in the area of residency restrictions pertaining to sexual offenders. They have argued that residency restrictions are popular, but ineffective, and may actually disrupt community reintegration (Levenson, D'Amora, & Hern, 2007). As a result, it has been suggested that poor community integration may actually serve to inflate rates of recidivism. Most studies fail to demonstrate any significant reduction in recidivism due to community notification, though a Washington study found that offenders subject to community notification were apprehended more quickly when new crimes did occur (Schram & Milloy, 1995). Research literature (Levenson & Cotter, 2005a; Levenson, D'Amora, et al., 2007; Tewksbury, 2002) has shown a significant amount of error on registry websites and has called into question the accuracy of sex offender registries. In many cases, address information for the offender was incorrect, with offenders living elsewhere, incarcerated, and in some cases, even dead. Thus, although the public may cite public notification and offender registries as important public safety measures, this perception is not based on actual recidivism rates or even current information in the registries.

Employment

Postincarceration adjustment is often a source of significant stress to offenders as they adjust to the less regimented aspects of daily living, while still conforming to the mandates of the court, supervised release, probation agents, and an often hostile social climate (especially in regards to sexual offenders). Poor reentry and reintegration planning may be a risk factor for recidivism (Willis & Grace, 2009). Offenders often have difficulty acquiring employment and suffer severe economic hardships. A criminal record makes an offender a poor candidate for employment. Many employers, especially larger or national companies, have blanket policies that prohibit the hiring of felons. Some companies, though hiring felons, will not hire sexual offenders. As a result, the offender will very likely face tremendous difficulty obtaining and maintaining employment upon release. The offender may be prohibited from working in his or her prior field, especially if the work in that field was related to the sexual offense. For example, a released child molester will very likely be required to work in a vocation that does not involve children or supervision over children.

Many offenders also face restrictions on computer usage, further impeding the ability of the offender to search for employment or apply for jobs. Restriction on computer usage is often a blanket condition of probation or conditional release regardless of whether a computer was a factor in the sexual offense. Many employers have moved past the traditional paper job application and now only accept job applications via the Internet. Many employers only post employment openings on websites. If an offender is prohibited from using a computer or accessing the Internet, many, if not most, potential jobs are in effect unavailable. This even holds true, though to a lesser extent, in the temporary employment ("temp work") industry, an area of employment historically more available to felons. Many temporary services post openings on the Internet. An offender unable to access the Internet must personally appear at a temporary employment service daily and wait, often for hours, to obtain work. If no temporary work is available, he or she has effectively lost a day to search for other employment.

Summary and Conclusions

Legislative, correctional, criminal justice, and mental health professionals are tasked with making every dollar count and accounting for the use of every resource. This means determining which sex offenders should be incarcerated and for how long, integrating technology with appropriate expectations into effective supervision models, and reallocating money from prisons to community corrections where appropriate. They are also responsible for ensuring that public policy related to sex offender treatment is not painted as "preventing" sexual abuse.

Depending on their risk level, sex offenders require varying degrees and intensities of community supervision and treatment. Specialized supervision skills, monitoring or prohibiting computer use, understanding and working with offenders with regard to residency restrictions where they exist, interfacing with treatment providers, skill with dynamic risk assessment—all must be brought to bear to maximize the likelihood of successful return to the community.

Ward, Gannon, and Vess (2009) argue for a human rights perspective in the management of sexual offenders. They propose an integrative framework of codified ethical principles, including core values of human rights and allowing sexual offenders the opportunity to further their own valued personal projects without interference from others. This is consistent with the principles found in the *Ethical Principles of Psychologists and Code of Conduct* (American Psychological Association, 2002) and the *Standards and Guidelines* of the Association for the Treatment of Sexual Abusers (2005). These principles do not argue against the legitimate curtailment of some basic rights as a response to an offender's behavior, but they promote a structure of ethical sensitivity and social responsibility to ultimately promote the core values of freedom and well-being.

KEY TERMS

Paraphilia

Classical conditioning

Sexual offender civil commitment

Risk-Needs-Responsivity Model (RNR)

Good Lives Model (GLM)

Community notification

Sexual offender registration

Dynamic risk factors

Stable dynamic factors

Acute dynamic factors

Static risk factors

The Adam Walsh Act

Prison Rape Elimination Act (PREA)

Electronic monitoring

Relapse prevention

Motivational interviewing

Penile plethysmograph (PPG)

DISCUSSION QUESTIONS

1. After reading this chapter, how has your understanding of sex offenders and the nature of their offenses changed?

2. Is progress being made in the assessment and treatment of sex offenders? Explain your answer.

3. What concerns, if any, do you have about the legal rights of sex offenders who are committed to treatment at the conclusion of their prison sentences?

4. Are sex offender treatment programs "designed to fail," in the sense of ensuring that sex offenders are either kept in secure settings or fail in the community and returned to prison? Is this what the public truly wants?

5. Which of the various treatment approaches—Risk-Needs-Responsivity, Good Lives Model, cognitive-behavior therapy, relapse prevention, or a combined approach— seems to you most likely to be effective in preventing further sexual offending? Why do you think so?

6. Imagine that you are a probation officer with a sex offender on your caseload. What advice would you give him or her about basic matters related to community reentry like finding housing or employment? How would this be different from advice you might give to someone else, perhaps a paroled drug dealer or other nonviolent criminal?

7. As is noted in the chapter, most sex offenses are never reported. Why do you think this might be, and how might this relate to the recidivism rates cited in the research literature?

References

Abel, G., Becker, J., Cunningham-Rathner, J., Mittelman, M., Murphy, M., & Rouleau, J. (1987). Self-reported sex crimes of nonincarcerated paraphiliacs. *Journal of Interpersonal Violence, 2*, 3–25.

Abel, G. G., Becker, J. V., Cunningham-Rathner, J., Mittelman, M. S., & Rouleau, J. L. (1988). Multiple paraphilic diagnoses among sex offenders. *Bulletin of the American Academy of Psychiatry and the Law, 16*, 153–168.

Abel, G. G., & Osborn, C. A. (1992). The paraphilias: The extent and nature of sexually deviant and criminal behavior. *Psychiatric Clinics of North America, 15*, 675–687.

Adam Walsh Child Protection and Safety Act of 2006, Pub. L. No. 109-248, 120 Stat. 587-650 (2006).

Ahlmeyer, S., Heil, P., McKee, B., & English, K. (2000). The impact of polygraphy on admissions of victims and offenses in adult sexual offenders. *Sexual Abuse: Journal of Research and Treatment, 12*, 123–138.

American Psychiatric Association. (2000). *Diagnostic and statistical manual of mental disorders* (4th ed., Text Revision). Washington, DC: Author.

American Psychological Association. (2002). Ethical principles of psychologists and code of conduct. *American Psychologist, 57*, 1060–1073.

Andrews, D. A., & Bonta, J. (2001). *The psychology of criminal conduct* (3rd ed.). Cincinnati, OH: Anderson.

Andrews, D. A., & Dowden, C. (2006). Risk principle of case classification in correctional treatment. *International Journal of Offender Therapy and Comparative Criminology, 50*, 88–100.

Association for the Treatment of Sexual Abusers. (2005). *Practice standards and guidelines for the evaluation, treatment, and management of adult male sexual abusers.* Beaverton, OR: Author.

Barbaree, H. E., Seto, M. C., Langton, C. M., & Peacock, E. J. (2001). Evaluating the predictive accuracy of six risk assessment instruments for adult sex offenders. *Criminal Justice and Behavior, 28*, 490–521.

Berlin, F. S., Saleh, F. M., & Malin, H. M. (2009). Mental illness and sex offending. In F. M. Saleh, A. J. Grudzinskas, J. M. Bradford, & D. J. Brodsky (Eds.), *Sex offenders: Identification, risk assessment, treatment and legal issues* (pp. 119–129). New York, NY: Oxford University Press.

Brown, S. L., & Forth, A. E. (1997). Psychopathy and sexual assault: Static risk factors, emotional precursors, and rapist subtypes. *Journal of Consulting and Clinical Psychology, 65*, 848–857.

Buffington-Vollum, J., Edens, J. F., & Johnson, J. (2002). Psychopathy as a predictor of institutional misbehavior among sex offenders: A prospective replication. *Criminal Justice and Behavior, 29*, 497–511.

Carnes, P. (1983). *Out of the shadows.* Minneapolis, MN: CompCare.

Coleman, E. (1996). What sexual scientists know, . . : About love. *The Society for the Scientific Study of Sexuality, 2*(1). Retrieved January 5, 2010, from http://www.sexscience.org/publications/index.php?category_id=440&subcategory_id=334&printable=1

Cumming, G., & Buell, M. (1996). Relapse prevention as a supervision strategy for sex offenders. *Sexual Abuse: A Journal of Research and Treatment, 8*, 231–241.

English, K., Jones, L., Pasini-Hill, D., Patrick, D., & Cooley-Towell, S. (2000). *The value of polygraph testing in sex offender management* (Research Report Submitted to the National Institute of Justice, No. D97LBVX0034). Denver: Colorado Department of Public Safety, Office of Research and Statistics.

Fagan, T. J., Wennerstrom, D., & Miller, J. (1996). Sexual assault of male inmates: Prevention, identification, and intervention. *Journal of Correctional Health Care, 3*(1), 49–65.

Finkelhor, D., & Ormrod, R. (2001, December). *Offenders incarcerated for crimes against juveniles* (Bureau of Justice Statistics Special Report NCJRS 191028). Washington, DC: National Criminal Justice Reference Service.

Firestone, P., Bradford, J., Greenberg, D., Larose, M., & Curry, S. (1998). Homicidal and non-homicidal child molesters: Psychological, phallometric, and criminal features. *Sexual Abuse: A Journal of Research and Treatment, 10*, 305–323.

Frost, A. (2004). Therapeutic engagement styles of child sexual offenders in a group treatment program: A grounded theory study. *Sexual Abuse: A Journal of Research and Treatment, 16*, 191–208.

Goodman, A. (1998). *Sexual addiction: An integrated approach.* Madison, WI: International Universities Press.

Greenfeld, L. (1997, February). *Sex offenses and offenders: An analysis of data on rape and sexual assault* (Bureau of Justice Statistics Special Report NCJRS 163392). Washington, DC: National Criminal Justice Reference Service.

Hanson, R. K. (1998). What do we know about sex offender risk assessment? *Psychology, Public Policy, and Law, 4*, 50–72.

Hanson, R. K., Broom, I., & Stephenson, M. (2004). Evaluating community sex offender treatment programs: A 12-year follow-up of 724 offenders. *Canadian Journal of Behavioural
Science, 36,* 87–96.

Hanson, R. K., & Bussiere, M. T. (1998). Predicting relapse: A meta-analysis of sexual offender
recidivism studies. *Journal of Consulting and Clinical Psychology, 66,* 348–362.

Hanson, R. K., & Harris, A. J. R. (2000). Where should we intervene? Dynamic predictors of sexual assault recidivism. *Criminal Justice and Behavior, 27,* 6–35.

Hanson, R. K., & Morton-Bourgon, A. (2004). *Prediction of sexual offender recidivism: An updated
meta-analysis.* Ottawa, Ontario, Canada: Public Works and Government Services.

Hanson, R. K., & Morton-Bourgon, K. (2005). The characteristics of persistent sexual offenders:
A meta-analysis of recidivism studies. *Journal of Consulting and Clinical Psychology, 73,*
1154–1163.

Hare, R. D. (1999). Psychopathy as a risk factor for violence. *Psychiatric Quarterly, 70,* 181–197.

Hare, R. D. (2006). Psychopathy: A clinical and forensic overview. *Psychiatric Clinics of North
America, 29,* 709–724.

Harkins, L., & Beech, A. R. (2007). A review of factors that can influence the effectiveness of sexual offender treatment: Risk, need, responsivity, and process issues. *Aggression and Violent
Behavior, 12,* 615–627.

Harris, G. T., Rice, M., Quinsey, V., Lalumière, M., Boer, D., & Lang, C. (2003). A multi-site comparison of actuarial risk instruments for sex offenders. *Psychological Assessment, 15,* 413–425.

Heil, P., Ahlmeyer, S., & Simons, D. (2003). Crossover sexual offenses. *Sexual Abuse: A Journal of
Research and Treatment, 15,* 221–236.

Heil, P., & Simons, D. (2008). Multiple paraphilias: Prevalence, etiology, assessment and treatment. In R. Laws & W. Donohue (Eds.), *Sexual deviance* (2nd ed., pp. 527–556). New York,
NY: Guilford.

Hildebrand, M., de Ruiter, C., & de Vogel, V. (2004). Psychopathy and sexual deviance in treated
rapists: Association with sexual and nonsexual recidivism. *Sexual Abuse: A Journal of
Research and Treatment, 16,* 1–24.

Irons, R., & Schneider, J. (1996). Differential diagnosis of addictive sexual disorders using the
DSM-IV. *Sexual Addiction & Compulsivity, 3,* 7–21.

Jacob Wetterling Crimes Against Children and Sexually Violent Offender Registration Act, Pub.
L. No. 103-322, 42 USC § 14071 et seq. (1994).

Långström, N., & Grann, M. (2000). Risk for criminal recidivism among young sex offenders.
Journal of Interpersonal Violence, 15, 855–871.

Långström, N., Sjöstedt, G., & Grann, M. (2004). Psychiatric disorders and recidivism in sexual
offenders. *Sexual Abuse: A Journal of Research and Treatment, 16,* 139–150.

Laws, D. R. (1999a). Harm reduction or harm facilitation? A reply to Meletzky. *Sexual Abuse:
Journal of Research and Treatment, 11,* 233–241.

Laws, D. R. (1999b). Relapse prevention: The state of the art. *Journal of Interpersonal Violence, 14,*
285–302.

Laws, D. R., Hudson, S. M., & Ward, T. (Eds.). (2000). *Remaking relapse prevention with sex offenders.* Thousand Oaks, CA: Sage.

Levenson, J. (2007). Residence restrictions and their impact on sex offender reintegration, rehabilitation, and recidivism. *ATSA Forum, 19*(2). Retrieved January 4, 2010, from
http://newsmanager.commpartners.com/atsa/issues/2007–03–15/1.html

Levenson, J., Becker, J., & Morin, J. (2008). The relationship between victim age and gender
crossover among sex offenders. *Sexual Abuse: A Journal of Research and Treatment, 20,* 43–60.

Levenson, J., Brannon, Y., Fortney, T., & Baker, J. (2007). Public perceptions about sex offenders
and community protection policies. *Analyses of Social Issues and Public Policy, 7,* 1–25.

Levenson, J., & Cotter, L. (2005a). The effect of Megan's law on sex offender reintegration. *Journal
of Contemporary Criminal Justice, 21,* 49–66.

Levenson, J., & Cotter, L. (2005b). The impact of sex offender residence restrictions: 1,000 feet
from danger or one step from absurd? *International Journal of Offender Therapy and
Comparative Criminology, 49,* 168–178.

Levenson, J., & D'Amora, D. (2007). Social policies designed to prevent sexual violence: The
emperor's new clothes? *Criminal Justice Policy Review, 18,* 168–199.

Levenson, J., D'Amora, D., & Hern, A. (2007). Megan's law and its impact on community re-entry for sex offenders. *Behavioral Sciences & the Law, 25,* 587–602.

Levenson, J., & Hern, A. (2007). Sex offender residence restrictions: Unintended consequences and community re-entry. *Justice Research and Policy, 9,* 59–73.

Lieb, R., Quinsey, V., & Berliner, L. (1998). Sexual predators and social policy. In M. Tonry (Ed.), *Crime and justice* (pp. 43–114). Chicago, IL: University of Chicago Press.

Marshall, L. E., & Marshall, W. L. (2006). Sexual addiction in incarcerated sexual offenders. *Sexual Addiction and Compulsivity, 13,* 377–390.

Marshall, W. L., Marshall, L. E., Serran, G. A., & Fernandez, Y. M. (2006). *Treating sexual offenders: An integrated approach.* New York, NY: Routledge.

McGrath, R., Cumming, G., & Holt, J. (2002). Collaboration among sex offender treatment providers and probation and parole officers: The beliefs and behaviors of treatment providers. *Sexual Abuse: A Journal of Research & Treatment, 14,* 49–65.

McMurran, M., & Ward, T. (2004). Motivating offenders to change in therapy: An organizing framework. *Legal and Criminological Psychology, 9,* 295–311.

Mercado, C., Alvarez, S., & Levenson, J. (2008). The impact of specialized sex offender legislation on community re-entry. *Sexual Abuse: A Journal of Research and Treatment, 20,* 188–205.

Morgan, D., & Glover, D. (2008, February). *GPS tracking of sex offenders.* Presented at the 16th annual conference on the Management of Adults and Juveniles With Sexual Behavior Problems, Galveston, TX.

Motivans, M., & Kyckelhahn, T. (2007, December). *Federal prosecution of child sex exploitation offenders, 2006* (Bureau of Justice Statistics Special Report NCJRS 219412). Washington, DC: National Criminal Justice Reference Service.

Mustaine, E. E., Tewksbury, R., & Stengel, K. M. (2006). Residential location and mobility of registered sex offenders. *American Journal of Criminal Justice, 30*(2), 177–192.

O'Connell, M. (1998). Using polygraph testing to assess deviant sexual history of sex offenders. *Dissertation Abstracts International, Section A: Humanities and Social Sciences, 58*(8-A), 3023.

Pam Lychner Sexual Offender Tracking and Identification Act of 1996, 42 USC 14072 et seq. (1996).

Peugh, J., & Belenko, S. (2001). Examining the substance use patterns and treatment needs of incarcerated sex offenders. *Sexual Abuse: A Journal of Research and Treatment, 13,* 179–195.

Pew Center on the States. (2009, March). *One in 31: The long reach of American corrections.* Retrieved January 3, 2010, from http://www.pewcenteronthestates.org/uploadedFiles/PSPP_1in31_report_FINAL_WEB_3-26-09.pdf

Porter, S., Fairweather, D., Drugge, J., Hervé, H., Birt, A., & Boer, D. (2000). Profiles of psychopathy in incarcerated sexual offenders. *Criminal Justice and Behavior, 27,* 216–233.

Prison Rape Elimination Act of 2003, Pub. L. No. 108-79, 117 Stat. 972-989 (2003).

Quinsey, V. L., Rice, M. E., & Harris, G. T. (1995). Actuarial prediction of sexual recidivism. *Journal of Interpersonal Violence, 10,* 85–105.

Rice, M. E., & Harris, G. T. (1997). Cross-validation and extension of the Violence Risk Appraisal Guide for child molesters and rapists. *Law and Human Behavior, 21,* 231–241.

Rice, M. E., Harris, G. T., & Quinsey, V. (1990). A follow-up of rapists assessed in a maximum-security psychiatric facility. *Journal of Interpersonal Violence, 5,* 435–448.

Schram, D., & Milloy, C. (1995). *Community notification: A study of offender characteristics and recidivism.* Olympia: Washington Institute for Public Policy.

Serin, R., Malcolm, P., Khanna, A., & Barbaree, H. (1994). Psychopathy and deviant sexual arousal in incarcerated sexual offenders. *Journal of Interpersonal Violence, 9,* 3–11.

Sjöstedt, G., & Långström, N. (2002). Assessment of risk for criminal recidivism among rapists: A comparison of four different measures. *Psychology, Crime and Law, 8,* 25–40.

Snyder, H. N. (2000, July). *Sexual assault of young children as reported to law enforcement: Victim, incident, and offender characteristics* (Bureau of Justice Statistics Special Report NCJ 182990). Washington, DC: National Criminal Justice Reference Service.

Soothill, K. (2009). Foreword. In A. R. Beech, L. A. Craig, & K. A. Browne (Eds.), *Assessment and treatment of sex offenders: A handbook* (pp. xxv–xxvii). Malden, MA: Wiley-Blackwell.

Tewksbury, R. (2002). Validity and utility of the Kentucky sex offender registry. *Federal Probation, 66*(1), 21–26.

U.S. Sentencing Commission. (2009). *U.S. Sentencing Commission preliminary quarterly data report: 2nd quarter release, preliminary fiscal year 2009 data through March 31, 2009.* Retrieved August 23, 2009, from http://www.ussc.gov/sc_cases/USSC_2009_Quarter_Report_2nd.pdf

Ward, T. (2002). Good lives and the rehabilitation of offenders: Promises and problems. *Aggression and Violent Behavior, 7,* 513–528.

Ward, T., & Brown, M. (2004). The good lives model and conceptual issues in offender rehabilitation. *Psychology, Crime and Law, 10,* 243–257.

Ward, T., & Gannon, T. (2006). Rehabilitation, etiology, and self-regulation: The comprehensive good lives model of treatment for sexual offenders. *Aggression and Violent Behavior, 11*(1), 77–94.

Ward, T., Gannon, T., & Vess, J. (2009). Human rights, ethical principles, and standards in forensic psychology. *International Journal of Offender Therapy and Comparative Criminology, 53,* 126–144.

Ward, T., & Stewart, C. (2003). The treatment of sex offenders: Risk management and good lives. *Professional Psychology: Research and Practice, 34,* 353–360.

Weekes, J., Pelletier, G., & Beaudette, D. (1995). Correctional officers: How do they perceive sex offenders? *International Journal of Offender Therapy and Comparative Criminology, 39,* 55–61.

Wilcox, D., Sosnowski, D., Warberg, B., & Beech, A. (2005). Sexual history disclosure using the polygraph in a sample of British sex offenders in treatment. *Polygraph, 34,* 171–181.

Willis, G. M., & Grace, R. C. (2009). Assessment of community reintegration planning for sex offenders: Poor planning predicts recidivism. *Criminal Justice and Behavior, 36,* 494–512.

Wormith, J. S., Althouse, R., Simpson, M., Reitzel, L. R., Fagan, T. J., & Morgan, R. D. (2007). The rehabilitation and reintegration of offenders: The current landscape and some future directions for correctional psychology. *Criminal Justice and Behavior, 34,* 879–892.

CHAPTER 13

Juvenile Offenders

Debra K. DePrato and Stephen W. Phillippi

Introduction

Today, juvenile offenders may be detained in a number of facility types, with most housed in detention centers, residential facilities, correctional centers, and adult prisons. Detention centers are short-term facilities for youth awaiting trial or disposition, in violation of probation, serving short-term dispositions, or awaiting placement. Residential facilities are long-term facilities that may specialize in treatment of certain populations of youth, such as those with substance abuse problems and mental illness. Juvenile correctional centers are long-term facilities for housing juvenile offenders secondary to a court-ordered disposition. Youth who have been transferred to adult court, if incarcerated, would be housed at an adult facility, with many of the same issues as youth in a juvenile facility, but likely fewer resources.

The first juvenile court was established in 1899 in Cook County, Illinois. This court was based upon the legal concept of "*parens patriae*," in which the state acts as "parent of the child," thereby allowing the state to take guardianship of the juvenile offender. By the 1950s and 1960s, juvenile courts were not seen as effective, as youth were often treated as adults, but without the ability to exercise the same rights as adults. Several landmark U.S. Supreme Court cases followed as a result of the lack of rehabilitation and punitive nature of juvenile courts, such as *In re Gault* (1967), which afforded youth due process rights in cases in which incarceration may result. In 1968, Congress passed the Juvenile Delinquency Prevention and Control Act, followed by the Juvenile Justice and Delinquency Prevention Act of 1974. These acts were significant in delineating status offenders versus juvenile offenders, emphasizing community-based diversion interventions, incorporating the concept of "disproportionate minority confinement," and creating the Office of Juvenile Justice and Delinquency Prevention (OJJDP; Snyder & Sickmund, 2006). Beginning in the 1980s, the "tough on crime" legislative approach led to changes in law enforcement, harsher sentencing, greater use of incarceration, and increased transfer of youth to adult court. Conditions in juvenile facilities worsened. Facilities experienced overcrowding, increased numbers of youth with mental illness, adult-oriented philosophy, isolation of youth, and little family interaction. Reacting to these issues, Congress passed legislation that led to legal remedies (Trupin, 2006). The Civil Rights of Institutionalized Persons Act of 1980 (CRIPA) enabled the U.S. Department of Justice to protect the rights of youth in juvenile detention and correctional facilities via investigation and litigation and has become one means of system reform.

Mental health professionals working within juvenile facilities should have a specialized knowledge of the behavioral/mental health assessment and treatment issues of the juvenile population. In addition, because treatment is conducted within a facility to which the youth has been committed for an offense, a working knowledge of the relevant legal issues is also important. This chapter will focus on juvenile correctional/residential facilities. However, as noted, youth may be housed in other settings, such as detention centers and adult facilities; therefore, it is important to understand the population of youth and the administrative and legal parameters in each type of setting.

Population Description

Juvenile Justice Statistics

In the OJJDP's *Juvenile Offenders and Victims: 2006 National Report* (Snyder & Sickmund, 2006), almost half (45%) of all youth in custody were housed in long-term secure facilities. The daily number of youth committed to facilities increased 28% from 1991 to 2003, peaking in 1999. The average custody rate in 2003 was 307 juvenile offenders for every 100,000 juveniles in the population, with 15% being female. The most frequently reported ages for females in custody were 15 and 16, and for males, 16 and 17; however, youth in secure care range in age from less than 12 to more than 18. In regards to race, the custody rates per 100,000 were 754 for Black youth, 348 for Hispanic youth, and 190 for White youth. Length of stay varied, with 80% of youth remaining at 30 days, 57% at 90 days, and 13% after 1 year.

A common outcome measurement of juvenile justice system success or failure is recidivism. Recidivism rates of juvenile offenders are measures of repetition of criminal behavior after release from a facility or other type of juvenile justice supervision such as probation or a treatment program (Snyder & Sickmund, 2006). It is measured differently by states, local jurisdictions, and treatment programs, as there is currently no standard measurement. Recidivism may be measured by rearrest, adjudication on a new offense, incarceration, or even self-report of criminal activity by juveniles. It is important to know the length of time utilized to measure recidivism, as well as the known number and severity of offenses. The most accurate recidivism rates capture many variables and allow for an adequate time period following release into the community. Well defined, recidivism can be a valid measure of the success of a juvenile justice program or intervention. In other words, the program should improve the successful reentry of youth while also protecting public safety. In general, Snyder and Sickmund (2006) describe 12-month recidivism rates to show rearrest rates as higher than readjudication rates, and readjudication rates as higher than reconfinement rates (55%, 33%, and 24%, respectively).

Mental Health Characteristics

Numerous studies have shown evidence that youth in the juvenile justice setting are at elevated risk for mental health and substance abuse issues as compared to the general population (Cauffman, 2004; Domalanta, Risser, Roberts, & Risser, 2003; Teplin, Abram, McClelland, Dulcan, & Mericle, 2002; Wasserman, McReynolds, Lucas, Fisher, & Santos, 2002). A recent analysis by Fazel, Doll, and Langstrom (2009) confirmed the high rates of symptoms and disorders in the juvenile justice population, with psychotic illness reported in 3.3% of boys and 2.7% of girls, major depression reported in 10.6% of boys and 29.2% of girls (much higher than the general population or adult prisoners), and ADHD in 11.7% of boys and 18.5% of girls. In a multistate study of the prevalence of mental health disorders, Shufelt and Cocozza (2006) gathered data on 1,437 youth from group homes, detention, and correctional facilities in three states using the Diagnostic Interview Schedule for Children–Present State Voice Version (V-DISC) and screening with the Massachusetts Youth Screening Instrument–Second Version (MAYSI-2). The findings were consistent with other studies. More than two thirds (70.4%) of the youth had at least one diagnosable mental disorder, and more than 60% of youth met criteria for three or more disorders. Table 13.1 summarizes the gender-specific findings of this study.

Table 13.1	Prevalence of Psychiatric Disorders Among Detained or Incarcerated Juvenile Delinquents

DSM *Diagnosis*	Male %	Female %
Any listed disorder	66.8	81.0
Any mood disorder	14.3	29.2
Any anxiety disorder	26.4	56.0
Any disruptive behavior disorder	41.4	45.6
Any substance use disorder	43.2	55.1

Source: Adapted from Shufelt and Cocozza (2006).

Note: DSM = Diagnostic and Statistical Manual of Mental Disorders–Fourth Edition, Text Revision.

Examining gender and race effects using the MAYSI-2 screening instrument, Vincent, Grisso, and Terry (2007) analyzed a national sample of 70,423 juvenile justice–involved youth. Across all sites, regardless of race, age, and legal status, females had higher rates of clinical elevations of mental health problems than males. Females also had higher rates of clinically significant problems with drug and alcohol use than their male counterparts, but only among younger youth. Across all sites, White youth had higher rates of clinically significant problems with alcohol and drug abuse and suicide ideation than African American or Hispanic youth, but there were no significant race differences for other forms of mental health problems.

Suicide/Self-Injurious Behaviors

OJJDP recently commissioned one of the first studies of suicides of youth within confinement. The study, *Characteristics of Juvenile Suicide in Confinement* (Hayes, 2009), examined the common characteristics of the youth and the circumstances leading to suicide. Of these youth, greater than two thirds were White, 80% were male, 70% were between the ages of 15 and 17, and most were confined for nonviolent offenses (70%). Other common youth factors found in the study were a history of substance abuse, mental illness (especially depression), and a history of suicidal behavior; however, no youth were under the influence of drugs or alcohol at the time of the incident. Almost half (42%) of the incidents occurred in secure facilities, and about one third occurred within 1 to 4 months of admission, with less than 4% occurring within the first 24 hours. Most of the suicides occurred by hanging during normal waking hours. Most youth were assigned to a single room, and half were on room confinement. Most facilities did not conduct a mortality review, but of those that did, the most common factors seen as precipitating events were fear of waiver to adult court, fear of transfer to a less desirable facility, death of a family member, a parent's failure to visit, and/or failure in the program.

In addition to suicidal behavior, self-mutilation behavior is also common in facilities and is often associated with major depression, borderline personality traits/disorder, and a history of suicidal behavior. In a recent study by Penn, Esposito, Schaeffer, Fritz, and Spirito (2003), almost one third (30%) of the confined youth reported self-mutilating behavior during their psychiatric assessment. This behavior was often accompanied with depression, anger, or anxiety.

Risk/Protective Factors

All mental health professionals working within juvenile justice settings must be mindful of the literature on risk and protective factors specific to youth violence and juvenile delinquency, including gender and age differences. The clinician should develop effective interventions that address the youth's risk factors while enhancing the youth's protective factors. Whereas no one factor causes certain behaviors, the cumulative effect of multiple risk factors and the severity of each place the youth at increased risk of offending. Factors are generally grouped into the following categories: individual, family, community/school, and environmental (see Table 13.2). Factors may be static or dynamic. Static factors are those that do not change or cannot be influenced, such as age and gender. Dynamic factors are those that may change over time such as school performance, peer group, family characteristics, and neighborhood. Effective treatment will reduce dynamic risk factors while increasing or strengthening protective factors.

Males and females share a number of similar risk and protective factors, but there are also important differences. Risk factors that are common to both sexes include family conflict and abuse, antisocial socialization, lack of school involvement/achievement, neighborhood disorganization (in addition to neighborhood crime, drug use, and weapons availability), and lack of availability of programs and resources in the community (e.g., impoverished neighborhoods; Office of the Surgeon General, 2001). Enhanced risk factors for girls include early puberty, sexual assault/abuse, greater prevalence of depression/anxiety, and the negative influence of a significant other (Hawkins, Graham, Williams, & Zahn, 2009). Interestingly, in girls, the single most important protective factor is the involvement and support of a caring adult (Hawkins et al., 2009).

| Table 13.2 | Risk/Protective Factors Associated With Delinquent Behavior |

Risk Factors
Individual
<ul><li>Low intelligence; cognitive, learning, and language problems</li><li>Poor impulse control</li><li>Not taking responsibility for behavior</li><li>Admiration for antisocial behavior</li><li>Perception of others as hostile</li><li>Early onset of delinquency</li><li>Child working more than 20 hours per week</li><li>Poor social skills</li></ul>
Family
<ul><li>Poverty</li><li>Low education levels</li><li>Conflict and hostility at home</li><li>Ineffective parental discipline and monitoring</li><li>Physical/sexual abuse</li><li>Familial substance abuse and psychiatric problems</li><li>Parental criminal history</li><li>Lack of warmth and affection between parents and child</li></ul>
Peers
<ul><li>Association with delinquent youth (for older youth/adolescents)</li><li>Peer rejection (for younger children)</li><li>Association with youth who use drugs or alcohol</li><li>Gang membership</li><li>Poor achievement/grades</li></ul>
School
<ul><li>Falling behind same-age peers</li><li>Poor attendance</li></ul>
Community
<ul><li>Availability of drugs and weapons</li><li>Poor support network</li><li>Isolation from neighbors</li><li>Living in "dangerous" neighborhoods</li><li>Frequent family moves</li></ul>

(Continued)

Table 13.2   (Continued)

Factors increasing girls' risk more than boys'
• Early puberty • Sexual abuse or maltreatment • Depression and anxiety • Affiliation with delinquent romantic partner
Protective Factors
• Resilient temperament • Positive social orientation • Intelligence • Positive relationship with adult(s) • Consistent system of recognition • Opportunities for active prosocial involvement • Belief in child's competence to succeed in school and to avoid drugs and crime are voiced, and clear expectations for rules governing such behavior are stated
Factors highlighted for decreasing girls' risk
• Perception of the presence of caring adult • School connectedness • School success • Religiosity (placing high importance on religion during adolescence)

Source: Adapted from Catalano and Hawkins (1995); Wasserman et al. (2003); and Zahn, Hawkins, Chiancone, and Whitworth (2008).

Common Presenting Problems and Issues

Many youth are referred to a mental health professional for screening and/or assessment for mental health, substance abuse, and suicidality on entry into the facility. Unfortunately, less than half of facilities in the United States screen all youth within a week of arriving at a facility (Snyder & Sickmund, 2006). Regardless, youth continue to enter facilities with a history of mental illness, psychiatric hospitalization, and suicidal behavior and are frequently on psychiatric medications with no accompanying paperwork. Additionally, many youths' mental disorders remain undiagnosed prior to entering a facility.

Most often, youth will be referred to treatment providers when entering the facility or at some point during their stay to address disruptive behavior in school or living areas, discipline issues, or self-mutilation. Some youth will complain of feeling sad, angry, or anxious. The majority of the population will also be dealing with some type of withdrawal from substance use because they likely used alcohol, tobacco, and/or illicit drugs (primarily marijuana) prior to incarceration. Youth may not have the cognitive skills to effectively deal with the demands of living in a secure environment. They may be on room confinement or protective custody status requiring by policy a mental health assessment. Regardless of the path for referral to a mental health provider, most youth will be identified at admission or later during the course of confinement with some type of behavioral or emotional issue.

Issues Particular to Youth in Correctional Environments

There are three areas to which the mental health professional should pay particular attention in their approach to working within juvenile facilities: *administrative, treatment,* and *legal.* Administrative issues and facility operations directly affect care and should be known to the clinician. These would include the juvenile's schedule of activities, protocols for when and where youth are treated, family visits, and who may have access to records. It also includes seclusion and restraint policies and protocols for the use of medications. Clinicians must understand their role as it relates to verbal and written reports to courts, probation/parole officers, and other juvenile justice professionals as part of the youth's ongoing assessment and treatment. Clinicians should have a working knowledge of all areas within a facility, such as school, dormitories, medical, and recreation, as well as a working relationship with the staff who interact with the youth on a regular basis. Security and safety of all youth and staff are paramount, so the clinician must always be aware of any potential compromises of these institutional missions and their responsibilities under such circumstances.

Special treatment issues arise in juvenile correctional facilities. Youth are involved in multiple systems, and the clinician should be a crucial part of a treatment team to aid in the development of an individualized treatment plan, including behavior management. A key component of the plan is for all staff to work toward the goals of the plan in conjunction with the youth. The clinician should take every opportunity to educate staff about the youth's intervention plan and reduce staff bias or misconceptions concerning mental illness.

Facilities are often large and resources are few, so the clinician must advocate for the needs of particular youth, while balancing these with the safety of other youth and staff. The clinician must be cognizant of the age of the youth, developmental capacity, and any evidence of secondary gain. A thorough understanding of normal adolescent behavior is needed, as adolescent risk-taking behavior is often mistaken by staff for "delinquent behavior." All youth should receive regular screening or monitoring for substance abuse, mental health issues, and suicide. Youth may not wish to attend the mental health clinic (and when they do, the time in treatment is limited) or take medication, so monitoring and communication between clinicians and custody staff who spend the most time with the youth is crucial.

Unique boundary and ethical issues frequently arise in the course of work in a facility that may include youth, family, and facility staff; therefore, all clinicians should receive adequate supervision with access to consultation as needed. Examples include:

- Negative or judgmental attitudes of the clinician toward the offender or the offender's family, which may interfere with engagement and treatment.
- Friendships and romantic relationships between staff and the offender, as staff and youth are often close in age.
- Breach of youth's confidentiality (beyond the scope of facility guidelines/legal policies).
- Inadequate reporting of coercive or negligent behavior by facility staff toward youth.
- Inadequate clinical assessment and/or provision of mental health services below a minimum standard of care.
- Dual or conflicting roles, as facility mental health staff often may be trained in aspects of security or disciplinary procedures at the facility (e.g., searching of youth's dorm for contraband is a role for security; participation in disciplinary hearings by mental health staff should be educational, aiding the understanding of youth's disorder, limitations, and recommendations for behavior plan).

Finally, clinicians should be aware of their state statutes and facility guidelines on guardianship, confidentiality, informed consent, forced treatment, parental rights, reporting of abuse, and the rights of juveniles versus adults. The state typically assumes guardianship of the youth while in custody, but policies differ on how a facility might consent to treatment for the youth, especially in emergency situations. In some settings, parents may retain some of their rights, or the facility may have the policy of obtaining parental consent on a routine basis. Because youth vary in age, some youth are at an age statutorily where they can consent to treatment. Full informed consent should always be given and documented. Parents and youth should be made aware of any court-ordered components of treatment as well as any limits to confidentiality.

The clinician should document carefully and routinely, as facility records are legal documents. It is necessary for a team of staff to be aware of a youth's problems; however, differing levels of access to details and to the youth's records should be based upon the role of each staff member. Clinicians are legally mandated reporters of abuse or excessive force to youth by either another youth or staff. They should be cognizant of staff-youth and youth-youth interactions that seem punitive, or aggressive, or coercive. Violations of incarcerated juveniles' constitutional rights are the basis of investigation and litigation by the U.S. Department of Justice Civil Rights Division, via CRIPA. Youths' rights are commonly found to have been violated when they are denied humane conditions, they are not protected from harm, they cannot access an education, or they fail to receive rehabilitative treatment. Table 13.3 summarizes CRIPA-identified areas of concern relevant to mental health.

Table 13.3	Protection of Juveniles' Rights: Common Areas of Mental Health Concern

Suicide Prevention Concerns:

- Insufficient assessment of suicide risk
- Inadequate mental health services for youth on precautions
- Unsafe housing of youth at risk of self-harm
- Inadequate supervision of youth on suicide precautions and in seclusion
- Lack of staff preparedness for suicide attempts and acts of self-harm

Inadequate Mental Health and Substance Abuse Services Concerns:

- Inadequate screening, identification, and assessment
- Inadequate follow-up clinical assessment, treatment planning, and case management
- Inadequate psychotropic medication management
- Inadequate mental health and substance abuse counseling (i.e., evidence-based practices)
- Lack of family involvement
- Failure to place youth in court-ordered treatment such as sex offender or substance abuse treatment
- Inadequate staff training in behavior management principles

Inadequate Transition Planning Concerns:

- Rehabilitative needs/achievements inadequately communicated to parole counselors, families, and community providers
- Inadequate transition of youth to community mental health and substance abuse services

Source: Adapted from Trupin (2006).

Case History

The following case history is fictional and is a compilation of typical scenarios of incarcerated youth in need of mental health intervention.

Eric was having a difficult time adjusting to life within a juvenile correctional facility. Within the first month, he had several disciplinary infractions and was having difficulty getting along with others in his living unit. He had angry outbursts, frequently ignored instructions, and did not engage with staff members. Finally, Eric was placed on room confinement as a consequence of his behavior, which required by policy that a mental health evaluation be performed.

The mental health professional noted that Eric, a 14-year-old African American male, had no prior documented history of mental illness; however, he had been diagnosed with marijuana dependence and conduct disorder. Although he had no history of violence, he was incarcerated for the first time due to a property offense and subsequent violation of probation. Eric had consistently used marijuana off and on since he was 12 years old. While on probation, he was involved in "drug treatment" that primarily consisted of a 12-step program, drug screens, and probation supervision. Eric grew up in an impoverished neighborhood with rampant crime, and he was born the fifth of six children to a single working mother.

Eric spoke very little to the mental health professional and seemed content to be confined to his room. By interviewing others, the mental health staff learned that Eric had a documented 10-pound weight loss since his admission and was having difficulty sleeping at night. At school, he kept his head on his desk the majority of the time, and the angry outbursts tended to occur when other residents teased or bullied him. (He was small in size and was teased frequently by both facility staff and youth.) The mental health staff also learned that Eric had had no visitors or calls since his admission.

Following the clinical assessment of Eric and a review of records and collateral information, Eric was diagnosed with a depressive disorder. During the assessment, Eric frequently drew pictures to illustrate his feelings, and it was evident that he had an artistic gift that had thus far been untapped.

The mental health team did a thorough assessment that included a review of all risk and protective factors. His treatment plan included treatment of his target symptoms of depression with medication, accompanied by cognitive-behavioral therapy (CBT). Family engagement was a key component to Eric's treatment plan, so that caring adults from his family, particularly his mother, could gradually become more involved with Eric's life and his reentry plan.

Eric gradually responded to treatment (as confirmed by monitoring his behavior at school, in the living unit, and with staff/peers). He was able to join the facility's graphics art class, which became a motivating factor in his daily schedule. Eric's treatment progressed, and once his symptoms of depression improved, it was an appropriate time to address the drug dependence via a relapse-prevention program. Eric had a few setbacks along the way, as drug dependence had been his predominant coping and problem-solving skill to deal with everyday life. Learning and practicing new replacement skills were key to his relapse prevention.

A reentry plan was developed in which Eric would be followed by a mental health provider who could address both his depression and his marijuana dependence and continue family engagement strategies. At the recommendation of the mental health team, he was able to have a few furloughs to practice his skills at home prior to his release.

A clinical note: Eric was referred to the clinician secondary to a facility policy requiring any youth placed on room confinement to be assessed by a mental health professional. Although Eric had no previous known history of a mental health disorder, a targeted assessment uncovered a major depression, as well as inadequate treatment of his substance abuse disorder. Prioritized treatment strategies were undertaken such as medication management and monitoring of target psychiatric symptoms, the proactive engagement of family, and development of a prosocial activity (his artistic ability). Eric's depression improved, allowing him to focus on long-term goals such as substance abuse, relapse prevention, and peer and family issues.

Treatment Goals/Strategies

Screening and Assessment

Institutional care should always be considered a measure of last resort, so ideally, before a youth ever enters the institution, a number of documents have been generated in the field through predispositional investigations and assessments by community providers. Whether a community meets this ideal standard or not, a few key guidelines regarding screening and assessment should be maintained. A thorough and accurate assessment of the youth entering care, or transitioning due to factors occurring during his or her care (e.g., transfer to an honors dorm, completion of secure care services, removal from activities due to violence, etc.), is key to adequately addressing the treatment and placement needs of the child. That assessment is often driven by an initial screen.

Screening instruments should be used at initial contact with the institution (within minutes to a few hours of first entry) to identify issues that may require immediate attention for the safety of the youth and staff (e.g., suicidal thoughts and behaviors) or to highlight areas that need in-depth assessment. The screening of youth allows the institution to quickly identify the subset of youth that may have mental health diagnoses (e.g., anxiety, depression, thought disorders), behavior problems (e.g., aggression), or problems in functional areas (e.g., school, peer, family) to then more fully assess those at risk (Vincent et al., 2007). According to Grisso (2005),

> The objective is similar to triage in medical settings, where incoming patients are initially classified indicating their level of urgency. Like triage, screening is useful in systems that have limited resources and therefore cannot respond comprehensively or immediately to every individual's particular needs. (p. 13)

It is also important to recognize the temporary nature of the information gleaned from screening instruments. Screens are not designed to provide a clinically valid diagnosis, identify the etiology of behavioral or mental health problems, or afford the institution enough information for long-range treatment or rehabilitation planning (Vincent et al., 2007). What screening results can offer is a current portrayal of acute symptoms and potential problem areas of a youth in the institution, which can then be further assessed. To illustrate just a few of the screening options, the following tools constitute an abbreviated list of research-supported instruments described in Vincent et al. (2007):

- Trauma Symptom Checklist for Children (TSCC)
- Suicide Ideation Scale (SIS)
- Massachusetts Youth Screening Instrument (MAYSI)
- Global Appraisal of Individual Need–Short Screener (GAIN-SS)
- Child and Adolescent Functional Assessment Scale (CAFAS)
- Child and Adolescent Needs and Strengths–Juvenile Justice (CANS-JJ)
- Diagnostic Interview Schedule for Children–Present State Voice Version (V-DISC)

- Practical Adolescent Dual Diagnosis Interview (PADDI)
- Global Appraisal of Individual Needs–Quick (GAIN-Q)

Evidence-based screening is a rapidly emerging field in juvenile justice. Clinicians are encouraged to remain current on the literature regarding both the validity and reliability of these instruments as they pertain to the youth in their particular setting.

After initial screening, "the purpose of assessment is to gather a more comprehensive and individualized profile of a youth" (Vincent et al., 2007, p. 275). Clinicians need to carefully assess delinquency risk and protective factors that are salient to a youth's developmental stage, paying attention to which combination of risk factors increases risk and which factors (typically dynamic factors) may protect the youth from future delinquency if properly addressed (Phillippi & DePrato, 2009). Identifying these factors provides the principal targets for intervention services to be formulated in the youth's treatment plan (Phillippi & DePrato, 2009).

In addition to the risk and protective factors associated with the potential for prompting further delinquent behaviors, a thorough assessment of youth in secure care settings should include the identification of any mental disorders, substance use disorders, educational problems, intellectual capacity, developmental disorders, known physical limitations, social problems, family history, and legal history. Information on each of these is achieved through approaching the evaluation with a broad ecological perspective, including a thorough investigation of the juvenile's behavior prior to placement at detention, in the home, school, workplace, and neighborhood (Melton, Petrila, Poythress, Slobogin, & Lyons, 1997). Ideally, probation staff and preplacement caregivers are a resource for this information; however, assessment staff should be prepared to collect collateral information from the child's preplacement residence as needed (see Table 13.4).

Table 13.4 Initial Mental Health Assessment Guidelines for Secure Care

1. Be well versed in all relevant administrative policies/procedures, including time frames governing intake mental health screening and assessments.

2. Understand confidentiality rules that apply to the assessment, as well as whom the information will be available to, and relate the information to both the youth and his or her guardian.

3. Review all records as part of the intake assessment, including all medical, psychiatric, psychological, school, probation, and detention records from prior stays at the facility. Request any records that are important to the assessment.

4. Include as part of the final diagnostic workup other assessment findings that may have occurred during intake, such as educational and medical, including psychiatric.

5. Youth whose screening or past history indicate that a mental health assessment is warranted should receive a full assessment that addresses the following areas: their functioning within all domains of their environments (family, school, other placements, detention, etc.), a thorough mental status examination, assessment of all cognitive domains, suicidality, premorbid functioning prior to incarceration, past legal history, acute or chronic stresses in their lives, a weapons and violence history, substance abuse, sexual or physical abuse, medical problems, and risk/protective factors.

(Continued)

Table 13.4   (Continued)

6. The assessment should include the primary caretakers of the youth (to whom he or she is returning) to develop family engagement strategies in treatment and as part of aftercare plan: Identify style of parenting as well as evidence of mental health or substance abuse disorders that may interfere with parenting, ability to interact with the youth's environment (such as school, probation, peer group, and neighborhood), family's support system, and strengths of family system.

7. Collateral interviews should be conducted whenever possible with the youth's prior mental health provider, probation officer, and pertinent others.

8. Targeted and relevant psychological testing should be performed as clinically indicated as part of the overall mental health assessment to address specific issues.

9. A thorough diagnostic opinion should be rendered that includes *Diagnostic and Statistical Manual of Mental Disorders* diagnosis, if present (inclusive of symptomatology), youth's and family's level of functioning, risk and protective factors, and acute/chronic stressors.

10. Specific and realistic short-term and long-term treatment recommendations should be made that address the needs of the youth while in care: Target mental health symptoms if mental illness is present, interventions in dynamic risk factors, enhancement of protective factors, addressing family factors for successful reentry of youth into the community.

One very important task at the completion of the assessment is the question of advocacy for the youth related to placement. Clinicians have a role in protecting youth from the potential harms of secure care placement and in advocating for the most appropriate treatment in the least restrictive setting, with a higher likelihood for better youth outcomes, and where risk to community safety can be minimized. Research has found that community-based treatment programs are generally more effective than incarceration or residential placement in reducing recidivism, even for some serious and violent juvenile offenders, and are more cost-effective, so it is recommended that every attempt be made to avoid incarceration if at all possible (Henggeler, Melton, Smith, Schoenwald, & Hanley, 1993; Lipsey, Chapman, & Landenberger, 2001). Clinicians should be aware of community-based best practice treatment, not only to advocate for the youth, but as part of the assessment in determining if the youth actually received effective treatment prior to incarceration and to plan for postincarceration services. These same general principles regarding placement advocacy also apply to reassessment of youth while in secure care. Examples of a few evidence-based community alternatives to secure corrections are provided in Table 13.5.

A best practice assessment should drive the youth's individualized treatment plan that results. In juvenile correctional settings, it is important to note that a wide range of professionals may access the assessment report and treatment plan. This might include psychiatrists, psychologists, social workers, licensed counselors, physicians, corrections administrators, security staff, case managers, probation officers, parole officers, judges, teachers, and nurses. For that reason, mental health assessment reports should be written in a clear, logical, and user-friendly manner. The assessment report should include a

| Table 13.5 | Alternatives to Secure Care Placement: Model Evidence-Based* Delinquency, Drug, and Violence Prevention Programs |

Program	Description
Functional Family Therapy (FFT)	Targets youth ages 11 to 18 at risk for and/or manifesting delinquency, violence, substance use, oppositional defiant disorder, or conduct disorders, and their families. Focuses on family relations and communication; builds on strengths as motivation for change. Flexibly delivered to clients in home, clinic, school, juvenile court, or other community settings.
Multisystemic Therapy (MST)	Targets chronic, violent, and substance-abusing delinquents ages 12 to 18 at high risk for out-of-home placement. Focuses on the entire ecology of the youth including family, school, peer, and community relations. Strives for behavior change in the youth's natural environment, using the strengths of each system (e.g., family, peers, school, neighborhood) to facilitate change.
Multidimensional Therapeutic Foster Care (MTFC)	Targets juveniles ages 12 to 17 with histories of chronic and severe delinquent behavior and/or severe mental health problems at risk of incarceration or psychiatric hospitalization who need residential placement. Recruits and supports host families with program goal to return youth to permanency placement (e.g., biological family). Emphasizes behavior-management methods with the youth in a structured, therapeutic living environment while also working with the parents during weekly group meetings.

Source: Adapted from information at http://www.colorado.edu/cspv/blueprints/index.html.

*Evidence-based practices are those that have been tested using rigorous research designs, have demonstrated consistent positive effects in favor of the experimental treatment, and for which there is a high level of standardization (a manual or standardized training materials are available).

clear opinion regarding the youth's problems; the information that the opinion was based on (objective and subjective); and realistic, prioritized recommendations for addressing, containing, or accommodating each of the youth's identified issues. For example, a comprehensive psychological "write-up" between two psychologists might be helpful, but it will have limited utility beyond their professional dialogue. A well-written assessment will impart the necessary information to the youth's multidisciplinary team, who should be able to quickly and easily access understandable, practical key recommendations, strategies, and priorities for interventions with youth in their care.

Treatment Planning

After thorough assessment, individualized treatment planning is the next step in intervention. For incarcerated youth, treatment plans should target specific behaviors for change and address at least five domains. These domains include plans for case management, physical health, mental health, and education/vocation interventions at a minimum. Each area should target specific need areas, identify risks and strengths in each domain, clearly list short- and long-term goals in behaviorally measurable language, and convey any accommodations needed for the youth to have the best opportunity to succeed at achieving his or her goals. Furthermore, physical health and mental health sections should clearly identify diagnosis, precautions, and all medications (for both psychiatric and physical health). Treatment plans should be regularly updated to accurately reflect the youth's progress and new issues and information.

Of particular emphasis should be the identification of short-term measurable goals that can be clearly communicated to the youth, custody staff, and parents. Short-term goals should be drafted and individualized in such a way that they are attainable; that is, within the particular youth's capacities. For example, the youth would work on reducing the number of incidents of disregarding teacher requests per day in the correctional school environment. This is all part of shaping the youth's behaviors to achieve more complex, difficult-to-reach, overarching goals eventually. For example, decreasing the incidents in the correctional school environment might translate to a larger goal of avoiding confrontation with authority figures upon release. Each success a youth experiences with short-term goals decreases both the frustration of the youth and the staff and, in turn, increases motivation. This will help increase the speed of treatment and increase the success rate of most treatment. Change is hard, and long-term, overarching goals often seem unattainable to youth; thus, their success in measurable, achievable increments is crucial.

Managing and Treating Youth in Secure Care

The outcomes associated with incarceration overall are consistently poorer than those of youth not institutionalized (Snyder & Sickmund, 2006); however, the literature does suggest that when services are delivered in community-based facilities, their effectiveness tends to increase (Krisberg, Austin, & Steele, 1989). Institutional programs are noted to be more effective when they are paired with comprehensive treatment services, including intensive aftercare (Latessa, 1999). Latessa (1999) specifically noted that CBT approaches appear most effective and argued that mental health treatment for offenders is only effective when coupled with the treatment of co-occurring delinquency risk factors. Otherwise, he reports finding the poorest outcomes in the group treated solely for their mental health symptoms. Similar findings, supporting a CBT approach with a combination of mental health and delinquency risk interventions, were produced in a Washington State study. According to the Washington State Institute for Public Policy (WSIPP; 2002), after implementing a Dialectical Behavioral Therapy (DBT) model in Washington's secure care facilities, youth in the treatment group recidivated less, particularly at the felony level (10% of those receiving DBT vs. 24% of the comparison group). Additionally, Palmer (1994) and Lipsey, Wilson, and Cothern (2000) offered that interventions found most successful include cognitive-behavioral, skills-oriented, and family-oriented treatment. Overall, the literature describing the best structured approaches for working with youth in secure care supports a comprehensive system of individual cognitive-behavioral approaches; family inclusion therapies; strong contingency management; educational and interpersonal skills development; and employment training (Andrews et al., 1990; Garrett, 1985; Lipsey, 1999; Lipsey et al., 2000; Palmer, 1994). On the other hand, psychodynamic, general milieu/group approaches without specific structure to limit delinquent modeling, programs that relied less on structured academic or vocational services, drug abstinence programs, and scared-straight models were least effective and often associated with more negative outcomes, specifically higher rates of recidivism (Andrews et al., 1990; Lipsey et al., 2000).

Suicide Prevention Programming

With the higher risk of suicide attempts in juvenile facilities, it is imperative that an adequate treatment program include a comprehensive suicide prevention/intervention component. National correctional care standards consistently require a detailed and written suicide prevention policy. According to the Council of Juvenile Correctional Administrators (2003), Hayes (2000), the National Commission on Correctional Health Care (2004), and Roush (1996), these standards of programming should consist of training, identification/screening methods, communication plans, housing standards, supervision levels, intervention processes, reporting procedures, and follow-up/mortality review processes. Each of these program elements is elaborated in *Characteristics of Juvenile Suicide in Confinement* (Hayes, 2009).

Research-Supported Treatment Approaches

As mentioned in the previous section regarding the management and treatment of youth in correctional environments, all treatment for juvenile offenders is not equal, and some interventions are harmful. It is the obligation of all clinicians to be sure they are recommending treatment that will address the problems presented by the youth and not recommend treatment that will increase the risk of reoffending. To that end, current science offers clinicians guidance.

A growing number of programs, commonly known as evidence-based practices, have program evaluations using strong research designs, offer evidence of significant deterrent effects, demonstrate sustained effects, and are often shown to be cost-effective. Most successful programs have treatment manuals designed around sound theoretical rationale for targeting known risk factors, structured staff training, written training curricula, methods for monitoring implementation of and fidelity to the treatment process, service delivery documentation procedures, routine structured supervision, outcome monitoring, and quality improvement procedures (Phillippi & DePrato, 2009). Specifically, research offers evidence of clinical practices that are effective in working with delinquent youth. Those research-driven approaches include motivational engagement, cognitive-behavioral treatment, and systems/ecological approaches.

Motivational Engagement

Motivational engagement emerged from the work of William Miller known as Motivational Interviewing, which has been found to be an effective treatment approach with highly resistant clients (Miller & Rollnick, 2002). Youth and their families are not expected to enter the juvenile justice system and its intervention programs motivated and ready to receive treatment from juvenile justice staff. It is the staff's responsibility to help elicit the patient's and his or her family's motivation for change.

Preliminary data from several studies support motivational engagement as an effective approach with adolescents in juvenile justice settings (Feldstein & Ginsberg, 2006). Models like Motivational Interviewing recognize that change is influenced by biological and psychological factors and individual values that each person brings to the change process. Motivational Interviewing draws out the youth's personal goals for change instead of imposing external measures that the youth cannot relate to or apply to his or her individual situation. For example, adolescents often do not desire total abstinence from drugs and alcohol, so risk or harm reduction may be a more realistic goal for a 16- or 17-year-old, and, most importantly, a goal that places him or her in a posture that is at least receptive to treatment (J. R. McKay, 1996). Simply being open to allowing the youth to identify personal change goals actually increases the success of both harm reduction and abstinence-based programs.

Motivational engagement approaches are gaining acceptance for their success in fostering positive relationships between counselors and clients and retaining clients in treatment (Baer & Peterson, 2002; Dodgen & Shea, 2000). These approaches respect the youth's autonomy by acknowledging and accepting choices. Motivational techniques assume that motivation is critical to change, is a dynamic and fluctuating state, is interactive, is influenced by a counselor's style, and can be modified. Motivational treatment may be all that is needed for some clients to successfully change or recover. Thus, the counselor's task is to elicit and enhance motivation to change (Center for Substance Abuse Treatment, 2002). Motivational engagement strategies minimize arguing, blaming, and coercive treatment by making use of the youth's own goals, values, and ambivalence to develop his or her own arguments for change.

Cognitive-Behavioral Treatment

Through the principles of psychology, clinicians are taught that if one can understand behavior, one can predict it, and that if one can predict behavior, one can also change it. CBT works to reduce problem behaviors and increase positive, adaptive behaviors. Interventions typically come in the form of challenging thinking patterns, teaching skills, and establishing a system of reinforcement for desired behavior. Success in intervening and changing one targeted behavior is then generalized to assist in targeting other problems and issues (Phillippi & Schroeder, 2006).

There are a number of manualized cognitive-behavioral treatment packages to assist clinicians in teaching specific skill sets. This type of treatment has been shown to be effective in treating not only behavior disorders common with juvenile delinquents but also depression, substance abuse, and anxiety disorders (Lipsey et al., 2001; M. McKay, Wood, Brantley, 2007; Najavits, 2002; Turner, 1996). The following are common elements of CBT approaches.

Skill Acquisition. An effective treatment program should help youth become more skilled at managing relationships, academics, vocations, and life events. If such a program were to rely strictly on punishment as a means for instituting behavioral change, that change would not last; a strategy that only suppresses undesired behaviors without teaching transferable replacement skills is unsustainable. Thus, skills development, enhanced coping, and building of positive social relationships and communications abilities will be rewarded through positive praise; positive rewards; and ongoing chances to practice new learning in a safe, supportive environment. Specific interventions to advance, cultivate, and build retention of learning start with a strong assessment process that provides structured learning vehicles and can include teaching skills, reinforcing the learning of new skills, shaping behaviors as they approach the desired product, coaching, contingency management, and skill generalization.

Skill Generalization. An effective treatment program should teach problem solving. Youth should be instructed on how to match the context of a situation with a set of skills. The program should incorporate the overlearning ("practicing") of new skills in a low-stress, lower risk environment. A treatment program should allow youth to practice using new skills while treatment staff coach them, and consultation is available to assist the youth in understanding and complying with cue exposure. Skill generalization is a vital and essential component to youths' learning processes, as well as a major factor in building the chances of real and lasting success upon return to the community. A process for ensuring that skills will transfer (i.e., generalize) as the youth leaves the intensive treatment program is essential.

Structuring the Environment. An effective treatment program needs to structure the environment so youth can invest and participate in a comfortable way to learn new skills while they progressively move away from previously manifested problem behaviors. Ultimately, an effective program should structure the environment (e.g., managing contingencies) to promote client success. An intended outcome of treatment is to teach youth to structure and manage their personal environments for adaptive behavior; such a strategy allows the youth the best possible chances for short- and long-term success.

Systems/Ecological Treatment

Juvenile offenders, like most adults, do not operate in isolation, even in the confines of a secure care institution. Juvenile offenders are impacted both positively and negatively by their ecology, or the world around them. These systems can also be key to effectively intervening in the life of a troubled youth and typically include family, school, peers, and others. Helping the youth to see how his or her behavior (both desirable and undesirable) fits within the context of his or her environment is critical. Intervention then takes the form of assisting the youth in reshaping his or her environment to better fit with prosocial goals and in helping the environment support him or her in pursuit of these goals. In other words, treatment takes place in the youth's ecology (e.g., institutional dorms, schools, cafeteria, recreation yards, family meeting spaces, furloughs off campus).

Group Therapy

There is evidence that grouping delinquent and antisocial youths together for group treatment purposes may produce a negative effect (Arnold & Hughes, 1999). The literature shows little evidence, or inconsistent evidence at best, of long-term improvement in youths after treatment in groups (Beelmann, Pfingsten, & Losel, 1994; Lipsey et al., 2000). As described earlier in the section on risk and protective factors associated with delinquency, there is a strong association between delinquent youth and their peer groups, which includes evidence that offenders with less serious behavior problems often become worse when grouped with other youth who have more serious behavior problems. Arnold and Hughes (1999) noted that "homogeneous group treatment of delinquent or at-risk youth opens up the possibility for reinforcement of deviant values, affiliation with peers who model antisocial behavior and values, increased opportunities for criminal activity, [and] stronger identification with a delinquent subculture" (p. 110). Group therapy is often offered in correctional settings; however, better outcomes were noted when family therapy was utilized (Latimer, 2001; Lipsey et al., 2000).

Although groups may not be the preferred method of treatment, there are group models that are promising with specific juvenile justice populations, particularly to treat specific psychiatric conditions and teach or practice skills. For example, *Seeking Safety* (Najavits, 2002) is a promising manualized treatment model that can be offered in either individual or group settings. Developed by Lisa Najavits under support from the National Institute on Drug Abuse, this treatment is described as a present-focused therapy to address co-occurring trauma/PTSD and substance abuse disorders. Similarly, the Cannabis Youth Treatment Series (Sample & Kadden, 2001; Webb, Scudder, Kaminer, &

Kadden, 2001), developed through the support of the Substance Abuse and Mental Health Services Administration (SAMHSA), combines motivational engagement, cognitive-behavioral treatment, and family therapy approaches with substance abuse treatment and has been shown to be effectively delivered via group methods.

Family Engagement

While in secure care, the youth will ideally gain significant individual skills that will assist him or her in demonstrating improved cognitive, behavioral, and emotional functioning in his or her environment (including the larger community, following discharge). Beyond the individual's development, family involvement has been correlated with successful transition and reduced recidivism (Dague & Tolin, 1996; Palmer 1996). Increasing the probability of extinguishing delinquent behavior requires strong family and/or community support networks with adult caregivers. However, due to competing demands of correctional staff and administrators, coupled with the inherent challenges of family participation in the institution's processes, family involvement may not be at the forefront of correctional program planning.

Thornberry (1994) reported a significant correlation between youth experiencing family conflict and poor outcomes when family issues remain unaddressed. These included the youth facing further delinquency, committing violent acts, failing to achieve in school, demonstrating poorer mental health, and/or experiencing higher rates of teen pregnancy. Conversely, as a protective factor, families can offer supportive, modeling relationships, positive discipline methods, good supervision, advocacy for the youth, and information gathering and sharing (Kumpfer & Alvarado, 1998).

According to Brock, Burrell, and Tulipano (2006), with the National Evaluation and Technical Assistance Center for the Education of Children and Youth Who Are Neglected, Delinquent or At-Risk (NDTAC), the question is not whether to include the family in the juvenile justice process but rather *how* to include them. In a 2006 NDTAC survey, both facility practitioners and family members indicated that family involvement was not yet a priority for interventions offered in institutions. According to the survey, facility practitioners viewed the absence of parents from their facilities as a lack of interest on the part of the family, yet the parents described discomfort in attempts to engage facility staff and did not perceive the institutions as welcoming them as a valued part of their child's treatment. Real challenges exist for parents that limit access to visitation, information, and treatment. As examples, Brock et al. (2006) explain that many parents live a long distance from facilities and often lack transportation; furthermore, parents are often not contacted when an incident or issue takes place involving their child at the facility.

Families must be encouraged to visit the youth and treatment staff on campus. Many institutions encourage family participation in treatment, and some even provide the transportation to facilitate their attendance. When this is not possible, phone contact should be attempted frequently, and mail and e-mail could be used to send out information to families on a regular basis. Youth should also be encouraged by the treatment staff to share progress and other matters with their families during their personal phone calls and visits. As a practical measure, clinicians can incorporate a phone call with parents/guardians during treatment sessions to promote a supervised, positive encounter between youth and family.

Researchers and advocates emphasize a number of vital components of family involvement. First, family members must be viewed, included, and supported as valuable members of the youth's treatment team (Osher & Hunt, 2002; Walker & Friedman, 2001). Second, families need information about the juvenile justice system pertaining to their children's involvement as well as their children's right to access services (Osher &

Hunt, 2002; Walker & Friedman, 2001). Third, when families are unable or unwilling to be involved, extended family, surrogates, or mentors should be identified and included to work with the youth and staff (Walker & Friedman, 2001). Finally, Larson and Turner (2002) specify that family treatment that is

carefully structured, teaches skills, and focuses on family problems or youth needs is shown to reduce recidivism. . . . [A] combination of cognitive problem solving training and parent training has been found to be the most effective approach for reducing antisocial behavior in youth and in reducing stress and depression in parents. (p. 20)

Specialized Treatment for Specific Subgroups

Treatment for Female Offenders

The research on effective gender-specific programs for girls is sparse (Chesney-Lind & Pasko, 2004; Zahn et al., 2008). A few common issues emerge from the limited literature that suggest some shaping of programming for girls. Chesney-Lind and Pasko (2004) describe the need for girls' programs to address physical and sexual violence (from parents, boyfriends, and others), pregnancy and motherhood, drug and alcohol dependency (especially as a coping mechanism for abuse), family problems, stress, and development of self-efficacy and empowerment through a variety of means including education and vocational training. To address these, Acoca (1999) summarizes that effective programs for girls should have highly structured phases linked to clearly defined tasks, privileges, and consequences.

According to Acoca and Dedel (1998), a combination of victimization and substance abuse correlates highly with risky behaviors such as truancy, unsafe sexual activity, and gang involvement. Although research is still forthcoming, one promising treatment based on cognitive-behavioral principles, as mentioned in the section on CBT above, for addressing this combination of issues specifically in female offenders, is *Seeking Safety* (Najavits, 2002). Additionally, Chesney-Lind and Pasko (2004) describe comprehensive programming that addresses the needs of both pregnancy and teenage motherhood. Treatment should focus on wellness during pregnancy and postpartum, parenting skills to reduce the higher likelihood of child abuse in this population, and the reduction of risky behaviors that could lead to another pregnancy before the girl reaches adulthood. For teens choosing to mother their children, access to their child postpartum to form critical attachments and practice parenting skills is critical.

Substance Abuse Treatment

Given the high prevalence of substance use disorders, the screening, evaluation, and treatment of substance-abusing youth in the care of secure juvenile facilities is essential; however, it is important to note that not all adolescents who abuse substances will become dependent. Thus, labeling or otherwise imposing the disease concept may do more harm than good (Estroff, 2001). When warranted, a comprehensive substance abuse treatment program should focus on increasing motivation for change and building skills that will assist to reduce the hindering effects of substance use disorders in correctional, educational, family, and social/peer settings. Clinicians and caseworkers might engage youth by relying on motivational interviewing skills to draw out the youth's personal goals for change instead of imposing external measures that the youth cannot relate to or apply to his or her individual situation (Miller & Rollnick, 2002). Once engaged, cognitive-behavioral therapies focus on the nature of an individual's beliefs, expectations, perceptions, and attributions about themselves and others regarding substance use. The role of the treatment provider then is to assist the youth in uncovering issues in cognitive processes, understand the underlying purpose of his or her substance-abusing behaviors, and facilitate learning experiences that provide alternate skills and/or ways to process and respond to the environment in which he or she must function. Relapse prevention then involves the teaching of skills to cope with high-risk substance abuse situations, as well as situations placing youth at risk for other high-risk situations (e.g., self-harm, aggression to others, victimization) when co-occurring mental illnesses are present. There are well-written manuals based on cognitive-behavioral principles to guide relapse prevention. Examples are the *Adolescent Relapse Prevention Workbook: A Brief Strategic Approach* (Gorski, 1996) and the Cannabis Youth Treatment Series (Sample & Kadden, 2001; Webb et al., 2001). Table 13.6 highlights recommended elements for substance abuse treatment.

Table 13.6	Recommended Components of Substance Abuse Treatment

- Provision of specialized substance abuse treatment services that encourage each youth to fully explore and recognize his or her substance use behaviors, as well as associated behaviors and consequences, and make a commitment to positive life change
- The provision of interventions designed to improve the youth's judgment and ability to manage impulsive behaviors that include substance use and delinquency
- The improvement of each youth's ability to successfully manage anger or other feelings that trigger substance use
- The development in each youth of an understanding of the antecedents of his or her substance use behavior, including the chain of thoughts, feelings, and events that led to substance use and delinquency
- Family inclusion in treatment as part of support system and relapse prevention planning
- The development of a relapse prevention plan that delineates each youth's high-risk factors, including situations that should be avoided, and coping skills that can be utilized to successfully manage situations that arise, including a return to substance use (relapse)

Source: Adapted from Stewart (2009).

Treating Serious Mental Illness

The treatment of youth with serious mental illness who are housed in secure juvenile facilities is extremely important given what is currently known about the prevalence of such disorders. Identification and intervention, with the goal of reducing the disabling effects of serious mental illness, are critical elements necessary for maximizing the potential of each youth in educational, correctional, and social settings. To effectively intervene in the lives of these youth, both cognitive-behavioral and psychotropic interventions targeting symptom reduction and management are key, in addition to strengthening family support and understanding of mental illness.

One particular model that has shown evidence of effectiveness with youth in secure care is a form of cognitive-behavioral treatment called DBT (Linehan, 1993). DBT is a comprehensive treatment approach for individuals with complex and difficult-to-treat mental disorders (WSIPP, 2002). DBT was originally developed to treat chronically suicidal individuals (Linehan, 1993). It has since been adapted for youth who have difficulty regulating their emotions and focuses on three functions: (a) enhancing behavioral skills to deal with difficult situations, (b) motivating youth to change dysfunctional behaviors and dysregulated emotions, and (c) ensuring new skills are used in daily institutional life (WSIPP, 2002). The treatment model emphasizes behavioral analysis, cognitive modification, skills coaching, skill acquisition, skills strengthening, skill generalization, exposure-based procedures, and contingency management to change maladaptive behaviors (WSIPP, 2002). Families, parole officers, and caseworkers are taught methods to reinforce new skills youth learn while receiving treatment in the institution.

Psychotropic medications are also commonly utilized and sometimes exclusively utilized as the treatment for mentally ill youth in correctional settings. This is often due to a lack of human resources for treatment, especially those treatments that can be time- and labor-intensive or require specialized training and supervision like CBT. However, research has suggested medication-only interventions are not as effective as medication coupled with CBT. In one study, results showed that almost 90% of those receiving the combination of CBT and antidepressant medication sustained their level of improved functioning after a 36-week period, compared to 82% in the medication-only group and 75% of those in the CBT-only group (Rohde et al., 2008). When medications are utilized for psychiatric disorders, both target symptoms of the medication and potential side effects should be understood by the youth and treatment team. They should be monitored and documented by the treatment team and reported back to the treating psychiatrist on a regular basis.

Barriers to Effective Treatment

The mental health provider will likely encounter frequent barriers to the effective treatment of youth in juvenile facilities. Barriers to treatment can occur at several levels, such as at the individual skill level of the therapist, supervision/management of the clinical staff, and at facility/administrative levels. A structure should be in place to recognize barriers that are present, to promote effective problem-solving, and to offer effective solutions on both an individual and institutional level. Table 13.7 offers examples of barriers to effective treatment that are commonly encountered in juvenile facilities.

Table 13.7 Barriers to Effective Treatment

Barriers	Potential Solutions
Lack of effective screening procedures	Screen all incoming youth with validated best practice screening tools.
Lack of appropriate follow-up from screening	Perform targeted mental health assessment on all youth screening positive for mental health and substance abuse issues.
Lack of effective treatment interventions	Clinicians educated and supervised in techniques and treatment interventions proven to be effective for juvenile offenders.

(Continued)

Table 13.7 (Continued)

Barriers	Potential Solutions
Lack of clinical supervision	Adoption of proven supervision strategies and models.
Redundant and irrelevant testing	Targeted testing based on the current needs of the youth.
Punitive institutional philosophy	Institutional behavior management plans should be based on a system of rewards and consequences and target skills development. They should also have adequate flexibility to adapt to youth with mental illness, developmental disabilities, etc.
Treatment plans are not individualized	Plans should have both short-term prioritized achievable goals as well as clear long-term goals with measurable behavioral outcomes that can be understood by the youth and family.
Lack of communication between professional staff	One mental health treatment plan that incorporates social work, psychology, and psychiatry with routine clinical staffing.
Difficulty in monitoring psychiatric medications	Mental health team, nursing staff, and youth understand why medication is given, target symptoms that should be monitored, and important side effects.
Family or significant others not included in treatment from onset of institutional care	Treatment staff are proactive in engaging families as part of treatment planning, for visits, therapeutic phone calls, and preparing youth for discharge.
Lack of human resources	Judicious use of incarceration for violent or serious offenders, while mental health staff also make appropriate recommendations for community-based treatment when possible or early release of youth completing treatment programming. Mental health staff should know the minimum standard of care that is expected (such as the Civil Rights of Institutionalized Persons Act [CRIPA] and professional practice standards).
Lack of reentry planning and practice	Begin reentry aftercare planning at the onset of care in the institution (e.g., assessment). Create policies that allow for furloughs and other methods to practice and demonstrate skills learned in the institution. Involve community resources, such as churches and businesses, in transition planning and support for youth. Arrange necessary follow-up appointments prior to release and provide adequate discharge medications at time of release.

Aftercare and Reintegration

Effectively transitioning juvenile offenders from incarceration to the community is critical. According to Gies (2003), juvenile reentry encompasses programs, services, and supports intended to assist youth to transition from residential placement back into the community. This includes preparing confined offenders for reentering the specific communities to which they will return, establishing the needed collaborative arrangements and linkages with agencies and individuals in the offender's community in direct relation to known risk and protective factors, and ensuring the delivery of required services and supervision after discharge (Altschuler & Armstrong, 2001; Gies, 2003).

Ideally, aftercare, reintegration, reentry, and discharge planning for the youth should begin postdisposition and prior to placement or, at least, as soon as he or she is admitted to an institution. Aftercare is an essential component of treatment with emphasis on long-term goals and relapse prevention. This includes successfully reintegrating large numbers of youth who, according to Snyder (2004), are more likely to come from single-parent homes and to have relatives who have also been incarcerated; lag significantly behind in terms of their levels of educational attainment; have significant alcohol and substance abuse problems; have prior criminal histories, including prior adjudications and placements; and have high rates of mental health needs. These youth are also likely to be parents themselves (Snyder & Sickmund, 2006). Most of these youth will also return to communities of concentrated disadvantage with high crime rates and few opportunities for education and employment (Mears & Travis, 2004). As argued by Mears and Travis (2004), the development of reentry services is critical to stem the high rates of juvenile recidivism, ensure community safety, and provide youth with the services and supports needed to facilitate a smooth and successful transition home. Discussion of placement possibilities, family inclusion, engagement and motivation, skill assessment/development, and reduction of symptom severity while in residential care should all be geared toward getting a youth ready to function more effectively in the facility and, more importantly, the larger community.

Reintegration preparation should include engaging the youth, the youth's family, and the youth's aftercare staff to promote continuity of treatment, while also attempting to build a positive support system for the youth. Altschuler and Armstrong (1994) describe an intensive aftercare model that should guide reentry program efforts for high-risk juveniles to include a number of key principles. Programs should prepare the youth for progressively increased responsibility and freedom in the community. Programs should facilitate youth-community interaction and involvement and work with the youth and targeted community support systems, such as schools and family, on qualities needed for constructive interaction and the youth's successful community adjustment. Programs should also monitor and test the youth and community on their ability to effectively deal with each other. To support these principles, staff should generate a coordinated and comprehensive transition plan, facilitate information exchange, ensure continuous and consistent access to services, and plan or provide monitoring in the community (Weibush, McNulty, & Le, 2000).

For youth with mental health needs, the challenges of transitioning from placement to the community may be even greater due to what Roskes, Feldman, Arrington, and Leisher (1999) describe as a "double stigma." These youth have a delinquent background as well as a mental health disorder, which may make accessing services even more difficult. The National Center for Mental Health and Juvenile Justice (Skowyra & Cocozza, 2007) points out that such youth face problems in leaving a structured environment with clear behavioral expectations for a less structured and often less consistent home environment.

Summary and Conclusions

Deprivation of liberty through incarceration is usually thought to be the most severe sanction that can be delivered by the juvenile justice system (McCord, Wisdom, & Crowell, 2001). It is easy to forget that almost all the youth entering a juvenile secure care institution will be out on the streets, back in neighborhoods, and in society within a few years or possibly even months. What they learn and what they are exposed to in the institution will likely influence their outcome. Having access to safe living conditions, positive mentors (i.e., staff) and peer interaction, appropriate educational and vocational training, and mental and physical health services may make all the difference between successful reintegration into society and reoffending.

As highlighted in this chapter, the best practices for correctional care are:

1. Screening practices utilizing validated tools.

2. Assessment practices that drive well-written individualized treatment plans that target specific behavior changes and are written in language that is understandable by practitioners, youth, and families.

3. Whenever possible, considering public safety and available best practice alternatives to incarceration, recommend noninstitutionalized care and/or care in less restrictive environments.

4. Engage and involve families and/or other surrogate mentors and supportive persons and systems from the youth's community.

5. Offer treatment that includes motivational engagement, cognitive-behavioral methods, and systems/social ecological approaches.

6. Focus on skills teaching, practice, demonstration, reinforcement, and generalization.

7. Plan and work towards successful reentry/aftercare from the initiation of treatment at the facility.

8. Target both delinquency risk factors and mental health symptoms for intervention and change, and enhance protective factors to increase success of treatment.

KEY TERMS

Juvenile Delinquency Prevention and Control Act of 1968

Juvenile Justice and Delinquency Prevention Act of 1974

Juvenile delinquent/ offender

Juvenile justice

Civil Rights of Institutionalized Persons Act (CRIPA)

Recidivism

Co-occurring mental illness and juvenile delinquency

Delinquency risk and protective factors

Screening vs. assessment

Alternatives to incarceration

Evidence-based practice

Behaviorally targeted treatment planning

Motivational engagement

Cognitive-behavioral treatment

Systems/ecological treatment

Family inclusion

Aftercare and reintegration

"*Parens patriae*"

Disproportionate minority contact/confinement

Status offender

Individualized treatment plan

DISCUSSION QUESTIONS

1. What are delinquent risk and protective factors, and how should they be utilized to influence intervention decisions?

2. What are the steps to develop an individualized treatment plan, and what are the key components of the final plan? How should this plan be utilized to provide effective interventions?

3. What are evidence-based practices? What research practices are available to improve the likelihood of positive outcomes for youth in correctional environments?

4. What improved outcomes are expected when including family and guardians in treatment? What are the barriers commonly experienced?

5. Why is aftercare/reintegration a critical component to juvenile secure care? What are the essential components of adequate aftercare planning and implementation?

References

Acoca, L. (1999). Investing in girls: A 21st century strategy. *Juvenile Justice, 6*(1), 3–13.

Acoca, L., & Dedel, K. (1998). *No place to hide: Understanding and meeting the needs of girls in the California juvenile justice system.* San Francisco, CA: National Council on Crime and Delinquency.

Altschuler, D. M., & Armstrong, T. L. (1994). *Intensive aftercare for high-risk juveniles: A community care model.* Washington, DC: U.S. Department of Justice, Office of Justice Programs, Office of Juvenile Justice and Delinquency Prevention.

Altschuler, D. M., & Armstrong, T. L. (2001). Reintegrating high-risk juvenile offenders into communities: Experiences and prospects. *Corrections Management Quarterly, 5,* 79–95.

Andrews, D. A., Zinger, I., Hoge, R., Bonta, J., Gendrew, P., & Cullen, F. (1990). Does correctional treatment work? A clinically relevant and psychologically informed meta-analysis. *Criminology, 28,* 369–404.

Arnold, M. E., & Hughes, J. N. (1999). First do no harm: Adverse effects of grouping deviant youth for skills training. *Journal of School Psychology, 37,* 99–115.

Baer, J. S., & Peterson, P. L. (2002). Motivational interviewing with adolescents and young adults. In W. Miller & S. Rollnick (Eds.), *Motivational interviewing: Preparing people for change* (2nd ed., pp. 320–332). New York, NY: Guilford.

Beelmann, A., Pfingsten, U., & Losel, F. (1994). Effects of training social competence in children: A meta-analysis of recent evaluation studies. *Journal of Clinical Child Psychology, 23,* 260–271.

Brock, L., Burrell, J., & Tulipano, T. (2006). *Family involvement* (NDTAC Issue Brief). Retrieved June 11, 2009, from www.neglecteddelinquent.org/nd/docs/NDTAC_issuebrief_family.pdf

Catalano, R. F., & Hawkins, J. D. (1995). *Risk focused prevention. Using the social development strategy.* Seattle, WA: Developmental Research and Programs, Inc.

Cauffman, E. (2004). A statewide screening of mental health symptoms among juvenile offenders in detention. *Journal of the American Academy of Child and Adolescent Psychiatry, 43,* 430–439.

Center for Substance Abuse Treatment. (2002). *Enhancing motivation for change in substance abuse treatment* (Treatment Improvement Protocol Series 35). Rockville, MD: U.S. Department of Health and Human Services.

Chesney-Lind, M., & Pasko, L. (2004). *The female offender: Girls, women, and crime* (2nd ed.). Thousand Oaks, CA: Sage.

Council of Juvenile Correctional Administrators. (2003). *Performance-based standards (PbS) for youth correction and detention facilities: PbS goals, standards, outcome measures, expected practices and processes.* Braintree, MA: Council of Juvenile Correctional Administrators.

Dague, B., & Tolin, C. (1996). *Developing parent supports within the juvenile justice setting: One community's experience.* Paper presented at the Family Strengths Meeting, Portland State University, Portland, OR.

Dodgen, C. E., & Shea, W. M. (2000). *Substance use disorders: Assessment and treatment.* San Diego, CA: Academic Press.

Domalanta, D., Risser, W., Roberts, R., & Risser, J. (2003). Prevalence of depression and other psychiatric disorders among incarcerated youth. *Journal of the American Academy of Child and Adolescent Psychiatry, 42,* 477–484.

Estroff, T. W. (2001). *Manual of adolescent substance abuse treatment.* Washington, DC: American Psychiatric Publishing.

Fazel, S., Doll, H., & Langstrom, N. (2009). Mental disorders among adolescents in juvenile detention and correctional facilities: A systematic review and metaregression analysis of 25 surveys. *Journal of the American Academy of Child & Adolescent Psychiatry, 47,* 1010–1019.

Feldstein, S. W., & Ginsberg, J. (2006). Motivational interviewing with dually diagnosed adolescents in juvenile justice settings. *Brief Treatment & Crisis Intervention, 6,* 218–233.

Garrett, C. (1985). Effects of residential treatment on adjudicated delinquents: A meta-analysis. *Journal of Research in Crime and Delinquency, 22,* 287–308.

Gies, S. (2003). *Aftercare services.* Washington, DC: U.S. Department of Justice, Office of Juvenile Justice and Delinquency Prevention.

Gorski, T. (1996). *Adolescent relapse prevention workbook: A brief strategic approach.* Independence, MO: Herald.

Grisso, T. (2005). Why we need mental health screening and assessment in juvenile justice programs. In T. Grisso, G. Vincent, & D. Seagrave (Eds.), *Mental health screening and assessment in juvenile justice* (pp. 3–21). New York, NY: Guilford.

Hawkins, S. R., Graham, P. W., Williams, J., & Zahn, M. A. (2009). *Resilient girls: Factors that protect against delinquency.* Washington, DC: U.S. Department of Justice, Office of Justice Programs, Office of Juvenile Justice and Delinquency Prevention.

Hayes, L. (2000). Suicide prevention in juvenile facilities. *Juvenile Justice, 7,* 24–32.

Hayes, L. (2009). *Characteristics of juvenile suicide in confinement.* Washington, DC: U.S. Department of Justice, Office of Justice Programs, Office of Juvenile Justice and Delinquency Prevention. Retrieved June 5, 2009, from www.ncjrs.gov/pdffiles1/ojjdp/214434.pdf

Henggeler, S. W., Melton, G. B., Smith, L. A., Schoenwald, S. K., & Hanley, J. H. (1993). Family preservation using multisystemic treatment: Long-term follow-up to a clinical trial with serious juvenile offenders. *Journal of Child and Family Studies, 2,* 283–229.

In re Gault, 387 U.S. 1, 14 (1967).

Krisberg, B., Austin, J., & Steele, P. (1989). *Unlocking juvenile corrections.* San Francisco, CA: National Council on Crime and Delinquency.

Kumpfer, K. L., & Alvarado, R. (1998). *Effective family strengthening interventions* (Juvenile Justice Bulletin). Washington, DC: U.S. Department of Justice, Office of Juvenile Justice and Delinquency Prevention.

Larson, K. A., & Turner, K. D. (2002). *Best practices for serving court involved youth with learning, attention and behavioral disabilities.* Washington, DC: U.S. Department of Education and U.S. Department of Justice.

Latessa, E. J. (1999). What works in correctional intervention. *Southern Illinois University Law Journal, 23,* 415–425.

Latimer, J. (2001). A meta-analytic examination of youth, delinquency, family treatment, and recidivism. *Canadian Journal of Criminology, 43,* 237–253.

Linehan, M. (1993). *Cognitive-behavioral treatment of borderline personality disorder.* New York, NY: Guilford.

Lipsey, M. W. (1999). Can intervention rehabilitate serious delinquents? *Annals of the American Academy of Political and Social Science, 564,* 142–166.

Lipsey, M., Chapman, G., & Landenberger, N. (2001). Cognitive-behavioral programs for offenders. *Annals of the American Academy of Political and Social Science, 578,* 144–157.

Lipsey, M., Wilson, D., & Cothern, L. (2000). *Effective intervention for serious juvenile offenders* (Juvenile Justice Bulletin). Washington, DC: U.S. Department of Justice, Office of Justice Programs, Office of Juvenile Justice and Delinquency Prevention.

McCord, J., Wisdom, C., & Crowell, N. (Eds.). (2001). *Juvenile crime, juvenile justice* (National Research Council and Institute of Medicine, Committee on Law and Justice and Board on Children, Youth and Families, Panel on Juvenile Crime: Prevention Treatment, and Control). Washington, DC: National Academy Press.

McKay, J. R. (1996). Family therapy techniques. In F. Rotgers, D. Keller, & J. Morgenstern (Eds.), *Treating substance abuse: Theory and technique* (pp. 143–173). New York, NY: Guilford.

McKay, M., Wood, J. C., & Brantley, J. (2007). *Dialectical behavior therapy workbook.* Oakland, CA: New Harbinger.

Mears, D., & Travis, J. (2004). *The dimensions, pathways, and consequences of youth re-entry.* Washington, DC: Urban Institute.

Melton, G. B., Petrila, J., Poythress, N. G., Slobogin, C., & Lyons, P. M. (1997). *Psychological evaluations for the courts: A handbook for health professionals and lawyers* (3rd ed.). New York, NY: Guilford.

Miller, W. R., & Rollnick, S. (2002). *Motivational interviewing* (2nd ed.). New York, NY: Guilford.

Najavits, L. (2002). *Seeking safety: A treatment manual for PTSD and substance abuse.* New York, NY: Guilford.

National Commission on Correctional Health Care. (2004). *Standards for health services in juvenile detention and confinement facilities.* Chicago, IL: Author.

Office of the Surgeon General. (2001). *Youth violence: A report of the surgeon general.* Washington, DC: U.S. Department of Health and Human Services, Office of the Secretary, Office of Public Health and Science, Office of the Surgeon General. Retrieved May 4, 2009, from www.surgeongeneral.gov/library/youthviolence

Osher, T., & Hunt, P. (2002). *Involving families of youth who are in contact with the juvenile justice system* (Research and Program Brief). Washington, DC: National Center for Mental Health and Juvenile Justice.

Palmer, T. (1994). *A profile of correctional effectiveness and new directions for research.* Albany: State University of New York Press.

Palmer, T. (1996). Programmatic and nonprogrammatic aspects of successful interventions. In A. T. Harland (Ed.), *Choosing correctional options that work: Defining the demand and evaluating the supply* (pp. 131–182). Thousand Oaks, CA: Sage.

Penn, J. V., Esposito, C. L., Schaeffer, L. E., Fritz, G. K., & Spirito, A. (2003). Suicide attempts and self-mutilative behavior in a juvenile correctional facility. *Journal of the American Academy of Child and Adolescent Psychiatry, 42,* 762–769.

Phillippi, S., & DePrato, D. (2009). Assessment and treatment of juvenile offenders. In E. Benedek, P. Ash, & C. Scott (Eds.), *Principles and practice of child and adolescent forensic mental health.* Washington, DC: American Psychiatric Publishing.

Phillippi, S., & Schroeder, J. (2006). Addressing the needs of mentally ill juvenile offenders: An integrated treatment model. *Forensic Therapist, 5*(2), 9–13.

Rohde, P., Silva, S., Toney, S., Kennard, B., Vitiello, B., Kratochvil, C., et al. (2008). Achievement and maintenance of sustained response during the treatment for adolescents with depression study continuation and maintenance therapy. *Archives of General Psychiatry, 65,* 447–455.

Roskes, E., Feldman, R., Arrington, S., & Leisher, M. (1999). A model program for the treatment of mentally ill offenders in the community. *Community Mental Health Journal, 35,* 461–472.

Roush, D. (1996). *Desktop guide to good juvenile detention practice.* Washington, DC: U.S. Department of Justice, Office of Justice Programs, Office of Juvenile Justice and Delinquency Prevention.

Sample, S., & Kadden, R. (2001). *Motivational enhancement therapy and cognitive behavioral therapy for adolescent cannabis users: 5 sessions* (Cannabis Youth Treatment Series, Vol. 1, Document BDK384). Washington, DC: U.S. Substance Abuse and Mental Health Services Administration.

Shufelt, J. S., & Cocozza, J. C. (2006). *Youth with mental health disorders in the juvenile justice system: Results from a multi-state, multi-system prevalence study.* Delmar, NY: National Center for Mental Health and Juvenile Justice.

Skowyra, K., & Cocozza, J. (2007). *Blueprint for change: A comprehensive model for the identification and treatment of youth with mental health needs in contact with the juvenile justice system.* Delmar, NY: National Center for Mental Health and Juvenile Justice.

Snyder, H. (2004). *Juvenile arrests 2002.* Washington, DC: U.S. Department of Justice, Office of Justice Programs, Office of Juvenile Justice and Delinquency Prevention.

Snyder, H., & Sickmund, M. (2006). *Juvenile offenders and victims: 2006 national report.* Washington, DC: U.S. Department of Justice, Office of Justice Programs, Office of Juvenile Justice and Delinquency Prevention.

Stewart, D. G. (2009, July). *Causes and consequences of adolescent substance abuse: Current scientific perspectives.* Presentation to the Louisiana Association of Substance Abuse Counselors and the Louisiana Office of Addictive Disorders, Shreveport, LA.

Teplin, L., Abram, K. M., McClelland, G., Dulcan, M. K., & Mericle, A. A. (2002). Psychiatric disorders in youth in juvenile detention. *Archives of General Psychiatry, 59,* 1133–1143.

Thornberry, T. P. (1994). *Violent families and youth violence* (Fact Sheet No. 21). Washington, DC: U.S. Department of Justice, Office of Juvenile Justice and Delinquency Prevention.

Trupin, E. (2006, Summer). *Investigation and litigation in juvenile justice* (Focal Point: Research, Policy, and Practice in Children's Mental Health: Corrections). Portland, OR: Portland State University.

Turner, F. J. (1996). *Social work treatment: Interlocking theoretical approaches* (4th ed.). New York, NY: Free Press and Macmillan.

Vincent, G. M., Grisso, T., & Terry, A. (2007). Mental health screening and assessment in juvenile justice. In C. L. Kessler & L. J. Kraus (Eds.), *The mental health needs of young offenders: Forging paths toward reintegration and rehabilitation* (pp. 270–287). Cambridge, MA: Cambridge University Press.

Walker, J., & Friedman, K. (2001). *Listening and learning from families in juvenile justice.* Columbia: Maryland Coalition of Families for Children's Mental Health. Retrieved May 27, 2009, from www.mdcoalition.org/jjustice.pdf

Washington State Institute for Public Policy. (2002). *Preliminary findings for the juvenile rehabilitation administration's dialectic behavior therapy program* (Document No. 02-07-1203). Olympia: Washington State Government.

Wasserman, G. A., Keenan, K., Tremblay, R. E., Cole, J. D., Herrenkohl, T. I., Loeber, R., et al. (2003). *Risk and protective factors of child delinquency* (Child Delinquency Bulletin). Washington, DC: U.S. Department of Justice, Office of Juvenile Justice and Delinquency Prevention.

Wasserman, G., McReynolds, L., Lucas, C., Fisher, P., & Santos, L. (2002). The Voice DISC-IV with incarcerated male youths: Prevalence of disorder. *Journal of the American Academy of Child and Adolescent Psychiatry, 41,* 314–321.

Webb, C., Scudder, M., Kaminer, Y., & Kadden, R. (2001). *The motivational enhancement therapy and cognitive behavioral therapy supplement: 7 sessions of cognitive behavioral therapy for adolescent cannabis users* (Cannabis Youth Treatment Series, Vol. 2, Document BKD385). Washington, DC: U.S. Substance Abuse and Mental Health Services Administration.

Weibush, R. G., McNulty, B., & Le, T. (2000). *Implementation of the intensive community-based aftercare program.* Washington, DC: U.S. Department of Justice, Office of Justice Programs, Office of Juvenile Justice and Delinquency Prevention.

Zahn, M. A., Hawkins, S. R., Chiancone, J., & Whitworth, A. (2008). *The girls study group: Charting the way to delinquency prevention for girls.* Washington, DC: U.S. Department of Justice, Office of Juvenile Justice and Delinquency Prevention.

CHAPTER 14

Managing Disruptive Offenders

A Behavioral Perspective

Steven J. Helfand

Introduction

Chronically disruptive offenders present both treatment and management challenges to mental health, medical, and correctional staff. Disruptive inmates display a heterogeneous set of behaviors that can endanger themselves (e.g., self-injury, suicide threats) or others (e.g., assaultive behavior) and threaten the safety, security, and long-term stability of the correctional systems in which they reside. Each institution typically has a small number of inmates who engage in extreme behaviors that interrupt normal operations and place themselves, other inmates, and staff at risk.

Many of the behaviors that occur within jails and prisons are quite specific to these settings and are not typical of violent and/or disruptive behaviors seen in the community. Often, disruptive behaviors may be conceptualized as tools of last resort for achieving a sense of control within restrictive environments like prisons (Skeem, Miller, Mulvey, Tiemann, & Monahan, 2005). Such offender behaviors may include cell-flooding or fire-setting; refusing to exit cells, perhaps with the intention of provoking a forced cell extraction and/or scuffle with staff; self-harm, such as threatening to or actually mutilating themselves via cutting or insertion of objects into their bodies; physically assaulting others; throwing feces or urine; or spitting at others.

It is common for institutional staff to debate whether these disruptive behaviors are driven by mental illness (i.e., "madness") or volitional choice with disruptive intent (i.e., "badness"). Tucker (1999) noted that the definition of "mad" typically includes the diagnoses of schizophrenia; major mood disorders; disabling anxiety disorders, such as obsessive-compulsive disorder and post-traumatic stress disorder; and several severe personality disorders, typically with marked functional impairment. In the prison context, a "bad" person is often defined as a person who intentionally disrupts prison routines for criminal and/or instrumental purposes (Toch, 2008). Many of the extreme reactions by officials (e.g., placement in a bare isolation cell) are in response to the disruptive impact of the inmate's behavior. From the psychological perspective, Tucker noted that "badness" can also be equated to the construct of psychopathy (Hare, 2006). Because the psychopath's often explosive and cruel behavior elicits strong emotional reactions, it is understandable how these feelings can manifest themselves among correctional staff and lead to extreme interventions.

However, in reality, this "mad" versus "bad" dichotomy often reflects a desire to assign primary responsibility for handling the problem to either the mental health or correctional staff. Other terms used for similar purpose include "Axis I" versus "Axis II," "mental health" versus "behavioral," and "mental health" versus "custody." Whereas many inmates meet criteria for Axis II Cluster B personality disorders such as antisocial personality disorder and borderline personality disorder (Trestman, Ford, Zhang, & Wiesbrock, 2007), such disorders do not in and of themselves place the onus of management solely on custodial staff. These categorizations may be helpful in understanding the etiology of these disruptive behaviors, but they do not promote the coordination and collaboration needed between mental health, medical, and custody disciplines to reduce and perhaps ultimately extinguish these problem behaviors.

This chapter explores the phenomenon of extremely disruptive behaviors within the correctional setting and highlights several mental health diagnoses and/or symptoms that are commonly associated with them. This chapter also focuses on the importance of detailed functional assessment (i.e., a careful analysis of antecedent conditions and behavioral consequences), the development of individualized behavioral treatment plans (BTPs), and the need for interdisciplinary cooperation in executing these plans. Lastly, this chapter discusses obstacles to the implementation of such behavioral treatment strategies in the correctional setting. Although the obstacles to successful formulation and implementation of BTPs in correctional settings can be considerable, they offer an alternative to established correctional strategies that are not always effective with this subset of disruptive inmates.

Behavioral Treatment Versus Behavioral Management: An Important Distinction

Although the terms *behavioral treatment plans/programs* and *behavioral management plans/programs* are sometimes used interchangeably in correctional settings, there are a few fundamental differences that should be clarified early in this chapter. Specifically, with behavioral management programs, the administration or correctional system is the primary client, a set of conditions is imposed as imperatives or ultimatums on the inmate whose behaviors are unacceptable, and inmate consent may not be requested or obtained. Punishment is more likely to be emphasized with behavior management plans (e.g., placement in segregation or loss of good time), and inmate resistance and resentment are possible outcomes (Toch, 2008). Behavioral management plans assume a more or less adversarial stance between the institution and the inmate and are relatively standardized. They are sometimes useful and appropriate in correctional settings, but their discussion is beyond the scope of this chapter.

Behavioral treatment plans/programs, on the other hand, have the inmate as the primary client, actively engage the inmate in formulating the plan or treatment contract, and emphasize reward or positive reinforcement. This approach has the advantage of being more ethical from a professional perspective and, from an empirical standpoint, is more likely to work. It is this more positive behavioral treatment strategy that will be the focus of this chapter. This approach relies on behavioral science principles and is focused on pragmatic, empirical, best practice solutions. Treatment plans based on behavioral principles are tailored to each inmate and each facility and may offer an effective alternative to current management strategies, which have not been shown to be very effective with more disruptive offenders.

Mental Health Problems Associated With Disruptive Institutional Behavior

Although there are a number of mental health diagnoses and/or symptoms that are associated with disruptive institutional behavior, this section will feature a few illustrative examples that are most relevant in correctional settings.

Personality Disorders

Personality disorders are defined as long-term, rigid patterns of inner experience and/or outer behavior that are pervasive in nature and result in either personal distress or dysfunction/impairment in one or more domains of functioning (e.g., social, relational, cognitive, and affective). Personality disorders are divided into three categories or clusters—the odd, dramatic, and anxious clusters. Each of these clusters can be subdivided into specific diagnosable mental disorders (American Psychiatric Association, 2000). Within the dramatic personality disorder cluster, there are two diagnostic categories, antisocial personality disorder and borderline personality disorder, which are commonly associated with violent and/or disruptive behaviors.

Antisocial Personality Disorder

Antisocial personality disorder is marked by a pervasive pattern of disregard for and violation of the rights of others occurring since age 15 that may include failure to conform to the law, deceitfulness, impulsivity or failure to plan ahead, irritability and aggressiveness, reckless disregard for safety of self or others, consistent irresponsibility, and lack of remorse (American Psychiatric Association, 2000). Prevalence rates for antisocial personality disorder in the community are about 3% for males and 1% for females. Rates are often higher in substance abuse treatment and correctional settings (American Psychiatric Association, 2000). In one comprehensive study of jail inmates, Trestman et al. (2007) found that 34.6% of their participants met the full diagnostic criteria for antisocial personality disorder. Regardless of the setting, the aggression and violence perpetrated by antisocial personality disordered individuals pose significant problems for both mental health and criminal justice systems, as well as for both perpetrators and their victims (Daffern & Howells, 2007).

Borderline Personality Disorder

Borderline personality disorder is defined by "a pervasive pattern of instability of interpersonal relationships, self-image, affects, and marked impulsivity that begins by early childhood and is present in a variety of contexts" (American Psychiatric Association, 2000, p. 706). These contexts may include frantic efforts to avoid real or imagined abandonment; identity disturbance; impulsivity in at least two areas that are self-damaging; recurrent suicidal behavior, gestures, or threats of self-mutilating behavior; affective instability due to marked reactivity of mood, chronic feelings of emptiness, inappropriate, intense anger or difficulty controlling anger; and transient, stress-related paranoid ideation or severe dissociative symptoms (American Psychiatric Association, 2000). Although all of these potential symptoms can contribute to unrest in the correctional setting, it is recurrent suicidal or self-mutilating behavior that typically strains the resources of the facility (Fagan, Cox, Helfand, & Aufderheide, 2010; Holton, 2003).

In a comprehensive study of jail inmates, Trestman et al. (2007) found that 16.6% of their participants met the criteria for borderline personality disorder, and 12.9% of males met criteria for borderline personality disorder as compared to community prevalence rates of less than 0.5%. In a study of 220 male and female offenders entering a state prison system, it was found that 26.8% of men and 54.5% of women met the full criteria (Black et al., 2007). Furthermore, 90% of those assessed had at least one self-reported borderline personality disorder symptom, the most frequent being impulsivity, followed by displays of inappropriate anger, unstable mood, suicidal thoughts/behaviors, and transient paranoid ideation. This study also found that nearly 57% of the offenders with borderline personality disorder met criteria for antisocial personality disorder.

Of all the mental illnesses seen in corrections, borderline personality disorder most requires the use of an integrated multidisciplinary treatment strategy to reduce an inmate's symptoms as well as to minimize the disruptive impact on the correctional environment (Holton, 2003). For these inmates, a combination of behavioral and cognitive treatment, skills training, close collaboration with custody to avoid staff splitting (i.e., an offender's attempt to play one staff member against another in an effort to achieve a particular goal), and medication strategies should be considered. This use of combined or adjunctive treatments will be discussed further below. It is absolutely essential that the offender, medical/mental health staff, and custody staff consult and agree on a plan for behavioral treatment. All parties must then follow through on what has been agreed to in the plan in an effort to reduce maladaptive behavior patterns that may result in self-harm, staff splitting, violent acting out, or other disruptive behaviors (Holton, 2003).

Consider the case of an offender with borderline personality disorder who is stressed by his total loss of personal control. He refuses to exit his cell when requested to do so by custody staff and frequently self-injures when asked to vacate his cell. A BTP in these circumstances might call for custody staff to allow the inmate 5 minutes to exit the cell, giving him a semblance of control over his circumstances. Additionally, during episodes of self-injury, medical staff might be instructed to address the injury without rewarding the inmate with peripheral conversation secondary to the medical treatment. Additionally, mental health staff may offer the inmate skills training to assist him in managing his anger when he feels controlled by others. All parties might also verbally reward the inmate for instances of compliance with cell exits and for increasing time intervals between episodes of self-injury. If all parties (i.e., the offender, custody staff, and medical/mental health treatment staff) agreed to this strategy, it is possible that the inmate might comply more with custody requests, self-injure less, and develop more effective coping strategies. The result is a situation where both the inmate and staff benefit.

Self-Injury

Self-injurious behavior (SIB) and borderline personality disorder have been found to be associated (Trestman, 2000). SIB by an inmate is often more disruptive to the orderly operation of a correctional facility than simply having an inmate on observation for suicide. Additionally, the potential for staff frustration and burnout is high when inmates repeatedly engage in SIBs or threaten to self-injure (Holton, 2003).

Generally, SIB, such as cutting, within prison settings has been viewed as an attention-seeking act (i.e., under the volitional control of the offender) rather than as a symptom of a diagnosable mental disorder (i.e., borderline personality disorder; Karten, 1991). However, Karten (1991) suggests that SIB is a symptom of borderline personality disorder among inmates and occurs more frequently during incarceration because inmates are unable to utilize the other maladaptive stress relievers like substance abuse that they employed in the community. Being under institutional control presents these offenders with unique situational stressors such as separation from family, dependency on others, and loss of control. Given their inability to easily acquire new strategies to problem-solve and cope with the stress associated with living in prison or to utilize usual strategies such as asking for a transfer or an extra phone call, these offenders may turn to SIB as a means of expressing their frustration. Regardless, staff responses to SIB often include irritation, frustration, and anger (Trestman, 2000).

Prevalence and Types of Self-Injury

Based on a review of the literature on SIB in correctional settings, Brooker, Repper, Beverley, Ferriter, and Brewer (2002) reported that an estimated 30% of all inmates engaged in SIB of some type during their incarceration. Shea (1993) reported prevalence rates between 6.5% and 25% among male inmates. Fifty-one percent of female prisoners have one or more instances of self-injury over their lifetime, and 29% reported more than one incident of self-injury (Borrill, Snow, Medlicott, Teers, & Paton, 2005). The differences in prevalence rates among these studies likely relate to varying definitions of SIB across different populations as well as the absence of a registration process for SIBs (Lohner & Konrad, 2006).

In a study of staff responses to SIB by inmates, DeHart, Smith, and Kaminski (2009) found that SIB occurred regularly in correctional settings and that a subset of inmates was responsible for recurrent events. They collected data from 54 correctional mental health professionals. Their data indicated that cutting was the most frequently witnessed SIB, followed by scratching, opening old wounds, and inserting objects.

There are many factors that contribute to SIB. These include psychosis, tension relief, impulsivity, manipulation for goal attainment, and the presence of a personality disorder. In a pilot study of self-injuring female offenders, Snow (1997) suggested that rather than SIB being mere attention-seeking, it was more often performed impulsively as a "cry for help" during periods of extreme emotional distress. In another study (DeHart et al., 2009), mental health staff reported manipulative ends as the primary motivation for SIB, followed by the perception that it was a strategy to cope with stress. The tendency to equate manipulation or malingering to SIB is one that might prohibit ideal interventions. It is paramount to maintain awareness that regardless of the motivation, the inmate is in some distress, is attempting to meet his or her needs, and is at continued risk of self-harm or violence toward others if his or her needs go unmet. The challenge is to balance meeting the needs of the inmate with those of the institution. It is clear from research and experience that blindly following institutional directives does not change these extreme behaviors. It is important to promote a collaborative and flexible approach based on the reality that continuing "as is" is not effective.

Impulsivity

Impulsivity is related to various forms of psychopathology and maladaptive behavior and is a core symptom of both antisocial and borderline personality disorders (Komarovskaya, Loper, & Warren, 2007). It has been defined as a tendency toward having a short latency period before acting on urges (Oquendo & Mann, 2000). The linkage between impulsivity and aggression has been well documented (Komarovskaya et al., 2007). Impulsive aggression may emerge in response to provocation or punishment and is often accompanied by frustration, fear, irritability, or anger. A biological link is also hypothesized between SIB and impulsive aggression (Oquendo & Mann, 2000).

In a study of 590 female inmates at a state prison, it was found that impulsive inmates, as measured by the Barratt Impulsiveness Scale (BIS), committed more violent prison infractions than those who were not impulsive. The impulsive inmates were also more likely to meet the diagnoses of borderline and antisocial personality disorders (Komarovskaya et al., 2007). Along with anger, hostility, and antisocial personality traits, impulsivity has been shown to be a strong predictor of institutional aggression, violence, and adjustment issues among incarcerated male offenders (Fornells, Capdevila, & Andres-Pueyo, 2002; Wang & Diamond, 1999).

Aggression

Within correctional environments, a single episode of other-directed aggression such as an inmate-on-inmate fight or an inmate-on-staff assault is probably best addressed through traditional correctional practices. However, continued instances of aggression should involve mental health consultation, including an assessment for psychiatric and/or medical conditions that may underlie the aggressive behaviors and then appropriate treatment to facilitate behavioral improvement (Lewis, 2000). While incarcerated, violent behaviors by male inmates are often used to gain or maintain control. Wagaman (2003) suggested that the "violent behavior demonstrated by female inmates is more often an expression of perceived loss of control and an effort to regain personal identity and/or maintain survival" (p. 128). Aggressive behaviors are often reinforced by the environment despite traditional correctional sanctions such as loss of privileges. Daffern and Howells (2007) cite the example of the patient in a secure setting who may become angry and aggressive when directed to participate in a unit activity and is then praised by his peers, thus rewarding his avoidance of the activity.

Generalized Maladaptive Behaviors

Severe and repetitive SIBs share many features associated with recurrent and nontraditional aggressive acts in the facility. For example, in a study of randomly selected male offenders receiving mental health treatment in prison, Young, Justice, and Erdberg (2006) found that those who self-injured were more than 8 times as likely to assault treatment staff as those who did not. Hillbrand, Krystal, and Sharpe (1994) found that self-mutilating patients were significantly more verbally and physically aggressive towards people and objects than those who did not self-mutilate. This suggests that a maladaptive behavior syndrome exists for some within the correctional population and that attention should be given to both types of behavior in planning interventions. These overlapping maladaptive behaviors are illustrated by the five composite cases of extreme behavior presented in Table 14.1.

Table 14.1	Cases of Extreme Behaviors in Correctional Settings

1. The inmate flooded her cell and then scratched her forearm with the fastener from the safety gown and then ripped the smoke detector from the ceiling and attempted to scratch her forearm with it.

2. The inmate broke his toilet and cut his wrist with the porcelain. He then threatened to cut staff with the porcelain and placed his mattress against the door in preparation for a use of force.

3. The inmate taped a plastic bag around his head. He then flooded his cell, utilized a cup to scoop feces and urine out of the toilet, and threw this mixture under the door prior to covering his window with toilet paper.

4. The inmate complained about not getting a double portion for dinner. He ripped his sheet, wrapped it around his neck, and stated that he was going to kill himself if not sent to the hospital unit. He then started flooding his cell and threatened to throw urine on any staff who entered his cell.

5. The inmate tied a torn piece of his shirt around his neck and then banged his hands and fists on the door and subsequently covered his cell window with feces.

In closing this section on mental health problems associated with disruptive institutional behaviors, two summary points are worth noting. First, a small group of inmates engage in these types of behaviors repetitively. The motivation for engaging in these behaviors varies across inmates, although most involve some degree of behavioral dysregulation. Second, such episodes may result in a use of force by custody staff (e.g., a forced cell removal). This is often followed with placement in restrictive settings or being shuttled back and forth between disciplinary and psychiatric units or between correctional institution and outside hospitals. Although such interventions may temporarily stop the behavior, they do nothing to address the motivations and reinforcement that led to its occurrence and may, in fact, be reinforcing the disruptive behavior in some instances.

Behavioral Treatment Plans

As noted earlier, this chapter conceptualizes BTPs as any planned set of interventions, treatments, and/or restrictions designed to increase desired behaviors and/or to eliminate problematic behaviors. For present didactic purposes, BTPs are defined as individualized and flexible interventions that emphasize the use of positive reinforcement rather than punishment and that involve the inmate as participant, including obtaining his or her informed consent. With BTPs, inmates are considered clients or patients and have input into formulating treatment goals. Here, the BTP is discussed as a best practice.

In formulating a BTP, a careful behavioral assessment is necessary. In conducting a behavioral assessment, formal diagnoses are not ignored so much as considered secondary. Notwithstanding, for example, that an inmate-patient may have a diagnosis of schizophrenia, or be characterized as "impulsive," the observable behaviors to be modified, and those measurable environmental contingencies that may be manipulated toward that end, are the primary variables of interest. As will be discussed below, functional behavioral assessment and treatment may complement other (e.g., pharmacological, cognitive) approaches.

The fundamentals of a behavioral intervention are fairly straightforward, at least in theory. Starting with the specification and measurement of the target behavior, in this case an undesirable behavior, and therefore one to be reduced or eliminated, its causes or determinants must be identified, as changing these conditions will be largely the means by which the target behavior will be modified. Measuring behavior means quantifying it in some fashion so that the effectiveness of an intervention can be assessed. For example, one might choose to measure how often an inmate-patient cuts himself or herself (provided the cutting is not so severe that restraint and medical treatment are necessary), and/or how severe the cut is when it occurs. However, to emphasize positive behavior, one could also measure time units (e.g., hours or days) *without* self-cutting. Once a baseline level of behavior is measured, the intervention (the reinforcement provided for positive behavior) is introduced, and the change in the target behavior is measured.

The environmental stimuli, which according to behavior theory control behavior, can be considered to be of two basic kinds: antecedents and consequences. Antecedents are those stimuli that elicit the behavior and the consequences are those which reinforce it: maintaining or increasing its occurrence.

Successful treatment will require an understanding of the function of the behavior (i.e., what it is supposed to accomplish from the inmate's perspective; Jeglic, Vanderhoof, & Donovick, 2005; Lovell, 2008). Therefore, the first step in completing a BTP should be to conduct a targeted evaluation to assess the function of the behavior. When assessing self-injury or other maladaptive behavior, each distinct act should be evaluated, and motivation, intent, lethality, and context (e.g., pending transfer to another facility) should be examined. This assessment would best be accomplished through a structured interview with the inmate, review of the health record, and collateral information from incident reports and witnesses. It is important to assess motivation to see if it was reward-seeking or avoidant behavior. As part of a good functional analysis, it is also important to assess the ways that the system or correctional environment reinforces the target behavior(s) from the inmate's perspective (Webb, 2001). Martinez (1980) noted that many inmates who engage in SIBs in correctional environments appear to do so to elicit desired consequences and that the intentional component of these behaviors becomes more salient when the antecedents and consequences surrounding the event are reviewed. Martinez (1980) referred to a "double bind" situation whereby treatment staff are forced to respond with actions that further reinforce the target problem, such as providing attention or forcibly removing the inmate from his or her cell. In such instances, these staff responses clearly reinforce the behavior, as do increased disciplinary sanctions (Martinez, 1980; Toch, 2008).

If this seems confusing, it will be helpful to recall that the definition of positive reinforcement is any consequence that increases or maintains an individual's behavior, not what someone else thinks it should be. If SIB, feces smearing, destruction of institutional property, or other problem behaviors increase subsequent to disciplinary measures, then a functional analysis of behavior would lead to the conclusion that the individual finds being removed from his or her cell or receiving staff attention (even in an adversarial context, as in a disciplinary hearing) reinforcing.

Formulating a Treatment Plan

Camilleri and McArthur (2008) indicate that a focus on the inmate's needs is central to the formulation of a BTP. The use of labels such as "malingering," "manipulating," "bad," "Axis II," "behavioral," "medication seeking," or "not seriously mentally ill" only serve to keep staff away from exploring underlying motivations for the behavior and developing more creative proactive solutions. These labels should be avoided in both written and verbal communications. Staff must accept that not meeting the inmate's needs in some form will only result in a continuation of maladaptive behaviors. Webb (2001) speaks about the formulation of an appropriate individualized treatment plan that addresses the behaviors at a point where the inmate's wants intersect with the facility's needs. In other words, it is possible to both provide the inmate with a reasoned approximation of what he or she wants and enforce facility rules. This is where compromises and agreements can often be made.

The first step in developing a BTP is to identify the motivation behind the maladaptive behavior. Staff should establish if the inmate is attempting to gain something such as medication, staff contact, or a specific housing unit or is attempting to avoid something such as debt, undesired transfers, or placement in segregation. If the behavior is self-reinforcing and driven by reduction of anxiety, psychiatric interventions should be considered, along with other interventions that may help reduce anxiety (e.g., deep-muscle relaxation or breathing exercises). If inmates are simply asked what they need, they may be able to articulate specific goals, and this can help form the therapeutic contract. Whether or not this is helpful, careful observation and measurement of what precedes the target behavior (the antecedents) and what follows it (the consequences) will be necessary.

The BTP should be jointly created by all parties, including the inmate, and framed as a written plan in clear, understandable language to minimize misunderstanding or sabotage later on. It should include parameters that are clear to everyone and should be specific to the inmate-patient. It should not be a boilerplate strategy used for others. It can be seen as a working contract that may be open to renegotiation as needed (i.e., if the initial plan fails). Lane (2009) proposes that correctional mental health clinicians consult with correctional administrative, custodial, and healthcare staff to communicate and use the information gained from motivational/behavioral assessments as part of a multidisciplinary decision-making process that would affect an inmate's housing, management, programming, and treatment disposition.

When developing a BTP, it is crucial to help the inmate recognize potential options that he or she has in choosing behaviors. This highlights that the inmate has some control and responsibility and can exercise this control to slow things down and adjust his or her behaviors. It is perfectly acceptable for the treatment team to propose or consider nontraditional rewards that are contingent on the absence of maladaptive behaviors. When the inmate adjusts his or her behavior, it becomes clear to everyone, including the inmate-patient, that the behavior is manageable. With the disruptive inmate, successful BTPs require flexibility. Those relatively few inmates in any correctional setting whose behavior is of the nature and frequency described in this chapter will ultimately exert a degree of control over staff's behavior (e.g., forcing them to respond with attention or other interventions) through these actions unless such flexible responses can disrupt their rigid behavioral patterns.

The challenge to staff is to develop progressive strategies to reinforce more adaptive behaviors according to an arrangement upon which all parties have agreed. This strategy is consistent with the National Commission on Correctional Health Care's (NCCHC; 2008) National Standard MH-G-06, which specifies that it is appropriate for mental health staff to provide behavioral consultation to staff on mental health issues including behavioral and disciplinary problems. This strategy is also consistent with legal mandates that speak to collaboration when dealing with the mentally ill and potential discipline within correctional settings. Inmates who self-injure or are otherwise seriously disruptive often respond poorly to delayed gratification or reinforcement, and therefore BTPs are most likely to be effective when they provide short-term reinforcement and have clear operational definitions (Martinez, 1980). The descriptions of the behaviors and contingencies must be written in language that is clear, consistent, and understandable to all. Finalized BTPs should be copied and, at a minimum, provided to the warden or administrator, shift commander, nursing director, and mental health director so that all are aware of what has been agreed upon and so that rewards can be provided consistently and promptly.

Agreed-upon behavioral goals and expectations must be attainable based on a review of the inmate's history and other individual factors. It is not realistic to expect an inmate who self-injures daily or who is disruptive at least every 2 days to be able to go 90 days within the same environment without engaging in these behaviors. BTPs should begin with very short-term expectations of behavioral control (e.g., 2 hours, one shift). As control is demonstrated and rewards provided, these time frames should be expanded as agreed upon. BTPs should also include explicit provisions for rewarding verbalization of needs rather than behavioral displays. Creativity is to be encouraged in identifying potential rewards such as an extra shower, recreation time despite security status, additional recreation time, recreation time outside of the segregation unit, taking a walk outside of the unit, individual time with a staff member, access to magazines and books, and property items such as a radio.

Many of the disruptive behaviors described in this chapter often occur in segregation units to protest being housed there, or are prompted by efforts to avoid placement in these units. Placement in segregation units is typically for a set period of time such as 30 days but may last for many months. For some inmates, their impulsivity and inability to employ adaptive problem-solving skills lead to continued disruptive behaviors and, consequently, increased lengths of stay in these units. This fixed approach to segregation placement is not effective for the few who engage in such extreme behaviors. Several alternative strategies are presented next. In general, however, BTPs should be reward-focused and emphasize a shorter time frame to disrupt the cycle of frustration, acting out, and further sanctions. In cases that include extreme physical risk, negative consequences such as removal of potentially dangerous items, such as eating utensils, may be appropriate as long as there is a contingency for returning such items as soon as possible; that is, once the danger of further harm has been eliminated. Table 14.2 contains a summary of the benefits of BTPs.

Table 14.2   Benefits of Behavioral Treatment Plans

- Foster inmate collaboration versus resistance
- Increase positive relations between correctional and mental health staff
- Increase positive relations with multiple disciplines
- Increase appropriate utilization of inpatient cells/outside hospitalization
- Stop pushing against maladaptive behaviors
- Build trust between inmate and staff
- Increase frustration tolerance of the inmate and the system

Sample Behavioral Treatment Strategies

Although currently considered nontraditional, below are several unique sample behavioral treatment strategies that might be considered when working with disruptive inmates.

In some cases, eliminating maladaptive behaviors may be achieved by not responding to the inmate's disruptive behavior or by giving the inmate's disruptive behavior minimal attention, a process known as *extinction*. For example, returning a self-injuring inmate to the same cell following an episode of self-injury may reduce the reinforcing value of placing the inmate in the infirmary. Early recommendations included never returning a self-injuring inmate to his or her original cell (Martinez, 1980). However, inmates can self-injure in any setting, and a lack of transfer actually may limit the reinforcement and be more likely to extinguish the behavior.

The maintenance of a behavior is the product of reinforcing stimuli such as social attention from staff (Webb, 2001). Webb (2001) describes a successful case in a super-max setting where the BTP involved the careful nonreinforcement (i.e., through selective nonattention) of problem behaviors along with the careful and clear reinforcement of the target behaviors when they occurred. Attention for adaptive behavior should be included in the plan. In this manner, timely and individually developed BTPs can reduce morbidity and extinguish behaviors, resulting in a safer environment for all (Jeglic et al., 2005).

Another option is to utilize infirmary and/or outside hospital placements, where economically feasible, as a planned respite for a period of adaptive functioning, if this appeals to the inmate-patient. This is an intervention that makes the transfer contingent on a defined period of adaptive functioning whereby the desired reward is achieved through inmate-initiated adaptive behaviors. The rationale is that without inmates' feeling a sense of control, they will probably manage to get to these desired settings through escalating the very behaviors that correctional workers are seeking to extinguish. Accordingly, when such a strategy is proposed, it must be explained clearly that such placement will be contingent on bed space and that the inmate can expect the ability to use this strategy to become less frequent.

Another strategy is to make adjustments to segregation times, whether through reductions or staggered segregation schedules. Many disruptive inmates owe tremendous amounts of segregation time that have been accumulated over time. For these inmates, it may be helpful to make a deal whereby 15 days could be completed rather than 6 months. Such reward would be contingent on an absence of the maladaptive behaviors for that time period. Allowing inmates to receive 2 or 3 days' credit for each adaptive day is also an option. Effectiveness has also been shown in allowing inmates to be housed in segregation during the week and in general population during the weekend.

All of these strategies are designed to instill a sense of control within the inmate-patient based on behaving appropriately, that is, as specified in the treatment plan. With an opportunity to achieve rewards, the inmate-patient will learn how to control some features of his or her environment appropriately, which will lead to a reduction in the experience of punishment and perhaps generalize to other situations. Table 14.3 contains a sample BTP that incorporates a sampling of the strategies described above.

Table 14.3   Sample Behavioral Treatment Plan

Maladaptive (Target) Behaviors:
 	
Identify and measure baseline (preintervention) rates of occurrence:
 	
  1. Fecal smearing (one time/day)
  2. Cutting (up to 10 times/day, but without bleeding)
  3. Flooding of the cell (three times/week)

Formulate Treatment Contract:
 	
  Identify staff involved; include inmate-patient in writing of plan
 	
  All parties identify and agree on specific behavior changes and contingencies (rewards for appropriate behavior; consequences for inappropriate behavior)

Short-Term Goals: Reduce the maladaptive behaviors by 50% over the next 7 days

Long-Term Goals:
 	
  Elimination of maladaptive behaviors
 	
  Eliminate utilization of infirmary unit
 	
  Eventual return to general population

Plan:
 	
• Cell placement nearest to officers' station on segregation unit
• Attention to be given to inmate-patient whenever he or she is observed *not* to be engaging in any inappropriate behavior
• Reading materials after one shift of adaptive behavior
• Institutional clothing after 1 day of adaptive behavior
• Upon no maladaptive behavior Monday through Friday, the inmate will be housed in the infirmary for the weekend at his request. This will be offered four times contingent on available bed space
• After 1 week of adaptive behavior, inmate will be allowed:
    ○ Access to art materials
    ○ Work out with gym equipment
• For each day of adaptive behavior, 3 days of segregation time will be suspended
• Upon transfer to general population, inmate will
    ○ Receive a job of his or her choice if available
    ○ Be able to attend all available programming

Other Contingencies (Nonreinforcement of Inappropriate Behavior):
 	
  If inmate requires medical attention, responding staff will only engage in conversation necessary to providing physical treatment to reduce reinforcing inappropriate behavior as much as possible
 	
  If placed on continuous observation, the assigned staff conducting the watch will have only necessary conversation with the inmate

Combined Interventions

Although BTPs can be effective, their effectiveness may be increased substantially when they are combined with other treatment modalities including medication and more cognitively oriented interventions. These additional treatment strategies might be helpful in increasing impulse control, in overcoming skill deficits, or in addressing underlying mental health issues. For example, breathing exercises, deep muscle relaxation, challenging irrational assumptions, and/or behavioral skills training (e.g., social skill training or assertiveness training) may each assist the inmate in gaining more control over impulses. Pharmacological interventions with or without hospitalization might be appropriate where psychosis is involved, especially when command hallucinations to act aggressively towards oneself and/or others are involved (see Chapter 7 for more information about psychopharmacological interventions). Linehan's (1993) book, *Cognitive-Behavioral Treatment of Borderline Personality Disorder*, provides an excellent conceptual integration of a range of cognitive and behavioral interventions, as well as the use of psychotropic medications, for patients with borderline personality disorder, although the practical applicability of this treatment-intensive approach to a general population correctional setting is questionable.

Obstacles to Best Practices

In this section, some of the potential obstacles to developing and implementing BTPs are discussed.

Past Practices: Finding an Alternative to Punishment

Consistent with the admonition to be firm, fair, and consistent in the treatment of inmates, correctional systems have guidelines that mandate specific, standardized procedures, including the imposition of penalties, in response to institutional rule violations. This approach works in most situations with most inmates, at least over the short term (Byrne & Hummer, 2007). However, it is well documented that punishment is not effective for promoting long-term behavioral changes (e.g., Amos, 2004).

In fact, punishment of disruptive institutional behaviors sometimes results in an ongoing power struggle and an escalation of the problem behaviors. This has largely to do with the emphasis on controlling the behavior of an unwilling participant and/or the emphasis on punishing unwanted behavior rather than rewarding appropriate behavior. Toch (2008) suggests that behavioral management plans (i.e., behavior control strategies implemented by staff without inmate consent) that emphasize punishment serve to intensify inmates' resentment and solidify their resistance, even when they lead to surface compliance. There certainly is little reason to expect an "ah-ha" moment with the extremely disruptive or aggressive inmate unless the situational circumstances within the institution change for the inmate.

Therefore, in planning behavioral interventions, it is the task of the mental health professional to consult with and convince wardens and other staff stakeholders that the inmate is ultimately controlling things through disruptive behaviors, and that a departure from traditional responses, that is, a collaborative approach that emphasizes positive reinforcement, is necessary. Standards of care, such as those offered by NCCHC (2008) and the American Correctional Association (2004), as well as features of settlement agreements and consent decrees from other jurisdictions, provide useful leverage for moving correctional systems away from sole reliance on traditional punitive custodial practices and toward the development of more flexible and effective behavioral treatment strategies. A collaborative approach that appreciates and incorporates both effective custody and mental health practices tailored to the inmate's functional level can result in successful and long-lasting behavioral change for the inmate and a smoother, more efficient correctional operation.

Staff Resistance

There may be potential differences between the assumptions under which mental health providers approach offenders and the standard correctional management approach. The former focuses on individual differences, whereas the latter stresses uniformity (i.e., equal standards and treatment for all). These philosophies can sometimes be difficult to reconcile in practice; it is often difficult for correctional workers to serve mental health care and correctional functions simultaneously. In particular, mental health care providers are likely to prioritize the institution's rehabilitation mission and a positive approach (as consistent with the learning theory emphasis on reward rather than punishment), broadly speaking. Most staff, particularly those in custody, must consider safety and security as paramount. As a result, they are likely to rely on short-term, punishment-oriented approaches, as dictated by institutional policy and applied consistently and objectively; and they are likely to resist deviations from these policies suggested by mental health clinicians.

Mental health care providers should bear in mind that BTPs depend on the cooperation of other staff, for whom the concept of the prisoner as patient, or healthcare consumer, may be utterly foreign. Hence, in formulating BTPs, it is vital to bear in mind that staff must be persuaded that BTPs have value and will benefit both the inmate and the institution. Additionally, staff must be reinforced for their cooperation. Ideally, wardens and other high-level administrators support these programs and recognize staff for their contributions.

Mental health, medical, and correctional staff may express apprehension that meeting one inmate's needs and making exceptions to standard correctional practices via BTPs will result in other inmates doing the same thing, the perceived failure of the system, the perception of inmates being in control, and the perception of giving in. However, this apprehension can easily be countered with the notion that when these behaviors are not properly treated, they can have a dramatic impact on facility operations, including increased staff injury and the canceling of visits, programs, recreation, and other activities important to inmates. Additionally, with regard to control issues, it is the chronically disruptive inmate who ultimately controls things anyway (e.g., provoking use of force, compelling staff to expend more time in paperwork) through his or her behavior. The key is to accept that current punitive strategies are not effective with this group of disruptive offenders and to attempt strategies that may prove more effective.

Cost-Benefit

The time and labor investments in BTPs are greater over the short term, that is, during the baseline and early implementation phases, whereas the reward to staff, in terms of improved behavior, may take considerable time. For example, assessment is continuous and requires ongoing observation and recording of the target behavior(s), so that the effectiveness of the intervention, once introduced, can be determined. During the earlier phases of the program, there may be no improvement in behavior or even an exacerbation of the problem, until and unless the inmate-patient responds favorably to the changed circumstances, that is, the intervention. Hence, staff should be prepared to exercise patience and consistency, and rewards (positive reinforcement) for *staff* involvement (e.g., through awards, letters of commendation placed in personnel files) should be built into these programs.

Obtaining Informed Consent

Finally, there is the challenge of obtaining the inmate-patient's cooperation in the BTP. Without the inmate's cooperation, any attempt at behavioral change would be considered a traditional behavior management plan, and as previously noted, with such plans there is the danger of increasing inmate resistance, the frequency of disruptive behaviors, and an adversarial relationship between staff and inmates. If the inmate can be persuaded to become an active partner in the treatment process; can see value in developing alternative, more acceptable behavioral patterns; and can be convinced to work collaboratively with staff, then behavioral change through BTPs becomes possible and more likely to succeed. Hence, if the inmate's cooperation cannot be obtained, perhaps because maintaining the control that exercising the problem behavior affords him or her is extremely reinforcing, or because no adequate reinforcement for more appropriate behavior can be found, it is recommended that a BTP be introduced on a much smaller scale. Perhaps in this instance, a first step would be to build trust through a small verbal agreement such as providing out-of-cell time for a shift of adaptive behaviors. Whereas formal signed contracts may not be needed if a verbal agreement can be obtained, it is important to ensure that the inmate is involved in the plan. As previously noted, improperly designed behavioral interventions can exacerbate problem behaviors.

Summary and Conclusions

This chapter has focused on disruptive inmate behaviors as well as possible motivations for these behaviors. It has reviewed treatment strategies designed to ensure safety and security through a collaborative approach designed to reduce these behaviors. The challenge for correctional staff is to reshape inmate demands into something acceptable to the institution through the reinforcement of appropriate, adaptive behaviors. Most systems can find the balance between care and safety in the service of change and good outcomes, as long as there is collaboration and clear communication. It is clear that in addition to those who meet typical criteria for serious mental illness, there is a small group of inmates with personality disorders or other mental health symptoms whose extreme behaviors require unique interventions based on behavioral principles. Although these interventions may be time- and labor-intensive and may meet initial resistance from correctional staff, their long-term benefits may warrant their use with some offenders when more traditional correctional management techniques prove ineffective.

While the "mad" versus "bad" dilemma has a long history in corrections, behaviors attributed to either must be addressed collaboratively and based, at least in part, on behavioral principles. Recent standards of care, legal cases, and heightened awareness are moving correctional facilities toward making accommodations for those whose mental illness or symptoms (e.g., impulsivity) prohibit them from progressing within the framework of traditional correctional practices. This is leading to best practices as detailed in this chapter. Although several obstacles still exist, mental health professionals are encouraged to consult with other staff to promote innovative and flexible strategies for treatment of the chronically disruptive inmate. These extreme behaviors present an opportunity to unite staff on behalf of successful behavioral interventions rather than divide them with continued frustration.

KEY TERMS

Disruptive behavior

"Mad" versus "bad" dichotomy

Antecedent conditions

Behavioral consequences

Positive reinforcement

Punishment

Behavioral treatment program/plan

Behavioral management program/plan

Personality disorder

Antisocial personality disorder

Borderline personality disorder

Self-injury

Impulsivity

Maladaptive behavior syndrome

Functional behavioral assessment

Baseline behavior

Informed consent

DISCUSSION QUESTIONS

1. Differentiating between inmates whose behavior is determined by serious mental illness versus criminal intent has been a long-standing correctional practice. Discuss the benefits and problems with using this approach.

2. You are the mental health provider responsible for developing a behavioral treatment plan (BTP) for an inmate who displays a variety of disruptive behaviors, including self-injurious behavior (SIB). When you propose your plan, the warden says, "We shouldn't give extra rewards to inmates to get them to follow the rules." What would you say to convince the warden to try your plan?

3. When you propose your BTP, the captain (the chief of custody) says, "That's too much work. My staff is already very busy." What would you say to convince the captain to try your plan?

4. An inmate repeatedly cuts himself, sometimes seriously enough to require stitches. You propose a BTP and ask him to agree on treatment goals. He says, "The only thing I want is to go back to the psychiatric hospital, because it's better than doing time here. I'll keep cutting myself until you send me or until I bleed out." What do you do? Should you revise the proposed BTP, send him to the hospital, or do something else?

5. An inmate who engages in disruptive behavior (including, but not limited to, SIB) agrees to a BTP, but is known to have a psychotic disorder. How might this affect your plan?

References

American Correctional Association. (2004). *Performance-based standards for adult local detention facilities* (4th ed.). Alexandria, VA: Author.

American Psychiatric Association. (2000). *Diagnostic and statistical manual of mental disorders* (4th ed., Text Revision). Washington, DC: Author.

Amos, P. A. (2004). New considerations in the prevention of aversives, restraint, and seclusion: Incorporating the role of relationships into an ecological perspective. *Research & Practice for Persons With Severe Disabilities, 29,* 263–272.

Black, D. W., Gunter, T., Allen, J., Blim, N., Arndt, S., Wenman, G., et al. (2007). Borderline personality disorder in male and female offenders newly committed to prison. *Comprehensive Psychiatry, 48,* 400–405.

Borrill, J., Snow, L., Medlicott, D., Teers, R., & Paton, J. (2005). Learning from "near misses": Interviews with women who survived an incident of severe self-harm in prison. *The Howard Journal, 44,* 57–69.

Brooker, C., Repper, J., Beverley, C., Ferriter, M., & Brewer, N. (2002). *Mental health services and prisoners: A review.* Sheffield, UK: Mental Health Task Force.

Byrne, J., & Hummer, D. (2007). In search of the "tossed salad man" (and others involved in prison violence): New strategies for predicting and controlling violence in prison. *Aggression and Violent Behavior, 12,* 531–541.

Camilleri, P., & McArthur, M. (2008). Suicidal behaviour in prisons: Learning from Australian and international experiences. *International Journal of Law and Psychiatry, 31,* 297–307.

Daffern, M., & Howells, K. (2007). Antecedents for aggression and the function analytic approach to the assessment of aggression and violence in personality disordered patients within secure settings. *Personality and Mental Health, 1,* 126–137.

DeHart, D. D., Smith, H. P., & Kaminski, R. J. (2009). Institutional responses to self-injurious behavior among inmates. *Journal of Correctional Health Care, 15,* 129–141.

Fagan, T. J., Cox, J., Helfand, S., & Aufderheide, D. (2010). Self-injurious behavior in correctional settings. *Journal of Correctional Health Care, 16,* 48–66.

Fornells, A. R., Capdevila, J. M. L., & Andres-Pueyo, A. (2002). Personality dimensions and prison adjustment. *Psicothema, 14*(Suppl.), 90–100.

Hare, R. D. (2006). Psychopathy: A clinical and forensic overview. *Psychiatric Clinics of North America, 29,* 709–724.

Hillbrand, M., Krystal, J. H., & Sharpe, K. S. (1994). Clinical predictors of self-mutilation in hospitalized forensic patients. *Journal of Nervous and Mental Disease, 182,* 9–13.

Holton, S. M. B. (2003). Managing and treating the mentally ill offender in jails and prisons. In T. J. Fagan & R. K. Ax (Eds.), *Correctional mental health handbook* (pp. 101–122). Thousand Oaks, CA: Sage.

Jeglic, E. L., Vanderhoof, H. A., & Donovick, P. J. (2005). The function of self-harm behaviors in a forensic population. *International Journal of Offender Therapy and Comparative Criminology, 49,* 131–142.

Karten, S. J. (1991). The relationship of borderline personality disorder, problem-solving ability, and anxiety to self-cutting behavior of prison inmates. *Dissertation Abstracts International, 52,* 4977.

Komarovskaya, I., Loper, A. B., & Warren, J. (2007). The role of impulsivity in antisocial and violent behavior and personality disorders among incarcerated women. *Criminal Justice and Behavior, 34,* 1499–1515.

Lane, E. (2009). Identification of risk factors for self-injurious behavior in male prisoners. *Journal of Forensic Sciences, 54,* 692–698.

Lewis, C. F. (2000). Successfully treating aggression in mentally ill prison inmates. *Psychiatric Quarterly, 71,* 331–343.

Linehan, M. (1993). *Cognitive-behavioral treatment of borderline personality disorder.* New York, NY: Guilford.

Lohner, J., & Konrad, N. (2006). Deliberate self-harm and suicide attempt in custody: Distinguishing features in male inmates' self-injurious behavior. *International Journal of Law and Psychiatry, 29,* 370–385.

Lovell, D. (2008). Patterns of disturbed behavior in a supermax population. *Criminal Justice and Behavior, 35,* 985–1004.

Martinez, M. E. (1980). Manipulative self-injurious behavior in correctional settings: An environmental treatment approach. *Journal of Offender Counseling, Services and Rehabilitation, 4,* 275–283.

National Commission on Correctional Health Care. (2008). *Standards for mental health services in correctional facilities.* Chicago, IL: Author.

Oquendo, M. A., & Mann, J. J. (2000). The biology of impulsivity and suicidality. *Psychiatric Clinics of North America, 23,* 11–25.

Shea, S. (1993). Personality characteristics of self-mutilating male prisoners. *Journal of Clinical Psychology, 49,* 576–585.

Skeem, J. L., Miller, J. D., Mulvey, E., Tiemann, J., & Monahan, J. (2005). Using a five-factor lens to explore the relation between personality traits and violence in psychiatric patients. *Journal of Consulting and Clinical Psychology, 73,* 454–465.

Snow, L. (1997). A pilot study of self-injury amongst women prisoners. *Issues in Criminological and Legal Psychology, 28,* 50–59.

Toch, H. (2008). Punitiveness as behavioral management. *Criminal Justice and Behavior, 35,* 388–397.

Trestman, R. L. (2000): Behind bars: personality disorders. *Journal of American Academy of Psychiatry and Law, 28,* 232–235.

Trestman, R. L., Ford, J., Zhang, W., & Wiesbrock, V. (2007). Current and lifetime psychiatric illness among inmates not identified as acutely mentally ill at intake in Connecticut's jails. *Journal of the American Academy of Psychiatry and Law, 35,* 490–500.

Tucker, W. (1999). The "mad" vs. the "bad" revisited: Managing predatory behavior. *Psychiatric Quarterly, 70,* 221–230.

Wagaman, G. L. (2003). Managing and treating female offenders. In T. J. Fagan & R. K. Ax (Eds.), *Correctional mental health handbook* (pp. 123–143). Thousand Oaks, CA: Sage.

Wang, E., & Diamond, P. (1999). Empirically identifying factors related to violence risk in corrections. *Behavioral Sciences and the Law, 17,* 377–389.

Webb, L. R. (2001). *Addressing severe behavior problems in a "super-max" prison setting.* Retrieved August 1, 2008, from National Institute of Corrections: http://www.nicic.gov/Library#016869

Young, M. H., Justice, J. V., & Erdberg, P. (2006). Risk of harm: Inmates who harm themselves while in prison psychiatric treatment. *Journal of Forensic Sciences, 51,* 156–162.

CHAPTER 15

Understanding the Broad Corrections Environment

Responding to the Needs of Diverse Inmates

Alix M. McLearen and Philip R. Magaletta

Introduction

As the number of incarcerated persons continues to increase, diverse groups within the inmate population begin to emerge and reflect aspects of diversity appearing within the general U.S. community. Although certain socioeconomic or racial groups are overrepresented in prison settings (Clear, 2007), correctional populations remain anything but homogeneous. Although the corrections literature is now replete with well-articulated best practice approaches for the general treatment and management of offenders (e.g., the use of cognitive-behavioral therapy [CBT]), these principles and standards are broad-based at best. In addition, corrections scholars are placing increased emphasis on the importance of individualized treatment based on effective principles and responsive application of these principles to the emergent, diverse inmate groups and their specific needs (Andrews & Bonta, 1998; Clements & McLearen, 2003).

For today's correctional mental health practitioners, developing an understanding of the emergent and diverse inmate groups they will be called upon to serve is essential. The corrections literature in this area continues to expand, and this volume is a testament to the vast amount of information now available. Nonetheless, a broad range of subgroups—both related to psychiatric diagnosis and not—exist within correctional populations about whom little has been considered or written.

The views expressed in this chapter are those of the authors only and do not necessarily reflect the views or opinions of the Department of Justice or the Federal Bureau of Prisons. Special appreciation is extended to Dr. Robert K. Ax, who provided the content of a text box in this chapter. Views expressed by Dr. Ax are his alone and do not necessarily represent those of the authors or the Federal Bureau of Prisons.

This chapter identifies several of these diverse inmate groups and suggests areas where intervention may be needed. The perspective is taken that understanding the literature concerning emergent, diverse inmate groups helps guide corrections practitioners. It does so by supporting the clinical considerations and custodial concerns that these practitioners are challenged with daily as they serve these groups of inmates. Because the most expensive and labor-intensive resources for the clinical care and custody of any inmate group are *human resources*, special consideration is given to the training of staff and the need to generate further information and knowledge that can be later used to refine and develop coherent treatment approaches and systems of care.

As noted, the U.S. correctional population is incredibly diverse and multifaceted. Numerous diagnostic, socioeconomic, and issue-driven groups and subgroups exist. In selecting geriatric, death penalty, traumatic brain injury (TBI), military, noncitizen, and terrorist groups, the authors attempt to describe those that have the greatest impact on resource utilization from both clinical and management perspectives. In addition, these groups have been explored in the literature, thus allowing relevant data to be provided to the reader. Future investigation into the diversity of correctional subpopulations may include, for example, such groups as transgendered inmates, which are not discussed in this chapter. In each section of this chapter, the population is introduced via demographic and other relevant background information. Clinical and management concerns are then presented, although they vary significantly among groups. Finally, training needs related to the care and custody of each population are discussed. Clearly, enhanced partnerships between the correctional and academic communities would lead to greater knowledge on all of these populations. Thus, the chapter concludes with a tabular display of potential research directions for each group covered herein (see Table 15.1 on page 344).

Geriatric Inmates

Demographic and Background Issues

One inmate group that has grown significantly over time is the elderly. As life spans outside the correctional setting have lengthened, so too have those within the prison walls. Longer sentences resulting from policy changes in the 1980s such as the "War on Drugs" and "three strikes" legislation have led to larger numbers of persons spending significantly longer periods of time under correctional supervision. Thomas, Thomas, and Greenberg (2005) also cite mandatory minimum sentencing guidelines and "get tough on crime" policies as adding to this outcome. Older inmates face a host of issues both different from and in addition to those of their younger counterparts. Aside from health issues associated with aging, they may begin to examine life choices that led to prolonged incarceration. In addition, victimization and assisted living needs may need to be addressed with these inmates, and although they may or may not have been sanctioned with a life sentence, end-of-life issues are common.

Prior to detailed discussion of the clinical considerations that may appear in response to this inmate group, it is important to define the inmates being discussed. A 2008 Pew Center on the States study noted that 1 in 100 Americans is presently incarcerated, but only 1 in 837 adults over the age of 55 fits into this category. For some racial or ethnic groups, this number is much higher. For example, among African American males, 1 in 115 persons over the age of 55 was incarcerated in 2006 (Sabol, Minton, & Harrison, 2007). Thomas et al. (2005) cite a 300% growth in the number of prisoners over age 50 between 1990 and 2005. Such a change is not consistent with the overall proportion of elderly in the American population, which remained relatively constant between 1990 and 2000 (Centers for Disease Control and Prevention, 2004). In reporting information pertaining to geriatric issues in prisons, definitional criteria vary. For the remainder of this section, geriatric inmates will be considered to be those aged 50 or older, with specific ages used when referencing empirically derived data.

Often referred to as the "graying" of the inmate population, the phenomenon of increasing numbers of elderly persons in prisons and jails has been associated with incremental increases in healthcare costs. In the community, older adults present with greater health-related needs, including hospitalization and prescription drug needs. In prison, these issues are magnified and accelerated, due to lifestyle issues such as drug use, violence, and poverty often associated with those incarcerated (Walters, 1999). Thus, issues commonly addressed in the community during a later developmental period (i.e., age 85 or older) may require intervention during an earlier developmental period with prison populations and/or may occur at a higher rate. For example, high rates of HIV/AIDS, hepatitis, and other blood-borne or sexually transmitted diseases and pathogens occur in correctional populations (see Allen, 2003; Hogben & Lawrence, 2000; Kaiser Network, 2008). Mitka (2004) argues the combination of harsh living conditions and inadequate preventative service utilization over the lifetime accelerates the process of aging among prisoners, such that a 50-year-old inmate may be biologically equivalent to a noninmate 10 to 15 years senior.

Clinical and Management Concerns

It is common knowledge that healthcare needs are correlated, albeit indirectly, with age. For example, hospitalization days increase threefold in the community among persons aged 65 and older compared to younger persons (American Hospital Association, 2003). In the aftermath of *Estelle v. Gamble* (1976), nearly all hospitalization, outpatient and other healthcare costs required by the inmate are the responsibility of the incarcerating body. Recent findings suggest significant growth in prison healthcare costs, which now account for a large proportion of correctional spending (Pew Center on the States, 2008). Some authors have suggested inmates in prison actually live longer than community counterparts due to increased access to healthcare and monitored quality of that care (Winkelman, 2007).

As noted, healthcare needs of the aging inmate may be myriad. Thomas et al. (2005) divide these healthcare needs into a dichotomy of those brought to the prison environment as a result of the criminal lifestyle and those that occur as a result of the aging process. Regardless of etiology, the care of the inmate becomes the responsibility of the prison as a whole whether the presenting problem is cancer, AIDS, or syphilis. It has been suggested that the average older offender suffers from at least three chronic health problems (Aday, 1994). Although physicians and their staff primarily treat many of these illnesses, associated features of these issues often become the focus of mental health professionals. For example, mental health clinicians in correctional settings may be tasked with developing interventions for chronic pain, sleep disturbance, and mood symptoms occurring secondary to the medical diagnosis.

Aside from psychological facets of medical syndromes, elderly inmates also may require treatment or mental health contact related to life-stage issues. For example, aging models (e.g., Erikson, 1963) suggest older adults reach a point in life where reexamination of life choices and/or search for purpose and meaning become paramount. Although these stages are considered to be normal parts of the aging process, it is suggested that prisoners who are aging, possibly dying in prison, and are separated from families may find the search for meaning more troubling than their free-world cohorts. Familiarity with such models and empirically supported interventions related to these issues may not be common among correctional providers, given findings suggesting fewer than 5% of psychologists specialize in geriatric service provision (Gatz, Karel, & Wolkenstein, 1991).

Another area in which correctional mental health professionals may provide treatment to older prisoners is actual psychiatric diagnosis. A fairly robust finding in correctional samples relates to the prevalence of major mental illnesses. Specifically, up to 15% to 16% of incarcerated persons are thought to meet criteria for major depressive disorder, bipolar disorder, or schizophrenia (Diamond, Wang, Holzer, Thomas, & Cruser, 2001; Ditton, 1999; Magaletta, Diamond, Faust, Daggett, & Camp, 2009). What is not known, however, is what proportion of these individuals are among the geriatric population of the prison. Ditton (1999) estimated mental illness occurs at a rate of 8.9% to 15.6% in prison inmates over age 55, with higher rates in jails. Disorders with chronic courses are known to lessen with regard to positive symptom display with age, which should not be taken to mean that intervention or monitoring is no longer needed. In addition, in community samples, rates of depression, including new onset of mood disorder symptoms, are fairly high among elderly persons. Thienhaus (2007) summarizes empirical findings suggesting the presentation of depressive symptoms among older adults may appear significantly different from the constellation observed among middle-aged persons. For example, depressed mood and anhedonia may be replaced with anger and anxiety. Pain is the primary somatic complaint, and nearly all cognitive functions are likely to show some kind of decline or decrease (Thienhaus, 2007). In elderly patients, failure to intervene appropriately with depressive issues can lead to other serious medical conditions, including death (House, Knapp, Bamford, & Vail, 2001).

Other mental health conditions associated with the aging process fall into the spectrum of cognitive disorders. Elderly inmates may be at increased risk for victimization or falling, resulting in potential TBI (discussed later in this chapter). Dementia or other symptoms of cognitive decline typically seen in nursing home settings may need to be addressed among geriatric inmates. Thienhaus (2007) notes that demented inmates typically come to the attention of mental health professionals as a result of disruptive behavior associated with cognitive decline. Intervention techniques require significant environmental controls (Cohen-Mansfield, 2001).

In prison, the eldest members of geriatric inmate groups also may be at increased risk of victimization due to inability to defend themselves. Figures on elder abuse in noncorrectional settings show staggering rates of victimization and neglect and include financial, physical, or even self-victimization (see Office of Justice Programs, 2008). Although data are not available, one can surmise that confused or physically weak persons would be at significant disadvantage in a correctional setting and, therefore, subject to potential physical, sexual, or financial predation.

Even those inmates who serve much of their sentences without physical or mental health abnormalities eventually may show signs of deterioration in extreme old age. Little data are available on the functionality of these individuals in prison settings, but clinical considerations for long-term care of elderly inmates by correctional mental health practitioners can be drawn from community-based literature. Hartz and Splain (1997) address three therapeutic approaches for managing long-term care residents: supportive therapy, reminiscence therapy, and validation therapy. The two former approaches may be considered for persons trying to make sense of their existence, grappling with their life choices and with growing old in prison. The authors suggest such interventions may be of assistance in moderating depressive symptoms. Validation therapy, on the other hand, is described as being developed specifically for patients with dementia. This information is not to suggest providers move away from evidence-based

CBT approaches with correctional patients but simply to note that in much older inmates, the focus of treatment may shift from targeting criminogenic needs to solving problems, finding meaning, and tolerating discomfort.

The mental and physical well-being needs of geriatric inmates typically integrate well with the clinical care and custodial concerns regarding assisted living and palliative care needs. Federal and state prisons have documented hospice care programs in which inmates are trained to care for one another much as in community hospice settings. Such a program at the Louisiana State Penitentiary has provided anecdotal evidence of the positive effect this sort of care has on both the dying inmate and his caregiver (Stolberg, 2001). Although data collection is needed, other factors identified as being key to palliative care program success are not beyond the scope of prison settings (Boothby, 2007; Byock, Twohig, Merriman, & Collins, 2006).

With regard to confinement issues that may require additional attention among the elderly, it is clear that nearly all areas of functioning are affected by age. Thienhaus (2007) identifies nine core areas on which to focus, many of which have been addressed in this chapter: medical care, diet/nutrition, disability needs, victimization, inmate assistance, work and exercise, disciplinary procedures, transitional services, and end-of-life care. In addition, the author suggests that an interdisciplinary approach involving mental health, medical, food service, recreation, religious service, correctional, and management staff is most likely to lead to the best outcomes for geriatric inmates. If at all possible, specialty units and/or facilities should be considered, particularly given the projected growth of this segment of the inmate population. Many facilities already offer some sort of separate housing for geriatric inmates (Aday, 1994), but little current data exist on the availability, functionality, or effectiveness of such models.

Training Needs

Curricula on issues related to eldercare should be considered for inclusion in annual or initial training sessions for all staff. As noted, even within mental health fields, few practitioners specialize in eldercare, and those persons are not necessarily employed in the correctional setting. Thus, specialty training for mental health and medical professionals needs to be requested and represents a best practice. Such training should include general training on the needs of elderly persons not specific to the correctional environment, as well as training on applying this information to the prison setting (Knight, Karel, Hinrichsen, Qualls, & Duffy, 2009). Custody and other correctional personnel also must receive basic training on geriatric needs. For example, an officer working in a housing unit for elderly inmates may be required to perform more frequent area checks, work more closely with medical staff, or supervise inmate workers and prevent predation. Staff must also be made aware of such phenomena as sundowning (increased confusion as the day progresses into evening) and understand the difference between purposeful defiance and organically caused confusion and irritability.

Death Penalty Inmates

Demographic and Background Issues

At the end of 2008, 3,309 individuals were on death row in the United States (Death Penalty Information Center [DPIC], 2009a).[1] Thirty-five states, the U.S. military, and the federal government presently have statutes allowing for execution. Pursuant to the

Kennedy v. Louisiana (2008) decision, there continues to be conflict relating to imposition of the death penalty for nonhomicide offenses (DPIC, 2009a). In 2008, 37 executions occurred in the United States, marking the lowest number in a 14-year downward trend (DPIC, 2009a).[2]

As of April 2009, 131 death row inmates had been exonerated for their crimes (DPIC, 2009a). In addition, since 1973, exonerations from death row have occurred at a rate of three to five per year (DPIC, 2009a). Despite these many exonerations, the number of persons on death row remains relatively constant over time, given that the average time spent on death row is 11 years, 5 months (Policy Almanac, n.d.).

In looking at the demographics of U.S. death row inmates, conventional wisdom holds that African American defendants are overrepresented. Although it is true that a large number of African Americans have been executed, the majority of death row inmates are White (DPIC, 2009a). Males constituted approximately 98.3% of death row inmates in 2006 (Bureau of Justice Statistics [BJS], 2006). Much like the graying of the prison population, statisticians are finding a graying of death row inmates, and in 2005, 137 inmates awaiting capital punishment were aged 60 or older (DPIC, 2009b). Other demographic information regarding death row inmates from 2006 include a mean education level of 11th grade and an average age of 28 at time of arrest (BJS, 2006). Most were divorced or had never been married, and 65.5% had prior felony convictions (BJS, 2006).

With regard to case law, death penalty issues are addressed regularly in state and federal venues. Of particular interest to mental health professionals are cases such as *Roper v. Simmons* (2005), which finally removed the United States from the company of China, Iran, and Pakistan by prohibiting the execution of minors. The Supreme Court also has banned the execution of mentally retarded individuals (*Atkins v. Virginia*, 2002), but although execution of mentally ill persons has been limited (*Ford v. Wainwright*, 1986), it has not been banned. An exhaustive review of the many legal issues surrounding the death penalty in the United States and the international community is beyond the scope of this chapter. Instead, the focus here will be on describing the needs of the individuals on death row, the types of clinical work that may occur with them, and the range of issues such work may raise for the correctional mental health practitioner.

Clinical and Management Concerns

For the mental health practitioner, death penalty cases often involve ethical considerations. Both psychological and medical/psychiatric professional association codes contain language relating to beneficence, but members are not barred specifically from any involvement in death penalty cases. In fact, historically, physicians were involved in the development of early execution practices. The guillotine was developed by a medical doctor as a humane form of implementing the death penalty, and in 1887, American physicians fought to replace hanging with electrocution for similar reasons (Matthews & Wendler, 2006). In modern practice, clinicians can be involved in mitigation or consultation, but they are most likely involved in death penalty cases as pretrial evaluators, postconviction treatment providers, or competency to be executed examiners (Eisenberg, 2004; McLearen & Zapf, 2007).

Pretrial (competency to stand trial) evaluators are cautioned to be thoroughly familiar with ethical and legal standards, as well as to have obtained training commensurate with the seriousness of the matter in potential death penalty cases. Eisenberg (2004) recommends such evaluations should be comprehensive and address all areas of competency, not simply competency to proceed with the trial. Once the inmate has been convicted, evaluation again is often required to determine whether the individual is competent to face execution. As noted, the Supreme Court held that persons incapable of understanding the nature of the penalty should not be executed (*Ford v. Wainwright*, 1986). No clear standard of incompetence was set, resulting in differing jurisdictional definitions of who is and is not eligible to be executed. Several authors have suggested specific standards for the completion of such examinations (Heilbrun, 1987; Zapf, Boccaccini, & Brodsky, 2003). Although some have espoused all participation in such proceedings to be unethical, more commonly, persons are simply encouraged to be well trained and to examine personal values prior to engaging in these professional activities (Bonnie, 1990; Eisenberg, 2004).

With more than 3,000 inmates currently on death row, one can conclude that many correctional staff and mental health professionals work with inmates facing death. Although the methods are somewhat different, correctional mental health professionals may be involved with both the management and treatment of this population. Woodford, Petrakis, and Stojkovic (2005) devote significant attention to successful management of inmates in a death row unit based on the model utilized in the California penal system. These authors highlight "incentive-based programming, strict adherence to safety and security safeguards, and an interdisciplinary approach" as necessary components of effective management of this population (Woodford et al., 2005, p. 17). In addition, legal access, visiting privileges, and phone usage are noted as being necessary (Woodford et al., 2005). Even within a death penalty unit, classification procedures are needed. Based on risk factors, inmates should be allotted time out of cell or other privileges involving social interaction. Training of staff who will work with these inmates is very important, and emphasis should be placed on understanding the difficulty both inmates and staff face in promoting dignity and hope in such a setting.

Earlier in this section, it was pointed out that the average death-sentenced inmate spends more than a decade awaiting execution after sentencing. During this time, it is conceivable that inmates on death row would be subject to at least the same level of medical and mental health problems as inmates in the general population. Clinicians should also remain cognizant of other issues that may arise. For example, similar to other populations facing death in prison, inmates on death row may seek supportive or grief counseling to deal with their impending death, the loss of loved ones, or guilt over their criminal activities. The DPIC (2009b) also describes a condition known as "Death Row Syndrome" in which lengthy periods of time between sentencing and punishment of death row inmates result in suicidality, delusional ideation, or loss of contact with reality. Suicide risk is a legitimate concern among death row inmates, despite the fact that many are seeking to remain alive. Thus, clinicians in this setting must be skilled in suicide risk assessment and able to rely on information regarding behavioral change provided by correctional staff.

The nexus between evaluation and treatment of death row inmates occurs with regard to cases in which an individual begins to demonstrate psychological deterioration while on death row. At some point, without proper intervention, such an individual could become incompetent for execution. In this scenario, the provider is faced with choosing to participate in treatment, which could ultimately lead to a person's death, or refusing treatment, which could allow the person to potentially suffer or commit suicide. In *Singleton v. Norris* (2003), the Eighth Circuit Court of Appeals supported the forcible medication of inmates solely for the purpose of restoring competency for execution. Matthews and Wendler (2006) discuss the ethicality of both positions and find support for treating and not treating incompetent death row inmates, but they ultimately return the decision to the moral and ethical standards of the individual practitioner.

Self-awareness and self-care are important components of being a competent treatment provider, and ethical practice warrants that clinicians recognize limits and burnout. Nonetheless, there are few settings in which these issues take on more importance than in death penalty work. Persons engaging in these professional activities are encouraged to seek supervision and/or counsel on a regular basis and to participate in regular, continuing education to ensure they remain abreast of current laws, trends, and ethical updates.

Training Needs

Mental health professionals involved with death penalty inmates should be trained in this area via both coursework and supervised clinical experience. Given the serious nature of this work, ongoing supervision/discussion with a colleague is an advised practice. Knowledge of the legal system and understanding of the limits of confidentiality must be sound. Providers should be required to participate in regular training on these issues. Staff who are not mental health professionals also should participate in training regarding the special needs of this population as well as ways in which to manage anxiety about working in a capital sentence unit. (See Text Box 15.1 for the views of one clinical psychologist who has worked on death row.)

TEXT BOX 15.1
BEST PRACTICES IN PROVIDING SERVICES TO DEATH-SENTENCED OFFENDERS

As a psychologist (and death penalty opponent) who worked on a capital sentence unit (for the State of New Jersey Department of Corrections), I believe this population presents some unusual ethical concerns that should be considered carefully prior to accepting an assignment to work with death-row inmates. This is a group, who, in the state's eyes, is beyond rehabilitation. Hence, to seek mutually acceptable goals as the basis of psychotherapy implies the possibility of working in opposition to the government's interest in merely managing inmates until appeals are exhausted and they can be executed. A particular example is that of collaborating toward the instillation of hope for survival (e.g., a commutation of sentence) with patients who may need to do the bulk of their legal work themselves: To achieve therapeutic success is to challenge the legal system.

Psychologists and other psychotherapists who choose to take on such work should first have a clear and explicit understanding with all parties concerned as to the nature and purpose of the assignment. For example, the expectations of and legal obligations to the administration and the state with respect to issues of confidentiality, such as record-keeping and consultation with colleagues, must be well defined. Therapeutic contracts should be explicit. The avoidance of one particular dual relationship is important to note in this case: Capital-sentence unit mental health care providers must be excluded from assessing these inmates, whether or not they have been patients, for competence to be executed. (Robert K. Ax, personal communication, August 21, 2009)

Inmates With Traumatic Brain Injury

Demographic and Background Issues

Recent findings suggest inmates with a history of TBI may be more common than was once thought (e.g., Slaughter, Fann, & Ehde, 2003). This section seeks to identify who these inmates are, how they may come to the attention of correctional staff, and what interventions may be effective with them given their presence in correctional settings.

The brain is the center for all human thought, behavior, and emotion. Thus, a person who has incurred a brain injury may display deficits in any number of areas including memory, motor activity/coordination, concentration, impulse control, affective stability, planning, intrapsychic resource management/self-awareness, learning, and aggression. Injury to the brain can occur prenatally, a phenomenon often referred to as congenital damage. Although similar impairments may be noted in individuals with these sorts of injuries, these individuals are typically diagnosed in childhood and therefore may avail themselves of interventions. In contrast, individuals with acquired brain injury, of which TBI is one example, are often underdiagnosed and therefore may not even know they have experienced brain damage (Sosin, Sniezek, & Thurman, 1996; Thurman, Alverson, Dunn, Guerrero, & Sniezek, 1999).

TBI generally refers to injury that is either caused by a significant or forceful blow to the brain (closed-head injury) or one in which the head or brain is penetrated by an object (open-head injury). Injury classification can range from mild to severe, and multiple injuries can have a cumulative effect, increasing functional impairment (Levin et al., 1987). TBI rates are highest among males and low-income groups. Violence, firearms, and substance use are often correlated with TBI (Corrigan, 1995; Thurman et al, 1999; Turkstra, Jones, & Toler, 2003). Often crime and TBI are interrelated. The very behaviors and situations involved in criminal activity are often the causes of TBI. For example, consider gangs, which often require physical violence as a prerequisite to membership, or the number of substance-induced accidents often found in an inmate's psychosocial history. In addition, there has been some suggestion that head injury may be a precursor to criminal activity. Studies involving minors convicted of crimes show a pattern of preexisting head injury (Leon-Carrion & Ramos, 2003; Timonen et al., 2002).

Large-scale, quality epidemiological studies related to TBI in correctional populations have yet to be conducted. Instead, most studies to date are from small and/or biased samples, use divergent operationalizations of brain injury, and rely heavily on self-report data. Keeping these limitations in mind, the fact remains that large numbers of inmates appear to have experienced TBI. In a study of jail inmates, 87% reported a past TBI, with 29% reporting having experienced a moderate to severe injury (Slaughter et al., 2003). In this same sample, inmates with TBI were more likely to experience comorbid mental health conditions and to score higher on anger and aggression measures. Barnfield and Leathem (1998) found similar rates of TBI in a New Zealand prison population, where 86.4% of the sample described at least one head injury and 56.7% reported more than one TBI.

Clinical and Management Concerns

As noted, the severity of head injury can vary significantly, and thus the resulting manifestations of the trauma may vary as well. Due to individual differences, the same injury could impact two brains differently. Barring significant injuries that lead to disfigurement or obvious deficits, many lasting effects of TBI go undetected or are misdiagnosed. Thus, correctional personnel may overlook the possibility that a seemingly defiant, lazy, or otherwise problematic inmate may, in fact, be coping with the outcome of a TBI.

Correctional staff may notice TBI effects in three areas of inmate behavior: motor ability, cognition, and mood (Magaletta, Diamond, McLearen, & Denney, 2010). These areas overlap to a degree, but each presents separate challenges to the officer or mental health practitioner attempting to manage an already complex and volatile population. Delays in motor ability may impact both speech and other gross motor behaviors. Responses to direction may appear slow or inaccurate, and staff may not have the knowledge or time to parse deficit from defiance. Other inmates, as well, may be less than tolerant of such deficits. Consider, for example, the high premium placed on sanitation in correctional settings. Inmates with TBI may be less capable of conforming to such standards and may face not only sanctions from staff for procedural violations but also informal ostracism or even violence from other inmates for their deficiencies.

Perhaps more common and more disruptive are compromised executive functioning abilities, which fall under the domain of cognition. For example, attention or memory issues may cause impairment in the ability to understand and follow instructions or even long-standing procedures. Inmates who fail in these areas may be seen as behavior management problems and find themselves in segregation or higher security facilities, where they are even less likely to demonstrate adaptive success. Due to problems of engaging in planning, these individuals also may show decreased rates of appropriate community reintegration or even time management while incarcerated.

Mood issues resulting from TBI also may pose significant problems for the correctional environment. Studies have suggested that aggression may increase after head injury (Brooks, Campsie, Symington, Beattie, & McKinlay, 1986). Impulse control also may be compromised significantly (Young, Justice, & Erdberg, 2004). Thus, it is easy to envision a minor verbal altercation escalating into violence as the result of emotional liability caused by TBI. Furthermore, environmental cues may be misinterpreted due to TBI that predisposes toward aggression, and therefore violent responses may follow neutral stimuli.

Aside from domain-specific deficits, there is a complex relationship between mental illness and brain injury. Foremost, many of the same symptoms are seen resulting from organic and acquired brain injuries and illnesses. In addition, mentally ill or cognitively impaired persons are more likely to engage in the behaviors that cause brain injury, such as aggression. Finally, persons with mental illness show increased rates of mental disorder. For example, up to 80% of TBI patients develop some form of mental illness (Hibbard, Uysal, Kepler, Bogdany, & Silver, 1998; Koponen et al., 2002), and rates of psychosis, anxiety, and depression are particularly high. Thus, inmates with TBI often present with a complicated set of treatment needs.

Mental health professionals tasked with managing or treating this diverse inmate group should do so at two levels: screening and intervening. As noted earlier, many persons with TBI do not appear "different" in any way and often do not know themselves that a TBI could be at the root of some of their criminal or other maladaptive actions. Thus, medical and mental health departments need to work collaboratively to establish a process for identifying TBI (Fowles, 1988; Magaletta et al., 2010). It is suggested this screening occur, at a minimum, at intake and again in the aftermath of any violent incidents during the incarceration period. The screening should be conducted by qualified mental health and/or medical staff. Questionnaires exist for detecting and categorizing head injury in this population, such as the Traumatic Brain Injury Questionnaire (TBIQ; Diamond, Harzke, Magaletta, Cummins, & Frankowski, 2007). Although an empirically validated instrument is obviously the preferred measure, in the absence of such a tool, clinicians are advised to query inmates about their history of head injury in some standardized way. Caution should be expended with regard to the phrasing of clinical interview questions. For example, inmates are likely to provide vastly different responses to "Have you ever sustained a traumatic brain injury?" and "Have you ever hit your head really hard?"

Once a screening procedure has been established, it is important that the information gleaned from this process is put to use in treating or managing the inmates identified. Simply training staff to engage in universal sound correctional management (respectful, directive, simplified communications, for example) is likely to impact this population positively. For those inmates identified as having deficits related to TBI, the ideal solution is placement in a residential program designed specifically for brain-injured inmates and adhering to CBT principles. Given the lack of availability of such programs in most correctional systems, Magaletta et al. (2010) suggest that individual treatment with these individuals address impulse control, communication, and decision making. Monitoring of the adaptation these persons make to the prison environment is important to ensure problems are addressed early rather than after irreversible harm has occurred. Other strategies to consider are placement with inmate tutors/assistants or enrollment in structured groups related to deficit areas.

Training Needs

Although training of staff is important with all populations, it is a quintessential feature of the management of inmates with TBI. In fact, most staff are not likely to be familiar with the terminology, let alone the potential consequences, of brain injury. Certainly, it is not suggested officers engage in clinical assessment. Instead, broad-based training is suggested for all staff that includes definitional information as well as descriptions of the kinds of deficits most commonly observed in TBI populations. Curricula also should include simple tips for addressing those deficits and may be made easy by presentation in tabular form (see Magaletta et al., 2010). A particular piece of information worthy of highlighting is the need to consider defiance as a possible skill deficit and to respond accordingly. Consultative relationships between custodial staff and mental health professionals should be made clear as part of this training. With regard to mental health professionals, it is essential that these staff have knowledge of TBI. Although this condition may not have been an area of study during graduate training, it behooves any professional working in a correctional environment to seek advanced instruction or supervision in neuropsychological issues.

Training may apply to inmates as well. Outside of therapeutic contacts, custodial staff may be able to train inmates to engage in such adaptive techniques as development of routines to avoid forgetting or use of waiting periods to avoid impulsivity. Certainly, given the deficit of self-awareness associated with TBI, inmates detected during screening as having this condition should be educated about symptoms and provided an opportunity for skills training.

Military Inmates

Demographic and Background Issues

In this section, the characteristics and needs of persons sentenced to serve time in United States Military Prisons are discussed. These individuals typically are active members of the U.S. military who have been accused or convicted of a criminal offense.

Military veterans who were not on active military duty at the time of the offense are not discussed in this section, as they would be incarcerated in standard facilities.

In addition to being subject to the laws of all U.S. citizens, soldiers are responsible for adhering to the tenets of the Uniform Code of Military Justice (n.d.). Violations of any of these regulations can result in incarceration in holding facilities (sometimes referred to in military terminology as "brigs" or "stockades" depending on the branch of service) or, in the case of longer sentences, military prisons. Each branch of the armed forces administers correctional facilities, including some overseas or aboard floating vessels. Males convicted of particularly serious offenses or those serving lengthy sentences are often housed at the U.S. Disciplinary Barracks in Fort Leavenworth, Kansas (USDB), whereas females are housed at NAVCONBRIG Miramar in California. Military inmates may be transferred to the custody of federal facilities when serving longer sentences.

As of April 2001, 1.37 million citizens were on active duty in the U.S. military, and an additional 1.28 million were in ready or reserve status (Defense Almanac, 2003). Of those, only a small proportion is ever incarcerated. The USDB is equipped to hold 515 prisoners, including the nine presently on death row (DPIC, n.d.-a; United States Army Combined Arms Center, n.d.). The U.S. military has not executed a prisoner since 1961 (DPIC, n.d.-a). The small size of the military correctional population is likely related to the military's screening of persons interested in service. Richardson (2003) identifies several of these factors, including the ineligibility of developmentally delayed and seriously medically or mentally ill individuals.

Clinical and Management Concerns

In general, the needs of military prisoners do not differ significantly from those of inmates housed in other federal or state facilities. Educational and vocational programs are offered to inmates, and military correctional personnel may receive specialty training in correctional management (Leeson, 1997). Other unique programs for military prisoners include the service dog training programs offered at Camp Lejeuene (Hershman, 2008).

Facilities for short sentences may be small and are not likely to offer the diversity of groups or other treatment options offered at larger military prisons such as the USDB. Through the Directorate of Treatment Programs, all inmates at the USDB are screened initially by treatment staff, and psychosocial history and relevant assessments are completed (Leeson, 1997). Research conducted at the facility has helped to hone the assessment process (Leeson, 1997), and the Army Corrections Command adheres to best practices approaches, including the adoption of a CBT model for chemical dependency issues (Miller, 2008).

With regard to psychological and/or psychiatric treatment, certain mental health issues may be of particular concern in military populations in which combat experiences may have occurred, such as post-traumatic stress disorder or TBI. Recent media coverage of both these syndromes suggests the likelihood that military psychologists would encounter such conditions. In addition, three facilities specialize in the treatment of sex offenders (Hassenritter, 2008). The sex offender treatment program at Fort Sill, Oklahoma, is a 7-month structured program grounded in CBT for low- to moderate-risk prisoners (Heller, 2008). No data are presently published on the efficacy of this approach. Moral reconation therapy (MRT), another CBT approach originally intended for drug treatment among prison inmates, has been applied to more general criminal thinking among military prisoners. Among a sample of 35 inmates to start the MRT program, 22 completed it. Interpretation of outcome data suggested a possible positive impact but also a need for further intervention (Herndon, 2008).

Training Needs

Although a military correctional system is smaller in size than many other correctional systems, practices suggest staff remain abreast of current information and seek advanced certification. Nonetheless, it is suggested that mental health staff consider developing training partnerships with other, larger agencies to promote the acceptance of identity as correctional mental health professionals and to have access to the resources of larger agencies. The importance of training staff to recognize the manifestations of brain injury has already been discussed, and this standard applies to military settings as well. In addition, training on helping convicted felons on making the transition to civilian life may be useful to staff and could be offered to staff of federal facilities who take custody of military prisoners.

Non–U.S. Citizen Inmates

Demographic and Background Issues

In 2008, 1 in 17 inmates in U.S. federal and state prisons was not a citizen of the United States (West & Sabol, 2009). This number, which translates to 5.8% of the national prison population, represents a diverse group of individuals from numerous ethnicities, dialects, and cultures. Over time, the majority of these individuals have been confined in federal custody, although prison systems in states along the Mexico-U.S. border such as Texas and those with high illegal alien populations also housed a significant proportion of this group. Data from 1995 showed persons of Mexican, Colombian, and Dominican origin to be the most common illegal aliens in federal custody. State data from this same period suggest western states incarcerated large numbers of Mexicans, whereas eastern states had high numbers of persons from the Caribbean and South/Central America (Clark & Anderson, 2000).

Persons who are not native to the United States are subject to the laws of this country, whether they are here legally or illegally. With regard to prison settings, this population can be divided into three subgroups: noncitizens who are here legally and commit a crime, persons whose sole crime is their status as an illegal alien, and persons who are here illegally and have committed an additional crime. In the majority of correctional systems, however, these distinctions are not necessarily relevant to housing decisions, as all three groups will likely be mainstreamed within the general prison population until sentence completion, when transfer to the Department of Homeland Security's Immigration and Customs Enforcement (ICE) Agency for possible deportation will be considered.

This population has received much attention for the costs of incarceration imposed on the American public. In particular, data from the five states with the largest number of incarcerated illegal aliens (Arizona, California, Florida, New York, and Texas) in 2002 and 2003 show expenditures of $1.6 billion related to these individuals, whereas it is estimated $5.8 billion was spent by the federal government on illegal aliens in prison between 2001 and 2004 (Government Accountability Office, 2005). Due to the high costs of incarcerating this population, it may seem cost-effective to limit certain services to those persons not returning to U.S. society. To date, no correctional system has denied essential services to its population based on citizenship, and the authors caution strongly against doing so. Certainly, for mental health professionals, such a practice goes against core ethical principles. At the same time, as will be discussed later, some services in fact may not be offered to non–U.S. citizens.

Clinical and Management Concerns

Although the sociopolitical zeitgeist is important in creating the context of the noncitizen discussion, the focus in this section is on the particular clinical and management needs of the non–U.S. citizen prisoner. Although some generalizations are made with regard to this population, their significant heterogeneity also is highlighted. One shared trait of this population is the unreliability of records pertaining to their behavior, treatment, and care prior to incarceration. Federal and many state prison systems investigate the lifestyle of most prisoners prior to sentencing. This often includes review of mental and medical health records, which then can be used to dictate classification and management decisions. Due to a lack of reliable records, it is foreseeable that non–U.S. citizens may be housed at inappropriate facilities or may otherwise have some unmet needs, which could create problems for prison administration if not identified and addressed.

Two specific examples of problems that may not be initially detected relate to medical and mental health issues. With regard to medical needs, non–U.S. citizens undergo screening for infectious diseases similar to that of all other detainees. Potential problems arise when such issues are not immediately identified, as they can then spread quickly within the closed prison environment. An example can be seen in the H1N1 (swine flu) pandemic that began in early 2009. Given that the highest proportion of illegal aliens in jails is from Mexico, the country in which this illness originated, concern arose about the possibility that contamination could occur prior to the illness being detected. A related issue is the potential for poor healthcare prior to incarceration and/or to entering the United States. As noted in this chapter, healthcare costs constitute a large portion of the correctional budget, and inmates who have not had access to preventive measures are likely to present with a greater number of minor and major illnesses.

With regard to mental health issues, diagnostic taxonomies often rely on time frames, for which historical data are needed. Appropriate interventions may be missed when this information is not available. In addition, in a field where verbal interaction is a primary modality of information sharing, language barriers become of particular significance. This is true not only in reference to diagnosis but also to intervention with mental illness or more minor adjustment issues. The use of a translator, when available, is a remedy, but even then subtle yet important nuances may be missed (see Chapter 6 for further discussion of this point).

The language barrier is not only a concern with regard to treatment. General management requires that inmates understand the rules and directions provided to them. Many facilities now translate most major inmate-related publications into Spanish, but it is financially and otherwise practically unfeasible to translate all documents into hundreds of languages and dialects. Even simple commands and instructions given by unit officers and/or work detail supervisors must be understood, and the inability of correctional staff to communicate with any member of the inmate population clearly represents a fundamental safety concern. An important practice of some agencies is the offering of intensive foreign language training to interested staff, but it is impossible to train all staff in all languages and dialects.

Due to a lack of bilingual staff, certain programs may require English proficiency, thereby disallowing the participation of some foreign-born inmates. Similarly, most correctional systems have a focus on release planning or skills training related to community reentry. Although non–U.S. citizens may be allowed to enroll in such programs, it is not clear whether such programs will benefit these persons. First, many will be deported from this country, and the skills or plans developed will not translate into utility in the country of origin. One program that is attempting to remedy this problem is offered through the country of Mexico and allows U.S. prison inmates to obtain

Mexican education credentials while incarcerated. The success and availability of this program is not yet known.

A final concern, not unique to the non–U.S. citizen prison population, relates to the possibility of gang-related recruiting during incarceration. Gang activity is associated with much of the misconduct and violence that occurs in correctional settings. Certainly, many of the gangs originated in the United States and are made up of citizens of this country. It is of note, however, that many of the identified disruptive groups have high memberships among non–U.S. citizens (Conley & Zobel, 2007). For example, the Florida Department of Corrections identifies six major prison gangs, and four of them are known to recruit persons of Hispanic origin, many of whom may not be U.S. citizens (Florida Department of Corrections, n.d.). Clearly, the needs of this population are myriad, and corrections officials have little ability to follow up with this population after release.

Training Needs

The obvious training need in the management or treatment of non–U.S. citizen inmates relates to the language barrier. Given the diversity of languages spoken in the larger global community, it is not reasonable to expect each facility to have staff speaking every language spoken by inmates. At the same time, it is quite realistic to expect correctional systems to offer language immersion programs to staff in languages or dialects commonly spoken among prison populations (Spanish, for example). At the very least, staff should be trained on where to seek translation services, rather than relying on other inmates to translate for them.

A final, related training need is to focus on cultural competencies (see Chapter 6 for a more detailed discussion of this topic). Even when staff cannot understand the language of prisoners under their care, they should have some basic exposure to the different practices and behaviors of persons from other countries. Interpersonal and nonverbal behaviors (e.g., variations in eye contact) as well as common religious and spiritual beliefs should be considered for curriculum inclusion. With regard to mental health professionals in corrections and cultural issues, practitioners may benefit from increasing knowledge of the attitudes of various ethnicities and cultures regarding mental illness and ways to best meet the needs of diverse peoples.

Terrorist Inmates

Demographic and Background Issues

Globally, the number of critical incidents related to terrorism continues to grow, and the individuals responsible for planning and/or committing these acts are becoming increasingly part of the criminal justice systems in Western democratic nations. The corrections professionals within these systems will be challenged to consider the clinical and custodial features associated with the incarceration of these terrorist inmates (Dernevik, Beck, Grann, Hogue, & McGuire, 2009).

As a diverse inmate group, sentenced terrorists may share some features with non–U.S. citizens. Here it is important to recognize that custodial classifications and demographic information are relevant. Typically, a distinction is drawn between domestic and international terrorists, with both citizenship and location of the terrorist plan or act being considered. Whereas both domestic and international terrorists may be identified by similar underlying political motivations, the ideologies they have accepted and the networks they represent may be quite distinct. Importantly, many gradations and confounds with operationalizing terrorism/terrorists exist. Depending upon the operationalization, some authors describe terrorists as overlapping with other groups who commit crimes (Hallett, 2005), whereas others argue that they are distinct from networks of criminals such as gangs (Hamm, 2007; von Tangen Page & Ax, 2007).

Clinical and Management Concerns

What is important to understand from a practitioner perspective is that regardless of definitions, failure to consider the unique management and treatment needs of inmate terrorists can have profound consequences both immediately and over the long term. It should be acknowledged that the foundation of managing terrorist inmates in custody is congruent with the overall mission of corrections agencies. As either presentenced or convicted inmates, the best practices for housing terrorists begin with sound, basic, and exceptionally practiced correctional management techniques. Those clinical and custodial staff with considerable correctional experience and superior service records may have the experience to best manage this group, and this is an important consideration. Due to their militaristic training and lifestyles, terrorist inmates may appear well disciplined and respectful of staff in correctional settings. This raises the risk of lulling staff into a false sense of security. This must be seen against the backdrop that terrorist inmates may be trained to continue harmful activities against the government and its representatives while in custody.

It is also important to note that while in custody all relationships can be observed through correctional management techniques. This presents opportunities to yield valuable information concerning communications taking place and highlighting the networks terrorists represent. This may be used to confirm or explore the links between various individuals and their networks. This aspect of social networks and its appropriateness as a model for understanding how terrorism develops is nicely elaborated by Sageman (2004) and is recommended reading for those interested in deepening their knowledge on this topic.

These custodial concerns are raised first as mental health practitioners may find themselves involved in training and reminding staff to remain cognizant of the risks that terrorist inmates can represent. In addition, there are several other considerations to which practitioners may respond. Although it has been noted that terrorist inmates do not present a greater prevalence of mental health issues than other groups of inmates (Sageman, 2004; von Tangen Page & Ax, 2007), the literature is replete with accounts of such inmates succeeding in hunger strikes as a way of expressing their agenda and discontent (von Tangen Page & Ax, 2007). This is a place for which a mental health practitioner would be called on to assess an inmate's mental health status.

As is true with other specialty populations described in this chapter, the role of screening and assessment with terrorist inmates is paramount. In this area, both mental health status and risk for future violence should be considered. A proper understanding of the role of violence in a terrorist inmate's record, whether it is likely to be impulsive or planned, can lead to more informed strategies of clinical care and custodial approach and technique. Hallett (2005) proposes an interesting schematic that may be used as an exemplary model to understand the terrorist inmate at this individual level. By scaling terrorism acts on a gradient of criminality, a model emerges that suggests more criminally motivated terrorist inmates may benefit from stronger approaches to challenge criminal thinking as a rehabilitative ideal. Such an understanding and model also may be used to conceptualize and develop an understanding of those inmates who may be interested in sharing information with law enforcement (von Tangen Page & Ax, 2007). The emphasis here is on strong case conceptualization, as it may lead to more accurately informed strategies for individual change in the terrorist inmate. Such individual changes may be of benefit to law enforcement authorities and the larger community as a whole.

Training Needs

Clinicians should understand that terrorist inmates, as a group, require consideration at the individual, group, and cultural levels. Training for practice should include an understanding of these broad cultural factors. In particular, clinicians will need to understand how culture influences the degree to which Western mental health service constructs are familiar to the individual terrorist inmate. In the case of domestic terrorists, this issue may need less consideration, while focusing more on understanding if prior mental health services had been received. Training among clinicians should require a deeper understanding of the ways in which elements of the culture, for example, religious beliefs, influence implicit personality theories. This understanding may lead to more informed planning of services beneficial to the mental health of domestic and international terrorist inmates (Smither & Khorsandi, 2009).

As new information becomes available and research on terrorist inmates is conducted, change strategies for and with these inmates may need to be implemented. Because this area is so new, little to no training has ever been offered to practitioners. This is a situation that likely will change over the next decade as a clearer understanding of terrorist inmates unfolds, and it should be noted that continuing education in this area is likely to be the first place in which such training occurs.

Summary and Conclusions

This chapter has attempted to cover a broad range of diverse inmate groups and the ways in which correctional mental health practitioners respond to their needs. There is still much more to be studied, and this will lead increasingly to effective corrections management and treatment strategies. It also is acknowledged that a deeper understanding of what works in addressing the needs of these diverse groups will emerge through the daily work of corrections practitioners (Magaletta, Patry, Dietz, & Ax, 2007). The authors advocate for respecting this voice of practice-based evidence while encouraging corrections scholars, administrators, and practitioners to continue using and developing evidence-based practices.

Finally, new models for thinking about the competencies and skills that must be brought to bear on behalf of these diverse inmate groups are encouraged. This applies to both mental health and custodial practitioners. In the end, it is only through seeing the congruence between and the unique features within diverse inmate groups that effective practices can emerge. These practices require focusing of both clinical and management concerns. Understanding and using the reciprocal relationship between clinical and custodial perspectives, as well as the relationship between clinical skill and the correctional environment, remains the essence of contemporary correctional practice with all diverse and nondiverse inmate groups.

| Table 15.1 | Future Research Directions for Furthering Mental Health Practice Knowledge With Diverse Inmate Groups |

Inmate Group	*Future Research Direction*
Geriatric inmates	• Prevalence and description of certain elder-specific problems are needed. • Pilot work to develop screening instruments detecting certain elder-specific problems is needed. • Explore efficacy of any existing management strategies and treatment program efforts with this group to determine differential outcomes. Results may be useful in building and implementing new management programs. • Theoretically based end-of-life treatment models and how they might be applied to intervention with this population. • For those elderly inmates who will be releasing from prison, research on continuity of care (from prison to home) issues should be a priority.
Death-sentenced inmates	• Little has been written about the impact of death-sentenced inmates on the provider. Thus, the primary recommendation is to develop a mental health services provider perspective. Empirical exploration of these staff issues should be undertaken. • Data on effective therapeutic approaches would be of assistance to clinicians faced with the challenge of treating this population.
Inmates with traumatic brain injury (TBI)	• Given the limited sample sizes and jurisdictions of existing prevalence studies, the actual prevalence of TBI across the range of injury awaits completion. • Screening, assessment, and evaluations of staff training in identification and referral are needed. • Links between TBI and aggressive misconduct (including self-injurious behaviors) remains particularly important given their potential outcomes. • The possible interaction of TBI and treatment attrition from cognitive-behavioral correctional treatment programs, including substance abuse treatment program, should be explored.
Military inmates	• Comparative research on offense types, between branches and across time, is warranted. • Research to develop screening and assessment measures prior to military entry should be pursued.
Non–U.S. citizen inmates	• Barriers to correctional mental health care should be explored for this group. • The efficacy of educational interventions to educate this group about correctional mental health services should be explored and piloted.
Terrorist inmates	• Because aggregate data may be difficult to assemble, the initial development of theoretical models for understanding prevention and intervention within and across terrorist networks should be pursued. • Future research might explore these theoretical underpinnings and determine if they comport with what is known about unhealthy radicalized corrections contexts.

Endnotes

1. The sanction of death as a penalty for criminal wrongdoing has been codified formally since at least the 18th century BCE and was present in early Greek, Roman, and Hittite codes (Death Penalty Information Center [DPIC], n.d.-c; Lifton & Mitchell, 2002; Schabas, 2002). Since that time, executions have occurred by differing means and with varying frequencies throughout the world (see McLearen & Zapf, 2007, for a review). Since the early 17th century, more than 15,000 persons have been executed for crimes in the United States (Acker, Bohm, & Lanier, 1998; DPIC, n.d.-b).

2. The vast majority of executions continue to take place in the South, with approximately one third of capital punishment sentences carried out since 1973 taking place in Texas (DPIC, 2009a). Regardless of information suggesting the death penalty does not act as a deterrent and costs more than incarceration, citizens continue to support the use of the death penalty (DPIC, 2009a; Radelet & Akers, 1996; Urbina, 2009). Although public support for the death penalty remains high, it is declining, and there is a trend toward decreased imposition of capital sentences (DPIC, 2009a). In addition, legal and ethical challenges have led to moratoria on and/or reexamination of the use of the death penalty in several states, and three states have recently abolished the death penalty (see *Baze v. Rees*, 2008; DPIC, n.d.-d; *Hill v. McDonough*, 2006).

KEY TERMS

Cognitive behavioral therapy	Death Row Syndrome	Moral reconation therapy
Death penalty	Geriatric offender	Terrorist
Death row	Intake screening	Traumatic brain injury

DISCUSSION QUESTIONS

1. Which of the diverse inmate groups mentioned share common needs and issues? Explain your answer.

2. Which group is most taxing on the corrections environment and why?

3. Which group stands to benefit the most from increased interaction with mental health professionals?

4. What other groups do you think might pose clinical and/or management concerns for correctional administrators?

5. What management problems are presented when terrorists are housed with other inmates in the general prison population?

References

Acker, J. R., Bohm, R. M., & Lanier, C. S. (1998). Introduction: America's experiment with capital punishment. In J. R. Acker, R. M. Bohm, & C. S. Lanier (Eds.), *America's experiment with capital punishment: Reflections on the past, present, and future of the ultimate penal sanction* (pp. 5–12). Durham, NC: Carolina Academic Press.

Aday, R. H. (1994). Golden years behind bars: Special programs and facilities for elderly inmates. *Federal Probation, 82*, 47–54.

Allen, S. I. (2003, April). *Developing a systematic approach to hepatitis C for correctional systems: Controversies and emerging consensus.* Retrieved August 29, 2009, from http://www.thebody.com/content/art13076.html

American Hospital Association. (2003, July). *Trends affecting hospitals and health systems.* Washington, DC: Author.

Andrews, D. A., & Bonta, J. L. (1998). *The psychology of criminal conduct* (2nd ed.). Cincinnati, OH: Anderson.

Atkins v. Virginia, 536 U.S. 304 (2002).

Barnfield, T. V., & Leathem, J. M. (1998). Incidence and outcomes of traumatic brain injury and substance abuse in a New Zealand prison population. *Brain Injury, 12*, 455–466.

Baze v. Reese, 553 U.S. No. 07-5439 (2008).

Bonnie, R. J. (1990). Dilemmas in administering the death penalty: Conscientious abstention, professional ethics and the needs of the legal system. *Law and Human Behavior, 14*, 67–90.

Boothby, J. L. (2007). Contemporary United States correctional, mental health, and social policy. In R. K. Ax & T. J. Fagan (Eds.), *Corrections, mental health, and social policy: International perspectives* (pp. 41–60). Springfield, IL: Charles C Thomas.

Brooks, N., Campsie, L., Symington, C., Beattie, A., & McKinlay, W. (1986). The five year outcome of severe blunt head injury: A relative's view. *Journal of Neurology, Neurosurgery and Psychiatry, 49*, 764–770.

Bureau of Justice Statistics. (2006). *Capital punishment 2006 statistical tables.* Retrieved March 15, 2009, from http://www.ojp.usdoj.gov/bjs/pub/html/cp/2006/tables/cp06st05.htm

Byock, I., Twohig, J. S., Merriman, M., & Collins, K. (2006). Promoting excellence in end-of-life care: A report on innovative models of palliative care. *Journal of Palliative Medicine, 9*, 137–151.

Centers for Disease Control and Prevention. (2004). *Health care in America: Trends in utilization.* Retrieved April 9, 2009, from http://www.cdc.gov/nchs/data/misc/healthcare.pdf

Clark, R. L., & Anderson, S. A. (2000). *Illegal aliens in federal, state, and local criminal justice systems summary.* Washington, DC: Urban Institute. Retrieved on April 15, 2008, from http://www.urban.org/publications/410366.html

Clear, T. R. (2007). Impact of incarceration on community public safety and public health. In R. Greifinger (Ed.), *Public health behind bars* (pp. 13–24). New York, NY: Springer.

Clements, C. B., & McLearen, A. M. (2003). Research-based practice in corrections: A selective review. In T. J. Fagan & R. K. Ax (Eds.), *Correctional mental health handbook* (pp. 273–302). Thousand Oaks, CA: Sage.

Cohen-Mansfield, J. (2001). Nonpharmacologic interventions for inappropriate behaviors in dementia: A review, summary, & critique. *American Journal of Geriatric Psychiatry, 9*, 361–381.

Conley, J. K., & Zobel, D. (2007). Prison gangs. In R. K. Ax & T. J. Fagan (Eds.), *Corrections, mental health, and social policy: International perspectives* (pp. 275–294). Springfield, IL: Charles C Thomas.

Corrigan, J. (1995). Substance abuse as a mediating factor in outcome from traumatic brain injury. *Archives of Physical Medicine & Rehabilitation, 76*, 302–309.

Death Penalty Information Center. (2009a). *Facts about the death penalty.* Retrieved April 20, 2009, from http://www.deathpenaltyinfo.org/FactSheet.pdf

Death Penalty Information Center. (2009b). *Time on death row.* Retrieved April 20, 2009, from http://www.deathpenaltyinfo.org/time-death-row#drs

Death Penalty Information Center. (n.d.-a). *Executions in the military.* Retrieved April 25, 2009, from http://www.deathpenaltyinfo.org/executions-military

Death Penalty Information Center. (n.d.-b). *Executions in the U.S. 1608-2002: The Espy file.* Retrieved March 15, 2009, from http://www.deathpenaltyinfo.org/executions-us-1608-2002-espy-file

Death Penalty Information Center. (n.d.-c). *Part I: History of the death penalty.* Retrieved March 15, 2009, from http://www.deathpenaltyinfo.org/part-i-history-death-penalty

Death Penalty Information Center. (n.d.-d). *States with and without the death penalty.* Retrieved June 21, 2009, from http://www.deathpenaltyinfo.org/states-and-without-death-penalty

Defense Almanac. (2003). *DOD at a glance.* Retrieved April 21, 2009, from http://www.defensegov/pubs/almanac/

Dernevik, M., Beck, A., Grann, M., Hogue, T., & McGuire, J. (2009). The use of psychiatric and psychological evidence in the assessment of terrorist offenders. *Journal of Forensic Psychiatry & Psychology, 20,* 508–551.

Diamond, P. M., Harzke, A. J., Magaletta, P. R., Cummins, A. G., & Frankowski, R. (2007). Screening for traumatic brain injury in an offender sample: A first look at the reliability and validity of the Traumatic Brain Injury Questionnaire (TBIQ). *Journal of Head Trauma Rehabilitation, 22,* 330–338.

Diamond, P. M., Wang, E. W., Holzer, C. E., Thomas, C. R., & Cruser, D. A. (2001). The prevalence of mental illness in prison: Review and policy implications. *Administration and Policy in Mental Health, 29,* 21–40.

Ditton, P. M. (1999). *Mental health and treatment of inmates and probationers* (Bureau of Justice Statistics Special Report). Retrieved April 30, 2009, from http://www.ojp.usdoj.gov/bjs/pub/ascii/mhtip.txt

Eisenberg, J. R. (2004). *Law, psychology, and death penalty litigation.* Sarasota, FL: Professional Resource Press.

Erickson, E. H. (1963). *Childhood and society.* New York, NY: Norton.

Estelle v. Gamble, 429 U.S. 97 (1976).

Florida Department of Corrections. (n.d.). *Major prison gangs.* Retrieved May 9, 2009, from http://www.dc.state.fl.us/pub/gangs/prison.html

Ford v. Wainwright, 477 U.S. 399 (1986).

Fowles, G. P. (1988). Neuropsychologically impaired offenders: Considerations for assessment and treatment. *Psychiatric Annals, 18,* 692–697.

Gatz, M., Karel, M. J., & Wolkenstein, B. (1991). Survey of providers of psychological services to older adults. *Professional Psychology: Research and Practice, 22,* 413–415.

Government Accountability Office. (2005). *Information on criminal aliens incarcerated in federal and state prisons and local jails.* Washington, DC: Author.

Hallett, B. (2005). Dishonest crimes, dishonest language: An argument about terrorism. In F. M. Moghaddam & A. J. Marsella (Eds.), *Understanding terrorism* (pp. 49–67). Washington, DC: American Psychological Association.

Hamm, M. S. (2007). *Terrorist recruitment in American correctional institutions: An exploratory study of non-traditional faith groups.* Washington, DC: National Institutes of Justice.

Hartz, G. W., & Splain, D. M. (1997). *Psychosocial intervention in long-term care: An advanced guide.* New York, NY: Haworth.

Hassenritter, D. (2008). Military corrections and ACA evolve together. *Corrections Today, 70*(6), 8, 10.

Heilbrun, K. (1987). The assessment of competency for execution: An overview. *Behavioral Sciences and the Law, 5,* 383–396.

Heller, M. L. (2008). Sex offender rehabilitation: Educating correctional cadre. *Corrections Today, 70*(6), 42–45.

Herndon, B. T. (2008). Meaningful action and moral reconation therapy. *Corrections Today, 70*(6), 50–51, 55.

Hershman, C. L. (2008). Inaugural marine prison dog program assists wounded veterans. *Corrections Today, 70*(6), 46–49.

Hibbard, M. R., Uysal, S., Kepler K., Bogdany J., & Silver, J. (1998). Axis I psychopathology in individuals with traumatic brain injury. *Journal of Head Trauma Rehabilitation, 13,* 24–39.

Hill v. McDonough, 547 U.S. 573 (2006).

Hogben, M., & St. Lawrence, J. S. (2000). HIV/STD risk reduction in prison settings. *Journal of Women's Health and Gender-Based Medicine, 9,* 587–592.

House, A., Knapp, P., Bamford, J., & Vail, A. (2001). Mortality at 12 and 24 months after stroke may be associated with depressive symptoms at one month. *Stroke, 32,* 696–701.

Kaiser Network. (2008). *HIV in correctional settings: Implications for prevention and treatment policy.* Retrieved March 25, 2009, from http://img.thebody.com/kaiser/2008/prison_amfar.pdf

Kennedy v. Louisiana, 554 U.S. No. 07-343 (2008).

Knight, B. G., Karel, M. J., Hinrichsen, G. A., Qualls, S. H., & Duffy, M. (2009). Pikes Peak model for training in professional geropsychology. *American Psychologist, 64,* 205–214.

Koponen, S., Taiminen, T., Portin, R., Himanen, L., Isoniemi, H., Heinonen, H., et al. (2002). Axis I and Axis II psychiatric disorders after traumatic brain injury: A 30-year follow-up study. *American Journal of Psychiatry, 159,* 1315–1321.

Leeson, B. A. (1997). The United States Disciplinary Barracks and military corrections. In R. G. Lande & D. T. Armitage (Eds.), *Principles and practice of military forensic psychiatry* (pp. 239–268). Springfield, IL: Charles C Thomas.

Leon-Carrion, J., & Ramos, F. J. (2003). Blows to the head during development can predispose to violent criminal behavior: Rehabilitation of consequences of head injury is a measure for crime prevention. *Brain Injury, 17,* 207–216.

Levin, H. S., Mattis, S., Ruff, R. M., Eisenberg, H. M., Marshall, L. F., Tabaddor, K., et al. (1987). Neurobehavioral outcome following minor head injury: A three-center study. *Journal of Neurosurgery, 66,* 234–243.

Lifton, R. J., & Mitchell, G. (2002). *Who owns death? Capital punishment, the American conscience, and the end of executions.* New York, NY: HarperCollins.

Magaletta, P. R., Diamond, P. M., Faust, E., Daggett, D., & Camp, S. D. (2009). Estimating the mental illness component of service need in corrections: Results from the mental health prevalence project. *Criminal Justice and Behavior, 36,* 229–244.

Magaletta, P. R., Diamond, P., McLearen, A. M., & Denney, R. (2010). Traumatic brain injury in correctional populations. In S. Stojkovic (Ed.), *Managing special populations in jails and prisons* (Vol. 2, pp. 2–15). Kingston, NJ: Civic Research Institute.

Magaletta, P. R., Patry, M. W., Dietz, E. F., & Ax, R. K. (2007). What is correctional about clinical practice in corrections? *Criminal Justice and Behavior, 34,* 7–21.

Matthews, D., & Wendler, S. (2006). Ethical issues in the evaluation and treatment of death row inmates. *Current Opinions in Psychiatry, 19,* 518–521.

McLearen, A. M., & Zapf, P. A. (2007). The death penalty: A brief review of historical roots and current practices relevant to the correctional mental health practitioner. In R. K. Ax & T. J. Fagan (Eds.), *Corrections, mental health, and social policy: International perspectives* (pp. 295–319). Springfield, IL: Charles C Thomas.

Miller, K. N. (2008, December). The army corrections command: Bringing it all together. *Corrections Today, 70*(6), 52–54.

Mitka, M. (2004). Aging prisoners stressing healthcare system. *Journal of the American Medical Association, 292,* 423–424.

Office of Justice Programs. (2008). *Elder crime and victimization.* Retrieved from http://www.ojp.usdoj.gov/ovc/ncvrw/2005/pg5h.html

Pew Center on the States. (2008). *One in 100: Behind bars in America 2008.* Retrieved March 15, 2009, from http://www.pewcenteronthestates.org/uploadedFiles/8015PCTS_Prison08_FINAL_2-1-1_FORWEB.pdf

Policy Almanac. (n.d.). *Capital punishment 2000.* Retrieved September 27, 2006, from www.policyalmanac.org/crime/archive/bjs_capital_punishment.shtml

Radelet, M. L., & Akers, R. L. (1996). Deterrence and the death penalty: The views of the experts. *Journal of Criminal Law and Criminology, 87,* 1–16.

Richardson, L. (2003). Other special offender populations. In T. J. Fagan & R. K. Ax (Eds.), *Correctional mental health handbook* (pp. 199–216). Thousand Oaks, CA: Sage.

Roper v. Simmons, 543 U.S. 551 (2005).

Sabol, W. J., Minton, T. D., & Harrison, P. M. (2007). *Prison and jail inmates at midyear 2006.* Washington, DC: Bureau of Justice Statistics. Retrieved March 25, 2009, from http://ojp.usdoj.gov/bjs/pub/pdf/pjim06.pdf

Sageman, M. (2004). *Understanding terror networks.* Philadelphia: University of Pennsylvania Press.

Schabas, W. A. (2002). *The abolition of the death penalty in international law* (3rd ed.). Cambridge, UK: Cambridge University Press.

Singleton v. Norris, 319 F. 3d 1018 (8th Cir. 2003).

Slaughter, B., Fann, J. R., & Ehde, D. (2003). Traumatic brain injury in a county jail population: Prevalence, neuropsychological functioning and psychiatric disorders. *Brain Injury, 17,* 731–741.

Smither, R., & Khorsandi, A. (2009). The implicit personality theory of Islam. *Psychology of Religion and Spirituality, 1,* 81–96.

Sosin, D. M., Sniezek, J. E., & Thurman, D. J. (1996). Incidence of mild and moderate brain injury in the United States, 1991. *Brain Injury, 10,* 47–54.

Stolberg, S. G. (2001, April 1). Behind bars, new effort to care for the dying. *The New York Times,* p. 1.

Thienhaus, O. J. (2007). Geriatric patients. In O. J. Thienhaus & M. Piasekci (Eds.), *Correctional psychiatry: Practice guidelines and strategies* (pp. 16-1 to 16-10). Kingston, NJ: Civic Research Institute.

Thomas, D. L., Thomas, J. A., & Greenberg, S. (2005). The graying of corrections—The management of older inmates. In S. Stojkovic (Ed.), *Managing special populations in jails and prisons* (pp. 11-1 to 11-18). Kingston, NJ: Civic Research Institute.

Thurman, D. J., Alverson, C., Dunn, K. A., Guerrero, J., & Sniezek, J. E. (1999). Traumatic brain injury in the United States: A public health perspective. *Journal of Head Trauma Rehabilitation, 14,* 602–615.

Timonen, M., Mieuttunen, J., Hakko, H., Zitting, H., Veijola, J., & von Wendt, L. R. P. (2002). The association of preceding traumatic brain injury with mental disorders, alcoholism and criminality: The Northern Finland 1966 Birth Cohort Study. *Psychiatry Research, 113,* 217–226.

Turkstra, L., Jones, D., & Toler, H. L. (2003). Brain injury and violent crime. *Brain Injury, 17,* 39–47.

Uniform Code of Military Justice. UCMJ, 64 Stat. 109, 10 U.S.C., Chap. 47 (n.d.).

United States Army Combined Arms Center. (n.d.). *U.S. Disciplinary Barracks.* Retrieved April 25, 2009, from http://usacac.army.mil/CAC2/usdb/

Urbina, I. (2009, February 25). Citing cost, states consider end to death penalty. *The New York Times.* Retrieved March 4, 2009, from http://www.nytimes.com/2009/02/25/us/25death.html

von Tangen Page, M., & Ax, R. K. (2007). Prison policy and terrorism: Learning the lessons of the past. In R. K. Ax & T. J. Fagan (Eds.), *Corrections, mental health, and social policy: International perspectives* (pp. 259–274). Springfield, IL: Charles C Thomas.

Walters, G. D. (1999). *The addictions concept.* Needham Heights, MA: Allyn & Bacon.

West, H. C., & Sabol, W. J. (2009). *Prison inmates at midyear 2008—Statistical tables.* Washington, DC: Bureau of Justice Statistics. Retrieved April 18, 2009, from http://www.ojp.usdoj.gov/bjs/pub/pdf/pim08st.pdf

Winkelman, C. (2007, January 24). Prison death rate lower than population. *Oakland Tribune.* Retrieved April 5, 2009, from http://findarticles.com/p/articles/mi_qn4176/is_20070124/ai_n17151235/

Woodford, J. S., Petrakis, S. M., & Stojkovic, S. (2005). Managing death row. In S. Stojkovic (Ed.), *Managing special populations in jails and prisons* (pp. 17-1 to 17-16). Kingston, NJ: Civic Research Institute.

Young, M. H., Justice, J. V., & Erdberg, P. (2004). Assault in prison and assault in prison psychiatric treatment. *Journal of Forensic Science, 49,* 1–9.

Zapf, P., Boccaccini, M., & Brodsky, S. (2003). Assessment of competency for execution: Professional guidelines and an evaluation checklist. *Behavioral Sciences and the Law, 21,* 103–120.

The Future of Correctional Mental Health Practice

CHAPTER 16

Correctional Mental Health

A Best Practices Future

Robert K. Ax

Introduction

The ideas, facts, and recommendations presented in the preceding chapters form a solid foundation for an empirically grounded, "best practices" future of correctional mental health research and practice. What remains, a task necessarily limited by the complexity of the issue and the available space, is to offer a few final thoughts concerning two related questions:

- What are the social, economic, legal, and political factors—that is, the context—impacting the future of correctional mental health for better or worse?
- Given the real-world context in which mental health professionals must function, how could "best practices" prisons and jails be characterized, and how can "best practices" mental health services be provided there?

The Context of Correctional Mental Health

"That we are in the midst of crisis is now well understood. Our nation is at war, against a far-reaching network of violence and hatred. Our economy is badly weakened, a consequence of greed and irresponsibility on the part of some, but also our collective failure to make hard choices and prepare the nation for a new age. Homes have been lost; jobs shed; businesses shuttered. Our health care is too costly; our schools fail too many; and each day brings further evidence that the ways we use energy strengthen our adversaries and threaten our planet."

—From President Barack Obama's Inaugural Address
January 20, 2009

The American public expresses concern about inmates, and supports rehabilitation, according to recent survey results (Krisberg & Marchionna, 2006). A tentative consensus has emerged supporting prison reform across the political spectrum. For example, in addition to the liberal interests and groups that have been pressing a variety of reform issues for decades, the National Drug Control Strategy (Office of the White House, 2008), issued under the auspices of President George W. Bush, noted the importance and effectiveness of drug courts in diverting nonviolent offenders from incarceration and into treatment programs. Recent legislation, such as the Second Chance Act of 2007, cosponsored by both Democrats and Republicans, is another example of the bipartisan appeal of prison reform. This law promotes community reentry and rehabilitation and, to a lesser extent, alternatives to incarceration. More generally, this might be seen to augur well for the provision of a range of correctional services, including those characterized as "correctional mental health."

Yet the American prison population continues to rise. By a considerable margin, the United States has the world's highest incarceration rate, at 738 per 100,000. Second on the list is the Russian Federation with 607 per 100,000. Other Western nations' incarceration rates—for example, those of the United Kingdom (145 per 100,000), Australia (126 per 100,000), Canada (107 per 100,000), and France (88 per 100,000)—are considerably lower (Hartney, 2006). (More recent data put the U.S. incarceration rate at 762 per 100,000 at midyear 2008; West & Sabol, 2009.) Although some states have recently experienced small decreases in the numbers of prisoners in their correctional systems, trends in other state systems, as well as the federal prison system, have offset this decrease (West & Sabol, 2009). Why is this? In part, the answer lies in the fact that focusing on the treatment of individuals already in jail or prison does not in and of itself entail broader reforms of the laws and policies that produce these large numbers in the first place. If, for example, laws exist under which large numbers of drug users are charged with crimes that carry lengthy prison sentences, then many of these individuals will go to prison, and there they must depend on whatever drug treatment services are available in a setting where healthcare is necessarily subordinate to safety and security missions. Successful completion of prison programs—"rehabilitation"—may be unrelated to the prospect of earlier release where laws prohibit granting parole. Once such laws are passed, politicians may be reluctant to consider repealing them for fear of being considered "soft on crime." Where life sentences, particularly those without parole, are handed out, rehabilitation and reentry become irrelevant. As more such punishments are handed out, the prison census is further inflated by individuals who will be incarcerated for decades. In the United States, 1 in every 11 prison inmates is incarcerated on a life sentence. This figure included more than 6,800 juveniles, individuals who, unless granted relief, could spend 50 years or more in prison and contribute to the growth of the geriatric inmate population (Nellis & King, 2009). Notably, in 2010, a Supreme Court decision, *Graham v. Florida*, held that juveniles could not be sentenced to life without the possibility of parole for a crime not involving homicide. This made 129 of these individuals (the total number of individuals in prison with such sentences at the time of the decision) eligible for parole and will prevent future imposition of life-without-parole sentences for nonhomicide crimes for juvenile defendants.

It also seems that the public is ambivalent about prison reform in the sense of considering alternatives to incarceration, notwithstanding recent reform initiatives such as the Second Chance Act and drug and mental health courts (see Chapter 1), which may have more of an impact on the prison population given time. The recent experience of California, which has the nation's second largest prison system (after the federal prison system and slightly ahead of Texas's; West & Sabol, 2009), is a noteworthy example. In November 2008, despite a multi-billion-dollar budget shortfall and badly overcrowded prisons, the state legislature rejected a proposal for a drug court program that would have diverted many nonviolent, mainly younger offenders, from prison. It was estimated that the initial costs for expanded community drug rehabilitation programs would have been more than offset by long-term savings in prison construction and administration costs (Secretary of State, State of California, n.d.; The Real Cost of Prisons Weblog, 2008).

In behavioral terms, the predominant trend in the American criminal justice system over the past three decades can be characterized in terms of the removal of many rewards, such as parole (in many jurisdictions) and Pell Grants for education, and the enhancement of punishments, such as the increased use of life sentences. Perhaps most punitive have been the prison conditions in which many inmates have had to live: increasingly overcrowded and underresourced facilities. Such approaches have limited the options prison administrators have in dealing with inmates, as they have fewer incentives to offer, such as earlier release from prison for good behavior.

Some states have instituted reforms (e.g., increasing the amount of good time inmates can earn) intended to cut prison populations, in light of protracted budget difficulties caused by the downturn in the economy. Even California is considering such initiatives (Steinhauer, 2009b). Whether they will be implemented on a large scale and have an appreciable impact on the numbers incarcerated and, if so, be maintained when the economy recovers, remains to be seen. However, with respect to those prisoners with serious mental illness, to release them earlier than otherwise would have been the case or to divert them from prison altogether, without providing the community services they need to make their transitions successful, would simply replicate the conditions that led to their original incarcerations and thereby parallel the ill-considered deinstitutionalization phenomenon of the late 20th century. At present, it is not at all clear that these services will be provided. Related to this is what appears to be an emerging problem at the front end of the criminal justice system—a critical overload of public defenders' caseloads. This has led to a revolt in several states, with lawyers refusing to take new cases (Eckholm, 2008). Well-intentioned reform initiatives can be undercut by an increase in prison admissions when public sector budget cuts result in inadequate legal services to defendants who have no other options.

Obstacles to Prison Reform and Rehabilitation

Highly relevant to reforming prisons and providing best practice mental health services are obstacles to reform, some of which are discussed here. Chief among these is ignoring preventive approaches: failing to address the root causes of crime and mental illness that together lead to the incarceration of persons with serious thought and emotional disorders.

Preventing mental illness and incarceration in the first place, insofar as that is possible, is fundamental to real reform within the legal and healthcare systems and, therefore, to prison reform. Failure to do so, and instead incarcerating large numbers of those who do not threaten the public well-being, that is, who have committed nonviolent offenses, is the biggest obstacle to best prison practices, as it does little or nothing to break the cycle of crime, punishment, and recidivism. By default, it makes jails and prisons the main locus of mental health treatment and rehabilitation efforts for its residents, many of whose needs are too great for the available services to accommodate. This is the present state of affairs. As noted in Chapter 1, there are more persons with serious and persistent mental illness in correctional facilities than in psychiatric hospitals (see Figure 16.1). Persons admitted to prisons are also exposed to a range of potentially iatrogenic effects, as noted in Chapters 2, 9, and 12.

Figure 16.1	Photograph of Los Angeles County Jail, Known as the Largest Mental Institution in the United States

In principle, prevention is fairly straightforward. However, in fact, the fundamental causes of crime are deeply interwoven into the fabric of society and, to some extent, into the human condition, as data emerges citing the influence of genetics on criminal behavior (e.g., Vaughn, DeLisi, Beaver, & Wright, 2009).[1] Neither is the prevention of crime a new idea. Nearly 150 years ago, it was suggested, "The first in our series of establishments, looking to the repression of crime, should be institutions of a preventive character. Here, indeed, to our view, is the real field of promise" (Wines & Dwight, 1867, p. 63). Of recent note is the relationship between dropping out of school and both incarceration and pregnancy. For example, in 2006 and 2007, about 1 of every 10 males who dropped out of high school was incarcerated at any given time. The comparable figure for high school graduates was fewer than 1 in 33. Incarceration rates were highest for Black dropouts, more than 3 times that of any other group (Asian, Hispanic, or White). Among females, dropping out of high school was also related to a higher likelihood of being a single mother and living in or near poverty (Sum, Khatiwada, McLaughlin, & Palma, 2009). Although no cause-and-effect relationship can be determined based on these data, it appears that increased levels of education, at least through high school, greatly increase the odds of escaping the cycle of poverty and incarceration.

Clearly, the growth of the American prison systems is mute testimony to a long history of failed prevention and reform efforts, in which category can be included many mental health interventions, of which a recent example is the community mental health movement (see Chapters 1 and 2). The breadth of issues that must be addressed in prevention efforts makes the prospect daunting. It includes child abuse and neglect, poverty, the failure of schools to educate young people, unemployment, and the ready availability of firearms and illegal drugs.[2] When the social safety net fails, incarceration is the frequent result. However, when it succeeds, the benefits are many and wide-ranging. The weight of evidence suggests that prevention programs, particularly those aimed at earlier phases of development—at children and their parents, as well as juveniles—can be particularly cost-effective (Washington State Institute for Public Policy, 2006).

Certainly, cost issues are a factor in the decision to implement or forgo prevention programs. As noted above, initial costs for drug diversion programs being proposed in the state of California would have been appreciable, even though projected savings would ultimately have outweighed these. Other factors that may constitute obstacles to best practices are related directly or indirectly to economics: cost-shifting (Lamb & Weinberger, 2005; see also the discussion of federalization, below), tax benefits, and/or the profit motive that comes into play when the private sector is involved in prison construction and maintenance. Prison systems provide tangible benefits to the individuals who work in them, the localities whose tax bases they enhance, and, in some cases, corporations (Chen, 2008; Hallinan, 2001; Santos, 2008; Whitley, 2002).

Private vendors may reduce costs per inmate, relative to traditional government-operated facilities. In fact, as of this writing, the state of Arizona is considering privatizing all of its prisons as a cost-savings measure (Steinhauer, 2009a). Privatization may include economizing on staff, particularly, for present purposes, mental health treatment staff. Corporations also have an incentive to house more prisoners to increase profits, and an alliance between state politicians and these corporations may be created to promote this. The Institute on Money in State Politics (2006) reported,

> Companies favored states with some of the toughest sentencing laws, particularly those that had enacted legislation to lengthen the sentence given to any offender who was convicted of a felony for the third time. Private-prison interests gave almost $2.1 million in 22 states that had a so-called "three strikes law," compared with $1.2 million in 22 states that did not [between 2000 and 2004]. (p. 5)

In extreme cases, the profit motive may conduce to outright illegal behavior and the corruption of public officials. In Luzerne County, Pennsylvania, two juvenile court judges entered into a scheme where, over a period of 5 years, they sent thousands of adolescents to privately operated detention centers in return for kickbacks from the owner-operators. Many of these defendants appeared before the court without lawyers and were sentenced for minor crimes such as shoplifting; in one case, a young woman was remanded for lampooning the assistant principal of her high school on the Internet. The judges were eventually indicted and pled guilty (Juvenile Law Center, 2009; Urbina, 2009; Urbina & Hamill, 2009). The private prison industry may be necessary, given the current needs for housing the millions of individuals sentenced to confinement, but it requires careful oversight and can easily become an impediment to best practices.

The *federalization* of American corrections has also served to enlarge and maintain the prison population. Much of the overall census increase in American prisons is accounted for by the U.S. Federal Bureau of Prisons (FBOP). It is now the largest prison system in the nation, and between December 31, 2000, and December 31, 2007, it grew at more than twice the mean state incarceration rate (4.6% vs. 1.7%). Notably, during the same period, the number of federal inmates housed in private facilities increased at an average annual rate of 10.5% (West & Sabol, 2009). The expansion of the FBOP has allowed the states to shift much of the costs to the federal government that otherwise would have been involved in processing defendants through their criminal justice systems and then housing them in their prisons.

The federal government's role in corrections has expanded considerably over the past several decades as it has assumed new legal missions, continuing a trend that began early in the 20th century with Prohibition, which made criminals of those who made, sold, and consumed alcohol. Of recent note has been the prosecution of street crime, such as drug offenses, that were largely the province of the various states until the 1980s. The advent of the Internet has also brought with it new forms of computer crime: unauthorized access (hacking), fraud, theft, and child pornography, which often carry a federal sentence (Ax, 2007).

To be clear, this is no criticism of the FBOP per se, rather a comment on the policies that shape it. The mission and scale of the federal prison system constitute an obstacle to best practices in two ways. First, the availability of federal incarceration, as noted above, creates a safety valve for states with crowded prisons, allowing a sizeable percentage of those committing crimes in these states to be housed at federal expense instead of in state facilities. The federal budget is not constrained with respect to deficit spending to the extent those of the various states are. Without such an option, states might have been forced to consider alternatives sooner, such as diversion programs.

Second, federal incarceration impedes community reintegration. Individuals placed in federal prisons are commonly housed farther from their homes than they would have been had they been sentenced to state prisons. For example, Mumola (2000) found that 84% of federal inmates with children were housed more than 100 miles from their prior residences, whereas the comparable figure for state inmate-parents was 62%. Greater distance from home reduces the likelihood that inmates will receive regular family and lawyer visits. As a result, community connections may be impaired or destroyed, and legal rights and legitimate grievances may go unaddressed. Those with a direct interest in particular inmates cannot advocate as effectively for their proper treatment, such as prompt medical attention or enrollment in mental health programs in the facilities in which they are housed, if these sites are hundreds or thousands of miles away. Similarly, when caseloads include inmates from all over the United States (and many foreign countries), it becomes nearly impossible for case managers assisting inmates with pre-release planning to develop a working familiarity with the local resources potentially available to those individuals or to establish professional relationships with community corrections staff, such as probation officers and mental health service providers, or with local charities that may help ex-offenders.

Furthermore, there is now an entirely new domestic prison system, administered by another branch of the federal government: the Department of Homeland Security's Immigration and Customs Enforcement (ICE) agency, devoted to housing illegal residents of the United States. As of fiscal year 2007, according to a Government Accountability Office (GAO; 2008) report, there were approximately 300 of these facilities. They had a total average daily population in excess of 30,000, with relatively short stays, about 37 days on average, making them more similar to jails than prisons in that regard. The GAO report found that most ICE facilities were in compliance with standards of medical and mental care. Problems were noted at three of these institutions, including having sick call request forms available only in English and failing to obtain informed consent before providing psychiatric medications. However, there were some exemplars, including one facility at which an inmate was able to receive kidney dialysis. If one facility can provide best practices care, why not all?

The most pervasive problem noted by the GAO (2008) study was that of telephone access. Although this may seem to be a relatively trivial issue, use of the telephone is often the sole means by which inmates can stay in regular and timely contact with family and legal counsel, particularly when they are incarcerated far from their primary residence within the United States. Costs of using the phone can be prohibitive for an incarcerated population containing a high percentage of indigent persons.

Notably, the findings in a separate report, a joint project of the National Immigration Law Center and the American Civil Liberties Union of Southern California, contrasted sharply with the GAO (2008) report. Based partly on information only made public pursuant to a court order, the report specified violations of detainees' legal rights, for example, to due process, and of failures of oversight and monitoring, even going so far as to accuse ICE of seeking to avoid accountability by keeping the monitoring process and results secret. Specific violations relative to healthcare included some facilities with no medical staff on site and others that completed medical screenings without any medical staff involvement. The report recommended increased transparency by making public several measures of the functioning of the facilities within the system (Tumlin, Joaquin, & Natarajan, 2009).

Problems created by distance are not unique to federal prisons, however. As of July 2005, thousands of prisoners from more than 40 states were on transfer status to another system: a different state department of corrections, the FBOP, or a private prison. The most common reason was to relieve overcrowding (LIS, Inc., 2006). Notably, phone access has also been a problem in other prison systems. The American Bar Association has noted the growing and general problem of phone access by prison and jail inmates and has petitioned the Federal Communications Commission to require correctional systems to make telephones available at reasonable rates (Susman, 2009).

All other things being equal, transparency, the openness of prisons to review and scrutiny by outside entities—legislators, family members, nongovernmental organizations (NGOs) that advocate for prisoners' rights, and the media—will be greater when jails and prisons are local than when they are great distances from the communities from which inmates come. With greater geographic distance comes greater social distance for individuals and potentially greater opacity at the institutional level. Certainly, the lack of transparency, including the remoteness of the sites, helped create the climate in which the abuses at the military prisons in Abu Ghraib, Iraq; in Guantánamo Bay, Cuba; and at several secret CIA prisons took place. For example, a report by the International Community of the Red Cross (ICRC; 2007) concerning the treatment of 14 "high-value" detainees in CIA custody noted,

> As regards conditions of detention and treatment of the fourteen, the effects of their being in undisclosed detention were severe and multifaceted, as the present report shows. The absence of scrutiny by any independent entity—including the ICRC—inevitably creates conditions conducive to excesses that would not otherwise be permitted. Persons held in undisclosed detention are especially vulnerable to being subjected to ill-treatment. (p. 24)

Such conditions are a fairly extreme case of what may happen, even in a democracy, when opacity combines with a lack of oversight and accountability. In terms of the conditions and practices in prisons and jails located within the United States, these occurrences speak to the importance of oversight by a variety of internal and external (e.g., NGOs, the media) entities.

Further obstacles to broad-scale prison reform and best practice correctional mental health include competing priorities, cultural insularity, fewer options for persons with serious mental illness, and rehabilitation failures. As President Obama noted in his inaugural address, the nation faces a daunting array of challenges. High among these is that of providing healthcare. Forty-seven million Americans, disproportionately poor and ineligible for Medicaid, lacked even basic health insurance (Kaiser Commission on

Medicaid and the Uninsured, 2008), at least until the recent enactment of federal health-care legislation (Patient Protection and Affordable Care Act of 2010), which will cover most, but not all, Americans (Stolberg, 2010). A recent Rand Corporation (2008) report documented that 14% of veterans previously deployed to Iraq and/or Afghanistan screened positive for post-traumatic stress disorder (PTSD). The financial viability of Medicare, the federal government program that provides healthcare for the elderly, is also threatened (Goldstein, 2009; Pear, 2009a).

Hence, the need for resources for best practices treatment of prisoners must compete with other demands. Given that ordinary citizens, and so many veterans who have served our nation heroically in previous and current wars, have compelling healthcare needs, why should the care and treatment of criminals, even those with serious mental illness, be a priority? The extent to which this is a political question cannot be overemphasized. It would be naïve for mental health professionals to underestimate the influence of politics and emotion, as related, for example, to the desire for retribution, or a belief in the need for draconian punishment to ensure that justice prevails, in formulating prison policy. High-profile criminal cases in particular may damage general reform efforts. For instance, the August 2009, arrest of Phillip Garrido, a paroled sex offender, alleged to have kidnapped and repeatedly raped a young girl over an 18-year period, was thought by some California officials to have the potential to derail a bill aimed at reducing the state prison population and the budget deficit through an early parole program (see Chapter 12).

> "If we let someone out early, and that man commits a crime, the assembly members are worried that that will come back to haunt them like the old famous Willie Horton ads," said a prominent state politician, who asked not to be identified because of concerns about undermining legislative negotiations. (Pogash & Moore, 2009, p. A9)

Stated differently, it is vital to consider the *intangible* costs and benefits of incarceration—for example, political advantage to legislators, or among the citizenry an increased sense of safety and security or a sense that justice has prevailed, versus long-term separation of inmates from their families and communities, or perpetuation of cycles of incarceration and poverty—as well as the purely financial aspects. Accordingly, those wishing to advocate effectively on behalf of an increased prioritization of correctional mental health care must martial arguments that go beyond simple dollar cost-effectiveness to the public's fears of crime and their reasonable interests in justice and safety.

As noted in Chapter 3, there are competing priorities *within* correctional institutions: security, health, mental health, and so on. Corrections departments must compete at the state and federal levels for limited resources with which to meet their assigned missions. The success of such competition will partly depend on the effectiveness of advocacy both from within those departments and from outside entities: NGOs, the media, and sometimes the courts.

The United States is an increasingly diverse nation, although Whites are still the majority demographic group. However, ethnic and racial minorities are overrepresented among American prison populations. In particular, the incarceration rate for Black males is more than 6 times that of White males (West & Sabol, 2009). More than 14% of those persons housed in the FBOP are foreign-born (West & Sabol, 2009), and all of those in ICE detainee prisons are noncitizens. As noted in Chapter 6, substantial cultural barriers to the provision of even basic mental health services often exist, such as a fundamental distrust of Western medicine and concepts of mental health. Language barriers will be present to varying extents. Where mental health staff are unable to establish basic communication and trust with these groups of individuals, successfully attending to their mental health needs is unlikely. With minority populations expected to increase, such that Whites will become a minority group by 2050 (Bernstein & Edwards, 2008), this issue will only become more relevant until it is confronted and addressed effectively, or until it breaks the back of the criminal justice system. Such redress ideally emphasizes primary prevention (see below), but it must also include effective interventions for ethnic, racial, and national minorities currently incarcerated in American prisons.

There are presently fewer options for the disposition of those persons with serious mental illness who come into contact with the criminal justice system. As noted in Chapters 1 and 2, deinstitutionalization, beginning in the mid-20th century, was supposed to be accompanied by the resources necessary to treat persons released from psychiatric hospitals in the community. This effort failed on a broad scale, resulting in the "criminalization of mental illness," an increasing presence of these individuals in the criminal justice system. Yet in the intervening decades, there has been no reversal of this phenomenon. The availability of beds in state facilities has continued to decrease even as the prison system has grown (Lamb & Weinberger, 2005; see also Chapter 2), while community programs for persons with serious mental illness remain underfunded (see Chapter 9).

The history of correctional mental health includes repeated and regular efforts at prison reform: ensuring humane treatment and otherwise recognizing inmates' rights. Advocacy groups, often NGOs such as Amnesty International, Human Rights Watch, and the American Civil Liberties Union, have been instrumental in these ongoing efforts. Yet reforming prisons, such as by relieving harsh living conditions, is not to be confused with the related issue of reforming prisoners, helping them to modify their thoughts and behaviors to support a prosocial and productive lifestyle after their release. The latter is usually called "rehabilitation" now.

Notwithstanding that correctional mental health care includes other services (see especially Chapters 1 and 9), rehabilitation is traditionally the most visible and controversial of these, perhaps because it implies a return to the community and the attendant risk of further harm individuals released from confinement might cause. There is a long history in the United States of disappointing outcomes of rehabilitation efforts, measured in terms of recidivism rates, dating to the creation of the modern penitentiary, which was itself intended as an instrument of reform. This also speaks to the limits of assessment practices, as when individuals judged to be at low risk for future criminal acts reoffend after being given probation or early release from prison (see Chapter 4). (See Ax, 2007, for more about the history of correctional mental health services, including rehabilitation.) When rehabilitation efforts fail, and particularly when they fail visibly (such as when stories of particularly egregious offenses by recidivists are carried in the media), the public may lose faith in the capacity of social science to "fix" criminals and perhaps even become hostile to further efforts.

Arguments for Prison Reform and Best Practice Correctional Mental Health

Several arguments, not mutually exclusive, are commonly advanced for giving greater attention to conditions in prisons and jails and, implicitly or explicitly, to correctional mental health. Two of these are the moral or humanitarian argument and the pragmatic or economic argument.

In general, the moral or humanitarian argument asserts that every human life has value, and everyone deserves to be treated decently, even prisoners (e.g., Whitman, 2003).

To conduct ourselves otherwise debases us as a society, even extending to the treatment of prisoners. When individuals must be confined in jail or prison, the least an enlightened society can do is to treat them humanely and with dignity and, by implication, provide them with good quality mental health care.

A pragmatic or economic argument challenges the utility of mass incarceration: Incarceration does not solve society's problems, including the root causes of crime (e.g., Mauer, 1999). Many crimes, even serious ones, are never reported in the first place (see Chapter 12). In the long run, lengthy periods of incarceration on a large scale (except for violent, dangerous criminals) are a waste of human capital and economic resources that could be better spent elsewhere, such as on public education or healthcare. Such spending is particularly wasteful in an era of budget deficits. Given the fact of incarceration, prisoners' potential as wage-earners, as spouses and parents, and as generally productive citizens must be nurtured through appropriate services, including effective mental health treatment and community reintegration programs.

To these, counterarguments come readily to mind. Rehabilitation is only one of the missions of incarceration (along with punishment, incapacitation, and deterrence), and some would say the least important. Prison inmates are individuals who have victimized others. If they are not appropriately punished, justice is not served, and prospective offenders are less likely to be deterred. They are not productive members of society and are perhaps unlikely ever to be so. High recidivism rates have proven this, it may be asserted, and there is no better place for criminals than prisons and jails. Given the closure of mental hospitals and the failure of community mental health, this includes persons with serious mental illness, who should not be "coddled" with services unavailable to many law-abiding citizens. Longer sentences will assuredly incapacitate these individuals from victimizing others, a safer alternative to the risks attendant upon rehabilitation programs and earlier release policies, and one that will save money as well (for example, in terms of losses to individuals or businesses victimized by criminals who are given alternative dispositions or early release, or medical expenses secondary to violent crimes these persons would commit if released). Furthermore, as already noted, the costs of prisons may be partially defrayed by the direct economic benefits of jails and prisons to local economies (i.e., jobs and taxes). Hence, there are what many would consider sound arguments for keeping prisons and jails open and full.

There are two additional arguments in support of prison programs, including correctional mental health services, which are not so easily countervailed. The first is the public health argument. Prisons and prisoners are part of the larger community, and whether the general public likes it or not, the great majority of people who are arrested are eventually released. As noted in Chapter 1, more than 9 out of 10 prisoners are eventually released, and hundreds of thousands return to the community every year. Those accused of minor crimes may spend only a few hours or days in jail. The potentially iatrogenic, or harmful, effects of incarceration must be taken into account when considering the costs and benefits of large-scale incarceration. If individuals held in correctional facilities are exposed to communicable diseases, cannot get treatment for serious mental disorders, or become angrier and more antisocially oriented as a result of their experiences in the legal system, the community will suffer when they are released. Appropriate health, mental health, and other interventions benefit not only inmates but those living in the community as well. The iatrogenic effects of incarceration can extend to secondary victims. Families and even communities can be devastated (see Chavez, 2007; and Clements et al., 2007, for more information concerning public health and prisons). Yet it may be argued that longer sentences, particularly for those inmates considered most likely to cause harm (based on past behavior), do more to benefit the public in general than programs whose effectiveness cannot be fully assessed while the inmate participants remain incarcerated.

What is ultimately most meaningful is the legal argument. The Eighth Amendment to the United States Constitution states that "cruel and unusual punishments" may not be inflicted. The historic *Estelle v. Gamble* Supreme Court decision in 1976, based on the Eighth Amendment, provided constitutional guarantees of adequate healthcare to prisoners. A series of other decisions, such as *Ruiz v. Estelle* (1980), has since extended those protections to mental health care. As has been made clear during the recent controversy over the treatment of prison detainees in the U.S. military prison at Guantánamo Bay, Cuba, international law also provides protections for some inmates. The Supreme Court held, in *Hamdan v. Rumsfeld* (2006), that the Geneva Convention was relevant to the legal rights of detainees there.

That said, the law provides necessary but not sufficient conditions for best mental health practices in correctional settings. At best, laws are translated into institutional policies and codes of conduct that require high standards of behavior and competence by prison staff on a day-to-day basis. Existing laws cannot dictate what, exactly, constitutes best practices in each subsequent situation, although legal opinions may cite instances of clearly inadequate or abusive treatment. Recourse to "community standards" is of questionable utility; it is a nebulous criterion, varying across jurisdictions, and the access of millions of free-world Americans to health and mental health care, even with the new federal healthcare legislation, remains questionable (see Chapter 2). Furthermore, much of the law is codified morality. If the zeitgeist dictates harsher treatment—longer sentences, capital punishment—then even the legal argument for best mental health practices and programs is weakened. For health and mental health care professionals, however, there is another standard. All recognized healthcare professions have ethical codes, which typically compel a higher standard of conduct than that required by law or institutional policy, as will be discussed below. (See also "Ethical Codes" in the appendix of this book.)

Best Practice Environments: Policies, Prisons, and Jails

In this section, an environment is imagined in which best correctional mental health practices take place. These are conceptual benchmarks against which real-world approximations to best practice environments may be measured. A representative, if not comprehensive, list of principles consistent with such a state of affairs would include the following.

1. Program and treatment resources are adequate. Budgets are adequate and moneys allocated appropriately to provide needed services. In turn, these resources are utilized to maximum efficiency to minimize waste. This will mean employing innovative practices, for example, telehealth and electronic health records and, likely, expanded scope of practice for some healthcare professionals (see below). Certainly, it will mean adequate funding for community services, to prevent failures similar to those that attended deinstitutionalization.

2. Criminal justice policies are preventive, aspirational, and restorative. In this section, the discussion follows the prevention framework articulated by Eaton (1995), in which *primary* prevention refers to preventing the onset of psychopathology, *secondary* prevention to efforts at impacting its course, and *tertiary* prevention to mitigating its outcome. Here, the terms apply to both the criminal justice process and to psychopathology, broadly speaking. Best correctional mental health practice policies include appropriate attention to prevention and, where possible, primary prevention; that is, to preventing the development of antisocial attitudes and behaviors, serious mental illnesses, and addictions. Early interventions within the free-world community may focus on the prevention of unwanted pregnancy, child abuse and neglect, complemented with the provision of education and vocational training, as well as health services that help vulnerable persons attain lifelong medical and mental health. Secondary prevention efforts make drug and mental health diversion courts available, allowing defendants, where appropriate, to obtain treatment within the community and avoid incarceration. Psychoeducational programs in community mental health centers could teach persons with serious mental illness about their legal rights, for instance, the right to counsel in the event of arrest and the right not to incriminate themselves, even as adequate funding for public defender services is ensured. Tertiary prevention policies help individuals to avoid or minimize the iatrogenic effects of incarceration; ensure that adequate mental health treatment is available for incarcerated persons; and assist them in remaking their lives in productive, prosocial ways during and after incarceration.

Best practices are aspirational by definition. Accordingly, laws, agency policies and guidelines, and employee codes of conduct are consistent with and supportive of the highest standards and best practices in all departments, given the necessity for interdepartmental collaboration if best mental health practices are to take place (see Chapter 8). They promote fair and humane treatment at the institutional level. For example, for persons with serious mental illness having difficulty functioning in general population, "step-up" general population units and other resources are made available to prevent unnecessary placement in segregation, thereby avoiding the iatrogenic effects of such an experience (Kupers et al., 2009; Magaletta, Ax, Patry, & Dietz, 2005).

Finally, restorative policies foster reintegration of the offender with his or her community upon release: from providing aftercare, including any needed mental health services, to making him or her as nearly "whole" in the eyes of the law and society as possible and appropriate (Ax, 2003). This may involve making restitution, perhaps directly to victims of the offender's crimes. From a behavioral standpoint, ex-offenders are offered rewards for adopting and maintaining prosocial lifestyles. Persons convicted of felonies forfeit certain rights. Their loss constitutes a barrier to full citizenship, and some or all of these might be restored after specified periods of good behavior in the community. Examples include permitting ex-offenders to be bonded, obtain or regain professional and vocational licenses, get a passport, and vote in elections. Sometimes a fresh start is necessary. For example, individuals who seek to leave gangs may need to relocate to do this successfully, and for their own safety. Funds could be made available for this purpose.

3. Criminal justice systems are integrated with healthcare systems and the "free world" community. Two interrelated concepts, the continuity of care and the portability of information, are central to best practices correctional mental health. There is no unitary criminal justice or correctional system in the United States. Prisoners may move between and among local and regional jails, and state and federal prisons, with their incarcerations interspersed with periods of street time. Inmates with healthcare needs may be hospitalized at some point in a local community facility, usually for acute medical needs, and/or within a forensic medical center for long-term mental health care or chronic medical disorder. Similarly, healthcare and mental health care in prison should be continuous with community care, but too often this is not the case. In essence, state prisoners' healthcare involves three and possibly four disaggregated state systems: criminal justice, health, and mental health, with substance abuse services either autonomous or integrated with, most likely, the mental health system, depending on the state. There may also be federal systems involved: past incarcerations in the federal prison system and/or treatment in the military, through the Department of Veterans Affairs or Public Health Service.

Best practices would mean having access to all relevant health/mental health care information from each of these systems. Therefore, good communication is essential within and across systems. This must include portability of data: mechanisms for safe and protected electronic storage and transmission of health records. Fortunately, concerns about privacy and security are being raised and addressed by stakeholders, including health and mental health professionals (Lohr, 2009; Nordal, 2009; Pear, 2009b; see also Chapter 1). Continuity of care is not possible without the portability of this information.

There is, however, a further consideration: continuity of care and portability of information *within* correctional facilities. In correctional facilities of any size, a variety of obstacles can interfere with the provision of mental health care. For example, bad weather, a late or inaccurate count, or an institutional disturbance can keep the entire facility locked down, preventing inmates from keeping appointments for psychotherapy or getting to the pharmacy to receive their psychotropic medications. Worse are situations in which inmates are moved from general population to segregation, and this information fails to reach the medical and mental health departments immediately. Providers, perhaps overwhelmed with routine matters, assume for the moment that inmate-patients have simply failed to appear for psychotherapy and/or medication. If follow-up is not undertaken in a timely manner and the inmates' location in the segregation unit identified, treatment may be disrupted or even effectively discontinued. This is another example of how multiple departments must communicate effectively to ensure the continuity of care (see Chapter 7 specifically in regard to medication issues).

4. Prison and jail treatment outcomes are measured and positive results rewarded, making providers and facilities accountable. The effectiveness of a prison or jail is often measured in terms of the *absence* of undesirable incidents such as escapes, suicides and other deaths in custody, or documented cases of abuse or denial or rights. To the extent these do not occur, the general public and the legislature are usually satisfied that correctional facilities are functioning adequately. With regard to healthcare in general and mental health care in particular, some assessment mechanisms, including internal agency reviews, are already in place. Many agencies request reviews by independent auditing bodies. The Joint Commission (formerly the Joint Commission on Accreditation of Healthcare Organizations) conducts audits of correctional facilities' healthcare services and accredits (or denies accreditation) as appropriate. The National Commission on Correctional Health Care (NCCHC) publishes health and mental health care standards and accredits facilities based on compliance with these standards. The American Correctional Association (ACA) accreditation criteria also include various aspects of medical and mental health care (see Chapter 5).

However, these reviews commonly take place only once every few years. In a true best practice environment, correctional facility treatment and rehabilitation outcomes would be assessed and made public. Measurable outcomes such as compliance rates with screening requirements of new arrivals and other Level 1 services (see Chapter 2) could be measured and released on a daily, weekly, monthly, or (at most) yearly basis. Recidivism rates for persons released from jails and prisons would be regularly documented and publicly reported. There are foreseeable difficulties with such an arrangement, such as the fact that inmates may be moved among several different facilities during their incarceration, thus complicating the assessment process. Notwithstanding these, if exemplary facilities, programs, and practitioners were recognized and rewarded, it would provide system incentives for best practices by all staff (but particularly mental health and healthcare providers) and for innovative programming. This state of affairs would promote accountability and thereby improved outcomes.

Information about healthcare is regularly made available to the public by a variety of outlets, formal and informal. A recent PricewaterhouseCoopers Health Research Institute (2008) report documented waste in American healthcare, with more than a trillion dollars lost in three domains: behavioral (e.g., obesity, smoking), clinical (mainly defensive medicine), and operational (with claims processing and ineffective use of information technology the two costliest items). In sum, there is clearly a movement towards measuring healthcare outcomes as a means by which to improve outcomes and reduce waste. The popular periodical *U.S. News and World Report* annually provides a list of the nation's best hospitals (e.g., "America's Best Hospitals," 2009), and consumers can now find online government ratings of nursing homes (U.S. Department of Health and Human Services, n.d.).

Consumers also have an increasing voice in rating healthcare. Patient ratings of physicians are now being made available by the Zagat Survey group in partnership with WellPoint, an insurance company, to the latter's customers (Freudenheim, 2009). On Angie's list (2009), an Internet-based consumer service, "reviews" of physicians, psychiatrists, and other healthcare providers, as well as hospitals, may be obtained. This phenomenon is in some sense the 21st-century version of "word-of-mouth" recommendations. Similarly, the BOPWatch Internet listserv is a forum in which members—lawyers, ex-offenders, family members of prisoners, and others—discuss various aspects of the FBOP, including healthcare. A recent e-mail discussion, for example, involved inquiries and responses about finding good mental health treatment within the federal prison system (e.g., Bussert, 2009; see also Chapter 12 regarding consumer use and marketing of information about sex offenders).

It is well for correctional professionals to remember that consumers will seek out information they want if it is not forthcoming from established sources, including the criminal justice system, and perhaps attempt to hold those systems accountable through legal or administrative actions. A best practice would be to embrace this principle, identify as many measurable outcomes in the criminal justice system as possible, and then hold individuals and facilities accountable for those results, with an emphasis on rewarding favorable outcomes rather than punishing failure. Correctional systems are also healthcare systems, and their healthcare—and rehabilitation—outcomes can and should be measured. The National Committee on Vital and Health Statistics (2004) published a report that provided recommendations for assessing the quality of healthcare according to several criteria, all of which in general can be meaningfully applied to corrections: assessing quality of healthcare and outcomes, reducing related racial and ethnic disparities, building the data and information infrastructure (e.g., with respect to patient records) to support quality healthcare, and balancing healthcare consumers' interests in quality care and the confidentiality of their information.

5. Prisons and jails are more local, smaller, less densely populated, and transparent. In a best practices environment, one in which prevention programs have met with success, the prison population is smaller. Correctional facilities are more local, thus more readily linked to the community. This makes release planning easier given the proximity to the appropriate resources and personnel in the community to which an inmate will be released. Informal professional relationships can be developed more easily between case managers in jails and prisons and community services providers, such as probation officers and community mental health professionals. Proximity also makes it easier for inmates' family members and lawyers to visit, preserving community ties and helping to ensure that legal rights are respected. This arrangement would especially benefit indigent inmates, whose family members do not have the funds to travel long distances for visits and who must depend on public defenders for legal representation.

Overcrowding, in terms of square feet allotted per inmate, would not exist. The *Ruiz v. Estelle* (1980) opinion specifically cited "persuasive testimony relating to the incremental negative physical and psychological effects of inmates' continued close confinement in too-intimate proximity with their fellows" (p. 1282).

6. Prison populations are representative and accommodate diversity. The prison population is representative of those who commit crimes, reflecting fair and unbiased treatment within the criminal justice system. Currently, several ethnic minority populations are overrepresented in prisons relative to the degree to which they commit crimes (see Chapter 6).

In particular, it will be necessary for prison systems to be responsive to the needs of Hispanic inmates from foreign countries. In addition to those individuals in state prisons and the FBOP, the United States, as earlier noted, now has a new prison system, run by ICE, which houses foreign individuals who have entered the United States illegally. The majority of these individuals are from countries in which Spanish is the primary language, and many speak little or no English. It will be necessary for these facilities, if they are to function as best practices prison environments, to employ sufficient numbers of mental health and other treatment staff who are fluent in Spanish and other languages and are familiar with the various cultures represented among the prison populations.

7. Non–mental health care staff conduct and composition also exemplify best practices. The human component of best practice correctional environments is the most crucial. Staff are well trained; conduct themselves ethically; are present in adequate numbers; and possess the knowledge, skills, and abilities to respond to the globally diverse populations of our prisons and jails. As institutional CEOs, wardens and sheriffs have extremely difficult jobs (see Chapter 3). They hold the highest levels of on-site authority and responsibility and are simultaneously accountable to upper levels of state, federal, or municipal government hierarchies (and, in the case of private prisons, corporate boards) for the safe and orderly running of their respective prisons and jails. They must function under the scrutiny of the media, prisoners' rights groups, and family members ready to support inmates' grievances. Their conduct is the key component in determining how these institutions function. "Correctional leadership is the major component to developing a correctional culture that can manage special population prisoners" (Stojkovic, 2005, p. 1-11), a point also underscored in Chapter 3 of this book.

In social learning terms (Bandura, 1977), administrators can *model* best leadership practices. This will set the tone for an institution that is run in a fair and humane manner and in which staff understand that accountability is required at all levels for the quality of care inmates receive. Acting as an advocate (or "champion") to upper levels of agency management on behalf of well-run programs, such as by making adequate program staffing levels a priority, further promotes a best practices environment. Where leadership fails, drastic consequences can result. One high-profile example of this is the military prison at Abu Ghraib, site of abuses of detainees in 2003, which were later made public. In a subsequent investigation, a failure of leadership was noted on the part of several of the high-ranking officers at the facility, including the facility's commander, a brigadier general (Taguba, n.d.).

In some facilities, medical and mental health services may be combined in the same department. In others, they are independent. Regardless, cooperation, communication, and collaboration between medical and mental health service providers are crucial.

These services form the core around which other relationships are created to provide comprehensive services to inmates with serious mental illnesses. As noted in Chapter 1 and earlier in the present chapter, continuity of care is critical, particularly where inmate-patients move between correctional facilities and the community and/or from one correctional system to another. Lapses in communication within an institution can result in lost information such as prescriptions for psychotropic medications, referrals for medical or psychological tests and other services, or suicide watch referrals. Perhaps most importantly, from a biopsychosocial perspective, mental health interventions are likely to involve multiple modalities and may have to be coordinated between and among practitioners, particularly medical and mental health practitioners. Avoidance of silos is fundamental to best practices (see Chapter 8).

One practice deserves particular attention in this regard. It is fairly common for general population correctional facilities to employ psychiatrists on a contract, part-time, basis. In practical terms, they become the interface between medical, pharmacy, and mental health staff. If necessary communication, including documentation of appointments, prescriptions, and referrals for medical or psychological tests, is not handled appropriately between and among all staff involved, best practices cannot be provided.

In a best practices correctional environment, custody staff, the "eyes and ears" of mental health staff within the institutions, and often the first responders in the event of a mental health emergency, are well trained in dealing with inmates with serious mental illness (see Chapter 3). They can refer inmates to mental health staff and, through their professional conduct, earn the trust of these individuals, who may be willing to approach such exemplary officers with their concerns, including mental health issues. To be effective, correctional officers must be present in adequate numbers. In particular, they can protect vulnerable inmates. Notwithstanding the desirability of changing prison culture to prevent sexual and other assaults on vulnerable inmates (Zweig & Blackmore, 2008), it is ultimately the presence of sufficient numbers of concerned, highly professional custody/security staff that discourages and ultimately prevents inmate-on-inmate assaults. Furthermore, even the U.S. Department of Justice concedes, "There is not yet a solid body of evidence as to what strategies and interventions prevent rape" (Zweig & Blackmore, 2008, p. 8). The *Ruiz v. Estelle* (1980) decision noted the increased risk of physical and sexual assaults when there are inadequate numbers of custody staff present in an institution. A best practices environment is not only one that provides high-quality mental health care; it is also one in which the iatrogenic effects of incarceration are prevented as much as possible.

"Real-World" Best Practices for Correctional Mental Health Practitioners

In this section, a different perspective is adopted in considering the possibilities for best practices by correctional mental health professionals, given the current obstacles presented by the realities of limited correctional budgets and other resources. Aside from those presented within the criminal justice and political systems, healthcare system issues, such as shortages and geographic maldistribution of providers (resulting in an oversupply in some areas and an undersupply in others), can present impediments to best practices. The needs of patients in correctional settings, and their growth in absolute numbers, threaten to overwhelm the capacity of the various American correctional systems to respond adequately. Under these circumstances, it becomes especially important for providers of these services, as individuals and as members of particular professions, to maintain the aspirational stance referred to earlier in this chapter with regard to their own competence and practice.

Adding Value: Scope of Practice Issues

In one fundamental respect, this translates to the necessity for mental health care providers to expand their scope of practice by improving what is known in bureaucratic terms as "knowledge, skills, and abilities" and thereby regularly adding value to their work. This is particularly important in an era where shortages of some healthcare professionals, particularly physicians and nurses, exist.

Recognizing the need for improved access to healthcare (including mental health care) in America, the Pew Health Commissions published a report in which they concluded,

> United States health care consumers need a regulatory system that bases authority to practice on the practitioner's demonstrated initial and continuing competence— acknowledging that differently trained and differently named professions may deliver the same services—so long as they demonstrate competence. Professionals should be allowed and encouraged to provide services to the full extent of their current training, experience and skills. A regulatory system that maintains its priority of quality care, while eliminating irrational monopolies and restrictive scopes of practice would not only allow practitioners to offer the health services they are competent to deliver, but would be more flexible, efficient, and effective. (Finocchio, Dower, McMahon, & Gragnola, 1995, p. 13)

Indeed, it is the norm rather than the exception for healthcare professions to evolve in accordance with scientific advances and with marketplace needs and opportunities. For correctional psychologists, this may mean adopting a primary care model or something closely approximating it, so that care can be better coordinated and provided more effectively (Fagan, Brandt, & Kleiver, 2007).

Given the decline in the numbers of psychiatrists being trained (Rao, 2003) and their shortages in some parts of the country (Fraher, Swartz, & Gaul, 2006; Office of Rural Health & Primary Care, Minnesota Department of Mental Health, 2003; Thomas & Holzer, 2006), it is understandable that organized psychology would seek prescriptive authority for those psychologists receiving specialized training in clinical psychopharmacology. Indeed, this has been at the forefront of the American Psychological Association's (APA's) agenda for several years now. However, as of this writing, only two states, New Mexico and Louisiana, have passed enabling legislation, and the future of the initiative seems uncertain (Fox et al., 2009). As noted in Chapter 7, clinical pharmacists can prescribe in some states. Other professionals, nurse practitioners or physician assistants, for example, could "train up," becoming skilled in mental health assessment, diagnosis, and psychological interventions. Added to their current skills and knowledge of clinical pharmacology, these professionals could provide health/mental health primary care in correctional settings.

Certainly, this is consistent with a biopsychosocial model of practice. In particular, this implies the emerging understanding that mental and somatic health are interrelated and speaks to issues of collaboration and evolution in the scopes of practice of the various healthcare professions. This means potential turf wars but also the possibility to maximize the value of a cadre of staff who are already highly trained and critical to the proper function of correctional facilities. Integration at the theoretical level could parallel the integration of medical and mental health services at administrative and practice levels, as mental and medical healthcare staff collaborate in support of health promotion/disease prevention efforts, a particularly important initiative in prisons, where dysfunctional lifestyles have left many with or vulnerable to illnesses. In particular, substance abuse has contributed to chronic infectious diseases, organ compromise, and other health problems (Chavez, 2007; Fagan et al., 2007; see also Chapter 11). Such collaborations can act as "competence multipliers" to assist inmates in regaining medical health lost to unhealthy lifestyles common among prison populations, in concert with more stable mental functioning.

"Train up or work down and lose out" might be a useful maxim for health and mental health care professionals. Those who fail to upgrade their skills regularly risk being marginalized, spending more of their time performing lower skilled tasks, or losing jobs altogether, as other professions collectively enhance their knowledge and skill sets and become available to perform similar assessment and treatment services, perhaps doing so at equivalent quality levels and at lower cost. This is likely to be more urgent in prison systems, where healthcare is a subordinate mission, and safety and security concerns reliably rank as higher priorities. Lower priority missions must accordingly be increasingly cost-effective. It is also a matter of advocacy. The ultimate success or failure of psychology's prescriptive authority initiative, for example, will be largely determined by the degree of political involvement and persistence of its members in promoting legislative initiatives in other states and in making a case for the usefulness of this skill in public agencies on behalf of underserved patient populations, such as prisoners. "Psychologists must understand that our obligations transcend guild concerns and must ultimately address the fundamental concern of expanded patient access to expert mental health services" (Fox et al., 2009, p. 267).

In many state correctional systems, the modal mental health provider is a master's-level "psychologist" (Boothby & Clements, 2000). However, "best practices" is not to be confused with "doctoral-level provider." Where doctoral-level mental health practitioners, psychiatrists and psychologists, are unavailable to provide needed services, it is desirable that others, following Finocchio et al. (1995), should be given the training and authority to do so. Best practices cannot be divorced from cost-effectiveness issues, especially in the current, economically challenging environment.

In correctional settings, particularly for mental health professionals, who depend on the quality of their therapeutic relationships with their patients for the success of their work, cultural responsiveness is crucial (see Chapter 6). Although it is not possible for them to be conversant with the entire range of cultures represented in prison populations, a willingness to engage with patients in identifying, addressing, and resolving cultural differences that may affect therapeutic work is crucial. More basically, correctional mental health providers who can speak a foreign language, particularly Spanish, will add considerable effectiveness to their work and value to their agencies.

Role Issues

By definition, the conduct of best practices involves high ethical standards. In correctional practice, this can be particularly difficult. Role conflict is always a possibility in an environment in which treatment missions are subordinate to those of safety and security. Practitioners must sometimes face complex situations involving unrealistic demands from the administration and other staff, on the one hand, and often hostile inmate-patients, on the other, who may refuse or misuse services, demand inappropriate treatments (e.g., preferred psychoactive medications), or malinger. Providers may need to advocate for improved treatment with administrators or other staff who may be hostile to particular best correctional mental health practices, for example, reduced reliance on the use of segregation or introducing mitigating or exculpatory information about an inmate's mental status in disciplinary hearing cases. Best practice often involves consulting with colleagues familiar with such situations and the ethical conundrums they present. In keeping with the dictum to "do no harm," practitioners must acknowledge the limits of their own competence. Sometimes practitioners must decline to perform an action if to do so would be unethical and potentially harm a patient, even when such actions are requested by the patient (e.g., denying sleep medication when not indicated). It may also be the best practice to do nothing when the alternative is to exceed the scope of one's competence or to impose treatment on a powerless inmate. Similar to this is the need to refrain from making unrealistic claims for the validity of assessment procedures or the effectiveness of treatments.

Problems with prison practice often result when too much time is spent considering what is permissible under the circumstances, rather than what is best. This contributed to the recent controversy the APA experienced in its attempts to create a policy that permitted psychologists to be involved in the interrogations of detainees at the Guantánamo Bay Naval Base and other facilities housing alleged terrorists. Amid growing concerns about allegations of torture, a grassroots movement among members protested this policy, eventually forcing a vote that banned all such involvement (Martin, 2008). Regarding the revised policy, Dr. Alan E. Kazdin, then-President of the American Psychological Association, wrote, in part, to President George W. Bush,

> The emphasis of this new policy is to *prohibit psychologists from any involvement in interrogations or any other operational procedures at detention sites that are in violation of the U.S. Constitution or international law* (e.g., the Geneva Conventions and the U.N. Convention Against Torture) [emphasis in the original]. (Kazdin, 2008b, p. 1)

Even alleged terrorists, perhaps the most devalued persons in any American prison system, are entitled to fair and humane treatment under the law and no less so to ethical treatment by health and mental health care providers.

However, role flexibility is often vital to best practice in an environment with limited resources. As has been discussed at many points throughout this book, collaboration across disciplines is central to all prison missions, including safety and security, as well as mental health treatment. Mental health practitioners must be willing to assist in preserving the more fundamental correctional missions that involve safety and security, including the prevention of assaults, escapes, contraband trafficking, and so forth. Where these missions are compromised, mental health services suffer. At the same time, innovative practices and new technologies also allow new roles, for example, the collaboration of mental health practitioners with medical personnel, in addressing the behavioral health aspects of health promotion and disease prevention.

Not all correctional mental health professionals work in prisons. They may work in academia, developing new interventions relevant to correctional populations. They may serve as clinicians in the community, providing preventive care for at-risk individuals and families, or care for those who have been released from prison and require ongoing treatment. They also work in the policy arena, as administrators, as legislators, or with NGOs.

Science and Technology

There is now clear evidence for the effectiveness of mental health interventions. "The challenge of yesteryear about whether psychological treatments are better than no treatment has been put to rest" (Kazdin, 2008a, p. 211). This holds true for many disorders that are the focus of mental health and rehabilitative intervention in criminal justice systems (Clements & McLearen, 2003). Prominent among the relevant literature is the "What Works" canon of Paul Gendreau and his colleagues (e.g., Gendreau, 1996; Smith, Gendreau, & Goggin, 2007; see Chapter 9). There has been a proliferation of research journals in the corrections and criminal justice fields, including *Criminal Justice and Behavior, Journal of Child Sexual Abuse, Journal of Correctional Health Care, Law & Human Behavior, Journal of Interpersonal Violence*, and *Psychology, Crime, and Law* (see the appendix to this volume for a larger list of these journals). A database of empirically supported preventive interventions is emerging (Washington State Institute for Public Policy, 2006). Evidence-based interventions are beginning to gain attention in the probation and parole disciplines (Cadigan, 2008; McGrath, 2008). Ax and Fagan (2007) provided an overview of effective interventions in other nations' criminal justice systems. As noted in Chapter 7, psychotropic medications have proven effective in treating many of the disorders that contribute to incarceration.

Employing empirically supported treatments is consistent with best practices from both an ethical and an accountability standpoint, which further speaks to the issue of risk management. As health and mental health care outcomes, including those in the criminal justice system, are increasingly measured and scrutinized, patients, providers, and correctional institutions benefit from interventions of proven clinical effectiveness in terms of patient well-being, institutional security, and protection of institutions and staff from litigation. More accurate risk assessment can promote greater credibility and thereby acceptance of mental health providers' recommendations for treatment, diversion from incarceration, or early release (see Chapter 4).

Technology can leverage the utility of existing staff resources and provide access to specialty care. Telehealth (or telemedicine), as discussed in Chapter 5, has become increasingly popular in criminal justice systems. Prisons are often built in rural areas where healthcare providers may be unavailable for face-to-face consultations (Magaletta, Dennery, & Ax, 2005). Technology can also support continuity of care, which, as previously discussed, can be a particular problem in corrections, both between institutions and in terms of the institutional-community link. The safe and confidential maintenance and transmission of electronic health records will support best practices as inmate-patients move between institutions and return to the community. It also supports the portability, quality, and economy of treatment *within* institutions, particularly when inmates are confined in segregation or are on suicide watch. In these settings, it may be difficult for practitioners to bring paper files, but it is crucial for them to be able to access treatment data during contacts. For example, when mental health practitioners conduct reviews in special housing units, they may see 20 or 30 inmates who have a range of concerns and mental health needs. Portable electronic databases carried by psychologists, psychiatrists, and other mental health providers visiting these restricted access areas would allow them to retrieve treatment records, including diagnoses, recent contacts, and medication histories.

Summary and Conclusions

More than two decades ago, the historian Paul Kennedy (1987) wrote about how great nations had declined when their ambitions and international obligations had outstripped their economic, military, and technological resources. He suggested then that the United States was facing a watershed moment similar to that of Imperial Spain in 1600 and the British Empire at the dawn of the 20th century—that our resources were becoming overtaxed as theirs had been when their declines began. Similarly, a recent report from the National Intelligence Council (2008) projected that in the world of 2025, the United States's international influence will have diminished. "Shrinking economic and military capabilities may force the U.S. into a difficult set of tradeoffs between domestic and foreign policy priorities" (p. iv). As this is being written, the United States is facing an ongoing series of crises, not the least of which is economic, as President Obama noted in his inaugural address. These may resolve in full or in part with a return of the United States to a position of economic, military, and political preeminence.

In light of these ongoing challenges, however, it remains to be seen whether America has both the capacity and the will to provide adequate mental health services for those under the care, custody, and control of the various American prison systems. In particular, America must confront its willingness to invest in preventive interventions, to take calculated risks on alternatives to incarceration for those marginalized individuals who are clearly not a threat to public safety, and to support other initiatives aimed at reintegrating ex-offenders into their communities. The nation has considerable resources available to it in terms of well-educated health and mental health care providers and new electronic and pharmacological technologies. However, in large part, it will be up to members of the health and mental health care professions to prove the worth of their specialized knowledge, skills, and abilities in the court of public opinion and so create a more favorable, best practice environment.

Endnotes

1. Readers interested in more information about the biological aspects of antisocial behavior are referred to the November 2009 issue of *Criminal Justice and Behavior*. This is a special issue with the theme "Biosocial Criminology," in which the Vaughn et al. article appears, along with several others on related topics.

2. Related to the issues of prevention, prison reform, and alternatives to incarceration is that of the reform of drug laws. An extensive discussion of this controversial topic is beyond the scope of this chapter. Suffice it to say at this point that some reconsideration of the often harsh penalties for drug use is occurring as of this writing. Notably, U.S. Attorney General Eric Holder recently announced that that the federal government would not prosecute users of medical marijuana who are in compliance with the laws of those states permitting its use (U.S. Department of Justice, 2009). Also, many of the penalties pursuant to the so-called "Rockefeller Drug Laws," enacted in New York State in 1973 under then-Governor Nelson Rockefeller, have been moderated by more recent legislation, which took effect in April 2009 (Drug Policy Alliance, 2009). These small-scale legal reforms may provide an opportunity to assess the relationship between drug laws, the prison census, and the incidence rates of drug abuse and addiction and thereby have a significant impact on related law and policy in the next decade.

KEY TERMS

Biopsychosocial model of practice

Ethical codes

Federalization

Private prisons

Public health

Primary prevention

Portability (of treatment and information)

Scope of practice

DISCUSSION QUESTIONS

1. Should the missions of prisons and jails be confined to punishment, deterrence, and incapacitation? Can prisons rehabilitate criminals, or should rehabilitation be abandoned as a correctional mission?

2. Was deinstitutionalization a good idea, or did it do more harm than good, and on what standards is your answer based? How might the mental health system be re-created so as to respect the civil rights of persons with serious mental illness while providing an effective alternative to incarceration?

3. Are the iatrogenic effects of prison an appropriate part of punishing crimes? Do these effects promote rehabilitation (e.g., by convincing inmates never to return to such a harsh environment)? Are there iatrogenic effects from prison that inmates should not experience, and if so, what can be done to minimize or eliminate them?

4. Should some or all currently illegal drugs be legalized or decriminalized as a means of reducing the prison population? Would this be a more humane, scientific way to treat the problem of drug abuse and addiction, or would it create even greater problems?

5. Imagine that you are a provider of mental health services in a prison and that you are asked to do something you believe to be unethical, such as occasionally to act as a correctional officer—potentially a dual role. What steps would you take in deciding what to do? Would your professional code of ethics be helpful?

References

America's best hospitals. (2009, August). *U.S. News and World Report, 146*(7), 84–86, 89, 90, 92, 95, 96, 98, 100, 102, 104, 106, 108, 111–112.

Angie's list. (2009). Retrieved November 11, 2009, from http://www.angieslist.com/AngiesList/Default.aspx

Ax, R. K. (2003). A viable future for correctional mental health care. In T. J. Fagan & R. K. Ax (Eds.), *Correctional mental health handbook* (pp. 303–327). Thousand Oaks, CA: Sage.

Ax, R. K. (2007). An international history of correctional mental health: The Enlightenment to 1976. In R. K. Ax & T. J. Fagan (Eds.), *Corrections, mental health and social policy: International perspectives* (pp. 5–40). Springfield, IL: Charles C Thomas.

Ax, R. K., & Fagan, T. J. (Eds.). (2007). *Corrections, mental health and social policy: International perspectives.* Springfield, IL: Charles C Thomas.

Bandura, A. (1977). *Social learning theory.* Englewood Cliffs, NJ: Prentice Hall.

Bernstein, R., & Edwards, T. (2008, August 14). *An older and more diverse nation by midcentury.* Washington, DC: U.S. Census Bureau. Retrieved October 2, 2009, from http://www.census.gov/newsroom/releases/archives/population/cb08-123.html

Boothby, J. L., & Clements, C. B. (2000). A national survey of correctional psychologists. *Criminal Justice and Behavior, 27,* 716–732.

Bussert, T. (2009, June 1). Re [FBOPWatch] FBOP facility "good" for vulnerable mentally ill prisoners. Message posted to FBOPWatch@yahoogroups.com [listserv].

Cadigan, T. P. (2008). Evidence-based practices in federal pretrial services. *Federal Probation, 72*(2), 87–90.

Chavez, R. S. (2007). U.S. prisons: A public health perspective. In R. K. Ax & T. J. Fagan (Eds.), *Corrections, mental health and social policy: International perspectives* (pp. 61–84). Springfield, IL: Charles C Thomas.

Chen, S. (2008, November 19). Larger inmate population is boon to private prisons. *The Wall Street Journal*. Retrieved April 10, 2009, from http://online.wsj.com/article/SB122705334657739263.html

Clements, C. B., Althouse, R., Ax, R. K., Magaletta, P. M., Fagan, T. J., & Wormith, S. J. (2007). Systemic issues and correctional outcomes: The impact of context on professional performance. *Criminal Justice and Behavior, 34*, 919–932.

Clements, C. B., & McLearen, A. M. (2003). Research-based practice in corrections: A selective review. In T. J. Fagan & R. K. Ax (Eds.), *Correctional mental health handbook* (pp. 273–302). Thousand Oaks, CA: Sage.

Drug Policy Alliance. (2009, August). *New York's Rockefeller Drug Laws: Explaining the reforms of 2009*. Retrieved November 11, 2009, from http://www.drugpolicy.org/docUploads/Explaining_the_RDL_reforms_of_2009_FINAL.pdf

Eaton, W. W. (1995). Studying the natural history of psychopathology. In M. T. Tsuang, M. Tohen, & G. E. P. Zahner (Eds.), *Textbook in psychiatric epidemiology* (pp. 157–177). New York, NY: Wiley-Liss.

Eckholm, E. (2008, November 9). Citing workload, public lawyers reject new cases. *The New York Times*, pp. A1, A33.

Estelle v. Gamble, 429 U.S. 97 (1976).

Fagan, T. J., Brandt, S. M., & Kleiver, A. L. (2007). Future directions. In R. K. Ax & T. J. Fagan (Eds.), *Corrections, mental health and social policy: International perspectives* (pp. 337–385). Springfield, IL: Charles C Thomas.

Finocchio, L. J., Dower, C. M., McMahon, T., & Gragnola, C. M. (1995, December). *Reforming health care workforce regulation: Policy considerations for the 21st century*. Retrieved January 2, 2007, from http://www.futurehealth.ucsf.edu/pdf_files/reforming.pdf

Fox, R. E., DeLeon, P. H., Newman, R., Sammons, M. T., Dunivin, D. L., & Baker, D. C. (2009). Prescriptive authority and psychology: A status report. *American Psychologist, 64*, 257–268.

Fraher, E., Swartz, M., & Gaul, K. (2006, January). *The supply and distribution of psychiatrists in North Carolina: Pressing issues in the context of mental health reform*. Retrieved September 3, 2007, from http://www.shepscenter.unc.edu/hp/Psychiatrist_Brief.pdf

Freudenheim, M. (2009, February 15). Noted rater of restaurants brings its touch to medicine. *The New York Times*. Retrieved on November 11, 2009, from http://www.nytimes.com/2009/02/16/business/media/16zagat.html?_r=1

Gendreau, P. (1996). Offender rehabilitation: What we know and what needs to be done. *Criminal Justice and Behavior, 23*, 144–161.

Goldstein, A. (2009, May 13). Alarm sounded on social security. *The Washington Post*, pp. A1, A6.

Government Accountability Office. (2008, June 4). *Alien detention standards: Observations on the adherence to ICE's medical standards in detention facilities* (GAO Report No. GAO-08–869T). Retrieved June 13, 2009, from http://www.gao.gov/htext/d08869t.html

Graham v. Florida, 560 U.S. (2010).

Hallinan, J. T. (2001). *Going up the river: Travels in a prison nation*. New York, NY: Random House.

Hamdan v. Rumsfeld, 05-184 U.S. (2006).

Hartney, C. (2006, November). *US rates of incarceration: A global perspective*. Retrieved June 3, 2009, from National Council on Crime and Delinquency: http://www.nccdcrc.org/nccd/pubs/2006nov_factsheet_incarceration.pdf

The Institute on Money in State Politics. (2006, April). *Policy lock-down: Prison interests court political players*. Retrieved June 7, 2009, from http://www.followthemoney.org/press/Reports/200605021.pdf

International Community of the Red Cross. (2007, February). *ICRC report on the treatment of fourteen "high value detainees" in CIA custody* [Limited distribution document]. Washington, DC: Author.

Juvenile Law Center. (2009, February 26). *Juvenile Law Center files federal class action complaint on behalf of affected Luzerne County children and families*. Retrieved on March 16, 2009, from http://jlc.org/news/luzernelawsuit/

Kaiser Commission on Medicaid and the Uninsured. (2008, August). *Five basic facts on the uninsured*. Retrieved September 1, 2008, from http://www.kff.org/uninsured/upload/7806.pdf

Kazdin, A. E. (2008a). Evidence-based treatments and delivery of psychological services: Shifting our emphases to increase impact. *Psychological Services, 5,* 201–215.

Kazdin, A. E. (2008b, October 2). *Letter to President George W. Bush.* Retrieved May 10, 2009, from http://www.apa.org/releases/kazdin-to-bush1008.pdf

Kennedy, P. (1987). *The rise and fall of the great powers.* New York, NY: Random House.

Krisberg, B., & Marchionna, S. (2006, April). *Attitudes of US voters toward prisoner rehabilitation and reentry policies.* Retrieved November 2, 2009, from National Council on Crime and Delinquency: http://www.nccd-crc.org/nccd/pubs/2006april_focus_zogby.pdf

Kupers, T. A., Dronet, T., Winter, M., Austin, J., Kelly, L., Cartier, W., et al. (2009). Beyond supermax administrative segregation: Mississippi's experience rethinking prison classification and creating alternative mental health programs. *Criminal Justice and Behavior, 36,* 1037–1050.

Lamb, H. R., & Weinberger, L. E. (2005). The shift of psychiatric inpatient care from hospitals to jails and prisons. *Journal of the American Academy of Psychiatry and the Law, 33,* 529–534. Retrieved October 31, 2009, from http://www.jaapl.org/cgi/content/full/33/4/529

LIS, Inc. (2006, February). *Interstate transfer of prison inmates in the United States.* Longmont, CO: U.S. Department of Justice, National Institute of Corrections Information Center. Retrieved June 7, 2009, from http://nicic.org/Downloads/PDF/Library/021242.pdf

Lohr, S. (2009, March 26). Doctors raise doubts on digital health data: Concern that effort may not improve care. *The New York Times,* p. B3.

Magaletta, P. R., Ax, R. K., Patry, M. W., & Dietz, E. F. (2005). Clinical practice in segregation: The crucial role of the psychologist. *Corrections Today, 67*(1), 34–36.

Magaletta, P. R., Dennery, C. H., & Ax, R. K. (2005). Telehealth—A future for correctional mental health care. In S. Stojkovic (Ed.), *Managing special populations in jails and prisons* (pp. 20-1 to 20-14). Kingston, NJ: Civic Research Institute.

Martin, S. (2008, November). *Members say no to psychologist involvement in interrogations in unlawful detention settings.* Retrieved October 31, 2009, from Monitor on Psychology: http://www.apa.org/monitor/2008/11/interrogations.html

Mauer, M. (1999). *Race to incarcerate.* New York, NY: New Press.

McGrath, M. P. (2008). Making "what works" work for rural districts. *Federal Probation, 72*(2), 50–53.

Mumola, C. (2000, August). *Incarcerated parents and their children* (Bureau of Justice Statistics Special Report NCJRS 182335). Retrieved November 11, 2009, from http://www.ojp.usdoj.gov/bjs/pub/pdf/iptc.pdf

National Committee on Vital and Health Statistics. (2004, May). *Measuring health care quality: Obstacles and opportunities.* Retrieved November 8, 2009, from U.S. Department of Health and Human Services: http://www.ncvhs.hhs.gov/040531rp.pdf

National Intelligence Council. (2008, November). *Global trends 2025: A transformed world* (NIC 2008-003). Retrieved November 22, 2008, from http://www.dni.gov/nic/PDF_2025/2025_Global_Trends_Final_Report.pdf

Nellis, A., & King, R. S. (2009, July). *No exit: The expanding use of life sentences in America.* Retrieved August 22, 2009, from The Sentencing Project: http://www.sentencingproject.org/doc/publications/inc_noexitseptember2009.pdf

Nordal, K. C. (2009, March). Protecting privacy in an electronic world. *Monitor on Psychology, 40*(3), 53.

Obama, B. H. (2009, January 20). *President Barack Obama's inaugural address.* Retrieved November 2, 2009, from http://www.whitehouse.gov/blog/inaugural-address/

Office of Rural Health & Primary Care, Minnesota Department of Mental Health. (2003, October). *Mental health and primary care in rural Minnesota.* Retrieved September 12, 2007, from http://health.state.mn.us/divs/chs/rhac/mhprofile.doc

Office of the White House. (2008, February). *National drug control strategy.* Retrieved November 2, 2009, from http://www.ncjrs.gov/pdffiles1/ondcp/221371.pdf

Patient Protection and Affordable Care Act, Pub. L. No. 111-148 (2010).

Pear, R. (2009a, October 20). Basic Medicare premium to rise by 15%. *The New York Times,* p. A20.

Pear, R. (2009b, January 18). Privacy issue complicates push to link medical data. *The New York Times,* p. 11.

Pogash, C., & Moore, S. (2009, August 31). California officials fear abduction case may hurt efforts on parole. *The New York Times*, p. A9.

PricewaterhouseCoopers Health Research Institute. (2008). *The price of excess: Identifying waste in healthcare spending.* Retrieved November 11, 2009, from http://pwchealth.com/cgi-local/ hregister.cgi?link=reg/waste.pdf

Rand Corporation. (2008). *Invisible wounds of war: Psychological and cognitive injuries, their consequences, and services to assist their recovery.* Retrieved November 7, 2009, from http://www.rand.org/pubs/monographs/2008/RAND_MG720.pdf

Rao, N. Y. (2003). Recent trends in psychiatry residency workforce with special reference to international medical graduates. *Academic Psychiatry, 27,* 269–276.

Ruiz v. Estelle, 503 F. Supp. 1265 S.D. Texas (1980).

Santos, F. (2008, January 27). Plan to shut prisons stirs worry in towns that depend on them. *The New York Times*, p. 22.

Second Chance Act of 2007, Pub. L. No. 110-199 (2008).

Secretary of State, State of California. (n.d.). *Text of proposed laws: Proposition 5 [Nonviolent Offender Rehabilitation Act of 2008].* Retrieved November 6, 2008, from http://www.voterguide .sos.ca.gov/past/2008/general/text-proposed-laws/text-of-proposed-laws.pdf

Smith, P., Gendreau, P., & Goggin, C. (2007). "What works" in predicting psychiatric hospitalization and relapse: The specific responsivity dimension of effective correctional treatment for mentally disordered offenders. In R. K. Ax & T. J. Fagan (Eds.), *Corrections, mental health and social policy: International perspectives* (pp. 209–233). Springfield, IL: Charles C Thomas.

Steinhauer, J. (2009a, October 24). Arizona may put all state prisons in private hands. *The New York Times*, pp. A1, A13.

Steinhauer, J. (2009b, March 25). To trim costs, states relax hard line on prisons. *The New York Times*, pp. A1, A16.

Stojkovic, S. (2005). Special populations in the context of jail and prison management. In S. Stojkovic (Ed.), *Managing special populations in prison and jails* (pp. 1-1 to 1-12). Kingston, NJ: Civic Research Institute.

Stolberg, S. J. (2010, March 23). Obama signs health care overhaul bill, with a flourish. *The New York Times.* Retrieved March 23, 2010, from http://www.nytimes.com/2010/03/24/ health/policy/24health.html?hp

Sum, A., Khatiwada, I., McLaughlin, J., & Palma, S. (2009, October). *The consequences of dropping out of high school: Joblessness and jailing for high school dropouts and the high cost for taxpayers.* Retrieved October 9, 2009, from Center for Labor Market Studies, Northeastern University: http://www.clms.neu.edu/publication/documents/The_Consequences_of_Dropping_ Out_of_High_School.pdf

Susman, T. H. (2009, January 15). *Letter to M. H. Dortch* [Communication from the American Bar Association to the Federal Communications Commission]. Retrieved June 13, 2009, from http://www.abanet.org/poladv/letters/crimlaw/2009jan15_fcc_1.pdf

Taguba, A. M. (n.d.). *Article 15-6 investigation of the 800th Military Police Brigade* [U.S. Army internal document]. Retrieved May 5, 2004, from http://www.npr.org/iraq/2004/prison_ abuse_report.pdf

The Real Cost of Prisons Weblog. (2008, November 10). *CA: Prop. 5 and 6 defeated in election.* Retrieved June 8, 2009, from http://realcostofprisons.org/blog/archives/2008/11/ca_ prop_5_and_6.html

Thomas, C. R., & Holzer, C. E. (2006). The continuing shortage of child and adolescent psychiatrists. *Journal of the American Academy of Child & Adolescent Psychiatry, 45,* 1023–1031.

Tumlin, K., Joaquin, L., & Natarajan, R. (2009, July). *A broken system: Confidential reports reveal failures in U.S. immigrant detention centers.* Retrieved July 30, 2009, from http://www.nilc.org/immlawpolicy/arrestdet/A-Broken-System-2009-07.pdf

Urbina, I. (2009, March 28). Despite red flags about judges, a kickback scheme flourished. *The New York Times*, pp. A1, A13.

Urbina, I., & Hamill, S. D. (2009, February 13). Judges guilty in scheme to jail youths for profit. *The New York Times*, pp. A1, A20.

U.S. Department of Health and Human Services. (n.d.). *Nursing home compare.* Retrieved December 18, 2008, from http://www.medicare.gov/NHCompare/Include/DataSection/

Questions/SearchCriteriaNEW.asp?version=default&browser=IE%7C7%7CWinXP& language=English&defaultstatus=0&pagelist=Home&CookiesEnabledStatus=True

U.S. Department of Justice. (2009, October 19). *Attorney general announces formal medical marijuana guidelines.* Retrieved November 11, 2009, from http://www.justice.gov/opa/pr/2009/October/09-ag-1119.html

Vaughn, M. G., DeLisi, M., Beaver, K. M., & Wright, J. P. (2009). DAT1 and 5HTT are associated with pathological criminal behavior in a nationally representative sample of youth. *Criminal Justice and Behavior, 36,* 1103–1114.

Washington State Institute for Public Policy. (2006, October). *Evidence-based public policy options to reduce future prison construction, criminal justice costs, and crime rates* (Document No. 06-10-1201). Retrieved January 7, 2009, from http://www.wsipp.wa.gov/rptfiles/06–10–1201.pdf

West, H. C., & Sabol, W. J. (2009, March). *Prison inmates at midyear 2008: Statistical tables* (Bureau of Justice Statistics Special Report NCJRS 225619). Retrieved August 22, 2009, from http://www.ojp.usdoj.gov/bjs/pub/pdf/pim08st.pdf

Whitley, T. (2002, August 30). Southside rallies for prisons: Community fights against closures. *Richmond Times-Dispatch*, pp. A1, A12.

Whitman, J. Q. (2003). *Harsh justice: Criminal punishment and widening divide between America and Europe.* New York, NY: Oxford University Press.

Wines, E. C., & Dwight, T. W. (1867). *Report on the prisons and reformatories of the United States and Canada.* Albany, NY: Van Benthuysen & Sons' Steam Printing House.

Zweig, J. M., & Blackmore, J. (2008, October). *Strategies to prevent prison rape by changing the correctional culture.* Washington, DC: U.S. Department of Justice, Office of Justice Programs, National Institute of Justice. Retrieved October 29, 2008, from http://www.ncjrs.gov/pdffiles1/nij/222843.pdf

Appendix

General Readings and Websites

The reference material included in this appendix represents a sampling of materials that the reader might find useful. The appendix is not meant to be a complete or even representative list of reference materials relevant to correctional mental health but, rather, may serve as a starting point for the reader interested in pursuing additional information about particular correctional and/or mental health topics.

Sample Articles, Book Chapters, and Documents

American Psychiatric Association. (2006, December). *The use of restraint and seclusion in correctional mental health care.* Retrieved February 17, 2010, from http://archive.psych.org/edu/other_res/lib_archives/archives/200605.pdf

American Psychological Association Presidential Task Force on Evidence-Based Practice. (2006). Evidence-based practice in psychology. *American Psychologist, 61,* 271–285.

Hayes, L. (2009). *Characteristics of juvenile suicide in confinement.* Available from www.ncjrs.gov/pdffiles1/ojjdp/214434.pdf

Human Rights Watch. (2003). *Ill-equipped: U.S. prisons and offenders with mental illness.* New York, NY: Author.

Office of the Surgeon General. (2001). *Youth violence: A report of the surgeon general.* Available from www.surgeongeneral.gov/library/youthviolence

Scott, W., & Crime and Justice Institute. (2008). *Effective clinical practices in treating clients in the criminal justice system.* Washington, DC: U.S. Department of Justice, National Institute of Corrections.

Severson, M., & Duclos, C. W. (2005, June). *American Indian suicides in jail: Can risk screening be culturally sensitive?* Washington, DC: U.S. Department of Justice, Office of Justice Programs, National Institute of Justice. Available from http://www.ncjrs.gov/pdffiles1/nij/207326.pdf

Task Force on Transforming Juvenile Justice. (2009, December). *Charting a new course: A blueprint for transforming juvenile justice in New York State.* Retrieved February 15, 2010, from http://www.vera.org/download?file=2944/Charting-a-new-course-A-blueprint-for-transforming-juvenile-justice-in-New-York-State.pdf

Warren, J. (2009, March). *One in 31: The long reach of American corrections.* Retrieved March 2, 2009, from Pew Center on the States: http://www.pewtrusts.org/uploadedFiles/wwwpewtrustsorg/Reports/sentencing_and_corrections/PSPP_1in31_report_FINAL_WEB_2-27-09.pdf

Warren, J., Gelb, A., Horowitz, J., & Riordan, J. (2008). *One in 100: Behind bars in America 2008.* Retrieved January 11, 2009, from Pew Center on the States: http://www.pewcenteronthestates.org/uploadedFiles/One%20in%20100.pdf

Washington State Institute for Public Policy. (2006, October). *Evidence-based public policy options to reduce future prison construction, criminal justice costs, and crime rates* (Document No. 06-10-1201). Retrieved January 7, 2009, from http://www.wsipp.wa.gov/rptfiles/06-10-1201.pdf

Young, M. (2001). *Victim rights and services: A modern saga.* Retrieved April 26, 2009, from National Organization for Victim Assistance: http://www.trynova.org/victiminfo/readings/VictimRightsandServices.pdf

Sample Books

American Psychiatric Association. (2000). *Diagnostic and statistical manual of mental disorders* (4th ed., Text Revision). Washington, DC: Author. (Note: *DSM-V* is in preparation.)

Andrade, J. (2009). *Handbook of violent risk assessment and treatment: New approaches for mental health professionals.* New York, NY: Springer.

Ax, R. K., & Fagan, T. J. (Eds.). (2007). *Corrections, mental health and social policy: International perspectives.* Springfield, IL: Charles C Thomas.

Boesky, L. (2002). *Juvenile offenders with mental health problems.* Alexandria, VA: American Correctional Association.

Braithwaite, J. (2002). *Restorative justice and responsive regulation.* New York, NY: Oxford University Press.

Carlson, P. M., & Garrett, J. S. (Eds.). (2008). *Prison and jail administration: Practice and theory* (2nd ed.). Sudbury, MA: Jones and Bartlett.

Cohen, F. (2008). *The mentally disordered inmate and the law* (2nd ed.). Kingston, NJ: Civic Research Institute.

Correia, K. M. (2009). *A handbook for correctional psychologists: Guidance for the prison practitioner* (2nd ed.). Springfield, IL: Charles C Thomas.

Dobbert, D. L. (2004). *Halting the sexual predator among us: Preventing attack, rape and lust homicide.* Alexandria, VA: American Correctional Association.

Fagan, T. J., & Ax, R. K. (Eds.). (2003). *Correctional mental health handbook.* Thousand Oaks, CA: Sage.

Gideon, L., & Sung, H. (2010). *Rethinking corrections: Rehabilitation, reentry, and reintegration.* Thousand Oaks, CA: Sage.

Greifinger, R. (Ed.). (2007). *Public health behind bars: From prisons to communities.* New York, NY: Springer.

Grisso, T., Vincent, G., & Seagrave, D. (Eds.). (2005). *Mental health screening and assessment in juvenile justice.* Alexandria, VA: American Correctional Association.

Haney, C. (2006). *Reforming punishment: Psychological limits to the pains of imprisonment.* Washington, DC: American Psychological Association.

Kupers, T. (1999). *Prison madness: The mental health crisis behind bars and what we must do about it.* San Francisco, CA: Jossey-Bass.

Marshall, W. L., Fernandez, Y., Marshall, L., & Serran, G. (Eds.). (2005). *Sexual offender treatment: Issues and controversies.* Alexandria, VA: American Correctional Association.

Mauer, M., & Chesney-Lind, M. (Eds.). (2002). *Invisible punishment: The collateral consequences of mass imprisonment.* New York, NY: New Press.

Megargee, E. I. (2006). *Using the MMPI-2 in criminal justice and correctional settings.* Minneapolis: University of Minnesota Press.

Mills, J. F., Kroner, D. G., & Morgan, R. D. (2011). *The clinician's guide to violence risk assessment.* New York, NY: Guilford.

Ruiz, A., Dvoskin, J., Scott, C., & Metzner, J. (Eds.). (2010). *Manual of forms and guidelines for correctional mental health.* Arlington, VA: American Psychiatric Association.

Schabas, W. A. (2002). *The abolition of the death penalty in international law* (3rd ed.). Cambridge, UK: Cambridge University Press.

Scott, C. (Ed.). (2010). *Handbook of correctional mental health* (2nd ed.). Arlington, VA: American Psychiatric Association.

Sims, B. (Ed.). (2007). *Substance abuse treatment with correctional clients.* London, UK: Taylor & Francis.

Thienhaus, O. J., & Piasecki, M. (Eds.). (2007). *Correctional psychiatry: Practice guidelines and strategies.* Kingston, NJ: Civic Research Institute.

Toch, H., & Adams, K. (2002). *Acting out: Maladaptive behavior in confinement.* Washington, DC: American Psychological Association.

Torrey, E. F. (2008). *The insanity offense: How America's failure to treat the seriously mentally ill endangers its citizens.* New York, NY: Norton.

Weiner, I. B., & Hess, A. K. (Eds.). (2006). *The handbook of forensic psychology* (3rd ed.). Hoboken, NJ: John Wiley.

Whitman, J. Q. (2003). *Harsh justice: Criminal punishment and the widening divide between America and Europe.* New York, NY: Oxford University Press.

Correctional Practice Standards

Althouse, R. (Ed.). (2010). Standards for psychology services in jails, prisons, correctional facilities, and agencies [Special Issue]. *Criminal Justice and Behavior, 37*(7), 752–808.

American Psychiatric Association. (2000). *Guidelines for psychiatric services in jails and prisons* (2nd ed.). Washington, DC: Author.

The Association for the Treatment of Sexual Abusers. (2004). *ATSA practice standards and guidelines for the evaluation, treatment and management of adult male sexual abusers.* Beaverton, OR: Author.

National Association of Social Workers. (2004). *NASW standards for palliative and end of life care.* Washington, DC: Author.

National Association of Social Workers. (2005). *NASW standards for social work practice with substance use disorders.* Washington, DC: Author.

National Commission on Correctional Health Care. (2004a). *Standards for health services in juvenile detention and confinement facilities.* Chicago, IL: Author.

National Commission on Correctional Health Care. (2004b). *Standards for opioid treatment programs in correctional settings.* Chicago, IL: Author.

National Commission on Correctional Health Care. (2008a). *Standards for health services in jails.* Chicago, IL: Author.

National Commission on Correctional Health Care. (2008b). *Standards for health services in prisons.* Chicago, IL: Author.

National Commission on Correctional Health Care. (2008c). *Standards for mental health services in correctional facilities.* Chicago, IL: Author.

Relevant Journals

Addiction Research

Aggression and Violent Behavior

American Journal of Law & Medicine

American Journal of Public Health

Behavioral Sciences and the Law

British Journal of Criminology

Canadian Journal of Criminology and Criminal Justice

Community Mental Health Journal

Crime & Delinquency

Criminal Behavior and Mental Health

Criminal Justice and Behavior

Criminal Justice Policy Review

Criminal Justice Studies: A Critical Journal of Crime, Law, & Society

Criminology

Criminology & Public Policy

European Journal of Criminology

Federal Probation

Forum on Corrections Research

International Journal of Forensic Mental Health

International Journal of Law and Psychiatry

International Journal of Offender Therapy and Comparative Criminology

Journal of Addictions and Offender Counseling

Journal of Applied Rehabilitation Counseling

Journal of Contemporary Criminal Justice

Journal of Correctional Health Care

Journal of Criminal Justice

Journal of Criminal Law and Criminology

Journal of Drug Issues

Journal of Forensic Sciences

Journal of Health Care for the Poor and Underserved

Journal of Interpersonal Violence

Journal of Law, Medicine, and Ethics

Journal of Offender Counseling, Services, and Rehabilitation

Journal of Offender Rehabilitation

Journal of Substance Abuse Treatment

Journal of the American Academy of Psychiatry and the Law

Justice Quarterly

Law and Human Behavior

Psychiatric Services

Psychological Services

Psychology, Crime, & Law

Psychology of Addictive Behaviors

Psychology, Public Policy, and Law

Punishment & Society

Sexual Abuse

The British Journal of Forensic Practice

The Journal of Research in Crime and Delinquency

The Journal of Sex Research

The Journal of Sexual Aggression

The Prison Journal

Criminal Justice/Corrections/ Mental Health Websites

Government Sites

Bureau of Justice Statistics: http://www.ojp.gov/bjs/

Centers for Disease Control and Prevention: www.cdc.gov

Civil Rights of Institutionalized Persons Act (CRIPA): www.usdoj.gov

The CMHS National GAINS Center, effective mental health and substance abuse services for people with co-occurring disorders in contact with the justice system: http://gainscenter.samhsa.gov/html/default.asp

Correctional Service of Canada: http://www.csc-scc.gc.ca/

FBI Research Page: http://www.fbi.gov/research.htm

Federal Bureau of Investigation: http://www.fbi.gov/

Federal Bureau of Prisons: http://www.bop.gov/

Federal Bureau of Prisons, APA-accredited psychology internship programs: http://www.bop.gov/jobs/students/psychology.jsp

National Center for Mental Health and Juvenile Justice: www.ncmhjj.com

National Criminal Justice Reference Service: http://www.ncjrs.gov/

National Institute of Corrections: http://nicic.org/

National Youth Screening and Assessment Project: http://www.umassmed.edu/nysap/

Office of Juvenile Justice and Delinquency Prevention: www.ojjdp.ncrjs.gov

Substance Abuse and Mental Health Services Administration: www.samhsa.gov

Nongovernmental Organizations (NGOs)

Amnesty International: http://www.amnesty.org/

Canadian Association of Elizabeth Fry Societies: http://www.elizabethfry.ca/

The Center for Behavioral Health Services & Criminal Justice Research: http://www.cbhs-cjr.rutgers.edu/

Criminal Justice, Mental Health Consensus Project: http://consensusproject.org/about-the-project

Families Against Mandatory Minimums: http://www.famm.org/

Fortune Society: http://www.fortunesociety.org/

Frontline, *The New Asylum* and *Released*: http://www.pbs.org/wgbh/pages/frontline/released/view/

Human Rights Watch: http://www.hrw.org/

John Howard Society of Canada: http://www.johnhoward.ca/jhsmiss.htm

Just Detention International: http://www.justdetention.org/

Juvenile Detention Alternatives Initiative: www.jdaihelpdesk.org

National Alliance on Mental Illness: http://www.nami.org/

National Commission on Correctional Health Care: www.ncchc.org

Pennsylvania Prison Society: http://www.prisonsociety.org/index.shtml

The Sentencing Project: http://www.sentencingproject.org

Vera Institute of Justice: http://www.vera.org/

Victims' Rights Organizations

Canadian Resource Centre for Victims of Crime: http://crcvc.ca/en

KlaasKids Foundation: http://www.klaaskids.org/vrights.htm

National Center for the Victims of Crime: http://www.ncvc.org/ncvc/main.aspx?dbID=dash_Home

National Organization for Victim Assistance: http://www.trynova.org/

Office for Victims of Crime, U.S. Department of Justice: http://www.ojp.usdoj.gov/ovc/welcovc/welcome.html

See also local, state/provincial, regional organizations, e.g., Missouri Victim Assistance Network: http://mova.missouri.org/

Professional Organizations

American Academy of Child and Adolescent Psychiatry: www.aacap.org

American Academy of Psychiatry and the Law: http://www.aapl.org/org.htm

American Correctional Association: www.aca.org

American Jail Association: http://www.aja.org/default.aspx

American Psychiatric Association: http://www.psych.org

American Psychological Association, Division 18 (Psychologists in Public Service Sector), Criminal Justice Section: http://ap.org/divisions18/

American Psychological Association, Division 41 (American Psychology-Law Society): http://www.ap-ls.org/

Canadian Psychological Association, Criminal Justice Section: http://www.cpa.ca/sections/criminaljustice/

International Association of Correctional and Forensic Psychology: http://ia4cfp.org

National Association for Addiction Professionals: http://www.naadac.org/

National Association of Social Workers: http://www.socialworkers.org/

Registered Nurses' Association of Ontario, Ontario Nurses' Interest Group: http://www.rnao.org/Page.asp?PageID=924&ContentID=1452

Professional Ethical Codes

A list of links to various professional codes of ethics may be found on http://kspope.com/ethcodes/index.php

In particular, see:

American Academy of Psychiatry and the Law: http://www.aapl.org/ethics.htm

American Correctional Association: http://www.aca.org/pastpresentfuture/ethics.asp

American Correctional Health Services Association: http://www.achsa.org/displaycommon.cfm?an=9

American Jail Association: http://www.aja.org/ethics.aspx

American Medical Association: http://www.ama-assn.org/ama/pub/physician-resources/medical-ethics/code-medical-ethics.shtml

American Nurses Association: http://www.med.howard.edu/ethics/handouts/american_nurses_association_code.htm

American Psychiatric Association: http://www.psych.org/MainMenu/PsychiatricPractice/Ethics.aspx

American Psychological Association: http://www.apa.org/ethics/code2002.html

American Public Health Association: http://www.apha.org/programs/education/progeduethicalguidelines.htm

Association for the Treatment of Sexual Abusers: http://www.atsa.com/pdfs/COE.pdf

Canadian Psychological Association: http://www.cpa.ca/cpasite/userfiles/Documents/Canadian%20Code%20of%20Ethics%20for%20Psycho.pdf

College of Registered Psychiatric Nurses: http://www.crpnbc.ca/competency.html

National Association of Social Workers: http://www.socialworkers.org/pubs/code/default.asp

Society of Correctional Physicians: http://www.corrdocs.org/framework.php?pagetype=aboutethics&bgn=2

Universal Declaration of Ethical Principles for Psychologists: http://www.cpa.ca/cpasite/userfiles/Documents/Universal_Declaration_asADOPTEDbyIUPsySIAAP_July2008.pdf

Corrections/Mental Health Conferences

Academic and Health Policy Conference on Correctional Health: http://www.umassmed.edu/commed/ch_conference09/index.aspx

American Correctional Association: http://www.aca.org/Conferences

American Psychology-Law Society Conference: http://www.ap-ls.org/conferences/Conferences.php

Association for the Treatment of Sexual Abusers Annual Conference: http://www.atsa.com/conf.html

See also: http://www.atsa.com/confOther.html

Forensic Mental Health Association of California Conference: http://www.fmhac.net/conference.html

Mental Health in Corrections Conference: http://mhcc.forest.edu/

National Association for Addiction Professionals, National Conference on Addiction Disorders: http://www.naadac.org/index.php?option=com_content&view=article&id=351&Itemid=117

National Commission on Correctional Health Care: http://www.ncchc.org/education/index.html

North American Correctional and Criminal Justice Psychology Conference: http://tinyurl.com/ddobyv

Other Electronic Learning Resources

Some criminal justice websites now offer online conferences, web-based seminars and forums, and so forth. The numbers may be expected to expand with the capabilities and reach of the Internet. A few such sites that offer information relevant to correctional mental health concerns are:

National Criminal Justice Reference Service Office for Victims of Crime, e.g., http://ovc.ncjrs.gov/ovcproviderforum/index.asp

National Institute of Corrections Video Learning Opportunities: http://nicic.org/Videos

National Institute of Justice: Online "expert chats": http://www.ojp.usdoj.gov/nij/events/expert-chats/welcome.htm and training links (including web-based training): http://www.ojp.usdoj.gov/nij/training/welcome.htm

Index

About the Editors

Thomas J. Fagan, Ph.D., is currently an associate professor of psychology and the director of the Division of Social and Behavioral Science at Nova Southeastern University in Ft. Lauderdale, Florida. For 23 years he was a psychology practitioner and administrator with the Federal Bureau of Prisons, where he was an active participant in developing correctional mental health programs; creating mental health policies and procedures; and training professional, paraprofessional, and correctional staff. Dr. Fagan was also the Bureau's chief hostage negotiator and coordinator of its crisis negotiation training program. Over the years, he has served as a consultant to numerous federal, state, and local law enforcement agencies in the areas of crisis negotiation, critical incident stress debriefing, and management of correctional mental health services and programs.

Dr. Fagan has published regularly in correctional and psychological journals, has authored several book chapters, and coedited two books with Robert K. Ax, Ph.D.—*Correctional Mental Health Handbook* (2003) and *Corrections, Mental Health, and Social Policy: International Perspectives* (2007). He also published a book on crisis negotiation in correctional settings—*Negotiating Correctional Incidents: A Practical Guide* (2003).

Since 1997, Dr. Fagan has served as the American Psychological Association's (APA's) representative on the Board of Directors of the National Commission on Correctional Health Care (NCCHC)—a national organization dedicated to ensuring quality health and mental health care to incarcerated individuals. He served as NCCHC's board chair from 2002 to 2003. He is a fellow in APA's Divisions 12 and 18. Division 18 recognized his work in correctional mental health with a special achievement award in 1993, and he received APA's Award for Distinguished Contributions to Practice in the Public Sector in 2006. He received his bachelor's degree from Rutgers University and his master's and doctoral degrees from Virginia Tech.

Robert K. Ax, Ph.D., received his doctorate in clinical psychology from Virginia Polytechnic Institute and State University and practiced in state and federal corrections for more than 20 years. He is a licensed clinical psychologist (Virginia), a fellow of the American Psychological Association (APA), a member of the Canadian Psychological Association (CPA), and a former president of the APA Division of Psychologists in Public Service (18). He has twice been the recipient of Division 18's Distinguished Service Award, and in 2009 he received its highest honor, the Harold Hildreth Award. He was the training director of the Federal Bureau of Prisons' first APA-accredited internship program at the Federal Correctional Institution, Petersburg, Virginia. Dr. Ax is the coeditor, with Dr. Thomas J. Fagan, of two previous volumes, the *Correctional Mental Health Handbook*, published by Sage in 2003; and *Corrections, Mental Health, and Social Policy: International Perspectives*, published by Charles C Thomas in 2007.

He has published articles on mental health training and correctional issues; currently serves on the editorial board of the journal *Criminal Justice and Behavior*; and has served as an invited reviewer for other journals, including *American Psychologist, Psychological Services*, and *Professional Psychology: Research and Practice.*

Dr. Ax has published several articles on organized psychology's prescriptive authority initiative as well. He delivered an invited address on this issue at the annual CPA convention in 2008 and served as a content expert (1998–1999) for the development of the APA College of Professional Psychology's Psychopharmacology Examination for Psychologists. Dr. Ax received the American Society for the Advancement of Pharmacotherapy's (APA's Division 55) National Leadership Award in 2006.

About the Contributors

Biographical information about contributing authors is in alphabetical order.

Dean Aufderheide, Ph.D., is a licensed psychologist specializing in clinical and forensic psychology in the state of Florida. After graduating with a master's degree in theology, he obtained his Ph.D. in clinical psychology, and he is currently working toward a master's degree in public administration.

Dr. Aufderheide has more than 20 years of experience in the provision, management, and oversight of mental health services across various levels of care in military, state government, and private settings. He has 15 years of experience in the criminal justice system and has authored numerous publications on mental health issues. A popular speaker, he has lectured on mental health issues in correctional settings at national conferences throughout the United States.

Dr. Aufderheide has been the director of mental health services for the Florida Department of Corrections for the past 6 years. He serves on the Board of Directors for the International Association of Correctional and Forensic Psychology and is a member of the Education Committee for the National Commission on Correctional Health Care. He is a member of the National Register of Health Care Providers in Psychology, American Psychological Association, Florida Psychological Association, and American Correctional Association. Dr. Aufderheide is passionately committed to ensure individuals with mental illness in America's prisons receive appropriate treatment and aftercare planning for successful reentry into our communities.

Dyona Augustin, B.S., received her degree in psychology from Nova Southeastern University (NSU) in May 2010. In addition to working on a number of research projects with her fellow undergraduate classmates, she also had the privilege of working as an undergraduate research assistant at the Center for Psychological Studies, NSU's psychology graduate school. Her primary research interests include forensic psychology and minority mental health issues. She is also interested in abnormal psychology and trauma psychology. She is currently enrolled in a clinical psychology doctoral program.

Rebecca L. Bauer, M.A., is currently a doctoral student in the Counseling Psychology program at Texas Tech University. She received her master of arts degree in forensic psychology from John Jay College of Criminal Justice and her bachelor of science degree in criminal justice from St. John's University. As a result of her outstanding academic performance, she received the St. John's University College of Professional Studies Silver Medal and the Robert S. Morrow Psychology Award from John Jay College of Criminal Justice. Ms. Bauer is a graduate student affiliate of Division 41 (American Psychology-Law Society) of the American Psychological Association. Her research interests are mainly focused in the area of correctional mental health. She recently coauthored two peer-reviewed publications examining barriers to offender employment. Her dissertation is investigating the impact long-term incarceration has on offenders with severe mental illness. Recently, utilizing the *Changing Lives and Changing Outcomes* program (Morgan, Kroner, Mills, & Bauer, manuscript in preparation), Ms. Bauer led two psychotherapy groups with offenders with co-occurring mental illness and substance abuse.

John D. Baxter, Ed.D., joined Corrections Corporation of America (CCA) in March 2008 as director of mental health services. Prior to joining CCA, he served as the psychology services administrator for the Federal Bureau of Prisons. Dr. Baxter's successful correctional mental health career spans 26 years of state, federal, and private sector service. During this time he has provided direct services to mentally ill patients as a psychologist examiner, psychologist intern, staff psychologist, and chief psychologist. He has provided administrative oversight regarding mental health care as regional psychology administrator and agency psychology administrator in the Federal Bureau of Prisons. His clinical and administrative work has included implementing substance abuse treatment programs, implementing treatment and risk assessment programs for sex offenders, expanding treatment programs for mentally ill and behaviorally disordered offenders, oversight of management development and distance training programs for a large correctional system, and administrative management of mental health and substance abuse treatment services. In his current role as director of mental health services for CCA, he provides leadership and administrative oversight to mental health teams in the largest private corrections system in the nation.

Dr. Baxter graduated from George Peabody College of Vanderbilt University with a doctoral degree in education (human development counseling). He also holds a master's degree from Harding School of Religion and a bachelor's degree from David Lipscomb University.

Shelia M. Brandt, Psy.D., earned her doctorate in clinical psychology from the Minnesota School of Professional Psychology in 1998. She completed her predoctoral internship at the Federal Correctional Institution in Petersburg, Virginia. She subsequently worked for the Virginia Department of Corrections as the director of a residential mental health unit within a medium-security prison. Subsequently, Dr. Brandt was employed as a senior doctoral psychologist with the Wisconsin Resource Center. In 2001, Dr. Brandt returned to Minnesota, where she worked as a forensic evaluator for both the Federal Bureau of Prisons and the state of Minnesota. In 2006, she became the psychology director for Minnesota State Operated Services, where she supervised psychologists providing forensic evaluations and risk assessments. Since 2009, Dr. Brandt has served as the legislative and stakeholder relations director for the Minnesota Sex Offender Program, interfacing with policy makers and community stakeholders (i.e., victim advocates, county attorneys) to shape policy and statutes related to sexual violence.

Dr. Brandt has served as an adjunct professor at St. Mary's University and at Gustavus Adolphus College. She has published several book chapters related to the provision of psychological services to individuals in jails and prisons. She served as associate editor for the journal *Psychological Services* for 4 years and presently serves as a reviewer. Dr. Brandt received the Distinguished Service Award from Division 18 (Psychologists in Public Service) of the American Psychological Association (APA) in 2009. Her current interests include civil commitment and alternatives for sex offenders; sentencing alternatives for the seriously mentally ill; international perspectives on criminal justice systems; and encouraging psychologists to use the science of psychology to inform public policy and legislation related to classification, sentencing, and treatment of criminal offenders. She is a licensed psychologist and is a member of APA, the Association for the Treatment of Sex Offenders, and the Minnesota Association for the Treatment of Sex Offenders.

Peter M. Carlson, D.P.A., is a professor in the Department of Government at Christopher Newport University, Newport News, Virginia. He is retired from a 30-year career with the U.S. Department of Justice, Federal Bureau of Prisons (FBOP), where he served as the assistant director of the agency, regional director of the Western Region, and warden of three federal prisons. He received his doctorate in public administration from the University of Southern California.

Dr. Carlson is the author of many professional publications in the field of prison administration and is the coeditor of the best-selling contributed text *Prison and Jail Administration: Practice and Theory*, a college textbook that is currently published in its second edition. Dr. Carlson was recently elected by his peers to serve as the chair of the University Faculty and president of the Faculty Senate of his university.

Debra DePrato, M.D., is an associate clinical professor of public health and preventive medicine at Louisiana State University (LSU) Health Sciences Center in New Orleans. She is board-certified in adult and forensic psychiatry and board-eligible in child and adolescent psychiatry. Dr. DePrato currently serves as the project director for the John T. and Catherine T. MacArthur Foundation's Louisiana *Models for Change*, a 5-year (2006–2011), $10 million commitment toward Louisiana juvenile justice community-based grants.

Dr. DePrato served as program director for the LSU Health Sciences Center Juvenile Justice Program, which developed and provided all medical, dental, and mental health care to Louisiana's incarcerated youth, from 2000 until 2006. During the same time, she served as chief of the Section of Juvenile Justice for the School of Public Health. Dr. DePrato founded the Division of Law and Psychiatry at LSU Medical Center and developed an accredited forensic residency program.

Dr. DePrato received her M.D. in 1984 from LSU Health Sciences Center–Shreveport and completed her adult and child psychiatry residency training at Albert B. Chandler Medical Center in Lexington, Kentucky. She completed a forensic psychiatry fellowship at Yale University in 1992, and then joined the faculty at the LSU School of Medicine in New Orleans, Department of Psychiatry.

Dr. DePrato has served as an expert in forensic and child psychiatry in numerous states and courts. In 2005, she was awarded the Exemplary Psychiatrist Award by the National Alliance on Mental Illness (NAMI). Dr. DePrato is a distinguished fellow in the American Psychiatric Association and served on the APA Psychiatry and the Law Council. Dr. DePrato is also a member of the American Academy of Psychiatry and the Law and of the Louisiana Psychiatric Medical Association, also serving in many capacities in these organizations. Dr. DePrato currently is an Advisory Board member to the National Institute of Drug Abuse and to the Governor's Juvenile Justice and Delinquency Prevention Board. She provides mental health expert/consultation services for the U.S. Department of Justice Civil Rights Division.

Dr. DePrato coauthored a book chapter in *Principles and Practice of Child and Adolescent Forensic Mental Health* (American Psychiatric Publishing, Inc., 2010).

Andrew Gray is a behavioral science technologist who has completed three 90-day contracts as an offender counselor with the Correctional Service of Canada. He holds a diploma in behavioral science technology, is a student member of the Criminal Justice Section of the Canadian Psychological Association, and is currently completing the final year of his honors B.A. in psychology at Carleton University. Although his main research interests lie within the realm of offender self-report and violence risk assessment, Andrew has assisted in research focusing on antisocial attitudes and associates in psychopathic offenders, the interrater reliability of risk appraisal guides in clinical settings, risk factors for offender suicide, and attitudes towards sexual coercion. Andrew's long-term goal is to obtain a Ph.D. in clinical psychology.

Steven J. Helfand, Psy.D., C.C.H.P., is currently regional vice president of operations for Correct Care Solutions, where he oversees the mental health and health services to multiple jail and prison systems. He previously served 4 and one half years as statewide director of mental health services for the University of Connecticut Health Center's Correctional Managed Health Care program, where he was responsible for the services provided to a daily population of approximately 20,000 inmates. Prior positions include director of forensic mental health for Nassau County Correctional Center in New York and deputy director/acting director of mental health services at Rikers Island in New York City. Other experience includes 4 years as director of mental health and health services at the New York City Department of Juvenile Justice and consultant to the New York City Department of Probation. Dr. Helfand has been working in corrections since 1993.

Dr. Helfand received his Psy.D. from Pace University and is currently a licensed psychologist in the states of New York and Connecticut. He has taught undergraduate and graduate courses at Pace University since 1997.

Dr. Helfand is a member of the National Commission on Correctional Health Care's Mental Health Task Force, which has completed comprehensive standards for jail and prison mental health services. He is recognized as a certified correctional health professional and is the former chair and current member of the Academy of Correctional Health Professionals Board of Directors as well as a member of their education committee. Dr. Helfand has served as a member of the National Governor's Association public programs task force addressing electronic health information exchange. He is a frequent presenter at conferences in the areas of behavioral management, self-injury, sex offenders, and correctional mental health care delivery. Dr. Helfand has published in the areas of self-injury in corrections and managing disruptive and aggressive inmates. He currently maintains a limited private consulting practice providing mental health oversight and expert services to jails, prisons, and attorneys.

Daryl G. Kroner, Ph.D., C.Psych., was employed as a correctional psychologist from 1986 to 2008. During this time he worked at maximum-, medium-, and minimum-security facilities. He received his Ph.D. from Carleton University and is a licensed psychologist in the province of Ontario. Dr. Kroner has taught university forensic courses; consulted with hostage negotiating teams; and conducted critical incident stress management workshops, risk assessment workshops, and in-house training sessions on a variety of topics. Dr. Kroner is the past-chair of Criminal Justice Psychology of the Canadian Psychological Association. He is also a fellow of the Canadian Psychological Association. His research interests have centered on assessment issues within corrections. This has included, in collaboration with Dr. Jeremy Mills, the development of several instruments, including the Measures of Criminal Attitudes and Associates (MCAA); Depression, Hopelessness and Suicide Scale (DHS); Criminal Attribution Inventory (CRAI); Release and Reintegration Inventory (RRI); and the Measures of Criminal and Antisocial Desistance (MCAD).

In the fall of 2008, Dr. Kroner joined the Department of Criminology and Criminal Justice at Southern Illinois University–Carbondale. He is a co-principal investigator on a National Institute of Justice research grant examining dynamic risk in community supervision. Current research interests include risk assessment and management issues among mentally ill offenders and criminal desistance.

Lacey Levitt, M.Ed., received her bachelor's degree from the Johns Hopkins University and her master's degree from the University of Virginia. She is currently a doctoral candidate in clinical psychology in the University of Virginia's Curry School of Education. Ms. Levitt has conducted research on forensic psychology issues and has facilitated psychoeducational groups in a women's prison, a jail, and a juvenile detention center. She has coauthored articles that have appeared in the *American Journal of Orthopsychiatry* and in the *Journal of Offender Rehabilitation*. She is a member of the Animal-Human Interaction Section of the American Psychological Association's Division 17 (Counseling Psychology) and is currently involved in a federal research project on the link between animal cruelty and interpersonal violence.

Ann Booker Loper, Ph.D., is a clinical psychologist and professor at the University of Virginia's Curry School of Education. She received her Ph.D. in psychology from the University of Texas in Austin in 1972. Dr. Loper is a licensed clinical psychologist in Virginia and fellow of the Academy of Cognitive Therapy. Her research focuses on mental health and adjustment of prisoners, with a particular interest in understanding the experiences of incarcerated parents and their families. In concert with her graduate students, Dr. Loper developed *Parenting From the Inside: Making the Mother-Child Connection*, a psychoeducational curriculum for mothers in prison that focuses on positive means of dealing with parenting stress in prison and effective ways of staying connected with children during incarceration. Dr. Loper has collaborated with prison, jail, and community partners in each of her research efforts and is currently undertaking an evaluation of jail transitional programming. Dr. Loper has also conducted research concerning the needs and characteristics of female juvenile offenders. During her tenure at the University of Virginia, Dr. Loper served as director of the Center for Clinical Psychology Services as well as director of the Curry School Programs in Clinical and School Psychology.

Philip R. Magaletta, Ph.D., has administered and practiced correctional psychology for more than a decade with the Federal Bureau of Prisons (BOP). He currently serves the agency as the clinical training coordinator for the Psychology Services Branch and is a faculty associate at the Johns Hopkins University. A graduate of the University of Scranton, Magaletta earned his master's degree in 1992 from Loyola College in Maryland and his doctorate in clinical psychology in 1996 from St. Louis University. He is an active member of several professional associations, and his research and work have been published in several journals and books. He is a member of the BOP's national Institutional Review Board and has earned a number of awards for his federal service, including the Myrl E. Alexander Award, a national award issued by the BOP for developing new techniques in correctional programs and implementing innovative correctional procedures. His areas of research include mental health services delivery to incarcerated populations, addictions counseling, spirituality, telehealth, and organizational approaches to behavioral sciences research in prisons.

Jon T. Mandracchia, Ph.D., is an assistant professor of psychology at the University of Southern Mississippi. He obtained his doctorate in counseling psychology from Texas Tech University. His research interests are in criminal thinking, suicide in correctional environments, public perceptions of criminal justice issues, and training in correctional and forensic psychology. His work has been published in such journals as *Criminal Justice and Behavior* and *Psychological Services*.

Alix M. McLearen, Ph.D., is a licensed clinical psychologist with the Federal Bureau of Prisons. After obtaining her master's degree from Missouri State University, she went on to complete a predoctoral internship at the United States Medical Center for Federal Prisoners, and received her doctorate in clinical psychology and the law from the University of Alabama in 2003. She has held a variety of positions in correctional psychology, including developer and administrator of a residential treatment program for inmates with cognitive deficits resulting from brain injury or mental illness. Presently, she serves as chief of psychology services at the Federal Correctional Institution in Memphis, Tennessee. In this capacity, she provides oversight of the facility's mental health services, conducts staff training on topics such as suicide prevention, and supervises the practicum training of graduate students. In addition, she was appointed as the institution's reentry coordinator, implementing initiatives to enhance societal reintegration opportunities for ex-offenders. Dr. McLearen has presented at national conferences on issues such as treatment of incarcerated offenders and malingering. She is the author or coauthor of a number of professional publications on topics related to the practice of forensic and correctional psychology, including recent pieces in *Corrections Today* and the book *Detection of Deception* (Professional Resource Press, 2006).

Jeremy F. Mills, Ph.D., C.Psych., is a licensed psychologist in the Province of Ontario, who, in addition to working within a correctional system, maintains a private practice and is an adjunct research professor at Carleton University. Dr. Mills holds an M.A. from Queen's University and a Ph.D. from Carleton University. He is the past chair of the Criminal Justice Section of the Canadian Psychological Association. Dr. Mills is a member and fellow of the American Psychological Association and has received the Distinguished Service Award from Division 18 (Psychologists in Public Service). He is the past and current chair of the North American Correctional and Criminal Justice Psychology Conference (2007, 2011).

Dr. Mills's research interests lie primarily within four areas: the assessment of risk for violence, antisocial attitudes and associates, assessing depression and risk for suicide, and the perception of criminal risk. His research has resulted in more than 30 peer-reviewed publications, and he regularly conducts workshops on the assessment of violence risk. He and his colleagues are currently under contract with Guilford Publications for a forthcoming book on violence risk assessment. He is a coinvestigator on a National Institute of Justice grant examining dynamic risk assessment within the Texas Department of Criminal Justice. He has authored and coauthored the development of several new instruments for use with correctional populations, including the Measures of Criminal Attitudes and Associates (MCAA); the Attributions of Crime Inventory; and the Depression, Hopelessness and Suicide Screening Form (DHS). The latter instrument has been adopted for inclusion within the Mental Health Screening Protocol for use nationwide within the Correctional Service of Canada.

Catherine Moffitt, Ph.D., is the director of evaluation research for Central New York Psychiatric Center (CNYPC). CNYPC is a comprehensive mental health service delivery system providing a full range of care and treatment to persons incarcerated in the New York State and County correctional systems. CNYPC consists of a 210-bed maximum-security inpatient facility located in Marcy, New York. It also provides services via a statewide network of mental health units located in designated New York State Department of Correctional Services facilities. Dr. Moffitt received her doctorate in clinical psychology from the University of Hawai'i at Manoa.

Robert D. Morgan, Ph.D., is an associate professor in the Department of Psychology at Texas Tech University. He is also director of forensic services at Lubbock Regional Mental Health Mental Retardation services. Dr. Morgan is a fellow and president (2009–2010) of Division 18 (Psychologists in Public Service) of the American Psychological Association. He publishes in the area of correctional mental health, forensic psychology, and professional development and training. He has authored or coauthored more than 35 peer-reviewed publications and coauthored/coedited three books: *Life After Graduate School in Psychology: Insider's Advice from New Psychologists, Careers in Psychology: Opportunities in a Changing World* (3rd ed.), and *The Clinician's Guide to Violence Risk Assessment* (2011). A fourth book, *Treating the Mentally Disordered Offender*, is in progress and under contract with Oxford University Press. He also codeveloped and served on the steering committee for the North American Correctional and Criminal Justice Psychology Conference (2007, 2011 [pending]).

Corinne N. Ortega, Ph.D., is a psychologist for the Federal Bureau of Prisons. She has more than 17 years of experience working in corrections and other criminal justice settings. Her professional and research interests focus on the application of culturally appropriate interventions in forensic settings and the reintegration and reentry of the offender into the community. Her research also focuses on the maintenance of paternal relationships during incarceration. As a fellow of the APA Minority Fellowship Program, Dr. Ortega has been recognized for her work with underserved populations. She is also a two-time recipient of both the Royce Ronning Memorial Award for Cultural Diversity in the Department of Educational Psychology and the Larson Minority Fellowship at the University of Nebraska–Lincoln. Dr. Ortega has also served as an adjunct professor of psychology at John Jay College of Criminal Justice. She completed her predoctoral internship with the Federal Bureau of Prisons at the Federal Medical Center in Devens, Massachusetts. Dr. Ortega received her Ph.D. in psychological and cultural studies at the University of Nebraska–Lincoln. She holds a B.A. in sociology and psychology from the University of Nebraska–Lincoln and an M.A. in forensic psychology from John Jay College of Criminal Justice in New York City. Dr. Ortega is a licensed psychologist in New York.

Stephen W. Phillippi, Ph.D., L.C.S.W., received his Ph.D. from Louisiana State University. Dr. Phillippi is a licensed clinical social worker, board-approved clinical supervisor, and clinically certified forensic counselor. He has a 20-year history of developing, managing, and providing direct care services along the full range of the juvenile justice system continuum of care. This includes work with Juvenile Drug Court, Families in Need of Services, adolescent substance abuse treatment, community-based intervention, family-based intervention, school-based services, and mental health programming in the community and juvenile correctional/secure-care facilities. In his current role with the Louisiana State University Health Sciences Center–School of Public Health, Dr. Phillippi is the project director for a MacArthur Foundation grant to assist in bringing evidence-based practices to local communities as part of their Louisiana Models for Change in Juvenile Justice initiative. The goal is to identify, train, and develop capacity to implement and sustain evidenced-based practices in screening, assessment, and treatment of youth and families involved in the juvenile justice system at the community level. Dr. Phillippi is also the chair of the Louisiana Mental Health and Juvenile Justice Network, which is part of a national network of states and professionals supported by the MacArthur Foundation to address mental health and behavioral health issues that impact a large proportion of the youth involved with the juvenile justice system. In addition to these activities, Dr. Phillippi performs research, teaches, writes, consults, participates in a number of professional and public service boards, and maintains a small private clinical practice in his hometown, just outside New Orleans.

Robert J. Powitzky, Ph.D., is a licensed psychologist who received his Ph.D. in clinical psychology from the University of Texas Health Science Center, Dallas. He has served in his current position of chief mental health officer of the Oklahoma Department of Corrections since 1999. During that same time period, he has also been an adjunct professor in the University of Oklahoma Health Science Center, Department of Psychiatry and Behavioral Sciences. His experience in the criminal justice system spans more than 37 years, 12 of those years in various positions for the Federal Bureau of Prisons, including as the chief of psychology services for the entire Federal Bureau of Prisons. He has also served as assistant director, Health and Correctional Programs, in the Arkansas Department of Corrections, and later worked 15 years in his own private forensic psychology practice in Dallas, Texas. Dr. Powitzky has served as an expert consultant to more than 18 prison and jail correctional systems, as well as various federal law enforcement, correctional, and mental health agencies. He has been elected to leadership positions in numerous professional organizations, including the American Psychological Association Division 18, the American Association of Correctional Psychologists (now the International Association of Correctional and Forensic Psychology), and the Oklahoma Psychological Association. He has served on boards of various non-profit agencies and has received numerous awards for his professional contributions, the most recent being the Oklahoma Psychological Association's 2003 Distinguished Contribution by a Psychologist in the Public Service Award and 2007 Distinguished Administrative Service Award. In 2005, he received the Commissioner's Bridging Award from the Oklahoma Department of Mental Health and Substance Abuse. He has authored several professional publications and is currently serving on the editorial boards of the *Correctional Mental Health Report* and *Psychological Services.*

Donald A. Sawyer, Ph.D., M.B.A., is chief executive officer of Central New York Psychiatric Center, New York State Office of Mental Health. He is a licensed psychologist in New York State who holds a Ph.D. in clinical psychology from the University of Ottawa and a master's in business administration from Syracuse University. Central New York Psychiatric Center employs more than 1,400 staff and is the sole provider of inpatient and corrections-based mental health services to the 59,000 inmates in the 65 New York State Department of Corrections prisons. In addition, Central New York Psychiatric Center is the primary location in New York for the treatment of civilly committed sex offenders. He has more than 30 years of experience in both the delivery of direct care services and in the administration of human service programs and has served as co-coordinator of rural affairs for the NYS Office of Mental Health. He is a past president of the National Association for Rural Mental Health and has been the lead investigator for research projects sponsored by the Center for Mental Health Services of the U.S. Department of Health and Human Services and the Federal Office of Rural Health Policy. He is also currently an assistant professor of psychiatry at Upstate Medical University in Syracuse, New York.

Gollapudi Shankar, Pharm.D., M.S., Ph.C., B.C.P.P., C.G.P., received his Pharm.D. from Creighton University, Omaha, Nebraska, and also holds an M.S. degree in public health from the University of Northern Colorado. He is board certified in psychiatric pharmacotherapy and is certified as a pharmacist clinician (Ph.C.) by the New Mexico Board of Pharmacy. He is a fellow of the Australian College of Pharmacy Practice. He is currently an associate professor of pharmacy practice-psychiatry at Western University College of Pharmacy, Pomona, California. Prior to this appointment, he worked for several years as a treatment review consultant and clinical pharmacist with the California Department of Mental Health and was a member of the statewide psychopharmacology advisory committee during that period. Dr. Shankar also worked as a treatment review consultant for the acute psychiatric program at the California Medical Facility (State Prison) in Vacaville for 12 years.

David J. Stephens, Psy.D., received his doctorate from the University of Denver. He is a licensed psychologist in four states (Colorado, Missouri, Wyoming, Kansas), with extensive experience in correctional mental and behavioral health. He has been the director of mental health for the Wyoming and Missouri Departments of Correction and the chief of behavioral health for the Colorado Department of Corrections. He is a member of the American Psychological Association and the International Association for Correctional and Forensic Psychology. He has also been the corporate director of mental health for Correctional Healthcare Management—a correctional health care company that specializes in providing behavioral health services to jails of all sizes throughout the United States. He has taught undergraduate and graduate psychology courses at the Colorado State University–Pueblo and at Denver Seminary.

He is a regular presenter at national conferences on correctional mental health and co-occurring disorders. He has presented at National Commission on Correctional Healthcare National Conferences and at the GAINS Center National Conferences. He has provided mental health training for community organizations and has appeared on local radio and television programs addressing issues related to sex offender treatment. In addition to these presentations, Dr. Stephens has authored a chapter in the book *Broken Wings: A Clergy Manual for Addressing Domestic Violence* (Heritage Christian Center, Aurora, Colorado, 1992).

Dr. Stephens participates in numerous professional and community activities. He has been invited or appointed to serve on several committees and boards, including the Colorado Governor's Executive Order Task Force on Traumatic Brain Injury; the Advisory Board, FOREST Program, Colorado Department of Corrections/Aurora Community Mental Health Center; the Developmental Disabilities/Mental Health Consortium; the Human Rights Committee (served as chairman), Colorado Developmental Disabilities Community Board; the Colorado Co-Occurring Disorders Committee; the Management Team, Missouri Department of Corrections Reentry Process; and the Colorado State Assembly on Co-Occurring Disorders and the Criminal Justice System.

Kelly O. N. Talbert is currently an undergraduate student at Southern Illinois University–Carbondale. After graduation, she plans to seek her Ph.D. in clinical psychology. Her major research interests are in the dynamics of the public's opinion of mentally ill offenders and how these perceptions are affected by current or anticipated professions, and juvenile delinquent behavior. She is a McNair Scholar and is currently active in several organizations for students, including the Association of Black Psychologists; PsiChi, the national psychology honor society; and the Psychology Student Association and Criminal Justice Association, both at Southern Illinois University–Carbondale.

Michael Thompson, Psy.D., M.S.W., earned his master's degree in clinical social work from Fordham University in 1995 and his doctorate in clinical psychology from Pacific University in 2001. He completed a doctoral internship in clinical and forensic psychology at Mendota Mental Health Institute and the University of Wisconsin, both in Madison, Wisconsin. His doctoral dissertation, *Sexual Arousal Patterns in Admitting and Denying Sexual Offenders*, examined differential arousal between men who admitted and men who denied their adjudicated sexual offenses. This research was presented at the annual conference of the Western Psychological Association, in Maui, Hawaii, in 2001.

Dr. Thompson has worked primarily in the area of sexual offender evaluation and treatment since 1996. Prior to completion of his doctoral work, Dr. Thompson worked as a foster care social worker in New York City, supervising foster homes and the welfare of children in foster care in the boroughs of Brooklyn, Queens, Manhattan, and the Bronx, and in several suburban counties. Dr. Thompson served as an adjunct instructor in psychology, social work, and education departments at several colleges and universities, including Marymount Manhattan College, the University of Portland, Augsburg College, and the University of Wisconsin at River Falls.

Dr. Thompson is a forensic psychologist in private practice in Minneapolis. He is also employed as an outpatient therapist at Alpha Human Services, also in Minneapolis. A licensed psychologist, Dr. Thompson is a clinical member of the Association for the Treatment of Sexual Abusers (ATSA). He currently serves on the ATSA Education and Training Committee and previously chaired the Credentialing Subcommittee of ATSA's Education and Training Committee. Dr. Thompson served on the board of directors and as the president of the Minnesota chapter of ATSA. He is also a member of the American Psychological Association, the Minnesota Psychological Association, the Sex Offender Civil Commitment Programs Network and the Minnesota Community Corrections Association.